INSTRUCTOR'S RESOURCE GUIDE

to accompany

Management

Sixth Edition

John R. Schermerhorn, Jr.
Ohio University

Prepared by

William L. Gardner III
Michael S. Starnes Professor of Management
University of Mississippi

John Wiley & Sons, Inc.
New York • Chichester • Weinheim • Brisbane • Singapore • Toronto

ISBN 0-471-29994-4

Printed in the United States of America

10 9 8 7 6 5 4 3 2

Printed and bound by Victor Graphics, Inc.

CONTENTS

UNIT 1

General Philosophy and Design of the Text

Just like the mosaic featured on the cover of **Management 6/E**, today's workplace offers a rich mix of colors, forms and impressions. Consistent with these changing times, the philosophy and design of **Management 6/E** reflects the author's commitment to create a true management mosaic which provides learning experiences for students that are intellectually sound and practical. This mosaic consists of the core text, informative videos, and a comprehensive web site with additional interactive case studies, self-assessments, career tools, and teaching resources drawn from the author's own classroom.

Like its predecessors, the sixth edition of **Management** introduces the essentials of management as they apply within the contemporary work environment. Its first goal is to cover the appropriate topics in sufficient depth for the introductory student. Its second goal is to do so in an interesting and applied way -- one that holds the students' attention and stimulates them to relate actively to the material at hand. Moreover, as the author notes in the **Preface**, it strives for balance between research insights and introductory education, management theory and practice, present understandings and future possibilities, and what "can" be done with what is "right" to do. In the spirit of these and related themes, **Management/6E** is offered as the management textbook for today...and tomorrow!

The subject matter of **Management/6E** remains carefully chosen to meet AACSB accreditation guidelines while allowing extensive flexibility to fit various course designs and class sizes. The book is thorough from a curriculum standpoint while written to meet the needs of the introductory student. Importantly, this is done with special attention to the environment, quality operations, cultural diversity, the global economy, and ethics and social responsibility and the growing influence of new information technologies as paramount concerns and themes of our day.

Management/6E also shows a healthy respect for the needs of practicing managers. Core theories, research insights, and key concepts are balanced with current trends and practical developments. Frequent real-world examples are used to help readers clearly relate the subject matter to actual applications of both large and small, local and global, and manufacturing and service organizations.

DESIGN OF THE TEXT

Management/6E can be used in business and management curricula or in general education curricula where only one management course is offered. The text is designed for an introductory management course and assumes no prerequisites. In a business and management curricula, the text would be appropriate for a management course that precedes courses in organizational behavior and personnel administration. In settings where no such course exists to follow a management course, the text would be additionally valuable since it covers organizational behavior and personnel activities.

There are many new things to look for in this edition. Along with updates of core material, the new edition of **Management** offers a number of changes in the organization, content, and design that respond to current themes and developments in the theory and practice of management.

Organizational Changes

* The book is reorganized into five parts with clear application to core themes relevant to today's organizations: Management Today, Context, Mission, Organization, Leadership.

* The fundamentals of the management process are integrated through core chapters on these action themes: Planning — To Set Direction; Organizing — To Create Structures; Leading — To Inspire Effort; Controlling — To Ensure Results.

* Part 1 opens the book with a clear focus on the exciting and dynamic new workplace, the importance of environment and competitive advantage, and the importance of information technology and decision making.

* Part 2 sets the context for management by reviewing the historical foundations, highlighting the importance of the global economy, and offering a strong reminder of the importance of ethics and social responsibility.

* Part 3 integrates both planning and controlling as management functions, and includes an all-new treatment of strategic management and entrepreneurship.

* Part 4 covers the essentials of organizing as a management function, with special attention to new developments in organization designs and work systems.

* Part 5 offers extensive coverage of leadership as a managerial function, including in-depth coverage of motivation and rewards, individual performance and job design, communication and interpersonal skills, teams and teamwork, and innovation and change management.

Content Additions

Throughout the book every effort is made to bring in the latest thinking and concepts facing managers and organizations today. In addition to core themes of diversity, competitive advantage, quality, globalization, and empowerment, specific coverage has been added in this edition on all of the following topics and more:

multi-cultural organizations, ethnocentrism, cultural relativism, self-management, customer-driven organizations, electronic commerce, Intranets, entrepreneurship, organizational learning, life-long learning, horizontal organizations, cross-functional teams, virtual teams, virtual organizations, process value analysis, re-engineering, informal learning, work-life balance, strategic human resource planning, performance-based rewards, job stress, alternative work environments, communication barriers, conflict management, negotiation, teamwork, innovation processes, and change leadership.

Design Features

The design of **Management 6/E** has been created in specific response to the author's experience as a classroom instructor and with the assistance of helpful feedback from management educators using the prior edition. With a clean and open look in a four-color format, the design is our attempt to provide introductory management students with a book that is consistent in style with the professional literature they can and should be reading.

Taking the benchmark of the professional literature, the new edition introduces each chapter with a "Headlines" feature that provides a variety of anecdotal vignettes to draw the reader into chapter content. The chapters themselves reflect a variety of additional features that visually present the material in an attractive and engaging manner. The design has been selected to help bring the best chapter features to the reader's clear and complete attention.

Chapter Features

Management/6E is an integrated learning tool that uses basic principles of learning theory to offer an effective learning experience for the reader. Basic pedagogical features that enhance the overall learning potential of the book include:

* **Opening Headline:** To emphasize the importance of learning as much as we can about the role of managers in this dynamic environment, we open each chapter with a *Headline* that calls out a key issue or point regarding management today. This is accompanied by a short vignette offering a timely report or example relevant to the chapter and to the new workplace of the 21st century. The vignettes feature real-world people and organizations. They have been carefully chosen to offer a stimulating view of the real challenges facing today's managers.

* **Planning Ahead:** The chapter opener provides a brief **Planning Ahead** statement which helps orient the reader to the chapter topic. This includes a set of **study questions** that are linked to the major subject headings of the chapter. They serve as learning objectives and create a framework for the later chapter summary.

* **Embedded Boxes:** *Diversity, quality, ethics, social responsibility, benchmarking, the global economy* -- these are all themes that managers must deal with on a daily basis. To exemplify the importance of these three themes, we have provided in-depth examples that are embedded by both content and design in the general text discussion. The examples chosen range from large, multinational organizations to small, local businesses, representing for-profit, nonprofit and manufacturing and service organizations. The embedded boxes are visually illustrated with engaging photographs that bring them to life and each features a visual icon which describes the overall theme of the box.

* **Manager's Notepads:** *Manager's Notepads* are concise lists of helpful hints -- the "do's and don't's" of managerial behavior. They are designed as useful theory-in-practice summaries, and to assist readers with understanding the action implications of material being studied. The Manager's Notepads appear as boxed inserts throughout the text as appropriately designed to resemble the familiar "yellow pads" used by most everyone.

* **Margin Photos:** Additional, briefer real-world examples are called out in the margin of the text and illustrated with photos. The captions to these photos highlight the ways in which the concepts and theories presented in the text apply in day-to-day managerial practices in a wide selection of organizations. These dynamic, real-world examples of management in action add further applications to text discussion, without distracting the reader. Where applicable, these margin photos also include the corporate Web addresses that can be used by students to pursue further research on the web.

* **Margin List Identifiers:** *Margin list notes* are provided throughout the text to identify key bulleted or numbered lists of information. The margin notes provide a convenient outline for students to use in studying chapter content and reviewing for examinations.

* **Margin Running Glossary:** Boldfaced key terms from the text are called out and defined in the margin, forming a **running glossary** of the key concepts of the discussion.

* **Chapter Summary:** The *chapter summary* is tied specifically to the study questions presented at the beginning of each chapter. The summary repeats each study question and offers, in concise bullet-list form, an overview of key points from that section of the chapter. It helps put the chapter into overall perspective, providing in depth answers to the study questions posed at the beginning of the chapter.

* **Chapter List of Key Terms:** The end-of-chapter list of key terms allows the student to double-check familiarity with basic concepts and definitions. Page numbers are included for easy access to the textual reference.

* **Chapter Self-Test:** The end-of-chapter self-test has been continued from the last edition. It provides a built-in study guide the student can use to prepare for examinations. Multiple-choice, true-false, short-answer, and application questions reflect the type of questions the student may be expected to answer on examinations. The author's answers to the self-test questions, including the short-answer and application questions, are found in the back of the book.

Career Readiness Workbook

An important innovation in *Management 6/E* is the inclusion of the *Career Readiness Workbook* as part of the hard-bound text. The workbook consists of six components, each of which has been designed to maximize learning opportunities for the student and provide a range of stimulating pedagogical options for the instructor. The complete portfolio of rich learning activities is presented in an easy-to-use format that is geared directly toward career and professional development. They can help students to evaluate their managerial capabilities and are suitable for either in-class or out-of-class assignments and for individual or group use. All materials are well-supported in a separate section of this Manual. The elements in the workbook are: *Career Advancement Portfolio, Cases for Critical Thinking, Integrative Learning Activities, Exercises for Teamwork, Self-assessments*, and *Research and Presentation Projects*.

* **Career Advancement Portfolio:** The unique *Career Advancement Portfolio* provides the template for students to build a career portfolio that documents, in paper or electronic form, their academic and personal accomplishments for external review. This resource can help them frame and summarize their credentials for potential internship sources and full time employers. There is a special option for building an electronic career portfolio and putting it on-line. In both print and on-line formats, the Career Advancement Portfolio can be easily maintained and updated for purposes of outcome assessment within a course or program of study, as well as for the student's personal and development.

* **Cases for Critical Thinking:** The *Critical Thinking Cases* brings to life the decisions managers must make every day in these dynamic times, on both a national and global level. Sometimes these choices are wise; other times they have proven to be erroneous. The case studies describe both the benefits and consequences of managers' decisions. Each case concludes with a list of questions for the student to answer concerning the in-depth scenarios they are given. Interactive versions of each case are available on-line through the *Management 6/E* web site. These on-line cases will be updated regularly and new cases posted to enrich the alternatives for classroom use.

* **Integrative Learning Activities:** Integration is one of the important thrusts in management education today. Included in the workbook are two easy-to-use and highly involving integrative learning activities that can supplement various aspects of a course. The *In-Basket Exercise* places

students in decision making situations that test their leadership and managerial capabilities, with an opportunity to stress written and oral communication skills. The *Integrative Video Case on Outback Steakhouse* further allows for various parts of the management process to be examined in the context of a real situation and a highly competitive environment. The case can be used in whole or in parts to best fit the instructor's course design.

* **Exercises in Teamwork:** The exercises offer opportunities to explore in the team setting a variety of issues and topics from chapters and class discussions. The team exercises present situations that provide the basis for group discussion or individual analytical exercises. Instructions are clear and self-explanatory; formats for group discussion and class interaction are provided. Additional team exercises are found among the instructional materials available on-line through the *Management 6/E* web site.

* **Managerial Skills Assessments:** A diverse selection of self-assessments are also included in the workbook. These self-assessment instruments ask the students to analyze their knowledge of management issues and their possession of the skills necessary to tackle these issues in daily life. Each assessment is broken down into *instructions* on how to complete the assessment; directions for *scoring*; and an *interpretation* of the score along with guidelines for its meaning in a larger context. Additional self-assessments are available on-line through the *Management 6/E* web site.

* **Managerial Skills Assessments:** The workbook offers a number of research and presentation projects on timely topics relating to the chapter discussions. The projects are designed to enhance students' research skills, including those involving the Internet and Electronic Data Bases. Importantly, the projects also offer important opportunities for students to refine their written and oral presentation skills. Each project is introduced with a brief scenario and hypothetical situation. A question is then posed about the situation. The scenario can be used as the basis for a wide variety of course assignments, including individual and group work. Students are pointed toward outside research sources that may help them solve the managerial dilemma, including library sources, local case studies of nearby organizations, and comparative field research they can conduct on their own. The responses can be used as the foundation for a professional individual research paper or group project.

Management 6/E Web Site

An extensive website has been developed in support of *Management 6/E* users. The site is available at *http://www.wiley.com/college/scherman6e,* and offers a range of information which includes the following special resources for instructional enrichment:

* Powerpoint downloads for supplementary figures and class presentations materials.

* Interactive on-line versions of all cases.

* Supplementary in-class exercises and activities.

* Special "quick-hitters" for use with various chapters, and with special value for large-lecture class sizes.

* Internet links to all organizations referenced in the textbook.

Additionally, the web site features a unique resource — "The Author's Classroom." This feature takes you inside the author's actual classroom and provides additional teaching ideas and resources for each chapter. An alternative to this Instructor's Manual, this on-line resource provides teaching tips and class enhancements for treating the core topics of each chapter, and as they are used in the author's classroom. By using this resource you have access to the author's personal PowerPoint presentations, special in-class activities, unique websites for Internet browsing during class, and more.

If you enjoy teaching, you'll enjoy working with The Author's Classroom. And if you stay in touch with this site, you will have access to new materials and resources as they become available from the author's own classes.

Conclusion

Overall, the text reflects the state of the art in management curricula and teaching. In this respect the author subscribes to four important principles in the design of a management course:

1. The management course in which the text is used should be designed rather than proprietary;

2. The course should provide cumulative knowledge for further course work;

3. The course should be part of an integrated pattern involving a broad definition or organizational behavior or management; and

4. The course should have real and apparent value for application.[1]

---

[1] Alan C. Filley, Lawrence W. Foster and Theodore Herbert, *Current Practices in Organization Behavior, Curricula and Teaching,* an Unpublished Report, Academic Program Committee, Organizational Behavior Division, Academy of Management, August, 1977.

LEARNING/TEACHING IDEAS FOR MANAGEMENT COURSES

The text's design features highlighted above, provide students with both didactic and heuristic instruction. Didactics is a form of teaching which is highly structured. Assignments are definite and clear, and follow a logical and precise format. Exams, primarily objective in nature, cover only material covered in class, individually-assigned, or both. The primary use of this method is to impart knowledge. According to Broudy[2], "as much as 80 percent of all undergraduate collegiate instruction is didactical."

A major problem with didactics, according to Broudy, is that the method is not very closely related to student interests at the time of teaching. Knowledge tends to packaged in a logical but not necessarily psychological order. Simple elements are typically used to build up to more complex ideas. Often, however, this logical presentation is abstract and boring. Student may tend to see the presentation as irrelevant to their current interests.

Heuristics, by contrast, requires students to think and discover solutions to problems on their own. The teacher forces creative thinking by refusing to reveal the "answer." The Socratic method and John Dewey's problem-solving approach are mentioned by examples from the management teaching area. In this text, a variety of heuristic learning opportunities are available such as cases, class exercises and "thinking through the issues."

---

[2]Harry S. Broudy, "Didactics, Heuristics and Philetics," *Educational Theory,* (Summer 1972), pp. 251 - 261.

UNIT 2

Teaching Ideas from Learning Theory and Research

Based on a summary of learning theory and research by Craig Schneier[3] the following modified ideas should be useful to you as you plan your course content and methods.

IDEAS FROM LEARNING THEORY

The Learning Environment

1. Teachers learn a great deal about their learners when actually teaching and given responsibility. The instructor, by using various participatory learning activities, gives students a chance to become in-class teachers in some respects, and, thus, the students learn more.

2. Objectives and success criteria for the course should be specified and communicated to learners, but don't lose flexibility and creativity in the process.

3. Assessment of learner progress and feedback should be done regularly to help students.

4. The teacher conditions emotional reactions in the learning program, as well as behavioral responses, and should, therefore, attempt to condition favorable reactions to himself/herself and to the subject matter.

Characteristics of the Learner and Learning Activity

1. People not only learn at different rates, but each person brings a different emotional state to the learning situation. Of course, the larger the class, the more difficult it can be to determine individual differences. Working in small groups may help you in monitoring individuals.

2. The motivational level of the learner is relevant to the type and amount of stimuli to which he/she will respond. The variety of applied learning activities offered in the text should be

---

[3]Craig Eric Schneier, "Training and Development Programs: What Learning Theory and Research Have to Offer," *Personnel Journal,* April 1974.

9

intrinsically rewarding to students when they get involved and therefore motivational in value.

3. Interest and attention come from successful experiences. These, in turn, facilitate learning as they are seen as rewarding experiences. Through your adaptation of material you can help students have successful experiences.

4. Active participation on the part of the student has been emphasized, but remember learning can also occur by simply observing. Too much student participation may be excessively time consuming and interfere with your teaching objectives.

5. There are several ways to learn: Trial and error, perception-organization insight, and modeling another's behavior. All are effective under certain conditions. Try a variety of approaches over the term.

6. Complex human learning includes a proper degree of discrimination and generalization. The integrating cases are particularly helpful to students in discriminating--distinguishing between quite similar stimuli which require different responses, or in generalizing--noting similar, but not exactly the same stimuli often require the *same* response.

Reinforcement of Learning

1. Knowledge of results of performance is basic to learning and is often a reinforcer. It provides necessary feedback for corrective action. Feedback on performance should be given to students regularly.

2. Social reinforcement (e.g. approval by others) can be effective in improving performance. Small group activities can provide a setting for social reinforcement.

3. For positive reinforcement and negative reinforcement to be most effective, they should be dispensed immediately and be appropriate in intensity for the particular response they follow. Regular verbal feedback from the instructor to students should be done when students do well in the class activities.

Summary

In summary, *Management/6E* was designed to:

1.   Deal with a widely-accepted set of management topics,

2.   Provide a cumulative knowledge base for further coursework,

3.   Provide a broad treatment of management topics by dealing with micro and macro aspects,

4.   Provide an applications emphasis,

5.   Link management topics to worker productivity and human resource maintenance as key work results, and

6.   Mix effectively theory and practice.

UNIT 3

Sample Course Outlines

The text is designed as a learning instrument which captures and maintains student interest via a mixture of real life examples, cases, self-assessments, and exercises. Additional exercises, self-assessments, and other learning aids are provided at the *Management 6/E web site.* This broad selection should help you create a course which fits your specific needs. It should also help you experiment over several offerings to keep the course fresh and interesting.

THE FLEXIBILITY OF THE TEXT

The text is designed to accommodate your preferences regarding the sequencing of major topics. The four major management functions -- planning, organizing, leading and controlling -- are covered in the parts labeled mission (which encompasses planning and controlling), organization, and leadership. If desired, the leadership function could be covered first. Or, Part 2, which deals with the management context might be preferred by some to be inserted after the other parts of the text. If necessary, some chapters may also be omitted at the discretion of the instructor. Sample omissions are not given here since omissions can only be made on the basis of your own particular situation. Normally chapters or parts should not have to be cut out in a full-term quarter or semester course.

The text is also designed to accommodate your preferences regarding the level and methods of treatment. By selectively using cases, assessments, exercises, and research and presentation projects from the *Career Readiness Workbook* or the *Management 6/E web site,* the instructor can shift emphasis between introductory and more advanced treatments of management topics. These instructional aids can also facilitate choosing among more didactic and more experiential classroom methods.

What follows is a set of sample course outlines showing how various topic sequences can be used in both semester and quarter systems, and with both two and three class meetings per week. These outlines can help you to plan your preferred sequence; they also show different mixes of case work, lecture and class discussion. These outlines can be revised in many separate ways as you see fit. They are only a few of the many ways the text can be used in a introductory management course. Many other sequences and mixes in addition to the ones shown in the sample outlines are possible. You are urged to develop the course outline most consistent with your needs and goals.

Please note that one special outline for an evening course meeting only once per week is also included.

SAMPLE COURSE SYLLABUS

Semester/Quarter/Year
Course Number:
Course Title:
Meeting Days & Times:
Meeting Place:
Instructor:
Office Location:
Office Hours:

Catalog Description

(As officially published.)

Course Objective

(Sample provided for modification as desired)

The objective of this course is to familiarize you with the knowledge, roles, responsibilities, and skills required of modern managers. The material covered will be relevant to you, regardless of your career objectives. In all likelihood, you will either be a manager or work with one in any occupation you choose. Indeed, in the final analysis, we are all managers of our own lives and can benefit by studying to be better managers.

Course Textbook

Management/6E, by John R. Schermerhorn, Jr. (New York: John Wiley & Sons, 1999).

Required Examinations

(Sample provided for modification as desired)

All exams are required. Each will consist of multiple-choice and true-false questions which will relate to assigned reading and lecture material, as well as any assigned cases and other supplemental work.

The exams will be administered according to the following timetable. Please note that the hour exams are not given during normal class times. Students are required to take each exam at its formally scheduled time.

September 16	Hour Exam 1	100 points
October 10	Hour Exam 2	100 points
November 11	Hour Exam 3	100 points
University Scheduled	Final Exam	200 points

Grading Procedures

(Sample provided for modification as desired.)

Final grades will be determined by multiplying total points earned on the three hour exams and final exam by 2, and then applying the following interpretations:

Total Points Earned	Final Grade
900 - 1000	A
800 - 899	B
700 - 799	C
699 - 600	D
599 or less	F

Course Rules and Procedures

(Sample provided for modification as desired.)

Prerequisite Rule: The Department of Management strictly enforces all course requirements. Concurrent enrollment does **not** satisfy prerequisites. Students who register for a course without meeting its requirements will automatically have their enrollment canceled. Prerequisites for this course are: Junior Standing (56 or more hours passed).

Make-Up Exams: No make-up exams will be given for other than instructor-approved absences. There are no excused absences from exams other than physician documented illness, official university travel, religious holiday, documented personal emergency, or absolute conflict with a regularly scheduled class. A request for a make-up exam must be approved **two weeks in advance** of the regularly scheduled exam. All make-ups will be essay exams scheduled at the instructor's convenience.

Class Attendance: Students are strongly encouraged to attend all class sessions. Exams will cover material from the textbook and class session presentations.

Late Class Arrivals: Late arrivals to class should enter a rear door and take a seat in the back of the room. The two rows of seats will be reserved each day for this purpose.

Academic Honesty: All university, college, and department policies on academic honesty will be strictly enforced. The usual consequence of academic dishonesty is failure of the course and referral of the case to the Dean of the College for additional disciplinary action. Examinations are individual and are to be completed **without** outside assistance of any sort. Persons observed cheating will receive a failing grade in the course.

Tentative Course Outline

NOTE: All reading is from *Management6/E,* by John R. Schermerhorn, Jr. (New York: John Wiley & Sons, 1999).

(SEE SAMPLE COURSE OUTLINES WHICH FOLLOW)

SAMPLE COURSE OUTLINE A
(10 week quarter; 2 meetings/week; 75 minutes/meeting)

Week	Meeting	Topic	Chapter
1	1	Course and Textbook Introduction	---
	2	The Dynamic New Workplace	1
2	1	Environment and Competitive Advantage	2
	2	Information Technology and Decision Making	3
3	1	Historical Foundations of Management	4
	2	Global Dimensions of Management	5
4	1	Ethical Behavior and Social Responsibility	6
	2	Planning — To Set Direction	7
5	1	Strategic Management and Entrepreneurship	8
	2	Controlling — To Ensure Results	9
6	**1**	**EXAMINATION**	1 - 9
	2	Organizing — To Create Structures	10
7	1	Organizational Design and Work Processes	11
	2	Human Resource Management	12
8	1	Leading — To Inspire Effort	13
	2	Motivation and Rewards	14
9	1	Individual Performance and Job Design	15
	2	Communication and Interpersonal Skills	16
10	1	Teams and Teamwork	17
	2	Innovation and Change Management	18

FINAL EXAMINATION AS OFFICIALLY SCHEDULED

NOTE: In the 75 minute class sessions, the instructor can find several opportunities to use case discussions/class exercises to supplement the assigned reading topics. Other options include: guest speakers on selected topics, and the use of instructional videotapes.

SAMPLE COURSE OUTLINE B
(15 week semester; 3 meetings/week; 50 minute/meeting)

Week	Meeting	Topic	Chapter
1	1	Course and Textbook Introduction	---
	2	The Dynamic New Workplace	1
	3	Case Discussion or Class Exercise	1
2	1	Environment and Competitive Advantage	2
	2	Environment and Competitive Advantage	2
	3	Information Technology and Decision Making	3
3	1	Information Technology and Decision Making	3
	2	Case Discussion or Class Exercise	2,3
	3	Historical Foundations of Management	4
4	1	Historical Foundations of Management	4
	2	Flexible Day (Instructor's Option)	
	3	**EXAMINATION # 1**	**1 - 4**
5	1	Global Dimensions of Management	5
	2	Global Dimensions of Management	5
	3	Ethical Behavior and Social Responsibility	6
6	1	Ethical Behavior and Social Responsibility	6
	2	Planning — To Set Direction	7
	3	Planning — To Set Direction	7
7	1	Strategic Management and Entrepreneurship	8
	2	Strategic Management and Entrepreneurship	8
	3	Case Discussion or Class Exercise	7, 8
8	1	Controlling — To Ensure Results	9
	2	Controlling — To Ensure Results	9
	3	**EXAMINATION # 2**	**5 - 9**
9	1	Organizing — To Create Structures	10
	2	Organizing — To Create Structures	10
	3	Organizational Design and Work Systems	11
10	1	Organizational Design and Work Systems	11
	2	Human Resource Management	12
	3	Human Resource Management	12
11	1	Leading — To Inspire Effort	13
	2	Leading — To Inspire Effort	13
	3	Case Discussion or Class Exercise	13

12	1	Motivation and Rewards	14
	2	Motivation and Rewards	14
	3	**EXAMINATION # 3**	**10 - 14**
13	1	Individual Performance and Job Design	15
	2	Individual Performance and Job Design	15
	3	Communication and Interpersonal Skills	16
14	1	Communication and Interpersonal Skills	16
	2	Teams and Teamwork	17
	3	Teams and Teamwork	17
15	1	Innovation and Change Management	18
	2	Innovation and Change Management	18
	3	Course Summary and Review	1 - 18

FINAL EXAMINATION AS OFFICIALLY SCHEDULED

NOTE: With three 50 minute class sessions per week, the instructor can find several opportunities to use case discussions/class exercises to supplement the assigned reading topics, as the sample syllabus indicates. Other options include: guest speakers on selected topics, and the use of instructional videotapes.

SAMPLE COURSE OUTLINE C
(15 week semester; 1 meeting/week; 2 1/2 hours/meeting)

Week	Topic	Chapter
1	The Dynamic New Workplace	1
2	Environment and Competitive Advantage;	2
	Information Technology and Decision Making	3
3	Historical Foundations of Management	4
4	Ethical Behavior and Social Responsibility	5
5	Global Dimensions of Management	6
6	**EXAMINATION # 1**	**1 - 6**
	Planning — To Set Direction	7
7	Strategic Management and Entrepreneurship	8
8	Controlling — To Ensure Results	9
9	Organizing — To Create Structures;	10
	Organizational Design and Work Processes	11
10	Human Resource Management	12
11	**EXAMINATION # 2**	**7 - 12**
	Leading — To Inspire Effort	13
12	Motivation and Rewards	14
13	Individual Performance and Job Design;	15
	Communication and Interpersonal Skills	16
14	Teams and Teamwork	17
15	Innovation and Change Management	18

FINAL EXAMINATION AS OFFICIALLY SCHEDULED

NOTE: In the 2 1/2 hour class sessions, the instructor can find several opportunities to use case discussions/class exercises to supplement the assigned reading topics. Other options include: guest speakers on selected topics, and the use of instructional videotapes.

UNIT 4

Sample Assignments

This part of the *MANUAL* contains assignments which might be used as part of your course. The assignments are briefly explained below. Actual handout masters for each assignment follow. You can reproduce these handouts directly from the *MANUAL* or modify them to fit your special needs. You should require most assignments to have prior approval before the students begin serious work on them. A general "Project Approval Form" is the first handout to follow.

INDIVIDUAL ASSIGNMENTS

Library Term Paper

This assignment requires library research using secondary data sources. Appropriate topics are limited only by the students' imagination. Let students pick a topic of interest to them. It is helpful also to hand out the "List of Useful Periodicals," and to use the "Grading Sheet" as a formal means of feedback.

Write and Analyze a Case

This assignment is especially useful when your students have work experience. It requires them to summarize a real work situation and to analyze it from a managerial perspective.

Research Project

On occasion students should do an empirical research project. It is a time consuming effort and is probably best reserved for your most advanced and serious students.

Journal Reviews

This is a mini-project that can be used in the form shown in the instructions, or as modified to become a weekly or bi-weekly effort. For example, you can require one journal review per week turned in on a 5 x 8 card. This assignment is designed to get students into the more recent research literature.

Personal Growth Assignment

This is an end-of-semester assignment that helps pull the course together. It emphasizes self-analysis and career planning for personal growth and development.

GROUP ASSIGNMENTS

Modified Individual Assignments

Each of the individual assignments can be modified into a group activity. Other suggestions for group assignments are found throughout the "Chapter Highlights and Teaching Suggestions" included later in this MANUAL.

The Classroom-As-Organization Pedagogy

The classroom-as-organization pedagogy is an approach to management education in which the class is structured as an organization complete with work groups and a CEO. The purpose of this approach is to provide students with first hand experience with a variety of course concepts such as division of labor, coordination, leadership, group processes, performance appraisal, formal and informal communication, and control. Through this approach student learning can be greatly enhanced as students are provided with the opportunity to immediately apply theory into practice.

Group Development Project

This team-building project can easily accompany other assigned group work. You'll find it easier to use it in the middle of a term and after students have already done at least one other Group assignment together. The project works best when the "Group Formation Exercise" is used early in the term, and when the "Personal Reaction Paper" is used to bring closure to the total group experience.

Personal Reaction Paper

This is an end-of-term assignment used to summarize students' experiences in their course work groups. Use of this assignment helps bring closure to the group work by reinforcing its learning value and personal implications. It is most helpful to require the "Peer Rating" and "Group Rating" forms as part of this assignment.

INDIVIDUAL ASSIGNMENT HANDOUTS

- Project Approval Form

- Library Term Paper Assignment

- Term Paper Grading Sheet

- List of Useful Periodicals

- Write and Analyze a Case Assignment

- Research Project

- Journal Reviews Project

- Personal Growth Assignment

PROJECT APPROVAL FORM

Title of Project _____   **Your Name** _____

I.   Summarize in about one half page the major direction which you plan to take in the project. If it is a case briefly summarize the problem(s) and give an idea of important background material. If the project is a term paper or research paper, indicate as specifically as possible the topic area, direction, and importance of the topic to management. Attach this completed approval to the final draft of your project turned in to the instructor.

II.   If the project is a term paper, list below (in correct writing form) at least six references representative of those you plan to use.

III. If the project is a research paper, see the Instructions for Research Project Form.

Instructor comments:

_____

_____

_____

_____

_____

_____

_____

_____

_____

_____

_____

Instructor signature of approval _____

LIBRARY TERM PAPER ASSIGNMENT

I.   The term paper should include: (1) a definition or discussion of a problem, its importance and managerial implications; (2) a review of the literature related to the problem; (3) a summary or conclusion which indicates possible solutions to the problem or extensions of research on the problem.

The review should be as thorough as possible and should be restricted to literature which you personally have been able to obtain. The review should include empirical studies and avoid armchair speculations. It should also use journals of the type indicated by your instructor.

II. All papers are due by _____. Papers may be submitted any time prior to the due date. You must have the instructor's signed approval before proceeding with this paper. Submit the completed "Project Approval Form" along with the paper on the due date.

III. Your paper should be typewritten, double-spaced, and follow proper report writing procedures (proper spelling, grammar, etc.). If you are in doubt about proper report writing procedures obtain a copy of one of the many guides to writing research papers. The use of headings, subheadings and summary lists is encouraged. All written work submitted by an individual implies that it was his/her work. All assistance received or references obtained from others should be documented in accordance with good reporting practice. Papers will be graded on both content and grammar.

IV. The "Term Paper Grading Sheet" should be turned in along with your paper on the due date. Complete the "My Rating" column and Question 7. The instructor will complete the rest and return it to you as feedback.

TERM PAPER GRADING SHEET

Title of Paper _____ **Name** _____

<u>Grade (A+ to F-)</u>
My Rating   Inst. Rating

1. Adequacy of statement and development of problem   _____   _____

_____

_____

2. Adequacy of discussion of managerial implications   _____   _____

_____

_____

3. Adequacy of conclusions concerning the problem   _____   _____

_____

_____

4. Adequacy of literature utilized   _____   _____

_____

_____

5. Following acceptable report writing procedure   _____   _____

     Format_____

     References_____

6. Style grammar, spelling, typing errors, etc.   _____   _____

_____

_____

7. Overall, how willing would I be to turn this report in to my boss if this were a "real world" assignment?

Extremely Willing	Quite Willing	Slightly Willing	Slightly Unwilling	Quite Unwilling	Extremely Unwilling
_____	_____	_____	_____	_____	_____

Overall Grade _____.   General comments on reverse side.

LIST OF USEFUL PERIODICALS

The following periodicals may be helpful in your library research efforts.

Trade Journals: These are oriented primarily toward practitioners.

Academy of Management Executive
Across the Board
Advanced Management Journal
American Management Association Research Reports
Business Horizons
Business and Society Review
California Management Review
Canadian Business
Columbia Journal of World Business
Dun's Review
Fortune
Futurist
Harvard Business Review
Industry Week
Journal of Contemporary Business
Journal of Long Range Planning
Management International Review
Management Record
Management Review
Managerial Planning
Monthly Labor Review
Nation's Business
Organizational Dynamics
Personnel
Personnel Administrator
Personnel Journal
Personnel Series
Production and Inventory Management
Psychology Today
Public Administration Review
Public Personnel Management
SAM Advanced Management Journal
Sloan Management Review
Social Science Reporter
Supervision
Supervisory Management
Training and Development Journal

Unit 4: Sample Assignments

Scholarly Journals: These are oriented primarily towards the academician or specialist.

Academy of Management Journal
Academy of Management Review
Administrative Science Quarterly
American Journal of Sociology
American Political Science Review
American Sociological Review
Behavioral Science
Decision Sciences
Group and Organization Management
Human Organization
Human Relations
Human Resource Management
Industrial and Labor Relations Review
Industrial Relations
International Studies of Management and Organization
Journal of Applied Behavioral Sciences
Journal of Applied Psychology
Journal of Applied Social Psychology
Journal of Business
Journal of Business Research
Journal of Business Strategy
Journal of Conflict Resolution
Journal of Management Studies
Journal of Small Business Management
Journal of Vocational Behavior
Management Science
Occupation Psychology
Operational Research Quarterly
Operating Research
Organization and Administrative Sciences
Organizational Behavior and Human Performance
Personnel Management
Personnel Psychology
Psychological Bulletin
Public Administration Review
Sociology
Sociometry
Strategic Management Journal

Abstracting Services: These are useful for finding relevant material in journals and books.

Business Periodicals Index
Employment Relations Abstracts
Management Abstracts
Management Research
Personnel Management Abstracts
Psychological Abstracts
Sociological Abstracts
Wall Street Journal Index

WRITE AND ANALYZE A CASE ASSIGNMENT

I.   A case must be based on a current or recent work experience of yours and from which you can obtain the kind of information shown in the cases used in class. It should include one or more managerial problems. You should be able to obtain enough information so that you can describe the case background and surroundings in considerable detail. Check text chapters and class notes to review the kind of background information that might be useful. The information in the case description does not have to be organized as in the chapters, it merely needs to be included in narrative form. Do not do your analysis in the case narrative; save that for the formal analysis section in Part II below.

II.   Analyze your case in the same way as your usual case analyses.

III.   All cases are due by:_____. They may be submitted any time prior to the due date. You must have the instructor's signed approval before doing this project and submit the completed "Project Approval Form" along with the case.

IV.   Your case and case analysis should be typewritten, double-spaced and follow proper report writing procedures (proper spelling, grammar, etc.). The use of headings, subheadings and summary lists are encouraged. All written work submitted by an individual implies that it is his or her own work. All assistance received or references obtained from others should be documented in accordance with good reporting practice. Papers will be graded on both content and grammar.

INSTRUCTIONS FOR RESEARCH PROJECT

I. While it is left up to you to determine the exact format of your paper, it should include at least the following information: (1) discussion of the problem, its importance and managerial implications; (2) review of literature related to the problem; (3) specific hypotheses or questions investigated; (4) brief discussion of instruments used, how developed, reliability, validity, etc.; (5) discussion of data analysis including statistical techniques, etc.; (6) report of results; and (7) discussion of results, summary and conclusions. Be sure to include a thorough discussion of the managerial implications of your results either here or in a separate section.

II. *Before* writing the report and *before* gathering your data you should formulate the specific hypotheses or key questions to be investigated. These, together with an example of appropriate supporting literature should be included on the Project Approval Form.

III. You must use appropriate statistical techniques in analyzing your data.

IV. All papers are due by _____. Papers may be submitted any time prior to the due date. You must have the instructor's signed approval before doing this project and submit the completed "Project Approval Form" along with the report.

V. Your paper should be typewritten, double-spaced, and follow proper report writing procedures (proper spelling, grammar, etc.). If in doubt about proper report writing procedures obtain a copy of one of the many guides to writing research papers. The use of headings, subheadings and summary lists is encouraged. All written work submitted by an individual implies that it is his/ her work. All assistance received or references obtained from others should be documented in accordance with good reporting practice. Papers will be graded on both content and grammar.

INSTRUCTIONS FOR JOURNAL REVIEWS PROJECT

I.   Select four trade and four scholarly journals from those indicated by your instructor:

     A.   Choose two representative articles from a different issue of each journal and briefly summarize them. If you are doing a term paper, these articles must be different from those included in that paper.

     B.   Based on these summaries and your perusal of several issues of each of these journals, summarize the general character of *each journal as you see it* (not as summarized by your instructor or the journal itself).

     C.   Based on your answer in B, describe where, when and if you might use these journals when faced with an actual problem as a manager.

II.   Your paper should be typewritten, double-spaced, and follow proper report writing procedures (proper spelling, grammar, etc.). If in doubt about proper report writing procedures obtain a copy of one of the many guides to writing research papers. The use of headings, subheadings and summary lists is encouraged. All written work submitted by an individual implies that it is his/ her work. All assistance received or references obtained from others should be documented in accordance with good reporting practice. Papers will be graded on both content and grammar.

III. The paper is due by: _____.

PERSONAL GROWTH ASSIGNMENT

The Personal Growth Assignment (PGA) is an opportunity for each individual to assess personal managerial strengths and weaknesses, and to establish a plan for continued professional growth and development. The PGA counts a total of

____% of the final course grade and is due at the beginning of the class period. Your PGA should include:

1. **Career Objectives:** A statement of your immediate post graduation employment plans. A statement of your post graduation career objectives for five and ten years in the future.

2. **Work Setting:** A description of your anticipated work settings for two time frames: (A) immediate upon graduation, and (B) five years post graduation. These descriptions should be as complete as possible including type of organization in which you expect to be employed, its location, your job description and number of subordinates. List any characteristics of this work setting which you feel may create special challenges to your managerial skills.

3. **Assessment of Managerial Strengths and Weaknesses:** A statement of personal assessment regarding strengths and weaknesses in dealing with the managerial responsibility associated with both work settings described in #2 above. Special attention should be given to anticipated challenges that stem from problems at the individual, group and organizational levels, and in acting more generally in a leadership capacity. Any insights gained through participation in class-related activities throughout the term should be highlighted. References to managerial models or theories from the scholarly literature may be used to add depth to your analysis.

4. **Professional Development Plan:** This plan should be a statement of what you intend to do in the five year period immediately post graduation in order to build upon your strengths and overcome weaknesses. Very specific activities should be detailed (e.g. continuing education, reading, training, special job assignments, personal activities, etc.). In general, you should answer the question: "What should I do to build strengths and overcome weaknesses so that my five year career objective will be achieved?" The format of your plan should be of the type indicated on the following page. Details and elaboration should be added in a supporting narrative.

Name

Professional Development Plan

(sample)

5 Year Career Objectives: To become regional sales manager for a major insurance company.

Time	Activity	Goal
Fall ????	Attend NTL workshop on group dynamics	Increase personal skills as a participant in task-oriented work groups
Jan. ????	Formal assignment as Sales Mgr.	Experience direct supervisory responsibility and test anticipated strengths and weaknesses

and so on . . .

Support and Justification:

5.   **A letter addressed to yourself assuming it will be opened in 5 years:** You choose what you want to say. Somewhere in the letter reference should be made to "checkpoints" which could be used to evaluate your career progress and professional development as a manager.

The PGA is a very *personal* assignment. There are no right or wrong answers. The assignment will be evaluated purely on the depth of your reflections and on the apparent rigor and sincerity which you apply in analyzing your managerial strengths and weaknesses. This is a chance to demonstrate that you have thought most seriously about the various learning activities included in the course. It is also a time for final one-to-one communication with your instructor. A sincere, reflective, analytical and well written PGA will receive high credit; superficial and/or inadequately written PGAs will suffer accordingly.

GROUP ASSIGNMENT HANDOUTS

- Group Formation Exercise

- Group Development Project

- Personal Reaction Paper

INSTRUCTIONS FOR THE GROUP FORMATION EXERCISE[4]

You have been assigned to a work group that requires your participation during the coming weeks. As with any new team, committee or task force, you and your group need to accomplish four things as soon as possible.

1. To become acquainted with one another as individuals.

2. To develop a shared understanding of one another's priorities or degree of commitment in regards to participation in the group.

3. To share expectations regarding what the group should be like.

4. To establish a shared sense of group purpose.

The following exercise is designed to help your group meet each of the above requirements. This exercise should be completed by the total group as soon as possible. It is strongly urged that this exercise be completed in one group meeting held in a quiet and private environment suitable for both task-oriented efforts and just plain old "having fun."

A summary of all written assignments included in the exercise is due in class on _____ .

Part 1:   Getting Acquainted

Pair off with a person whom you do not already know. Spend 5-10 minutes in conversation learning as much about the other person as possible. Jot down notes on the person's name, major, interests, special skills, work experience, and any other bits of enlightening information. Reassemble with the total group and introduce your partner to the other members.

---

[4]Prepared by John R. Schermerhorn, Jr. as an instructional exercise. Adapted, in part, from William G. Dyer, *Team Building: Issues and Alternatives*. (Reading, Mass.: Addison-Wesley, 1977), pp.76-78.

Written Assignment: Someone in the group should write a brief biographical sketch of each person in the group from notes provided by each of the interviewers.

Part II: Sharing Priorities

Use the diagram shown below to mark the point from 0 to 100 that identifies where this group stands in terms of your total work requirements and priorities. For example, you might say that the group has only a very minor priority (e.g. 10) based on your other time commitments. On the other hand, the possible learning value of the group may seem very high to you and thus deserve a score of 90.

Also write in the blank space below the diagram the total number of hours you have available to allocate to group activities in a typical week.

```
0                          50                          100
_____

  Zero                                            Highest
Priority                                          Priority
```

Number of hours available per week _____

Now share your priority and number of available work hours with the other members of the group. Each of you should explain why you made the choices you did, and discuss what they mean in terms of the group tasks ahead.

Written Assignment: Someone in the group should tabulate the results for each individual. A summary diagram showing the priority points for each group member should be prepared. Also, the frequency distribution of hours available, the total number of hours available, and the average number of hours available per person should be listed.

Part III: Sharing Expectations

Take five minutes to think about the group, its future and your place in it. Try to answer the following questions,
- What do you want as a result of participating?
- What worries you about the group?
- What do you think the group should do to insure the most positive outcomes?

Now share your answers with those of the other group members. Be sure to express yourself clearly, and to listen carefully to what others are saying. Try to make sure that everyone participates and that you learn as much about one another's views of the forthcoming group experience as possible.

Written Assignment: Someone in the group should summarize the thoughts shared during this phase of the exercise. Every comment need not be listed, but the range of ideas and general mood of the group members should be fully expressed.

Part IV: The Group Goal

Now that you have gotten acquainted and shared some personal information with one another, it is time to clarify the group's purpose. Obviously, you are part of a group because the instructor requires it. What do you think the ultimate goal of the group should be, however, as it faces its formally assigned tasks? Write your goal statement in the space below.

Goal statement:

Share your goal statement with the other group members. As a group, prepare one goal statement that everyone feels a sense of ownership in and attachment to. This goal should become a unifying force in the work ahead.

Written Assignment: Someone in the group should write down the formal statement of the group's goal.

WRITTEN SUMMARY

All written summaries should be typed and compiled in the following format for submission to the instructor.

- Cover Page: group identification and group goal
- Group Biographic Profile: names and profiles
- Member Priorities: date summaries
- Member Expectations: summary of discussion
- Any additional comments deemed appropriate

As with all written assignments, this material should be presented in a highly professional, neat, typed, error-free and grammatically precise fashion. Make sure you use the appropriate subheads and transition from one section to the next. Do not treat this as either an essay with no subheads or as a series of disjointed questions.

A Final Note

There is more to an effective work group than "work." As long as you're together, have a little "fun,' too. Chances are, it will pay off in the long run!

INSTRUCTIONS FOR THE GROUP DEVELOPMENT PROJECT[5]

Previously, your group participated in the "Group Formation Exercise" and also was involved in various class assignments. Now, it is time to assess the status of the group *as a work unit,* and to take action designed to increase both its task performance and the satisfaction of its members. The mechanism through which you can accomplish these goals is described below as the "Group Development Project."

Due Date: The final summary report on the group development project is due during the week of _____ and at a time mutually agreed upon between the group and your instructor.

PROJECT DETAILS

The group is to complete each of the development activities described below. Then, a meeting is to be scheduled with your instructor at a place of *your choosing.* During this meeting the group will communicate the results of the project activities in terms of both 1) a group assessment summary, and 2) a set of future action plans. *No written report is required.* However, *visual aids* to improve communications during the meeting will certainly be useful. A final evaluation will be made by the instructor according to:

* the apparent completeness with which the project activities were accomplished,
* the ability of the group to communicate the results of its assessment and planning efforts, and,
* the quality of the assessment and action plans.

Activity #1

Review the results of the "Group Formation Exercise." Ascertain where the group has progressed according to or different from your original expectations. Identify the implications of this analysis. Reestablish priorities, expectations, and goals where appropriate.

Activity #2

Each member of the group should complete the "Criteria of Group Maturity." Summarize these responses using appropriate descriptive statistics. Assess the meaning of the data in terms of group development. Use those results constructively.

---

[5]Prepared by John R. Schermerhorn, Jr. as an instructional exercise.

Activity #3

Prepare *two* group sociograms. One sociogram should reflect member responses to the question, "who is the most influential person in terms of group **task** concerns?" The second sociogram should reflect the question, "who is the most influential person in terms of group **maintenance** concerns?"

A sample sociogram is diagrammed below. To make a sociogram, have each member choose one or more persons in response to each question. Then draw arrows from each member *to* the persons chosen. The result is a diagram such as the following.

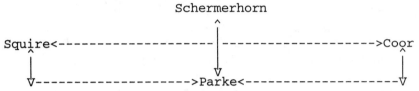

Analyze the implications of the two sociograms for group functioning. Use the sociogram information as part of your group development effort.

Activity #4

Consider your group to be an open system with two outputs -- task performance and member satisfaction. Use the following outline as an aid for analyzing how these two outputs are affected by the nature of your group's inputs and operational structure.

A. **Inputs:** In respect to inputs, focus on the impact on group performance and satisfaction caused by the nature of the tasks faced and differential traits, backgrounds, needs and values of group members.

B. **Operational Structure:** In respect to group operations, consider the impact on group performance and satisfaction caused by norms, cohesion, group maintenance and task roles, communications, decision-making and conflict. Relevant questions include:

1) What **norms** emerged in the group? How did these norms relate to the task at hand? How were they perceived by various group members? How did they influence group performance?

2) What level of **cohesiveness** was achieved in the group? What factors determined this level of cohesiveness? How did this level of cohesiveness influence group performance?

3) To what extent were **group task and maintenance roles** performed during the various phases of the group experience? Who performed these roles at various times? Why? To what degree of effectiveness? How did the ability of the group to account for these task and maintenance roles influence group performance?

4)   How would you characterize the quality and levels of **interpersonal communications** in the group? What were some of the primary barriers and/or facilitators? How did interpersonal communications influence group performance?

What **communications network or structure** was implemented by the group to accomplish its tasks? How did the communications structure influence group outcomes?

5)   How were **decisions** made in your group? Were they decisions by majority, minority, vote, or consensus? How did the various members feel about certain key decisions? Was there an identifiable pattern for your decision-making activities? How did the way the group handled decisions influence group performance?

6)   Was there **conflict** in the group? Over what? To what extent? Was conflict limited to certain individuals? Factions? How did the group handle conflict? Did it? How did conflict in the group influence (positively *or* negatively) group performance and satisfaction?

C.   **Outputs:** The group should recognize that the type of analysis detailed above requires some determination of what its actual performance to date has been. *As a group* you should consider the **productivity** question and decide where you came out. Was your productivity high or low and why?

As individuals you must also contribute to the group some measure of individual satisfaction. Are group members satisfied with what has been accomplished and with what is taking place? Why?

Analyze how these input-operations-output factors have changed for your group over time as you pass through the various stages of group development outlined in lecture.

Use the results of this activity to make constructive changes in the group's inputs and/or operational structure.

Activity #5

Each member should *write* a personal contract with the group stating what he/she will a) do more of, b) do less of, and c) continue to do in order to insure the success of the group in its remaining work during the course. These contracts should be shared, discussed, and then modified to obtain maximum relevancy.

INSTRUCTIONS FOR A PERSONAL REACTION PAPER

I.   Think about your experiences in your course work group. Prepare detailed written comments on each of the following topics.

    1.   **You as a group member.** Describe your behavior in the group and how the group did or did not help meet your needs. Discuss how the group influenced you and vice versa.

    2.   **Other group members.** (a) Assess each group member using the attached "Peer Rating" form. Briefly discuss your justification for each of these ratings. Summarize the background of each group member and the roles played by each. Discuss the positive or negative impact of each group member. (b) Complete the attached "Group Rating" form. Briefly discuss your justification for the rating. Show how this group description ties in with your discussion in (a).

    3.   **Improving group functioning.** Discuss in detail your group's evolution through the group development. Discuss things you could do as a member to make your group more effective. Do the same thing assuming you are formally appointed as the group leader.

    4.   **Other observations.** Include anything else which you feel is relevant in understanding the functioning of your group.

II. In preparing this paper make sure you integrate your personal reactions with material from the text and course. Your paper should be typewritten, doublespaced, and follow proper report writing procedures (proper spelling, grammar, etc.). If in doubt about proper report writing procedures obtain a copy of one of the many guides to writing research papers. The use of headings, subheadings, and summary lists is encouraged. All written work submitted by an individual implies that it is his/her work. All assistance received or references obtained from others should be documented in accordance with good reporting practice. Papers will be graded on both content and grammar.

III. Your paper is due by _____.

PEER RATING FORM

GROUP #_____

Rank order each of the members of your group except yourself on each of the items below (1 is best, 2 is next best, etc.).

	A	B	C	D	E	F
Quality of contribution to group discussions						
Quality of contribution to writing the assignments						
Quality of contribution to organizing assignments						
Quality of initiative when things needed to be done						
Reliability in completing assigned responsibilities						
Amount of effort put forth						
Commitment to the group						
Leadership, inspiration provided to the group						
Emphasis on task functions						
Emphasis on relationship functions						
Would want to work with again						

Group Members: A _____

B _____

C _____

D _____

E _____

F _____

GROUP RATING FORM[6]

Group # _____

Please place a check mark in the most appropriate space below for each of the nine pairs of adjectives best describing your feeling about members in your group.

Members in my group are ....

Cooperative _____:_____:_____:_____:_____:_____:_____ Uncooperative

Cordial _____:_____:_____:_____:_____:_____:_____ Noncordial

Quarrelsome _____:_____:_____:_____:_____:_____:_____ Congenial

Selfish _____:_____:_____:_____:_____:_____:_____ Unselfish

Combative _____:_____:_____:_____:_____:_____:_____ Friendly

Active _____:_____:_____:_____:_____:_____:_____ Passive

Competent _____:_____:_____:_____:_____:_____:_____ Incompetent

Wise _____:_____:_____:_____:_____:_____:_____ Foolish

Reliable _____:_____:_____:_____:_____:_____:_____ Unreliable

---

[6]This rating form is based on one originally developed by William E. Scott and Kendrith M. Roland in "The Generality and Significance of Semantic Differential Scales as Measures of Morale," *Organizational Behavior and Human Performance,* Vol. 5 (1970), pp. 576-591.

UNIT 5

Innovative Instructional Designs

In this section, three innovative instructional designs which can be used in conjunction with *Management/6E*, are described. The first approach is the "Classroom-As-Organization" pedagogy which is best suited for a relatively small class size of between 20 to 35 students. The second focuses on the other end of the spectrum in terms of class size as it involves a "Planned Fading" technique for introducing case analyses in a large lecture setting. The final approach involves using the "In Search of Excellence" video module to illustrate relevant course concepts. The specific details of each of these approaches are described in more detail below.

THE CLASSROOM-AS-ORGANIZATION MODEL

One of the most powerful pedagogies for teaching management is the "Classroom as an Organization" approach to instruction[7]. By structuring the classroom as an organization, the instructor can explicitly demonstrate a variety of aspects of organizational life such as division of labor, coordination, leadership, group processes, performance appraisal, formal and informal communication, and control. Students' understanding of course concepts is greatly enhanced since they are able to immediately apply theory to practice[8].

Applying the classroom-as-organization model to a typical management class involves setting up six to eight work groups with four to six members each. The objectives of these groups are to apply course concepts to the analysis of cases and other group exercises in order to obtain high quality solutions while ensuring human resource maintenance. The instructor serves as the chief executive officer (CEO) and is responsible for the overall functioning of the organization. In addition, each of the work groups have managers who report to the CEO on the activities and progress of the group.

Responsibilities of the CEO

The CEO has the ultimate authority and responsibility for the instruction and evaluation of class members. Much of the instruction is accomplished through the usual lectures and class exercises typical of college courses. While the use of the classroom-as-organization model encourages considerable learning within student work groups, it does require additional planning and time commitment from

---

[7]For another description of the "Classroom-As-Organization" model See A. R. Cohen, "Beyond Simulation: Treating the Classroom as an Organization," *The Organizational Behavior Teaching Journal,* 1976, *2*(1), 13-19.

[8]Portions of this discussion are excerpted from William L. Gardner's and Lars L. Larson's article entitled "Practicing Management in the Classroom: Experience *is* the Best Teacher," *The Organizational Behavior Teaching Review,* 1987-1988, *12*(3), 12-23.

the instructor. The CEO is responsible for selecting the team managers, oversee-ing the team formation process, communicating roles and responsibilities, assigning group tasks, and evaluating the performance of the various work groups by measuring the quality of group products (i.e., grading case analyses and the group development project).

Team Formation and Responsibilities

During the initial weeks of the semester, all students are required to submit an employment application to the CEO. This application identifies the student's career objective, position objective (manager versus subordinate), work experience, educational background, courses taken in management, at least three persons who can be contacted to provide references, and any other information the student considers pertinent. Students who apply for managerial positions are also required to provide the CEO with a brief summary of their managerial objectives, style, and philosophy.

Managerial Selection. The CEO examines the job applications of the students who apply for managerial positions and selects the candidates who are considered to be most qualified to be team managers. The criteria used in selecting team managers include scholastic performance, extra-curricular activities, work experience, number of business courses taken, communication skills, apparent motivation and professionalism. Importantly, managerial experience is not included as a criterion for selection since the purpose of this approach is to *provide* managerial experience. Indeed, if two candidates were equivalent in every respect expect managerial experience, we would favor the less experienced candidate. All persons who apply for managerial positions are provided with feedback on the reasons why they were or were not selected to be managers. The purpose of this feedback is to better prepare the students for securing a desired position upon graduation.

Responsibilities of Team Managers. While the chief executive is ultimately responsible for student instruction and evaluation, some authority for directing and evaluating group members is delegated by the CEO to the group managers. To increase the realism of the manager's role, managers are given the authority to select team members, assign tasks, evaluate member performance, and distribute rewards.

Member Selection. The job applications of students who either applied to be subordinate members or were not selected to be managers are assembled into job applicant packets. These packets are made available to the team managers after they are informed of their selection. The managers are provided with an opportunity to review the job applications and identify students they would like to have on their teams. Within one week after distributing the applicant packets, a managerial meeting is held to further orient the managers and provide them with an opportunity to select their team members.

The process used to hire team members can best be described as a "draft." A die is rolled, and the manager who rolls the highest number receives first pick, the manager with the second highest number receives second pick, etc. Four to five "rounds" of the draft are held until all students have been picked to serve as group members. Importantly, the CEO instructs managers *not* to tell students about the stage of the draft at which they were selected. To date, we have had no trouble keeping this information confidential.

Responsibilities of Team Members. Once selected, the members of the work teams are required to cooperate with each other and the team manager in performing assigned activities. The work group setting is designed to provide members with experience in working with a "boss" and their peers to accomplish specified goals. The contributions of each member are required to achieve "synergy," goal accomplishment, and high levels of member satisfaction. Typical member activities include reading relevant materials, completing group exercises, contributing and critiquing ideas, writing case sections, preparing audiovisual aids, making presentations, typing, proofreading, and editing. Team members are also responsible for providing written and numerical evaluations of their manager's performance to the CEO.

Managerial Meetings

Throughout the semester, four to five meetings between the CEO and the team managers are held outside of class to discuss the progress of the groups and develop strategies for improving team performance. To schedule a meeting, the instructor periodically checks with the team managers to see if a meeting would be helpful. On those occasions when a meeting is considered desirable, a mutually convenient time and location is arranged and a formal memo confirming the time and place is forwarded to the group leaders.

The managerial meetings serve to familiarize the CEO with the teams' operations and improve communications between the CEO and the team managers. During these meetings, managers often ask the CEO for clarification of an assignment or inquire about methods of motivating a low performing member. In addition, these meetings facilitate planning, provide greater control at both levels of management and serve as a formal arena for decision making activities.

Performance Appraisals

Another characteristic of our application of the classroom-as-organization model is the process employed to evaluate the performance of managers and team members. The grade assigned by the instructor for a particular group project serves as the starting point in determining individual grades for both managers and team members. The overall project grade is subsequently weighted by the manager's evaluations of the team member and the members' ratings of the manager.

Project Evaluations. For each of the two case analyses projects, the instructor assesses the degree to which the teams effectively completed the following case analysis activities: (1) statement of the problem(s), (2) analysis of possible causes, (3) solution and implementation, and (4) justification of the proposed solution. We prefer this format for case analysis because of its clarity, logic and parsimony. Other instructors, however, could effectively implement this approach to the classroom-as-organization using whatever case analysis procedure or project evaluation schema they prefer. For the group development project, the main evaluation criteria include the insights the team gains from its analysis of group processes and the quality of its presentation to the CEO.

Member Evaluations. At the conclusion of each assigned project, team managers are required to determine the percentage of the group grade their team members should receive. These evaluations are supplied to the CEO in writing at the time each project is submitted.

The individual grades of group members are calculated as follows: (Project Grade) X (Grade Assigned by the Manager). For example, suppose Steve is the manager of the "Better Solutions" group which earned an 88 on their group project. After considering that Sally attended most of the group meetings and made a number of valuable contributions to the final product, Steve decides she should receive 95% of the group grade. Sally's individual grade is thus 88 X .95 = 83.6. In contrast, in evaluating a second member named Jim, Steve notes that Jim missed two meetings and contributed far less than the other members and decides Jim should receive 80% of the group grade. Jim's individual grade would be 88 X .80 = 70.4. It is the job of the manager to communicate final individual grades on each project to the group members.

Manager Evaluations. At the conclusion of each assigned project, all team members other than the manager are required to jointly determine the percentage of the project grade the manager should receive. This evaluation is forwarded to the CEO in writing at the time a group project is submitted. The manager's grades are calculated as follows: Manager's Grade = (Project Grade) X (Grade Assigned by Team Members) + (0 to 5 Discretionary Points awarded by the CEO). This grade is communicated to the manager by the CEO.

The discretionary points represent bonus points which the CEO can use to reward team managers who excel. Managers who do an exceptional job of managing their teams and producing high quality products are typically awarded five bonus points. The bonus points could potentially increase the manager's final course grade by five percent. Managers who do an unusually poor job of managing their group, however, receive zero bonus points.

Conflict Resolution Procedures

Grievance Procedures. Students with complaints about the operations of their group, or the work of their manager or teammates have the opportunity to voice their complaint by filing a grievance. The grievance procedure is similar to that used by unionized organizations. Grieving students must first meet with the team managers and make them aware of the grievance. If a member is not satisfied with the manager's response, he/she is required to submit a 1-page written summary of the grievance to the CEO. The CEO examines the grievance and assesses its merit. If the CEO considers the grievance to be valid, a meeting between the CEO and the work team (including the team manager) is held and an equitable solution is sought. The CEO may convene a panel to hear both sides of the argument and provide additional advice.

Subordinate Termination. To enhance the realism of the manager's role we have provided group leaders with the authority to terminate members who are consistently negligent at performing their assigned duties. Member termination is used only as a last resort for dealing with a problem subordinate. Before a manager can terminate a subordinate, a formal performance appraisal must be conducted and documented. Upon firing the member, the manager is required to submit a written justification of the termination which includes the documentation from the performance appraisal. The terminated member can in turn file a grievance under the procedures outlined above. Terminated members are required to submit job applications to the managers of the remaining teams. Managers who are interested in hiring these members may choose to interview them. Students who are selected through this process become members of the hiring manager's team. Subordinate members who are not selected are required to complete the group projects on their own.

Leadership Changes. Any work group may petition the CEO for a change in leadership if the members feel such a change is necessary. A request for a change in leadership must be submitted in writing to the CEO and signed by a majority of group members. The request must include an explanation of the need for the change. Upon receiving a request for a leadership change, the CEO meets with the group as a whole and attempts to resolve the conflict. Frequently, this step is incorporated into the group development project. If it is impossible to resolve the conflict without a change in leadership, the CEO seeks a solution which is acceptable to both parties. For example, the manager may choose to resign but remain a part of the group with the group's approval. Alternatively, the manager may choose to leave the group and join another group which is willing to accept him or her as a member. By meeting with the team as a whole prior to a change in leadership, the CEO insures that the manager obtains feedback from the group and thus gains insight into potentially dysfunctional aspects of his or her leadership style. The CEO also meets separately with the disposed leader and emphasizes the lessons to be learned from this unpleasant experience.

Once the leader resigns, the group may choose to nominate a successor. The nominee must complete an application for the management position and the CEO scrutinizes this application using the same criteria employed during the initial selection process. A nominee who meets these criteria would then be formally appointed and oriented by the CEO. If the group is unable to identify an acceptable nominee, the CEO may nominate a group member or select a qualified student from another group to take over as manager.

Summary

The team management process described above represents an attempt to provide students with first hand experiences of several organizational characteristics such as work groups, manager-subordinate relations, evaluation processes, grievance procedures and organizational structures. It is believed that the students can "learn by doing" and that such learning will complement well the other types of instructional methods used in this course.

"PLANNED FADING" AS A TECHNIQUE FOR INTRODUCING CASE ANALYSIS METHODS IN LARGE-LECTURE CLASSES

There are a number specific problems which are often encountered in large lecture classes including difficulties in eliciting student participation, a lack of individual student attention in and out of the classroom, and difficulties in generating and maintaining student interest in lecture presentations. However, rather than dwelling on this negative view of the large lecture environment, a more positive perspective views large lectures as providing both a challenge and an opportunity to achieve more effective and efficient instruction through innovative techniques.

"Planned fading" is an instructional approach developed to facilitate the introduction of case analysis methods in large-lecture classes[9]. The "planned fading" of the instructor's role takes place during the semester until there is a substantial shift in responsibility for the analysis of assigned cases from the instructor to the student. The approach can be used and further developed in other large-lecture class settings covering a wide variety of subject matters. "Planned fading" was developed to provide a means through which Introduction to Management students in a large lecture setting could be initially exposed to case analysis methods. The basic premises underlying "planned fading" are: 1) students can learn from positive demonstrations, and (2) they can gradually assume increasing personal responsibility for using the knowledge and techniques so demonstrated.

Planned fading seeks to achieve vicarious student learning by first having the instructor explain a structured case analysis procedure and then completely demonstrating its application to an initial case. On subsequent case analyses, the instructor systematically delegates progressively larger amounts of responsibility for the procedure to students until a final case is reached for which they are held accountable for nearly all of the analysis. In keeping with the special demands of large-lecture class sizes, a set of multiple-choice/true-false questions is used for examination purposes on each case throughout the fading sequence. Thus, the basic elements of the planned fading approach are:

1. A structured case analysis format.
2. Planned fading of the instructor's responsibility for applying the format to actual cases.
3. Objective examination of student learning.

---

[9]Portions of this discussion are excerpted from an article by Dale Brown, John R. Schermerhorn, Jr., and William L. Gardner entitled " 'Planned Fading' as a Technique for Introducing Case Analysis Methods in Large-Lecture Classes," *The Organizational Behavior Teaching Review,* 1986-1987, *11*(4), 31-41.

Structured Case Analysis Format

To begin the planned fading process, the structured case analysis format described elsewhere in this MANUAL is presented and explained to students. This model is used because of its clarity, parsimony and logic. Instructors may implement planned fading, however, using any structured case analysis procedure of personal choice. The important thing is that the procedure allow for a clear and concise classroom presentation and demonstration of actual case analyses, even in a large lecture setting. Students need an analytical framework they can easily understand and remember as they assume increasing personal responsibility for analyzing assigned cases. The instructor needs a framework which can be initially presented and then periodically "drilled" in class through demonstrated applications to actual cases.

To illustrate an application of this model, a sample case (Tom Coronado[10]) and the corresponding analysis of this case are provided at the end of this reading.

"Planned Fading" of the Instructor's Responsibility

"Planned fading" basically means that the analysis of cases during a course proceeds on the continuum of responsibility shown in Figure 1. This continuum begins with the instructor taking full responsibility for presenting, discussing and explaining the application of the structured format to analyze an assigned case. For the initial demonstration, a case is selected which is fairly straight forward and yet illustrates a variety of relevant course concepts. Students are instructed to read the case before class, and are encouraged to come to class with thoughts and ideas on each step of the format as it applies to the case. The instructor in turn carefully prepares to jointly analyze the case with the class in a step-by-step fashion and prepare supporting visual aids.

First Case Analysis Class Session. During the actual case analysis session, the instructor assumes full responsibility for leading students through the entire case analysis. As part of this process the instructor asks leading questions and generates student participation to complete each step in the structured format. The nature of student participation varies. To inventory background facts and identify key actors, students are encouraged to spontaneously "volunteer" information while the instructor writes on an overhead transparency. Because later steps become more complicated, the large class is usually managed through a direct question-and-answer format.

For this first case the instructor's role is to clearly demonstrate a *good application* of the structured case analysis format. "Good" does not mean that the instructor's analysis is *the only* correct one for this case, but simply means that it is a strong one based upon the use of both current course concepts and the analytical format. To accomplish this successfully, the instructor must skillfully assimilate divergent student inputs into a case analysis which is

---

[10]This case appears in both the first and second editions of *Management for Productivity*.

consistent with the format, understandable, and relevant to the course. This includes serving as the final "authority" in sorting through and elaborating class suggestions to provide correct information, specify the problem(s), identify potential causes, and propose and justify viable solutions.

The first classroom demonstration of the planned fading approach sets the stage for subsequent case analyses and helps to clarify for students the shared roles between the faculty member and themselves. This session ends with the students being reminded about future case assignments, and the importance of coming to class prepared to actively follow the analysis and discussion. The instructor also reviews the planned shift in future responsibilities by explaining that students will be held accountable for a greater portion of the analysis on the next case. It is also a good idea to stress that the skills students acquire in solving the assigned cases will benefit them in other courses as well as life in general. The instructor can reinforce this by pointing out subsequent courses in the curriculum in which case analysis is likely to be a major component, as well as the fact that they will encounter problems in their future careers for which similar problem solving approaches will be critical.

Subsequent Case Analysis Class Sessions. The analysis of subsequent cases involves a progressive sharing of responsibilities between the instructor and student for the different steps in the case analysis format. This is where planned fading occurs, and it can be done over any number of cases. As Figure 1 shows, the approach can be applied to a total of three cases. In this example, in the second case the students and instructor share responsibility for the facts, problem(s), and causes steps and students are held accountable for completing the solutions and justification steps on their own. The instructor must once again thoroughly analyze the case prior to class to ensure that the steps discussed in class properly prepare students for completing the analysis. During the class period, the instructor guides the case discussion through the first three steps and then alerts students to their responsibility for the final steps. Advice and suggestions for completing the analysis are provided, as is a reminder that the coming exam will cover *all* steps of the analysis.

By the time the third and final case would be used, almost total responsibility for the complete five-step analysis is shifted to the students. The instructor assists the students in identifying the problem(s), answers clarifying questions in class, and encourages students to complete a thorough analysis of the case prior to the examination. The rationale for assisting the students in identifying the problem(s) is to ensure that everyone begins the analysis from the same perspective, since all of the subsequent steps in the structured format are tied to the problem statement. This is especially important in the large lecture setting where opportunities for "give-and-take" discussion on various problem statements are limited and testing is done in a closed-ended objective format. Students are also reminded that more than one problem statement is possible in any case, but that one has been selected (a "major problem") or two (a "major" and a "minor" problem) to focus their attention and facilitate learning within the course context. It is also important to reiterate before the class ends that students must complete the remainder of the final case analysis on their own.

Objective Examinations

A special feature of the planned fading approach as it is applied in the large-lecture setting is its use of an objective testing format. Because of large student enrollments, it is often necessary to test students in introductory management courses using computer-scored objective exams. Rather than rule out the use of cases in this setting, objective testing is both feasible and reasonable in combination with the planned fading approach just described. Accordingly, a test bank can be created by writing questions on--

1. **Each step in the structured case analysis model:** These questions should test students on their comprehension of the format itself, including the five steps, and the logic and meaning of each.

2. **The case analysis steps as applied to each assigned case:** These questions should test students on their comprehension of how the various steps in the model could specifically be applied to each assigned case.

In respect to the latter set of questions, having the five-step format as a frame of reference helps to create a more meaningful and complete set of questions for each case. For example, students can be asked to certify if certain case "facts" are true or false, or to select an appropriate "problem statement" from a list of alternatives. More analytical questions would ask them to identify potential "causes" of the problem. Sample test items for the "Tom Coronado Case" include --

In the Tom Coronado case, the increasing occurrence of payroll errors was:
    a. a major problem
    b. a minor problem
    c. a cause of the problem
    d. a symptom of the problem
    e. a justification of the problem

In the Tom Coronado case, there are at least two possible causes of the major problem. These are _____ and _____.
    a. computer system deficiencies, office procedure deficiencies.
    b. computer system deficiencies, Tom's management style.
    c. computer system deficiencies, human resource deficiencies
    d. Tom's management style, human resource deficiencies
    e. unreliability of Tom's secretary, poor quality control procedures

Naturally, objective test questions for case analysis segments which include direct instructor responsibility are chosen directly from class discussion of the case; questions on those segments falling in the zone of students' responsibility are not specifically covered in class. The instructor must exercise particular care in writing these latter questions. It is essential that the "correct" response be clear and identifiable to persons who have thoroughly analyzed the case, but not be obvious to others. Overall, this testing approach has proven to be workable and reasonable within the planned fading approach and the objectives of our course.

Sample Class Meetings

The following class meeting outlines show how the planned fading approach has been employed in one large-lecture setting. Class meeting A usually takes place in the third session of the semester; Class meeting B follows as the fourth session. The two sessions together complete the treatment of the initial assigned case. Sessions dealing with later cases are modified from these agendas.

CLASS MEETING A: During the last 25 minutes of a class session
1. Explanation of the use of cases in the business curriculum
2. Presentation of the five step CASE ANALYSIS FORMAT
3. Explanation of the PLANNED FADING APPROACH (Figure 1)
4. Assignment of Case # 1 for class meeting B. Students are asked to read the case prior to the next class and come prepared to volunteer responses to the following questions:
   a. What are the important FACTS of the case?
   b. What are the major PROBLEMS in this case?
   c. What are the possible CAUSES of these problems?

CLASS MEETING B: Using an entire class session (50 minutes)
1. Instructor quickly reviews the CASE ANALYSIS FORMAT presented in Class Meeting A;
2. Instructor provides a brief overview of the assigned case;
3. Instructor generates participation on *Step 1: Inventory of Facts* and lists suggestions from class on transparency or chalkboard;
4. Instructor discusses list, circles the key facts (adding them where necessary) and provides positive reinforcement;
5. Instructor generates student participation on *Step 2: Statement of Problem* and again lists suggestions.
6. Instructor discusses list, reviews the logic of "problem statements" as presented in Class Meeting A, and presents a good problem statement(s) for the assigned case.
7. Students are requested to share their thoughts on possible causes of the problems as defined--the instructor listens, lists suggestions, and encourages participation.
8. Instructor provides a good analysis of possible causes, and carefully explains the reasoning for selecting one or more for further attention.
9. Steps #7 and #8 are repeated to generate and select potential solutions and their justifications.
10. Instructor summarizes the case analysis, stresses the benefits of a structured approach and reminds students of their increasing responsibility as the planned fading progresses later in the course.
11. Instructor reminds students that some questions on the next examination will be taken from class Meetings A and B on the case analysis format and its application to the first case.

Benefits

Specific benefits of this approach to large lecture teaching via the case analysis method are described below.

Introduction of the Case Analysis Approach. While the level of expectation of students regarding case analyses is certainly not as rigorous in the large introductory course as it typically is in smaller, more advanced courses, planned fading provides an effective means of exposing students to cases early in their curriculum. Simply put, it allows a reasonable and substantive initial exposure to case analyses which might otherwise be forgone because of the large lecture setting. In addition, students are presented with a model analytical process which can serve them well in other courses and experiences.

A Systematic Process. Planned fading presents a structured approach to case analysis that exposes students to the benefits of systematic thinking as a component in the problem-solving process. By demonstrating and applying a logical step-by-step application of the problem solving process, planned fading of case analyses nicely complements lecture presentations on this process.

Modeling. The literature on vicarious learning suggests that modeling can be a particularly powerful means of instruction (Manz & Sims, 1981). Planned fading allows the instructor to take an active role in serving as a positive model for the case analysis process. The instructor's expertise is mobilized for student learning in an entirely appropriate and useful way. In addition, students are initially provided with the "correct" information during the learning of this process. In essence, students receive guidance regarding appropriate case analysis but retain the opportunity to "learn by doing" as the planned fading process takes place.

More Class Interaction. Discussion and interaction are important side effects of the case analysis process. Students observe that the instructor remains open to their insights into the case while providing them with the benefits of his or her expertise and guidance. In addition, knowledge of the structured case analysis format and the natural desire to express one's views helps the students overcome some of the intimidating factors of large lecture classes which too often discourage participation. The fact that class participation takes place in response to specific questions from the instructor (e.g., "What are the important facts in this case?", "What is the major problem?") helps generate and facilitate participation in the large lecture setting. Tying the questions to the specified case analysis helps students prepare ahead of time and gives them greater confidence to speak out in class. Knowing that the instructor will step in with an "expert's" view further adds to the class enthusiasm in the expectation that a true sense of closure will be gained by the time the class session ends.

Positive Reinforcement. Students have an opportunity to get immediate feedback in class discussion to their ideas and thinking. The instructor plays a legitimate role as "expert" for all case analysis steps to be covered in class at each point in the planned fading sequence. As a consequence, the instructor is able to reinforce students in class for correct analyses, advise them on incorrect or less useful ones, and encourage them to apply similar systematic thinking to subsequent cases. Of course, this requires that the instructor be thoroughly prepared for the case analysis.

Shared Responsibility and Cooperation. A high degree of communication by the instructor of class expectations and goals provides guidance to the students. In addition, students have from the onset the idea that they are expected to take responsibility for class involvement and learning the process of case analysis. Time would not allow the instructor to take full responsibility for completely "teaching" very many cases in an introductory large-lecture course. Through this approach, students are expected to take more responsibility for learning the case analysis process while at the same time they are provided with assistance and insight from the instructor.

Benefits for Later, More Advanced Courses. Later, more advanced courses which employ cases should be able to spend more time on case analysis content and less on the general process of case analysis by virtue of the learning achieved by students passing through the planned fading approach in introductory large-lecture classes. Additionally, students having positive case experiences early in their academic careers should have more confidence in their ability to systematically approach the case as a meaningful opportunity to apply concepts in later more involved case-oriented courses.

"Planned Fading" Using the Five-Step Case Analysis Format in a Large-Lecture Class Setting

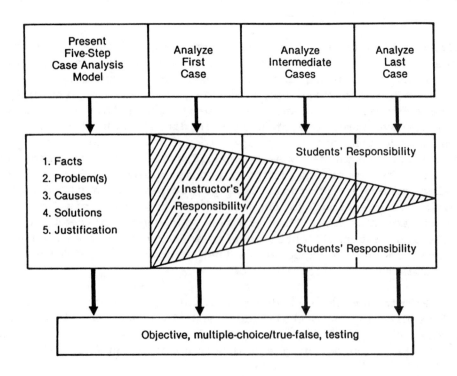

TOM CORONADO[11]

True to form, Tom Coronado - manager of employee relations for Huse Manufacturing Company - pulled into his reserved company parking space early. It was 7:30 Monday morning - usually the most hectic day of the week, with more than its share of problems. But the first good news: Friday had been payday. Now the bad news: Monday of every week turned up Friday's payroll errors. With new hires, overtime work, and different wage-rate categories, there always seemed to be mistakes in figuring wages and paychecks.

To make matters worse, in recent weeks, these errors had been on the increase. Reason: a new computerized payroll system. Long live progress, Tom thought. He was also thinking, with concern, about a 10 o'clock meeting scheduled with the executive vice-president on this very subject. Tom would have to report on how the new system was working out. Right now, though, he needed to find at least an hour of quiet to get his report together.

Fortunately, his office was quiet, and Tom was able to review a couple of computer printouts. But shortly after 8 o'clock the phone began to ring. His secretary wasn't in yet, so Tom had to take six calls personally in 20 minutes. The first five were about errors in the payroll checks; two calls were from shop supervisors, one was from a worker on the night shift, one from the production superintendent, and one from the local union president. This last one was the most sweat; the union leader's parting shot was, "When in blazes are you going to straighten out this payroll mess?" The sixth call was from Tom's secretary. She wouldn't be in today.

Over the next hour, Tom was able to correct most of the payroll errors - with a little help from his friends. These included payroll clerks, the production superintendent, a junior systems analyst, and one hourly paid worker. By 9:30, Tom thought he was ready to stick his phone in a filing cabinet and sit down with his materials for a last review before the 10 o'clock meeting. Five minutes later the phone started ringing. It was Ted Brokenshire, president of the Metropolitan Personnel Association. Would Tom be willing to give a talk at the association's next meeting?

By the time he hung up the phone, Tom realized he had talked away the rest of his prep time before the meeting. It was 9:57. Quickly, he pulled together his notes and materials and walked into the two corridors to the vice-president's office. The secretary waved him right in to a meeting that lasted two hours. But they were two hours well spent, Tom thought. The problems and the progress of putting in the new payroll system were taken apart, gone over, and put together again. And despite the recent increase in mix-ups, implementation was actually two weeks ahead of schedule.

---

[11]From Lawrence J. Gitman and Carl McDaniel, Jr., *Business World* (New York: Wiley, 1983, p. 98.

Unit 5: Innovative Instructional Designs

Tom came out of the meeting feeling good and ready to go ahead on the assignment. As he entered his office, it also occurred to him that he had a few more ingredients for that talk he had agreed to give Metro Personnel. Then his eye caught the clock: 12:20. Now for some lunch, he thought. He remembered that he hadn't had breakfast, and how he felt like having a big plate of shrimp lo mein. Then the phone rang.

Tom finally left for lunch at 2:30. As he pulled into the parking lot of the Shanghai Dynasty, he recalled that they were closed on Mondays.

SAMPLE CASE ANALYSIS: TOM CORONADO

I. **Facts of the Case:** Tom Coronado is the manager of employee relations for Huse Manufacturing Company. He has a very hectic monday. His secretary is out and he is bombarded with calls about a number of payroll errors that have arisen as a result of the implementation of a new, computerized payroll system. Although Tom wanted to have at least an hour to prepare a report on implementation for his 10:00 meeting with the vice president, he instead spent his time on the phone ironing out the payroll errors. Nevertheless, the meeting was a success.

II. **Problem Identification:** The fact that many payroll errors are occurring with increasing frequency is the *primary problem* in this case. Thus there is a deviation from the desired state of affairs (no errors) and the actual state of affairs (many errors). The fact that Tom spends a great deal of his time "firefighting" is a *secondary problem*. Specifically, the gap between the desired state of few interruptions and the actual state of many interruptions, suggests that Tom is not using his time efficiently.

III. **Causes:** The possible causes of the *primary problem* (kinks in the computerized payroll system) can be grouped into two broad categories: (a) *computer system deficiencies*, and (b) *human resource deficiencies*. Potential computer shortcomings include technical deficiencies or malfunctions (e.g., inappropriate hardware, equipment breakage) and design deficiencies (e.g., inappropriate software, collecting and inputting the wrong data). Alternatively, human resource inadequacies arising from poor selection, training or preparation of personnel could be the cause of the payroll errors. That is, the personnel who are using the system may lack the skills required to operate it, or they may be resistant to implementation. Tom needs to investigate of these possibilities and pinpoint the precise cause before he can solve the primary problem.

With regards to the *secondary problem* (inefficient use of Tom's time), a number of potential causes are apparent. These include the absence of Tom's secretary, his reluctance to delegate routine tasks, and an inability to follow through on his plans (e.g., spending an hour on his report). Thus it appears that Tom lacks time management skills.

IV. **Solution(s):** The solution to the *primary problem* depends upon which of the potential causes described above are found to be responsible for it. If the problem stems from a technical deficiency of the system, then it will be necessary to purchase new equipment or repair the existing hardware. If a poor design is to blame, it will be critical to redesign the system with the help of its users, upgrade the software, and/or change the data collection/input procedures. Similarly, if Tom concludes that human resource deficiencies have contributed to the problem, he may find it necessary to hire better qualified personnel, provide better training, and/or directly address the workers' concerns about the system.

With regards to the *secondary problem*, there are several actions which Tom should take to gain more control of his time. First, he should receive some time management training by attending a workshop or reading a book on this subject. Second, he needs to make arrangements with a temporary service so that he will have someone to fill in for his secretary when she is out. Third, he needs to delegate routine tasks to his subordinates. Finally, he needs to budget quiet time into his work routine.

V. **Justification:** The actions recommended for dealing with the *primary problem* of increasing payroll errors are appropriate because they directly address the problem causes. In order for a management information system (MIS) to function effectively, the right equipment must be configured in the right way to supply the right people with the right information at the right time. If the design, the equipment, and/or the human resources are deficient, the system will likewise be deficient in its performance. Because the recommended solution focuses on each of these areas, it should be successful in removing the causes and solving the primary problem.

The actions recommended for solving the *secondary problem* -- Tom's inefficient usage of his time -- likewise focus directly on the key causes of this problem. Time management training has helped many an executive to use his/her time more effectively. In addition, the hiring of a temporary service will ensure that Tom has a secretary to screen his calls and appointments, even when his regular secretary is out. Finally, the delegation of routine tasks and the scheduling of quiet time are tried and true time management practices that are designed to free up time for more important job responsibilities. If Tom follows these recommendations, he will be able to use his time more efficiently and effectively.

UNIT 6
Instructional Support Package

    Management 6/E is supported by a comprehensive learning package that assists the instructor in creating a motivating and enthusiastic environment. It also provides the student with additional instruments for understanding and reviewing management concepts and with the opportunity to see these concepts in practice.

* This *Instructor's Resource Guide* is a unique, comprehensive guide to building a system of customized instruction. The manual offers helpful teaching ideas, advice on course development, sample assignments, and chapter-by-chapter text highlights, learning objectives, lecture outlines, class exercises, and lecture notes. This version of the *Instructor's Resource Guide* also includes a section entitled "Use of Cases" and the "Case Method." The entire guide is also available on disk.

* A comprehensive *Test Bank* is available, consisting of 3000 multiple-choice, true-false, and essay questions categorized by pedagogical element (margin notes, margin terms, or general text knowledge), page number, and type of question (factual or applied). Each question has been subjected to educational testing standards to ensure that the test bank is both valid and reliable and written according to Bloom's taxonomy, which outlines several ways that a good exam can test knowledge. The entire test bank is also available in a computerized version, MICROTEST, for use on MS-Windows based platforms.

* *PowerPoint Slides* are available for use in class and management training programs. Full-color slides highlight key figures from the text as well as many additional lecture outlines, concepts, and diagrams. Together, these provide a versatile opportunity to add high-quality visual support to lectures.

* The comprehensive *Video Package* offers video selections from the highly respected business news program, *Nightly Business Report (NBR)*. These video clips tie directly to the theme of the management mosaic and bring to life many of the case examples used in the text as well as others from outside sources. Also available is an *Integrated Video Case on Outback Steakhouse* which corresponds to the integrated case in the text.

* A *Student Video CD-ROM*, included in each copy of the book, offers selected video cases for personal student use and study. Students will have the ability to view the video and instantly link to the interactive on-line cases on the text web site. A set of viewing questions prompts students to think critically about the issues on the case.

* The *Business Extra Program*, a partnership between Wiley and Dow Jones Company, offers an exciting new way to extend your textbook beyond the walls of the classroom. The Business Extra Program is comprised of the *On-Line Business Survival Guide* — which includes a special password for

Wiley's **Business Extra web site**, through which your students get instant access to a wealth of current articles, as well as a special offer for the *Wall Street Journal Interactive Edition*. The **On-Line Business Survival Guide** can be packaged with the text by using the set IBSN 0471-33019-1.

A **web-based course management tool** is available for on-line teaching and learning. Wiley will provide basic content based upon material accompanying the text. Instructors have the option of uploading additional material and customizing existing content to fit their needs.

UNIT 7
Use of Cases and the Case Method

The *Career Readiness Workbook* component of the text provides a variety of cases and situations in which to use them. The *Cases for Critical Thinking* section, for example, brings to life the decisions managers must make every day in these dynamic times, on both a national and global level. Sometimes these choices are wise; other times they have proved to be erroneous. The case studies describe both the benefits and consequences of managers' decisions. Each case concludes with a list of questions for the student to answer concerning the in-depth scenarios they are given. Interactive versions of each case are available on-line through the *Management 6/E web site*. These on-line cases will be updated regularly and new cases posted to enrich the alternatives for classroom use.

The *Cases for Critical Thinking* can be assigned as outside learning responsibility, and then in-class discussion can be done through individual student input. In some instances where cases are particularly complex or controversial, it is helpful to form small groups of four to five students in class, let them discuss and debate what they believe to be the problems and appropriate solutions; and then hold open forum to see what the groups decided, why, and how they arrived at the decision or solution.

Since there are more cases in the text than would normally be assigned students in a single term, you might also initiate case discussions in class without the written responsibility.

The *Integrative Video Case on Outback Steakhouse* further allows for various parts of the management process to be examined in the context of a real situation and a highly competitive environment. The case can be used in whole or in parts to best fit the instructor's course design.

Why are cases a valuable method? Managers must work effectively both in terms of being individual, self-sufficient problem solvers and decision-makers and in terms of being effective team members and participatory problem solvers. The use of case problems can contribute to students' development of both self-sufficient skills as well as the interpersonal skills that they will need if they are to be effective managers. When requiring students to write solutions on their own and present them in a class discussion, you should evaluate them in terms of specific criteria. Barach[12] suggests that seven performance objectives for the case-method be used by professors in assessing the ability students demonstrate via the cases in the application of course content.

---

[12]Jeffrey A. Barach, "Performance Criteria Used in the Evaluation of Case Course," *Collegiate News and Views*.

Performance Objective I

The student must be able to make the required decisions in the case. This means in a big-issue business, society, and the individual case, that the immediate applied decision required in the case must be attended to. A long philosophical discussion which passes the buck on the concrete situation shows the student incapable of applying his long, philosophical discussion. That's bad. In a marketing and management context, a beautiful theoretical discussion which does not provide concrete recommendations as called for, is also bad. In both cases the performance objective stressed throughout the course is that the student be able to make concrete decisions and to apply what he knows to the concrete situation. A passion for passing the buck in favor of discussing profundities is inadequate performance.

Performance Objective II

The student must demonstrate the ability to think logically, clearly, and self-consistently. In the support of his recommendations and his analysis, his conclusions should follow from his assumptions, his reasoning should be self-consistent. This statement is not dependent on subject matter, but the definition of what is consistent, what is logical, is subject-matter dependent. A student must show a knowledge of what are appropriate facts, assumptions, realities, and the determination of this is subject-matter dependent.

Performance Objective III

The student must be able to present his analysis in a cogent and convincing manner.

Performance Objective IV

The student must have common sense defined as the capacity to see the obvious and the relevant. A student should be capable of recognizing and putting appropriate weight on the fundamental issues and factors relevant to the case. This objective is so crucial, that it has been said that the total impact of the Harvard Business School education can be summed up as teaching one to apply his common sense in an administrative context.

Performance Objective V

The student must demonstrate his willingness and ability to apply analytical muscle and quantitative analysis where relevant. A coherent, self-consistent, basically relevant argument which ignores the fundamental tools of managerial problem analysis is deficient. If a company is losing money, and this can be perceived from ratio analyses, or profit-and-loss and balance about information, a student should be able to do this. If a company owns ten acres of downtown Dallas, which is evaluated on a balance sheet at a trifling figure because it was acquired when Dallas was only a cow town, a student should know that the real estate represents a major financial resource for the corporation. Albeit, many exams' require no more than slide-rule technology and common sense, nonetheless, that's a performance objective.

Performance Objective VI

The student should be capable of transcending the concrete situation adding perspective, and demonstrating competence. This is more a criterion for an "A" paper, and more applicable in some courses than in others. Many cases are springboards to broader discussions. In some situations, the ability to jump from that springboard to an intelligent discussion of the broader context represented by the situation at hand may be relevant.

Performance Objective VII

A student should be able to make use of available data to form a fairly detailed and well-argued analysis of situations requested for analysis. While this is similar to some of the objectives above, it is different in the sense that simply making a decision and arguing for it without filling in the concrete details, the many little decisions which make the main decision meaningful, does not represent a fully successful case analysis. There is a quality of follow-through required.

There may be many more appropriate performance objectives for case analyses, but these are seven salient ones. In the strictest sense, they are objectives in terms of written and/or oral performance on a specific instance, given a case simulation. They are not guarantees that the student can and will be able to perform in the real world. Thus, performance objectives are map reading and writing objectives necessarily.

CASE PROBLEM TEACHING TOOLS

Case Grading

There are different ways of grading cases ranging from an overall global assessment to a breakdown into components. Two such breakdowns are shown in the grading sheets that follow. They use categories and weightings similar to those indicated in our case analysis handout. You can get even more specific by adding subcomponents under each category.

Note that the first grade sheet divides each area into a weighted portion of 100 points. The second grade sheet divides the grading scale as follows:

A+	A	A-	B+	B	B-	C+	C	C-	D+	D	D-	F+	F	F-
97	93	90	87	83	80	77	73	70	67	63	60	57	53	50

Attach a letter grade to each section. These should then be translated into the percentages above and averaged to provide a total grade. They can be differentially weighted, if desired. The above scale should be useful anytime you need to translate letter grades into percentages.

The second grade sheet also asks the students to make two ratings at the time the case is turned in. These can then be compared with the instructor's rating and are useful in helping students take personal responsibility for their completed cases.

CASE GRADE AND FEEDBACK FORM

Name _____ Case _____

Group No. _____

GRADING AREAS	MAXIMUM	OBTAINED POINTS
	POINTS	
1. SUMMARY OF FACTS	5	_____
2. STATEMENT OF THE PROBLEM	10	_____
3. CAUSES (# & Clarity)	20	_____
4. ALTERNATIVE SOLUTIONS (# & Clarity)	20	_____
5. BEST SOLUTION, ITS IMPLEMENTATION & JUSTIFICATION	25	_____
6. CITATION OF THEORIES/CONCEPTS	15	_____
7. WRITING: GRAMMAR, SPELLING, CLARITY	5	_____
TOTAL	100	_____

NOTE: The above grade is for the group case. Individual Members' grades will be given later.

GENERAL FEEDBACK ON THE CASE ANALYSIS

GRADE SHEET FOR WRITTEN CASE ANALYSIS

Name _____ Case _____ Group No. _____

                                              Grade (A+ to F-)
                                              My Rating   Inst. Rating

1. Adequacy of statement and causes of the problem(s)   _____   _____

   _____

   _____

2. Adequacy of alternative solutions to problem(s)   _____   _____

   _____

   _____

3. Adequacy of alternative chosen and justification   _____   _____

   _____

   _____

4. Adequacy of implementation of chosen alternative   _____   _____
   and statement of assumptions used here and in 3.

   _____

   _____

5. Incorporation of course material in analysis   _____   _____

6. Style grammar, spelling, typing errors, etc.   _____   _____

   _____

   _____

7. Overall, how willing would I be to turn this report in to my boss if this
   were a "real world" assignment?

Extremely Likely	Quite Likely	Slightly Likely	Slightly Unlikely	Quite Unlikely	Extremely Unlikely
____	____	____	____	____	____

	A+	A	A-	B+	B	B-	C+	C	C-	D+	D	D-	F	F	F-
Points	97	93	90	87	83	80	77	73	70	67	63	60	57	53	50

General comments on the back.   Average (points/6) _____

66

FORMAT FOR WRITTEN CASE ANALYSIS[13]

Objectives

The purposes of a written analysis of a case situation are to:

1. Test your ability to view a management situation in terms of the concepts we have studied.
2. Test your ability to apply the knowledge you have acquired to a specific concrete situation.
3. Test your ability to present your ideas and opinions in a well thought out, readable form.
4. Test your ability to identify managerial approaches that are most appropriate for given organizational situations and (for problem-oriented cases, as indicated below).

Please keep these objectives in mind while preparing your analysis of the assigned cases.

Format

Many organizations specify a format for reports, memos, etc. Your written analysis of the cases should include the parts indicated below. The format will vary depending upon whether the case is a problem-oriented one or an analytical one. The problem-oriented one involves more steps and is listed first.

Problem-Oriented Approach

The approach is reflected in the following example concerning a boss and subordinate.

Boss:	Becomes concerned about the crucial facts in an incident which occurred in his/her department *(Summary of facts)*. Discusses these with subordinate to determine the problem.
Subordinate:	Boss I think the problem is ... *(Statement of the problem)*.
Boss:	What leads you to think that's the problem?
Subordinate:	*(Causes of the problem)*.
Boss:	*What* are some different things we could do and what are some strong and weak points of each?
Subordinate:	(Possible Solutions).
Boss:	Which solution do you recommend?
Subordinate:	(Recommended Solution).

---

[13]This is a modification of a handout originally prepared by Lars L. Larson, Southern Illinois University at Carbondale combined with ideas on the Analytical Approach" developed by R.D. Willits, University of New Hampshire and discussed in "One Man's Model for Case Analysis, pp. 113-114 in Cohen, et al., *Teacher's Manual for Use with Effective Behavior in Organizations.*

Boss:	*How* should we go about carrying out the solution?
Subordinate:	(Implementation portion of the solution).
Boss:	*Why* do you think that will work?
Subordinate:	*(Justification).*

I.   Summary of the Facts

This section should present a brief listing of the key facts with page numbers from the case in ( ), where appropriate. It should not exceed *two* pages. Therefore, there is little room for a long-winded presentation of each fact. Important *assumptions* should also be listed here and labeled as such.

II.   Statement of the Problem

This section should present a brief treatment of the major problem or problems. It should include a *concise* statement of the major problem or problems you see in the case. This part of your analysis should not exceed one-half page in length and may be shorter. Remember, the more problems you identify, the more solutions are likely to be necessary or the more complex a given solution is likely to be.   Thus, you will want to be careful about identifying too many problems.

Some questions to ask when formulating your definition of the problem are:

1.   Have I identified the basic problem(s) or am I dealing with the symptoms?
2.   If I have identified more than one problem, are they separate or related?
3.   Am I putting myself in the manager's shoes and looking toward future actions?

III. Causes of the Problem

This section should provide a detailed analysis of the causes of the problem(s) you identified in Section II. A major objective is to illustrate clearly how you are using course concepts to better understand the causes of the problem.   Show that you are *applying course material!!!*   An example of application is: According to Maslow's hierarchy of needs, a satisfied need does not motivate an individual. Sam's need for security is apparently satisfied as is evidenced by his comments to Dale when he says ... Therefore, the current attempts to motivate Sam are not directed at the right needs level. Again, where appropriate, it is useful to include in () a page number or other reference.

Some questions to ask when writing your causes of the problem section are:

1. Have I applied the appropriate course material?

2. Do the causes I have identified relate to the problem(s) stated in Section II?

3. When I draw conclusions or make assumptions do I *support* these conclusions or assumptions with a sentence from the case or a quote or paraphrase from the readings or an example from class?

IV. Possible Solutions

This section should indicate a number of possible solutions. Each solution should also have listed the pros and cons (strong and weak points) which relate to it.

V. Solution and Its Implementation

This section should outline your recommended solution to the problem(s). The solution will be one or a combination of the ones listed in IV above. It should be specific stating *what* should be done, by *whom*, and in *what sequence*. In short, it will include not only *what* should be done but *how* it should be done.

Some questions and concerns to keep in mind when writing your solution and implementation section are:

1. Have I indicated an awareness of the problem of implementation (the how aspect)?
2. Have I been too general? For example, a general solution might state: "The manager needs to realize that he/she should match his/her style to the situation." A specific solution would indicate *what* style is most appropriate for the situation and *how* you will attempt to have the manager "realize" the appropriate style. Note the emphasis on *how* as well as *what*.
3. Does my solution and implementation address the problems and *causes* identified in the previous sections? Does my solution take into account the pros and cons listed earlier?

VI. Justification

This section of your analysis should, using course concepts, tell why your solution and implementation will work. A major objective of this section is to show clearly how you are applying course concepts to arrive at a workable solution and implementation to the problem you have identified. Please stress the *application of course concepts!* Thus, course concepts are crucially important here as well as in Section III.

Some questions to ask when writing your justification section are:

1. Have I applied the appropriate course material?

2. Do I support my conclusions with appropriately referenced facts, quotes, explanations from the case, readings and class activities?

3. Does my justification recognize the pros and cons listed earlier?

Analytical Approach

Some cases aren't really problem-oriented and thus they do not call for a solution. Rather, they call for an emphasis on analytical skills. The following steps are important.

1. *What are the Facts in the Case?*

2. *What can be Inferred from the Facts?*

    This section should focus on the inferences to be drawn from the facts, such as:

    a. People's attitudes, values, etc.
    b. Relative power and influence
    c. Relationships among individuals and groups
    d. Job requirements (e.g. high finger dexterity, etc.)
    e. Key success criteria (e.g., delivery more important than cost, quality more important than quantity, etc.)
    f. Other important inferences

These inferences should reflect your knowledge of theories of management and other relevant areas. They form the basis for hypotheses or educated conjectures about linkages among key variables. Managers typically make decisions and take action on the basis of inferences.

An alternative to Section II is to analyze what is happening and why. This is particularly useful in terms of human behavior.

III. What General Ideas Can be Drawn from this Case?

Among the things a case may suggest are: (1) an illustration of a model or theoretical concept; (2) limitations of a model or concept; (3) crucial questions that need further consideration; or (4) propositions or hypotheses that may be useful in the future. Be specific concerning the above things and make sure you *tie in course concepts* with appropriate references.

Grades

Evaluation of performance is always a potential conflict area. The Boss (instructor) has certain standards of performance and it is not always possible to convey these standards in an unambiguous way to Subordinates (students). The differential weighting of grades for the assigned cases is in part a recognition of the fact that standards are articulated through a feedback process. The following is a first attempt to outline instructor expectations.

1. The group analysis of case assignments will represent your own group's effort. Individual analysis will represent your own individual effort.

2. The analysis will follow the format outlined in this handout and will be typed (double spaced). Correct spelling and grammar are expected and errors in these will be penalized.

3. The case will be handed in on time. Cases are due at the *beginning of the class period* on the date assigned. Late cases will be penalized.

Major weight in grading your problem-oriented case assignments is given to *Section III*, causes of the problem, *Section V*, solution and implementation, and *Section VI* justification. A major objective of the assignment is to test your ability to apply course concepts to the situation presented in the case. Grading of these sections is based on:

1. Your ability to correctly use *appropriate course concepts*. Do you use the appropriate concepts? Do you apply the concepts correctly?
2. Do you support your conclusions?
3. Is your solution workable? Do you recognize the steps necessary to implement your solution and the likely trouble spots?

Secondary emphasis is placed on the statement of the problems section. Do you identify the obvious problems? Do you recognize the "not so obvious problem"?

Major weight in grading your analytical case assignments is given to *Section II* (what can be inferred? or what is happening?) and *Section III* (what general ideas can be drawn from the case?).

For both problem-oriented and analytical case assignments, use clearly labelled headings and subheadings in your paper, together with appropriate transitional material as you move from one section to another.

In Conclusion

Perhaps the biggest single thing to be on guard against is mistaking a *restatement of the case* for the kind of problem-solving and analytical requirements set forth above. *Do not* simply write a "he did this and they did that" paper. A paper which never *analyzes* why people behave as they do, nor suggests what might be done, nor applies concepts from the book or class, nor draws any general lessons, etc. will not receive a good grade!

GOOD LUCK!

Unit 8
TEXT HIGHLIGHTS AND TEACHING SUGGESTIONS

This section of the *MANUAL* offers a guide for each part of the book and for each chapter in the parts. There is a brief outline and overview for each part. Within each part, the highlights and teaching suggestions are offered for each chapter. This consists of the following:

* Study questions.
* Chapter learning objectives.
* Chapter overview.
* A chapter lecture outline which describes the teaching objective of the chapter, indicates the suggested time for presenting it, identifies supporting materials from the text supplements and *Management 6/E web site*, and lists major chapter headings.
* A detailed set of chapter lecture notes which include numerous lecture enhancements.
* Chapter Summary.
* Definitions for Key Terms.

CHAPTER 1: THE DYNAMIC NEW WORKPLACE

CHAPTER 1 STUDY QUESTIONS

o   What are organizations like in the new workplace?
o   Who are managers and what do they do?
o   What is the management process?
o   What are the challenges of working in the 21st century?

CHAPTER 1 LEARNING OBJECTIVES

After completing this chapter, students should be able to:

1.   Define organization and explain how organizations operate as open systems.
2.   Define productivity and explain the relationships between productivity, performance effectiveness, and performance efficiency.
3.   Discuss the changing nature of organizations, and explain the concepts of total quality management (TQM), virtual organizations, cross-functional teams, and self-managing teams.
4.   Define the terms manager and management, and discuss the manager's role in the dynamic new workplace.
5.   Describe the different levels and types of managers and discuss the activities and responsibilities associated with each.
6.   Define accountability and explain how and why managers are held accountable for performance, quality of work life, and valuing diversity.
7.   Discuss the changing nature of managerial work, and explain how emerging concepts such as the "upside-down pyramid" reflect these changes.
8.   Describe the management process and explain the interrelationships among the four functions of management.
9.   Identify and describe key managerial activities and roles.
10.   Discuss the importance of managerial agendas and networks.
11.   Identify and describe key managerial skills and competencies and explain how they vary across management levels.
12.   Explain the managerial implications of important environmental trends, including the global economy, heightened expectations for managerial ethics and social responsibility, workforce diversity, changing employment values and human rights, rapid information and technological change, and the increased emphasis placed on careers and career portfolios.

CHAPTER 1 OVERVIEW

The world of work is undergoing dynamic and challenging changes that provide great opportunities along with tremendous uncertainty, as the *Headline* opener on *Fast Company* magazine titled, **Smart People Create Their Own Future,** indicates. Today, individual and organizational success must be forged within workplaces that are constantly reinventing themselves. Themes such as "empowerment", "involvement", "participation", "self-management", and "teamwork" are common, as people manage careers described as "flexible" and "entrepreneurial." To excel in such settings, organizations must deliver in terms of operating efficiency, product quality, technology utilization, and customer satisfaction as they make a positive contribution to society.

Management is a pervasive element of modern life and key to organizational performance. Organizations need managers to guide the activities of their members toward goal accomplishment. The chapter begins by describing the changing nature of organizations, and the roles that managers play in meeting the challenges of the modern workplace. The terms manager and management are defined, and the responsibilities of different levels and types of managers are discussed. The notion of accountability, and the fact that managers are held accountable for not only performance, but the quality of work life and valuing diversity, is considered. Further insights into the manager's job are provided through a discussion of managerial work, the four functions of management -- planning, organizing, leading and controlling -- and the nature of managerial activities, roles, agendas, networks, skills and competencies.

The chapter concludes with a discussion of the many challenges facing organizations and managers as we enter the 21st century. These include the global economy, heightened expectations for managerial ethics and social responsibility, workforce diversity, changing employment values and human rights, rapid information and technological change, and the increased emphasis placed on careers and career portfolios. Finally, the pedagogical framework for learning provided by **Management/6E** is described.

CHAPTER 1 LECTURE OUTLINE

Teaching Objective: To increase awareness of how a dynamic and changing environment affects organizations, managers, and the management process in the new workplace.

Suggested Time: Two to three hours of class time is recommended to present this chapter. Attempts to cover the material in less time are discouraged since this introductory chapter serves as a foundation for subsequent topics.

Organizations and the New Workplace
> What is an Organization?
> Organizations as Systems
> Productivity and Organizational Performance
> Changing Nature of Organizations

Managers and the New Workplace
> Types of Managers
> Accountability and Managerial Performance
> Changing Nature of Managerial Work

The Management Process
> Functions of Management
> Managerial Activities and Roles
> Managerial Agendas and Networks
> Managerial Skills and Competencies

The Challenges Ahead: Working in the 21st Century
> A Global Economy
> Ethics and Social Responsibility
> Workforce Diversity
> Employment Values and Human Rights
> Information and Technological Change
> Careers and Career Portfolios

Management/6E: A Framework for Learning

CHAPTER 1 SUPPORTING MATERIALS

Textbook Inserts

Headline: Smart People Create Their Own Future
Margin Photos: Whole Foods Market, Solectron Corporation, Hudson Institute, Reebok, Ritz-Carlton
Embedded Boxes: Whirlpool, Ohio University
Manager's Notepad 1.1: Nine Responsibilities of Team Leaders and Supervisors
Manager's Notepad 1.2: Personal Competencies for Managerial Success

Multi-Media Resources

NBR Video Report:
    Coca-Cola (Available on Videotape Supplement & Video Cases CD-ROM)

PowerPoint Presentations (Website):
    Figures 1.1 to 1.6 from the Textbook plus Supplemental Figures
    NBR Video Viewing Questions: Coca-Cola & Kodak

In-Class Activities

Cases for Critical Thinking (Career Readiness Workbook & Website):
    The Coca-Cola Company (Primary Case)
    Kodak (Alternate Case)

Exercises:
    First-day Icebreaker — My Best Manager (Career Readiness Workbook)
    What Managers Do (Career Readiness Workbook)

Assessments:
    A 21st Century Manager (Career Readiness Workbook & Website)

Research and Presentation Projects:
    What Do Managers Really Do? (Website)

Self-Test 1 (Textbook and Website)

CHAPTER 1 LECTURE NOTES

ENHANCEMENT

To supplement the *Headline* opener on *Fast Company* magazine titled, **Smart People Create Their Own Future,** consider visiting the website for this company; the link is provided from the ***Management 6/E website***. Together, the opener and website emphasize the dynamic and challenging changes that are occurring in the world of work today, and the great opportunities -- and tremendous uncertainty -- that such changes create for individuals seeking career and organizational success.

I.   **Organizations and the New Workplace**

    A.   *What is an Organization?*

        1.   An **organization** is a collection of people working together in a division of labor to achieve a common purpose.

        2.   The **purpose** of any organization is to produce goods and/or services to satisfy the needs of customers.

    B.   *Organizations as Systems*   **FIGURE 1.1**

        1.   A **system** is a collection of interrelated parts that function together to achieve a common purpose.

        2.   As **Figure 1.1** illustrates, an **open system** interacts with its environment; a **closed system** does not.

        3.   Because the **environment** provides organizations with **resources** and **feedback**, it has a significant impact on their operations.

    C.   *Productivity and Organizational Performance*   **FIGURE 1.2**

        1.   As open systems, the notion of **value-added** is very important to organizations. If operations add value, then (1) a business organization can earn a profit (sell a product for more than it costs to make it), or (2) a nonprofit organization can add wealth to society (provide a public service that is worth more than it costs).

        2.   **Productivity** is a summary measure of the quantity and quality of work performance with resource utilization taken into account.

        3.   **Performance Effectiveness** is a measure of task output or goal accomplishment.

4. **Performance Efficiency** is a measure of the resource cost associated with goal accomplishment -- that is, outputs realized compared to inputs consumed.

5. Use **Figure 1.2** to illustrate various combinations of performance effectiveness and efficiency.

D. *Changing Nature of Organizations*

1. **Total quality management (TQM)** involves managing with an organization-wide commitment to continuous improvement and meeting customer needs completely.

2. **Virtual organizations** operate with the support of extensive computer networks, and, in so doing, are able to work across vast geographic distances with a minimum number of full-time workers.

3. **Cross-functional task forces** bring people together from different parts of an organization to share problem-solving expertise and coordinate operations.

4. The continuing emphasis on participation is evidenced by **job enrichment** programs for individuals and **autonomous work groups** or **self-managing work teams** for groups of workers.

II. **Managers and the New Workplace**

A. *What is a Manager?*

1. A **manager** is someone in an organization who is responsible for the work performance of one or more other persons.

2. These other people, usually called *direct reports*, *team members*, or *subordinates*, are the important and essential **human resources** of organizations.

ENHANCEMENT

To illustrate the pervasiveness of management, ask students to raise their hands for each of the following questions if the answer is yes.

1. Are you a manager right now? (Record the names of these students and note their place in the room.)
2. Have you ever been a manager? (Depending on the size of your class, you may wish to record the names of these students as well.)
3. Have your parents ever been managers?
4. Do you have friends that are managers?
5. Do you know a manager?

ENHANCEMENT (Continued)

Now ask everyone who answered yes to any of the above questions to raise their hand. Almost everyone in the class will have their hand raised. Make the point that this illustrates the pervasiveness of management. Also point out that management is something they experience in their own lives; it is thus very tangible and highly relevant.

The *Exercise* titled **My Best Manager** which is included in **Career Readiness Workbook** represents an alternative "ice-breaking" exercise which can be used to get students thinking about managers and management.

> B.   *What is Management?*
>
>> 1.   **Management** is formally defined as planning, organizing, leading, and controlling the use of resources to accomplish performance goals.

ENHANCEMENT

Ask the students identified during the preceding exercise as having managerial experience, to describe the type of managerial job they had and the nature of the organization they worked in. Then, use the students' examples to distinguish between the levels and types of managers listed below.

> C.   *Levels and Types of Management*
>
>> 1.   **Levels of Management**
>>
>>> a.   **Top managers** ensure that major performance objectives are established and accomplished in accord with the organization's purpose. **Examples:** CEO, president, vice-president, senior managers, executives.
>>>
>>> b.   **Middle managers** report to top managers while they themselves are in charge of relatively large departments or divisions consisting of several smaller work units. **Examples:** clinic directors, college deans, division managers.
>>>
>>> c.   **First-line managers** ensure that their work teams or units meet performance objectives that are consistent with the plans of middle and top management. **Example:** A first job in management typically occurs as an assignment as **team leader** or **supervisor** — someone in charge of a smaller work unit composed of nonmanagerial workers.

ENHANCEMENT

Students who were identified in the opening exercise as having first line managerial experience can be asked about their jobs. After this discussion, the following list of **Nine Responsibilities of a Team Leaders and Supervisors** from **Manager's Notepad 1.1** can be reviewed.

1. Plan meetings and work schedules.
2. Clarify goals and tasks and gather ideas for improvement.
3. Appraise performance and counsel team members.
4. Recommend pay raises and new assignments.
5. Inform team members about organizational goals and expectations.
6. Inform higher levels of work unit needs and accomplishments.
7. Recruit, train, and develop team members to meet performance standards.
8. Encourage and maintain enthusiasm for job performance and teamwork.
9. Coordinate with other teams and support their work efforts.

2. **Types of Managers**

   a. **Line managers** are responsible for activities which contribute directly to providing the product or service.

   b. **Staff managers** use their special technical expertise to support the efforts of line personnel.

   c. **Functional managers** have responsibility for a single area of activity.

   d. **General managers** are responsible for complex subunits that include many functional areas of activity.

   e. **Administrators** are managers of public and nonprofit organizations.

D. *Accountability and Managerial Performance*

   1. **Accountability**

      a. **Accountability** is the requirement of one person to answer back to another and show results achieved for assigned duties.

      b. Every manager's daily challenge is to fulfill this **performance accountability** for a team or work unit while depending on the accomplishments of others to make this performance possible.

81

c. **Effective managers** utilize organizational resources to achieve *both* high levels of task performance *and* high levels of personal satisfaction among people doing the required work.

2. **Quality of Work Life**

a. The term **quality of work life (QWL)** is frequently used as an indicator of the overall quality of human experiences in the workplace.

b. A **high quality of work life** is one that offers the individual such things as:

  * Adequate and fair pay for a job well done.
  * Safe and healthy working conditions.
  * Opportunity to learn and use new skills.
  * Room to grow and progress in a career.
  * Protection of individual rights.
  * Pride in the work itself and the organization.

3. **Valuing Diversity**

a. **Workforce diversity** is a term used to describe demographic differences -- principally in respect to age, gender, race, national origin, and physical characteristics -- among members of the workforce.

b. **"Cultural bias"** is still a limiting factor in too many settings. It can take the form of:

  * <u>Prejudice</u> -- negative, irrational attitudes towards members of minority groups; and

  * <u>Discrimination</u> - when prejudice results in actual disadvantage to minorities by denying them full benefits of organizational membership.

c. The **glass ceiling effect** refers to an invisible barrier that may prevent women, blacks, and minority workers from rising above a certain level of organizational responsibility.

d. **Example:** Less than 3% of top executives in large firms at the time of this writing are women; less than 2% are from a racial minority; and, only one black heads a *Fortune 1,000* company.

E.   *Changing Nature of Managerial Work*   **FIGURE 1.3**

1.   **Figure 1.3** illustrates the **"upside-down pyramid,"** which reflects a new way of looking at organizations where the operating workers are at the top of the pyramid, and supported by the activities and efforts of managers at the bottom.

2.   Each individual is a **value-added worker**, i.e., someone who must do something that creates eventual value for the organization's customer or client.

3.   The **job of managers is to support these workers' efforts** to add value to the good or service.

4.   Because of these **trends in management**, the best managers are often known for "coaching," "helping," and "supporting" rather than "directing" and "order-giving"; moreover, the title manager is being replaced on some organizational charts with terms such as "coordinator," "coach," and "team leader."

III. **The Management Process**

A.   *Four Functions of Management*   **FIGURE 1.4**

1.   **Planning** - The process of setting objectives and determining what should be done to accomplish them.

2.   **Organizing** - The process of assigning tasks, allocating resources, and arranging activities to implement plans.

3.   **Leading** - The process of arousing enthusiasm and directing human resource efforts toward organizational goals.

4.   **Controlling** - The process of measuring performance and taking corrective action to ensure desired results.

B.   *Managerial Activities and Roles*

ENHANCEMENT

The *Website Followup Assignment* titled **What Do Managers Really Do?** can be used very effectively to further illustrate the nature of managerial work. In this project, students interview managers to obtain estimates of how managers spend their time, and the types of activities, roles, agendas, networks, and skills that they use. After summarizing the managers' responses to the students' interviews, share with them the results of research into managerial work that are included in the *Instructor's Notes* for the **What Managers Do** exercise in Unit 9 of this *Manual*. Discuss with students the extent to which these results are consistent with their own conclusions.

1.   **Managerial Roles**   **FIGURE 1.5**

   a.   <u>Interpersonal roles</u> (figurehead, leader, liaison): These
        roles all involve interactions with others.

   b.   <u>Informational   roles</u>   (monitor,   disseminator,
        spokesperson): These roles involve giving, receiving and
        analyzing information.

   c.   <u>Decisional roles</u> (entrepreneur, disturbance handler,
        resource allocator, negotiator): These roles involve
        making decisions to solve problems and/or take advantage
        of opportunities.

2.   Henry Mintzberg is a management researcher who identified the
     following characteristics of managerial work.

   a.   <u>Managers work long hours</u> - 50-90 per week;

   b.   <u>Managers work at an intense pace</u> - hundreds of separate
        incidents per day;

   c.   <u>Managers work at fragmented and varied tasks</u> - they
        experience frequent interruptions and engage in a wide
        variety of activities;

   d.   <u>Managers work with many communication media</u> including
        face-to-face conversations, telephone calls, written
        memos, electronic mail, etc.;

   e.   <u>Managers work largely through interpersonal
        relationships</u> - About 80% of time spent interacting with
        others.

C.   *Managerial Agendas and Networks*

1.   **Agenda setting** involves managers' efforts to develop action
     priorities for their jobs that include goals and plans
     spanning long and short time frames.

2.   **Networking** is the process of building and maintaining positive
     relationships with people whose cooperation may be needed to
     implement one's work agendas.

D.   *Managerial Skills and Competencies*   **FIGURE 1.6**

1.   A **skill** is an ability to translate knowledge into action that
     results in desired performance.

2. A **technical skill** is the ability to apply a special proficiency or expertise to perform particular tasks.

3. A **human skill** is the ability to work well in cooperation with other persons.

4. A **conceptual skill** is the ability to think analytically and solve complex problems.

5. Use **Figure 1.6** to show that as one moves up the managerial hierarchy, technical skills decrease in importance and conceptual skills increase; the importance of human skills remains constant.

6. **Directions in Managerial Competencies**

    a) A <u>managerial competency</u> is a skill or personal characteristic that contributes to high performance in a management job.

ENHANCEMENT

One way to introduce your discussion of managerial competencies to the class is to have students first complete the *Assessment* entitled **A 21st Century Manager?** which is included in the *Career Readiness Portfolio*. For students who are willing to share their scores, you can have an open discussion regarding their standings on, and the importance of, the managerial skills and competencies this assessment measures. **Manager's Notepad 1.2** provides a summary of the competencies examined through *Assessment*. Further discussions of these assessments are included in Unit 9 of this *Manual*.

    b) **Manager's Notepad 1.2** summarizes the following <u>Personal Competencies for Managerial Success</u>

    *   *Leadership:* Ability to influence others to perform tasks.

    *   *Self-objectivity:* Ability to evaluate one's self realistically.

    *   *Analytic thinking:* Ability to interpret and explain patterns in information.

    *   *Behavioral flexibility:* Ability to modify personal behavior to reach a goal.

* *Oral presentations:* Ability to express ideas clearly in oral presentations.

* *Written communication:* Ability to express one's ideas clearly in writing.

* *Personal impact:* Ability to create a good impression and instill confidence.

* *Resistance to stress:* Ability to perform under stressful conditions.

* *Tolerance for uncertainty:* Ability to perform in ambiguous situations.

IV.   The Challenges of Ahead: Working in the 21st Century

A.   *A Global Economy*

1.   We are fast becoming a **borderless world** of intense business and economic competition for global markets.

2.   Competition and the global economy are changing business, industry, and national economic strategies.

B.   *Ethics and Social Responsibility*

1.   Modern society is growing very strict in expecting its social institutions to be **socially responsible**, i.e., to conduct their affairs according to high moral standards.

2.   Managers of these institutions are likewise expected to set high standards of **managerial ethics**.

ENHANCEMENT

Since examples of both socially responsible and irresponsible corporate behavior are increasingly in the news, you may want to conduct a brainstorming session with students to identify recent examples of each. The textbook points to alternatives to the "longbox" packaging for CDs and the efforts of fast-food franchises to eliminate waste as examples of socially responsible behavior. The Exxon Valdez oil spill and the controversy of Dow Corning's silicone breast implants provide examples of less desirable corporate conduct. Students will typically have little trouble thinking of many other examples.

C.   *Workforce Diversity*

   1.   **Changing demographics** are making the workforce increasingly diverse with respect to differences in people with respect to gender, age, race and ethnicity, and able-bodiedness.

   2.   **Trends in workforce diversity** identified by the *Hudson Institute's Workforce 2000* report include:
        a.   The size of the workforce is growing more slowly.
        b.   The available pool of younger workers is shrinking.
        c.   The average age of workers is rising.
        d.   More women are entering the workforce.
        e.   The proportion of ethnic minorities in the workforce is increasing.
        f.   The proportion of immigrants in the workforce is increasing.

   3.   The *Hudson Institute's Workforce 2020* report warns of a continuing loss of low-skill high-wage jobs and a shortage of workers for high-skill jobs.

   4.   *Workforce 2020* calls for major changes in public education systems, employer human resource systems, and government policies to meet such challenges.

D.   *Employment Values and Human Rights*

   1.   **Forces affecting supervisor-subordinate relationships** include:

        a.   Pressures for equal employment opportunity.
        b.   Pressures for equity of compensation and benefits.
        c.   Pressures for participation and employee involvement.
        d.   Pressures for privacy and due process.
        e.   Pressures for freedom from sexual harassment.
        f.   Pressures for job security and occupational health and safety.

E.   *Information and Technological Change*

   1.   The Internet, World Wide Web, notebook computers, supercomputers, computer-assisted design (CAD) and production, expert systems, group-decision software, facsimile (fax) mail, and related developments, are all part of our **"information-intensive" workplace** and work lives.

   2.   Futurist *Alvin Toffler* foresees a world complicated by power differences based not only economic development, but also over access to information technology.

3. This is the age of the **"knowledge worker"** — someone whose mind is a critical asset; computer literacy is a knowledge component to be mastered as a foundation for career success.

F. *Careers and Career Portfolios*

1. Charles Handy identifies an **organizational shamrock** with three leaves to describe the career orientations of today's employees.

    a. <u>Full-time employees</u> pursue career paths with a traditional character; with success and the maintenance of critical skills, these core employees can advance with the organization and remain employed for a long time.

    b. <u>Contract workers</u> perform specific tasks as needed by the organization and are compensated on a contract or fee-for-service basis rather than a continuing wage or salary.

    c. <u>Part-time workers</u> are hired only as needed and for only the number of hours needed.

2. Today's careers require a **"portfolio of skills"** that are continually developed and well communicated to potential employers.

ENHANCEMENT

Emphasize to students that the textbook and *website* provide a *Career Readiness Workbook* which includes a **Career Advancement Portfolio** designed to help them develop their managerial skills and competencies. Encourage them to take this resource seriously and use it to full advantage to better prepare themselves for the career challenges they will face in the dynamic new workplace.

V. **Management/6e: A Framework for Learning**

A. The text is divided into six parts to provide a *framework for learning:*

    1. Part 1: Management Today
    2. Part 2: Context
    3. Part 3: Mission
    4. Part 4: Organization
    5. Part 5: Leadership
    6. Part 6: Career Readiness Workbook

CHAPTER 1 SUMMARY

What are organizations like in the new workplace?

* Organizations are collections of people working together to achieve a common purpose.
* As open systems, organizations interact with their environments in the process of transforming resource inputs into product outputs.
* Productivity is a measure of the quantity and quality of work performance, with resource utilization taken into account.
* Organizations should achieve both performance effectiveness, in terms of goal accomplishment, and performance efficiency, in terms of resource utilization.
* The best organizations today include a focus on total quality management (TQM) among their productivity and performance objectives.
* In today's dynamic environment organizations are adopting new forms and practices to meet the challenges of new technology, intense competition, and demanding customers.

Who are managers and what do they do?

* Managers facilitate work accomplishments by people in organizations.
* Top managers concentrate on long-term concerns; middle managers help coordinate activities across the organization; team leaders and supervisors focus on group or work-unit objectives.
* Functional managers work in one business area, such as marketing or finance; general managers are responsible for multiple functions; administrators are managers in non-profit organizations.
* The manager's challenge is to fulfill a performance accountability while being dependent upon team members or subordinates to do the required work.
* Managers must respect the quality of work life (QWL) and value diversity in supporting the work efforts and experiences of others.
* The focus of managerial work is increasingly on "coaching" and "supporting" others rather than simply "directing" and "order-giving."

What is the management process?

* The management process consists of the four functions of planning, organizing, leading, and controlling.
* Managerial work is intense and stressful and places a great emphasis on the ability to perform well in interpersonal, informational, and decision-making roles.
* Effective managers create and maintain interpersonal networks that facilitate the accomplishment of task agendas.
* Managers must develop and maintain essential technical, human, and conceptual skills to succeed in a dynamic environment.

What are the challenges ahead?

* Today's turbulent environment challenges managers and organizations in complex and demanding ways.
* Competition and the global economy are changing business, industry, and national economic strategies.
* Strong values demand ethical behavior and social responsibility within, and by, organizations.
* Demographics are making the workforce increasingly diverse with respect to differences among people in gender, age, race and ethnicity, and able-bodiedness.
* Pressures on employment relationships call for the protection of individual rights to privacy, due process, and freedom from sexual harassment, among other rights.
* Information and technological change are modifying organizations as computers and related information technologies exert their influence on the workplace.
* Careers today require "portfolios" of skills that are continually developed and well communicated to potential employers.

CHAPTER 1 KEY TERMS

Accountability The requirement for a subordinate to show results of assigned duties to a supervisor.

Administrators Managers who work in public or nonprofit organizations as opposed to business concerns.

Conceptual skill The ability to think analytically and solve complex problems.

Controlling The process of measuring performance and taking corrective action to ensure desired results.

Discrimination An active form of prejudice that disadvantages people by denying them full benefits of organizational membership.

Functional managers Managers who are responsible for one area of activity such as finance, marketing, production, personnel, accounting, or sales.

General managers Managers who are responsible for a complex organizational unit that includes many areas of functional activity.

Glass ceiling effect An invisible barrier that limits the advancement of women and minorities to higher level responsibilities in organizations.

Human resources The people, individuals, and groups that help organizations produce goods or services.

Human skill The ability to work well in cooperation with other persons.

Leading The process of arousing enthusiasm and directing human resource efforts toward organizational goals.

Line managers Managers who have direct responsibility for activities making direct contributions to the production of the organization's basic goods or services.

Management The process of planning, organizing, leading, and controlling the use of resources to accomplish performance goals.

Manager Persons in an organizations who are responsible for the work performance of one or more other persons.

Middle managers Managers who report to top-level management, oversee the work of several units, and implement plans consistent with higher-level objectives.

Open system A system that transforms resource inputs from the environment into product outputs.

Organization A collection of people working together in a division of labor to achieve a common purpose.

Organizing The process of assigning tasks, allocating resources, and arranging coordinated activities to implement plans.

Performance effectiveness An output measure of a task or goal accomplishment.

Performance efficiency A measure of the resource cost associated with goal accomplishment.

Planning The process of setting objectives and determining what should be done to accomplish them.

Prejudice The holding of negative, irrational attitudes toward individuals because of their group identity.

Productivity A summary measure of the quantity and quality of work performance, with resource utilization taken into account.

Quality of working life (QWL) The overall quality of human experiences in the workplace.

Skill The ability to translate knowledge into action that results in the desired performance.

Staff managers Managers who use special technical expertise to advise and support the efforts of line workers.

Supervisor Someone in charge of a smaller work unit composed of nonmanagerial workers.

Team leader Someone in charge of a team of nonmanagerial workers.

Technical skill The ability to use a special proficiency or expertise in one's work.

Top managers The highest level managers who work to ensure that major plans and objectives are set and accomplished in accord with the organization's purpose.

Total quality management (TQM) An organization-wide commitment to continuous work improvement, product quality, and meeting customer needs completely.

Workforce diversity A term used to describe demographic differences (age, gender, race and ethnicity, and able-bodiness) among members of the workforce.

CHAPTER 2: ENVIRONMENT AND COMPETITIVE ADVANTAGE

CHAPTER 2 STUDY QUESTIONS

o   What is the environment of organizations?
o   What is a customer-driven organization?
o   What is the quality commitment in operations?
o   Why is organizational culture important?
o   What are current directions in organizational cultures?

CHAPTER 2 LEARNING OBJECTIVES

After completing this chapter, students should be able to:

1.   Define competitive advantage and explain its importance to effective management.
2.   Distinguish between the general and specific environments within which organizations operate, and identify and discuss key elements of each.
3.   Define environmental uncertainty, identify its underlying dimensions, and explain its implications for management.
4.   Discuss the notion of the customer-driven organization, explain how customer service can be an important source of competitive advantage.
5.   Explain the distinction between external and internal customers, and the importance of both to an organization's quest for customer service and quality outcomes.
6.   Define operations management (OM) and explain how it can enhance quality and competitive advantage.
7.   Define total quality management (TQM) discuss ISO 9000 certification, and identify the criteria for total quality commitment as specified by the Malcolm Baldridge National Quality Awards.
8.   Discuss Crosby's four absolutes of management for total quality control.
9.   Describe Deming's approach to quality control, and discuss the 14 points in Deming's path to quality.
10.   Define the concept of continuous improvement and the utility of quality circles, benchmarking, and cycle times in achieving such improvements.
11.   Define organizational culture and corporate culture and explain what "strong" cultures can do.
12.   Describe the ingredients of organizational culture, including the observable and core cultures, as well as the role of leadership in establishing and maintaining organizational culture.
13.   Define the term multi-cultural organization, and identify its characteristics.
14.   Define subculture and describe common subcultures found in organizations.
15.   Explain how an organization's ethical culture impacts the expectations and behavior of its members.

CHAPTER 2 OVERVIEW

With the year 2000 upon us, the old ways of management aren't good enough anymore. The best of the past must be combined with new thinking to lead organizations of tomorrow to real "competitive advantage" -- having a unique product or process that makes it hard for competitors to duplicate organizational performance in the marketplace. This chapter examines how organizations, such as the **Customer Foot's** eastcoast stores described in the *Headline* opener titled, ***Make Technology Work for You,*** manage quality and competitive advantage to address the challenges of the 21st century head on.

The chapter begins by defining competitive advantage and considering the relevance of the external environment for organizational efforts to secure it. Next, both "general" and "specific" aspects of the external environment that influence, and pose special challenges, for modern organizations are examined. The role that environmental uncertainty plays in challenging managers and their organizations to be flexible and responsive to new and changing conditions is also considered.

The customer-driven organization is described as one that recognizes customer service and product quality as foundations of competitive advantage. Customer service is identified as a core ingredient of total quality operations, which includes concerns for both external and internal customers. Operations management is noted to be the branch of management concerned with the physical production of goods and services; it is increasingly viewed from a strategic perspective and with close attention to the demands for productivity, quality, and competitive advantage. Specific manifestations of the quality commitment in operations are examined next, including total quality management (TQM), Crosby's four absolutes of management for total quality control, the 14 points in Deming's path to quality, continuous improvement, and quality circles.

At this point, the focus of the chapter shifts to organizational culture. This section begins by defining organizational culture as the system of shared beliefs and values that develops within an organization and guides the behavior of its members. A discussion of what "strong" cultures can do follows. The ingredients and leadership of organizational culture are then described, including specific elements of the observable and core culture. Finally, emerging directions in organizational cultures, such as worker empowerment, subcultures, multi-cultural organizations, and ethics, are considered.

CHAPTER 2 LECTURE OUTLINE

Teaching Objective: To familiarize students with the environmental challenges they will face in managing for quality and competitive advantage in the 21st century. The key components of an organization's culture, and emerging trends in this area, are also examined.

Suggested Time: Two hours of class time is recommended to present the material in this chapter. Depending on your objectives, however, the chapter can be presented in as little as one hour or as much as three hours.

External Environments of Organizations
>   What is Competitive Advantage?
>   The General Environment
>   The Specific Environment
>   Environmental Uncertainty

Customer-Driven Organizations
>   What do Customers Want?
>   Internal and External Customers
>   Customers and Operations Management

Commitment to Quality Operations
>   Total Quality Management
>   Deming's Path to Quality
>   Quality and Continuous Improvement
>   Quality and Technology Utilization
>   Quality and Product Design

The Nature of Organizational Culture
>   What Strong Cultures Can Do
>   Levels of Organizational Culture
>   Leadership and Organizational Culture

Directions in Organizational Culture
>   Culture and Empowerment
>   Multicultural Organizations
>   Organizational Subcultures
>   Ethical Cultures

CHAPTER 2 SUPPORTING MATERIALS

Textbook Inserts

Headline: Make Technology Work for You
Margin Photos: Speedway Motor Sports, Hewlett-Packard, Jaguar, Nordstrom,
     Service Performance Corporation, Stride Rite
Embedded Boxes: Vermont Teddy Bear Company, Tennant Company, Bell Atlantic,
     Patagonia
Manager's Notepad 2.1: Deming's 14 Points to Quality

Multi-Media Resources

NBR Video Report: Saturn (Available on Videotape Supplement & Video Cases CD-ROM)

PowerPoint Presentations (Website):
     Figures 2.1 to 2.5 from the Textbook plus Supplemental Figures
     NBR Viewing Questions: Saturn & Tom's of Maine

In-Class Activities

Cases for Critical Thinking (Career Readiness Workbook & Website):
     Saturn (Primary Case)
     Tom's of Maine (Alternate Case)

Exercises:
     Defining Quality (Career Readiness Workbook)
     Why Do Customers Leave (Website Quick Hitter)
     Classroom Culture Graphs (Website Exercise)

Assessments:
     Which Organizational Culture Fits You? (Career Readiness Workbook)

Research and Presentation Projects:
     Corporate Culture — Can it be Changed? (Career Readiness Workbook)

Self-Test 2 (Textbook and Website)

CHAPTER 2 LECTURE NOTES

I.   **External Environments of Organizations**

   A.   *What is Competitive Advantage?*

      1.   **Competitive advantage** involves the utilization of a *core competency* that clearly sets an organization apart from competitors and gives it an advantage over them in a marketplace.

   B.   *The General Environment*

      1.   The **general environment** consists of all the background conditions in the external environment of an organization.

      2.   The **components of the general environment** include:

         a)   <u>Economic conditions</u> --- general state of the economy in terms of inflation, income levels, gross domestic product, unemployment, and related indicators of economic health.

         b)   <u>Sociocultural conditions</u> --- general state of prevailing social values on such matters as human rights and environment, trends in education and related social institutions, as well as demographic patterns.

         c)   <u>Legal-political conditions</u> --- general state of the prevailing philosophy and objectives of the political party or parties running the government, as well as laws and government regulations.

         d)   <u>Technological conditions</u> --- general state of the development and availability of technology in the environment, including scientific advancements.

         e)   <u>Natural environment conditions</u> --- general state of nature and conditions of the natural or physical environment, including levels of environmentalism.

   C.   *The Specific Environment*   **FIGURE 2.1**

      1.   The **specific environment** (or *task environment*) consists of all the actual organizations, groups, and persons with whom an organization must interact in order to survive and prosper.

      2.   The specific environment is often described in terms of **stakeholders** — the persons, groups, and institutions who are affected by the organization's performance.

3.   Important **elements in an organization's specific environment**, as depicted in **Figure 2.1**, include:

    a)   <u>Customers</u> --- specific consumer or client groups, individuals and organizations, that purchase the organization's goods and/or use its services.

    b)   <u>Suppliers</u> --- specific providers of the human, information, and financial resources and raw materials needed by the organization to operate.

    c)   <u>Competitors</u> --- specific organizations that offer the same or similar goods and services to the same consumer or client groups.

    d)   <u>Regulators</u> --- specific government agencies and representatives, at the local-state-national levels, that enforce laws and regulations affecting the organization's operations.

D.   *Environmental Uncertainty*   **FIGURE 2.2**

1.   **Environmental uncertainty** means that there is a lack of complete information regarding what developments will occur in the external environment; this makes it difficult to predict future states of affairs and to understand their potential implications for the organization.

2.   **Figure 2.2** describes environmental uncertainty along two dimensions:

    a)   <u>Complexity</u>, or the number of different factors in the environment, and

    b)   the <u>rate of change</u> in these factors

3.   In general, the **greater the environmental uncertainty**:

    a)   the more <u>attention</u> management must direct to the external environment, and

    b)   the more need there is for <u>flexible</u> and <u>adaptible</u> organizational designs and work practices.

II.   Customer-Driven Organizations

A.   *What Do Customers Want?*

1.   **Customers sit at the top** when the organization is viewed as an upside-down pyramid.

2.   Customer service can be an important source of **competitive advantage.**

You can use the *Website Quick Hitter* titled, ***Why Do Customers Leave?***, to solicit student input on what customers want, and don't want, from organizations.

B.   *Internal and External Customers*   **FIGURE 2.3**

1.   **External customers** are the final customers or clients who buy the organization's products.

2.   **Internal customers** are the persons/groups in the organization who "use" or otherwise depend on the results of another person or group in order to do their jobs well.

3.   **Figure 2.3** illustrates the **importance of both "external" and "internal" customers in an organization's workflows.**

4.   **Example:** At Hewlett-Packard, a new quality control system was designed to make sure things are done right at every step in production. Each person in the workflow works directly with their "suppliers" and "customers" to make sure everyone has the quality materials they need to pass a quality product on to the next work station. This provides accountability for results to one's co-workers, not just supervisors.

C.   *Customers and Operations Management*

1.   **Operations management (OM)** is a branch of management theory specifically concerned with the activities and decisions through which organizations transform resource inputs into product outputs.

2.   The **transformation process** is the actual set of operations or activities through which various resources are utilized to produce finished goods or services of value to customers or clients.

3.   Today, OM is increasingly viewed in a **strategic** perspective, and with close attention to the demands of productivity, quality, and competitive advantage.

4.   **Figure 2.4** illustrates a **customer-driven view of operations.**

III. Commitment to Quality Operations

A. *ISO 9000 Certification* indicates that a company meets the quality standards set by the International Standards Organization in Geneva, Switzerland, which have been adopted by many countries of the world. Increasingly, the ISO 9000 "stamp of approval" is viewed as a necessity in international business.

B. *Total Quality Management*

   1. **Total quality management (TQM)** involves the process of making quality principles part of the organization's strategic objectives, applying them to all aspects of operations, committing to continuous improvement, and striving to meet customers' needs by doing things right the first time.

   2. TQM is often associated with the work of the quality pioneers *W. Edwards Deming* and *Joseph Juran*, whose ideas have been popular in Japan since the early 1950s.

ENHANCEMENT

To get students to more thoroughly consider the meaning of quality, assign the *Exercise*, **Defining Quality** from the *Career Readiness Workbook*. In addition, the *Research Project*, **The Best of Total Quality Management** from the same portfolio can be assigned to deepen student knowledge of TQM. Additional discussion of this assignment is included in this Manual in Unit 9.

---

   3. An organization's success in achieving productivity *with* quality can be evaluated using the following **Quality Essentials for the Malcolm Baldridge National Quality Award:**

      a) Top executives incorporate quality values into day-to-day management.
      b) The organization works with suppliers to improve the quality of their goods and/or services.
      c) The organization trains workers in quality techniques and has systems to ensure products are of high quality.
      d) The organization's products are as good or better than those of its competitors.
      e) The organization meets customers' needs and wants, and gets customer satisfaction ratings equal to or better than those of competitors.
      f) The organization's quality system yields concrete results, such as increased market share and lower product-cycle times.

ENHANCEMENT

To introduce your presentation on **competitive advantage through quality**, include a discussion of **USAA** here. Technology and people serve as the keys to the "customer service comes first" approach at USAA, an insurance and investment firm for military officers and their dependents. Computer programmers at USAA are kept busy developing innovative software. One of the programs developed with IBM sorts documents, arranges them in order of importance, and assigns them to an employee qualified to process them. Employees can access assignments electronically rather than remove papers from an in-basket. Another program is designed for policy representatives who deal with customers by telephone. Each rep's computer terminal is set up so that the rep can call up any customer's compete record as soon as customers identify themselves. Equipped with this information, reps can often settle matters on the first call. Robert McDermott, USAA's CEO, believes that such technology can improve customer service and increase customer satisfaction. McDermott must be doing something right -- under his leadership close to 99 percent of USAA policy holders renew their policies annually. In addition, in a *Consumer Reports* opinion poll ranking 51 car insurers, customers gave the company second-place honors for quick and fair claims settlement.

(Source: Ronald Henkoff, "Make Your Office More Productive," *Fortune,* February 25, 1991, pp. 72-84.)

4.   **Crosby's "Four Absolutes" of Management for Total Quality Control**

 a)   <u>Quality means conformance to standards</u> -- Workers must know exactly what performance standards they are expected to meet.

 b)   <u>Quality comes from defect prevention, not defect correction</u> -- Proper leadership, training, and discipline must prevent defects in the first place.

 c)   <u>Quality as a performance standard must mean defect-free work</u> -- The only acceptable quality standard is perfect work.

 d)   <u>Quality saves money</u> -- Doing things right the first time saves the cost of correcting poor work.

5.   **Example:** At Tenant Company, top management realized the firm's survival was threatened by the poor quality of the motorized sweepers being shipped to Japan, and impending competition from Toyota. Consultant Philip Crosby pointed out that the product had to be made right the first time. Managers and workers met in small groups to brainstorm how to improve quality. They changed the shape of the assembly line, rerouted parts deliveries, and revised production procedures. They were also taught statistical quality control techniques to monitor defects and set goals for reducing their frequency.

C. *Deming's Path to Quality*

1. What began in 1951 as a visit to Japan by *W. Edwards Deming* to share **quality-control techniques** developed in the U.S., became a life-long relationship epitomized by the **"Deming" prize for quality control.**

2. The **precepts of Deming's method** are:
    a) Tally defects.
    b) Analyze and trace them to the source.
    c) Make corrections.
    d) Keep a record of what happens afterwards.

3. **Deming's basic proposition** is that the cause of a quality problem may be some component of the production/operations process, like an employee or a machine, or it may be internal to the production/operations system itself.

4. **Deming's 14 Points to Quality**   **MANAGERS' NOTEPAD 2.1**
    1) Create a consistency of purpose in the organization to innovate, put resources into research and education, and put resources into maintaining equipment and new production aids.
    2) Learn a new philosophy of quality to improve every system.
    3) Require statistical evidence of process control and eliminate financial goals and quotas.
    4) Require statistical evidence of control in purchasing parts; this will mean dealing with fewer suppliers.
    5) Use statistical methods to isolate the sources of trouble.
    6) Institute modern on the job training.
    7) Improve supervision to develop inspired leaders.
    8) Drive out fear and instill learning.
    9) Break down barriers between departments.
    10) Eliminate numerical goals and slogans.
    11) Constantly revamp work methods.
    12) Institute massive training for employees in statistical methods.
    13) Retrain people in new skills.
    14) Create a structure that will push, every day, on the above 13 points.

5. **Implications:** If it is caused by an employee, that person should be retrained or replaced. If the cause lies within the system, blaming an employee only causes frustration. Instead the system must be analyzed and constructively changed.

ENHANCEMENT

As an example of Deming's approach, you can discuss the solution obtained by Genesco, a middle-sized hosiery plant, following a study which traced many defects to the "looping" department where toes were closed. Inspectors found that a few workers produced most of the defects. So, a worker responsible for 20% of the defects was persuaded to take early retirement. Others did fine once they got new glasses. Another improved her work once she realized management cared. In seven months, the plant cut its rejects from 11,500 to 2,000 out of weekly output of 120,000. Productivity climbed 4% virtually cost-free.

(Source: Jeremy Main, "Under the Spell of Quality Gurus" *Fortune,* August 18, 1986, pp. 30-34).

D.   *Quality and Continuous Improvement*

    1.   **Continuous improvement** is the attempt to maintain the quality advantage over time by always looking for new ways to incrementally improve upon current performance.

    2.   A **quality circle** is a group of workers (usually no more than 10) who meet regularly to discuss ways of improving the quality of their products or services by applying every member's full creative potential.

    3.   **Benchmarking** involves identifying other "high performance" organizations or subunits and then systematically comparing them to one's own ways of doing things.

    4.   Total quality operations also focus on **cycle times** -- the elapsed time between receipt of an order and delivery of the finished product; the objective is to find ways to quickly develop new products, reduce costs, raise quality, and increase customer loyalty.

E.   *Quality and Technology Utilization*

    1.   **Lean production** whereby new technologies and streamlined systems allow work to be performed with fewer workers and smaller inventories.

    2.   **Flexible manufacturing** wherein manufacturing processes can be changed quickly and efficiently to produce different products or modifications of existing ones; production efficiencies are maintained while the special needs of customers -- such as a small order -- are being met.

    3.   **Agile manufacturing** and the advent of **mass customization** where individualized products are made quickly and with the production efficiencies once only associated with mass production of uniform products.

4. **Computer-based technologies** are used in modern production systems to better integrate the various aspects of manufacturing as well as allow modifications to be made quickly and in a cost-efficient fashion.

F. *Quality and Product Design*

1. **Product design** is a very timely and important strategic issue in operations management.

2. A **"good" design** is one that has eye appeal to the customer *and* is easy to manufacture.

3. **Example:** At David Kelley Design, a Palo Alto based consulting firm, customers are corporations who want ideas on how to get new products to work both in the marketplace and the factory. Kelley and his team try to satisfy production concerns while retaining the designer's original concept. When working with the "mouse" for Apple computers, they reduced the number of parts in the prototype to make manufacturing easier.

4. A **robust design**, as pioneered by the Japanese consultant Genichi Taguchi, is a design that is "production proof" and can withstand manufacturing fluctuations that might otherwise cause defects.

5. **Example:** If a kiln is producing warped tiles because of humidity or temperature variations, Taguchi would try to adjust ingredients in the clay before spending large amounts to upgrade equipment.

6. Progressive manufacturers now emphasize **design for manufacturing** in their quests for competitive advantage; this means that products are styled to lower production costs and smooth the way toward high-quality results in all aspects of the manufacturing process.

7. **Design for disassembly** involves the design of products with attention to how their components will be used when product life ends.

IV. The Nature of Organizational Culture

A. *Organizational culture* or *corporate culture* is the system of shared beliefs and values that develops within an organization and guides the behavior of its members.

B.   *What Strong Cultures Can Do*

1.   **Strong cultures** have a clear and positive influence on the behavior of organizational members.

2.   A strong culture **commits and reinforces members** to do things for and with one another that are in the best interests of **organizational objectives**.

ENHANCEMENT

A discussion of the *Margin Photo* on **Bell Atlantic** can be included here to provide students with an example of a strong corporate culture. Bell Atlantic grew out of the old, highly regulated Bell System. CEO Raymond Smith and his predecessor began to establish a new culture by involving over 1400 managers in a series of "design seminars" to think through the corporate values. Eventually, the following core values were identified: integrity, respect and trust, excellence, individual fulfillment, and profitable growth. Smith then spent a year working with 50 top managers to examine their obligations to the corporation. Next, quality was made a corporate imperative in the strategic plan, and a quality improvement program was begun. Now the Bell Atlantic Way is clearly identified in employees' minds as "an organized, participative method of working together that allows us to get the most out of our own efforts and maximize our contribution to team goals."

C.   *Levels of Organizational Culture*   **FIGURE 2.5**

1.   **Observable culture** is what one sees and hears when walking around an organization as a visitor, customer, or employee.

2.   **Elements of the Observable Culture in Organizations**

a)   Stories: Oral histories and tales, told and retold among members, about dramatic sagas and incidents in the life of the organization.

b)   Heroes: The people singled out for special attention, and whose accomplishments are recognized with praise and admiration among members.

c)   Rites and rituals: The ceremonies and meetings, planned and spontaneous, that celebrate important occasions and performance accomplishments.

d)   Symbols: The special use of language and other non-verbal expressions to communicate important themes of organizational life.

105

3. The **core culture** consists of the *core values* or underlying beliefs that influence behavior and actually give rise to the aspects of observable culture.

4. **Values** are essential to strong culture organizations, and are often widely publicized in formal statements of corporate mission and purpose.

5. **Example**: IBM's founder, Tom Watson, Sr., based the firm's corporate culture on three fundamental values: respect for the individual, customer service, and excellence.

D. *Leadership and Organizational Culture*

1. **Leadership of the core culture** involves establishing and maintaining appropriate values.

2. This responsibility exists at the level of the **entire organization**, as well as for any manager in his or her **work unit**.

3. **Criteria for Evaluating Core Values**

    a) Relevance: The core values support key organizational objectives.

    b) Pervasiveness: The core values are known by organization members.

    c) Strength: The core values are accepted by organization members.

4. **Symbolic managers** use symbols well to establish and maintain a desired organizational culture.

5. Symbolic managers use **language metaphors** -- positive examples from another context -- to reinforce and communicate a desired culture.

6. **Example**: The culture of Disney, Inc. is still strongly influenced by Walt Disney and his initial business of movies. The core mission of the firm remains "making people happy." New employees are counseled by managers to think of themselves as key "members of the cast" who work "on stage."

7. Good symbolic managers tell key **stories** -- such as the **founding story**, or stories about **heroes** -- over and over, and encourage others to tell them.

8. **Rites and rituals** are also used to glorify the performance of the organization and its members.

9. **Example:** Mary Kay Cosmetics relies heavily on rites and rituals. The Gala events where top sales performers share their success stories are legendary; so too are the incentive awards, such as pink luxury cars.

ENHANCEMENT

To personalize your discussion of corporate culture, assign the *Assessment* from *Career Readiness Workbook*, titled **Which Organizational Culture Fits You?** Based on their responses, students may indicate that they would prefer to work in one of the following four different corporate cultures: (a) "a baseball team," (b) "a club," (c) "a fortress," or (d) "an academy." By completing this assignment, students can obtain personal insights regarding the type of culture they prefer, which should in turn enable them to better understand the chapter material on corporate culture. To provide additional insight into corporate cultures and various means whereby management can shape this culture, assign the *Research and Presentation Project* titled, **Corporate Culture -- Can It be Changed?** For additional discussion of these assignments, see Unit 9 of this *Manual*.

V. **Directions in Organizational Cultures**

A. *Culture and Empowerment*

1. Managers are finding that the best way to seek the advantages of a strong culture is with an underlying commitment to employee **participation**, **involvement**, and **empowerment.**

2. **Example:** Pepsico's CEO, D. Wayne Calloway's message to the firm's 300,000 employees is, "Act like an owner, not a hired hand." He wants every employee to feel empowered to make decisions, take actions, and create opportunities.

B. *Multicultural Organizations*

1. **Multiculturalism** involves pluralism and respect for diversity in the workplace.

2. **Characteristics of a Multicultural Organization**

    a) <u>Pluralism</u>: Members of both minority cultures and majority cultures are influential in setting key values and policies.

    b) <u>Structural integration</u>: Minority culture members are well-represented in jobs at all levels and in all functional responsibilities.

107

c) <u>Informal network integration</u>: Various forms of mentoring and support groups assist in the career development of minority culture members.

d) <u>Absence of prejudice and discrimination</u>: A variety of training and task force activities continually address the need to eliminate culture group bias.

e) <u>Minimum intergroup conflict</u>: Diversity does not lead to destructive conflicts between members of majority cultures and minority cultures.

C. *Organizational Subcultures*

1. Organizations contain **subcultures**, which are the cultures common to groups of people with similar values and beliefs based upon shared personal characteristics.

2. **Common Subcultures Found in Organizations**

    a) Occupational subcultures.
    b) Functional subcultures.
    c) Ethnic and racial subcultures.
    d) Generational subcultures.
    e) Gender subcultures.

3. **Occupational Subcultures**

    a) <u>Occupational subcultures</u> have "salaried professionals" such as lawyers, scientists, engineers, accountants.

    b) These professionals have <u>needs for work autonomy</u> which may conflict with traditional top-down management practices.

    c) Managers must recognize and respond appropriately to these needs, or these professionals may be difficult to integrate into the culture of the larger organization.

4. **Functional Subcultures**

    a) <u>Functional subcultures</u> embody people who develop strong identities with their work groups and specific areas of task responsibilities, such as "systems people", "marketing people", "manufacturing people", and "finance people."

    b) This results in tendencies to separate in-group people from the rest of the organization, to use jargon, and to compete with other people from other subsystems.

5.   **Ethnic and Racial Subcultures**

a)   Hofstede's research on national cultures can provide a broad-brush view of <u>ethnic cultures</u>.

b)   Hofstede's framework must be supplemented by other understandings gained through <u>direct contact</u>, <u>personal commitment</u>, and a genuine <u>openness to people with different ethnic backgrounds</u>.

c)   <u>Racial subcultures</u> of "African-Americans," "Asian-Americans," or "Caucasians" could learn to work better together by understanding each others' subcultures better.

6.   **Generational Subcultures**

a)   "<u>Generational gaps</u>" exist between people who grew up during different periods of history, and whose values have thus evolved under different influences.

b)   "Defiant 60's kids" have high needs for participative decision making.

c)   Their needs may clash with the top-down approach of higher-level managers, whose values were set in the 40's and 50's.

7.   **Gender Subcultures**

a)   When men work together, a <u>male group culture</u> forms, which typically has a competitive atmosphere and relies on "sports" metaphors.

b)   When women work together, a <u>female group culture</u> forms, which typically involves more personal relationships with an emphasis on collaboration.

ENHANCEMENT

Point out to students that countercultures, which reject the dominant culture, can also arise in organizations. Ask students to provide examples.

D.   *Ethical Cultures*

1.   The **ethical climate** is a shared set of understandings about what is considered ethically correct behavior in an organization.

2.   Organizations with **strong and positive ethical climates** set clear expectations for their members regarding what should be done when ethical dilemmas occur.

3.   Such organizations also remind everyone that **top management** and **organization policies** stand behind these expectations.

4.   **Example:** Over 20 years ago, the Stride-Rite Corporation -- a Massachusetts shoe manufacturer -- became the first U.S. company to have an on-site child care facility. Due to the program's success, the Stride-Rite Intergenerational Day Care Center was established to accommodate the elderly as well as the very young.

CHAPTER 2 SUMMARY

What is in the external environment of organizations?

* Competitive advantage and distinctive competency can only be achieved by organizations that deal successfully with dynamic and complex environments.
* The external environment of organizations consists of both general and specific components.
* The general environment includes background conditions that influence the organization, including economic, socio-cultural, legal-political, technological, and natural environment conditions.
* The specific environment consists of the actual organizations, groups, and persons that an organization deals with; these include suppliers, customers, competitors, regulators, pressure groups.
* Environmental uncertainty challenges organizations and their management to be flexible and responsive to new and changing conditions.

What is a customer-driven organization?

* Any organization must develop and maintain a base of loyal customers or clients, and a customer-driven organization recognizes customer service and product quality as foundations of competitive advantage.
  Customer service is a core ingredient of total quality operations, and it includes concerns for both internal and external customers.
* The "upside-down pyramid" is a symbol of how organizations of today are refocusing on customers and on the role of managers to support work efforts to continually improve quality and customer service.
* Operations management is specifically concerned with activities and decisions through which organizations transform resource inputs into product outputs.
* Today, operations management is increasingly viewed in a strategic perspective, and with close attention to the demands of productivity, quality, and competitive advantage.

What is the quality commitment to operations?

* To compete in the global economy organizations are increasingly expected to meet ISO 9000 certification standards of quality.
* Total quality management (TQM) involves making quality a strategic objective of the organization, and is supported by continuous improvement efforts.
* The use of quality circles --- groups of employees working to solve quality problems --- is a form of employee involvement in quality management.

Why is organizational culture important?

* The internal environment of organizations includes the notion of organizational or corporate culture.
* Organizational culture establishes a personality for the organization as a whole and has a strong influence on the behavior of members.
* The observable culture is found in the rites, rituals, stories, heroes, and symbols of the organization.

* The core culture consists of the shared values that underlie the organization.
* In organizations with strong cultures, members behave with shared understandings that support accomplishment of important organizational objectives.
* Symbolic managers are good at building shared values and using stories, ceremonies, heroes and language to reinforce these values in daily affairs.

What are the current directions in organizational culture?

* Organizational cultures typically include the existence of many subcultures, including those based on occupational, functional, ethnic, racial, age, and gender differences in a diverse workforce.
* People in organizations must learn to work together comfortably across subculture borders; they must avoid negative stereotyping and dysfunctional cross-cultural clashes.
* Multi-cultural organizations operate through a culture that values pluralism and respects diversity.
* The organizational culture should display a positive ethical climate, or shared set of understandings about what is considered ethically correct behavior.

CHAPTER 2 KEY TERMS

Benchmarking A process of comparing operations and performance with other organizations known for excellence.

Competitive advantage A special edge that allows an organization to deal with market and environmental forces better than its competitors.

Continuous improvement Searching for new ways to incrementally improve operations quality and performance.

Core values The underlying beliefs shared by members of the organizational culture and that influence their behavior.

Cycle time The elapsed time between the receipt of an order and delivery of a finished good or service.

Design for disassembly The design of products with attention to how their components will be used when product life ends.

Design for manufacturing Creating a design that lowers production costs and improves quality in all stages of the production process.

External customer The customer or client who buys the organization's products and/or services.

Flexible manufacturing The ability to change manufacturing processes quickly and efficiently to produce different products or modifications of existing ones.

General environment The cultural, economic, legal-political, and educational conditions in the locality in which an organization operates.

Internal customer Someone who uses or depends on the work of another person or group within the same organization.

ISO 9000 certification The certification granted by the Internationals Standards Organization to indicate that a business meets a rigorous set of quality standards.

Multicultural organization Pluralism and respect for diversity in the workplace.

Operations management A branch of management theory that studies how organizations transform resource inputs into product and service outputs.

Organizational culture The system of shared beliefs and values that develops within an organization and guides the behavior of its members.

Quality circle A group of employees who meet periodically to discuss ways of improving the quality of their products or services.

Specific environment The actual organizations and persons with whom the focal organization must interact in order to survive.

Subcultures Cultures common to a group of people with similar values and beliefs based upon shared personal characteristics.

Symbolic manager A manager who uses symbols well to establish and maintain a desired organizational culture.

Total quality management Managing with an organization-wide commitment to continuous work improvement, product quality, and meeting customer needs completely.

CHAPTER 3: INFORMATION TECHNOLOGY AND DECISION MAKING

CHAPTER 3 KEY STUDY QUESTIONS

o   How is information technology changing the workplace?
o   What are the current directions in information systems?
o   How is information used for problem solving?
o   How do managers make decisions?
o   How do learning and knowledge management create value?

CHAPTER 3 LEARNING OBJECTIVES

After completing this chapter, students should be able to:

1.   Define intellectual capital and explain how it serves as a major source of competitive advantage.
2.   Discuss the role of information technology in the new workplace, including its importance to electronic commerce, or e-business.
3.   Define information and discuss the external and internal information needs of organizations.
4.   Define information systems and management information systems (MIS), and discuss the following types of MIS: decision support systems (DSS), group decision support systems (GDSS), groupware, and expert systems.
5.   Compare and contrast the purposes, features, and applications of intraorganizational systems and intranets versus interorganizational systems and extranets.
6.   Define the term problem, and explain the difference between a performance deficiency and a performance opportunity.
7.   Compare and contrast structured versus unstructured problems, and programmed versus nonprogrammed decisions.
8.   Discuss crisis problems and describe the recommended approach to dealing with crises.
9.   Compare and contrast the attributes of alternative problem environments.
10. Compare and contrast the ways in which problem avoiders, problem solvers, and problem seekers approach managerial problems, as well as the differences between systematic, intuitive, and multidimensional thinking.
11. List and explain the steps in the problem-solving process.
12. Define cost-benefit analysis and identify the major criteria for evaluating alternatives.
13. Compare and contrast the classical, administrative and judgmental heuristics approaches to managerial decision-making.
14. Define escalating commitment and discuss the guidelines for avoiding the escalation trap.
15. Explain the importance of conducting an ethics double-check prior to choosing a decision.
16. Discuss the key considerations involved in implementing a solution and evaluating results.
17. Explain the importance of organizational learning, lifelong learning, and knowledge management to individual and organizational success.
18. Define and discuss the ingredients of learning organizations.

CHAPTER 3 SUMMARY

As rapid advances in information technology sweep through modern organizations, innovations in learning, problem solving, and knowledge management have arisen — including the types of virtual universities described in the chapter opener, **Welcome to the World of Virtual Learning.** This chapter describes the impact of information technology in management and decision making, and the opportunities and challenges that IT creates.

The chapter begins by considering the importance of intellectual capital to organizational success. Next, the roles that information technology plays in the new workplace, including the electronic office and electronic commerce of e-business are considered, along with the information needs of organizations. Developments in information systems including various forms of management information systems (MIS) such as decision support systems (DSS), group decision support systems (GDSS), groupware, expert systems, intraorganizational systems/intranets, and interorganizational systems/ extranets are also discussed.

The focus of the chapter then shifts to information and problem solving. The various types of problems and problem environments that managers encounter are examined, along with the ways in which managers deal with problems. A detailed discussion of the steps in the problem solving process follows. These include: 1) identifying and defining the problem; 2) generating and evaluating possible solutions; 3) choosing a solution and conducting an "ethics double-check"; 4) implementing the solution; and 5) evaluating results. Included in the discussion of step 3 is a description of the classical, administrative, and judgmental heuristic approaches to decision making. The chapter concludes by examining the importance of organizational learning and knowledge management.

CHAPTER 3 LECTURE OUTLINE

Teaching Objective: The objective of this chapter is to familiarize students with the roles that information, information systems, and information technology, play in the problem solving and decision making processes. The ways in which learning and knowledge management add value through the transformation process are also explored.

Suggested Time: Two or more hours of class time are recommended to present the material in this chapter.

Information Technology and the New Workplace
 Work and the Electronic Office
 Electronic Commerce
 Information Needs of Organizations

Developments in Information Systems
 Management Information Systems
 Intraorganizational Systems and Intranets
 Interorganizational Systems and Extranets

Information and Problem Solving
 Types of Managerial Problems
 Problem Environments
 How Managers Deal with Problems

The Decision-Making Process
 Step 1: Identify and Define the Problem
 Step 2: Generate and Evaluate Possible Solutions
 Step 3: Choose a Solution and Conduct the "Ethics Double Check"
 Step 4: Implement the Solution
 Step 5: Evaluate Results

Learning and Knowledge Management
 Organizational Learning
 Lifelong Learning
 Knowledge Management

CHAPTER 3 SUPPORTING MATERIALS

Textbook Inserts

Headline Opener: Welcome to the World of Virtual Learning
Margin Photos: John Wiley & Sons, Inc., D'Artagan, Inc., Pentagon Entertainment,
      Motorola, Ernst & Young
Embedded Boxes: Amazon. Com, Fidelity Investments
Manager's Notepad 3.1: Avoiding Common Information Systems Mistakes
Manager's Notepad 3.2: How to Avoid the Escalation Trap

Multi-Media Resources

NBR Video Report:
      Netscape (Available on Videotape Supplement & Video Cases CD-ROM)

PowerPoint Presentations (Website):
      Figures 3.1 to 3.5 from the Textbook plus Supplemental Figures
      NBR Viewing Questions: Netscape & Boeing

In-Class Activities

Cases for Critical Thinking (Career Readiness Workbook & Website):
      Netscape (Primary Case)
      Boeing (Alternate Case)

Exercises:
      Leading through Participation (Career Readiness Workbook)
      Demonstrating Computer Literacy (Website)

Assessments:
      Decision Making Biases (Career Readiness Workbook)
      Your Intuitive Ability (Career Readiness Workbook & Website)

Self-Test 3 (Textbook and Website)

CHAPTER 3 LECTURE NOTES

I. Introduction

ENHANCEMENTS

A discussion of the chapter opener titled, **Welcome to the World of Virtual Learning**, can be used as an intriguing and easy to relate to forum for introducing students to this chapter. The opener discusses the use of distance learning by Duke University, the University of Tennessee, and Florida Gulf Coast University, as well as the Western Governors University (which exists only as a virtual university), to reach geographically diverse students. These include executives living abroad, practicing physicians, and other types of nontraditional students. Ask students for their reactions to distance learning and "virtual universities." What challenges and advantages does this type of learning provide?

    A.   *Information*

        1.   **More** information about **more** things is being made available to **more** people in organizations **more** quickly than ever before.

        2.   **Intellectual capital** is the collective brainpower or shared knowledge of a workforce.

        3.   Information capital is a major source of **competitive advantage**.

II. Information Technology and the New Workplace

    A.   *Work and the Electronic Office*

        1.   Because of the growing importance of information and information technology to modern organizations, an increasing number have created a prominent position for the **chief information officer (CIO)** or **chief knowledge officer (CKO)**.

        2.   The **electronic office** uses computers and related technologies to facilitate operations in an office environment. It relies on:

            a)   "Smart" stations.
            b)   Voice messaging.
            c)   Data bases.
            d)   Electronic mail.
            e)   Facsimile transmission.
            f)   Electronic bulletin boards.
            g)   Computer and video conferencing.

ENHANCEMENTS

Ask students to compare this view of the electronic office with one, say, from fifty years ago. Keep in mind such tasks as answering the phone; preparing, editing, duplicating and storing documents; inter-office and intra-office communication; mail; meetings; etc.

B.   *Electronic Commerce*

1.   **Electronic commerce** or **e-business** is a business form in which commercial transactions take place through the use of advanced uses information technology (IT), including special telecommunications and computer mediation.

2.   The **steps in developing e-business**, as identified by IBM, include:

a)   <u>Step 1 in E-business</u> — establishing a web site and then using the site to publish information electronically.

b)   <u>Step 2 in E-business</u> — advancing the web site to "self-service" status, where customers can do things like check their account status or trace the location of a package for delivery.

c)   <u>Step 3 in E-business</u> — further advancing the web site to allow "transactions," including buying and selling of merchandise and managing resource supply and product distribution chains.

ENHANCEMENTS

The embedded box on **Amazon.com** provides an excellent example of *e-business* which students may readily relate to, especially if they are customers. Amazon.com advertizes the availability of over 400,000 titles with savings of 20 to 40 percent. The firm invites you to shop in their bookstore anytime you want, day or night, 365 days a year. By doing so, the firm has established a new level and form of competition in the bookstore industry.

C.   *Information Needs of Managers*   **FIGURE 3.1**

1.   **Information** is data that is made useful for decision making.

2.   **Informational exchanges with the environment.** Managers must monitor and interact with the external environment to:

a) Gather <u>intelligence information</u> on consumer tastes, competitor activities, etc. for use in decision making.

b) Gather <u>public information</u> to be disseminated to the appropriate external elements.

3. **Internal informational exchanges** to facilitate decision making and problem solving. **Figure 3.1** shows how the information needs vary by level of managerial responsibility.

a) At the <u>top management level</u>, information systems are used for strategic purposes to gain a competitive advantage.

<u>Example</u>: Fidelity Investments Corporation refined its information systems to become the first investment firm to provide its clients with hourly quotes on mutual funds.

b) At the <u>first level of management</u>, information systems are used to facilitate <u>operational control</u>.

<u>Example</u>: In the city garage of Salinas, Ca., a computer helps mechanics more efficiently manage the maintenance and repair of 150+ vehicles and 300 engine driven devices.

III. Developments in Information Systems

A. *Information Systems*

1. **Information systems** collect, organize, and distribute data in such a way that they become meaningful as information.

2. Effective managers and organizations use information systems to get the *right* information at the *right* time and in the *right* place.

3. **Three Keys to Information System Success**

a) <u>Technical quality of the system</u>: Information systems of higher technical quality produce more favorable user attitudes.

b) <u>Management support of the system</u>: Strong management support in systems development and implementation results in more favorable attitudes.

c) <u>Participation and involvement in systems design</u>: Individual involvement in systems design and operation results in more favorable user attitudes.

4. **Chief Information Officer (CIO)**

a) <u>CIO</u> is a senior executive responsible for IT and its utilization throughout an organization.

b) The CIO typically reports to the CEO and fulfills these functions:

* Oversees the *computer-based information and data processing systems*, as well as *office and telecommunications systems*.

* Plays a key role in *long-range and strategic decisions*.

* Manages the *information applications of computer technology* within the organization.

c) The CIO's job is to ensure that the organization always uses information in ways that help its workforce operate with <u>competitive advantage</u>.

B. *Management Information Systems (MIS)*   **MANAGER'S NOTEPAD 3.1**

1. A **management information system (MIS)** is specifically designed to meet the information needs of managers as they make a variety of decisions on a day-to-day basis.

2. **Manager's Notepad 3.1** provides the following tips for **avoiding common information systems mistakes:**

a) Don't assume more information is always better.
b) Don't assume that computers eliminate the need for human judgement.
c) Don't assume the newest technology is always the best.
d) Don't assume nothing will ever go wrong with your computer.
e) Don't assume that everyone understands how the system works.

3. **Decision Support Systems (DSS)**

a) <u>Decision support systems (DSS)</u> allow users to interact directly with a computer to create information helpful in making decisions to solve complex and sometimes unstructured problems.

121

b) <u>DSS applications</u> include:

* Merger and acquisition decisions.
* Plant expansions.
* New product developments.
* Stock portfolio management.
* Materials purchasing.
* Transportation systems.

c) <u>Examples</u>: At IBM, managers of one manufacturing plant use a DSS purchasing system to enter requirements and arrive at an optimal combination of vendors, parts, order quantities, and order times that will minimize all relevant costs over multiple time periods.

4. **Group Decision Support Systems (GDSS)**

a) A <u>GDSS</u> is an interactive computer-based information system that facilitates *group* efforts at solving complex and unstructured problems.

b) GDSSs use specialized software, called <u>groupware</u>, to facilitate information retrieval, sharing and usage among group members.

c) Continuing developments in groupware are expanding the presence and opportunities of <u>virtual teams</u> in organizations.

EXERCISE

To increase student awareness of some of the uses of virtual teams, assign the *Research and Presentation Project* titled, **Virtual Teams -- Does Groupware Work?** from the *Career Readiness Workbook*.

5. **Expert Systems (ES)**

a) <u>Artificial intelligence (AI)</u> is a field of study that is concerned with building computer systems with the capacity to reason the way people do, even to the point of dealing with ambiguities and difficult issues of judgement.

b) <u>Expert systems (ES)</u> are software systems that use AI to mimic the thinking of human experts and, in so doing, offer consistent and "expert" advice to the user.

c) <u>Example</u>: American Express uses an Authorization Assistant Expert System to perform required searches of company data bases on customer's with unusual credit requests, and makes the authorization decision in seconds, while the merchant is still on the telephone.

d) Most current ESs are "<u>rule-based</u>" systems that use a complicated set of "if ... then" rules to analyze problems; the rules are determined by specialists.

e) ESs free workers up to tackle more complex problems.

C. *Intraorganizational Systems and Intranets*

1. Central to the electronic office is the integration of computers and software into **networks** through computer-to-computer linkages.

2. **Intranets** are computer networks that allow persons working in various locations within the same organization to share data bases and communicate electronically.

3. An **enterprise-wide network** uses IT to move information quickly and accurately from one point to another within an organization.

D. *Interorganizational Systems and Extranets*   **FIGURE 3.2**

1. **Extranets** are computer networks that use the public Internet to allow communication between the organization and elements in its external environment.

2. **Interorganizational Information Systems**

a) Using new IT, <u>interorganizational information systems</u> are increasingly used to allow information transfers between two or more organizations.

b) They are the basic foundations for fast-paced developments occurring in <u>electronic commerce</u> or <u>e-business</u>.

c) Through <u>electronic data interchange (EDI)</u> companies communicate electronically with one another to move and share documents such as purchase orders, bills, receipt confirmations, and even payments for services rendered.

d) **Figure 3.2** provides an example of how extranets and interorganizational networking systems are contributing to the emergence of electronic markets for goods and services.

IV.   **Information and Problem Solving**

    A.   *Problems and Problem Solving*

        1.   A **problem** exists whenever there is a difference between an actual and a desired situation.

            a)   The most obvious problem encountered by managers is a <u>performance deficiency</u>, which occurs when actual performance is less than desired.

            b)   Some performance deficiencies which may require managerial attention include increases in employee <u>turnover</u> or <u>absenteeism</u>, <u>declining quality</u>, and <u>customer complaints</u> regarding service.

            c)   Managers also face <u>performance opportunities</u> whenever an actual situation turns out either better than anticipated or offers the opportunity to do so.

        2.   **Problem-solving** is the process of identifying a discrepancy between the actual and desired state of affairs and then taking *action* to resolve the discrepancy.

    B.   *Types of Managerial Problems*

ENHANCEMENT

To stimulate discussion of the following types of managerial problems, ask students to provide examples of each type. You can either solicit student examples as a prelude to your own illustrations, or present your examples first to get them started.

---

        1.   **Structured Problems**

            a)   <u>Structured problems</u> are ones that are familiar, straightforward, and clear in respect to the information needed to resolve them.

            b)   <u>Example</u>: A typical manager may expect to encounter "personnel" problems when making decisions on periodic staff pay raises and promotions, vacation requests, and committee assignments.

            c)   Managers can <u>plan ahead</u> for these problems and develop specific ways of dealing with them, or even take actions to prevent their occurrence.

d) <u>Programmed decisions</u> apply solutions from past experiences to the problem at hand.

* Programmed decisions are used for *structured and routine problems* that tend to arise on a regular basis.

* *Example:* The decision to reorder inventory automatically when on-hand stock falls below a predetermined level.

* An increasing number of programmed decisions are being handled by computers using *decision-support software*.

2. **Unstructured Problems**

a) <u>Unstructured problems</u> tend to occur as new or unexpected situations that involve ambiguities and information deficiencies.

b) Unstructured problems require <u>novel solutions</u>; astute and "proactive" managers (e.g., problem-seekers), are sometimes able to get a jump on them by realizing that the situation is problem prone and that contingency plans may be needed.

c) <u>Example</u>: The biggest fear of executives of *The Vanguard Group* is an investors' panic that overloads customer services during a major plunge in the bond or stock markets. In anticipation, the investment firm has trained its accountants, lawyers, and money-fund managers to staff the telephones if needed.

d) <u>Nonprogrammed decisions</u> develop unique solutions that are specifically tailored to the situation at hand.

* Nonprogrammed decisions are required when *new and unfamiliar problems* arise, and/or when standard responses have not been prepared.

* The information requirements for defining and resolving nonroutine problems typically are high; although computer support may assist in information processing, *the decision will be based primarily on human judgment*.

* Most problems faced by *higher-level managers* are nonprogrammed.

3.   **Dealing with Crisis**

a)   A <u>crisis problem</u> is an unexpected problem that can lead to disaster if it is not resolved quickly and appropriately.

b)   <u>Examples</u>: The Challenger disaster and Chernobyl nuclear plant explosion are good examples of crises.

ENHANCEMENT

To embellish your discussion of crisis situations, consider presenting the following **Guidelines for Taking Quick Action in Response to Crisis Situations.**

a)   *Prepare for action* by knowing as much as possible about all phases of the operation you are responsible for.
b)   *Build a network of reliable sources of information and advice,* and be willing to use them when needed.
c)   *Don't accept the problem as delivered;* acquire information quickly to confirm and define it for yourself.
d)   *Test your responses before acting* whenever possible, even if just with one or more key people.
e)   *Don't shirk your responsibility;* address the problem, even in the face of risk and incomplete information.
f)   *Remember to learn from the situation;* think about what can be done to keep it from happening the next time.

C.   *Problem Environments*   **FIGURE 3.3**

1.   **Certain Environment**

a)   <u>Certain environments</u> offer complete information on possible action alternatives and their consequences.

b)   Few managerial problems occur in certain environments, but steps can be taken to reduce uncertainty.

2.   **Risk Environment**

a)   <u>Risk environments</u> lack complete information, but offer "probabilities" of the likely outcomes for possible action alternatives.

b)   <u>Example</u>: In developing and marketing Airfon, telephone service for passenger airplanes, entrepreneur and CEO John D. ("Jack") Goekin, took a calculated risk that there would be demand for this service.

126

3. **Uncertain Environment**

   a) <u>Uncertain environments</u> are so poor in information that it is difficult even to assign probabilities to the likely outcomes of alternatives.

   b) <u>Example</u>: The creators of the "Teenage Ninja Mutant Turtles" played a "hunch" that paid off handsomely.

D. *How Managers Deal with Problems*

   1. **Problem-solving Styles**

      a) <u>Problem avoiders</u> - Managers who ignore information that would otherwise signal the presence of a problem; they are *inactive* and do not want to deal with the problem.

      b) <u>Problem solvers</u> - Managers who try to solve problems when they arise; they are *reactive* in responding to problems after they occur.

      c) <u>Problem seekers</u> - Managers who actively look for problems to solve or opportunities to explore as a matter of routine; they are *proactive* in anticipating problems before they occur.

   2. **Systematic versus Intuitive Thinking**

      a) <u>Systematic thinking</u> approaches problems in a rational and analytical fashion.

      b) <u>Managers who employ systematic thinking</u> tend to...

         ... make a plan for solving a problem.
         ... be very conscious of their approach.
         ... define specific constraints of the problem early.
         ... discard alternatives only after careful analysis.
         ... conduct an ordered search for additional
             information.
         ... complete any discrete analytical step they begin.

      c) <u>Intuitive thinking</u> approaches problems in a flexible and spontaneous fashion.

      d) <u>Managers who employ intuitive thinkers</u> tend to...

         ... keep the overall problem continuously in mind.
         ... rely on unverbalized cues, even hunches.
         ... defend the solution in terms of fit.
         ... consider a number of alternatives simultaneously.

... repeatedly jump from one step in analysis to
        another.
... explore and abandon alternatives very quickly.

ENHANCEMENTS

Ask students to raise their hands if they think that they rely predominantly on
systematic thinking. Make a note of these students. Do the same for those who
believe that they use *intuitive thinking* most often. From here, several
approaches to generating discussion of these alternative problem-solving styles
are available. For example, you may ask students who believe that they rely more
on systematic and intuitive thinking to elaborate on the ways in which they
typically make decisions. What do they consider to be the advantages of their
approach? The disadvantages? Or you could create panels of intuitive and
systematic thinkers to engage each other in a debate on the relative merits of
their problem-solving styles. Another option would be to create panels of
intuitive and systematic thinkers, but instead of having them debate one another,
you could instruct them to ask the students with alternative styles questions
about the ways in which they typically approach various problems. Any of these
options can be used to generate a lively discussion of the relative strengths and
weaknesses of the systematic and intuitive thinking.

   As an alternative approach to introducing this topic, consider assigning
the *Assessment* titled, **Your Intuitive Ability**, which is included in *Career
Readiness Workbook*. A discussion of this assessment can also be found in this
Manual in Unit 9.

   You may also want to share with students the results of a psychological
study of investors which suggest that investment decisions are primarily based
on judgements of the venture's management and unique business opportunity, and
that "gut feeling" strongly colors these judgements.

(Source: "Intuition in Venture Capital Decisions," Journal of Business Venturing, January 1990, p. 49).

3.   **Multi-Dimensional Thinking**

   a)   <u>Multi-dimensional thinking</u> is the capacity to view many
        problems at once, in relationship to one another, and
        across long and short time horizons. It becomes
        increasingly important as one moves up the management
        hierarchy.

   b)   <u>Strategic opportunism</u> involves remaining focused on
        long-term objectives while being flexible enough to
        resolve short-term problems and opportunities in a
        timely manner.

V.   The Problem-solving Process   FIGURE 3.4

A.   *Five Steps in the Problem-Solving Process*

1.   Identify and define the problem.
2.   Generate and evaluate possible solutions.
3.   Choose a solution *and* conduct the "ethics double check."
4.   Implement the solution.
5.   Evaluate results.

ENHANCEMENT

Illustrative Case: Tough Decision at Ajax Aluminum

To provide students with a example of the problem-solving process, review the five steps of this process using a real world example. For your convenience, a discussion of the decisions that *Ajax Aluminum* made in response to the problem described in the chapter is provided in the text and reiterated below.

Background Information: Ajax Aluminum had decided to close its Murphysboro, Illinois plant because of poor market conditions. A buyer could not be found.

Step 1: Identify and Define the Problem - Closing the plant would put many employees out of work, and negatively impact their families and the local community. The loss of the Ajax tax base will further hurt the community.

Step 2: Generate and Evaluate Possible Solutions - You can generate class discussion of this case by asking students to identify potential alternatives. The alternatives identified by Ajax's management included:

1. Simply closing the plant on schedule.
2. Delaying the plant closing until all efforts have been made to sell it to another firm.
3. Offering to sell the plant to the employees and/or local interests.
4. Closing the plant and offering transfers to other Ajax plants.
5. Closing the plant, offering some transfers, and actively helping employees find new jobs in the local area.

Ask students for their opinions on the advantages and disadvantages of each of these alternatives.

Step 3: Choose a Solution *and* Conduct the "Ethics" Double-Check -Ask students to indicate which alternative they would have selected. Ajax's management selected the fifth option because they thought it was most consistent with company values and most likely to solve the problem. Management also conducted an "ethics" double-check to ensure that this option was consistent with prevailing moral standards. Of the five options, the last is clearly the most ethical. It recognizes the reality that the plant is no longer viable, as well as the company's responsibilities to its employees, and attempts to find alternative employment for the workers.

Step 4: Implement the Solution - Ajax ran an ad in the local newspaper for 15 days at a cost of $2600 informing local employers of the skills and availability of the firm's employees.

Step 5: Evaluate Results - A substantial number of Ajax's employees were able to relocate in new jobs in the Southern Illinois area.

B.   *Step 1: Identify and Define the Problem*

1.   **Problem finding** involves identifying gaps between actual and desired states and determining their causes.

2.   Managers who are good at problem finding **continually scan** their work environment for indicators of potential problems or opportunities.

3.   **Problem symptoms** (e.g., an increase in absenteeism) are consequences of problems which signal the presence of a performance deficiency or opportunity; managers must look beyond symptoms to find out what is really wrong or how things could be improved.

4.   **Common Mistakes in Defining Problems**

ENHANCEMENT

━━━

To initially demonstrate the types of errors people often commit in defining problems, you may want to assign the *Assessment* titled, **Facts and Inferences**, which is included in the *Career Readiness Workbook*. Further discussion of the instructional use of this assessment is provided in this *Manual* in Unit 9.

━━━

a)   Mistake Number 1 -- Defining the problem too broadly or too narrowly - The problem stated as "build a better mousetrap" might better be stated as "get rid of mice." Similarly, at Volvo the problem defined as "redesign the assembly line" was better defined as "create more flexibility for workers in the assembly process."

b)   Mistake Number 2 -- Focusing on symptoms instead of causes - Symptoms (e.g., an increase in absenteeism) are consequences of problems which alert managers to deviations from the desired state. They should not, however, be confused with the underlying *causes* (e.g., an undesirable change in job duties) or the problem (e.g., a decline in worker morale and performance).

c)   Mistake Number 3 -- Choosing the wrong problem - Knowing which problems to focus on at any given time is a key to effective problem-solving. Managers must *prioritize* problems and attack those which represent the greatest threats or opportunities. "No action" -at least for the time being - can be a very legitimate response, particularly if a number of problems demand attention simultaneously.

    C.   *Step 2: Generate and Evaluate Possible Solutions*

        1.   **Criteria for Analyzing Alternatives**

           a)   <u>Benefits</u> -- What are the "benefits" of using the alternative to solve a performance deficiency or taking advantage of opportunity?

           b)   <u>Costs</u> -- What are the "costs" to implement the alternative, including direct resource investments as well as any potential negative side effects?

           c)   <u>Timeliness</u> -- How fast will the benefits occur and will a positive impact be achieved?

           d)   <u>Acceptability</u> -- To what extent will the alternative be accepted and supported by those who must work with it?

           e)   <u>Ethical soundness</u> -- How well does the alternative meet acceptable ethical criteria in the eyes of multiple stakeholders?

        2.   **Cost-benefit analysis** involves the comparison of what an alternative will cost in relationship to the expected benefits; at a minimum, the benefits should exceed the costs.

    D.   *Step 3: Choose a Solution and Conduct the "Ethics Double Check"*

        1.   **Decision-making Models**   **FIGURE 3.5**

           a)   **Figure 3.5** summarizes the differences between the <u>classical</u>, <u>administrative</u>, and <u>judgmental heuristics approaches</u> to managerial decisions.

ENHANCEMENT

Ask students to indicate the approach they think most accurately reflects the ways in which managers typically make decisions. Students will typically argue that they consider the behavioral and judgmental heuristics approaches to be more realistic. If this occurs, you may want to ask them if they can think of situations where the assumptions of the classical approach are realistic. These questions usually generate discussion and assist students in distinguishing between these approaches.

---

           b)   The <u>classical decision model</u> views the manager as acting in a world of complete certainty. It assumes:

               *   A clearly defined problem.
               *   Knowledge of all possible action alternatives and their consequences.
               *   Choice of the "optimum" alternative; that is an *optimizing decision* is made, whereby the decision

maker chooses the absolutely best solution to the problem.

c)   The <u>administrative decision model</u>, which is perhaps best represented by the work of Nobel Prize winner, *Herbert Simon*, describes how managers act in situations of limited information and bounded rationality.

*   *Cognitive limitations*, or limits to our human information-processing capabilities, compromise the ability of managers to make perfectly rational decisions.

*   These limitations create a *bounded rationality* such that managerial decisions are rational only within the boundaries defined by the available information.

d)   The <u>administrative decision model</u>, accordingly, asserts that people act only in terms of what they perceive about a given situation.   It assumes that:

*   The problem is not clearly defined.
*   Knowledge is limited on possible alternatives and their consequences.
*   Decision makers rely on *satisficing* -- choosing the first satisfactory alternative that comes to your attention.

e)   The <u>classical decision model</u> is most appropriate for *relatively certain decision environments*, while the <u>administrative decision model</u> is better suited for *ambiguous problems in risky and uncertain conditions*.

ENHANCEMENT

To demonstrate the *judgmental heuristics* discussed below, assign the *Assessment* titled, **Decision-Making Biases** included in the *Career Readiness Workbook*, which presents students with a series of questions which typically elicit these heuristics, and thereby reveals their personal susceptibility to these biases. A discussion of this assessment as a pedagogical tool is included in Unit 9 of this *Manual*.

2.   **Judgmental heuristics** are strategies for simplifying decision-making; the use of such strategies can cause decision errors.

a)   The <u>availability heuristic</u> occurs when people use information "readily available" from memory as a basis for assessing a current event or situation.

132

        * *Potential bias:* The readily available information may be fallible and represent irrelevant factors.

        * *Example:* Deciding whether or not to invest in a new product based upon your recollection of how well similar new products have performed in the recent past.

b) The representativeness heuristic occurs when people assess the likelihood of something happening based upon its similarity to a stereotyped set of occurrences.

        * *Potential bias:* The representative stereotype may fail to discriminate important and unique factors relevant to the decision.

        * *Example:* Deciding to hire someone for a job vacancy simply because they graduated from the same school attended by your most successful new hire.

c) The anchoring and adjustment heuristic involves making decisions based on adjustments to a previously existing value or starting point.

        * *Potential bias:* The decision may be inappropriately biased to move only incrementally from the starting point.

        * *Example:* Deciding on a new salary level for an employee by simply adjusting upward their prior year's salary by a reasonable increment.

3. **Escalating Commitments**   MANAGER'S NOTEPAD 3.2

a) Asking and answering these questions can help managers avoid escalating commitment -- the tendency to pursue a course of action that is not working in the vain hope that more effort and perhaps more resources will reverse the trend.

ENHANCEMENT

Explain to students that *escalating commitment* is encouraged by the popular saying, "If at first you don't succeed, try, try again." Current wisdom supports an alternative view, illustrated in this quote by the late W.C. Fields: "If at first you don't succeed, try, try again. Then quit. No use being a damn fool about it."

A useful exercise for demonstrating escalating commitment titled, *"Competitive Escalation: The Dollar Auction"* is provided in Roy J. Lewicki, Donald D. Bowen, Douglas T. Hall, and Francine S. Hall, *Experiences in Management and Organizational Behavior*, John Wiley & Sons, New York, 1988, pp. 91-94.

  b) **Manager's Notepad** 3.2 provides the following tips on <u>How to Avoid the Escalation Trap</u>

    * *Set limits on your involvement and commitments* to a particular course of action; stick with these limits.

    * *Make your own decisions*; don't follow the lead of others, since they are also prone to escalation.

    * *Carefully determine just why you are continuing a course of action*. If there are insufficient reasons to continue, don't.

    * *Remind yourself what a course of action is costing*; consider the savings of such costs as a reason to discontinue.

    * *Watch for escalation tendencies*; be on guard against their influence on both you and others involved in a course of action.

 4. **Ethics Double-Check**

  a) Before implementing any potential solution, it should be <u>reexamined</u> to make sure that it is completely ethical.

  b) This step should result in better decisions and <u>prevent ethical mistakes</u> that can result in costly litigation.

E. *Implement the Solution*

 1. **Implementation** involves taking action to make sure the solution decided upon becomes a reality.

 2. **Lack of participation** is a common implementation difficulty. To ensure a successful implementation, the manager must involve those individuals whose support is required for success in the problem-solving process.

F. *Evaluate Results*

 1. **Evaluation** involves comparing the actual and desired results to insure that the problem has really been solved. If not, the manager needs to start the problem-solving process again. It may also reveal ways of improving the original solution.

2. Although, this step is often neglected, it is essential to effective problem-solving.

VI. Learning and Knowledge Management

A. *Organizational Learning*

1. A **learning organization** is an organization that "by virtue of people, values, and systems is able to continuously change and improve its performance based upon the lessons of experience."

2. In *The Fifth Discipline*, Peter Senge identifies the following **core ingredients of learning organizations:**

a) <u>Mental models</u> — everyone sets aside old ways of thinking.

b) <u>Personal mastery</u> — everyone becomes self-aware and open to others.

c) <u>Systems thinking</u> — everyone learns how the whole organization works.

d) <u>Team learning</u> — everyone works together to accomplish the plan.

B. *Lifelong Learning*

1. **Lifelong learning** is the process of continuously learning from our daily experiences and opportunities which helps us build a portfolio of skills that are always up to date and valuable to an employer.

C. *Knowledge Management*

1. **Knowledge management** is a term used to describe the processes through which organizations develop, organize, and share knowledge to achieve competitive advantage.

2. The significance of knowledge management as a strategic and integrating force in organizations is represented by the emergence of a new executive job title — **Chief Knowledge Officer (CKO)**

3. The **CKO** is responsible for energizing learning processes and making sure that an organization's portfolio of intellectual assets and pool of knowledge are well managed and continually update.

CHAPTER 3 SUMMARY

How is information technology changing the workplace?

* Continuing advances in computers and information technology (IT) bring many opportunities for improving the workplace by utilizing information better.
* Today's "electronic" offices with e-mail, voice messaging, and networked computer systems, are changing the nature of office work.
* The many information needs in organizations are served by a variety of information systems using the latest in computer and information technologies.
* An information system collects, organizes, and distributes data so that they become useful information.
* To be effective, an information system must be designed to meet the needs of end users.

What are the current directions in information systems?

* A management information system, or MIS, collects, organizes, stores, and distributes data in a way that meets the information needs of managers.
* Decision-support systems (DSSs) provide information and help managers make decisions to solve complex problems.
* Group-decision support systems utilize groupware to allow the computer-mediated exchange of information and decision making by group members.
* Intraorganizational information systems use intranets and networks to allow persons within an organization to share databases and communicate electronically.
* Interorganizational information systems use extranets and the public Internet for communication between the organization and its environment.

How is information used for problem solving?

* Information is data that are made useful for decision making and problem solving.
* A problem is a discrepancy between an actual and desired state of affairs. Managers face structured and unstructured problems in environments of certainty, risk, and uncertainty.
* The most threatening type of problem is the crisis, which occurs unexpectedly and can lead to disaster if not handled quickly and properly.

How do managers make decisions?

* The steps in the decision-making process are find and define the problem, generate and evaluate alternatives, choose the preferred solution, implement the solution, and evaluate results.
* An optimizing decision, following the classical model, chooses the absolute best solution from a known set of alternatives.
  A satisficing decision, following the administrative model, chooses the first satisfactory alternative to come to attention.
* Judgemental heuristics, such as the availability heuristic, the anchoring and adjustment heuristic, and the representativeness heuristic, can bias decision making.

How do learning and knowledge management create value?

* The old ways of management aren't good enough anymore; an age of transformation demands that the best of the past be combined with new thinking so organizations can be competitive in the 21st century.
* A learning organization is one in which people, values, and systems support continuous change and improvement based upon the lessons of experience.
* Lifelong learning involves a personal commitment to continuously seek learning opportunities in one's work.
* Knowledge management ·is the process of capturing, developing, and utilizing the knowledge of an organization to achieve competitive advantage.

CHAPTER 3 KEY TERMS

Administrative decision model A model of decision-making that describes how managers act in situations of limited information and bounded rationality.

Certain environment A problem environment in which the information is sufficient to predict the results of each alternative in advance of implementation.

Classical decision model A model of decision-making that describes how managers should ideally make decisions using complete information.

Cost-benefit analysis An analysis that involves comparing the costs and benefits of each potential course of action.

Crisis problem An unexpected problem that can lead to disaster if not resolved quickly and appropriately.

Decision-making A process that involves the identification of a problem and the choice of preferred problem-solving alternatives.

Enterprise-wide networks Networks that move information quickly and accurately from one point to another within an organization.

Escalating commitment The tendency to continue to pursue a course of action, even though it is not working.

Extranet A computer network that uses the public Internet to allow communication between the organization and elements in its external environment.

Heuristics Strategies for simplifying decision-making.

Information system A system that collects, organizes, and distributes data regarding activities occurring inside and outside an organization.

Intellectual capital The collective brainpower or shared knowledge of a workforce that can be used to create wealth.

Intranet A computer network that allows persons within an organization to share data bases and communicate electronically.

Interorganizational information system An information system that facilitates information transfers among two or more organizations.

Intuitive thinker Someone who tends to approach problems in a flexible and spontaneous fashion.

Knowledge management The processes through which organizations develop, organize, and share knowledge to achieve competitive advantage.

Multidimensional thinking The capacity to view many problems at once, in relationship to one another, and across long and short time horizons.

Nonprogrammed decision A decision which is unique and specifically tailored to a problem at hand.

Optimizing decision A decision that occurs when a manager chooses an alternative that gives the absolute best solution to a problem.

Problem The difference between an actual situation and a desired situation.

Problem-solving The process of identifying a discrepancy between an actual and desired state of affairs and then taking action to resolve the discrepancy.

Problem symptoms Signs of the presence of a performance deficiency or opportunity, which should trigger a manager to act.

Programmed decision A decision that is available from past experience and appropriate to the task at hand.

Risk environment A problem environment in which information is lacking, but some sense of the "probabilities" associated with action alternatives and their consequences exists.

Satisficing Choosing the first satisfactory alternative that comes to your attention.

Strategic opportunism The ability to remain focused on long-term objectives by being flexible in dealing with short-term problems and opportunities as they occur.

Structured problem A problem that is familiar, straightforward, and clear in its information requirements.

Systematic thinker Someone who approaches problems in a rational and analytical fashion.

Uncertain environment A problem environment in which information is so poor that it is difficult even to assign probabilities to the likely outcomes of known alternatives.

Unstructured problem A problem that involves ambiguities and information deficiencies.

CHAPTER 4: HISTORICAL FOUNDATIONS OF MANAGEMENT

CHAPTER 4 KEY STUDY QUESTIONS

o   What can be learned from classical management thinking?
o   What ideas were introduced by the human resource approaches?
o   What is the role of quantitative analysis in management?
o   What is unique about the systems view and contingency thinking?
o   What are the continuing themes as we enter the 21st century?

CHAPTER 4 LEARNING OBJECTIVES

After completing this chapter, students should be able to:

1.   Discuss the evolution of management thought and identify and briefly describe the four major schools of management thought.
2.   Describe the assumptions and major lessons of the classical management approach.
3.   Identify the major contributors to the scientific management, administrative principles, and bureaucratic organization branches of the classical management approach; discuss the key contributions of these individuals to management theory and practice.
4.   Describe the assumptions and major lessons of the human resources approach to management.
5.   Explain the contributions of the Hawthorne experiments, Maslow's Hierarchy of Needs, McGregor's Theory X and Theory Y, and Argyris' Theory of Personality and Organization, to the human resources approach.
6.   Discuss the assumptions and major lessons of the quantitative approach to management; identify and describe the foundations, techniques and applications which characterize this approach.
7.   Describe the assumptions and implications of the modern approach to management.
8.   Describe the major components of systems and contingency theory and explain their contributions to the modern approach to management.
9.   Identify continuing trends that are impacting management theory and practice as we enter the 21st century.

CHAPTER 4 OVERVIEW

Historical records indicate that people have been "getting things done through others" since at least biblical times. In all likelihood, prehistoric people practiced management as well in order to secure shelter, direct hunting expeditions, and cultivate the land. The systematic study of management through the use of the scientific method, however, is a relatively recent development. Today's managers can benefit from the organized body of knowledge we call "management" as a source of theories to guide their actions.

This chapter outlines the historical evolution of management thought. The *Headline* opener on *Mary Parker Follett* titled, **Don't Neglect the Wisdom of History,** describes some of the valuable insights into successful management which she provided to management thinking; her writings directly relate to many of the current trends and issues in management. The relevance of Follett's work reminds us not to ignore the past as we search for answers to today's and future management challenges.

The systematic study of management as a science began in earnest with the classical approaches. Individuals such as Frederick Taylor, Henry Fayol, and Max Weber contributed greatly to the development of the scientific management, administrative principles, and bureaucratic organization branches of the classical approaches. The theories and ideas of these individuals are discussed in detail along with the "lessons learned" from these approaches.

With the advent of the human resource approaches, the assumptions of management theory shifted away from the notion that people are rational, toward the idea that people are social and self-actualizing. The impetus for this shift was provided by the Hawthorne studies and Maslow's Hierarchy of Needs, and manifest in McGregor's Theory X and Theory Y and Argyris' ideas regarding worker maturity. The chapter provides a thorough discussion of the contributions and insights provided by these human resource approaches.

Next, the foundations, techniques and applications of the quantitative approaches are explored. While the benefits of these approaches are clearly presented, the need for managers to exercise judgement and consider human factors in applying quantitative techniques is emphasized.

The chapter then considers the modern approaches to management. Systems theory contributes to the modern perspective by providing managers with an appreciation for the complexity and dynamic nature of organizations and their environment. Contingency theory attempts to guide the manager in dealing with this complexity by identifying the situations in which various classical, human resource, quantitative and modern management techniques are most appropriate.

Finally, continuing trends in management theory and practice are considered. One trend is reflected in the commitment to meet customer needs 100 percent of the time, which guides organizations toward total quality management and continuous improvements in operations. The global economy also serves as a dramatic influence on organizations today, and opportunities abound to learn new ways of managing from practices in other cultures. It is pointed out that leadership is a demanding responsibility for all managers, especially so in today's challenging times. New managers must accept and excel at responsibilities to perform as global strategists, technology masters, consummate politicians, and leader/motivators.

CHAPTER 4 LECTURE OUTLINE

Teaching Objective: The purpose of this chapter is to expose students to the historical roots of management theory and practice. By understanding the theoretical foundations for modern management, students can develop a greater appreciation for the concepts advanced in subsequent chapters.

Suggested Time: A minimum of 2 hours of class time is required to thoroughly present this chapter.

Classical Approaches to Management
> Scientific Management
> Administrative Principles
> Bureaucratic Organization

Human Resource Approaches to Management
> The Hawthorne Studies
> Human Relations Movement

Quantitative Approaches to Management
> Management Science Foundations
> Quantitative Analysis Today

Modern Approaches to Management
> Systems Thinking
> Contingency Thinking

Continuing Management Themes
> Quality and Performance Excellence
> Global Awareness
> Leadership, Knowledge Workers, and the New Management

CHAPTER 4 SUPPORTING MATERIALS

Textbook Inserts

Headline: Don't Neglect the Wisdom of History
Margin Photo: Four Seasons Hotel, Xerox
Embedded Boxes: United Parcel Service, Digital Equipment Corporation,
       Mercedes Benz
Manager's Notepad 4.1: Practical Lessons from Scientific Management
Manager's Notepad 4.2: Eight Attributes of Performance Excellence

Multi-Media Resources

NBR Video Report:
       Harley-Davidson (Available on Videotape Supplement & Video Cases CD-ROM)

PowerPoint Presentations (Website):
       Figures 4.1 to 4.4 from the Textbook plus Supplemental Figures
       NBR Viewing Questions: Harley-Davidson & UPS

In-Class Activities

Cases for Critical Thinking (Career Readiness Workbook & Website):
       Harley-Davidson (Primary Case)
       UPS (Alternate Case)

Exercises:
       What Would the Classics Say? (Career Readiness Workbook)
       The Great Management History Debate (Career Readiness Workbook)

Assessments:
       What are Your Managerial Assumptions (Career Readiness Workbook)

Self-Test 4 (Textbook and Website)

CHAPTER 4 LECTURE NOTES

ENHANCEMENT

One way to introduce this chapter is to ask students, "Why do we bother to study management history?" Students are quick to point out that we can learn from the experiences of others to capitalize on their successes and avoid their mistakes. After all, those who are "ignorant of history are doomed to repeat it."

You may also want to discuss the growing interest among both practitioners and management historians in corporate archives. Indeed, the Winthrop Group, a firm that consults on corporate history, has been commissioned to write ten full length histories in recent years. The purpose of these histories is to document the collective wisdom of past managers so that their modern counterparts can learn from their successes as well as their failures. Most students will find the notion of treating company records as history to be a novel and intriguing idea. (*Source*: As reported in Amanda Bennet, "For Those Who Write Business History, It Helps to Have the Skills of a Detective," *Wall Street Journal*, May 27, 1988, p. 15).

I.   **Introduction**

A.   Today's managers can draw on *management theory* to guide their actions; they can learn from the insights of people throughout history who have thought about effective management.

B.   *Early Management Thinking* - Early management thinking began with the ancient Sumerian civilization in 5000 B. C. and evolved through many subsequent civilizations such as the Egyptians, and Babylonians.

C.   *The Industrial Revolution and Beyond - Adam Smith* established the principles of **specialization** and **division of labor**; these principles were further popularized by *Henry Ford*.

D.   *Major Schools of Management Thought*

1.   The **classical approaches** focus on developing universal principles for use in various management situations.

2.   The **human resource approaches** focus on human needs, the work group, and the role of social factors in the workplace.

3.   The **quantitative** or **management science approach**es focus on the use of mathematical techniques for management problem-solving.

4.   The **modern approaches** focus on the systems view of organizations and contingency thinking in a dynamic and complex environment.

5. Management **trends and directions** include a continuing emphasis on quality and performance excellence, global awareness, and respect for learning and knowledge workers.

II. **Classical Approaches to Management**   **FIGURE 4.1**

A. **FIGURE 4.1** depicts the *major branches of the classical approach to management*.

B. *Assumption: People are Rational* - Classical management theory assumes that people will rationally consider the opportunities available to them and do whatever is necessary to maximize their economic gain.

C. *Scientific Management*

1. **Taylor's contributions** - as "The father of scientific management," Taylor advocated the following **four principles of scientific management**:

   a) Develop a "science" for every job, including rules of motion, standardized work implements, and proper working conditions.

   b) Carefully select workers with the right abilities for the job.

   c) Carefully train these workers and providing proper incentives.

   d) Support workers by carefully planning their work and by smoothing the way as they go about their jobs.

ENHANCEMENT

Students can appreciate Taylor's work better if they understand that since his youth he looked for the "one best way" of doing things. For example, he searched for the "best way" to take cross country walks. At Bethlehem Steel, Taylor searched for the "best way" to do various jobs. He studied the job of loading 92 pound "pigs of iron ore," found a husky volunteer named Schmidt, and showed him the "best way" to load the ore. Interestingly, he told Schmidt to rest 58% of the time. The amount he could load rose from 12.5 to 47.5 tons per day and his wages rose 60%. In telling this story, you may ask a muscular student to load a mock pig of ore (use a moderately heavy object) before showing how to do so using fewer motions. This example illustrates the power of scientific management. Taylor popularized this approach and its impact on manufacturing is still apparent. (*Source:* Daniel A. Wren, *The Evolution of Management Thought*, New York: The Ronald Press Company, 1972, pp. 112-133).

2. **Manager's Notepad 4.1** summarizes the following **Practical Lessons from Scientific Management:**

    a) Create a consistency of purpose in the organization to innovate, put resources into research and education, and put resources into maintaining equipment and new production aids.

    b) Make results-based compensation a performance incentive.

    c) Carefully design jobs with efficient work methods.

    d) Carefully select workers with abilities to do these jobs.

    e) Train workers to perform jobs to the best of their abilities.

    f) Train supervisors to support workers so they can perform jobs to the best of their abilities.

3. **Contributions of the Gilbreths** - The Gilbreths pioneered **motion study**, the science of reducing a job or task to its basic physical motions; wasted motions are eliminated to improve performance. As the text indicates, UPS currently uses many of the techniques developed by the Gilbreths to achieve maximum efficiency in its package sorting centers.

ENHANCEMENT

You may also want to point out to students Henry Gantt's contributions, which include: a) an innovative **task and bonus wage scheme** in which workers and supervisors received bonuses for exceeding standards, and b) the **Gantt Chart** which graphically depicts the scheduling of tasks required to complete a project.

D. *Administrative Principles*

1. **Henry Fayol's Rules and Principles of Management**

    a) Fayol was a French executive who advanced five "rules" of management: <u>Foresight</u>, <u>organization</u>, <u>command</u>, <u>coordination</u>, and <u>control</u>. Note the similarity of these "rules" to the management functions introduced in Chapter 1.

    b) Fayol also introduced 14 general <u>principles of management</u> such as division of work, scalar chain, unity of command and unity of direction.

2. **Mary Parker Follett: Dynamic Administration**

    a) Follett brought an <u>understanding of groups</u> and a <u>deep commitment to human cooperation</u> to her writings about businesses and other organizations.

b)   She anticipated many modern management concepts and practices such as <u>employee-ownership</u>, <u>systems theory</u>, and <u>social responsibility</u>.

E.   *Bureaucratic Organization*

1.   *Max Weber*, a German intellectual, introduced **bureaucracy** as an organizational structure which promotes efficiency and fairness.

2.   Weber viewed a **bureaucracy** as an **ideal organizational form**, which includes the following attributes:

a)   Clear division of labor.
b)   Clear hierarchy of authority.
c)   Formal rules and procedures.
d)   Impersonality.
e)   Careers based on merit.

ENHANCEMENT

At this point you could summarize the following advantages and disadvantages of Weber's bureaucracy.

Expected Advantages	**Possible Disadvantages**	
Efficiency	Red Tape	Apathy
Fairness	Rigidity	Resistance

Modern management theory does not consider bureaucracy to be appropriate or inappropriate for all situations; instead, the bureaucratic structure is recommended for simple and stable environments, while more flexible structures are suggested for dynamic and complex environments.

III. **Human Resource Approaches to Management**   **FIGURE 4.2**

A.   *Assumption: People are Social and Self-Actualizing*

B.   **Figure 4.2** depicts the *foundations in the human resource approaches to management*.

C.   *The Hawthorne Studies*

1.   **The Illumination Studies**

a)   These studies started off as <u>scientific management experiments</u> designed to identify the optimal relationship between illumination and productivity.

b)   Despite repeated efforts, however, <u>no consistent relationship</u> was found. In one group of subjects, production increased even though illumination was reduced to "moonlight"!

2.   **The Relay Assembly Test-Room Studies**

    a)   *Elton Mayo* and his associates manipulated physical work conditions to assess their impact on output. Once again, output increased regardless of the changes made.

    b)   Mayo concluded that increases arose from the <u>group atmosphere</u> which fostered pleasant social relations, and the <u>participative supervision</u> found in the experimental groups.

3.   **Employee Attitudes, Interpersonal Relations, and Group Services**

    a)   Interviews with employees revealed that they had <u>differing sources of satisfaction</u>.

    b)   The final study in the <u>bank wiring room</u> showed that workers would <u>restrict their output to satisfy group norms</u>, even if this meant reduced pay.

ENHANCEMENT

To the Hawthorne researchers' surprise, the workers in the Bank Wiring Room established an informal group norm regarding the quantity of output which was below the standard set by management. Output was restricted despite a group incentive plan which rewarded each worker on the basis of the total output of the group. The restriction of output norm was enforced by such disciplinary devices as sarcasm, ridicule, ostracization and "binging." For fun, ask students if they know what "binging" means; chances are they won't. Then find a volunteer for a demonstration. Pretend that you are going to "bing" the student by punching him or her in the arm but stop short before making contact. This amuses the class while demonstrating the lengths that groups will go to in enforcing norms. Wrap up the demonstration by noting the contribution of the Hawthorne studies in revealing these subtle group processes.

4.   **Lessons from the Hawthorne Studies** - The Hawthorne researchers concluded that:

    a)   People's feelings, attitudes and relationships with co-workers influence their performance, and therefore;

    b)   Managers using good human relations will achieve productivity.

      c)   In addition, the <u>Hawthorne effect</u> was identified as a tendency of persons who are singled out for special attention to perform as anticipated merely because of the expectations created by the situation.

D.   *Human Relations Movement*

    1.   The Hawthorne studies contributed to the emergence of the **human relations movement** during the 1950s and 1960s, which asserted that managers who used good human relations in the workplace would achieve productivity.

    2.   The insights of the human relations movement set the stage for what has now evolved as the field of **organizational behavior**, the study of individuals and groups in organizations.

    3.   **Maslow's Theory of Human Needs**   **FIGURE 4.3**

        a)   Maslow's hierarchy identifies five levels of human needs: <u>physiological</u>, <u>safety</u>, <u>social</u>, <u>esteem</u>, and <u>self-actualization</u>. Use **FIGURE 4.3** to illustrate Maslow's hierarchy of needs and explain the following principles.

        b)   <u>The deficit principle</u> states that people act to satisfy "deprived" needs - that is, needs for which a satisfaction "deficit" exists; conversely, <u>a satisfied need is not a motivator</u> of behavior.

        c)   <u>The progression principle</u> states that the five needs exist in a <u>hierarchy of prepotency</u>; a need at any level only becomes activated once the next lower-level need is satisfied.

    4.   **McGregor's Theory X and Theory Y**

        a)   *Douglas McGregor* was influenced heavily by the Hawthorne studies and Maslow's work to propose that managers devote more attention to subordinates social and self-actualizing needs.

        b)   He asserted that managers must shift their perspective from "<u>Theory X</u>" to "<u>Theory Y</u>" assumptions.

ENHANCEMENT

Consider assigning the *Assessment* titled **What are Your Managerial Assumptions?** which is included in *Career Readiness Workbook*. This assessment enables students to determine if their assumptions about people are more consistent with Theory X or Theory Y, and thereby makes this topic more personally meaningful.

    c)   <u>Theory X Managers</u> assume subordinates:
* Dislike work.
* Lack ambition.
* Are irresponsible.
* Resist change.
* Prefer to be led than to lead.

    d)   <u>Theory Y Managers</u> assume subordinates are:
* Willing to work.
* Capable of self-control.
* Willing to accept responsibility.
* Capable of imagination, ingenuity, creativity.
* Capable of self-direction.

    e)   McGregor believed that mangers who hold either set of assumptions can create <u>self-fulfilling prophesies</u> — that is, through their behavior they create situations where subordinates act to confirm their expectations.

ENHANCEMENT

Once you have presented the assumptions of Theory X and Theory Y managers, ask students to think about managers they have had in the past and to indicate if they seemed to make Theory X or Theory Y assumptions. Then ask "How did they treat their employees?" "Do you consider them to be a good or a bad manager?" McGregor argued that Theory X assumptions often became self-fulfilling prophecies and that workers respond more positively and productively to Theory Y assumptions.

    5.   **Argyris' Theory of Personality and Organization**

    a)   Argyris asserts that some <u>classical management principles</u> such as task specialization, chain of command and unity of direction <u>inhibit worker maturation</u> by discouraging independence, initiative and self-actualization.

    b)   He advocates management practices which accommodate the mature personality by increasing a) <u>task responsibility and variety</u>, and b) <u>participative decision making</u>.

ENHANCEMENT

The *Exercise* titled **What Would the Experts Say?** from *Career Readiness Workbook*, can serve as a fun approach to reviewing the contributions made by Taylor, Fayol, Weber, Maslow, and Argyris. The *Exercise* titled the **The Great Management History Debate** can also be used to achieve the same outcome. Instructor's notes on each of these exercises are provided in Unit 9 of this *Manual*.

IV.   **Quantitative Approaches to Management**

A.   *Assumption: Applied Mathematics Can Help Solve Management Problems* - The quantitative approaches share the assumption that mathematical techniques can be used as tools to solve managerial problems.

B.   *Management Science Foundations*

1.   **Management Science** and **Operations Research** are interchangeably terms used as labels for these approaches.

2.   **Techniques and Applications** - Quantitative decision techniques and applications include:

a) mathematical forecasting.
b) inventory modeling.
c) linear programming.
d) queuing theory.
e) network models.
f) simulations.

3.   **Common Characteristics of the Quantitative Approaches**

a)   Focus on decision making, with ultimate implications for management action.
b)   Use of "economic" decision criteria.
c)   Use of mathematical models.
d)   Use of computers.

C.   *Quantitative Analysis Today*

1.   **Desk-top personal computers** have greatly expanded the potential applications of quantitative techniques to managerial problems.

2.   It is important to keep these tools in perspective; **good judgement** and an **appreciation for human factors** is required to use these techniques effectively.

V.   **Modern Approaches to Management**

A.   *Assumption: People Are Complex* - The modern approaches to management assume that people:

1.   Attend to multiple and varied needs;
2.   Change over time these patterns of needs, action tendencies, and desires; and
3.   Respond to a wide variety of managerial strategies.

151

B.   The modern approaches to management attempt to *extend the other approaches* by delineating the situations in which they can be used most appropriately and productively.

C.   *Systems Thinking*   **FIGURE 4.4**

1.   A **system** is a collection of interrelated parts that function together to achieve a common purpose.

2.   A **subsystem** is a smaller component of a larger system.

3.   An **open system** interacts with its environment; a **closed system** does not.

ENHANCEMENT

To provide students with some historical background on the **systems approach** you could include a brief discussion of the contributions of **Chester Barnard** here. Barnard served for many years as CEO of the New Jersey Bell Telephone Company. His book, *The Functions of the Executive*, is a highly respected account of management theory viewed from the manager's perspective.   Barnard viewed organizations as "cooperative systems" which he defined as "a complex of physical, biological, personal, and social components which are in a specific relationship by reason of the cooperation of two or more persons for at least one definite end."   (*Source:* Chester I. Barnard, *The Functions of the Executive*, Cambridge: Harvard University Press, 1938, p. 65).

---

4.   Because the **environment** provides organizations with **resources** and **feedback**, it has a significant impact on their operations.

5.   **Figure 4.4** uses the case of a regional electric utility to illustrate the complexity of organizations as open systems; the different subsystems must work together so the firm can produce and sell electric power to its customers.

6.   This example also shows the president, public relations department, engineering & design group, purchasing unit, and sales & distribution section acting as **boundary-spanners**.

7.   As the environment changes over time, it is the manager's job to stay informed of these changes and ensure that the organization responds in a productive way.

D.   *Contingency Thinking*

1.   **Contingency thinking** tries to match managerial responses with the problems and opportunities unique to different situations, particularly those posed by individual and environmental differences.

2. Contingency approaches to management assert that there is **no one best way to manage**, and that what is best depends in any given circumstance on the nature of the situation.

3. In short, the best way to manage **depends upon the situation**.

ENHANCEMENT

Students often find contingency theory easier to understand if it is described as IF-->THEN thinking. In essence, contingency theory asserts that IF a manager is confronted with situation A, THEN response X is most appropriate. IF, however, situation B occurs, THEN response Y is more appropriate. This type of thinking can be further illustrated by using **FIGURE 13.5** to preview **Fiedler's Contingency Theory of Leadership** as follows: IF the situation facing the leader is **extremely** favorable or unfavorable, THEN a **task-oriented style** of leadership is most effective; conversely, IF the situation is **moderately** favorable or unfavorable, THEN a **relationships-oriented** style is more likely to be successful. Let students know that the details of this theory are not essential at this point; it is the <u>logic</u> of this perspective which is important.

VI. Trends and Directions

A. *Quality and Performance Excellence*   MANAGER'S NOTEPAD 4.2

1. **Quality** is usually defined as the ability to meet customer needs 100 percent of the time.

2. Managers in truly progressive organizations are **"quality conscious"**; they understand the basic link between **competitive advantage** and the ability to always deliver quality goods and services to their customers.

3. A push for **total quality management**, which is a comprehensive approach to continuous quality improvement that is lead by top management and supported throughout the organization, has emerged in recent years.

4. Inspired by Tom Peters and Bob Waterman's book *In Search of Excellence*, the quest for **performance excellence** has also emerged as a key management theme.

5. **Manager's Notepad 4.2** summarizes the following **Eight Attributes of Performance Excellence**

   a) <u>A bias toward action</u> -- making timely decisions and getting things done.

   b) <u>Closeness to the customer</u> -- knowing customer needs and valuing customer satisfaction.

> c) <u>Autonomy and entrepreneurship</u> -- supporting innovation, change, and risk taking.
>
> d) <u>Productivity through people</u> -- respecting human resources as the keys to quality and performance.
>
> e) <u>Hands-on and value-driven</u> -- having a clear sense of organizational purpose.
>
> f) <u>Sticking to the knitting</u> -- focusing on activities that the organization does well.
>
> g) <u>Simple form and lean staff</u> -- minimizing levels of management and the use of staff personnel.
>
> h) <u>Simultaneous loose-tight properties</u> -- allowing worker flexibility while maintaining overall control.

B.   Global Awareness

1.   The drive to performance excellence has lead to major changes in American businesses, such as **process reengineering, virtual organizations, agile factories,** and **network firms,** among other "topics of the moment."

2.   Much of the pressure for quality and performance excellence is created by a **highly competitive global economy.**

3.   Closely related to the quality theme is continuing interest in **Japanese management practices.**

4.   **Theory Z,** as derived from *William Ouchi's* book of that title, is used to describe a management framework based on the Japanese example.

5.   **New** managers — those who deliver under the high performance expectations of these dynamic times — must be **well educated,** and they must **continue their education** throughout their careers.

6.   **New** managers succeed in turbulent times only through **continuous improvement;** they must also possess **"the ability to make things happen."**

C.   *Leadership, Knowledge Workers, and the New Management*

1.   **Leadership** is perhaps the most important component of "the new management."

2.   Managers of the 21st century will have to excel as never before to meet the expectations held of them and the organizations they lead.

ENHANCEMENT

The *Website Quick Hitter* titled, **Job of A Global Manager,** can be used here to generate student discussion about the requirements of a global manager.

3.   **Requirements of the 21ˢᵗ Century Executive**

   a)   <u>Global strategist</u> — who recognizes interconnections among nations, cultures, and economies in the world community and is able to plan and act with due consideration of them.

   b)   <u>Master of technology</u> — who is comfortable with existing high technology, and who understands technological trends and their implications and is able to use them to best advantage.

   c)   <u>Consummate politician</u> — who understands the growing complexity of government regulations and the legal implications and is able to work comfortably at the interface between them and the interests of the organization.

   d)   <u>Leader/motivator</u> — who is able to attract highly motivated workers and inspire their enthusiasm by creating a high-performance climate where individuals and teams can do their best work.

4.   In a society where knowledge workers are increasingly important, new managers must be well educated, and they must continue to engage in **life-long learning** to upgrade their knowledge throughout their careers.

CHAPTER 4 SUMMARY

What can be learned from classical management thinking?

* Frederick Taylor's four principles of scientific management focused on the need to carefully select, train, and support workers for individual task performance.
* Henri Fayol suggested that managers should be trained to take on the responsibilities now known as the management functions of planning, organizing, leading, and controlling.
* Max Weber described bureaucracy with its clear hierarchy, formal rules, and well-defined jobs as an ideal form of organization.

What ideas were introduced by the human resource approaches?

* The human resource approaches shifted attention toward the human factor as a key element of organizational performance.
* The historic Hawthorne studies suggested that work behavior is influenced by social and psychological forces and that work performance may be improved by better "human relations."
* Abraham Maslow's hierarchy of human needs introduced the concept of self-actualization and the potential for people to experience self-fulfillment in their work.
* Douglas McGregor urged managers to shift away from Theory X and toward Theory Y thinking, which views people as independent, responsible, and capable of self-direction in their work.
* Chris Argyris pointed out that people in the workplace are adults and may react negatively when constrained by strict management and rigid organizational structures.

What is the role of quantitative analysis in management?

* The availability of high-power desktop computing provides many opportunities for mathematical methods to be used for problem solving.
* Many organizations employ staff specialists with expertise in quantitative management science and operations research to solve problems.
* Quantitative techniques in common use include various approaches to forecasting, linear programming, and simulation, among others.

What is unique about the systems view and contingency thinking?

* Organizations are complex open systems that interact with their external environments to transform resource inputs into product outputs.
* Resource acquisition and customer satisfaction are important requirements in the organization-environment relationship.
* Organizations are composed of many subsystems that must work together in a coordinated way to support the organization's overall success.
* Contingency thinking recognizes the need to understand situational differences and respond appropriately to them.

What are the continuing themes as we enter the 21st century?

* The commitment to meet customer needs 100 percent of the time guides organizations toward total quality management and continuous improvements in operations.

* The global economy has a dramatic influence on organizations today, and opportunities abound to learn new ways of managing from practices in other cultures.
  This is the age of information in which knowledge and knowledge workers are major resources of modern society.
* New managers must accept and excel at responsibilities to perform as global strategists, technology masters, consummate politicians, and leader/motivators.

KEY CHAPTER 4 DEFINITIONS

Bureaucracy An intentionally rational, and efficient form of organization founded on principles of logic, order, and legitimate authority.

Contingency thinking An approach of modern management theory that argues that there is no one best way to manage, and that what is best depends in any given circumstance on the nature of the situation.

Hawthorne effect The tendency of persons who are singled out for special attention to perform as anticipated merely because of the expectations created by the situation.

Human relations movement A movement based on the viewpoint that managers who use good human relations in the workplace will achieve productivity.

Management science A scientific approach to management that uses mathematical techniques to analyze and solve problems.

Motion study The science of reducing a job or task to its basic physical motions.

Need A physiological or psychological deficiency a person feels the compulsion to satisfy.

Open system A system that interacts with its environment and transforms resource inputs into outputs.

Operations research A scientific approach to management that uses mathematical techniques to analyze and solve problems.

Organizational behavior The study of individuals and groups in organizations.

Quality A degree of excellence, often defined in management terms as the ability to meet customer needs 100 percent of the time.

Scientific management An approach to management that involves developing a science for every job, including rules of motion and standardized work instruments, careful selection and training of workers, and proper supervisory support for workers.

Self-fulling prophesies Situations in which a person acts in ways that confirm another's expectations.

Theory X A set of managerial assumptions that people in general dislike work, lack ambition, are irresponsible and resistant to change, and prefer to be led than to lead.

Theory Y A set of managerial assumptions that people in general are willing to work and accept responsibility, and are capable of self-direction, self-control, and creativity.

Theory Z A term that describes a management framework used by American firms following Japanese examples.

CHAPTER 5: GLOBAL DIMENSIONS OF MANAGEMENT

CHAPTER 5 STUDY QUESTIONS

o   What are the challenges of management in a global economy?
o   What are the forms and opportunities of international business?
o   What complicates the environment for global operations?
o   How does culture create global diversity?
o   How do management practices and learning transfer across cultures?

CHAPTER 5 LEARNING OBJECTIVES

After completing this chapter, students should be able to:

1.   Discuss international management and the managerial significance of the global economy.
2.   Distinguish between different forms of international business.
3.   Define the term multinational corporation, and distinguish between different types of multinational corporations (MNCs).
4.   Identify and explain the environmental challenges MNCs face in the global economy.
5.   Discuss the pros and cons of MNCs in the global economy, their relations with their host and home countries, and ethical concerns about MNCs.
6.   Define the concepts of culture shock and ethnocentrism, and describe the stages in adjusting to a new culture.
7.   Discuss the popular dimensions of culture, and their implications for international management.
8.   Discuss Geert Hofstede's research on national culture and its implications for international management.
9.   Discuss the patterns of cultural differences identified by Fons Trompenaars, and explain their implications for international management.
10   Define comparative management and explain its importance to the field of management.
11.   Explain the ways in which the basic management functions are employed across cultures.
12.   Describe and depict schematically two multinational organizational structures.

CHAPTER 5 OVERVIEW

As the initial chapter makes clear, the global economy represents an important trend which students of management must understand to meet the challenges of the 21st century. Indeed, the likelihood that students will engage in or be affected by some form of international operations is extremely high. This chapter considers the obstacles and opportunities faced by managers of international activities and provides practical advice for meeting these challenges.

The chapter begins by discussing economic developments in the European Union, the Americas, Asia and the Pacific Rim, and Africa. Next, various forms of international business are described and the roles that multinational corporations (MNCs) play in the world, host and home country economies are presented.   Included in this discussion is consideration of the environmental challenges multinational corporations face from the economic, legal, and educational sectors. From here, the managerial implications of popular dimensions of culture are explored, followed by the dimensions of national culture identified by the Dutch scholar and researcher, Geert Hofstede. The patterns of cultural differences in the ways relationships are handled among people, attitudes toward time, and attitudes toward the environment identified by Fons Trompenaar, are also examined. This research helps to introduce the field of comparative management, including its objectives and implications.

Throughout the chapter, it is emphasized that management techniques developed in one culture, be it American, Japanese, or another, cannot be unconditionally transferred to other cultures.   Importantly, the need to adapt specific practices to the local culture is stressed.

CHAPTER 5 LECTURE OUTLINE

Teaching Objective: To sensitize students to the impact of international activities on management practices and to provide guidelines for effective management in an international arena.

Suggested Time: Two hours of class time are recommended for this chapter.

The Global Economy
> The New Europe
> The Americas
> Asia and the Pacific Rim
> Africa

Forms of International Business
> Market Entry Strategies
> Direct Investment Strategies

Environment and Global Operations
> Types of Multinational Corporations
> Environmental Challenges in the Global Economy
> Pros and Cons of Multinational Corporations
> Ethical Issues in Multinational Operations

Culture and Global Diversity
> Popular Dimensions of Culture
> Values and National Cultures
> Understanding Cultural Differences

Management Across Cultures
> Planning and Controlling Global Operations
> Organizing and Leading Global Operations
> Are Management Theories Universal?
> Global Organizational Learning

CHAPTER 5 SUPPORTING MATERIALS

Textbook Inserts

Headline: Live and Work in a Global Village
Margin Photos: Quicksilver Enterprises, SBC Communications/Telekom Malaysia,
    Kemet Electronics, Nike, Honda
Embedded Boxes: Petofi Printing and Packaging, Mozambique,
    Ford Motor Co., British Airways, Digital Equipment Corporation
Manager's Notepad 5.1: Checklist for Joint Ventures
Manager's Notepad 5.2: Stages in Adjusting to a New Culture

Multi-Media Resources

NBR Video Report:
    Kodak (Available on Video Supplement & Video Cases CD-ROM)

PowerPoint Presentations (Website):
    Figures 5.1 to 5.5 from the Textbook plus Supplemental Figures
    NBR Viewing Questions: Kodak & Harley Davidson

In-Class Activities

Cases for Critical Thinking (Career Readiness Workbook & Website):
    Kodak (Primary Case)
    Harley Davidson (Alternate Case)

Exercises:
    What do You Value in Work? (Career Readiness Workbook)
    Less and More Corrupt Countries for Doing Business (Website Quick Hitter)
    Competencies for Global Success (Website Quick Hitter)
    Job of a Global Manager (Website Quick Hitter)

Assessments:
    Global Readiness Index (Career Readiness Workbook)

Research and Presentation Projects:
    Foreign Investment in America — What are the Implications (Career
    Readiness Workbook)

Self-Test 5 (Textbook and Website)

CHAPTER 5 LECTURE NOTES

I. **Introduction**

    A. The modern manager steps directly into a *complex global arena.*

    B. *International management* is a term used to describe management that involves the conduct of business and other operations in foreign countries.

    C. *Reasons for Going International*

        1) **Profits:** Global operations may offer profit potential.

        2) **New markets:** Global operations may offer new locations to sell products.

        3) **Raw materials:** Global operations may offer access to needed raw materials.

        4) **Financial capital:** Global operations may offer access to financial resources.

        5) **Lower labor costs:** Global operations may offer lower costs of labor.

ENHANCEMENT

One way to bring home the topicality and relevance of this chapter, is to make a transparency or handout of recent newspaper or magazine headlines which relate to international management issues. These can easily be found in business publications such as *The Wall Street Journal, Business Week*, and *Forbes*, as well as many other publications such as the "Money" section of *USA Today*, or popular magazines such as *Time* and *Newsweek*. These headlines can also be revisited whenever course concepts that are relevant to a particular story are presented.

    The **Global Readiness Index** from the *Career Readiness Workbook* can also provide for a stimulating means of introducing the chapter. This exercise can serve as a real "eye-opener" for many students who have a limited knowledge of international business. Explore with students the implications and potential detrimental consequences of being unaware of important international issues, events and places. For many students, this assessment can serve as the impetus for increasing their awareness of international business events.

II. **The Global Economy**

    A. The *global economy* is one based on worldwide interdependence of resource supplies, product markets, and business competition.

B.   *The New Europe*

    1.   The **European Union(EU)** is a grouping of 15 countries who agreed to support mutual economic growth by removing barriers that previously limited cross-border trade and business development.

    2.   The **EU** is expected to expand to at least 25 members in the near future; at present, only Switzerland and Norway from Western Europe remain outside the group; at least a dozen others, including several new republics from the former Soviet Union, have applied or expressed an interest in joining.

    3.   Important **European Community (EC) agreements** include:

        a)   Eliminating frontier controls and trade barriers.
        b)   Creating uniform minimum technical product standards.
        c)   Opening government procurement to businesses from all member countries.
        d)   Unifying financial regulations and lifting competitive barriers in banking and insurance.
        e)   The creation of a common currency — the "Euro."

C.   *The Americas*

    1.   The **North American Free Trade Agreement (NAFTA)** largely frees the flow of goods and services, workers, and investments within North America.

    2.   Implementation of this agreement was delayed by **protectionism**, or government legislation and support to protect domestic industries from foreign competition.

    3.   **Maquiladoras** are manufacturing plants that are allowed to operate in Mexico with special privileges in return for employing Mexican labor.

    4.   The possibility of a **Free Trade of the Americas (FTAA)** agreement would create a free-trade zone from Alaska to Chile.

D.   *Asia and the Pacific Rim*

    1.   This "megamarket" already represents a superpower in the global economy, which possesses considerable growth potential.

    2.   This does not refer to just Japan, China and the "four Tigers" of South Korea, Hong Kong, Taiwan and Singapore; in Southeast Asia, growth in Malaysia, Thailand, and Indonesia is already significant, the Philippines is making progress, and Vietnam is gaining special attention.

3. Still, Japan's economic power is ever-present; a large majority of *Fortune's* "Pac-Rim 150" are Japanese firms.

4. Even with recent economic crises taken into account, Pacific Rim economies are expected to be larger than those of the current EU. Indeed, the **Asian-Pacific Economic Forum (APEC)** is gaining prominence as the platform of a regional economic alliance; member countries already represent a third of the global marketplace, including being the world's top market for cars and telecommunications equipment.

5. Despite internal turmoil and controversy over human rights violations, China has emerged as a major exporter, and its markets have been quietly penetrated by many Multinational Corporations (e.g., RJR-Nabisco, Coca-Cola, Proctor & Gamble).

E. *Africa*   **FIGURE 5.1**

1. While foreign business interests tend to stay away from the risks in trouble spots, they are **focusing increased attention** on countries such as *Uganda*, the *Ivory Coast*, *Botswana*, *South Africa*, and *Ghana* because of their positive economic prospects.

2. Post-apartheid *South Africa*, undergoing **political revival**, is experiencing **economic recovery** and is proving highly attractive to outside investors.

III. **Forms of International Business**   **FIGURE 5.2**

A. An *international business* conducts for-profit transactions of goods and services across national boundaries.

B. *Market entry strategies* are most appropriate for a firm just getting started internationally; these strategies involve the sale of goods or services to foreign markets, but do not require expensive capital investments.

1. **Global sourcing** involves the manufacturing and/or purchasing of components from various parts of the world for use in a final product.

   Example: While the original IBM-PC was assembled in the U.S., the parts came from the following sources:
   * Monitor -- Korea.
   * Floppy disk drives -- Singapore.
   * The power supply, printer and keyboard -- Japan.
   * Case and semiconductors -- U.S.

2.   **Exporting** involves selling locally-made products in foreign markets.

3.   **Importing** involves buying foreign-made products and selling them in domestic markets.

4.   A **licensing agreement** occurs when a firm pays a fee for the rights to make or sell a foreign company's product (usually a special technology or brand name).

5.   **Franchising** is a form of licensing in which the licensee buys the complete "package" of support needed to open a particular business.

C.   *Direct investment strategies* require major capital commitments but create rights of ownership and control over operations in the foreign country.

1.   **Joint ventures** establish operations in a foreign country through joint ownership and local partners.

   Example: GM and Toyota's New United Motor Manufacturing Inc. (NUMMI).

2.   **Checklist for Joint Ventures**   **MANAGER'S NOTEPAD 5.1**

   a)   Choose a foreign partner whose activities relate closely to your firm's major business.
   b)   Choose a foreign partner with a strong local workforce.
   c)   Choose a foreign partner large enough to offer future expansion possibilities.
   d)   Choose a foreign partner with a strong local market for its own products.
   e)   Choose a foreign partner with good profit potential.
   f)   Choose a foreign partner in sound financial standing.

3.   **Wholly-owned subsidiaries** are subsidiary operations which are 100% owned by a foreign country.

IV.   Environment and Global Operations

A.   A *multinational corporation (MNC)* is a business firm with extensive international operations in more than one foreign country.

B.   *Multinational organizations (MNO)* are organizations like the International Red Cross, the United Nations, and the World Bank, whose nonprofit missions and operations span the globe.

ENHANCEMENT

An easy way to solicit student input and get them involved in the discussion at this point is to ask them to provide examples of MNCs. Students are able to quickly generate a long list of MNCs. You can then classify them into domestic and foreign based firms.

C.   *Types of Multinational Corporations*

1.   Based on the **approaches adopted in pursuing their global objectives**, MNCs can be classified as:

a)   An <u>ethnocentric MNC</u> exerts strict headquarters control over foreign operations, expects to operate the same way it does at home, and often creates local resentment by failing to respect local needs and customs.

b)   A <u>polycentric MNC</u> gives its foreign operations more operating freedom, respects market differences among countries, and pursues "multidomestic" plans, such as product design and advertising, that treat each country as a separate competitive domain.

c)   A <u>geocentric MNC</u> is more transnational and seeks total integration of global operations by operating without "home country" prejudices, making major decisions from a global perspective, and employing senior executives from many different countries.

2.   **Transnational corporations** or **global corporations** are MNCs that strive to operate on a borderless basis and without being identified with one national "home".

D.   *Environmental Challenges in the Global Economy*

1.   **Economic Environment**

a)   <u>Type of Economic System</u>

*   *Centralized-planning economies* require a central governmental body to make basic economic decisions for an entire nation (e.g., the old Soviet Union, China).

*   *Free-market economies* operate under an economic system governed by laws of supply and demand (e.g., U.S.).

b) <u>Former communist nations</u> face great difficulties as they shift toward market economies, including controversies of rising prices, unemployment, business competition, and the challenges of *privatization* --- the selling of state-owned enterprises into private ownership.

c) The <u>General Agreement on Trade and Tariffs (GATT)</u> and its successor the <u>World Trade Organization (WTO)</u> are international accords in which member nations agree to ongoing negotiations and reducing tariffs and trade restrictions.

2. **Legal Environment**

a) The more host country laws vary, the more difficult and complex it is for international businesses to adapt to local ways.

b) <u>Common legal problems</u> in international business involve incorporation practices and business ownership; negotiating and implementing contracts with foreign parties; protecting patents, trademarks, and copyrights; and handling foreign exchange restrictions.

3. **Educational Environment**

a) Differences in <u>educational systems, literacy levels, and the availability of skilled labor</u> affect international operations.

b) <u>Shortages in labor supplies</u>, along with skill deficiencies are forecast for the U.S., France, Spain, Germany, etc.

c) <u>Informed managers</u> are making greater investments in educational systems, training programs, and family-friendly workplaces to <u>support human resource development</u>.

E. *Pros and Cons of Multinational Corporations*   **FIGURE 5.3**

1. **Figure 5.3 summarizes what can go right and what can go wrong in MNC-host country relationships.**

2. **Host country complaints about foreign MNCs include:**
    a) Extract excessive profits.
    b) Dominate the local economy.
    c) Interfere with the local government.
    d) Fail to help domestic firms develop.
    e) Hire the most talented of local personnel.

> f)   Fail to transfer advanced technologies.
> g)   Fail to respect local customs, laws, and needs.

3.   **Concerns of "home" countries** include the possibilities that MNCs will:
   a)   Lose touch with domestic needs and priorities.
   b)   Shift jobs to cheaper foreign labor markets.
   c)   Export capital investments abroad.
   d)   Engage in corrupt practices abroad.

F.   *Ethical Issues in Multinational Operations*

1.   The **Foreign Corrupt Practices Act (1977)** is a controversial law intended to make "corrupt practices" such as bribery illegal for MNCs. Critics charge the law fails to recognize the "reality" of local business customs.

ENHANCEMENT

This is a good place to use the *Website Quick Hitter* titled, **Less and More Corrupt Companies for Doing Business**.

2.   **"Sweatshop" operations**, which employ local labor at low wages and often in poor working conditions, are another concern in the global business arena.

3.   **Global concerns for environmental protection** represent another ethical issue for MNCs.

V.   **Culture and Global Diversity**

A.   *Culture* is a shared set of beliefs, values, and patterns of behavior common to a group of people.

B.   *Culture shock* is the confusion and discomfort someone experiences when in an unfamiliar culture.

C.   *Ethnocentrism* is the tendency to consider one's culture as superior to all others.

D.   *Stages in Adjusting to a New Culture*   **MANAGER'S NOTEPAD 5.3**

1.   **Confusion:** First contacts leave you anxious, uncomfortable, and in need of information and advice.

2.   **Small victories:** Continued interactions bring some "successes" and form an initial confidence in day-to-day affairs.

3. **The honeymoon:** A time of wonderment, cultural immersion, and infatuation, where things are viewed most positively.

4. **Irritation and anger:** A time when "negatives" may overtake "positives," and the new culture becomes an object of criticism.

5. **Reality:** A time of rebalancing; you are able to enjoy the new culture while recognizing less desirable elements.

E. *Popular Dimensions of Culture*

1. **Language** - Foreign language training, or at the very least, a good translator, may be required to conduct business in the host country.

2. **Use of space** - Some cultures (e.g., Arabs and many Latin Americans) prefer to communicate at much closer distances than others (e.g., Americans).

3. **Time orientation** is different in many cultures.

   a) Monocrhronic *cultures* tend to do one thing at a time (e.g., schedule a meeting with one person).

   b) Polychronic *cultures* use time to accomplish many things at once (e.g., holding meetings with several different people simultaneously).

4. **Religion** has a major impact on people's lives which can extend to business practices regarding dress, eating, and interpersonal behavior, including ethical and moral teachings.

5. **Role of contracts** is another area along which cultures vary; while a contract is a final and binding agreement in the U.S., it may be viewed as more of a starting point in other countries, such as China.

ENHANCEMENT

To help students relate to *Hofstede's Dimensions of National Culture*, you may want to first have students complete and score the *Assessment* titled **Cultural Attitudes Inventory** which is included in *Career Readiness Workbook*. This inventory will provide students with a measure of their personal standing on each of Hofstede's dimensions, and serves to personalize the discussion of national culture. Further discussion of this assessment is provided in Unit 9 of this *Manual*.

F.   *Values and National Cultures*   **FIGURE 5.4**

1.   **Geert Hofstede**, identified the following dimensions of culture after studying the personnel of an MNC operating in 40 countries.

   a)   <u>Power distance</u> - The degree to which a society accepts the unequal distribution of power in organizations.

   b)   <u>Uncertainty avoidance</u> - The degree to which a society tolerates risk and situational uncertainties.

   c)   <u>Individualism-Collectivism</u> - The degree to which a society emphasizes individual self-interests, or the collective values of groups.

   d)   <u>Masculinity-Feminity</u> - The degree to which a society emphasizes assertiveness and material concerns, or relationships with others and concerns for feelings.

   e)   <u>Short-term---long-term orientation</u> - The degree to which a society emphasizes future considerations, versus greater concerns for the past and present.

2.   **Figure 5.4** shows how selected countries in Hofstede's study ranked on each of these four dimensions.

G.   *Understanding Cultural Differences*

1.   *Fons Trompenaar's* study of 15,000 respondents from 47 countries, has identified **systematic differences** in the ways relationships are handled among people, attitudes toward time, and attitudes toward the environment.

2.   **Relationships with People**

   a)   <u>Universalism vs. Particularism</u> - The degree to which a culture emphasizes rules and consistency in relationships or accepts flexibility and the bending of rules to fit circumstances.

   b)   <u>Individualism vs. Collectivism</u> - The degree to which a culture emphasizes individual freedoms and responsibilities in relationships or focuses more on group interests and consensus.

   c)   <u>Neutral vs. Affective</u> - The degree to which a culture emphasizes focused and in-depth relationships or broader and more superficial ones.

      d)   <u>Achievement vs. Prescription</u> - The degree to which a culture emphasizes an earned or performance-based status in relationships or ascribes status based on social standing and nonperformance factors.

  3. **Attitudes toward Time**

      a)   <u>Sequential view</u> - cultures that consider time to be a continuous and passing series of events; this somewhat casual view of time may be represented by a circle and the notion that time is recycling.

      b)   <u>Synchronic view</u> - cultures that view time as linear, with an interrelated past, present, and future; here, time takes on a greater sense of urgency.

  4. **Attitudes toward the Environment**

      a)   <u>Inner-directed</u> cultures include people who tend to view themselves as quite separated from nature, and the environment as something to be controlled or used for personal advantage.

      b)   <u>Outer-directed</u> cultures include people who tend to view themselves as part of nature, and hence try to blend with or go along with the environment, rather than trying to control it.

VI. Management Across Cultures

A. *Comparative management* is the study of how management practices systematically differ from one country and/or culture to the next.

B. A *global manager* works successfully across international boundaries.

C. *Planning and Controlling for Global Operations*

  1. The complexity of the international operating environment makes **global planning and controlling** even more important but difficult for managers.

  2. **Political-Risk Analysis** involves forecasting the probability of various events that can threaten the security of a foreign investment.

    Example: After China opened its borders to Western businesses, firms conducted political-risk analysis to assess the risk of a policy reversal.

D. *Organizing and Leading for International Operations*

1. **Multinational organizational structures**

    a) <u>Multinational geographic structure</u>   **FIGURE 5.5**

        *   In this structure, *producing and selling functions* are grouped under separate geographic units. Activities in each major area of the world are under the supervision of a line executive reporting to corporate management.

    b) <u>Multinational product structure</u>   **FIGURE 5.6**

        *   This structure *assigns product group managers* worldwide responsibilities for their products and/or services. Area specialists from the corporate staff provide guidance on the special needs of various countries or regions.

2. **Staffing International Operations**

    a) Organizations seeking success on a global scale must learn to fully utilize workers from different countries and cultures, including <u>competent locals</u>.

    b) MNCs also need some <u>expatriates</u> in foreign locations. <u>Expatriates</u> are workers sent on short-term or long-term assignments from home offices, or imported from abroad on special work contracts.

E. *Are Management Theories Universal?*

1. *Geert Hofstede* argues that American management theories do not apply abroad; he worries that many are ethnocentric and fail to take into account cultural differences.

2. **Example:** America's emphasis on *participation* in **leadership** reflects the culture's moderate stance on power distance; other countries with higher scores (e.g., France) are less participative.

3. Hofstede also argues U.S.-based **motivation theories** are value laden, with an emphasis on individual performance; he argues that this is consistent with the individualism found in Anglo-American countries such as the U.S.; elsewhere, where values are more collectivistic, the theories may be less appropriate.

4.   The U.S.'s focus on **individual** job enrichment as opposed to the focus on **groups** of workers in Europe, is also consistent with individualistic vs. collectivistic differences.

5.   Similarly, while some **Japanese practices** can be applied successfully abroad, others have meet with difficulties; typical practices include:

    a)   <u>Life-time employment</u>.
    b)   <u>Job rotation and broad career experience</u>.
    c)   <u>Shared information</u>.
    d)   <u>Collective decision making</u>, as evidenced by the *ringi* system, through which agreement is gained from individuals or groups affected by the decision before any actions are implemented.
    e)   <u>A quality emphasis</u>, as evidenced by the *kaizen*, or the quest for continuous improvement.

6.   **Keiretsu** are long-term industry alliances or business groups that link together various businesses ---manufacturers, suppliers, and finance companies --- for common interests.

7.   This practice is criticized by outsiders as a **potential trade barrier** that makes it hard to do business in Japan; it is also criticized as a source of **unfair competition** in the ways Japanese firms operate in other countries --- like the antitrust-conscious United States.

F.   *Global Organizational Learning*

1.   Kenichi Ohmae, noted Japanese management consultant and author, notes in *The Borderless World* that "Companies can learn from one another, particularly from other excellent companies, both at home and abroad."

2.   Still, **caution** should be exercised in transferring any culture-based management practice to a new culture; no management practices can be **universally** applied.

3.   **Comparative management research** seeks to delineate the circumstances under which particular management practices work best to lead to improved management worldwide.

4.   The best approach to comparative management is an alert, open, inquiring, but always cautious one. It is important to identify both the potential merits of management practices found in other countries *and* the ways cultural variables may affect their success or failure when applied elsewhere.

CHAPTER 5 SUMMARY

What are the management challenges in a global economy?
*   International management is practiced in organizations that conduct business in more than one country.
*   The global economy is making the diverse countries of the world increasingly interdependent regarding resource supplies, product markets, and business competition.
*   The global economy is strongly influenced by regional developments that involve more economic integration in Europe, the Americas, and Asia, and the economic emergence of Africa.

What are the forms and opportunities of international business?
*   Five forms of international business are global sourcing, exporting and importing, licensing and franchising, joint ventures, and wholly owned subsidiaries.
*   The market entry strategies of global sourcing, exporting/importing, and liscensing are common for firms wanting to get started internationally.
*   Direct investment strategies to establish joint ventures or wholly owned subsidiaries in foreign countries are substantial commitments to international operations.

What complicates the environment of global operations?
*   Global operations are influenced by important environmental differences among the economic, legal-political, and educational systems of countries.
*   A multinational corporation, or MNC, is a business with extensive operations in more than one foreign country.
*   True MNCs are global firms with worldwide missions and strategies, and who earn a substantial part of their revenues abroad.
*   MNCs offer potential benefits to host countries in broader tax bases, new technologies, and employment opportunities; MNCs can also disadvantage host countries if they interfere in local government, extract excessive profits, and dominate the local economy.
*   The Foreign Corrupt Practices Act prohibits American MNCs from engaging in corrupt practices in their global operations.

How does culture create global diversity?
*   Management and global operations are affected by the dimensions of popular culture, including language, space perception, time perception, religion, and the nature of contracts.
*   Management and global operations are affected by differences in national cultures including Hofstede's dimensions of power distance, uncertainty avoidance, individualism--collectivism, masculinity--femininity, and long-term--short-term orientation.
*   Differences among the world's cultures may be understood in respect to how people handle relationships with one another, their attitudes toward time, and their attitudes toward their environment.

How does management and learning transfer across cultures?

* The management process must be used appropriately and applied with sensitivity to the local cultures and situations.
* The field of comparative management studies how management is practiced around the world and how management ideas are transferred from one country or culture to the next.
* Cultural values and management practices must be consistent with one another, and that practices successful in one culture may work less well in others.
* The concept of global management learning has much to offer as the "borderless" world begins to emerge and as the management systems and practices of various countries become more visible.

CHAPTER 5 KEY TERMS

Asian-Pacific Economic Cooperation (APEC) A platform for regional economic alliance among Asian and Pacific Rim countries.

Comparative management The study of how management practices systematically differ from one country and/or culture to the next.

Culture A shared set of beliefs, values, and patterns of behavior common to a group of people.

Culture shock The confusion and discomfort a person experiences when in an unfamiliar culture.

Ethnocentrism The tendency to consider one's culture as superior to all others.

European Union (EU) A political and economic alliance of European countries that have agreed to support mutual economic growth and to lift barriers that previously limited cross-border trade and business development.

Expatriates Employees who live and work in a foreign country on a long- or short-term assignment.

Exporting The process of producing products locally and selling them abroad in foreign markets.

Franchising A form of licensing in which the licensee buys the complete "package" of support needed to open a particular business.

General Agreement on Tariffs and Trade (GATT) An international accord in which member nations agree to ongoing negotiations and reducing tariffs and trade restrictions.

Global economy An economic perspective based on worldwide interdependence of resource supplies, product markets, and business competition.

Global manager A manager who works successfully across international boundaries.

Global sourcing A process of purchasing materials or components in various parts of the world and then assembling them at home into a final product.

Importing The process of acquiring products abroad and selling them in domestic markets.

International business The conduct of for-profit transactions of goods and/or services across national boundaries.

International management Management that involves the conduct of business or other operations in foreign countries.

Joint ventures A form of international business that establishes operations in a foreign country through joint ownership with local partners.

Keiretsu A Japanese term describing alliances or business groups that link together various businesses -- manufacturers, suppliers, and finance companies -- for common interests.

Licensing agreement When a firm pays a fee to enter an agreement giving it the rights to make or sell another company's products.

Maquiladora A Mexican term describing foreign manufacturing plants that operate in Mexiço with special privileges in return for employing Mexican labor.

Monochronic cultures Cultures in which people tend to do one thing at a time.

Multinational corporation (MNC) A business firm with extensive international operations in more than one foreign country.

Multinational organizations (MNO) Organizations with nonprofit missions and operations in many countries.

North American Free Trade Agreement (NAFTA) A trade agreement that links Canada, the United States, and Mexico in a regional economic alliance.

Political risk The risk of losing one's investment in or managerial control over a foreign asset because of political changes in the host country.

Polychronic cultures Cultures in which time is used to accomplish many different things at once.

Privatization The selling of state-owned enterprises into private ownership.

Transnational corporation An MNC that operates world-wide on a borderless basis and without being identified with one national home.

Wholly owned subsidiary A local operation completely owned and controlled by a foreign firm.

World Trade Organization An international accord in which member nations agree to ongoing negotiations and reducing tariffs and trade restrictions; the successor to GATT.

CHAPTER 6: ETHICAL BEHAVIOR AND
SOCIAL RESPONSIBILITY

CHAPTER 6 STUDY QUESTIONS

o   What is ethical behavior in organizations?
o   How can ethical dilemmas complicate the workplace?
o   How can high ethical standards be maintained?
o   What is corporate social responsibility?
o   How does government regulation influence business behavior?

CHAPTER 6 LEARNING OBJECTIVES

After completing this chapter, students should be able to:

1.   Define ethics and ethical behavior, and the relationships between the law, values, and ethical behavior.
2.   Identify and discuss four alternative views of ethical behavior.
3.   Discuss the influence of culture on ethical behavior, and compare and contrast the notions of cultural relativism and ethical imperialism.
4.   Explain how companies can respect core and universal values across cultures.
5.   Define the term ethical dilemma and identify four rationalizations for unethical behavior.
6.   Identify and discuss the key factors influencing ethical behavior.
7.   List and discuss ways in which high ethical standards can be maintained.
8.   Explain the concept of corporate social responsibility and discuss contrasting views of social responsibility.
9.   Define the term social audit and describe the four criteria for evaluating corporate social performance.
10. Identify and explain four strategies of corporate social responsibility.
11. Explain the role of government agencies as regulators of business and the complex legal environment.
12. Explain how high ethical standards and social responsibility can be integrated as part of the manager's performance accountability.

CHAPTER 6 OVERVIEW

Ethical behavior and corporate social responsibility are critical issues for contemporary managers. This chapter seeks to make students aware of various ethical dilemmas they may face in their careers while encouraging them to adopt high ethical standards. It also takes a look at the arguments for and against social responsibility.

The chapter begins by defining key terms such as ethics and ethical behavior before considering these terms in a managerial context. The utilitarian, individualism, moral-rights, and justice views of ethical behavior are examined next. Ethical dilemmas faced by managers are then described, along with four rationalizations for unethical behavior. The factors influencing

179

ethical behavior are also considered together with various ways of maintaining high ethical standards.

From here, the focus shifts to the related topic of corporate social responsibility. A summary of the arguments "against" and "for" social responsibility is provided and four criteria for evaluating corporate social performance are also discussed. A continuum reflecting different strategies of social responsibility is also presented. Because government regulation influences and is in turn influenced by the level of social responsibility exhibited by corporations, the reciprocal relationship between businesses and government is described.

In your discussion of these issues, be sure to stress the long-term benefits of ethical managerial behavior and corporate social responsibility.

CHAPTER 6 LECTURE OUTLINE

Teaching Objective: To expose students to the issues of managerial ethics and corporate social responsibility and encourage them to adopt high ethical standards.

Suggested Time: Two hours of class time are typically required to present the material in this chapter.

What is Ethical Behavior?
      Law, Values, and Ethical Behavior
      Alternative Views of Ethical Behavior
      Cultural Issues in Ethical Behavior

Ethics in the Workplace
      What is an Ethical Dilemma?
      Rationalizations for Unethical Behavior
      Factors Affecting Managerial Ethics

Maintaining High Ethical Standards
      Ethics Training
      Whistleblower Protection
      Top Management Support
      Formal Codes of Ethics

Corporate Social Responsibility
      Social Responsibility and Corporate Performance
      Social Responsibility Audits
      Social Responsibility Strategies

Government Regulation of Business
      The Complex Legal Environment
      Integrating Ethics, Social Responsibility, and Performance

CHAPTER 6 SUPPORTING MATERIALS

Textbook Inserts

Headline: Make This World a Better Place
Margin Photos: The Council on Economic Priorities, Florist Directory Assistance/
      Florist Search, Inc., GE Plastics, The Gap, Inc., The City of San Francisco
Embedded Boxes: Tom's of Maine, Malden Mills, Levi Strauss, Quad/Graphics
Manager's Notepad 6.1: How Companies Can Respect Core or Universal Values
Manager's Notepad 6.2: Checklist for Making Ethical Decisions
Manager's Notepad 6.3: "Do" and "Don't" Tips for Whistleblowers

Multi-Media Resources

PowerPoint Presentations (Website):
      Figures 6.1 to 6.4 from the Textbook plus Supplemental Figures

In-Class Activities

Cases for Critical Thinking:
      Tom's of Maine (Primary Case)
      Ben and Jerry's Ice Cream (Alternate Case)

Exercises:
      Confronting Ethical Dilemmas (Career Readiness Workbook)
      Survey of Secretarial Loyalty (Website Quick Hitter)
      Corporate Social Responsibility and Campus Drinking (Website Quick Hitter)

Self-Assessments:
      Diversity Awareness (Career Readiness Workbook)

Research and Presentation Projects:
      Corporate Social Responsibility — What's the Status? (Career
          Readiness Workbook)
      Corporate Citizenship Survey (Website)

Self-Test 6 (Textbook and Website)

CHAPTER 6 LECTURE NOTES

I.   Introduction

ENHANCEMENT

The title of the chapter opener says it all: **"Make This World A Better Place"**. As the opener indicates, more and more organizations are adding a new job title -- Vice President of the Environment. These senior managers are concerned with everything from a company's recycling program to long-term corporate environmental policies. One way to introduce this chapter is to discuss the underlying causes behind this trend, as well as its implications. You can follow this discussion up with the bad news: not all reports from the corporate world are as positive as these examples. Here you can discuss the examples of corporate scandals from the first paragraph of the chapter, such as AT&T's use of confidential bid information, Hertz's admission that they overcharged consumers and insurers more than $13 million for repairs to damaged cars, the imprisonment of Beech-nut executives for selling adulterated apple juice.

    A.   *The Ethical Challenge*

        1.   The chapter opens with several examples of unethical business practices.

        2.   Archbishop Desmund Tutu's call for ethical managerial behavior presents the challenge facing students.

II.   What is Ethical Behavior?

ENHANCEMENT

One stimulating approach to introducing this chapter is to assign the *Exercise* titled, **Confronting Ethical Dilemmas** from the *Career Readiness Portfolio*. This exercise asks students to indicate their responses to several ethical dilemmas, and share these with a group of students to be designated by the instructor. After the group discussions, you may want to poll the class to see how students believe they would respond to each of the dilemmas presented. It is also a good idea to ask students espousing alternative responses to justify their stand. This usually results in a lively, and sometimes heated, debate regarding the ethical appropriateness of various responses to these dilemmas. Further discussion of this exercise is included in Unit 9 of this *Manual*.

        After this initial discussion, you can ask students for additional examples of ethical dilemmas that they expect to encounter in their careers. You may also want to solicit examples of corporate behaviors that are considered to be socially irresponsible, such as Dow Corning's marketing of silicone breast implants which were known to pose serious health risks. To bring the issue of

ENHANCEMENT *(Continued)*

social responsibility and ethics closer to home, discuss the ethical behavior of students at a university. Topics may include cheating, adherence to campus regulations, maintenance of the environment, or unauthorized use of materials or equipment. From here, you can present the definitions of ethics and ethical behavior which follow.

A.   *Ethics* can be defined as the code of moral principles that sets standards of good or bad, or right or wrong, in one's conduct and thereby guides the behavior of a person or group.

B.   *Ethical behavior* is behavior that is accepted as "good" and "right" as opposed to "bad" or "wrong" in the context of the governing moral code.

C.   *Law, Values, and Ethical Behavior*

1.   Any behavior considered **ethical** should also be **legal** in a just and fair society.

2.   **Legal behavior**, however, is **not necessarily ethical behavior.**

3.   What one considers to be **ethical** depends on personal **values** -- the underlying beliefs and attitudes that help determine individual behavior.

D.   *Alternative Views of Ethical Behavior*   **FIGURE 6.1**

ENHANCEMENT

Ask students for examples of each of the following views of ethical behavior. These can be either hypothetical examples, or situations they have encountered in their own lives. Ask them to indicate which view they think is the most valid, and why.

1.   **Utilitarian view:** ethical behavior delivers the greatest good to greatest number of people.

2.   **Individualism view:** ethical behavior is that which best serves long-term self interests.

3.   **Moral-rights view:** ethical behavior is that which respects the fundamental rights shared by all.

4.   **Justice view:** ethical behavior is impartial, fair, and equitable in treating people.

a)   <u>Procedural justice</u>: The degree to which policies and rules are fairly administered. <u>Example:</u> Does a sexual harassment charge receive the same full hearing if levied against a senior executive instead of a shop-level supervisor?

b)   <u>Distributive justice</u>: The degree to which people are treated the same regardless of individual characteristics based on ethnicity, race, gender, age, or other criteria. <u>Example</u>: Does a woman with the same qualifications and experience as a man receive the same pay for doing the same job?

E.   *Cultural Issues in Ethical Behavior*   **FIGURE 6.2**

1.   **Cultural relativism** is the notion that there is no one right way to behave and that ethical behavior is always determined by the cultural context.

2.   **Figure 6.2** contrasts this notion with the alternative position that suggests if a behavior is not okay in one's home environment it shouldn't be acceptable practice anywhere else' critics of such a **universal approach** claim that it is **ethical imperialism,** or the attempt to externally impose one's ethical standards on others.

3.   Business ethicist *Thomas Donaldson* argues instead that certain fundamental rights and ethical standards,or **"hyper-norms"** should transcend cultural boundaries; however, with a commitment to the core values underlying a trans-cultural umbrella, international business behaviors can be tailored to local and regional cultural contexts.

4.   Use **Manager's Notepad 6.1** to summarize how companies can show **respect for core or universal values** such as human dignity, basic rights, and good citizenship.

III. Ethics in the Workplace

A.   *What is an Ethical Dilemma?*

1.   An **ethical dilemma** occurs when someone must choose whether or not to pursue a course of action that, although offering the potential of personal and organizational benefit or both, is also unethical and/or illegal.

A good way to get students thinking about **ethical dilemmas** while generating some lively discussion, is to ask students how they would respond to the following three dilemmas. The range of student responses is likely to be quite broad. Next, you can present the results of the *Harvard Business Review* survey from which they were taken.

Case 1: Foreign Payment. The minister of a foreign nation asks you to pay a $200,000 consulting fee. In return for the money, the minister promises special assistance in obtaining a $100-million contract that would produce at least a $5-million profit for your company. The contract will probably go to a foreign competitor if not won by you. **Result:** 42% of the responding managers would refuse to pay; 22% would pay, but consider it unethical; 36% would pay and consider it ethical in a foreign context.

Case 2: Competitor's Employee. You learn that a competitor has made an important scientific discovery. It will substantially reduce, but not eliminate, your profit for about a year. There is a possibility of hiring one of the competitor's employees who knows the details of the discovery. **Result:** 50% would probably hire the person; 50% would not.

Case 3: Expense Account. You learn that an executive in your company who earns $50,000 a year has been padding his expense account by about $1500 a year. **Results:** 89% feel padding is okay if superiors know about it; 9% feel it is unacceptable regardless of the circumstances.

To generate more discussion, you may ask students to indicate how they would respond to the following additional example of an ethical dilemma.

(*Source:* Steven N. Brenner and Earl A. Mollander, "Is the Ethics of Business Changing?" *Harvard Business Review*, January-February 1977, Volume 55, p. 60).

Additional Example of an Ethical Dilemma. As a mortgage loan officer, you sign a customer up for an adjustable rate payment at 8.5 percent. The loan rate could rise to 10.5 in one year. Do you warn the customer how much, in dollars, his payment could increase? Ethical dilemmas like these are confronted daily in corporate America by everyone from hourly workers and janitors to secretaries and executive vice presidents.

(*Source:* "The Rise of the Corporate Credo." *Detroit Free Press*, Nov. 27, 1989, p. D1.)

B.   *Rationalizations for Unethical Behavior*

1.   **Convincing yourself that the behavior is not really illegal.** This rationalization is particularly common in ambiguous situations. A good rule of thumb is: When in doubt, don't do it.

2.   **Convincing yourself that the behavior is in everyone's best interest.** Look beyond this view to the long run implications. When asking "How far should I go?" the best answer is "Don't find out."

3. **Convincing yourself that nobody will ever find out what you've done.** This argument assumes no crime is committed unless discovered. To deter this view, make sure sanctions for wrongdoing are public.

4. **Convincing yourself that the organization will "protect" you.** This implies the organization will condone the practice, but organizational norms should not be put above the law or social morality.

C. *Factors Affecting Managerial Ethics*   **FIGURE 6.3**

1. **Figure 6.3** summarizes the following factors affecting ethical managerial behavior.

2. **The Person:** In developing <u>ethical frameworks</u> as personal strategies for ethical decision making, managers are influenced by the following factors:
    a) Family influences.
    b) Religious values.
    c) Personal standards and needs.

3. **The Organization:** The organization also plays a key role in shaping managerial ethics through:
    a) Policies, codes of conduct.
    b) Behavior of supervisors.
    c) Behavior of peers.

ENHANCEMENT

The *Website Quick Hitter* titled **Survey of Secretarial Loyalty** can be used here to emphasize the pressure that superiors can exert on subordinates to compromise their ethics. The exercise presents students with scenarios describing a set of ethically questionable directives from superiors, and then asks students to estimate the percentages of American and Canadian secretaries who indicated in a *Wall Street Journal* survey that they would report each of these unethical/incorrect acts. Before discussing the results, you can ask students (a) whether or not they consider the act to be unethical, and (b) why they believe secretaries might comply with requests from their bosses to do these things. Finally, after presenting the results, you can discuss what secretaries could do in these circumstances if they didn't want to comply with a boss's directive to do one or more of these things. Be sure to generalize the discussion to consider how anyone can cope with a directive to do something that is unethical.

4. **The Environment:** Managerial ethics are also shaped by the following components of the external environment:
    a) Government regulation.
    b) Norms and values of society.
    c) Ethical climate of the industry.

IV. Maintaining High Ethical Standards

A. *Ethics training* is designed to help people better understand the ethical aspects of decision making, and incorporate high ethical standards into their daily behaviors.

B. A *Checklist for Making Ethical Decisions*   **MANAGER'S NOTEPAD 6.2**

   1. Recognize the ethical dilemma.
   2. Get the facts.
   3. Identify your options.
   4. Test each option:
           Is it legal?
           Is it right?
           Is it beneficial?
   5. Decide which option to follow.
   6. Double-check your decision by asking:
       "How will I feel if my family finds out about my decision?"
       "How will I feel if my decision is printed in the newspaper?"
   7. Take action.

ENHANCEMENTS

Ask students to suppose that they are a manager facing an ethical dilemma--for example, a hospital administrator in charge of purchasing, who is offered a state-of-the-art personal computer system from a supplier in return for purchasing the hospital's new computerized billing system from that company. Ask students, either singly or as a group, to go through the checklist step by step in order to determine what to do.

C. *Whistleblower Protection*

   1. A **whistleblower** is someone who exposes the misdeeds of others in organizations to preserve ethical standards and protect against wasteful, harmful, or illegal acts.

   2. New state laws protect whistleblowers from **retaliatory discharge.**

   3. Nevertheless, **organizational blocks to whistleblowing** include:

       a) A strict chain of command which makes it difficult to report unethical practices to higher level managers.

       b) Strong work group identities. Group norms may support unethical practices. Violations of these norms through whistleblowing may result in group sanctions.

        c)   <u>Ambiguous priorities</u>. Formal policies may be inconsistent with day-to-day practices, thus making it difficult to determine if a behavior is unethical, let alone expose it.

4.   **Ethics advisors** and **moral quality circles** are two ways to overcome these barriers and encourage high ethical standards.

5.   **"Do" and "Don't" Tips for Whistleblowers**   MANAGER'S NOTEPAD 6.3

        a)   *Do* make sure you really understand what is happening and that your allegation is absolutely correct.

        b)   *Don't* assume that you are automatically protected by law.

        c)   *Do* talk to an attorney to ensure that your rights will be protected and proper procedures followed.

        d)   *Don't* talk first to the media.

        e)   *Do* keep accurate records to document your case; keep copies outside of your office.

        f)   *Don't* act in anticipation of a big financial windfall if you end up being fired.

D.   *Top Management Support*

1.   Because top managers serve as **role models,** their behavior can either encourage or discourage unethical behavior.

2.   *Too* much pressure to accomplish goals that are *too* difficult can also encourage unethical behavior. Surveys of executives suggest that most feel they are under pressure to compromise their ethics to achieve company goals.

ENHANCEMENT

Point out to students that, in a survey of business executives, respondents indicated that superiors were the most common source of pressures to compromise their personal ethics.

(Source: Steven N. Brenner and Earl A. Mollander, "Is the Ethics of Business Changing?" *Harvard Business Review,* January-February 1977, Volume 55, p. 60).

E.   *Formal Codes of Ethics*

1.   **Codes of ethics** document in writing the commitments to values and ethical conduct an organization expects of its employees.

ENHANCEMENT

A *Conference Board* study also indicates that in firms that adopt such codes, over 80% of top management executives get involved in the development of these codes. To add bite to these codes, many include penalties for violations that range in severity from terminations to comments in performance appraisals.

(Source: As reported in Amanda Bennett, "Ethics Codes Spread Despite Skepticism," *The Wall Street Journal,* July 15, 1988, p. 13).

2.   **Areas Often Covered in Written Codes of Ethics**

a)   Workforce diversity.
b)   Bribes and kickbacks.
c)   Conflicts of interest.
d)   Political contributions.
e)   Honesty of books or records.
f)   Customer/supplier relationships.
g)   Misappropriation of corporate assets.
h)   Confidentiality of corporate information.

V.   **Corporate Social Responsibility**

A.   *Corporate social responsibility* is an obligation of the organization to act in ways that serve both its own interests and the interests of its many external publics.

B.   These publics are considered *stakeholders* -- the persons and groups who are affected in one way or another by the behavior of an organization.

C.   *Social responsibility in corporate performance* is driven by leaders who hold special beliefs about the world, such as:

1.   The belief that people do their best in **healthy work environments** that allow for job involvement, respect for contributions, and a good balance of work and family life.

2.   The belief that organizations function best over the long run when located in **healthy communities** with high qualities of life.

3.   The belief that organizations realize performance gains and efficiencies when they **treat the natural environment with respect** in all aspects of their operations.

4. The belief that **organizations must be managed and led** for long-term success.

5. The belief that the **reputation** of an organization must be protected to ensure consumer and stakeholder support.

D. *Contrasting Views on Social Responsibility*

1. The **classical view** holds that management's only responsibility is running a business to maximize profits.

2. The **socio-economic view** holds that any organization must be concerned about the broader social welfare.

3. The arguments of the **classical view "against"** social **responsibility** and the arguments of the **socio-economic view "in favor of"** social **responsibility** are summarized below.

AGAINST	IN FAVOR OF
* Reduced business profits.	* Long-run profits for businesses.
* Higher business costs.	* Public expectations support
* Dilution of business	business social responsibility.
purpose.	* Better public image for businesses.
* Too much social power for	* Businesses may avoid more
businesses.	regulation.
* Lack of business	* Businesses have the resources.
accountability to the	* Businesses have the ethical
public.	obligation.
	* Better environment for everyone.
	* The public wants it.

ENHANCEMENT

An excellent example of the benefits of **social responsibility** is provided by Johnson & Johnson's (J & J) response in the wake of the discovery that cyanide had been maliciously placed in capsules of Tylenol. Following the philosophy of social responsibility reflected in J & J's **"credo,"** both corporate and local level managers decided, independently, to remove the product from store shelves. This was so even though it was quickly discovered that the contamination occurred after the shipments had left J & J's manufacturing and distribution centers, simply because it was the right thing to do to protect consumers.

E. *Social Responsibility Audits*

1. A **social audit** is a systematic assessment and reporting of an organization's resource and action commitments, and

performance accomplishments in these areas of social responsibility.

2. **Four Criteria for Evaluating Corporate Social Performance**

    a) Is the organization's <u>economic responsibility</u> met?

        * Its *economic responsibility* is met when it earns a profit through the provision of goods and services desired by customers.

    b) Is the organization's <u>legal responsibility</u> met?

        * Its *legal responsibility* is fulfilled when it operates within the law and according to the requirements of various external regulations.

    c) Is the organization's <u>ethical responsibility</u> met?

        * Its *ethical responsibility* is met when its actions voluntarily conform to legal expectations and the broader values of society.

    d) Is the organization's <u>discretionary responsibility</u> met?

        * Its *discretionary responsibility* involves its voluntary movement beyond basic economic, legal, and ethical expectations to providing leadership in advancing the well-being of stakeholders.

F.   *Social Responsibility Strategies*   **FIGURE 6.4**

ENHANCEMENT

Discuss some real-life examples of corporations using **obstructionist** or **defensive** strategies. Do these strategies tend to have a positive or negative financial impact on these firms? How about their corporate image?

---

1. **Figure 6.4** displays this continuum and the primary concerns of the following **strategies of social responsibility.**

    a) <u>Obstructionist</u> -- "Fight the social demands." Meet economic responsibilities.

    b) <u>Defensive</u> -- "Do the minimum legally required." Meet economic and legal responsibilities.

    c) <u>Accommodative</u> -- "Do the minimum ethically required." Meet economic, legal, and ethical responsibilities.

d) <u>Proactive</u> -- "Take leadership in social initiative." Meet direct economic, legal, ethical, and discretionary responsibilities.

ENHANCEMENT

Discuss ways in which businesses can protect the environment and save money at the same time, such as grocery stores selling low-priced canvas bags to replace paper or plastic ones; coffee shops encouraging patrons to bring in their own cups; and fast food restaurants providing recycling bins so customers can sort their trash. Ask students for other examples.

To further deepen students' knowledge of *strategies of corporate social responsibility* assign the *Research Project* titled **Corporate Social Responsibility Status Report** included in **Career Readiness Portfolio**. Additional discussion of this assignment is included in Unit 9 of this manual. An alternative project that can be used to achieve the same type of learning is the *Website Project* titled, **Corporate Citizenship Survey**.

VI. **Government Regulation of Business**   FIGURE 6.5

A. *Government Agencies as Regulators* - Government agencies such as the Federal Aviation Administration (FAA), Environmental Protection Agency (EPA), Occupational Safety and Health Administration (OSHA), and Food and Drug Administration (FDA) are charged with monitoring and ensuring compliance with government legislation.

B. *The Complex Legal Environment* - State and federal laws have lead to the following "quality-of-life" protections for U.S. workers.

1. **Organizational safety and health** is protected by the Occupational Safety and Health Act (OSHA) of 1970.

2. **Fair labor practices** are governed by such laws as the National Labor Relations Act (NLRA) and the Equal Employment Opportunity Act (EEOA) of 1972.

3. **Consumer protection** is provided by the Consumer Product Safety Act of 1972 which gives the government authority to remove from sale any product considered dangerous.

4. **Environmental protection** is provided by many laws including the Air Pollution Control Act of 1962.

C. *Integrating Ethics, Social Responsibility, and Performance*

1. **High ethical standards** and **corporate social responsibility** and **organizational performance** should be integrated.

CHAPTER 6 SUMMARY

What is ethical behavior?
* Ethical behavior is that which is accepted as "good" or "right" as opposed to "bad" or "wrong."
* Simply because an action is *not illegal* does not make it necessarily ethical in a given situation.
* Because values vary, the question of "What is ethical behavior?" may be answered differently by different people.
* Four ways of thinking about ethical behavior are the utilitarian, individualism, moral-rights, and justice views.
* Cultural relativism argues that no culture is ethically superior to any other.

How can ethical dilemmas complicate the workplace?
* When managers act ethically they can have a positive impact on other people in the workplace *and* on the social good performed by their organizations.
* An ethical dilemma occurs when someone must decide whether or not to pursue a course of action that, although offering the potential of personal or organizational benefit or both, may be considered potentially unethical.
* Managers report that their ethical dilemmas often involve conflicts with superiors, customers, and subordinates over such matters as honesty in advertising and communications, as well as pressure from their bosses for doing unethical things.
* Common rationalizations for unethical behavior include believing the behavior is not illegal, is in everyone's best interests, will never be noticed, and will be supported by the organization.

How can high ethical standards be maintained?
* Ethics training in the form of courses and training programs helps people better deal with ethical dilemmas in the workplace.
* Whistleblowers expose the unethical acts of others in organizations, even while facing career risks for doing so.
* Top management sets an ethical tone for the organization as a whole, and all managers are responsible for acting as positive models of appropriate ethical behavior.
* Written codes of ethical conduct are used increasingly to formally state an organization's expectations of its employees regarding ethical conduct in workplace affairs.

What is corporate social responsibility?
* Corporate social responsibility is an obligation of the organization to act in ways that serve both its own interests and the interests of its many external publics, often called stakeholders.
* Criteria for evaluating corporate social performance include economic, legal, ethical, and discretionary responsibilities.

* Corporate strategies in response to social demands include obstruction, defense, accommodation, and proaction, with more progressive organizations taking proactive stances.

How does government influence business?
* Government agencies are charged with monitoring and ensuring compliance with the mandates of law.
* Managers must be well informed about existing and pending legislation in a variety of areas --- including environmental protections and other quality-of-life concerns.
* All decisions made and actions taken in every workplace should allow performance accountability to be met by high ethical standards and socially responsible means.

CHAPTER 6 KEY TERMS

Accommodative strategy A strategy that accepts social responsibilities and tries to satisfy prevailing economic, legal, and ethical performance criteria.

Code of ethics A written document that states values and ethical standards to guide the behavior of employees.

Corporate social responsibility An obligation of an organization to act in ways that serve both its own interests and the interests of its many external publics.

Cultural relativism The notion that there is no one right way to behave; ethical behavior is always determined by the cultural context.

Defensive strategy A strategy that seeks to protect the organization by doing the minimum legally required to satisfy social expectations.

Distributive justice The degree to which people are treated the same regardless of individual characteristics such as ethnicity, race, gender, or age.

Ethical behavior Behavior that is accepted as "right" or "good" in the context of a governing moral code.

Ethical dilemmas Situations with a potential course of action that, although offering potential benefit or gain, is also unethical and/or illegal in the broader social context.

Ethical imperialism The attempt to externally impose one's ethical standards on other cultures.

Ethics The code of morals of a person or group that sets standards as to what is good or bad, or right or wrong in one's conduct.

Ethics training Training that seeks to help people better understand the ethical aspects of decision making and to incorporate high ethical standards into their daily behavior.

Individualism view A view of ethical behavior based on the belief that one's primary commitment is to the advancement of long-term self-interests.

Justice view A view of ethical behavior based on the belief that ethical decisions treat people impartially and fairly according to guiding rules and standards.

Moral-rights view A view of ethical behavior that seeks to respect and protect the fundamental rights of people.

Obstructionist strategy A strategy that avoids social responsibility and reflects mainly economic priorities.

Proactive strategy A strategy that meets all the criteria of social performance, including discretionary performance.

Procedural justice The degree to which policies and rules are fairly administered.

Social audit A systematic assessment and reporting of an organization's commitments and accomplishments in areas of social responsibility.

Stakeholders Members of the external environment who is directly involved with an organization and/or affected by its operations.

Utilitarian view A view of ethical behavior as that which delivers the greatest good to the greatest number of people.

Values Broad beliefs about what is or is not appropriate; they are the underlying beliefs and attitudes that help determine the behavior an individual displays.

Whistleblowers Individuals who expose the misdeeds of others in organizations to preserve ethical standards and protect against wasteful, harmful, or illegal acts.

CHAPTER 7: PLANNING — TO SET DIRECTION

CHAPTER 7 KEY STUDY QUESTIONS

o   Why is planning an essential management function?
o   What types of plans are used by managers?
o   What are the different approaches to planning?
o   What planning tools and techniques are useful?
o   How does Management by Objectives facilitate planning?

CHAPTER 7 LEARNING OBJECTIVES

After completing this chapter, students should be able to:

1.   Discuss the importance of planning to the practice of management.
2.   Explain the relationship between planning and the other management functions.
3.   List and describe the steps in the formal planning process.
4.   Identify and discuss the major benefits of planning.
5.   Discuss the importance of time management to planning and provide specific tips on managing one's time.
6.   Distinguish between and provide examples of short-, medium- and long-range plans, strategic and operational plans, and standing use and single use plans.
7.   Explain what a business plan is and describe what a typical business plan should include.
8.   Compare and contrast inside-out versus outside-in planning and top-down versus bottom-up planning.
9.   Discuss contingency planning and its benefits.
10.   Describe the role of forecasting in the planning process, and distinguish between qualitative and quantitative forecasting techniques.
11.   Explain how scenario planning, benchmarking, participation and involvement, and staff planners can contribute to planning effectiveness.
12.   Describe the management by objectives (MBO) process, distinguish between specific types of performance objectives in MBO, and discuss the things managers should do to make MBO successful.

CHAPTER 7 OVERVIEW

Through planning, managers attempt to look into the future and make decisions that will facilitate goal accomplishment. Planning thus serves as the primary management function, setting the stage and providing a foundation for the manager's efforts to organize, lead and control. The fundamentals of planning are presented in this chapter along with guidelines for good planning.

The chapter opener titled, **"Know What You Want to Accomplish,"** serves as an excellent introduction to the importance of planning at *Cypress Semiconductor Corp.*, and its relationship to control. The key to Cypress' success is described by its CEO, T.J. Rodgers as follows: "The way to win is to determine what your company has to do and do it --- all the time, every time, accepting no excuses along the way." In practice, this process of planning and control begins when employees set their own goals and enter them into a computer program that acts as an organizational inventory. Anyone in the company can review another person's goals by entering the program. Typically, there are over 10,000 goals on the system. Employees commit to achieving their goals by a target date and review them weekly with their managers. During these reviews, goals may be redefined and any needed corrective action or followups taken. Rodgers points out that while the system is designed for accountability, its emphasis is on finding problems before they interfere with performance.

The chapter begins by examining the role of planning as a management function, including its relationships with the other functions. The formal planning process and the benefits of planning are then discussed, along with the relationship between planning and time management. Next, the types of plans that managers employ and various approaches to planning, such as inside-out, outside-in, top-down, bottom-up and contingency planning, are described. A discussion of the planning tools and techniques follows. The chapter concludes with a description of the management by objectives (MBO) approach to planning and control, and recommendations for ensuring that the MBO process is successful.

CHAPTER 7 LECTURE OUTLINE

Teaching Objective: The purpose of this chapter is to teach students the fundamentals of managerial planning. These fundamentals include the planning process, the various types of plans, forecasting, and the ways in which lower, middle and top level managers contribute to organizational plans.

Suggested Time: Two or more hours of class time are recommended to present the material in this chapter. If time is limited, however, time can be saved by presenting some topics in conjunction with your lecture on Chapter 8, Strategic Management and Entrepreneurship. For example, inside-out versus outside-in planning can be incorporated into the discussion of the strategic planning process.

Planning as a Management Function
　　The Planning Process
　　Benefits of Planning

Types of Plans in Organizations
　　Short-Range and Long-Range Plans
　　Strategic and Operational Plans
　　Policies and Procedures
　　Budgets and Project Schedules
　　Business Plans

Approaches to Planning
　　Inside-Out versus Outside-In Planning
　　Top-Down versus Bottom-Up Planning
　　Contingency Planning

Planning Tools and Techniques
　　Forecasting
　　Use of Scenarios
　　Benchmarking
　　Participation and Involvement
　　Role of Staff Planners

Management by Objectives
　　The Concept of MBO
　　Performance Objectives in MBO
　　How to Make MBO Work for You

CHAPTER 7 SUPPORTING MATERIALS

Textbook Inserts

Headline: Know What You Want to Accomplish
Margin Photos: Hewlett-Packard, Lucent Technologies, McDonald's & Burger King, Xerox
Embedded Boxes: U.S. Healthcare, Meter Man, Inc., Royal Dutch/Shell
Manager's Notepad 7.1: Tips on How to Manage Your Time
Manager's Notepad 7.2: What to Include in a Business Plan
Manager's Notepad 7.3: Steps to Successful MBO

Multi-Media Resources

PowerPoint Presentations (Website):
    Figures 7.1 to 7.6 from the Textbook plus Supplemental Figures

In-Class Activities

Cases for Critical Thinking (Career Readiness Work & Website):
    Walmart (Primary Case)
    Boeing (Alternate Case)

Exercises:
    Beating the Time Wasters (Career Readiness Workbook)
    Personal Career Planning (Career Readiness Workbook)
    Karnak the Magnificent (Website Quick Hitter)

Assessments:
    Your Intuitive Ability (Career Readiness Workbook)
    Time Management Profile (Career Readiness Workbook & Website)

Self-Test 7 (Textbook and Website)

CHAPTER 7 LECTURE NOTES

I.   **Planning as a Management Function**

    A.   *Planning* is the process of deciding exactly what one wants to accomplish and how best to go about it.

    B.   *Planning and the Other Functions*   **FIGURE 7.1**

        1.   Planning **sets the stage** for the other functions; hence, it serves as the foundation for:

            a)   <u>Organizing</u> — allocating and arranging resources to accomplish essential tasks;

            b)   <u>Leading</u> — guiding the efforts of human resources to ensure high levels of task accomplishment; and

            c)   <u>Controlling</u> — monitoring task accomplishments and taking necessary corrective action.

        2.   **Figure 7.1** illustrates the relationship between planning and the other management functions, while simultaneously summarizing the planning process.

    C.   *The Planning Process*   **FIGURE 7.1**

        1.   **Define your objectives** -- identify desired outcomes or results in very specific ways. Know where you want to go; be specific enough that you will know when you have arrived, or how far off the mark you are at various points along the way.

ENHANCEMENT

The *Website Quick Hitter* titled, **Karnak the Magnificent**, can be used here to help students to develop more focused career objectives, while conveying the criteria of a good objective.

---

        2.   **Determine where you stand vis-a-vis objectives** -- Evaluate current accomplishments relative to the desired results. Know where you stand in reaching the objectives; know what strengths work in your favor and what weaknesses may hold you back.

        3.   **Develop premises regarding future conditions** -- Try to anticipate future events. Generate alternative "scenarios" for what may happen; identify things for each scenario that may help or hinder progress toward your objectives.

4. **Analyze possible action alternatives, choose the best among them, and decide how to implement** -- List and carefully evaluate the possible actions that may be taken. Choose the alternative(s) most likely to accomplish your objectives; decide step by step what must be done to follow the chosen course of action.

5. **Implement the action plan and evaluate results** -- Take action and carefully measure your progress toward objectives. Do what the plan requires; evaluate results; take corrective actions and revise plans as needed.

D. *Benefits of Planning*

1. **More Focus and Flexibility**

    a) An <u>organization with focus</u> knows what it does best, what its customers want, and how to serve them; an <u>individual with focus</u> knows where he or she wants to go in a career or situation and is able to retain that objective even in difficult circumstances.

    b) An <u>organization with flexibility</u> is willing and able to change in response to shifting circumstances and operates with an orientation toward the future; an <u>individual with flexibility</u> factors into career plans the problems and opportunities posed by new and developing circumstances.

2. Action Orientation

    Planning can <u>improve performance</u> because it is...

    .... *results oriented* -- it creates a performance-oriented sense of direction.
    .... *priority oriented* -- it focuses energies on the most important problems and opportunities.
    .... *advantage oriented* -- it helps allocate resources to best utilize strengths.
    .... *change oriented* -- it helps anticipate problems and opportunities so they can be best dealt with.

3. **Improved Coordination**   **FIGURE 7.2**

    a) A <u>hierarchy of objectives</u> is a series of objectives linked together such that each higher-level objective is supported by one or more lower-level ones.

    b) This creates a <u>means-ends chain</u> whereby the achievement of lower-level objectives serves as the *means* for accomplishing the higher-level objectives or *ends* with which they are clearly linked.

c)   **Figure 7.2** illustrates a sample hierarchy of objectives and means-ends chain for total quality management.

3.   **Better Control**   **FIGURE 7.3**

a)   Planning facilitates control by <u>defining objectives</u> -- desired performance results -- and <u>identifying specific actions</u> through which they are to be pursued.

b)   **Figure 7.3** offers a reminder that <u>planning and controlling</u> should work closely together; planning leads to controlling, which leads to further planning.

4.   **Better Time Management**   **MANAGER'S NOTEPAD 7.1**

ENHANCEMENT

The **Beating the Time Wasters** *Exercise* and the *Assessment* titled **Time Management Profile**, included in the *Career Readiness Portfolio* can be employed here to supplement this discussion of time management. Students typically enjoy these assignments and find them to be beneficial in helping them to better organize their time.

a)   Each day, managers are bombarded by a multitude of tasks and demands in a setting of frequent interruptions, crises, and unexpected events; it can be easy to lose track of objectives and fall prey to what consultants identify as "<u>time wasters</u>."

b)   **Manager's Notepad 7.1** summarizes several <u>Tips on How to Manage Your Time</u>
*   *Do* say "No" when requests will divert you from work you should be doing.
*   *Don't* get bogged down in details and routines that should be left to others.
*   *Do* establish a system for screening your telephone calls.
*   *Don't* let "drop-in" or unannounced vistors use too much of your time.
*   *Do* prioritize work tasks in order of importance and urgency.
*   *Don't* become "calender bound" by losing control of your schedule.
*   *Do* work tasks in priority order.

ENHANCEMENT

"People who dealt with David Rockefeller during his tenure as chairman of Chase Manhattan Bank agree that you could set your clock by his commitments. He walked into a 10 a.m. appointment precisely at 10. If the appointment was set for 20 minutes, he departed at 10:20." (The Orange County Register, February 24, 1992).

II. Types of Plans Used by Managers

A. *Short-Range and Long-Range Plans*

1. Draw the following continuum to illustrate the categorization of plans across the time dimension.

```
X-------------------------X-----------------------X
Short-Range          Intermediate-Range       Long-Range
Plans                     Plans                  Plans

< 1 year              1 to 2 years            2 to 5+ years

Daily "To Do"         Two-Year Capital        A general idea
Lists, Monthly            Budget              of the types of
Work Schedules                                products to be
                                              introduced over
                                              the next 5 years.
```

ENHANCEMENT

To generate discussion, ask students to identify their short-, intermediate-, and long-range career plans. Many students will be able to quickly identify and distinguish between these types of plans. For example, some students may express a long-term career objective of owning their own business. Their intermediate-range plans for achieving this goal may include obtaining a college degree and then working in a large corporation for a number of years to "learn the ropes" of a particular industry. Their short-range plans will most likely include detailed plans for completing this course as well as other relevant subjects.

2. *Elliot Jaques* suggests that people vary in their capability to think out, organize, and work through events of different time horizons.

3. Jaques believes that most people work with only 3-month time spans, a smaller group works well with a 1-year span, and only about 1 person in several million can handle a 20-year **time frame.**

4. Although a supervisor's planning challenges may rest mainly in the 3-month range, the next higher manager may deal with a 1-year range, while a vice president deals with 3 years, and a **CEO** is expected to have a vision extending 5 to 10+ years.

5. Career progress to higher management levels, therefore, clearly requires the **conceptual skills** to work well with longer-range time frames.

B. *Strategic and Operational Plans*   **FIGURE 7.4**

1. **Strategic plans** address long-term needs and set comprehensive action directions for an organization or subunit.

2. **Operational plans** define what needs to be done in specific areas to implement strategic plans and achieve strategic objectives.

3. **Figure 7.4** illustrates **typical operational plans:**

   a) <u>Production plans</u> -- dealing with the methods and technology needed by people in their work.

   b) <u>Financial plans</u> -- dealing with the money required to support various operations.

   c) <u>Facilities plans</u> -- dealing with facilities and layouts required to support task activities.

   d) <u>Marketing plans</u> -- dealing with the requirements of selling and distributing goods or services.

   e) <u>Human resource plans</u> -- dealing with personnel recruiting, selection, and placement to staff jobs.

C. *Policies and Procedures*

1. **Standing plans** are designed to be used again and again.

2. **A policy** is a standing-use plan that communicates *broad guidelines* for decisions and actions.

3. Policies often cover hiring, termination, layoffs, smoking, alcohol and drug abuse, employee discipline, illness and related issues.

4. **Rules** or **procedures** are plans that describe exactly what actions are to be taken in specific situations.

205

5.   **Examples**: SOPs - the standard operating procedures found in employee handbooks. "No Smoking" is an example of a rule which is often imposed in work places.

D.   *Budgets and Project Schedules*   **FIGURE 7.5**

1.   **Single-use plans** are only used once; they are designed to meet the needs of a unique situation.

2.   **Budgets** are single-use plans that commit resources to activities, projects or programs.

    a)   <u>Fixed budgets</u> allocate resources on the basis of a single estimate of costs.

    b)   <u>Flexible budgets</u> allow resource allocations to vary in proportion with various levels of activities.

    c)   <u>Zero-based budgets</u> allocate resources to projects or activities as if they were brand new; ongoing and newly proposed programs are forced to compete on an equal footing for funding.

3.   **Project schedules** are single-use plans that identify a set of activities required to accomplish a specific task objective, and which link these activities to specific time frames, performance targets, and resources.

    a)   **Figure 7.5** illustrates a <u>Gantt chart</u>, which is used to visually depict the expected progress of each required activity from start to finish in a large project; computer programs are now available to provide this type of project planning support.

4.   A **business plan** is a plan that describes all the details necessary to set direction for a new business and to obtain necessary financing to operate it.

    a)   **Manager's Notebook 7.2** summarizes **What to Include in a Business Plan** as follows:

       *   *Executive summary* — overview of business purpose and highlight of key elements of the plan.

       *   *Industry analysis* — nature of the industry, including economic trends, important legal or regulatory issues, and potential risks.

       *   *Company description* — mission, owners, and legal form.

206

* *Products and services description* — major goods or services, with special focus on uniqueness vis-a-vis competition.

* *Market description* — size of market, competitor strengths and weaknesses, five year sales goals.

* *Marketing strategy* — product characteristics, distribution, promotion, pricing and market research.

* *Operations description* — manufacturing or service methods, supplies and suppliers, and control procedures.

* *Staffing description* — management and staffing skills needed and available, compensation and human resource management systems.

* *Financial projection* — cash flow projections 1 - 5 years.

* *Capital needs* — amount of funds needed to run the business, amount available, amount requested from new sources.

III. Approaches to Planning

A. *Inside-Out versus Outside-In Planning*

1. **Inside-out planning** involves focusing future effort on what you are already doing but always trying to find ways of doing it better. Here, the organization *looks inward first* to its strengths and then uses these strengths to gain success in its environment.

2. **Outside-in planning** involves analyzing the external environment and looking for specific niches or opportunities that can be exploited. Here, the organization *looks outward first* to identify threats and opportunities and then responds accordingly.

3. **Use inside-out planning:** When you want to do what you and/or others are already doing, but want to do it better.

4. **Use outside-in planning:** When you want to find a unique niche for your activities--that is, to do something no one else is doing.

ENHANCEMENT

Squibb Corporation, a pharmaceutical giant, uses inside-out and outside-in planning together to achieve strategic advantages over its competitors. The inside-out planning involves the careful, realistic identification of product markets in which Squibb possesses considerable expertise. The outside-in component entails constant communication between Squibb's savvy marketers and the R&D staff to find new markets. (*Source*: As reported in "Squibb's Rx for Success: Find a Need and Fill It," *Business Week*, October 5, 1987, p. 80).

   B.   *Top-Down versus Bottom-Up Planning*

   1.   **Top-down planning** is where senior management sets the broad objectives and then allows lower management levels to make plans within these constraints.

   2.   **Bottom-up planning** begins with plans that are developed at lower levels without constraints before they are sequentially passed up the hierarchy of authority to top management.

   C.   *Contingency Planning*

   1.   **Contingency planning** involves identifying alternative courses of action that can be implemented if and when an original plan proves inadequate because of changing circumstances.

   2.   The key is early identification of possible shifts in future events that could affect current plans. This is accomplished by good forward thinking by managers and/or staff planners, by a "devil's advocate" method, or the development of "worst case" scenarios of future events.

IV.   **Planning Tools and Techniques**

   A.   *Forecasting* is an attempt to predict outcomes that will happen in the future. These predictions serve as premises which managers can use as a basis for planning.

   1.   **Qualitative forecasting** uses expert opinions to predict the future. Either a single expert or a panel of experts may be consulted.

   2.   **Example**: The *Delphi Technique* can be used to aggregate experts' opinions regarding future events or trends.

   3.   **Quantitative forecasting techniques** use mathematical and statistical analyses of data banks to predict future events. These techniques may be used to forecast GNP, interest rates, inflation, etc. Sample techniques include the following:

a) <u>Time-series analysis</u> makes predictions by using statistical routines such as regression analysis to project past trends into the future.

b) <u>Econometric modeling</u> builds complex computer models of variable interrelationships to simulate future events based on probabilities and multiple assumptions.

c) <u>Statistical surveys</u> use statistical analysis of opinion polls and attitude surveys, to forecast events (e.g., future consumer tastes, employee preferences, and political choices).

4. Because all forecasts rely ultimately on **human judgement, managers** must treat them with caution when making plans; all **forecasts** are subject to error.

5. Forecasting should not be confused with planning; planning involves deciding what to do in response to the forecasts.

B. *Use of Scenarios*

1. **Scenario planning** is a long-term version of contingency planning which involves identifying several alternative future "scenarios" or states of affairs, and then making plans to **deal** with each should they occur.

2. **Example**: Royal Dutch/Shell envisions two 20 year scenarios which it uses to prepare for "future shocks":

a) The *Sustainable World Scenario*, identifies a world with great concerns for global warming and the need for conservation, recycling, and emissions controls; and

b) The *Mercantilist World Scenario*, which sees increased protectionism, a de-emphasis of environmentalism, and slower world economic growth.

C. *Benchmarking*

1. **Benchmarking** refers to the use of external comparisons to gain an added perspective on current performance and help initiate the planning process.

2. **Example**: Xerox compares itself to its Japanese competitors to benchmark production costs in making manufacturing plans.

D.   *Participation and Involvement*

    1.   **Participative planning** actively includes in the planning process as many people as possible who will be affected by the resulting plans and/or will be asked to implement them.

    2.   Participation can increase the **creativity** and **information** used in planning as well as **understanding, acceptance** and **commitment** to the plan.

    3.   Use **Figure 7.6** to illustrate the importance of **building commitments to plans** throughout all phases of the planning process.

E.   *Role of Staff Planners*

    1.   **Staff planners** are persons who take responsibility for leading and coordinating the planning function for the total organization or one of its major components.

    2.   **Responsibilities of staff planners**
        a)   Assist line managers in preparing plans.
        b)   Develop special plans upon request.
        c)   Gather and maintain planning information.
        d)   Assist in communicating plans to others.
        e)   Monitor in-use plans and suggest changes.

V.   **Management by Objectives**

A.   *Management by objectives (MBO)* is a structured process of regular communication in which a supervisor and subordinate jointly set performance objectives for the subordinate and review results accomplished; MBO is also known by the terms *management by results, management by goals,* and *work planning and review.*

B.   *The Concept of MBO*   **FIGURE 7.7**

    1.   MBO involves a **formal agreement between a supervisor and subordinate** concerning:

        a)   The <u>subordinate's performance objectives</u> for a given time period;

        b)   The <u>plans</u> through which they will be accomplished;

        c)   <u>Standards</u> for measuring whether or not they have been accomplished; and

        d)   <u>Procedures for reviewing results</u>.

2. **Figure 7.7** depicts the **MBO process** described below.

    a) The <u>supervisor</u> and subordinate <u>jointly</u> establish plans and control results.

    b) The <u>subordinate</u> is responsible for <u>performing</u> the agreed upon tasks.

    c) The <u>superior</u> is responsible for providing necessary <u>support</u>.

3 The end product of MBO is a written agreement that documents the **subordinate's objectives.**

4. MBO fosters **understanding** and promotes subordinate **participation** in decision making.

C. *Performance Objectives in MBO*

1. **Types of Performance Objectives**

    a) <u>Improvement objectives</u> document a desire to improve a performance factor. <u>Example</u>: Reduce defects by 10%.

    b) <u>Personal development objectives</u> pertain to personal growth activities. <u>Example</u>: To pass a sales seminar.

    c) <u>Maintenance objectives</u> formally express intentions to continue performance at existing levels. <u>Example</u>: Maintain market share.

2. **Criteria of a "Good" Performance Objective**

    a) <u>Specific</u> -- Targets a key result to be accomplished.
    b) <u>Time defined</u> -- Identifies a date for achieving results.
    c) <u>Challenging</u> -- Offers a realistic and attainable challenge.
    d) <u>Measurable</u> -- Is as specific and as quantitative as possible.

3. When objectives can be stated in specific and quantifiable terms, the achievement can be ascertained by examining **measurable end products.**

4. Since some performance areas are hard to quantify, it is often necessary to agree on performance objectives stated as **verifiable work activities.**

D.   *How to Make MBO Work for You*

   1.   **Things to Avoid**

       a)   Tying MBO to compensation.
       b)   Focusing too much attention on objectives that are easily quantified.
       c)   Focusing too much attention on written documentation and forms.
       d)   Using a prepackaged program.
       e)   Telling subordinates their objectives.

   2.   **Steps to Successful MBO**

       a)   Step 1: An individual lists key performance objectives for a time period with target dates for accomplishing them.
       b)   Step 2: Objectives are reviewed and discussed with the supervisor, and an agreed upon set of objectives is documented.
       c)   Step 3: The supervisor and subordinate meet regularly to review progress and make revisions or update objectives as needed.
       d)   Step 4: At a specified time, such as after 6 months, the individual prepares a "performance report" that lists accomplishments and comments on discrepancies between expected and actual results.
       e)   Step 5: This self-appraisal is discussed with the supervisor with an emphasis on its implications for future performance.
       f)   Step 6: A new set of objectives is established for the next time period, as in Step 1, and the MBO cycle begins anew.

CHAPTER 7 SUMMARY

Why is planning an essential management function?
* Planning is the process of setting performance objectives and determining what should be done to accomplish them.
* A plan is a set of intended actions for accomplishing important objectives.
* Planning sets the stage for the other management functions---organizing, leading, and controlling.
* The steps in the planning process are (1) define your objectives, (2) determine where you stand vis-à-vis objectives, (3) develop your premises regarding future conditions, (4) identify and choose among alternative ways of accomplishing objectives, and (5) implement action plans and evaluate results.
* Good planning improves performance by better focus and flexibility, coordination, control and time management.

What types of plans are used by managers?
* Short-range plans tend to cover a year or less, while long-range plans extend up to 5 years or more.
* Strategic plans set critical long-range directions; operational plans are designed to implement strategic plans.
* Standing-use plans, such as policies and procedures, are used over and over again.
* Single-use plans, such as budgets and project schedules, are established for a specific purpose and time frame.
* A business plan sets forth the direction and financial requirements for a new business venture.

What are the different approaches to planning?
* Inside-out planning looks at internal strengths and tries to improve upon what is already being done.
* Outside-in planning looks for opportunities or "niches" in the external environment that can be pursued to advantage.
* Top-down planning helps maintain direction; bottom-up planning builds commitment.
* Contingency planning identifies alternative courses of action that can be implemented if and when circumstances change in certain ways over time.

What planning tools and techniques are useful?
* Forecasting, a prediction of what will happen in the future, is a planning aid but not a planning substitute.
* Scenario planning through the use of alternative versions of the future is a useful form of contingency planning.
* Planning through benchmarking utilizes external comparisons to identify desirable action directions.
* Participation and involvement open the planning process to valuable inputs from people whose efforts are essential to effective implementation of plans.

* Specialized staff planners can help with planning details, although care must be taken to make sure they work well with line personnel.

How does Management by Objectives help facilitate planning?
* Management by objectives is a process through which supervisors work with their subordinates to "jointly" set performance goals and review performance results.
* The MBO process is a highly participative form of integrated planning and controlling.
* MBO should clarify performance expectations for the subordinate and also identify support needed from the supervisor.
* Only when the MBO process is mutual and participative can the full benefits be realized.

KEY CHAPTER 7 DEFINITIONS

Benchmarking The use of external comparisons to gain added perspective on current performance and help initiate the planning process.

Bottom-up planning Planning that begins with ideas developed at lower management levels, which are modified as they are passed up the hierarchy to top management.

Budget A plan that commits resources to projects or programs; it is a formalized way of allocating resources to specific activities.

Business plan A plan that describes direction for a new business and the financing needed to operate it.

Contingency planning The process of identifying alternative courses of action that can be used to modify an original plan if and when circumstances change with the passage of time.

Forecast An attempt to predict outcomes; it is a projection into the future based on historical data combined in some scientific manner.

Inside-out planning Planning that focuses on internal strengths and trying to do better than what one already does.

Management by objectives (MBO) A process of joint objective setting between a superior and subordinate that can be done on an organization-wide basis.

Objectives The specific results or desired end states that one wishes to achieve.

Operational plan A plan of limited scope that addresses those activities and resources required to implement strategic plans.

Outside-in planning Planning that uses analysis of the external environment and makes plans to take advantage of oppotunities and avoid problems.

Participative planning The inclusion in the planning process of as many people as possible from among those who will be affected by plans and/or asked to help implement them.

Plan A statement of intended means for accomplishing a desired result.

Planning The process of setting objectives and determining what should be done to accomplish them.

Policy A standing plan that communicates broad guidelines for making decisions and taking action.

Procedures Standing plans that precisely describe what actions are to be taken in specific situations.

Project schedules Single-use plans that identify specific time frames, performance targets, and resources for activities required to accomplish a task objective.

Rules Standing plans that precisely describe what actions are to be taken in specific situations.

Scenario planning A long-term version of contingency planning, involves identifying several alternative future "scenarios" or states of affairs and then making plans to deal with each should it occur.

Single-use plan A plan that is used only once.

Standing plan A plan that is used more than once.

Strategic plan A comprehensive plan that reflects the longer term needs and directions of the organization or subunit.

Top-down planning Planning that begins with broad objectives set by top management, which then allows lower management levels to make plans within these constraints.

Zero-based budget A budget that allocates resources to a project or activity as if it were brand new and forces both ongoing and newly proposed programs to compete on an equal footing for available resources.

CHAPTER 8: STRATEGIC MANAGEMENT AND ENTREPRENEURSHIP

CHAPTER 8 STUDY QUESTIONS

o   What is strategic management?
o   What types of strategies are used by organizations?
o   How are strategies formulated?
o   What are the issues in strategy implementation and control?
o   What is entrepreneurship?

CHAPTER 8 LEARNING OBJECTIVES

After completing this chapter, students should be able to:

1.   Define strategy and discuss the notion of strategic intent.
2.   Explain how strategic management can be used to provide an organization with a competitive advantage.
3.   Explain how the competitive nature of organizational environments varies.
4.   Define strategic management, and explain the importance of strategy formulation and strategy implementation to the strategic management process.
5.   Identify and discuss five strategic management tasks.
6.   Explain the importance of the organizational mission, values, and objectives to strategic management, and identify several common operating objectives of a business.
7.   Discuss the importance of the analysis of organizational resources and capabilities, and the analysis of industry and environment to the strategic management process; include in your response a discussion of the technique known as SWOT analysis.
8.   Distinguish between different levels of strategies used by organizations.
9.   Identify, describe and provide examples of the four "grand" strategies used by organizations.
10. Identify the major opportunities for competitive advantage, and their relevance to strategy formulation.
11. Compare and contrast the following approaches to strategy formulation: portfolio planning, Porter's competitive strategies, adaptive strategies, product life-cycle approach, and emergent strategies.
12. Identify and discuss the keys to effective strategy implementation and common strategic planning pitfalls.
13. Explain how to double-check a strategy.
14. Discuss the importance of leadership, top management teams, and corporate governance to strategy implementation.
15. Define entrepreneurship and discuss the characteristics of entrepreneurs.
16. Discuss the role that entrepreneurship plays in contributing to the effectiveness of both small businesses and large enterprises.

CHAPTER 8 OVERVIEW

The chapter opener, **Get (and Stay) Ahead with Strategy**, demonstrates well the importance of strategic planning to organizational success. It describes how Wal-Mart's retail strategy -- consistently low prices and high customer service -- has enabled the firm to become America's largest retailer. Strategies such as this set critical directions for organizations and guide the allocation of their resources. This chapter focuses on strategic management and the role strategy plays in achieving organizational productivity.

The chapter begins by defining the key terms of strategy and strategic management, and describing the strategic management process, including the critical sub-processes of strategy formulation and strategy implementation. The utility of strategic management in gaining a competitive advantage is also discussed. Next, the importance of the analyses of 1) mission, values, and objectives, 2) organizational resources and capabilities, and 3) industry and environment, is considered, followed by a discussion of the various levels and types of grand strategies. Considerable attention is then devoted to several approaches to strategy formulation, including portfolio planning, Porter's competitive strategies, adaptive strategies, product life-cycle approach, and emergent strategies.

The chapter's focus shifts to the critical process of strategy implementation. The major pitfalls to avoid, the importance of leadership, top management teams, and corporate governance to this process are discussed. The chapter concludes by examining the nature of entrepreneurship, including its importance to both small businesses and large enterprises.

CHAPTER 8 LECTURE OUTLINE

Teaching Objective: The goal of this chapter is to provide students with a solid understanding of strategic management and entrepreneurship. The process of strategy formulation and implementation is emphasized.

Suggested Time: Because this chapter contains many concepts, two to three hours of class time is required to present this material. Additional time may be needed if the video and/or case enhancements are employed.

Strategy and Strategic Management
      Strategy and Competitive Advantage
      The Strategic Management Process
      Analysis of Mission, Values, and Objectives
      Analysis of Organizational Resources and Capabilities
      Analysis of Industry and Environment

Strategies Used by Organizations
      Levels of Strategy
      Types of Strategy

Strategic Formulation
      Portfolio Planning
      Porter's Competitive Strategies
      Adaptive Strategies
      Product Life Cycles
      Emergent Strategies

Strategy Implementation
      Management Practices and Systems
      Leadership and Top Management Teams
      Corporate Governance

Strategy and Entrepreneurship
      Who are the Entrepreneurs?
      Entrepreneurship and Small Business
      Small Business Development
      Entrepreneurship and Large Enterprises

CHAPTER 8 SUPPORTING MATERIALS

Textbook Inserts

Headline: Get (and Stay) Ahead with Strategy
Margin Photos: American West Airline, Worthington Industries, McDonald's,
        Bernard's Cape Cod Potato Chips
Embedded Boxes: Starbucks, Rubin Central Design Board, Endres Floral Company,
        Meter Man, Inc.
Manager's Notepad 8.1: Five Strategic Management Tasks
Manager's Notepad 8.2: How to Double-check a Strategy

Multi-Media Resources

NBR Video Report:
        Nucor (Available on Videotape Supplement & Video Cases CD-ROM)

PowerPoint Presentations (Website):
        Figures 8.1 to 8.6 from the Textbook plus Supplemental Figures
        NBR Viewing Questions: Nucor & AT&T

In-Class Activities

Cases for Critical Thinking (Career Readiness Workbook):
        Nucor (Primary Case)
        AT&T (Alternate Case)

Exercises:
        Strategic Scenarios (Career Readiness Workbook)

Assessments:
        Entrepreneurship Orientation (Career Readiness Workbook)

Research and Presentation Project:
        Entrepreneurship — Is it for You? (Career Readiness Workbook)

Self-Test 8 (Textbook and Website)

CHAPTER 8 LECTURE NOTES

I.   Introduction

ENHANCEMENT

A discussion of the *Headline* opener on *Wal-Mart* titled, **Get (and Stay) Ahead with Strategy** indicates, strategy can serve as a means of introducing the chapter and generating some enthusiastic class participation. As observers of Wal-Mart's phenomenal growth, students tend to be knowledgeable of the strategies this firm has employed to gain competitive advantages. You may also want to draw an analogy between a game or sport (e.g., football, chess, baseball, bridge) in which "strategies" are used to gain competitive advantages, and the strategies used by modern organizations. In each case, the strengths and weaknesses of the strategist and the competitor are analyzed, and a plan to capitalize on relative strengths while overcoming weaknesses is devised. Of course, the success of the strategy depends on the quality of implementation in both cases as well. This type of introduction provides a convenient lead into the following definition of strategy and strategic management.

II.   Strategy and Strategic Management

A.   A *strategy* is a comprehensive plan of action that identifies long-term direction and guides resource utilization to accomplish an organization's mission and objectives with sustainable competitive advantage.

B.   It is a plan for using resources with consistent *strategic intent*, that is with all organizational energies focused on a unifying and compelling target.

C.   *Strategy and Competitive Advantage*

   1.   Any strategy defines the direction an organization intends to take to move in a competitive environment; at the same time an organization tries to create a competitive advantage, they are doing likewise.

   2.   The **competitive nature of organizational environments** varies in the following ways:

      a)   <u>Monopoly environment</u> — An environment in which there is only one player and no competition; this creates absolute competitive advantage with a sustainable and most likely excessive business profit. <u>Example</u>: Microsoft is close to a monopoly as a supplier of computer operating systems.

221

    b)   <u>Oligopoly environment</u> — An environment that contains a few players who do not directly compete against one another; firms within an oligopoly sustain long-term competitive advantages within defined market segments. <u>Example</u>: The breakfast cereals market is dominated by three players — Kellogg's, Post, and Ralston Purina.

    c)   <u>Environment of hypercompetition</u> — An environment in which there are at least several players who directly compete with one another. <u>Example</u>: The fast food industry where McDonald's, Burger King, Wendy's and others compete for the same customers.

D.   *The Strategic Management Process*   **FIGURE 8.1**

1.   **Strategic management** is the process of formulating and implementing strategies to advance an organization's mission and objectives and secure competitive advantage.

2.   **Figure 8.1** describes the following **two major responsibilities in the strategic management process**:

    a)   <u>Strategy formulation</u> involves assessing existing strategies, organization, and environment to develop new strategies and strategic plans capable of delivering future competitive advantage. *Peter Drucker* associates this process with five strategic questions.

        *   *What is our business mission?*
        *   *Who are our customers?*
        *   *What do our customers value?*
        *   *What have been our results?*
        *   *What is our plan?*

    b)   <u>Strategy implementation</u> this is the responsibility for putting strategies and strategic plans into action.

3.   **Five Strategic Management Tasks**   **MANAGER'S NOTEPAD 8.1**

```
|------->  a)
|
|
|
| Strategy b)
| Formula-
|  tion
|
|          c)
|
|------->
```

a)   <u>Identify organizational mission and objectives</u>. *Ask*, What business are we in? Where do we want to be in the future?

b)   <u>Assess current performance vis-a-vis purpose and objectives</u>. *Ask*, "How well are we currently doing?"

c)   <u>Create strategic plans to accomplish purpose and objectives</u>. *Ask*, "How can we get where we really want to be?"

```
|------>    d)    Implement the strategic plans.  Ask, "Has everything
| Strategy        that needs to be done been done?"
| Implement-
|  ation    e)    Evaluate results and renew the strategic planning
|                 process as necessary.  Ask, "Are things working out as
|------>          planned, and what can be improved?"
```

E.   *Analysis of Mission, Values, and Objectives*   **FIGURE 8.2**

    1.   **Mission Statenents**

        a)   The <u>mission</u> or <u>purpose</u> of any organization may be described as its "reason" for existence; it reflects the organization's basic purpose as a supplier of goods and/or services to society.

        b)   A <u>mission statement</u> is a formal written statement of an organization's purpose.

        c)   A good mission statement is precise in identifying the <u>domain(s)</u> in which the organization intends to operate, including...
... the *customers* it intends to serve;
... the *products* and/or *services* it intends to provide;
... the *location* in which it intends to operate.
... the underlying *philosophy* that will guide employees in these operations.

        d)   <u>Example</u>: Baxter International's mission statement is: "We will be the leading health-care company providing the best products and services for customers around the world, consistently emphasizing innovation, operational excellence, and the highest quality in everything we do."

        e)   An important test of corporate purpose and mission is how well it serves the organization's <u>stakeholders</u> — employees, and members of the external environment, customers, shareholders, suppliers, creditors, community groups, and others who are directly involved with the organization and/or affected by its operations.

        f)   A <u>strategic constituencies analysis</u> involves a review of the interests of "stakeholders" along with the organization's record in responding to their interests.

        g)   **Figure 8.2** shows how stakeholders can be reflected in the mission statement.

2.   **Core Values**

a)   <u>Values</u> are broad beliefs about what is or is not appropriate. Through corporate cultures, the values of managers and other individuals are shaped and pointed in common directions.

b)   <u>Example</u>: IBM's "Respect for the Individual" is a key value reflected in its corporate culture.

c)   <u>Corporate culture</u> is the predominant value system for the organization as a whole.

ENHANCEMENT

Discuss with students the following quotation. "These builders {of the great early American corporations like IBM, Procter & Gamble, and Johnson & Johnson} saw their role as creating an environment--in effect a culture--in their companies in which employees could be secure and thereby do the work necessary to make the business a success."

(*Source:* Terrence E. Deal and Allan A. Kennedy, *Corporate Cultures*, Addison-Wesley, 1982).

3.   **Objectives**

a)   <u>Operating objectives</u> are specific ends toward which organizational resources are actually allocated; they identify *key results* that organizations pursue in their day-to-day activities.

b)   <u>Common Operating Objectives for Organizations</u>

* *Profitability*: Producing at a net profit in business.
* *Marketing share*: Gaining and holding a specific share of a product market.
* *Human talent*: Recruiting and maintaining a high-quality workforce.
* *Financial health*: Acquiring financial capital and earning positive returns.
* *Cost efficiency*: Using resources well to operate at low cost.
* *Product quality*: Producing high-quality goods or services.
* *Innovation*: Achieving a desired level of new product or process development.
* *Social responsibility*: Making a positive contribution to society.

F.   *Analysis of Organizational Resources and Capabilities*   **FIGURE 8.3**

   1.   **SWOT Analysis**

      a)   Two critical steps in the strategic process are analysis of the organization and analysis of the environment; they may be approached by a technique called a SWOT analysis, that is an analysis of **S**trengths, **W**eaknesses, **O**pportunities, and **T**hreats.

      b)   **Figure 8.3** indicates the types of questions typically asked in a SWOT analysis.

      c)   A major goal is to identify core competencies in the form of special strengths or things the organization does exceptionally well.

      d)   Potential Sources of Core Competencies

         (1) Technology
         (2) Human resources
         (3) Manufacturing approaches
         (4) Management talent
         (5) Financial strength

      e)   Organizational weaknesses may be found in the same areas.

   G.   *Analysis of Industry and Environment*

   1.   **Figure 8.3** indicates the types of questions asked in this second part of the SWOT analysis.

ENHANCEMENT

The *Exercise* titled **Strategic Scenarios** which is included in *Career Readiness Portfolio,* can be assigned to provide students with practice in identifying external threats to specific organizations. Further discussion of this exercise is provided in Unit 9 of this *Manual.*

   2.   Potential influences include **macro environmental** factors such as developments in areas likely technology, government, social structures and population demographics, the global economy, and the natural environment.

   3.   They also include the **industry environment** with respect to the organization's resource suppliers, competitors, and customers.

> 4. **Opportunities** may be found in such areas as possible new markets, a strong economy, weaknesses in competitors, and emerging technologies.
>
> 5. **Threats**, however, may be identified in such things as the emergence of new competitors, resource scarcities, changing customer tastes, and new government regulations.

III. Strategies Used By Organizations   FIGURE 8.4

A.   *Levels of Strategy*

1. **Corporate Strategy**

a)   <u>Corporate strategy</u> directs the organization as a whole toward sustainable competitive advantage.

b)   Corporate strategy answers the strategic question: <u>"In what businesses and markets should we compete?"</u>

c)   <u>Example</u>: A corporate strategy decision for the mass discount retailer, Target, is to cater to department store shoppers by emphasizing fashion apparel bargains, while matching other discounters on prices of everyday household items.

2. **Business Strategy**

a)   <u>Business strategy</u> sets the strategic direction for a single business unit or product line; in large conglomerates such as GE, the term <u>strategic business unit (SBU)</u> is used to describe such divisions when they operate with separate missions within a larger enterprise.

b)   The selection of a business strategy answers the strategic question: <u>"How are we going to compete for customers in this industry and market?"</u>

c)   <u>Example</u>: The three major business strategies at AT&T apply to the long distance services, computer, and international divisions.

3. **Functional strategy**

a)   <u>Functional strategy</u> guides the use of resources to implement business strategy; this level of strategy focuses on activities within a specific functional area of operations.

b) The strategic question to be answered in selecting functional strategies is: <u>"How can we best utilize resources to implement our business strategy?"</u>

B. *Types of Strategies*

1. **Growth strategies** seek an increase in size and the expansion of current operations. **Example:** Wal-Mart and Target are both pursuing highly aggressive growth strategies. Specific types of growth strategies include:

   a) <u>Concentration</u> - Using existing strengths in new and productive ways, but without taking the risks of great shifts in direction. Concentration strategies include market development, product development, and innovation. <u>Example</u>: McDonald's concentration on fast foods.

   b) <u>Diversification</u> involves the acquisition of new business in related or unrelated areas, or investment in new ventures. Common forms of diversification include horizontal integration, vertical integration, conglomerate diversification, and joint ventures. <u>Example</u>: General Electric buys and sells businesses in such diverse areas as household appliances, broadcasting, and military weaponry.

2. **Retrenchment**, sometimes called, **defensive strategies**, reduce the scale of operations in order to gain efficiency and improve performance.

   a) <u>Turnaround</u> is a strategy of "downsizing" to reduce personnel and other costs, and "restructuring" to streamline operations to correct problems and improve operating efficiency.

      <u>Example</u>: When Grand Metropolitan International bought Pillsbury, they laid off several thousand employees in Pillsbury's Minneapolis headquarters. These jobs were absorbed by Grand Met's existing staff, and operations were consolidated.

   b) <u>Divestiture</u> involves selling parts of the organization to cut costs, improve operating efficiency, and/or return to business areas of traditional strength.

      <u>Example</u>: Mobil Oil's sale of Montgomery Ward's.

   c) <u>Liquidation</u> involves closing down operations through complete sale of assets or declaration of bankruptcy.

> <u>Example</u>: Federated Department Stores, which owned Bloomingdale's, Abraham & Straus in New York, and Rich's in Atlanta, declared bankruptcy in 1990 due to cash-flow problems.

3. **Stability** -- pursuit of the **status quo**, or present course of action; used when firms are doing very well, when "low risk" is valued by decision makers, and when a rest period is needed before other strategies are pursued.

   Example: A profitable restaurant which continues to offer its popular entries in order to satisfy its loyal customers and preserve its market share.

4. **Combination** -- pursuit of two or more strategies at the same time.

ENHANCEMENT

Ask students to provide supplemental examples throughout the discussion of the various types of "grand strategies." Since corporate strategies receive substantial coverage in the popular press, students are quite capable of identifying examples of these strategies and enjoy doing so.

IV. **Strategy Formulation**

A. *Opportunities for Competitive Advantage*

1. **Cost and quality** — where strategy drives an emphasis on operating efficiency and/or product or service quality.

2. **Knowledge and timing** — where strategy drives an emphasis on innovation and speed of delivery to market for new ideas.

3. **Barriers to entry** — where strategy drives an emphasis on creating a market stronghold that is protected from entry by others.

4. **Financial resources** — where strategy drives an emphasis on investments and/or loss sustainment that competitors can't match.

B. *Portfolio Planning*

1. **Portfolio planning** is most useful for addressing corporate-level strategy in multi-business or multi-product situations.

2. The goal of a **portfolio strategy** is to identify a mix of investments that best serve organizational objectives.

3.   **The BCG Matrix**   FIGURE 8.5

   a)   The <u>BCG matrix</u> is a portfolio planning approach offered
        by the Boston Consulting Group, which ties strategy
        formulation to an analysis of business opportunities
        according to <u>market growth rate</u> and <u>market share</u>.

   b)   It also indicates <u>recommended strategies</u> for the
        following kinds of businesses.

        *   *"Stars"* are high share/high growth businesses.
            They enjoy a dominant competitive position in a
            growing industry. The preferred strategy is
            growth.

        *   *"Cash Cows"* are high share/low growth businesses.
            They occupy a dominant position in a low growth
            industry. The preferred strategy is *stability* or
            modest growth.

        *   *"Question Marks"* are low share/high growth
            businesses. They occupy a poor competitive
            position in a growing industry. The preferred
            strategies are *growth* for promising businesses
            and *retrenchment* for the rest.

        *   *"Dogs"* are low share/low growth businesses with a
            poor competitive position in a low growth
            industry; preferred strategy is *retrenchment*.

C.   *Porter's Competitive Strategies*   FIGURE 8.6

   1.   The **competitive strategies model** developed by *Michael Porter*
        begins with an analysis of an organization's current and
        potential competitive environment.

   2.   **Generic strategies** for gaining a strategic advantage.

   a)   <u>Differentiation</u>: Trying to distinguish one's products
        from those of the competition.

        <u>Example</u>: Rolex's production of gold and stainless steel
        watches that are hand-made and subjected to strenuous
        tests of reliability and quality.

   b)   <u>Cost leadership</u>: Using cost minimization to operate more
        efficiently than competitors.

<u>Example</u>: Wal-Mart gains a strategic advantage from its "productivity loop," which allows it to offer customers the lowest prices and still make a reasonable profit.

c) <u>Focus</u>: Concentrating on serving one special market or customer group.

<u>Example</u>: Stouffer's offering of its Lean Cuisine line of low-calorie, high quality frozen dinners.

D. *Adaptive Strategies*

1. The major premise of **Miles and Snow's adaptive model** is that organizations should pursue product/market strategies congruent with their external environments.

2. **Four Strategies in the Adaptive Model**

a) <u>Prospector strategy</u>: Taking risk, seeking opportunities, innovation and growth. This strategy is best suited for *dynamic and high growth environments*.

<u>Example</u>: 3M's efforts to develop new products.

b) <u>Defender strategy</u>: Avoiding change, seeking stability and perhaps retrenchment. This strategy is suited for a *stable environment*, and perhaps in declining industries.

<u>Example</u>: Small local retailers.

c) <u>Analyzer strategy</u>: Maintaining stability, while exploring limited innovation; a "follow-the-leader-when-things-look-good" approach.

<u>Example</u>: Makers of PC clones follow the successes of industry leaders.

d) <u>Reactor strategy</u>: Responding to events, but without a guiding strategy; this is really a non-strategy and "follow as last resort" approach.

<u>Example</u>: Public utilities operating in restricted environments under government regulation.

E. *Product Life Cycles*

1. A **product life cycle** is a series of stages a product or service goes through in the "life" of its marketability.

2. Four typical stages are (1) **introduction**, (2) **growth**, (3) **maturity**, and (4) **decline**.

3. This is a **contingency** approach which suggests that different business strategies should be used to support products in different stages of their life cycles.

4. Products in the **introduction** and **growth** stages lend themselves to **differentiation** and **prospector** strategies, and require investments in advertising and market research to establish a market presence and build a customer base.

5. In the **maturity** stage, the strategic emphasis shifts toward keeping customers and gaining production efficiencies, through **focus** and/or **cost leadership** strategies.

6. During **decline**, **defender** or **analyzer**, strategies may appear as strategic planners seek ways to extend product life.

7. **Example**: IBM is still grappling with the strategy implications of the maturation of its large mainframe computer products.

F. *Emergent Strategies*

1. *James Brian Quinn* describes the process of **logical incrementalism** in which incremental changes in strategy occur as managers learn from experience.

2. *Henry Mintzberg* and *John Kotter* see managers as planning and acting in complex interpersonal networks, and in hectic and fast-paced work settings.

3. Effective managers must have the capacity to stay focused on long-term objectives while still being flexible enough to master short-run problems and opportunities as they occur.

4. Mintzberg argues that **emergent strategies** develop over time as "streams" of decisions, as managers learn from, as well as respond to, their situations.

V. **Strategy Implementation**

A. *Management Practices and Systems*

1. In order to successfully put strategies into action, the entire organization and all of its resources must be **mobilized** to support them.

2.   **Common Strategy Pitfalls**

a)   <u>Failures of substance</u> reflect a lack of attention to the major strategic planning elements -- analysis of purpose/mission, core values and corporate culture, and the SWOT analysis.

b)   <u>Failures of process</u> reflect poor handling of the ways in which the various aspects of strategic planning were accomplished.

*   The *insufficient participation error* may stem from over-centralization of planning in top management, or too much delegation to staff planners.

*   *Goal displacement* can occur when the process gets so bogged down in details that the planning process becomes an end in itself.

3.   **How to Double-Check a Strategy**   **MANAGER'S NOTEPAD 8.2**

a)   Is the strategy consistent with your purpose and mission?

b)   Is the strategy feasible, given strengths and weaknesses?

c)   Is the strategy responsive to opportunities and threats?

d)   Does the strategy offer a sustainable competitive advantage?

e)   Is the risk in the strategy a "reasonable" risk?

f)   Is the strategy flexible enough?

B.   *Leadership and Top Management Teams*

1.   **Strategic management is a leadership responsibility** -- Effective strategy implementation and control depends on the full commitment of all managers to supporting and leading strategic initiatives within their areas of supervisory responsibility.

2.   A **top management team** is one that is headed by a chief executive officer or president and entails, at a minimum, the senior managers reporting directly to this position.

3.   Such teams are responsible for sharing information and working together to facilitate the strategic management of the enterprise.

C.   *Corporate Governance*

    1.   **Corporate governance** is the system of control and performance monitoring that is maintained by boards of directors and other major stakeholder representatives.

    2.   **Boards of directors** are formally charged with ensuring that an organization operates in the best interest of its owners and/or the representative public in the case of nonprofit organizations.

    3.   Controversies often arise over the role of **inside directors** who are chosen from the senior management of the organization and **outside directors** who are chosen from other organizations and positions external to the organization.

    4.   The current trend is toward **greater emphasis on corporate governance**, as top managers are held more accountable for performance by boards of directors and other stakeholder interest groups.

VI.   Strategy and Entrepreneurship

ENHANCEMENT

To make the following discussion of entrepreneurship more personally meaningful for students, assign the *Assessment* titled **Entrepreneurship Orientation** from *Career Readiness Portfolio*. You may also want to assign the *Research and Presentation Project* titled **Entrepreneurship -- Is it For You?**, to provide students with a greater appreciation for the issues involved in the strategic management process. Further discussion of these assignments is provided in Unit 9 of this *Manual*.

A.   *Entrepreneurship* is a term used to describe risk-taking behavior that results in the creation of new opportunities for individuals and/or organizations.

B.   *Who Are the Entrepreneurs?*

    1.   An **entrepreneur** is a risk-taking individual who takes action to pursue opportunities and situations others may fail to recognize as such, or may even view as problems or threats.

    2.   **Typical Characteristics of Entrepreneurs**

        a)   <u>Internal locus of control:</u> Entrepreneurs believe that they control their own destiny.

        b)   <u>High need for achievement</u>: Entrepreneurs are motivated to act individually to accomplish challenging goals.

        c)   <u>Tolerance for ambiguity</u>: Entrepreneurs are able to tolerate situations with high degrees of uncertainty.

        d)   <u>Self-confidence:</u> Entrepreneurs feel competent, believe in themselves, and are willing to make decisions.

        e)   <u>Action-oriented</u>: Entrepreneurs want to get things done quickly, and do not want to waste valuable time.

C.   *Entrepreneurship and Small Business*

1.   Entrepreneurship plays an important role in the **formation of smaller enterprises**.

2.   A **small business** is commonly defined as one with 500 or fewer employees; almost 99% of American businesses are small.

3.   Small businesses offer two major **economic advantages**:

        a)   They create many <u>job opportunities</u>.

        b)   They are the source of many <u>new goods and services</u>.

4.   Small businesses have a high **failure rate** -- 50 to 60 percent fail in their first 5 years.

5.   Success is more likely with a **business plan** -- a written document that describes the nature of the business as well as exactly how an entrepreneur intends to start and operate it.

D.   *Small Business Development*

1.   The **United States Small Business Administration** works with state and local agencies to support a network of over 1000 **Small Business Development Centers** nationwide. They offer guidance to entrepreneurs and small business owners.

2.   State governments also typically offer special assistance in helping small businesses get involved in **exporting**.

E.   *Entrepreneurship and Large Enterprises*

1.   In today's dynamic environment, **larger businesses** also depend on entrepreneurial managers willing to assume risk and encourage the creativity and innovation so important to continued success.

2. **Intrapreneurship** is entrepreneurial behavior displayed by people or subunits within large organizations.

3. Because success for large organizations sometimes depends on their ability to innovate like smaller ones, some create small subunits called **skunkworks**, in which groups of people are allowed to work together in a setting that is highly creative and free of many of the restrictions of large organizations.

4. **Example:** Apple Computer used skunkworks to create the MacIntosh computer -- a state-of-the-art, user-friendly personal computer.

CHAPTER 8 SUMMARY

Why is strategic management?

* A strategy is a comprehensive plan that sets long-term direction and guides resource allocation to accomplish an organization's mission.
* Strategic thinking involves the ability to understand the different challenges of monopoly, oligopoly, and hyper-competition environments.
* Strategic management is a responsibility for the formulation and implementation of strategies that support organizational mission and objectives in a competitive environment.
* The strategic management process begins with analysis of mission, clarification of core values, and identification of objectives.
* The strategic management process involves a SWOT analysis of organizational resources and capabilities and industry/environment opportunities and threats.

What types of strategies are used by organizations?

* Corporate strategy sets direction for an entire organization; business strategy sets direction for a business division or product/service line; functional strategy sets direction for the operational support of business and corporate strategies.
* The grand or master strategies used by organizations include growth -- pursuing expansion; retrenchment -- pursuing ways to scale back operations; stability -- pursuing ways to maintain the status quo; and combination — pursuing the strategies in combination.

How are strategies formulated?

* The BCG matrix is a portfolio planning approach that classifies businesses or product lines as "stars," "cash cows," "question marks," or "dogs."
* Porter's model of competitive strategy identifies the major generic strategic options: differentiation -- distinguishing one's products from the competition, cost leadership -- minimizing costs relative to the competition, and focus -- concentrating on a special market segment.
* The adaptive model focuses on the congruence of prospector, defender, analyzer, or reactor strategies with demands of the external environment.
* The product life-cycle model focuses on different strategic needs at the introduction, growth, maturity, and decline stages of a product's life.
* The incremental or emergent model recognizes that many strategies are formulated and implemented incrementally over time.

What are current issues in strategy implementation?

* Management practices and systems -- including the functions of planning, organizing, leading, and controlling -- must be mobilized to support strategy implementation.
* Among the pitfalls that inhibit strategy implementation are failures of substance, such as poor analysis of the environment, and failures of process, such of lack of participation in planning process.
* Increasingly, organizations utilize top management teams to energize and direct the strategic management process.

* Corporate governance, involving the role of boards of directors in the performance monitoring of organizations, is being addressed as an important element in strategic management today.

What is entrepreneurship?
* Entrepreneurship is risk-taking behavior that results in the creation of new opportunities for individuals and/or organizations.
* An entrepreneur is someone who takes strategic risks to pursue opportunities in situations others may view as problems or threats.
* Entrepreneurship results in the founding of many small business enterprises that offer job creation and other benefits to economies.
* In the United States, small businesses have access to a variety of forms of support and assistance, including Small Business Development Centers funded by government sources and business incubators.
* Intrapreneurship, or entrepreneurial behavior within larger organizations, is important in today's dynamic and competitive environments.

CHAPTER 8 KEY TERMS

Analyzer strategy A corporate competitive strategy that seeks to maintain the stability of a core business while selectively responding to opportunities for innovation and change.

Business strategy A strategy that identifies the intentions of a division or strategic business unit to compete in its special product and/or service domain.

BCG matrix A portfolio planning approach developed by the Boston Consulting Group that ties strategy formulation to an analysis of business opportunities according to market growth rate and market share.

Combination strategy A strategy that involves stability, growth, and retrenchment in one or more combinations.

Core competencies Special strengths that give an organization a competitive advantage in its domain.

Corporate culture The predominant value system for the organization as a whole.

Corporate governance The system of control and performance monitoring or top management.

Corporate strategy A strategy that sets the direction of and serves as a resource allocation guide for the total enterprise.

Cost leadership strategy A corporate competitive strategy that seeks to achieve lower costs than competitors by improving efficiency of production, distribution, and other organizational systems.

Defender strategy A corporate competitive strategy that emphasizes existing products and current market share without seeking growth.

Differentiation strategy A corporate strategy that seeks competitive advantage through uniqueness, by developing goods and/or services that are clearly different from those offered by the competition.

Entrepreneur A person who displays entrepreneurship and is willing to take action to pursue opportunities in situations others view as problems or threats.

Entrepreneurship Behavior that is dynamic, risk taking, creative, and growth oriented.

Focus strategy A corporate competitive strategy that concentrates attention on a special market segment to serve its needs better than the competition.

Functional strategy A strategy that guides the activities within various functional areas or organizational operations.

Growth strategy A grand strategy that involves expansion of the organization's current operations.

Intrapreneurship Entrepreneurial behavior displayed by people or subunits within large organizations.

Mission An organization's reason for existing as a supplier of goods and/or services to society.

Operating objectives The specific ends toward which organizational resources are actually allocated.

Portfolio planning A strategic planning approach that seeks to identify the best mix of investments among alternative business opportunities.

Product life cycle The series of stages a product or service goes through in the "life" of its marketability.

Prospector strategy A corporate competitive strategy that involves pursuing innovation and new opportunities in the face of risk and with the prospects of growth.

Reactor strategy A corporate competitive strategy that involves simply responding to competitive pressures in order to survive.

Retrenchment strategy A grand strategy that involves slowing down, cutting back, and seeking performance improvement through greater efficiencies in operations.

Small business A business with fewer than 500 employees and that is independently owned and operated and does not dominate its industry.

Stability strategy A grand strategy that maintains the present course of action.

Strategic business unit (SBU) A separate operating division that represents a major business area and operates with some autonomy vis-à-vis other similar units in the organization.

Strategic management The managerial responsibility for leading the process of formulating and implementing strategies that lead to longer term organizational success.

Strategy A comprehensive plan or action orientation that sets critical direction and guides the allocation of resources for an organization to achieve long-term objectives.

SWOT analysis The process that sets the stage for strategy formulation by analysis of organizational strengths and weaknesses and environmental opportunities and threats.

CHAPTER 9: CONTROLLING -- TO ENSURE RESULTS

CHAPTER 9 STUDY QUESTIONS

o   What is the control process?
o   What are the types of controls used in organizations?
o   How do organizational systems assist in control?
o   How can operations management improve control?

CHAPTER 9 LEARNING OBJECTIVES

After completing this chapter, students should be able to:

1.   Define controlling and explain its importance to effective management.
2.   List and explain the steps in the control process, and describe the characteristics of effective control systems.
3.   Identify and discuss different types of controls.
4.   Compare and contrast internal versus external control strategies
5.   Explain how key organizational systems promote control, including management process controls, compensation and benefit systems, employee discipline systems, and information and financial controls.
6.   Discuss areas of operations management that promote control, including purchasing control, inventory control, project management and control, and statistical quality control.
7.   Compare and contrast alternative approaches to inventory control, including economic order quantity, just-in-time scheduling, and materials requirements planning.

CHAPTER 9 OVERVIEW

Controlling is a process of monitoring performance and taking action to ensure desired results.   Management requires control in order to ensure goal accomplishment and to avoid chaos. The importance of control is well illustrated by *Headline* opener titled, **Facts Can be Your Best Friends,** which describes how a ski-maker applied process analyses to solve production problems and improve product quality This chapter describes the ways in which control systems, such as those employed by Volant, can be used to achieve high levels of quality and productivity.

The chapter begins with a discussion of the importance of controlling and the elements of the control process. Specific types of controls are described next before moving on to internal and external control strategies. Next, various organizational systems that facilitate control are discussed, including management process controls, compensation and benefit systems, employee discipline systems, and information and financial control systems. The chapter concludes by examining various areas where operations management techniques are applied to achieve control, including purchasing control, inventory control, project management and control, and statistical quality control.

CHAPTER 9 LECTURE OUTLINE

Teaching Objective: To acquaint students with the fundamentals of controlling, including the control process and the systems through which managers achieve control.

Suggested Time: Two full hours of class time is recommended to cover this chapter.

Controlling as a Management Function
> The Importance of Controlling
> Steps in the Control Process
> Characteristics of Effective Controls

Types of Controls
> Feedforward Controls
> Concurrent Controls
> Feedback Controls
> Internal versus External Control

Organizational Control Systems
> Management Process Controls
> Compensation and Benefits Systems
> Employee Discipline Systems
> Information and Financial Controls

Operations Management and Control
> Purchasing Control
> Inventory Control
> Project Management and Control
> Quality Control

CHAPTER 9 SUPPORTING MATERIALS

Textbook Inserts

Headline: Facts Can Be Your Best Friends
Margin Photos: General Electric, Society for Human Resource Management, U.S.
     Army, C & S Mystery Shoppers
Embedded Boxes: Bell Atlantic, Wal-Mart Stores, Steelcase, Sun Microsystems
Manager's Notepad 9.1: "Hot Stove Rules" of Employee Discipline
Manager's Notepad 9.2: Popular Financial Ratios
Manager's Notepad 9.3: Success Factors for JIT Systems

Multi-Media Resources

PowerPoint Presentations (Website):
     Figures 9.1 to 9.5 from the Textbook plus Supplemental Figures
     NBR Viewing Questions: UPS & Nucor

In-Class Activities

Cases for Critical Thinking (Career Readiness Workbook & Website):
     United Parcel Service (Primary Case)
     Nucor (Alternate Case)

Exercises:
     The MBO Contract (Career Readiness Workbook)

Assessments:
     Internal/External Control (Career Readiness Workbook)

Research and Presentation Project:
     Total Quality Management: Is It Working?

Self-Test 9 (Textbook and Website)

CHAPTER 9 LECTURE NOTES

A humorous way to introduce this chapter is to ask students if they have ever seen the old television series, **"Get Smart."** You can then ask those who are familiar with this show the name of the organization that employed the series' hero, **Maxwell Smart.** The answer, of course, is **"Control."** Next, ask for the name of the villainous organization which Maxwell battled against. The answer to this question is **"C.H.A.O.S."** From here, you can point out that while the series was a farcical comedy, managers share with Maxwell Smart the desire to maintain *control* and to avoid organizational *chaos*.

I.   **Controlling as a Management Function**

    A.   *Controlling* is a process of monitoring performance and taking action to ensure desired results.

    B.   *The Importance of Controlling*

        1.   **Figure 9.1** depicts controlling in relation to the other three management functions.

        2.   **Controlling** sees to it that the right things happen, in the right way, at the right time.

Point out to students that the importance of controlling is well illustrated by the chapter opener on *Volant, Inc.,* which describes how Volant Mark Soderberg addressed persistent production problems to improve product quality.

    C.   *Steps in the Control Process*   **FIGURE 9.2**

        1.   A **cybernetic control system** is one that is self-contained in its performance monitoring and correction capabilities; such an ideal state is rarely achieved in management practice.

Before you formally present the **steps in the control process**, you may want to solicit student input by asking them to identify some examples of controls that are used in organizations. You can simply record these controls on the chalkboard or overhead projector as they are offered. Students typically provide many examples ranging from a minimum GPA requirement, to liquor laws to shoplifting guards. You can then use one or more of the examples provided to illustrate the control process presented below. For instance, using the example

ENHANCEMENT (Continued)

of the minimum GPA requirement, you could point out that this requirement is a standard against which actual student performance is compared. When students' GPAs fall below this standard, they are placed on academic probation and counseled to improve their performance. If they remain below the standard, they are suspended from the program. Through this process, the quality of students who graduate from a program is maintained. Students who do exceptionally well, are also singled out for special attention in the form of awards and honors. An example such as this can make the control process more tangible to students.

2.   **Figure 9.2** summarizes the **four steps in the control process** listed below.

   a)   <u>Step 1</u>: Establish objectives and standards.
   b)   <u>Step 2</u>: Measure actual performance.
   c)   <u>Step 3</u>: Compare results with objectives and standards.
   d)   <u>Step 4</u>: Take corrective action as needed.

3.   **Step 1: Establishing Objectives and Standards**

   a)   The control process begins with <u>planning</u> and the establishment of <u>performance objectives</u>.

   b)   From a control standpoint, any <u>objective</u> should be associated with a measurement <u>standard</u> or "<u>benchmark</u>" for determining how well they are accomplished.

   c)   <u>Output standards</u> measure performance <u>results</u> in terms of quantity, quality, cost, or time.

   <u>Examples</u>: Percentage error rate, number of units produced.

   d)   <u>Input standards</u> measure the work <u>efforts</u> that go into a performance task.

   <u>Examples</u>: Efficiency in the use of resources, work attendance.

4.   **Step 2: Measuring Actual Performance**

   a)   During this step, attention is devoted to accurately measuring <u>actual</u> performance.

   <u>Example</u>: Calculating the quantity of units sold during a given time period.

5. **Step 3: Comparing Results with Objectives and Standards**

   a) The comparison made at this step is summarized by the following <u>control equation</u>:

   Need for action = *Desired* performance - *actual* performance

   b) A <u>historical comparison</u> uses past performance as a benchmark for evaluating correct performance.

   c) A <u>relative comparison</u> uses the performance of other persons, work units, or organizations as the evaluation standard.

   d) An <u>engineering comparison</u> uses engineered standards set scientifically through such methods as time and motion studies to analyze jobs to determine what outputs are possible and/or what inputs are most appropriate.

6. **Step 4: Taking Corrective Action**

   a) <u>Management by exception</u> involves focusing managerial attention on situations showing the most significant deviations between actual and desired performance.

   b) This practice can save the manager time, energy, and other resources, and concentrate efforts on areas showing the greatest need.

   c) <u>Two types of exceptions</u> can be recognized by the control equation:

      (1) A *problem situation* is one in which actual performance is less than desired, suggesting *corrective action* is needed.

      (2) An *opportunity situation* arises when actual performance exceeds the standard.

D. *Effective Control*

1 **Human Reactions to Controls**

   a) Excessive controls can <u>backfire</u>, causing people to "play the game" or "make their numbers."

   b) People sometimes <u>resent</u> and <u>reject</u> controls.

2. **Characteristics of Effective Controls**

    a)   Strategic and results oriented.
    b)   Understandable.
    c)   Encourage self-control.
    d)   Timely and exception oriented.
    e)   Positive in nature.
    f)   Fair and objective.
    g)   Flexible.

II. Types of Controls   FIGURE 9.3

ENHANCEMENT

If you solicited examples of controls as an enhancement, you can follow up on this discussion here by classifying the controls identified into the categories presented below.

A. **Figure 9.3** illustrates the following *three major types of controls*.

1. **Feedforward controls** or **Preliminary controls**

    a)   These controls are employed <u>before a work activity begins</u> to ensure that proper directions are set and the right resources are available to accomplish them.

    b)   <u>Example</u>: The quality of ingredients that go into a food product, such as a breakfast cereal, must meet precise specifications.

2. **Concurrent controls** or **Steering controls**

    a)   These controls <u>monitor operations and activities</u> to make sure things are being done correctly.

    b)   Ideally, these controls allow for corrective action to be taken <u>while the work is in process</u>.

    c)   <u>Example</u>: Students receive grades on exams and other assignments throughout the semester so that they can make the necessary adjustments and learn the material required to pass their courses.

3. **Feedback controls** or **Postaction controls**

    a)   These controls <u>focus on end results</u> and take place after an action is completed.

b) <u>Example</u>: Hotel questionnaires ask guests how they liked their stay ... after their visit is completed.

c) Postaction controls provide feedback that can be used to <u>evaluate and revise plans</u>.

B. *Internal versus External Control*

ENHANCEMENT

The *Assessment* titled **Internal/External Control** included in *Career Readiness Portfolio* is designed to indicate if a student possesses an *internal or external locus of control*. It can be used to provide students with some personal insights regarding their ability to control their own destiny. The *Assessment* titled **Empowering Others** can then be used to discuss ways in which managers can develop subordinates' self-control by empowering them. Additional discussions of each of these assessments are provided in Unit 9 of this *Manual*.

1. **Internal control** allows motivated individuals to exercise self-control in fulfilling job expectations.

2. **External control** occurs through personal supervision and the use of formal administrative systems.

ENHANCEMENT

Examples of External Control
Pacific Southwest Airlines and American Express use modern computer technologies to achieve **external control** by closely monitoring employee behavior. Similarly, Automatic Data Processing employs its keystroke monitoring system to measure and reward efficient data entry. Critics claim, however, that electronic monitoring is stress-inducing and counterproductive.

(Source: "Memo to Workers: Don't Phone Home," *Business Week*, January 28, 1988, pp. 88-89; and Stephen Koepp, "The Boss that Never Blinks," *Time*, July 28, 1986, pp. 46-47).

III. Organizational Control Systems

A. *Management Process Controls*

1. **Control via strategy and objectives** occurs when work behaviors are initially directed toward the right end results.

2. **Control via policies and procedures** occurs when good policies and procedures exist to guide behavior, thereby making it more likely that organizational members will act uniformly on important matters.

3. **Control via staff selection and training** occurs when capable people are hired and given the ongoing training needed to perform their jobs at high levels of accomplishment.

4. **Control via performance appraisal** occurs when individual performance is assessed and evaluated to ensure high performance results, and to identify areas where training and development is needed.

5. **Control via job design and work structures** involves putting people to work in jobs that are designed to best fit the job-holder's talents.

6. **Control through performance modeling** means that leadership sets the example and that workers have good models to follow in their jobs.

7. **Control via performance norms** occurs as group members support performance directions and work hard to accomplish them.

8. **Control via organization culture** occurs in similar fashion when shared values and continuous mutual reinforcement support individual performance efforts.

B. *Compensation and Benefit Systems*

1. **Base compensation** in the form of market-competitive salary or hourly wages is one means of obtaining a qualified workforce.

    a) The more the organization succeeds in <u>attracting qualified persons who exercise self-control</u>, the more it can <u>cut costs and boost productivity in the long run</u>.

    b) The <u>less capable the workforce</u> is to begin with, the greater the burden on <u>external controls</u>.

2. **Incentive compensation** such as "merit" pay, "pay-for-performance," and "performance-contingent pay" can serve as powerful means of influencing external control over workplace performance.

ENHANCEMENT

Example of Merit Pay
Lincoln Electric, a builder of welding machinery and electric motors in Cleveland, Ohio, uses **"pay for performance"** incentives to inspire workers. Each worker is paid only for what he or she produces, and workers must repair defects on their own time. One says, "The individual's own ability is the only factor limiting them." Turnover in the firm is only 3 percent.

3.   <u>Fringe benefits</u> can also help or hinder the attraction of capable workers.

ENHANCEMENT

To provide students with a deeper understanding of the issues surrounding fringe benefits, assign the *Research and Presentation Project* titled, **Fringe Benefits — Can they Be Managed?** from *Career Readiness Portfolio*. Further discussion of this assignment is provided in Unit 9 of this *Manual*.

This is also a good point to examine the *Embedded Box* on **Steelcase Incorporated**, a Michigan office furniture manufacturer. The essay describes how the growing number of two-career couples and intense competition for labor has contributed to the firm's emphasis on flexibility in employment relationships, including **a cafeteria benefits plan**. Employees may choose from a wide variety of benefits, such as a) a child-care referral service, b) health benefits, including those provided by the Steelcase Medical Center, Fitness Center, Wellness program, Food Service Department, Counseling and Referral Service, and substance abuse program, c) a tuition reimbursement plan, and d) a Pre-Retirement Planning program.

C.   *Employee Discipline Systems*

1.   **Discipline** involves influencing people through reprimands; it is a form of managerial control designed to influence the behavior of people at work.

2.   **Control Through Progressive Discipline**

a)   <u>Progressive discipline</u> ties reprimands to the severity and frequency of the employee's infractions.

b)   In most progressive discipline systems, the <u>least severe disciplinary action</u> is a *written or verbal warning*, and the <u>most severe</u> is a *discharge*.

c)   The <u>goal of progressive-discipline systems</u> is always to achieve compliance with organizational expectations through the *least* extreme reprimand possible.

3.   **Guidelines for Disciplinary Action**

a)   <u>"Hot Stove Rules" of Employee</u>   **MANAGER'S NOTEPAD 9.1**
      <u>Discipline</u>

      To be effective, a *reprimand should*...
      ...   be immediate.
      ...   be directed towards someone's actions, not their personality.
      ...   be consistently applied.

> ... be informative.
> ... occur in a warm and supportive setting.
> ... support realistic rules.

D. *Information and Financial Controls*   **MANAGER'S NOTEPAD 9.2**

1. When the utilization of resources is considered from the standpoint of managerial control, the **use of information in financial analysis** of firm or organizational performance is critical.

2. **Activity-based costing** attempts to assign true costs to products and services in respect to resources consumed by all activities associated with their creation and accomplishment.

3. The concept of **economic value added** pertains to attempts to measure financial performance by examining the value added by all activities a the level of each job, work unit, or business process.

4. **Important Financial Aspects of Organizational Performance**

   a) Liquidity -- ability to generate cash to pay bills.

   b) Leverage: -- ability to earn more in returns than the cost of debt.

   c) Asset management — ability to use resources efficiently and operate at minimum cost.

   d) Profitability — ability to earn a total profit.

5. The **Manager's Notepad 9.2** summarizes **Popular Financial Ratios** [with preferred directions ^ or v].

   a) Liquidity Ratios

      [^] *Current ratio* = Current assets/Current liabilities
      [^] *Acid test* = (Current assets - inventory)/Current liabilities

   b) Leverage Ratios

      [v] *Debt ratio* = Total debts/Total assets
      [v] *Times interest earned* Profits before interest and taxes/Total interest

    c)   <u>Asset Management Ratios</u>

        [^] *Inventory turnover* = Sales/Average inventory
        [^] *Total asset turnover* = Sales/Total assets

    d)   <u>Profitability Ratios</u>

        [^] *Net margin* = Net profit after taxes/Sales
        [^] *Return on investment (ROI)* = Net profit after taxes/ Total assets

IV. Operations Management and Control

A.   Control is an **essential** element in the **operations management process**, where the emphasis is always on utilizing people, resources, and technology to best advantage.

B.   *Purchasing Control*

    1.   Executives are recognizing that purchasing control is a **productivity tool.**

    2.   **Trends in Purchasing Control**

        a)   To <u>leverage buying power</u>, more organizations are centralizing purchasing to allow buying in volume.

        b)   Firms are committing to a <u>small number of suppliers</u> with whom they can negotiate special contracts, gain quality assurances, and get preferred service.

        c)   Firms are also finding ways to work together in <u>supplier-purchaser partnerships</u> to operate in ways that allow each partner to contain its costs.

C.   *Inventory Control*

    1.   **Inventory** is the amount of materials or products kept in storage; it is common for organizations to maintain inventories of raw materials, work in process, and/or finished goods.

    2.   **Economic Order Quantity (EOQ)**   **FIGURE 9.4**

        a)   <u>Economic order quantity (EOQ)</u> is a method of inventory control that involves ordering a fixed number of items every time an inventory level falls to a predetermined point; when this point is reached, a decision is automatically made (more and more frequently by computer) to place a standard order.

b) EOQ seeks to determine order sizes that <u>minimize two costs of inventory</u>:

    *   *Ordering costs* are the costs of placing an order, including the costs of communication, shipping, and receiving.

    *   *Carrying costs*, or *holding costs*, include the costs of storing and insuring the items in inventory, as well as any finance costs.

c) <u>EOQ Formula</u>

$$EOQ = 2DO/C$$

where

D = actual demand for inventory use
O = ordering cost of inventory
C = carrying cost of inventory

d) The <u>objective</u> is to always have new inventory arrive just as old inventory runs out; this minimizes total inventory costs.

3. **Just-in-Time Delivery**

a) <u>Just-in-time scheduling (JIT)</u> involves an attempt to reduce costs and improve workflows by scheduling materials to arrive at a work station or facility "just-in-time" to be used.

b) This approach involves <u>minimizing carrying costs</u> and maintaining almost no inventories by ordering or producing only as needed; it usually occurs in <u>extremely small lots</u>, possibly even on a unit-by-unit basis.

c) JIT can cut down carrying costs of inventories, maximize the use of space, and even contribute to improved quality of results.

d) <u>Kanban</u> is a Japanese word for the piece of paper that accompanies, for example, a bin of parts in a camera factory; when a worker first takes parts from a new bin, the kanban is routed back to the supplier and serves as an order for new parts.

e)   Success Factors for JIT   **MANAGER'S NOTEPAD 9.3**
      Scheduling

      *   High quality of supplies.
      *   Manageable supplier network.
      *   Geographical concentration.
      *   Efficient transportation and materials handling.
      *   Strong management commitment.

D.   *Project Management and Control*

1.   A **project** is an entire set of actions needed to create single
      products (goods or services) that are not complete until many-
      --perhaps hundreds---of individual tasks are finished in a
      particular sequence.

      Examples: Production of a nuclear submarine; construction of
      an athletic stadium.

2.   **Project management** is the responsibility for making sure that
      various activities are completed on time, in the order
      specified, and with a level of quality sufficient to guarantee
      the success of the final product.

3.   **Program Evaluation and Review Technique (PERT)** is a project
      management technique that identifies and controls the many
      separate events required to complete a project.

      a)   **Figure 9.5** depicts a PERT diagram which charts the
            relationships among various phases of a project, with
            key activities being identified according to anticipated
            time requirements.

      b)   The model makes it possible to plan for effective
            completion of a project by ensuring that activities on
            all paths get done in proper sequence and on time.

      c)   The critical path is the path requiring the longest time
            to accomplish. Any delays encountered in this path will
            lengthen the entire project and, most likely, increase
            costs.

      d)   Computer software is now available to help managers
            utilize PERT schedules for even very complex projects.

E.   *Statistical Quality Control*

1.   **Quality control** involves the process of checking products or
      services to ensure that they meet certain standards.

253

2. **Statistical quality control** is based on the establishment of upper and lower control limits that can be graphically and statistically monitored to ensure that products meet standards.

3. **Figure 9.6** depicts a **control chart**, which is used to graphically keep track of trends by displaying work results on a graph that clearly delineates **upper control limits (UCL)** and **lower control limits (LCL)**; a process is in or out of control depending on how well results remain within these established limits.

4. **Inspection by statistical sampling** involves extending this concept using statistical techniques to set upper and lower control limits and monitor product performance in respect to them; instead of checking every part, batches of a product or service are checked by taking a random sample from each.

5. **"Six Sigma" Control** — A quality standard developed by GE executives to benchmark quality against that achieved by two rivals known for their quality accomplishments — Motorola and Allied Signal. This program commits GE to always delivering quality goods within six standard deviations of a desired result. This means that statistically the firm's quality performance will tolerate no more than 3.4 defects per million — a perfection rate of 99.9997 percent!

CHAPTER 9 SUMMARY

What is the control process?
* Controlling --- the fourth management function --- is the process of monitoring performance and taking corrective action as needed.
* The four steps in the control process are: (1) establish performance objectives, (2) measure actual performance, (3) compare results with objectives, and (4) take necessary action to resolve problems or explore opportunities.
* Control must be done well in order to have a positive impact on behavior in organizations; unintended consequences sometimes interfere with the control process.
* Effective controls will be results oriented, clear, fair, flexible, and timely and include a substantial opportunity for self-control.

What types of controls are used in organizations?
* Feedforward controls, also called preliminary controls, are accomplished before a work activity begins; they ensure that directions are clear and that the right resources are available to accomplish them.
* Concurrent controls, sometimes called steering controls, monitor ongoing operations and activities to make sure that things are being done correctly; they allow corrective actions to be taken while the work is being done.
* Feedback controls, also called postaction controls, take place after an action is completed and focus on end results; they address the question: "Now that we are finished, how well did we do?"
* External control is accomplished through personal supervision and the use of formal administrative systems.
* Internal control occurs through individuals taking responsibility for their work; it allows motivated individuals and groups to exercise self-discipline in fulfilling job expectations and is consistent with many progressive developments in the new workplace.

How do organizational systems assist in control?
* Control through the management process is contributed when the management functions of planning, organizing, and leading are well implemented.
* Performance appraisal is an important element in the comprehensive control system of an organization.
* An organization's compensation and benefits system assists in control by helping to attract and retain a high quality workforce.
* Discipline, the process of influencing behavior through reprimand, is part of an organizational control system.
* Progressive discipline links reprimands to the severity and frequency of inappropriate behavior.
* Information and financial controls are essential in the control process, with useful financial ratios addressing liquidity, leverage, asset management, and profitability.

How can operations management improve quality control?
*   Effective operations management can improve the control of inventories, projects, and product quality.
*   The economic order quantity (EOQ) method controls inventories by ordering a fixed number of items every time inventory level falls to a given point.
*   Just-in-time scheduling (JIT) attempt to reduce costs and improve workflows by scheduling materials to arrive at a work station or facility "just in time" to be used.
*   Statistical quality control uses graphical and statistical control limits to ensure that products meet standards.

CHAPTER 9 KEY TERMS

Concurrent control A control that acts in anticipation of problems and focuses primarily on what happens during the work process.

Control chart A method for quality control in which work results are displayed on a graph that clearly delineates upper control limits and lower control limits.

Controlling The process of measuring performance and taking action to ensure desired results.

Cybernetic control system A control system that is entirely self-contained in its performance monitoring and correction capabilities.

Discipline The act of influencing behavior through reprimand.

Economic order quantity (EOQ) A method of inventory control that involves ordering a fixed number of items every time an inventory level falls to a predetermined point.

External control Control that occurs through direct supervision or administrative systems such as rules and procedures.

Feedback control A control that takes place after an action is completed.

Feedforward control Control that ensures proper directions are set and that the right resources are available to accomplish them before the work activity begins.

Input standards Standards that measure work efforts that go into a performance task.

Internal control Self-control that occurs through self-discipline and the personal exercise of individual or group responsibility.

Inventory The amount of materials or products kept in storage.

Just-in-time scheduling (JIT) A system popularized by the productivity of Japanese industry which attempts to reduce costs and improve workflows by scheduling materials to arrive at a work station or facility "just in time" to be used.

Management by exception Focusing managerial attention on situations in which differences between actual and desired performance are substantial.

Output standards Standards that measure performance results in terms of quantity, quality, cost, or time.

Preliminary control Control that ensures proper directions are set and that the right resources are available to accomplish them before the work activity begins.

Program evaluation and review technique (PERT) A means for identifying and controlling the many separate events involved in the completion of projects.

Progressive discipline The process of tying reprimands in the form of penalties or punishments to the severity of the employee's infractions.

Project management The responsibility for making sure that all activities in a project are completed on time, in the order specified, and with a high quality.

Quality control The process of checking products or services to ensure that they meet certain standards.

Statistical quality control The use of statistical techniques to assist in the quality control process.

CHAPTER 10: ORGANIZING — TO CREATE STRUCTURES

CHAPTER 10 STUDY QUESTIONS

o   What is organizing as a management function?
o   What are the major types of organization structures?
o   What are the new developments in organization structures?
o   What organizing trends are changing the workplace?

CHAPTER 10 LEARNING OBJECTIVES

After completing this chapter, students should be able to:

1.   Define organizing and explain its importance as a management function.
2.   Discuss the concepts of organization structure, restructuring, and formal structure, and describe the information that organizational charts convey about structure.
3.   Define informal structure and identify its potential benefits and disadvantages.
4.   Define departmentation and explain the properties and potential advantages and disadvantages of traditional means of departmentation, including functional, divisional, and matrix structures.
5.   Discuss recent developments in organization structures, including team and network structures.
6.   Explain how classical management principles regarding the chain of command, span of control, unity of command, delegation, centralization-decentralization, and line-staff relationships, are being refined by organizational trends in the workplace.
7.   List and explain the three steps in delegation and discus the ground rules for effective delegation.
8.   Define the terms specialized staff, personal staff, advisory authority, and functional authority and discuss the role of each in modern organizations.

CHAPTER 10 OVERVIEW

Organizing is the process of arranging people and other resources to work together to accomplish a goal. As such, organizing represents a major responsibility of all managers. The importance of organizing for managerial success is well illustrated by the chapter opener on *Edwards Jones Brokers* titled, **Structure Must Support Strategies**. This chapter introduces students to the fundamentals of organizing, including the alternative structural forms employed by modern organizations.

The chapter begins by discussing organizing and its importance to the other management functions, before proceeding to the topic of structure. The concepts of formal structure, as depicted by organization charts, and informal structure are both examined. Next, the traditional means of departmentation including functional, divisional, and matrix structures are explored, along with recent trends in organization structures. The chapter concludes with the organizing trends in the modern workplace, including: a) shorter chains of command, b) less unity of command, c) wider spans of control, d) more delegation and empowerment, e) decentralization with centralization, and f) less use of staff.

CHAPTER 10 LECTURE OUTLINE

Teaching Objective: The purpose of this chapter is to familiarize students with the fundamentals of organizing. To achieve this, the process of organizing is examined along with traditional and alternative organization structures, and organizing trends in the modern workplace.

Suggested Time: Two to three hours of class time are required to cover the material in this chapter. Although it is possible to present the material in less time, it is not encouraged since subsequent chapters build upon the fundamentals introduced here.

Organizing as a Management Function
     What is organization structure?
     Formal structure
     Informal structure

Traditional Organization Structures
     Functional Structures
     Divisional Structures
     Matrix Structures

Developments in Organization Structures
     Team Structures
     Network Structures

Organizing Trends in the Modern Workplace
     Shorter Chains of Command
     Less Unity of Command
     Wider Spans of Control
     More Delegation and Empowerment
     Decentralization with Centralization
     Reduced Use of Staff

CHAPTER 10 SUPPORTING MATERIALS

Textbook Inserts

Headline: Structures Must Support Strategies
Margin Photos: KPMG Peat Marwick LLP, Intel, H.J. Heinz, Delta Airlines
Embedded Box: Center for Workforce Development at Siemens, Jaguar,
        Appalachian Center for Economic Networks (ACEnet), Nucor
Manager's Notepad 10.1: What You Can Learn from an Organization Chart
Manager's Notepad 10.2: Ground Rules for Effective Delegation

Multi-Media Resources

PowerPoint Presentations (Website):
        Figures 10.1 to 10.6 from the Textbook plus Supplemental Figures
        NBR Viewing Questions: AT&T and UPS

In-Class Activities

Cases for Critical Thinking (Career Readiness Workbook & Website):
        AT&T (Primary Case)
        UPS (Alternate Case)

Exercises:
        The Future Workplace (Career Readiness Portfolio)

Assessments:
        Organizational Design Preference (Career Readiness Portfolio)

Self-Test 10 (Textbook and Website)

CHAPTER 10 LECTURE NOTES

I. **Organizing as a Management Function**

ENHANCEMENT

The **"Build an Organization" Exercise** included at the end of this unit of the *Instructor's Resource Guide* provides a unique way to introduce the organizing function to students. The exercise gets students directly involved in the presentation of a variety of chapter topics including *formal structure, organizational charts, division of labor, span of control, chain of command, departmentation, coordination and delegation.* Students typically find the exercise to be very memorable and fun.

    A.   *Organizing* is the process of arranging people and other resources to accomplish tasks in service of a common purpose; it involves dividing up the work to be done (division of labor) and coordinating results.

    B.   Use **Figure 10.1** to a) depict the *relationship between organizing and the other management functions,* and b) summarize the following *elements of organizing:*

        1.   Dividing up the work.
        2.   Arranging resources.
        3.   Coordinating efforts.

    C.   *What is Organization Structure?*

        1.   **Organization structure** is the system of tasks, workflows, reporting relationships, and communication that link together the work of diverse individuals and groups.

        2.   **Restructuring** is the process of changing an organization's structure in an attempt to improve performance.

    D.   *Formal Structure*

        1.   An **organization chart** is a diagram describing the basic arrangement of work positions within an organization.

        2.   An organization chart provides a representation of the organization's **formal structure**; that is, the structure of the organization in its official state.

3. **What You Can Learn from an Organization Chart**   MANAGER'S NOTEPAD 10.1

   a) The division of work.
   b) Supervisor-subordinate relationships.
   c) Communication channels.
   d) Major subunits.
   e) Levels of management.

E. *Informal Structure*

   1. The **informal structure** is a "shadow" organization made up of the unofficial, but often critical, working relationships between organization members.

   2. **Potential Benefits of Informal Structures**

      a) Helping people accomplish their work.
      b) Helping people overcome limits of the formal structure.
      c) Allowing people to communicate better with one another.
      d) Allowing people to support and protect one another.
      e) Satisfying people's needs for social interaction.

   3. **Informal learning** is learning that takes place as people interact informally throughout the work day and in a wide variety of unstructured situations.

   4. **Potential Disadvantages of Informal Structures**

      a) Susceptibility to rumor.
      b) Carry inaccurate information.
      b) Breed resistance to change.
      c) Diversion of work efforts from important objectives.
      d) Feelings of alienation by "outsiders," or persons who are left out of informal groupings.

III. **Traditional Organization Structures**

   A. *Departmentation* is the process of grouping together people and jobs into work units.

   B. *Functional Structures*   FIGURE 10.2

   1. **Functional structures** group together people with similar skills who perform similar tasks.

   2. **Figure 10.2** illustrates a functional structure for a business, which includes senior managers arranged by the functions of marketing, finance, production, and human resources.

3. **Potential Advantages of Functional Structures**

   a) Economies of scale with efficient use of resources.
   b) Task assignments consistent with technical training.
   c) High quality technical problem solving.
   d) In-depth training and skill development within functions.
   e) Clear-cut career paths within functions.

4. **Potential Disadvantages of Functional Structures**

   a) <u>Functional chimneys problem</u> -- a lack of communication, coordination, and problem solving across functions.
   b) Narrow view of performance objectives.
   c) Too many decisions referred upward in the hierarchy.
   d) Lack of clear responsibility for product or service delivery.
   e) Slow innovation in response to environmental changes.

C. *Divisional Structures*

1. **Divisional structures** group together in a unit people who work on the same product or process, similar customers, and/or are located in the same geographical region.

2. Divisional structures are useful:

   a) In <u>complex situations</u> where organizations are pursuing <u>diversified strategies</u>, or

   b) To meet pressures for <u>innovation</u> and <u>change</u> in <u>dynamic environments</u>.

3. **Potential Advantages of Divisional Structures**

   a) More flexibility in responding to environmental changes.
   b) Improved coordination across functional departments.
   c) Clear points of responsibility for product or service delivery.
   d) Expertise focused on specific customers, products, and regions.
   e) Greater ease in changing size by adding or deleting divisions.

4. **Potential Disadvantages of Divisional Structures**

   a) Duplication of resources and efforts across divisions.
   b) Competition and poor coordination across divisions.
   c) Overemphasis on division versus organizational goals.

5.   **Types of Divisional Structures**   FIGURE 10.3

a)   <u>Product structures</u> group together people and jobs working on a single product or service.

<u>Example</u>: IBM's Information Products Division has worldwide responsibility for typewriters, printers, copiers and associated supplies and programming.

b)   <u>Geographic structures</u> group together people and jobs performed in the same location.

<u>Example</u>: IBM has created domestic and worldwide divisions. The domestic division is divided into two marketing divisions -- North-Central and South-West. Its World Trade Corporation divides the world into two groups -- Asia/Pacific and Europe/Middle East/Africa.

c)   <u>Customer structures</u> group together people and jobs that are serving the same customers and clients.

<u>Example</u>: American Hospital Supply Corporation uses customer departmentation to give separate attention to its hospital and laboratory customers.

d)   <u>Process structures</u> group together jobs and activities that are part of the same processes.

A <u>process</u> is a group of tasks related to one another and that collectively create something of value to a customer.

<u>Example</u>: Product purchasing teams, order fulfillment teams, and systems support teams for the mail-order catalog business.

D.   *Matrix Structures*   FIGURE 10.4

1.   A **matrix structure** uses permanent cross-functional teams to blend the technical strengths of functional structures with the integrating potential of divisional structures.

2.   The nature of the matrix form of departmentation can be summarized using the equation:

Matrix = Functional X Divisional

3.   The matrix form is used in **manufacturing** (e.g., aerospace, electronics, pharmaceuticals), **service** (e.g., banking, brokerage, retailing), **professional** (e.g., accounting,

advertising, law), and **non-profit** (e.g., city, state, and federal agencies, hospitals, universities) organizations.

4. Matrix structures are often found in organizations pursuing **growth strategies** in **dynamic and complex environments**.

5. **Potential Advantages of Matrix Structures**

   a) Better interfunctional cooperation in operations and problem solving.

   b) Increased flexibility in adding, removing and/or changing operations to meet changing demands.

   c) Better customer service since there is always a program, product, or project manager who is fully informed and available to answer questions.

   d) Better performance accountability, also through the program, product, or project managers.

   e) Improved decision making as problem solving takes place at the team level, where the best information exists.

   f) Improved strategic management since top mangers are freed from unnecessary problem solving to focus time on strategic issues.

6. **Disadvantages of Matrix Structures**

   a) <u>Power struggles</u>: The "two-boss" system can result in power struggles as functional and program managers try to gain maximum advantage for personal perspectives.

   b) <u>"Groupitis"</u>: Program teams may become too focused on themselves and the group process, and lose sight of production goals.

   c) <u>Increased costs</u>: The matrix adds overhead in extra salaries for program managers; this creates problems when the need for a matrix is unclear and/or a matrix operation is made more complex than necessary.

IV. **Developments in Organization Structures**

   A. *Team Structures*   **FIGURE 10.5**

   1. **Team structures** use permanent and temporary cross-functional teams to improve lateral relations and solve problems throughout the organization.

      2.   **Cross-functional teams** are composed of members from different functional areas who work together to solve problems and explore opportunities.

      3.   **Potential Advantages of Team Structures**

         a)   Break down communication barriers.
         b)   Promote cross-functional interaction and comradery.
         c)   Improve the quality and speed of decision making.

      4.   **Potential Disadvantages of Team Structures**

         a)   Conflicting loyalties among members.
         b)   Excessive time spent in meetings.

B.   *Network Structures*   **FIGURE 10.6**

      1.   A **network structure** consists of a central core working with networks of outside suppliers of essential business services.

      2.   Network structures are contributing to the emergence of **boundaryless organizations** and **virtual organizations**

      3.   These organizations use a variety of **strategic alliances and contracts** to operate without having to "own" all of their supporting functions; such firms gain a *competitive advantage* through *reduced overhead* and *increased operating efficiency*.

      4.   **Electronic computer networks** greatly facilitate the establishment of network links, even across great distances.

      5.   **Control problems arising from network complexity** represent the *major disadvantage* of this structure; if any part of the network breaks down, the whole system suffers.

V.   **Organizing Trends in the Modern Workplace**

A.   *Shorter Chains of Command*

      1.   The **chain of command** links all persons with successively higher levels of authority.

      2.   A basic principle of the **classical school of management** is the **scalar principle**:

         There should be a clear and unbroken chain of command linking every person in the organization with successively higher levels of authority up to and including the top manager.

3. As organizations grow they tend to get **"taller"** as management levels are added to the chain of command; this increases overhead and distance between the top and lower levels.

4. **Current trend:** Organizations are being "streamlined" by cutting unnecessary levels of management; flatter structures are viewed as a competitive advantage.

B. *Less Unity of Command*

1. **Unity of command principle:** Each person in an organization should report to one and only one supervisor.

2. The objective of this classical management principle is to ensure that subordinates do not receive work directions from more than one source.

3. **Current trend:** Organizations are using more cross-functional teams, task forces, and matrix-type structures, and they are becoming more customer conscious; as they do so, employees often find themselves working for more than one "boss."

C. *Wider Spans of Control*   **FIGURE 10.7**

1. The **span of control** is the number of subordinates reporting directly to a manager.

2. When span of control is **"narrow"** only a few people are under a manager's direct supervision; a **"wide"** span of control indicates many people are supervised.

3. Classical management theorists searched in vain for the ideal span of control, and developed the **span of control principle:**

   There is a limit to the number of persons one manager can effectively supervise; care should be taken to keep the span of control within manageable limits.

ENHANCEMENT

Students are often interested in the efforts of classical management theorists to identify an **"ideal" span of control**. The work of **V. A. Graicunas**, a French management consultant, is representative of this effort (Daniel A. Wren, *The Evolution of Management Thought*, New York: The Ronald Press Company, 1972). Graicunas argued that "cross relationships" between subordinates must be

ENHANCEMENT (Continued)

considered in addition to "single direct relations" when establishing the span of control. You can illustrate Graicunas' point by drawing the following organizational charts. First, assume the span of control is one.

Here, there is only one direct relationship. The number of total relationships is therefore one. If only one subordinate is added, increasing the span of control to three, the number of "direct single relations" increases to three as shown below. Graicunas doesn't stop here, however. He argues that "direct group relations" must be considered also. There are three possible "group relations" between individuals and dyads in this example, bringing the total to six.

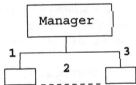

For fun, ask students to guess the number of relationships with **12** subordinates. The answer is **24,708**. How about **20** subordinates? Answer: **10 Million**. Graicunas concluded that while the span of control grew **arithmetically**, the number of potential relationships grew **exponentially**. He developed the following **mathematical formula** to illustrate this growth.

$$\text{Total relationships} = n(2^n/2 + n - 1)$$
$$n = \text{span of control}$$

Thus if the span of control in the above example was increased to **three**, the total number of relationships would be:

$$\text{Total} = 3(2^3/2 + 3 - 1), \text{ or } 3 \times 6 = 18.$$

To show the growth as subordinates are added:

n =	1	2	3	4	5	6	7	8	9	10	11	12	
Total =	1	6	18	44	100	222	490	1080	1376	5210	11374	24708	ETC.

Graicunas concluded that the ideal span of control is **five**. Ask students what they think of this argument. Students are usually quick to point out that there is a difference between the **potential** and **actual** number of relations a manager must be concerned about. The actual number will **depend** upon a number of **contingency variables**. This point provides a nice lead into the following discussion of factors influencing spans of control.

4. **Span of Control and Levels in the Hierarchy** - Use **Figure 10.7** to illustrate that, given the same number of subordinates, a narrow span of control will result in more levels of management than a wide span of control. Thus:

   a) Organizations with <u>wider</u> spans of control tend to be <u>flat</u> because they have fewer levels of management.

   b) Organizations with <u>narrow</u> spans of control tend to be <u>tall</u> because they have many levels of management.

5. **Current trend:** Many organizations are shifting to wider spans of control as chains of command are shortened and "empowerment" gains prominence; individual managers are taking responsibility for larger numbers of subordinates who operate with less direct supervision.

6. **Example:** After Alcoa's chairperson, Paul H. O'Neill eliminated several layers of management and broadened his span of control to 25 business heads, it became possible for these business heads to get their plans approved in just one meeting.

D. *More Delegation and Empowerment*

1. **Delegation** is the process of distributing and entrusting work to other persons.

2. The **three steps in delegation** are:
   a) The manager assigns <u>responsibility</u>.
   b) The manager grants <u>authority</u> to act.
   c) The manager creates <u>accountability</u>.

3. **Responsibility**, **authority**, and **accountability** are the foundation of vertical coordination through delegation.

   a) <u>Responsibility</u> is the obligation to perform that results when a subordinate accepts an assigned task.
   b) <u>Authority</u> is the right to assign tasks and direct the activities of other persons.
   c) <u>Accountability</u> is the requirement for a subordinate to show results of assigned duties to a supervisor.

4. **Authority-and-responsibility principle:** Authority should equal responsibility when work is delegated from supervisor to subordinate.

5. If this principle is violated, the supervisor will unfairly be held accountable for the work of people over whom he or she has no authority.

6. A common mistake is **failure to delegate**; it overloads the manager, robs others of opportunities to use their talents, and denies the organization the full value of other members' experiences and knowledge.

7. **Empowerment** involves giving others the freedom to contribute ideas and do their jobs in the best possible ways.

8. **Current trend:** Managers in progressive organizations are delegating more and finding more ways to empower people at all levels to make more decisions affecting them and their work.

9. **Example:** SAS gives employees the authority to make on-the-spot decisions in order to satisfy passenger needs.

10. **Ground Rules for Effective Delegation MANAGER'S NOTEPAD 10.2**

    a) Carefully choose the person to whom you delegate.
    b) Make the assignment clear.
    c) Agree on performance objectives and standards.
    d) Agree on a performance timetable.
    e) Allow the person to act independently.
    f) Show trust in the other person.
    g) Provide performance support.
    h) Give performance feedback.
    i) Recognize and reinforce performance progress.
    j) Help when things go wrong.
    k) Don't forget *your* accountability for performance results.

E. *Decentralization with Centralization*

1. **Centralization** is the concentration of authority for most decisions at the top level of an organization.

2. **Decentralization** is the dispersion of the authority to make decisions throughout all levels of the organization.

3. **Current trend:** Whereas empowerment and related forces are contributing to more decentralization in organizations, advances in information technology simultaneously allow for the retention of centralized control.

4. **Example 1:** CEO T. J. Rodgers of Cypress Computers uses a computer system to monitor the progress of a highly decentralized set of operations. Subordinates maintain computerized lists of 10-15 objectives, for which they update their progress on a daily basis. Rodgers reviews these lists each week and meets with persons who have trouble meeting their goals. This approach is taken throughout the firm.

5.   **Example 2:** IBM strives for "the centralization of control and decentralization of operations."

ENHANCEMENT

Check Point: Understanding Variable Interrelationships
To check on student understanding of the relationships between these variables, you may want to ask them to "fill in the blanks" in the following chart.

Students should understand that **as the amount of delegation ...**

	... increases.	... decreases.
Spans of Control...	... increase.	... decrease.
Chain of Command...	... decreases.	... increases.
Levels of Management...	... decrease.	... increase.
Centralization...	... decreases.	... increases.
Decentralization...	... increases.	... decreases.

A great illustration of these interrelationships is provided in the on-line case, **"Can Nucor Handle Growth and Control?",** which describes the successful management practices of Nucor Corporation. Nucor, the leader of the U.S. mini-mill steel industry, is an excellent example of a firm that has successfully realized the potential benefits of decentralization. As Nucor's CEO Ken Iverson explains, "The general managers are the ones who make the decisions. All I do is make sure everyone understands that's what we agreed on." This practice of delegation enables Nucor to employ a very flat structure with few levels of management, a short chain of command, and wide spans of control. Iverson attributes Nucor's success to its lean structure and argues that "the most important thing American industry needs to do is to reduce the number of management layers."

F.   *Reduced use of Staff*

1.   **Specialized staff** perform a technical service or provide special problem-solving expertise to other parts of the organization. **Example:** Personnel Department.

2.   **Personal staff** are "assistant-to" positions that provide special administrative support to higher-level positions. **Example:** Assistant to the President.

3.   **Functional authority** is the authority to act within a specified area of expertise and in relation to the activities of other persons or units lying outside the formal chain of command. **Example:** A personnel manager may require a line manager to follow EEOC guidelines.

4.   **Current trend:** Organizations are reducing the number of staff personnel; they are seeking increased operating efficiency by employing fewer and smaller staff units.

CHAPTER 10 SUMMARY

What is organizing as a management function?
* Organizing is the process of creating work arrangements of people and resources, be it for a small unit, a large division, or an entire enterprise.
* To organize a work setting, the manager must make decisions on how to divide up the work that needs to be done, allocate people and resources to do it, and coordinate results to achieve productivity.
* Structure is the system of tasks, reporting relationships, and communication that links the people and positions of an organization.
* Formal structure, such as shown on an organization chart, describes how an organization is supposed to work.
* The informal structure of organization is also very important, consisting of the unofficial relationships among members.

What are the major types of organization structures?
* Departmentation is the process of creating structure by grouping people together in formal work units.
* In functional structures, people with similar skills who perform similar activities work together under a common manager.
* In divisional structures, people who work on a similar product, work in the same geographical region, or serve the same customers are grouped together under common managers.
* A matrix structure combines the functional and divisional approaches to create permanent cross-functional project teams.

What are the new developments in organization structures?
* Increasing complexity and rates of change in the environment are challenging the performance capabilities of traditional organization structures.
* New developments include the growing use of team structures that create horizontal organizations using cross-functional teams and task forces to improve lateral relations and improve problem solving at all levels.
* New developments are also underway in respect to network structures, sometimes called boundaryless or virtual organizations, that cluster systems of contracted services and strategic alliances around a "core" business or organizational center.

What organizing trends are changing the workplace?
* Traditional vertical command-and-control structures are giving way to more horizontal structures strong on employee involvement and flexibility.
* Many organizations today are operating with shorter chains of command and less unity of command.

* Many organizations are operating with wider spans of control and fewer levels of management.
* The emphasis in more organizations today is on effective delegation and empowerment.
* Advances in information technology are making it possible to operate with decentralization while still maintaining centralized control.
* Reduction in the size of staff is a trend in organizations seeking greater efficiency and productivity.

CHAPTER 10 KEY TERMS

Centralization The concentration of authority for most decisions at the top level of an organization.

Chain of command An unbroken line of authority that vertically links all persons in an organization with successively higher levels of authority.

Cross-functional teams A team structure in which members from different functional departments work together as needed to solve problems and explore opportunities.

Customer structure A divisional structure that groups together jobs and activities that serve the same customers or clients.

Decentralization The dispersion of authority to make decisions throughout all levels of management by extensive delegation.

Delegation The process of distributing and entrusting work to other persons.

Departmentalization The process of grouping together people and jobs under common supervisors to form various work units or departments.

Divisional structure An organizational structure that groups together people with diverse skills and tasks but who work on the same product, with similar customers or clients, in the same geographical region, or on the same time schedule.

Formal structure The structure of the organization in its pure or ideal state.

Functional chimneys problem A lack of communication, coordination, and problem solving across functions.

Functional structure An organizational structure that groups together people with similar skills who perform similar tasks.

Geographical structure A divisional structure that groups together jobs and activities being performed in the same location or geographical region.

Informal learning Learning that takes place as people interact informally throughout the work day and in a wide variety of unstructured situations.

Informal structure The undocumented and officially unrecognized structure that coexists with the formal structure of an organization.

Matrix structure An organizational form that combines functional and divisional departmentation to take best advantage of each.

Network structure An organizational structure that consists of a central core with "networks" of outside suppliers of essential business services.

Organization chart A diagram that describes the basic arrangement of work positions within an organization.

Organization structure The system of tasks, reporting relationships, and communication that links people and groups together to accomplish tasks that serve the organizational purpose.

Organizing The process of mobilizing people and other resources to accomplish tasks that serve a common purpose.

Personal staff "Assistant-to" positions that provide special administrative support to higher level positions.

Process structure An organizational structure that groups together people and jobs that are part of the same processes.

Product structure An organizational structure that groups together jobs and activities working on a single product or service.

Span of control The number of subordinates reporting directly to a manager.

Specialized staff Positions that perform a technical service or provide special problem-solving expertise for other parts of the organization.

Team structure An organizational structure through which permanent and temporary teams are created to improve lateral relations and solve problems throughout an organization.

CHAPTER 10 CLASS EXERCISE: "BUILDING AN ORGANIZATION"

The **"Building an Organization"** exercise is a fun way to get students highly involved in the chapter material on organizing. The essence of the exercise is for students to submit proposals for a new business. One proposal is selected. The person who drafted the proposal is appointed "President" and given an opportunity to name the company and hire employees. The specific steps involved in conducting the exercise are presented below.

1. **Background Information.** Ask the students to imagine that you, the instructor, are an investment banker who is willing to lend money to prospective entrepreneurs with creative and feasible proposals for new products and/or services.

2. **Generating Ideas for New Products and/or Services.** Instruct the students to think for a minute about the type of business they would like to operate if given the opportunity. Encourage the students to be creative in identifying products or services they would like to market.

3. **Soliciting Business Proposals.** Tell the students that you would like to provide funds to support one new business. Ask them to write down their business proposals along with their names on a small piece of paper and that you will be collecting these proposals for review. Let the students know that you only have funds to support one business.

4. **Collecting the Business Proposals.** Have the students submit their proposals. If you have a large lecture class, you may consider collecting a "representative" sample of proposals. You can explain that you unfortunately don't have time to entertain all possible proposals.

5. **Evaluating the Proposals and Selecting a "Winner."** Take a couple of minutes to review the student's proposals. Students typically discuss their ideas and the suspense regarding the proposal to be chosen builds. Use your own discretion in selecting the criteria to be used in evaluating the proposals. You may want to select the idea you consider to be most thoroughly developed and most likely to succeed. Alternatively, you may want to select an unusual product or service which you think students are likely to find amusing. Another option is to select a subset of proposals using whatever criteria you consider to be appropriate and then informing the class that you'd like their input in selecting the proposal to be funded. The "finalists" could even be given opportunities to elaborate on their proposals. The class could then vote on the proposal to be funded.

6. **Appointing the "President" and Naming the Company.** Once the "winning" proposal has been selected, inform its creator that he or she will be the "President" of this new business. Ask this individual to name the company. Students often think of original and amusing company names.

7. **Hiring Employees.** To make the business a success, the president will naturally need some assistance. Inform the president that he or she has the opportunity to hire three individuals from the class to work in the organization. The class typically enjoys watching the president select employees from amongst them.

8. **Dividing up the Work.** Ask the president to identify the positions these new employees will occupy. The president then proceeds to assign titles and duties to these workers. Draw an organization chart for the company on the chalkboard or an overhead transparency. This chart will look something like the following.

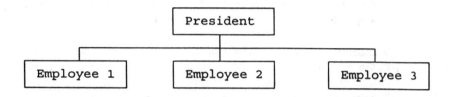

9. **Expanding Operations.** Ask the class to imagine that 5 years have transpired since the founding of the company. Inform them that the president did an excellent job of identifying a needed product or service and that demand has grown dramatically. With this growth, however, the responsibilities of each organizational member have grown to the point where they can no longer handle the work load by themselves.

10. **Hiring New Employees.** Tell the three employees selected by the president that they have now been promoted to vice presidents and that they have an opportunity to hire 2 new employees into their departments. The vice presidents proceed to hire the new workers. Draw the new organization chart on the chalkboard or on an overhead transparency. It should look something like the following chart.

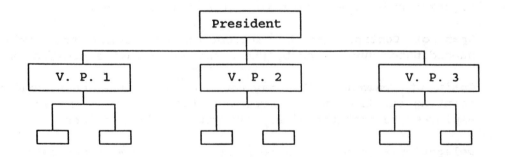

11. **Discussion.** Once the organization is built, the organization charts drawn earlier can be used to present a variety of course concepts including:

A.   The Basic Elements of An Organization

1.   <u>Collection of people</u> - In building this organization, a collection of people were hired and <u>synergy</u> was achieved through their combined efforts to produce a product or service they could not have otherwise provided.

2.   <u>Division of labor</u> - The president divided up the work to be done and assigned specialized tasks to the individuals he or she considered to be most qualified to perform them.

3.   <u>Working together</u> - The president and later the vice presidents coordinated the specialized activities of the employees to ensure goal accomplishment.

4.   <u>Common purpose</u> - The mission of the organization was to produce the product or provide the service proposed by the president in a profitable manner. This goal provided a sense of common direction for the organization.

B.   Organization Charts - Review the organization charts drawn earlier in this exercise. Point out that organization charts such as these are useful for illustrating the following.

1.   The division of work.
2.   The type of work performed.
3.   Supervisor-subordinate relationships.
4.   Formal communication channels.
5.   Major subunits.
6.   Levels of management.

C.   Departmentation - You may want to introduce the concept of departmentation by pointing out that as the organization grew, <u>departmentation</u> occurred as people and activities were grouped together under the supervision of a common manager.

D.   Span of Control can be introduced by noting the number of subordinates supervised by the president and vice presidents.

E.   Chain of Command - You may want to introduce this concept by pointing out the chain of command that runs from the lower level employees through the vice presidents to the president.

F.   Delegation - Point out to students that as the organization grew, authority to perform certain tasks was delegated to lower levels.

CHAPTER 11: ORGANIZATIONAL DESIGN AND WORK PROCESSES

CHAPTER 11 STUDY QUESTIONS

o   What are the essentials of organizational design?
o   How do contingency factors influence organization design?
o   What are the major issues in subsystems design?
o   How can work processes be reengineered?
o   How is operations technology influencing design?

CHAPTER 11 LEARNING OBJECTIVES

After completing this chapter, students should be able to:

1.   Define organizational design and describe it from a problem-solving perspective.
2.   List and explain the features of bureaucratic organizations, as well as the potential limitations of this design.
3.   Compare and contrast the features of mechanistic and organic design alternatives.
4.   Identify and discuss the various mechanistic design alternatives.
5.   Discuss adaptive organizations and describe the various organic design alternatives.
6.   Explain the contingency factors pertinent to appropriate organizational design and discuss the corresponding organizational design guidelines.
7.   Distinguish between the general and specific environments and discuss the implications of environmental uncertainty for organizational design.
8.   Define technology and explain the implications of the various types of technology for organizational design.
9.   Describe the four phases in the organizational life cycle and explain the implications of size and life-cycle for organizational design.
10.   Explain the implications of human resources for organizational design.
11.   Define the term subsystem and explain the role of differentiation and integration in subsystem design.
12.   Discuss specific means of improving subsystem integration.
13.   Describe the practice of process reengineering, and the relevance of the terms work process and workflow to this practice.
14.   Explain the implications of technology for operations design with respect to manufacturing applications, office systems and support, and enterprise-wide integration.

CHAPTER 11 OVERVIEW

Organizational design is the process of choosing and implementing structures that meet the needs of an organization and/or subunit. Drawing on the fundamentals of organizing presented in Chapter 9, this chapter presents a contingency perspective of organizational design. The utility of this perspective is apparent from the chapter opener titled, **Design for Integration and Empowerment**. Specifically, the opener describes some of the key factors that *Nestle* considered in creating a flexible organizational design to support the effective international marketing of its brands.

The chapter formally begins by defining organization design and describing current directions for change that are impacting organization design choices. After discussing the strengths and the weaknesses of bureaucratic organizations and mechanistic designs, the alternatives of adaptive organizations and organic designs are considered. Special attention is devoted to the contingency factors of environmental uncertainty, strategy, technology, size, organizational life-cycle, and people, which determine the appropriateness of the mechanistic and organic design alternatives. The research of Lawrence and Lorsch and its implications for subsystem design are discussed next. Throughout this discussion, guidelines for effective organizational and subsystem design are provided to assist current and future managers in choosing and implementing appropriate structures for their work units.

At this point, the focus of the chapter shifts to the practice of process reengineering, which involves a systematic and complete analysis of work processes and the design of new and better ones. The terms work process and workflow are introduced, and the typical steps involved in reengineering core processes are described. Finally, the relevance of technology to operations design is considered, including the implications of technology for manufacturing applications, office systems and support, and enterprise-wide integration.

CHAPTER 11 LECTURE OUTLINE

Teaching Objective: The purpose of this chapter is to provide students with a thorough understanding of the concepts of organizational design and work processes. To achieve this, several organization design alternatives are described, along with the circumstances under which they are most effective. The ways in which work processes can be reengineered, as well as the impact of operations technology on design, are also explored.

Suggested Time: This chapter typically requires a minimum of two hours to present.

Organizational Design Essentials
      Directions for Change
      Bureaucratic Designs
      Adaptive Designs

Contingencies in Organizational Design
      Environment
      Strategy
      Technology
      Size and Life Cycle
      People

Subsystems Design and Integration
      Differentiation
      Integration

Work Process Design
      What is a Work Process?
      How to Reengineer Core Processes

Operations Technology and Design
      Manufacturing Applications
      Enterprise-wide Integration

CHAPTER 11 SUPPORTING MATERIALS

Textbook Inserts

Headline Design for Integration and Empowerment
Margin Photos: Rickard Group, Inc., 3M, Patricia Seybold Group
Embedded Box: Visa International, Coleman Company, Dana Corporation
Manager's Notepad 11.1: Organizational Design Checklist
Manager's Notepad 11.2: How to Improve Subsystems Integration

Multi-Media Resources

NBR Video Report:
>   Price Waterhouse/Coopers and Lybrand (Available on Video Supplement & Video
>   Cases CD-ROM)

PowerPoint Presentations (Website):
>   Figures 11.1 to 11.6 from the Textbook plus Supplemental Figures
>   NBR Viewing Questions: Price Waterhouse/Coopers and Lybrand

In-Class Activities

Cases for Critical Thinking (Career Readiness Workbook & Website):
>   Price Waterhouse/Coopers and Lybrand (Primary Case)
>   Boeing (Alternate Case)

Exercises:
>   Dots and Squares Puzzle (Career Readiness Workbook)

Research and Presentation Projects:
>   Re-engineering — Does it Work? (Career Readiness Workbook)

Self-Test 11 (Textbook and Website)

CHAPTER 11 LECTURE NOTES

I.   **Organizational Design Essentials**

    A.   *Organizational design* is the process of choosing and implementing structures that best organize resources to serve mission and objectives.

    B.   Managers should view organizational design as a *problem-solving activity*, which requires a *contingency approach* to select and implement the right structure for the unique circumstances of the organization or subunit.

    C.   *Directions for Change*

        1.   As the **trends in organization and management practices** described in the prior chapter make their way into the operations of organizations, one finds more sharing of tasks, reduced emphasis on hierarchy, greater emphasis on lateral communication, more teamwork, and more decentralization of decision making.

        2.   Key directions for change today involve a basic shift in attention *away* from a **traditional emphasis on more vertical or authority-driven structures**, *to* one's that are **more horizontal and task-driven structures.**

    C.   *Bureaucratic Designs*

        1.   *Max Weber* viewed a bureaucracy as an **ideal organizational form** characterized by:
            a)   A clear-cut division of labor.
            b)   A strict hierarchy of authority.
            c)   Formal rules and procedures.
            d)   Promotion based on competency.

ENHANCEMENT
───

To stimulate discussion, ask students for "horror" stories regarding their experiences with *bureaucracies*. These examples will help illustrate the limitations of this structure summarized below.
───

        2.   **Limitations of Bureaucracies** - In practice, bureaucracies are prone to the following limitations:

            a)   Too rigid and formal.
            b)   Slow to respond to rapidly changing and uncertain environments.

  c) Too many levels in the hierarchy can cause higher-level managers to lose touch with lower-level operations.

  d) Overspecialization can reduce employee initiative and creativity, as workers conform to rules.

ENHANCEMENT

To enhance your discussion of organization design, assign the *Assessment* from *Career Readiness Portfolio,* titled **Organizational Design Preference**. The assessment measures student preferences for mechanistic versus organic design alternatives. By completing this assignment, students can obtain insights regarding the type of organizational design they prefer, which should increase the personal relevance of the organizational design topic. Further discussion of this exercise is provided in Unit 9 of this *Manual.*

3. **A Continuum of Organizational Design**   **FIGURE 11.1**
  Alternatives

  a) The <u>contingency perspective of organizational design</u> asks:

    * *When* is a bureaucratic form a good choice for an organization?
    * *What* alternatives exist when it is not a good choice?

  b) The key to effective organizational design is to "<u>match</u>" the appropriate organizational structure with the situation facing the organization.

  c) *Burns and Stalker* performed pioneering research designed to specify the <u>appropriate organizational structures</u> for different environments.

    * Burns and Stalker found that a bureaucratic or *"mechanistic"* form thrived when the environment was *stable.*

    * An *"organic"* form performed best when the environment was *rapidly changing* and *uncertain.*

4. **Mechanistic designs** are highly bureaucratic, with centralized authority, many rules and procedures, a clearcut division of labor, narrow spans of control, and formal coordination.

5. **Examples:** A local McDonald's restaurant; the U.S. Postal Service.

D.   *Adaptive Organizations*

1.   **Adaptive organizations** operate with a minimum of bureaucratic features and encourage empowerment and participation with team work.

2.   Adaptive organizations are often based upon **team structures** and **network structures.**

3.   **Example:** To become more flexible and competitive, Coleman Company, a manufacturer of stoves and camping equipment, replaced its bureaucratic form with an adaptive structure. Product development teams have cut the time it takes to bring a product to market in half. The firm can now produce and ship goods within a week, which has boosted its profits.

4.   **Organic designs** are decentralized with fewer rules and procedures, more open divisions of labor, wider spans of control, and more personal coordination.

5.   Organic designs are flexible and adaptable forms which perform best in **dynamic environments.**

6.   **Example:** Anchor Brewing Company in San Francisco is a small, flexible and adaptable brewery that is able to alter its production processes rapidly to produce different liquors.

ENHANCEMENT

Xerox is an example of an organization that has moved back and forth on the continuum of organizational structures. Under Xerox's founder, Joseph Wilson, the company was positioned on the organic end of the continuum as evidenced by its "loose organizational structure." Wilson's successor as CEO, Peter McClough moved Xerox toward the mechanistic end through the implementation of much-needed controls. When David Kearnes took over as CEO, however, he found that the bureaucratic culture McClough had implemented was characterized by slow decision making, unnecessary layers of management, and an inability to respond to face-paced market changes. Kearnes responded to these problems by moving Xerox back toward an organic design which included small product teams and encouraged diversification.

(Source: "Culture Shock at Xerox," *Business Week*, June 22, 1987; "Remaking the American CEO," *New York Times*, January 25, 1987, p. C-8).

II.   **Contingencies in Organization Design**

A.   *Organization Design Checklist*   MANAGER'S NOTEPAD 11.1

1.   **Check 1:** Does the design fit well with the major problems and opportunities of the *external environment*?

2. **Check 2:** Does the design support implementation of *strategies* and accomplishment of key *operating objectives*?

3. **Check 3:** Does the design accommodate and allow *core technologies* to be used to best advantage?

4. **Check 4:** Can the design handle changes in organizational size and different stages in the *organizational life cycle*?

5. **Check 5:** Does the design *empower workers* and allow their talents to be used to best advantage?

B. *Environment*   **FIGURE 11.2**

1. **Environmental uncertainty** is the rate and predictability of change associated with important environmental elements.

2. A **certain environment** is composed of relatively stable and predictable elements; as a result, **bureaucratic organizations** and **mechanistic designs** are quite adequate under such conditions.

3. An **uncertain environment** will have more dynamic and less predictable elements; as a result, **adaptive organizations** and **organic designs** are more appropriate.

4. **Figure 11.2** summarizes these relationships, showing how increasing uncertainty in organizational environments calls for more horizontal and adaptive designs.

C. *Strategy*

1. Structure must **support strategy** if desired results are to be achieved.

2. **Stability strategies** will be more successful when supported by **bureaucratic organizations** using **mechanistic designs; growth strategies** will be more successful when supported by **adaptive organizations** using **organic designs.**

3. Because **stability** strategies are based on the premise of little environmental change, they focus on achieving operating efficiencies and cost leadership; **mechanistic designs** are best suited for providing the desired level of certainty in the relationship between operations and plans.

4. Because **growth** strategies seek innovative and flexible responses to capitalize on changing environmental conditions, they are best supported by **organic designs.**

ENHANCEMENT

Matching Strategy and Structure
Sears was once a cost leader, but it has lost this advantage to K-mart and Wal-Mart. It has had difficulty moving from efficient centralized purchasing for lower costs, to decentralized purchasing for customer responsiveness in its clothing and fashion lines.

     D.   *Technology*

         1.   **Technology** is the combination of equipment, knowledge, and work methods that transforms inputs into outputs.

         2.   **Woodward's Classification of Manufacturing Technology**

             a)   <u>Small-batch production</u>: The production of a variety of custom products that are crafted to fit customer specifications.
                 <u>Example</u>: A bicycle shop.

             b)   <u>Mass production</u>: The production of a large number of uniform products with an assembly-line type of system.
                 <u>Example</u>: A personal computer assembly-line.

             c)   <u>Continuous-process technology</u>: The continuous feeding of materials into an automated system of production.
                 <u>Examples</u>: Oil refinery, brewery.

         3.   Woodward's **Technological Imperative** states that technology is a major influence on organizational structure.

         4.   **Service Technologies**

             a)   <u>Intensive technology</u>: A technology that focuses the efforts and talents of many people to serve clients.
                 <u>Examples</u>: Hospital emergency room, R & D laboratory.

             b)   <u>Mediating technology</u>: A technology that links together people in a beneficial exchange of values.
                 <u>Examples</u>: Banks, stockbrokers, real estate agencies.

             c)   <u>Long-linked technology</u>: A technology like mass-production where a client moves from point to point during service delivery.
                 <u>Example</u>: An automobile assembly-line.

    E.   *Size and Life Cycle*

        1.   **Organizational size** is typically measured by number of employees.

        2.   Although **larger organizations** tend to have more **mechanistic designs** than smaller ones, it is not clear that this *should* be the case.

        3.   **Organizational life-cycle** is the evolution of an organization over time through different stages of growth.

        4.   **Four Stages in the Organizational Life Cycle**

            a)   <u>Birth stage</u>: When the organization is founded by an entrepreneur; the founder runs things, a structure stays simple.

            b)   <u>Youth stage</u>: When the organization starts to grow rapidly; the simple structure begins to exhibit the stresses of change.

            c)   <u>Midlife stage</u>: When the organization has grown large with success; structure gets more complex and formal; numbers of managers, levels, and staff increase greatly.

            d)   <u>Maturity stage</u>: When the organization stabilizes at a large size. Size stabilizes, typically with a mechanistic structure; the organization risks becoming slow and nonresponsive in competitive markets.

        5.   **Ways of Managing Organizational Maturity and Large Size**

            a)   <u>Downsizing</u> involves reducing the size of an organization by eliminating workers.

            b)   <u>Simultaneous structures</u> use mechanistic and organic designs to accomplish both production efficiency and innovation.

                Figure 11.3 depicts how simultaneous structures can be used to facilitate *operating efficiency* and *continuing innovation*.

            c)   <u>Intrapreneurship</u> is the pursuit of entrepreneurial behavior by individuals and subunits within large organizations.

                <u>Example</u>: Apple Computer created a small project team to develop the MacIntosh.

F.   *People*

1.   A good organizational design provides **people** with the **supporting structures** they need to achieve both high performance and satisfaction in their work.

2.   Modern management theory addresses people-structure relationships in a contingency fashion, by arguing that there should be a good "fit" between organization structures and the people who staff them.

III.   Subsystems Design and Integration

A.   A *subsystem* is a work unit or smaller component within a larger organization.

B.   *Lawrence and Lorsch* studied 11 firms in three different industries with varying levels of environmental uncertainty.   They concluded:

1.   The **total system structures** of successful firms in each industry **matched** the challenges of their **environments**.

2.   *Subsystems* in a given firm faced **differing subenvironments**.

3.   The **subsystems** of successful firms **matched** the challenges of their **subenvironments**.

4.   **Subsystems** in the successful firms **worked well with one another**, even though some had very different structures.

C.   *Differentiation*

1.   **Differentiation** involves the degree of difference that exists among the internal elements of an organization.

2.   **Sources of Differentiation among Subsystems**

a)   <u>Differences in time orientation</u>: The planning and action horizons of managers vary from short to long term. Sometimes these differences become characteristic of work units themselves.

b)   <u>Differences in objectives</u>: The different tasks assigned to work units may also result in differences in objectives.

c)   <u>Differences in interpersonal orientation</u>: To the extent that patterns of communication, decision making, and social interaction vary, it may be harder for personnel from different subsystems to work together.

        d)   <u>Differences in formal structure</u>: Someone from a more organic setting who is used to flexible problem solving may find it very frustrating to work with a manager from a mechanistic setting bound by strict rules that limit individual discretion.

D.   *Integration*

1.   **Integration** is the level of coordination achieved among subsystems in an organization.

2.   **Organization Design Paradox:** Increased differentiation among organizational subsystems creates the need for greater integration. However, integration becomes more difficult to achieve as differentiation increases.

3.   **How to Improve Subsystem Integration** **MANAGER'S NOTEPAD 11.2**

        a)   <u>Rules and procedures</u>: Clearly specify required activities.

        b)   <u>Hierarchical referral</u>: Refer problems upward to a common superior.

        c)   <u>Planning</u>: Set targets that keep everyone headed in the same direction.

        d)   <u>Direct contact</u>: Have subunit managers coordinate directly.

        e)   <u>Liaison roles</u>: Assign formal coordinators to link subunits together.

        f)   <u>Task forces</u>: Form temporary task forces to coordinate activities and solve problems on a timetable.

        g)   <u>Teams</u>: Form permanent teams with authority to coordinate and solve problems over time.

        h)   <u>Matrix organizations</u>: Create a matrix structure to improve coordination on specific programs.

4.   The first three mechanisms for achieving subsystem integration rely more on **vertical coordination through the chain of command**, and hence work best when **differentiation is low.**

5.   The remaining mechanisms emphasize **horizontal coordination** and **improved lateral relations**, and hence are more appropriate when **differentiation is high.**

IV. **Work Process Design**

    A.   *Process reengineering* is defined by consultant *Michael Hammer* as the systematic and complete analysis of work processes and the design of new and better ones.

ENHANCEMENT

To help students to acquire in depth knowledge regarding the advantages and disadvantages of reengineering you may want to assign the *Research Project* titled, **Reengineering -- Does It Work?** from the *Career Readiness Portfolio*. Further discussion of this assignment is available in Unit 9 of this *Manual*.

    B.   *What is a Work Process?*

        1.   In *Beyond Reengineering*, Michael Hammer defines a **work process** as "a related group of tasks that together create a result of value for the customer." He goes on to define the following key words in this definition:

            a)   <u>Group</u> — tasks are viewed as part of a group rather than in isolation.
            b)   <u>Together</u> — everyone must share a common goal.
            c)   <u>Result</u> - the focus is on what is accomplished, not on activities.
            d)   <u>Customer</u> — processes serve customers and their perspectives are the ones that really count.

        2.   The concept of **workflow**, or the movement of work from one point to another in the manufacturing or service delivery process, is central to understanding processes.

        3.   An important starting point for a reengineering effort is to **diagram** or **map** these workflows as they actually occur; then each step can be systematically analyzed to determine whether or not it is adding value and to consider ways of streamlining to improve efficiency.

    C.   *How to Reengineer Core Processes*   **FIGURE 11.5**

        1.   Through a **process value analysis**, core processes are identified and carefully evaluated for their performance contributions. This approach typically involves the following steps:

            a)   Identify the core processes.
            b)   Map the core processes in respect to workflows.
            c)   Evaluate all tasks for the core processes.

      d)   Search for ways to eliminate unnecessary tasks or work.

      e)   Search for efficiencies in how work is shared and transferred among people and departments.

2. **Figure 11.5** offers a point of reference for both the process reengineering approach and its potential to streamline operations.

3. In reengineering a process can be viewed as a **"black box"** with inputs coming in and outputs coming out; the process is what turns inputs into outputs, and the outputs should have greater value than did the inputs.

4. **Example:** The process of fulfilling a customer order should result in at least three value-added outcomes: order delivery, a satisfied customer, and a paid bill. In between there are such things to be successfully accomplished as inventory handling, shipping, billing and collections. While traditional business systems often have each of these steps assigned to separate functions and people, a common reengineering solution is to have these activities addressed together as components of a core business process.

V.   Operations Technology and Design

A.   *Manufacturing Applications*

1. <u>Computer-aided design (CAD)</u>: Uses computers to help create engineering designs and rapidly change them as needed.

2. <u>Computer-aided manufacturing (CAM)</u>: Uses computers to monitor the production process, link various machines and operations to one another, and provide feedback for control.

3. <u>Computer-aided process planning (CPP)</u>: Uses computers to plan operations and determine the best routings for parts through a series of machines.

4. <u>Computer numerical control (CNC)</u>: Uses computers to store instructions on various machine operations, and control changes in machine settings and movements.

5. <u>Group technology (GT)</u>: Uses computers to help code and classify parts into families that get similar handling in storage and manufacturing.

6. <u>Robotics</u>: Uses computers to guide multifunctional robots in the performance of work tasks otherwise performed by human operators.

7.   <u>Rapid prototyping</u> or "RP" is an innovative software development which enables many designs developed in a CAD framework to be turned into prototypes with great time and cost savings.

8.   <u>Rapid manufacturing</u> uses innovative software to allow for the manufacture of salable end products directly from CADs.

C.   *Enterprise-Wide Integration*

1.   **Integration** is a key word in all aspects of organizational design today.

2.   In business operations, one of the hot developments is the **enterprise-wide integration system** offered by SAP, a German software company.

3.   **Figure 11.6** illustrates how SAP's powerful R/3 computer programs provide for **complex integration** of diverse processes and systems from point of order to inventory management to staffing requirements, to production scheduling, to materials purchasing and more.

CHAPTER 11 SUMMARY

What are the essentials of organizational design?

* Organizational design is the process of choosing and implementing structures that best arrange resources to serve organizational mission and purpose.
* Bureaucratic or mechanistic organizational designs are vertical in nature and perform best for routine and predictable environments.
* Adaptive or organic organizational designs are horizontal in nature and perform best in conditions requiring change and flexibility.

Which contingency factors influence organizational design?

* Environment, strategy, technology, size, and people are all contingency factors influencing organizational design.
* Certain environments lend themselves to more vertical and mechanistic organizational designs. Uncertain environments require more horizontal and adaptive organizational designs.
* Technology -- including the use of knowledge, equipment, and work methods in the transformation process, is an important consideration in organizational design.
* Although organizations tend to become more mechanistic as they grow in size, designs must be used to allow innovation and creativity in changing environments.

What are the major issues in subsystems design?

* Organizations are composed of subsystems that must work well together.
* Differentiation is the degree of difference that exists among various subsystems; integration is the level of coordination achieved among them.
* As organizations become more highly differentiated, they have a greater need for integration, but as differentiation increases integration is harder to accomplish.
* Low levels of differentiation can be handled through authority relationships and more vertical organizational designs.
* Greater differentiation requires more intense coordination through horizontal organizational designs, with an emphasis on cross-functional teams and lateral relations.

How can work processes be reengineered?

* A work process is a related group of tasks that together create value for a customer.
* Business process engineering is the systematic and complete analysis of work processes and the design of new and better ones.
* In reengineering the workflows of an organization are diagramed to identify how work moves from one point to another throughout a system.
* In process value analysis all elements of a process and its workflows are examined to identify their exact contributions to key performance results.

How is operations technology influencing design?

* Computer and information technologies are having an important impact on the design of organizations and their component operations.
* In manufacturing, the developments with computer applications include lean production, flexible manufacturing, mass customization, among other possibilities.
* In the important area of enterprise-wide integration of operating systems and process, the SAP computer programs are considered a source of potential competitive advantage.

CHAPTER 11 KEY TERMS

Adaptive organization An organization that operates with a minimum of bureaucratic features and encourages worker empowerment and participation with teamwork.

Continuous-process production Technology that involves the continuous feeding of materials into an automated system of production.

Differentiation The degree of differences that exists among people, departments, or other internal components of an organization.

Integration The level of coordination achieved among subsystems in an organization.

Intensive technology Technology that focuses efforts and talents of many people to serve clients.

Long-linked technology A technology like mass-production, where a client moves from point to point during service delivery.

Mass production The production of a large number of one or a few products with an assembly-line type of system.

Mechanistic design An organizational design that is highly bureaucratic, with centralized authority, many rules and procedures, a clear cut division of labor, narrow spans of controls, and formal coordination.

Mediating technology A technology that links together parties seeking a mutually beneficial exchange of values.

Organic design An organizational design that is decentralized with fewer rules and procedures, more open divisions of labor, wider spans of control, and more personal means of coordination.

Organizational design The process of choosing and implementing structures that best organize resources to serve mission and objectives.

Organizational life cycle The evolution of an organization over time through different stages of growth.

Process reengineering The systematical analysis of work processes to design new and better ones.

Process value analysis Identifying and evaluating core processes for their performance contributions.

Simultaneous structure An organizational design that involves the coexistence of mechanistic and organic structures within an organization in the attempt to accomplish both production efficiency and innovation.

Small-batch production The production of a variety of custom products that are tailor-made, usually with considerable craftsmanship, to fit customer specifications.

Technology The combination of equipment, knowledge, and work methods that allows an organization to transform inputs into outputs.

Workflow The movement of work from one point to another in a system.

Work process A related group of tasks that together create a result of value for the customer.

CHAPTER 12: HUMAN RESOURCE MANAGEMENT

CHAPTER 12 STUDY QUESTIONS

o   What is strategic human resource management?
o   How do organizations attract a quality workforce?
o   How do organizations develop a quality workforce?
o   How do organizations maintain a quality workforce?

CHAPTER 12 LEARNING OBJECTIVES

After completing this chapter, students should be able to:

1.   Define human resource management and discuss the activities involved in attracting, developing, and maintaining a quality workforce.
2.   Describe the influence of the complex legal environment on human resource management.
3.   Define strategic human resource planning and describe the human resource planning process.
4.   Discuss the recruitment process and effective recruiting practices, including external recruitment, internal recruitment, and realistic job previews.
5.   Identify and explain the key steps in the selection process.
6.   Define employee orientation and discuss the activities involved in orienting new employees.
7.   Explain the role of training and development in the human resource management process, and discuss alternative methods of training and development.
8.   Define performance management system and performance appraisal, and discuss alternative performance appraisal methods.
9.   Discuss the key areas involved in maintaining a quality workforce, including career development, work-life balance, retention and turnover, compensation and benefits, and organized labor.

CHAPTER 12 OVERVIEW

Human resource management is a term used to describe the wide variety of activities involved in attracting, developing, and maintaining quality personnel. As such, human resource management is an integral part of a manager's organizing responsibilities. Indeed, the activities of finding, hiring, orienting, training, developing, evaluating, compensating, and retaining the right people to perform the organization's work are all critical to productivity.

The chapter begins by defining human resource management, and describing the activities involved in the human resource management process. The importance of the complex legal environment to human resource management is examined, including legal requirements for equal employment opportunities and affirmative action programs. Detailed discussions of the major areas of human resource management, including strategic human resource planning, recruitment, selection, orientation, training and development, performance management, career development, compensation and benefits, retention and turnover, and organized labor, are provided.

CHAPTER 12 LECTURE OUTLINE

Teaching Objective: The purpose of this chapter is to thoroughly familiarize students with the human resource management process and the role of the manager in this process. To achieve this, the various activities involved in human resource management are examined in detail.

Suggested Time: Three hours of class time are recommended to present this chapter. However, the lecture can be shortened by providing overviews of the major elements of the staffing process and skipping some of the details.

Strategic Human Resource Management
> Human Resource Management
> Complex Legal Environment
> Strategic Human Resource Planning

Attracting a Quality Workforce
> The Recruiting Process
> External versus Internal Recruitment
> Realistic Job Previews
> Making Selection Decisions

Developing a Quality Workforce
> Employee Orientation
> Training and Development
> Performance Management

Maintaining a Quality Workforce
> Career Development
> Work-Life Balance
> Retention and Turnover
> Compensation and Benefits
> Organized Labor

CHAPTER 12 SUPPORTING MATERIALS

Textbook Inserts
Headline: Make People Your Top Priority
Margin Photos: Robert Goizueta of Coca-Cola, Southwest Airlines,
        Johnson and Johnson, Westt Inc.,
Embedded Box/Photo Essays: Mercedes, Walt Disney World, Autodesk
Manager's Notepad 12.1: How to Conduct Job Interviews
Manager's Notepad 12.2: Things to Remember when Handling a Dismissal

Multi-Media Resources

PowerPoint Presentations (Website):
        Figures 12.1 to 12.6 from the Textbook plus Supplemental Figures
        NBR Viewing Questions: Ben & Jerry's Ice Cream & Nucor

In-Class Activities

Cases for Critical Thinking (Career Readiness Workbook & Website):
        Ben & Jerry's Ice Cream (Primary Case)
        Nucor (Alternate Case)

Exercises:
        Interviewing Job Candidates (Career Readiness Workbook)
        Glass Ceiling Effects (Website Quick Hitter)

Assessments:
        Performance Appraisal Assumptions (Career Readiness Workbook)

Research and Presentation Projects:
        Affirmative Action — Where Do We Go From Here?
        Fringe Benefits — Can They be Managed?

Self-Test 12 (Textbook and Website)

CHAPTER 12 LECTURE NOTES

I.   **Strategic Human Resource Management**

A.   *Human resource management* is a term used to describe the wide variety of activities involved in attracting, developing and maintaining a talented and energetic organizational workforce.

B.   This is a *strategic* process whereby workers with relevant skills and enthusiasm are secured in order for corporate, business, and functional strategies to be implemented.

C.   The major elements of the *human resource management process* include:

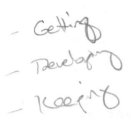

1.   **Attracting a quality workforce:** Human resource planning, recruitment, and selection.

2.   **Developing a quality workforce:** Orientation, training and development, and career planning and development.

3.   **Maintaining a quality workforce:** Managing employee retention and turnover, performance appraisal, compensation and benefits, and labor-management relations.

D.   *Complex Legal Environment*   **FIGURE 12.1**

1.   Human resource management must be accomplished within the framework of **government laws and regulations**, which cover activities related to pay, employment rights, occupational health and safety, retirement, privacy, vocational rehabilitation, and related areas.

2.   **Employment discrimination**, or the use of criteria that are not job-relevant when hiring or promoting someone into a position, is prohibited by the following laws.

a)   The *Civil Rights Act (1964)* and the *Equal Employment Opportunity Act (1972)*, which guarantee *equal employment opportunity (EEO)*, i.e., the right to employment without regard to race, color, national origin, religion, or gender. EEO is enforced by the Equal Employment Opportunity Commission (EEOC).

b)   *Affirmative-action programs* are designed to increase opportunities for women and other minorities including veterans, the aged, and disabled persons.

301

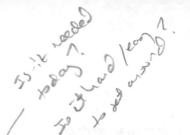

ENHANCEMENT

Example of an Affirmative Action Program
"At many companies, affirmative action programs are top-down projects, sparked by the chief executive officer's interest. Some companies, however, respond better to a bottom-up approach. At the New York headquarters of Avon Products Inc., for example, all minority employees belong to in-house race-based networks--- advocacy groups that have become a crucial part of minority relations at the company."

(Source: Business Week, July 8, 1991, p. 53.)

Given the current public debate regarding affirmative action, you may also want to assign the *Research and Presentation Project* titled, **Affirmative Action: Where Do We Go from Here?** from *Career Readiness Workbook*. This project requires students to thoroughly research the merits of arguments both for and against affirmative action. An in-class debate of students findings could provide an additional vehicle for stimulating an animated discussion of this topic. In addition, the *Website Quick Hitter* titled, **Glass Ceiling Facts,** can be used to generate debate regarding the need for affirmative action. Further discussion of this assignment is provided in Unit 9 of this *Manual*.

d) Employers have the right to establish *bona fide occupational qualifications*, which are criteria for employment that can be clearly justified as being related to someone's capacity to perform a job.

E. *Strategic Human Resource Planning*

1. **Strategic human resource planning** is the process of analyzing staffing needs and identifying actions to satisfy these needs in a way that best serves organizational mission, objectives, and strategies.

2. **Steps in the Human Resource Planning Process**   **FIGURE 12.2**

a) <u>Step 1: Review of organizational mission, objectives, and strategies</u>. This is done to create the frame of reference for human resource planning.

b) <u>Step 2: Review of human resource objectives and strategies</u>. This is conducted to establish and refine to human resource plans that complement strategic plans.

c) <u>Step 3: Forecast human resource needs</u>

(1) This step begins with a *job analysis* which is the orderly study of job requirements and facets that can influence performance results.

(2)   The job analysis is used to write and/or update:

*   *Job descriptions*, which are written statements detailing the duties and responsibilities of a job holder; and

*   *Job specifications*, which are lists of the qualifications required of any job holder.

d)   <u>Step 4: Assess current human resources</u>. This is done to determine the skills and abilities of the current personnel, their training needs, and their potential for promotion.

e)   <u>Step 5: Develop and implement human resource plans</u>. After *making a comparison* between human resource needs and supplies, managers *take action*.

(1)   If human resources *needs exceed supplies*, an active recruiting strategy is appropriate to *correct/avoid a personnel shortage*.

(2)   If human resource *supplies exceed needs*, a strategy of planned terminations and/or nonreplacement is appropriate to *correct/avoid a personnel surplus*.

II.   Attracting a Quality Workforce

A.   *The Recruitment Process*

1.   **Recruitment** is a set of activities designed to attract a qualified pool of job applicants to an organization.

2.   **Steps in the Recruitment Process**

a)   <u>Advertisement of a job vacancy</u>: The firm may advertise the vacancy through newspapers, job postings, or professional publications.

b)   <u>Preliminary contact with potential job candidates</u>: Short interviews (20 to 30 minutes) are scheduled during which applicants provide resumes and explain their qualifications, and the recruiter describes the position.

c)   <u>Initial screening</u>: The recruiter reviews the applicants' resumes and qualifications with appropriate line managers; a pool of qualified applicants is selected.

ENHANCEMENT

A good way to introduce the discussion of the **recruitment process** presented above is to see if any of your students are currently engaged in a job search. You can then ask students who respond affirmatively to describe their experiences with the college recruiting process. This discussion typically helps students to see more clearly the relevance of recruiting from both a management perspective and their own personal perspectives as prospective job candidates.

 B. *External versus Internal Recruitment*

  1. **External recruitment** involves the attraction of job candidates from outside the hiring organization.

   The **advantages** of external recruitment include:

   a) The fresh perspectives of outsiders.
   b) The provision of expertise or experience that may not be available from insiders.

  2. **Internal recruitment** seeks applicants from inside the organization; it involves making employees aware of job vacancies through job posting and personal recommendations.

   The **advantages** of internal recruitment include:

   a) Lower costs.
   b) Easy access to applicant performance records.
   c) Candidate familiarity with the organization.
   d) Promotional incentives for existing employees.

ENHANCEMENT

Example of Executive Succession and External Recruitment
To provide students with a practical example of the tradeoffs involved in external versus internal recruiting, you may want to share with them the following news story: "Chrysler passed over its own president and reached across an ocean into a rival company to find a replacement for its outgoing chairman, Lee Iacocca. The No. 3 automaker anointed Robert Eaton, 52, -- head of European operations for rival automaker General Motors -- as Chrysler's supreme commander in waiting ... The frustrated bridesmaid: Chrysler President Robert Lutz, 60. He is credited for a string of potentially hot new models that could dramatically revitalize Chrysler ... Chrysler wouldn't say so, but Lutz' fighter-pilot demeanor is widely believed to have been fatal in the race for the corner office."

(Source: James R. Healey and Micheline Maynard, *USA Today,* March 17, 1992, 1B-2B).

C.   *Realistic Job Previews*

1.   **Realistic recruitment** seeks to provide the job candidate all
      pertinent information (both positive and negative) about a
      prospective job and the employing organization.

      a)   In contrast, <u>traditional recruitment</u> often seeks to
            "sell" the organization by only communicating the most
            positive organizational features to potential
            candidates.

      b)   Realistic recruitment is used to foster a healthy
            perspective on the employment relationship, and thereby
            facilitate <u>job satisfaction</u>, while reducing the
            <u>premature turnover</u> which often occurs when expectations
            go unmet.

D.   *Making Selection Decisions*

1.   **Selection** is the process of choosing from a pool of applicants
      the person or persons who offer the greatest performance
      potential.

2.   **Validity** is a demonstrated link between a selection device and
      job performance; it is important to know that all aspects of
      the selection process meet the test of validity.

3.   **Steps in the Selection Process**   **FIGURE 12.3**

      a)   <u>Application forms</u>: A job-application form declares the
            individual as a formal job candidate; it summarizes the
            applicant's personal history and qualifications.
            Personal resumes may be attached. Candidates who lack
            the appropriate credentials are rejected at this stage.

      b)   <u>Interview or site visit</u>: Interviews allow job candidates
            and key persons from within the organization to learn
            more about one another.

      <u>How to Conduct Job Interviews</u>   **MANAGER'S NOTEPAD 12.1**

      (1)   *Plan ahead.* Review the job specifications and job
             description, as well as the candidate's
             application.

      (2)   *Create a good interview climate.* Allow sufficient
             time; choose a quiet place; be friendly and show
             interest; give the candidate your full attention.

305

(3)   *Conduct a goal-oriented interview.* Know what information you need, and get it; look for creativity, independence, and a high energy level.

(4)   *Avoid questions that may imply discrimination.* Focus all questioning on the job applied for and the candidate's *true* qualifications for it.

(5)   *Answer the questions asked of you ... answer others that may not be asked.* Do your part to create a realistic job preview.

(6)   *Write notes on the interview immediately upon completion.* Document details and impressions for later deliberation and decision making.

ENHANCEMENT

Assign the *preparation* segment of the *Exercise* titled, **Interviewing Job Candidates** from *Career Readiness Workbook* to students prior to class. You can then break the students into work groups to complete the in-class portion of the exercise. By the end of this exercise, students will have a much better understanding of the types of questions which are appropriate for an recruiter to ask during a job interview. Further discussion of this exercise is provided in Unit 9 of this *Manual*.

c)   <u>Employment tests</u> are used to further screen job applicants by gathering additional position-relevant information.

(1)   Some *common types of employment tests* include:
* Intelligence tests.
* Aptitude tests.
* Personality tests.
* Interest tests.

(2)   To be useful in predicting applicant job performance, employment tests must meet the criteria of *validity* and *reliability*.

* *Validity* refers to the ability of an employment test to measure exactly what it is supposed to.

* *Reliability* refers to the ability of an employment test to yield the same result over time if taken by the same person.

306

(3) An *assessment center* is a selection technique that examines candidates' handling of simulated job situations.

(4) *Computerized testing* employs specialized software that include interactive and multimedia approaches to assess an applicants' job-relevant skills; such computerized tests often ask the applicant to indicate how he or she would respond to a series of job-relevant situations.

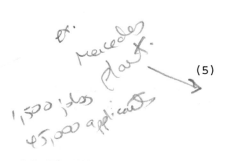

(5) *Work sampling* is a testing approach which assesses a person's performance on a set of tasks which directly replicate those required for the vacant position.

ENHANCEMENT

Ask your students if they have ever been evaluated at an assessment center. Students with work experience, or students who are currently seeking employment, may have direct experience with this selection tool. If so, ask them to describe their experiences to the rest of the class.

d) <u>Reference and background checks</u> are inquiries to prior employers, academic advisors, family members and/or friends regarding the qualifications, experience, or past work records of an applicant.

e) <u>Physical examinations</u> are used to ensure that the person is physically capable of fulfilling job requirements and as a basis for enrolling the applicant in life, health, and disability insurance programs.

f) <u>Final decisions to hire or reject</u>. Although the final decision to reject or hire a candidate usually rests with the manager, the best selection decisions tend to be information based and made in consultation with others, including potential coworkers.

III. **Developing a Quality Workforce**

A. *Socialization* is the process of systematically changing the expectations, behavior, and attitudes of a new employee in a manner considered desirable by the organization.

B.   *Employee Orientation*

    1.   Socialization **begins with initial orientation** and continues during later training and development activities as well as day-to-day supervisor-subordinate relations.

    2.   **Orientation** is a set of activities designed to familiarize new employees with their jobs, co-workers, and key aspects of the organization as a whole.

C.   *Training and Development*

    1.   **Training** is a set of activities that provides learning opportunities through which people acquire and improve job-related skills.

    2.   **Types of Training**

        a)   <u>On-the-job training</u> occurs in the work setting and during actual job performance. It includes:

            (1)   *Job rotation* allows people to spend time working in different jobs and thus expanding the range of their job capabilities.

            (2)   *Coaching* is the communication of specific technical advice to an individual.

            (3)   *Apprenticeship* involves an assignment to serve as an understudy or assistant to a person already having the desired job skills.

            (4)   *Modeling* is the process of demonstrating through personal behavior what is expected of others.

            (5)   *Mentoring* is the act of sharing experiences and insights between a seasoned executive and junior manager.

        b)   <u>Off-the-job training</u> is accomplished in an area away from the actual work setting.

            (1)   *Management development* is training to improve knowledge and skills in the fundamentals of management.

            (2)   *Management simulations* - This developmental tool places participants in "real-life" organizational situations that involve problem solving and

decision making in a hectic setting of frequent meetings, phone calls and interruptions.

(3) *Example:* The Center for Creative Leadership's "Looking Glass" simulation.

D. *Performance Management*

1. A **performance management system** sets standards, assesses results, and plans actions to improve future performance.

2. **Performance appraisal** is the process of formally assessing someone's work and providing feedback on performance.

3. **Two Purposes of Performance Appraisal**

a) <u>Evaluation</u>: Letting people know where they stand relative to objectives and standards. Evaluation focuses on *past* performance; it places the manager in a *judgmental role.*

b) <u>Development</u>: Assisting in the training and continued personal development of people. Development focuses on *future* performance; it places the manager in a *counseling* role.

ENHANCEMENTS

To provide students with insights into their own viewpoints regarding performance appraisals, assign the *Assessment* titled, **Performance Appraisal Assumptions** from ***Career Readiness Workbook***. The assessment is intended to measure the extent to which students see performance appraisals as being primarily used for *evaluation* versus *development* purposes. Further discussion of this assessment is provided on in Unit 9 of this *Manual.*

E. *Performance Appraisal Methods*

1. Like tests, any performance appraisal method must be **reliable** and **valid**.

2. **Graphic rating scales** offer checklists of traits or characteristics that are thought to be related to high performance outcomes in a given job.

a) **Figure 12.4** illustrates a sample <u>graphic rating scale</u>.

b) Graphic rating scales are relatively <u>quick and easy to complete</u>.

        c)   The <u>reliability</u> and <u>validity</u> of graphic rating scales are very *limited*.

3.   The **narrative technique** involves written essay descriptions of someone's job performance.

        a)   Free-form narratives <u>require good writing skills</u>.

        b)   They are often used in <u>combination</u> with other methods.

4.   **Behaviorally anchored rating scales (B.A.R.S.)** are based on explicit descriptions of actual behaviors that exemplify various levels of performance achievement.

See book

        a)   **Figure 12.5** illustrates a sample <u>B.A.R.S.</u>

        b)   Because <u>B.A.R.S.</u> anchor performance assessments to specific descriptions of work behavior, they are <u>relatively reliable</u> and <u>valid</u>.

        c)   The <u>behavioral anchors</u> can also be helpful in <u>training</u> people to master job skills of demonstrated performance importance.

5.   **Critical-incident techniques** involve a running log or inventory of effective and ineffective behaviors. Examples of incidents for a *customer service representative* follow:

        a)   <u>Positive example</u> - "Took extraordinary care of a customer who had purchased a defective item from a company store in another city."

        b)   <u>Negative example</u> - "Acted rudely in dismissing the complaint of a customer who felt that a 'sale' item was erroneously advertised."

6.   **Multiperson comparisons** compare one person's performance with that of one or more others. These techniques include:

        a)   <u>Rank ordering</u> - Ratees are ranked in order of performance.

        b)   <u>Paired comparisons</u> - Each person is compared to all other persons and rated as either superior or weaker; the sum of superior rankings provides an overall performance index.

        c)   <u>Forced distributions</u> - Each person is placed into a specified frequency distribution of performance classifications.

class discussion
on performance
Reviews.

<u>Example</u> - Grading on a "curve."

VI.   Maintaining a Quality Workforce

A.   *Career Development*

1.   A **career** is a sequence of jobs and work pursuits constituting what a person does for a living.

2.   A **career path** is a sequence of jobs held over time during a career.

3.   **Career planning** is the process of systematically matching career goals and individual capabilities with opportunities for their fulfillment; career planning involves answering questions such as *"Who am I?" "Where do I want to go?" "How do I get there?"*

4.   A **career plateau** is a position from which someone is unlikely to move to a higher level of work responsibility.

B.   *Work-Life Balance*

1.   **Work-life balance** involves balancing career demands with personal and family needs.

2.   **Dual-career couples** are couples where both adult partners are employed. They make up over 50% of U.S. married couples.

3.   The **single parent,** who must balance complete parenting responsibilities with a job, is also becoming increasingly important.

4.   "**Family-friendliness**" of an employer is now frequently and justifiably used as a screening criterion by job candidates.

C.   *Retention and Turnover*

1.   **Replacement** is the management of promotions, transfers, terminations, layoffs, and retirements.

2.   **Replacement Decisions that Lead to Movement Within the Organization**

a)   A <u>promotion</u> is a replacement decision which moves an employee to a higher level position.

b)   A <u>transfer</u> is a replacement decision which moves an employee to a different job at the same or similar level of responsibility.

3. **Replacement Decisions that Result in Employment Termination**

   a) <u>Retirements</u> represent voluntary decisions to end one's career. It is important for organizations to properly prepare employees for retirement.

   b) <u>Early retirements</u> involve retirement before formal retirement age but with special incentives; they are often offered by organizations which are downsizing.

   c) <u>Firings</u> involve the involuntary and permanent dismissal of an employee.

4. **Things to Remember When Handling a**   MANAGER'S NOTEPAD 12.2
   Dismissal

   a) Dismissal can be as personally devastating as divorce or death of a loved one.

   b) Dismissal should always be legally defensible and done in compliance with organizational policies.

   c) Dismissal should not be delayed unnecessarily; it is best done as soon as the inevitability of the dismissal is known.

   d) Dismissal should include offers of assistance to help the former employee reenter the labor market.

D. *Compensation and Benefits*

1. **Base compensation** in the form of salary or hourly wages, can make the organization a desirable place of employment.

2. **Fringe benefits** are the additional non-monetary forms of compensation provided to an organization's workforce. Typical benefit packages include various options on disability protection, health and life insurance, and retirement plans.

3. A **competitive wage and salary structure,** and a **good benefits program**, can help to *attract* and *retain* highly competent employees.

4. A **flexible benefits** (i.e., cafeteria benefits) program allows employees to choose from a range of benefit options within dollar limits.

ENHANCEMENT

To generate a lively and in depth discussion of the utility of providing employees with competitive levels of compensation and fringe benefits, assign the *Exercise* titled, **Compensation and Benefits Debate** from *Career Readiness Workbook*. The "preparation" portion of the exercise should be assigned to be completed before class, and the remainder of the exercise -- including the debate -- can be conducted in class. Further discussion of this exercise is provided in Unit 9 of this *Manual*.

      E.   *Organized Labor*

          1.   **Labor unions** are organizations to which workers belong and which collectively deal with employers on their behalf.

          2.   Unions act as bargaining agents who negotiate **labor contracts** which specify the rights and obligations of employees and management in respect to wages, work hours, work rules, and other conditions of employment.

          3.   **Typical Provisions of a Union Contract**

              a)   <u>Job specifications</u> regarding what workers are allowed to do.
              b)   <u>Seniority rules</u> for changing jobs, advancing in pay, choosing work shifts.
              c)   <u>Compensation</u> including wage rates and benefits.
              d)   <u>Grievance mechanisms</u> for handling complaints by workers and by management.
              e)   <u>Procedures</u> for hiring, promoting, transferring, and dismissing workers.

          4.   **Collective bargaining** is the process of negotiating, administering, and interpreting a formal agreement or labor contract between a union and the employing organization.

          5.   **Legislation Governing Labor-Management Relations**

              a)   The *Wagner Act (1935)* protects employees by recognizing their rights to join unions and engage in union activities.

              b)   The *Taft-Hartley Act (1947)* protects employers from unfair labor practices by unions, and allows workers to decertify unions.

              c)   The *Civil Service Reform Act (1978)* clarifies the rights of civil service employees to form labor unions.

6. **A Traditional *Adversarial* View of** **FIGURE 12.6**
   Labor-Management Relations

   a) <u>What unions can do to make things difficult for management</u>:

      (1) Strike.
      (2) Boycott.
      (3) Picket.

   b) <u>What managers can do to make things difficult for unions</u>:

      (1) Lockout.
      (2) Strike-breakers.
      (3) Injunctions.

7. The **adversarial approach** represents a *"win-lose" conflict situation*, in which labor and management expend a lot of energy in prolonged conflict.

8. A **new and more progressive era** of labor-management relations is emerging, *as many unions and employers try to work together for the common good.*

CHAPTER 12 SUMMARY

Why is human resource management important?
* The human resource management process is the process of attracting, developing, and maintaining a quality workforce.
* A complex legal environment influences human resource management, giving special attention to equal employment opportunity.
* Human resource planning is the process of analyzing staffing needs and identifying actions to satisfy these needs over time.
* The purpose of human resource planning is to make sure the organization always has people with the right abilities available to do required work.

How do organizations attract quality workers?
* Recruitment is the process of attracting qualified job candidates to fill vacant positions.
* Recruitment can be both external and internal to the organization.
* Recruitment should involve realistic job previews that provide job candidates with accurate information on the job and organization.
* Managers typically use interviews, employment tests, and references to help make selection decisions; assessment centers and work sampling is becoming more common.

How do organizations develop quality workers?
* Orientation is the process of formally introducing new hires to their jobs, performance requirements, and the organization.
* On-the-job training may include job rotation, coaching, apprenticeship, modeling, and mentoring.
* Off-the-job training may include a range of formal courses and programs, as well as simulations and other training specifically tailored to the needs of managers.
* Performance management systems focus on the establishment of work standards and the assessment of results through performance appraisal.
* Common performance appraisal methods are graphic rating scales, narratives, behaviorally-anchored rating scales, and multiperson comparisons.

How do organizations maintain a quality workforce?
* Career planning systematically matches individual career goals and capabilities with opportunities for their fulfillment.
* Programs that address work-life balance and the complex demands of job and family responsibilities are increasingly important in human resource management.
* Whenever workers must be replaced over time due to promotions, transfers, retirements, and terminations, the goal should always be to treat everyone fairly while ensuring that jobs are filled with the best personnel available.
* Compensation and benefits packages must be continually updated to maintain a competitive position for the organization in external labor markets.
* Where labor unions exist, labor-management relations should be positively approached, and handled in all due consideration of applicable laws.

CHAPTER 12 KEY TERMS

Affirmative-action program An organizational program designed to increase opportunities for women and other minorities including veterans, the aged, and disabled persons.

Apprenticeship A special form of training that involves a formal assignment to serve as understudy or assistant to a person who already has the desired job skills.

Assessment center A selection technique that engages job candidates in a series of experimental activities over a 1- or 2-day period.

Base compensation A salary or hourly wage paid to an individual.

Behaviorally anchored rating scale (BARS) A performance appraisal method based on explicit descriptions of actual behaviors that exemplify various levels of performance achievement.

Career planning The process of systematically matching career goals and individual capabilities with opportunities for their fulfillment.

Career plateau A position from which someone is unlikely to move to a higher level of work responsibility.

Coaching The communication of specific technical advice to an individual.

Collective bargaining The process of negotiating, administering, and interpreting a labor contract.

Critical-incident technique A performance appraisal method that involves a running log of effective and ineffective job behaviors.

Equal employment opportunity The right of people to employment and advancement without regard to race, sex, religion, color, or national origin.

Employment discrimination The use of criteria that are not job-relevant when hiring or promoting someone into a position.

Flexible benefits A program that allows employees to choose from a range of benefit options within certain dollar limits.

Fringe benefits Nonmonetary forms of compensation (e.g., health plans, retirement plans, etc.).

Graphic rating scale A performance appraisal method that uses a checklist of traits or characteristics thought to be related to high-performance outcomes in a given job.

Human resource management The process of attracting, developing, and maintaining a qualified workforce.

Human resource planning The process of analyzing staffing needs and identifying actions to fill those needs over time.

Job analysis An orderly study of job requirements and facets that can influence performance results.

Job description A written statement that details the duties and responsibilities of any person holding a particular job.

Job specification A list of the qualifications required of any job occupant.

Labor contract A formal agreement between a union and the employing organization, which specifies the rights and obligations of each party in respect to wages, work hours, work rules, and other conditions of employment.

Labor union An organization to which workers belong that collectively deals with employers on their behalf.

Management development Training directed toward improving a person's knowledge and skills in the fundamentals of management.

Mentoring The act of sharing experiences and insights between a seasoned and junior manager.

Modeling The process of demonstrating through personal behavior that which is expected of others.

Multiperson comparison A performance appraisal method that involves comparing one person's performance with that of one or more persons.

Narrative technique A performance appraisal method that uses a written essay description of a person's job performance.

Orientation Activities through which new employees are made familiar with their jobs, their coworkers, and the policies, rules, objectives, and services of the organization as a whole.

Performance appraisal A process of formally evaluating performance and providing feedback on which performance adjustments can be made.

Performance management system A system that ensures performance standards and objectives are set, that performance is regularly assessed for accomplishments, and that actions are taken to improve performance potential in the future.

Realistic job preview An attempts by the job interviewer to provide the job candidate with all pertinent information about a prospective job and the employing organization, without distortion and before a job offer is accepted.

Recruitment A set of activities designed to attract a qualified pool of job applicants to an organization.

Replacement The management of promotions, transfers, terminations, layoffs, and retirements.

Selection The process of choosing from a pool of applicants the person or persons who best meet job specifications.

Socialization The process of systematically changing the expectations, behavior, and attitudes of a new employee in a manner considered desirable by the organization.

Strategic human resource management A process of analyzing staffing needs and planning how to satisfy these needs in a way that best serves organizational mission, objectives, and strategies.

Training A set of activities that provide learning opportunities through which people can acquire and improve job-related skills.

Validity The ability of an employment test to measure exactly what they intend to relative to the job specification.

Work-live balance How people balance the demands of careers with their personal and family needs.

CHAPTER 13: LEADING — TO INSPIRE EFFORT

CHAPTER 13 STUDY QUESTIONS

o   What is leadership?
o   How do leaders gain and use power?
o   What are the important leadership traits and behaviors?
o   What can be learned from contingency theories of leadership?
o   What are current issues in leadership development?

CHAPTER 13 LEARNING OBJECTIVES

After completing this chapter, students should be able to:

1.   Define leadership and leading, and explain the differences between leadership and management.
2.   Define vision and discuss the five principles of visionary leadership.
3.   Define power and describe the key sources of power.
4.   Define empowerment and discuss its relationship to lateral leadership and bottom-up leadership.
5.   Compare and contrast the four general approaches to studying leadership.
6.   Discuss the focus, objectives, research findings and limitations of the trait approach to leadership.
7.   Describe the focus, theoretical foundations, research findings and limitations of the behavioral approach to leadership.
8.   Explain the focus, theoretical foundations and managerial implications of (a) Fiedler's contingency model of leadership, (b) Hersey-Blanchard situational leadership theory, (c) House's path-goal theory of leadership, and (d) the Vroom-Jago leader-participation theory.
9.   Compare and contrast transactional and transformational leadership and describe the attributes of transformational leaders.
10.   Discuss the three dimensions of good "old-fashioned" leadership as described by Peter Drucker.
11.   Discuss the ethical aspects of leadership.

CHAPTER 12 OVERVIEW

Leading is the process of inspiring others to work hard to accomplish important tasks. As such, the leading function is an essential component of effective management. The central role of effective leadership is made readily apparent from the *Headline* opener titled, **You Have to Believe in People**. The opener describes the approach to leadership practiced by Max Depree, the chairperson and son of the founder of Herman Miller, Inc., a Michigan-based office furniture maker. Depree advocates and practices a leadership style based on respect for others and diversity. Respect of this nature ensures that the organization benefits from everyone's contributions. Herman Miller's success at realizing such benefits is apparent from its ranking as one of *Fortune's* "most admired" American corporations.

This chapter focuses on the leading function and various theories of leadership. It begins by noting that while leading and managing are not the same thing, managers must be good leaders to be effective. The relationships between important sources of position and personal power, as well as the practice of empowerment, are discussed next. The chapter continues with a discussion of the trait, behavioral, contingency, and charismatic approaches to studying leadership. Under the contingency approach, particular attention is devoted to the managerial implications of Fiedler's contingency theory, House's path-goal theory, the Hersey-Blanchard situational leadership theory, and the Vroom-Jago leader-participation theory. The focus then shifts to current directions in leadership theory and practice which include transformational leadership, gender and leadership, and "good 'old-fashioned' leadership." The ethical aspects of leadership are also considered.

CHAPTER 13 LECTURE OUTLINE

Teaching Objective: To provide students with a solid understanding of leadership and its importance to management. To accomplish this, the role of power as a leadership resource and various approaches to the study of leadership are presented.

Suggested Time: A minimum of three hours of class time is required to present the material in this chapter. More time may be required depending on the number of enhancements incorporated into the lecture.

The Nature of Leadership
    Leadership and Vision
    Leadership and Power
    Turning Power into Influence
    Leadership and Empowerment

Leadership Traits and Behaviors
    Search for Leadership Traits
    Focus on Leadership Behaviors

Contingency Approaches to Leadership
    Fiedler's Contingency Model
    Hersey-Blanchard Situational Leadership Model
    House's Path-Goal Leadership Theory
    Vroom-Jago Leader-Participation Theory

Issues in Leadership Development
    What is Transformational Leadership?
    Gender and Leadership
    "Good Old-Fashioned" Leadership
    Ethical Aspects of Leadership

CHAPTER 13 SUPPORTING MATERIALS

Textbook Inserts

Headline: You Have to Believe in People
Margin Photos: Harley-Davidson, Bernard J. Ebbers - CEO of World Com, The Gap
Embedded Box/Photo Essays: Patricia Gallup - CEO of PC Connection,
      Faith Wohl - CEO of Child Care Action Campaign, W. L. Gore & Associates,
      Mary Kay Cosmetics
Manager's Notepad 13.1: Five Principles of Visionary Leadership
Manager's Notepad 13.2: Guidelines for Reaching Group Consensus

Multi-Media Resources

PowerPoint Presentations (Website):
      Figures 13.1 to 13.7 from the Textbook plus Supplemental Figures

In-Class Activities

Cases for Critical Thinking (Career Readiness Workbook & Website):
      Mike Krzyzewski (Primary Case)
      Tom's of Maine (Alternate Case)

Exercises:
      Sources and Uses of Power (Career Readiness Workbook)
      Empowering Others (Career Readiness Workbook)
      Leading through Participation (Career Readiness Workbook)
      Gender Differences in Management (Career Readiness Workbook)
      The FedEx Leadership Test (Website)

Assessments:
      "T-P" Leadership Questionnaire (Career Readiness Workbook)
      "T-T" Leadership Style (Career Readiness Workbook & Website)
      Least Preferred Coworker Scale (Career Readiness Workbook & Website)
      The Nine Faces of Leadership (Website)

Self-Test 13 (Textbook and Website)

CHAPTER 13 LECTURE NOTES

I. **The Nature of Leadership**

    A.   <u>*Leadership* is the process of inspiring others to work hard to</u> <u>accomplish important tasks.</u>

    B.   **Figure 13.1** depicts the relationship between *leading and the other management functions.*

ENHANCEMENT

A good way to introduce this section is to ask students, "Are leaders and managers the same thing?" and "If not, what are the differences between leaders and managers?" In their discussion of these questions, make sure that students identify the distinctions made by Warren Bennis, which are noted in the beginning of the chapter. A summary of these distinctions is provided below. You may also want to ask students if they can think of examples of individuals who are leaders but not managers or vice versa. Martin Luther, Jesse Jackson, Joan of Arc, Mother Theresa, John Lennon, are good examples of individuals who are seen as leaders even though they never formally held a management position. For an example of an administrator who was criticized for lacking leadership, you could refer students to Jimmy Carter's quote of a congressman in his famous "malaise" speech: "Mr. Carter, you are not leading the nation, merely managing the federal government."

    C.   *Leadership and Vision*

        1.   **Leading** builds the commitments and enthusiasm needed for people to apply their talents fully to help accomplish plans.

        2.   **Vision** is the term generally used to describe a clear sense of the future and the actions needed to get there ... successfully.

ENHANCEMENTS

Since the *Margin Photo* on **Harley-Davidson** illustrates the concept of *vision* extremely well, you may want to discuss it with students at this point. You can also embellish your discussion with the following information.

    In 1981 Vaughan L. Beals, Harley's chairperson, and James H. Paterson, then president of the motorcycle division, set out to make their vision of a rejuvenated Harley-Davidson a reality. To overcome a declining market share and lost sales to Japanese competitors, these executives came up with a plan to appeal to a new upscale market. They devised a special advertising campaign, gave Harley's name to products as diverse as cologne and wine coolers, instructed dealers to make their stores more inviting, built stereos and intercoms into helmets, and started the Harley Owners Group (HOG). Most importantly, the firm applied Japanese management techniques and the concept of teamwork to dramatically improve the quality of the motorcycles produced. The extent to which their vision of rejuvenation has been successfully realized, is readily apparent from the firm's domestic market share of 65 percent.

(Source: Harley-Davidson's 1990 Annual Report and other corporate literature).

3.   **Five Principles of Visionary**   MANAGER'S NOTEPAD 13.1
Leadership

a)   <u>Challenge the process</u>: Be a pioneer -- encourage innovation and people with ideas.

b)   <u>Be enthusiastic</u>: Inspire others through personal example to share in a common vision.

c)   <u>Help others to act</u>: Be a team player and support the efforts and talents of others.

d)   <u>Set the example</u>: Provide a consistent model of how others should act.

e)   <u>Celebrate achievements</u>: Bring emotion into the workplace and rally "hearts" as well as "minds."

II.   **Leadership and Power**   **FIGURE 13.2**

A.   *Power* is the ability to get someone else to do something you want done or to make things happen the way you want.

B.   As **Figure 13.2** indicates, managers acquire power from their **position** as well as **personal** sources.

Managerial Power = Position Power + Personal Power

C.   *Sources of Position Power*

1.   **Position power** is based on the things managers can offer to others.

2.   **Reward power:** The capability to offer something of value -- a positive outcome -- as a means of controlling people.

3.   **Coercive power:** The capability to punish or withhold positive outcomes as a means of controlling people.

4. **Legitimate power:** The capability to control other people by virtue of the rights of office. Legitimate power is equivalent to *formal authority*.

ENHANCEMENT

Assign the *Exercise* titled, **Sources and Uses of Power** which appears in the *Career Readiness Workbook*. This exercise provides students with useful insights regarding the sources of power they utilize most often, and the relative effectiveness of alternative bases of power in different situations. Further discussion of this exercise is provided in unit 9 of this *Manual*.

D. *Sources of Personal Power*

1. **Personal power** is power that the person brings to the situation in terms of unique personal attributes.

2. **Expert power:** The capability to influence other people because of specialized knowledge.

3. **Reference power:** The capability to influence other people because of their desires to identify personally and positively with the power source.

E. *Turning Power into Influence*

ENHANCEMENT

To help students relate to the discussion of **power bases** and **influence strategies** which follows, you may want to assign the *Exercise* titled, **Sources and Uses of Power** from the *Career Readiness Workbook*. Further discussion of this exercise is available in Unit 9 of this *Manual*.

1. Good managers build or enhance their **position power** by acting in the following ways.

    a) <u>Centrality</u>: Becoming a *"central"* link in the organization's information flows.

    b) <u>Criticality</u>: Making their jobs *"critical"* to the organization's performance

    c) <u>Visibility</u>: Staying *"visible"* as people the organization can't do without.

2. With respect to **personal power** it is important to remember that:

    a) There is no substitute for <u>expertise</u>.

    b) Likable <u>personal qualities</u> are very important.

    c) <u>Effort</u> and <u>hard work</u> breed respect.

    d) Personal behavior must <u>support expressed values</u>.

3. Chester Barnard's **acceptance theory of power** identifies four conditions that determine whether a leader's directives will be followed:

    a. The other person must truly understand the directive.
    b. The other person must feel capable of carrying it out.
    c. The other person must believe that the directive is in the organization's best interest.
    d. The other person must believe that the directive is consistent with personal values.

F. *Leadership and Empowerment*

    1. **Empowerment** is the process of giving people at all levels of responsibility the opportunity to act and make relevant decisions on their own.

ENHANCEMENT

An excellent example of a firm which **empowers** workers is provided by the chapter opener titled, **You Have to Believe in People.** The opener describes the approach to leadership practiced by *Max Depree*, the chairperson of **Herman Miller, Inc.,** a Michigan-based office furniture maker. In his book, *Leadership is an Art*, Depree, who is the son of the firm's founder, outlines a leadership style based on respect for others and diversity. Respect of this nature ensures that organization can benefit from everyone's contributions. DePree also makes a big deal about the difference between *"hierarchical"* and *"roving"* leadership. His point? Often it is the roving, or informal leader, who really counts. What does the hierarchical leader do? If smart, this person -- or manager -- "supports" the roving leader and helps him or her lead. DePree says: "Roving leadership is the expression of the ability of hierarchical leaders to permit others to share ownership of problems -- to take possession of the situation."

An example of how "roving," "lateral," and "bottom-up" leadership works at Herman Miller is provided by research manager Bill Foley's decision to forbid the use of rosewood and Honduran mahogany in one of the firm's hallmark products -- the $2,000 plus Eames chair, because use of these woods contributed to the destruction of the rainforests. While his decision lead to considerable debate,

325

it ultimately was supported. Foley claims the company's strong ethics and commitment to participatory management helped him feel empowered to make the decision. Herman Miller's success at capitalizing on these strengths is apparent from its ranking as one of *Fortune's* "most admired" American corporations.

2.   **How to Empower Others**   MANAGER'S NOTEPAD 13.2

  a.   Get others involved in selecting their work assignments and the methods for accomplishing tasks.

  b.   Create an environment of cooperation, information sharing, discussion, and shared ownership of goals.

  c.   Encourage others to take initiative, make decisions, and use their knowledge.

  d.   When problems arise, find out what others think and let them help design the solutions.

  e.   Stay out of the way; give others the freedom to put their ideas and solutions into practice.

  f.   Maintain high morale and confidence by recognizing successes and encouraging high performance.

III. **Leadership Traits and Behaviors**

  A.   **Figure 13.3** summarizes four alternative directions in the study of managerial leadership -- the *trait, behavioral, contingency, and charismatic approaches.*

  B.   *Traits* are relatively stable and enduring characteristics of an individual.

ENHANCEMENT

One way to demonstrate to students the objectives as well as the shortcomings of the **trait approach** to leadership is to ask them to identify the traits of effective leaders. You can do this by asking a generic question such as **"What are the traits of effective leaders?"** and then recording their responses. Alternatively, you could provide more direction and distinguish between physical and personality traits by respectively asking, **"What do leaders look like?"** and **"What personality characteristics do leaders typically possess?"** If you use the former approach, you may want to record the physical and personality traits the

ENHANCEMENT (Continued)

students identify separately. Once a reasonable number of traits are listed, you can review them and cross out physical traits such as tall, strong, and good looking, which have not been substantiated by research. You can also note that while the leadership traits of *drive, motivation, integrity, self-confidence, intelligence, knowledge* and *flexibility* are seen as desirable, researchers have not found a *definitive* profile of leadership traits.

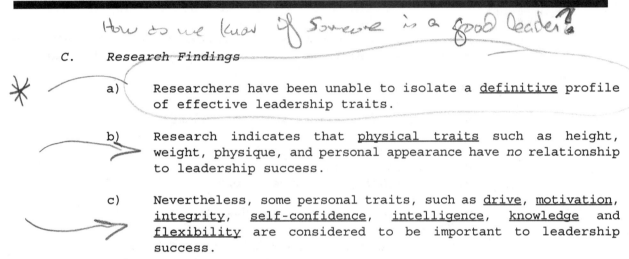

How do we know if someone is a good leader?

C.   *Research Findings*

   a)   Researchers have been unable to isolate a <u>definitive</u> profile of effective leadership traits.

   b)   Research indicates that <u>physical traits</u> such as height, weight, physique, and personal appearance have *no* relationship to leadership success.

   c)   Nevertheless, some personal traits, such as <u>drive</u>, <u>motivation</u>, <u>integrity</u>, <u>self-confidence</u>, <u>intelligence</u>, <u>knowledge</u> and <u>flexibility</u> are considered to be important to leadership success.

IV.   **Focus on Leadership Behaviors**

ENHANCEMENT

Point out that the advent of the leader behavior approach represented a shift in focus away from the question, *"What* makes a person an effective leader?," to the question, *"How* does an effective leader behave?"

   A.   *Leadership style* is the recurring pattern of behaviors exhibited by a leader.

   B.   *Task and People Concerns*

ENHANCEMENT

Consider assigning the *Assessment* from the **Career Readiness Workbook** titled **"T-P" Leadership Questionnaire"** for students to complete prior to your discussion of the behavioral approach. After scoring the instrument and learning about their own "leadership style", this discussion is typically much more relevant for students. You may also want to point out, however, that because only extreme responses such as "always" or "never" are counted will scoring this instrument, while the intermediate response of "occasionally" is not, their scores on

ENHANCEMENT (Continued)

either the "Task" or the "People" dimensions may be biased downward. Indeed, the "occasionally" response is actually more consistent with the contingency models discussed next, which recognize that the "best" leadership style depends on the characteristics of the followers and/or situation. This makes for a nice segue into the discussion of the contingency approaches.

1. Research on leadership behavior revealed two basic underlying dimensions: **concern for people**, and **concern for the task.**

2. **How a Task-oriented Leader Behaves**

    a) Plans and defines work to be done.
    b) Assigns task responsibilities.
    c) Sets clear work standards.
    d) Urges task completion
    e) Monitors performance results.

3. **How a People-oriented Leader Behaves**

    a) Acts warm and supportive toward followers.
    b) Develops social rapport with followers.
    c) Respects the feelings of followers.
    d) Is sensitive to followers' needs.
    e) Shows trust in followers.

4. Four **leadership styles** arise from the different **combinations of concern for task and concern for people** that leaders exhibit.

    a) <u>Abdicative or laissez-faire leadership</u>: Low concern for both people and task.

    b) <u>Directive or autocratic leadership</u>: Low concern for people, high concern for task.

    c) <u>Supportive or human relations leadership</u>: High concern for people, low concern for task.

    d) <u>Participative of democratic leadership</u>: High concern for both people and task.

ENHANCEMENT

Example of an Autocratic Leader
Walter J. Connolly, former CEO of the Bank of New England, grilled his top
executives at monthly meetings. The details he often demanded, reflected his
failure to remove himself from the bank's nitty-gritty operations. He ruled so
completely that many managers feared telling him anything he didn't want to hear.
(Source: Business Week, April 1, 1991, p. 58).

C.   *Research and Training Insights*

1.   Research by scholars at *Ohio State University* and the
       University of Michigan concluded that truly **effective leaders**
       are high in **both** concern for people and concern for task.

need to
be both

2.   **Figure 13.4** illustrates *Blake and Mouton's Managerial Grid*, a
       popular model for depicting this conclusion.

Fg. 269

ENHANCEMENT

At this point in your explanation of the **Managerial Grid**, you can refer students
chapter opener, **You Have to Value People**, and ask students to classify, *Max
Depree*, **Herman Miller's** chairperson, using the managerial grid. Most will
probably classify him as a team manager. You can also ask them if they see any
problems with the approach advocated by Blake and Mouton. Students are usually
quick to recognize that these authors' universal endorsement of the team
management style lacks a contingency perspective. This point provides a nice
introduction for the contingency theories of leadership outlined below.

a)   This approach uses <u>assessments</u> to determine managers'
       locations on the grid.

b)   A <u>training program</u> is implemented to shift the manager
       toward the "ideal" of a <u>team manager</u> or "9-9" leader who
       emphasizes both a high concern for people and task.

V.   Contingency Theoris of Leadership

A.   Modern leadership theories reflect a *contingency perspective* which
       attempts to match situational demands with appropriate leader
       behaviors.

Chapter 13: Leading — To Inspire Effort

B.   *Fiedler's Contingency Model* -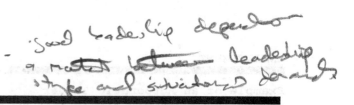

ENHANCEMENT

A good way to increase the relevance of **Fiedler's contingency theory** to students is to assign the *Assessment* titled, **Least-Preferred Coworkers Scale (LPC)** which is included in the **_Career Readiness Workbook_**. To conserve class time, assign the LPC Scale as homework prior to the period in which you intend to discuss Fiedler's theory. During your lecture on the theory, ask for a show of hands of students who scored as relationship-oriented, task-oriented or somewhere in between (use the LPC ranges provided below to assist students in determining their leadership styles). You may also want to ask students if they feel the LPC accurately measured their leadership style. While many will believe that it has, at least a few students will usually think otherwise. At this point you can point out that the skepticism of these students is shared by critics of Fiedler's theory, who contend that one's score on the LPC Scale is not necessarily indicative of leadership style. It is also important to note, however, that Fiedler has obtained empirical support for his theory. Further discussion of this assessment is provided in Unit 9 of this *Manual*.

1.   **Measuring Leadership Style**

   a)   The first step in applying Fiedler's theory is to understand one's predominant <u>leadership style</u>.

   b)   The <u>Least-Preferred Coworker Scale (LPC Scale)</u> is designed to measure a person's leadership style as follows.

      (1)   Persons scoring 73 or higher are classified as *high LPC leaders* who tend to view even their least-preferred coworker in favorable terms; Fiedler equates this tendency with a *relationship-oriented leadership style*.

      (2)   Persons scoring 64 or less are classified as *low LPC leaders* who view their least preferred coworker in less favorable terms; Fiedler equates this tendency with a *task-oriented leadership style*.

      (3)   Persons scoring in the 65-72 range should *use their best judgement* in determining their style.

2.   **Understanding Leadership Situations**   **FIGURE 13.5**

   a)   The second step in applying Fiedler's theory is to diagnose the amount of <u>situational control</u> available to the leader.

330

b)   <u>Situational control</u> is the extent to which a leader can determine what a group is going to do, and what the outcomes of its actions and decisions are going to be.

c)   The following <u>three contingency variables</u> are used to <u>diagnose situational control</u>:

      (1)   *Quality of leader-member relations* (good or poor) -- The degree to which the group supports the leader.

      (2)   *Degree of task structure* (high or low) -- The extent to which task goals, procedures, and guidelines are clearly spelled out.

      (3)   *Amount of position power* (strong or weak) -- The degree to which the position gives the leader power to reward and punish subordinates.

3.   **Matching Leadership Style and Situation**

a)   The third step in applying Fiedler's theory is to obtain a <u>match</u> between leadership style and the situation.

b)   **Figure 13.5** summarizes Fiedler's findings regarding the <u>situations in which task- and relationship-oriented leaders are most effective</u>.

      (1)   *Proposition No. 1:* A task-oriented leader will be most successful in either very favorable (high control) or very unfavorable (low control) situations.

      (2)   *Proposition No. 2:* A relationships-oriented leader will be most successful in situations of moderate control.

ENHANCEMENT

One means of enhancing students' understanding of Fiedler's theory is to provide them with various scenarios and ask them to apply the theory to determine the appropriate leadership style for each situation. Some sample scenarios and the corresponding analyses are provided below. (These scenarios were adapted from John R. Schermerhorn, Jr., James G. Hunt, and Richard N. Osborn, *Managing Organizational Behavior*, John Wiley & Sons, 1988).

ENHANCEMENT (Continued)

Scenario 1: You are an experienced supervisor of an assembly line with nonunion, supportive workers.

Analysis: Supportive subordinates means good leader-member relations. The structure of assembly line work is high, and you have experience, so the task structure is high. Finally, the nonunion nature of the job gives you the authority to reward and punish, and hence provides high position power. This is a <u>high control situation</u> and hence a <u>task-oriented leader</u> will be most effective.

Scenario 2: You are a well-liked university department chair with many tenured faculty, and you are responsible for enhancing the teaching, research and service of the department.

Analysis: There are good leader-member relations, but task structure is low since the "how" of the task is not very clear. Your position power is also not very high vis-a-vis the tenured faculty members. This is a <u>moderate control situation</u> and hence a <u>relationship-oriented leader</u> will be most effective.

Scenario 3: You are the chair of a student council committee of volunteers who are not happy about your appointment. The committee is to organize a program to improve university-parent relations.

Analysis: Task structure is low since it is unclear how the committee should go about improving university-parent relations. Leader-member relations are poor since the members don't want you to be chair. Finally, position power is weak since the members can quit at any time. This is a <u>low control situation</u> and hence a <u>task-oriented leader</u> will be most effective.

4. **Fiedler's Recommendations**

    a) Prospective leaders should actively seek situations which <u>match</u> their leadership style.

    b) When a <u>mismatch</u> occurs, leaders should:

        (1) First, engage in *situational engineering*; this involves changing the situational characteristics to better match one's leadership style.

        (2) As a last resort, *change one's leadership style* to match the situation; Fiedler feels this will be difficult because leadership style is strongly tied to personality factors that are not easy to change.

332

C.   *Hersey-Blanchard Situational Leadership Theory*

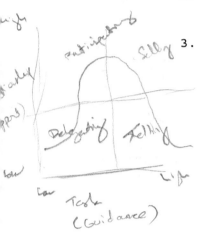

1.   This contingency theory suggests that successful leaders adjust their styles depending on the **readiness of followers to perform** in a given situation.

2.   **"Readiness"** refers to how able, willing, and confident followers are in performing required tasks.

3.   **Figure 13.6** illustrates the following alternative **leadership styles.**

   a)   <u>Delegating</u>: Allowing the group to make and take responsibility for task decisions; a low task, low relationship style.

   b)   <u>Participating</u>: Emphasizing shared ideas and participative decisions on task directions; a low task, high relationship style.

   c)   <u>Selling</u>: Explaining task directions in a supportive and persuasive way; a high task, high relationship style.

   d)   <u>Telling</u>: Giving specific task directions and closely supervising work; a high task, low relationship style.

4.   **Figure 13.6** also indicates the **contingent relationship between leadership style and follower readiness** described below.

ENHANCEMENT

Hersey and Blanchard's four levels of follower readiness can be compared to student classifications on a high school or college sports team. Freshmen are essentially low readiness subordinates who require a *telling* style of leadership. Sophomores are willing to assume more responsibility, but lack some of the skills; they respond well to a *selling* style. Juniors are able to handle more responsibility, but may lack confidence; they respond well to a *participating* style. Finally, since seniors are able, willing, and confident, they respond best to the *delegating* style.

---

   a)   The <u>delegating style</u> works best in <u>high readiness</u> situations.

   b)   The <u>telling style</u> works best in <u>low readiness</u> situations.

c) The <u>participating style</u> is recommended for <u>low to moderate readiness</u> situations.

d) The <u>selling style</u> for is recommended for <u>moderate to high readiness</u> situations.

5. Hershey and Blanchard believe the leader's style can and should be changed as followers **mature** over time.

6. If the **correct leadership styles are used in lower readiness** situations, followers will "mature" and **grow in ability, willingness** and **confidence.**

D. *House's Path-Goal Leadership Theory*

1. **Central thesis:** <u>Effective leadership clarifies the paths by which subordinates can achieve goals, helps them to progress along these paths, and removes barriers to goal accomplishment.</u>

2. **Four Leadership Styles**

a) <u>Directive leadership</u>:
* Letting subordinates know what's expected.
* Giving directions on what should be done and how.
* Clarifying the leader's role in the group.
* Scheduling work to be done.
* Maintaining definite standards of performance.

b) <u>Supportive leadership</u>:
* Showing concern for subordinates.
* Doing little things to make the work pleasant.
* Treating group members as equals.
* Being friendly and approachable.

c) <u>Achievement-oriented leadership</u>:
* Setting challenging goals.
* Expecting subordinates to perform at their highest level.
* Emphasizing excellence and improvements in performance.
* Displaying confidence that subordinates will meet high standards.

d) <u>Participative leadership</u>:
* Involving subordinates in decision making.
* Consulting with subordinates.
* Asking for suggestions from subordinates.
* Taking these suggestions seriously in making decisions.

3. **Predictions and Managerial Implications**

   a) The path-goal model advises managers to always use leadership styles that <u>compliment</u> the needs of situations.

   b) An <u>effective leader</u> contributes things that are *not* already present, i.e., avoids being <u>redundant</u>.

   c) The key <u>contingency variables</u> include --

      (1) *Subordinate characteristics:*

         * Ability.
         * Experience.
         * Locus of Control.

      (2) *Work Enviornment:*

         * Task structure.
         * Authority system.
         * Work group.

   d) <u>Examples</u>:

      (1) When *job assignments* are *ambiguous*, *directive leadership* is needed to clarify task objectives and expected rewards.

      (2) When *worker self-confidence* is low, *supportive leadership* is needed to clarify individual abilities and offer needed task assistance.

      (3) When *performance incentives* are poor, *participative leadership* is need to identify individual needs and appropriate rewards.

      (4) When *task challenge* is insufficient, *achievement-oriented leadership* is needed to clarify job challenges and raise performance aspirations.

E. *Substitutes for Leadership*

   1. **Substitutes for leadership** are aspects of the work setting and the people involved that can reduce the need for a leader's personal involvement.

   2. When "substitutes" are present, managers should **avoid redundant leadership** and act instead to **compliment** the situation by focusing on areas that require outside attention.

3. **Possible substitutes for leadership** include:

    a) <u>Subordinate characteristics</u>: Ability, experience, and independence.

    b) <u>Task characteristics</u>: Routineness, availability of feedback, and opportunities for intrinsic satisfaction.

    c) <u>Organizational characteristics</u>: Clarity of plans, formalization of rules and procedures, and influence of staff functions.

F. *The Vroom-Jago Leader-Participation Theory*

ENHANCEMENT

To better illustrate the **Vroom-Jago leadership participation theory**, assign the *Exercise* titled, **Leading through Participation** which is included in the *Career Readiness Workbook*. Further discussion of this exercise is provided in Unit 9 of this *Manual*.

1. **Alternative Decision-Making Methods**

    a) <u>Authority decision</u>: The manager makes the decision alone using available information.

    b) <u>Consultative decision</u>: The manager makes the decision after gathering information from others.

    c) <u>Group decision</u>: The manager shares information and works with the group to reach consensus.

2. **Choosing a Decision Method**

    a) Managers should use <u>group decision methods</u> when:

        (1) They *lack sufficient information* to solve a problem by themselves.

        (2) *The problem is unclear* and help is needed to clarify the situation.

        (3) *Acceptance of the decision by others is necessary* to achieve successful implementation.

        (4) *Adequate time is available* to allow for true participation.

b) Managers can make <u>individual decisions</u> when:

(1) *They have greater expertise* on a problem.

(2) They are *confident and capable* of acting alone.

(3) *Others are likely to accept the decision made.*

(4) *Little or no time is available* for discussion.

ENHANCEMENT

Compare and contrast the **four major contingency theories** discussed above using the following table. Point out that while Fiedler argues that its hard for leaders to change their style, the other theorists recommend that leaders be flexible in adjusting their styles to match the situation. Therefore, the theory which works best for a particular individual, may depend upon the extent to which he or she is capable of changing styles.

CONTINGENCY THEORIES

Comparison Points	Fiedler's Approach	House's Approach	Hersey & Blanchard's Approach	Vroom-Jago Approach
Concern	Situational Control	Situational Attributes	Situational Attributes	Problem Attributes
Diagnostic Focus	Task Structure, Position Power, Leader-member Relations	Subordinate Characteristics, Task Demands	Follower Readiness	Decision Quality, Subordinate Acceptance, Information & Time Availability
Leadership Styles	Task-motivated, Relationship-motivated	Directive, Supportive, Participative, Achievement-oriented	Telling, Selling, Participating, Delegating	Authoritative, Consultative, Participative
Managerial Implic-cations	Effective leader matches style with situation	Effective leader chooses style to complement situational attributes	Effective leader chooses style to complement situational attributes	Effective leader uses decision method best fitting the problem at hand

Chapter 13: Leading — To Inspire Effort

VI.   Issues in Leadership Development

   A.   *Charismatic Leaders*

      1.   **Superleaders** are leaders who, through vision and strength of personality, have a truly inspirational impact on other persons.

      2.   **Charismatic leaders** are leaders who develop special leader-follower relationships and inspire followers in extraordinary ways.

ENHANCEMENT

Assign the *Assessment* titled, **"TT" Leadership Style** which is included in the *Career Readiness Workbook*. Knowledge of their score should provide students with personal insight, while increasing the perceived relevance of *transformational leadership*. Further discussion of this assessment is provided in Unit 9 of this *Manual*.

   B.   *What is Tranformational Leadership?*

      1.   **Transformational leadership** is inspirational leadership that influences the beliefs, values, and goals of followers, and gets them to *perform above and beyond expectations*.

      2.   They create **"transformations"** that shift people and organizational systems into new and high performance patterns.

      3.   **Example:** Lee Iacocca is a business leader who exercised transformational leadership during the early eighties by turning around the bankrupt Chrysler Motor Company and making it profitable again.

      4.   **Transactional leadership** describes managers who apply the insights of the leader-behavior and contingency theories, particularly the path-goal theory.

      5.   Through task-oriented and/or people-oriented **"transactions"** with followers, the leader helps followers meet their needs and those of the organization in mutually satisfactory ways.

      6.   Transactional leadership **meets only part** of an organization's requirements.

ENHANCEMENT

The *Website Assessment and Exercise* titled, **The Fedex Leadership Test/Nine Faces of Leadership**, can be used here to familiarize students with the attributes of leaders that are considered to be essential at Fedex — many of which are listed below. This gives students yet another opportunity to assess their leadership potential.

7. **Attributes of Transformational Leaders** — *special qualities*
    transformational other characteristic of leader

    a) <u>Vision</u>: Having ideas and a clear sense of direction; communicating them to others; developing excitement about accomplishing shared "dreams."

    b) <u>Charisma</u>: Arousing others' enthusiasm, faith, loyalty, pride, and trust in themselves through the power of personal reference and appeals to emotion.

    c) <u>Symbolism</u>: Identifying "heroes," offering special rewards, and holding spontaneous and planned ceremonies to celebrate excellence and high achievement.

    d) <u>Empowerment</u>: Helping others develop, removing performance obstacles, sharing responsibilities, and delegating truly challenging work.

    e) <u>Intellectual stimulation</u>: Gaining the involvement of others by creating awareness of problems and stirring their imagination to create high-quality solutions.

    f) <u>Integrity</u>: Being honest and credible, acting consistently out of personal conviction, and meeting commitments by following through.

C. *Gender and Leadership*

    1. Research evidence clearly indicates that **both women and men can be effective leaders.**

    2. **Emerging results** suggest, however, that:

        a) <u>Women may be more prone toward interactive leadership</u> (i.e., democratic and participative leadership) which involves focusing on good interpersonal relations through communication and involvement.

        b) <u>Men may be more transactional</u>, acting more directive and assertive, and using authority in a traditional "command and control" sense.

3. Given the current emphasis on shared power, communication, cooperation, and participation in new-form organizations, **interactive leadership** appears to be an **excellent fit**.

4. Regardless of whether the relevant behaviors are displayed by men or women, it seems clear that future leadership success will rest more on one's capacity to lead through positive relationships and empowerment.

D. *Good "Old Fashioned" Leadership*

1. *Peter Drucker* views leadership as much more than charisma.

2. **Drucker's Three Essentials of Leadership**

   a) Establishing a <u>sense of mission</u>.

   b) Accepting leadership as a "<u>responsibility</u>" rather than a rank.

   c) Earning and keeping the <u>trust</u> of followers.

E. *Ethical Aspects of Leadership*

1. **Integrity** involves the leader's honesty, credibility, and consistency in putting values into action as an element of effective leadership.

2. *John Gardner* talks about the **"moral aspects"** of leadership, arguing that leaders have a moral obligation to supply the necessary spark to awaken the potential of each individual.

3. Good managers instill a sense of **"ownership"** in followers by being truly willing to let others do *their* best.

CHAPTER 13 SUMMARY

What is effective "managerial" leadership?

* Leadership is the process of inspiring others to work hard to accomplish important tasks.
* An effective leader influences other people to work enthusiastically in support of organizational performance objectives.
* Vision, or a clear sense of the future, is increasingly considered to be an essential ingredient of effective leadership.
* Visionary leaders are able to communicate their vision to others and build commitments to perform the work required to fulfill it.

How do leaders gain and use power?

* Power, the ability to get others to do what you want them to do, is an essential ingredient of effective leadership.
* Managerial power may be gained through the manager's formal position in the organization and/or through personal sources.
* Sources of position power are based on rewards, coercion, and legitimacy or formal authority.
* Sources of personal power are based on expertise and reference.
* Effective leaders empower others---that is, they help and allow others to take action and make decisions on their own.

What are the important leadership traits and behaviors?

* Early leadership research studied personal traits in the search for a profile that differentiated successful and unsuccessful leaders.
* Traits that seem to have a positive impact on leadership include drive, integrity, and self-confidence, among others.
* Research on leader behaviors focused on alternative leadership styles and their impact on followers.
* One suggestion of leader-behavior researchers is that effective leaders will be good at both initiating structure through task-oriented behaviors and showing consideration through people-oriented behaviors.

What can be learned from contingency theories of leadership?

* Contingency leadership approaches point out that no one leadership style works in all situations; rather, the best style is one that properly matches the demands of a situation.
* Fiedler's contingency theory describes how situational differences in task structure, position power, and leader-member relations may influence which leadership style works best.
* House's path-goal theory points out that leaders should add value to situations by responding with supportive, directive, achievement-oriented, and/or participative styles as needed.
* The Hersey--Blanchard situational theories recommends using task- and people-oriented behaviors depending upon the "maturity" of the group a manager is attempting to lead.
* The Vroom--Jago theory leader-participation theory advises leaders to choose different decision-making methods appropriate to the problems they are trying to resolve.

What are current issues in leadership development?
* Transactional leadership focuses on tasks, rewards, and structures to influence behavior.
* Charismatic leadership creates a truly inspirational relationship between leader and followers.
* Transformational leadership uses charisma and related qualities to inspire extraordinary efforts in support of innovation and large-scale change.
* The interactive leadership style seems consistent with the demands of the new workplace, and emphasizing communication, involvement, and interpersonal respect.
* All leadership is "hard work" that always requires a personal commitment to meet the highest ethical and moral standards.

CHAPTER 13 KEY TERMS

Authority decision A decision made by the manager and then communicated to the group.

Charismatic leader A leader who develops special leader-follower relationships and truly inspires her or his followers in extraordinary ways.

Coercive power The capability to punish or withhold positive outcomes as a means of influencing other people.

Consultative decision A decision made by a manager after receiving information, advice, or opinions from group members.

Expert power The capability to influence other people because of specialized knowledge.

Group decision A decision made with the full participation of all group members.

Leadership The process of inspiring others to work hard to accomplish important tasks.

Leadership style The recurring pattern of behaviors exhibited by a leader.

Legitimate power The capability to influence other people by virtue of formal authority or the rights of office.

Power The ability to get someone else to do something you want done or to make things happen the way you want.

Referent power The capability to influence other people because of their desires to identify personally and positively with the power source.

Reward power The capability to offer something of value -- a positive outcome -- as a means of influencing other people.

Substitutes for leadership Factors in the work setting that move work efforts toward organizational objectives without the direct involvement of a leader.

Transactional leadership Leadership that orchestrates and directs the efforts of others through tasks, rewards, and structures.

Transformational leadership The ability of a leader to get people to do more than they originally expected to do in support of large-scale innovation and change.

Vision The term used to describe a clear sense of the future and the actions needed to get there.

CHAPTER 14: MOTIVATION AND REWARDS

CHAPTER 14 STUDY QUESTIONS

o   Why is motivation important?
o   What are the different types of individual needs?
o   What are the insights of process theories of motivation?
o   What role does reinforcement play in motivation?
o   What are the trends in motivation and compensation?

CHAPTER 14 LEARNING OBJECTIVES

After completing this chapter, students should be able to:

1.   Define motivation and discuss its importance to management.
2.   List different types of work-related rewards and discuss the importance of rewards to motivation and performance.
3.   Identify and distinguish between the three general types of motivation theories, and discuss the integrated model of individual work motivation.
4.   Discuss the dynamics of Maslow's hierarchy-of-needs theory of motivation.
5.   Describe Alderfer's ERG theory and explain how it differs from Maslow's need theory.
6.   Identify and discuss the three acquired needs identified by McClelland and their implications for management.
7.   Compare and contrast the attributes and dynamics of Maslow's, Alderfer's Herzberg's and McClelland's human need theories of motivation.
8.   Indicate the dynamics and managerial implications of equity theory.
9.   Express the fundamentals of expectancy theory as an equation and describe the separate and joint impact which the components of this equation have on motivation.
10. Discuss Locke's goal-setting theory and explain how goals can be set to encourage high levels of individual motivation and performance.
11. Discuss the law of effect and the role of environmental consequences in reinforcement theory.
12. Explain the concepts and dynamics associated with reinforcement theory such as operant conditioning, organizational behavior modification (OB Mod), reinforcement strategies, shaping, reinforcement schedules, and the ethics of OB Mod.
13. List and discuss the guidelines for positive reinforcement and punishment.
14. Explain the relationship between motivation and compensation and describe the mechanics and issues associated with merit pay, incentive compensation systems, and other creative pay practices.

CHAPTER 14 OVERVIEW

Motivation to work is the term used describe the forces within the individual that account for the level, direction, and persistence of effort expended at work. While most people are very interested in the topic of motivation, they also tend to hold strong biases concerning the processes through which motivation is achieved. This chapter provides a well-rounded perspective of the different factors that motivate people.

The chapter begins by discussing the interrelationships between rewards, motivation, and performance. Next, the major theories of work motivation are examined in detail, including Maslow's, Alderfer's, Herzberg's, and McClelland's content or human needs theories, the process perspectives of equity, expectancy theory, and goal setting theory, as well as reinforcement theory. The chapter ends by focusing on the relationship between compensation and motivation, and the dynamics of merit pay, incentive compensation systems, and other creative pay practices.

CHAPTER 14 LECTURE OUTLINE

Purpose: To provide students with a thorough understanding of the dynamics of motivation and the ways in which rewards can be used to motivate employees.

Suggested Time: A minimum of three hours of class time is recommended to present this chapter. If many enhancements are used, more time may be needed.

Importance of Motivation
      Motivation and Rewards
      Rewards and Performance

Content Theories of Motivation
      Hierarchy of Needs Theory
      ERG Theory
      Two-Factor Theory
      Acquired-Needs Theory
      Questions and Answers on the Content Theories

Process Theories of Motivation
      Equity Theory
      Expectancy Theory
      Goal-Setting Theory

Reinforcement Theory of Motivation
      Reinforcement Strategies
      Positive Reinforcement
      Punishment
      Ethical Issues in Reinforcement

Motivation and Compensation
      Pay for Performance
      Incentive Compensation Systems

CHAPTER 14 SUPPORTING MATERIALS

Textbook Inserts

Headline: Value Diversity and Individual Differences
Margin Photos: Roppe Corporation, Silicon Graphics, Rocky Shoes & Boots,
      Pratt & Whitney
Embedded Box/Photo Essays: Lincoln Electric
Manager's Notepad 14.1: How to Make Goal Setting Work for You
Manager' Notepad 14.2: Guidelines for Positive Reinforcement... and Punishment

Multi-Media Resources

NBR Video Report:
      Black Entertainment Television (Available on Video Supplement & Video Cases
         CD-ROM)

PowerPoint Presentations (Website):
      Figures 14.1 to 14.8 from Textbook plus Supplemental Figures
      NBR Viewing Questions: Black Entertainment Network & Nucor

In-Class Activities

Cases for Critical Thinking (Career Readiness Workbook & Website):
      Black Entertainment Television (Primary Case)
      Nucor (Alternate Case)

Exercises:
      Why Do We Work? (Career Readiness Workbook)
      Why Do We Do the Things We Do? (Website Quick Hitter)

Assessments:
      Two-Factor Profile (Career Readiness Workbook)

Research and Presentation Project:
      CEO Pay — Is it Too High? (Career Readiness Workbook)

Self-Test 14 (Textbook and Website)

CHAPTER 14 LECTURE NOTES

I. **Importance of Motivation**

    A.   *Motivation* is the term used to describe the forces within the individual that account for the level, direction, and persistence of effort expended at work.

ENHANCEMENT

The *Exercise* from the *Career Readiness Workbook* titled, **Why Do We Work?**, can be used as an initial ice breaker to generate preliminary discussion of the reasons why people work. This discussion can then lead into a more detailed consideration of the motivation theories described below. A more detailed discussion of this exercise is provided in Unit 9 of this Manual. Alternatively, the *Website Quick Hitter* titled, **Why Do We Do the Things We Do?** can be used for the same purpose.

    B.   *Motivation and Rewards*

        1.   A **reward** is a work outcome of positive value to the individual.

        2.   **Extrinsic rewards** are externally administered (e.g., pay and verbal praise); the motivational stimulus originates *outside* the person.

ENHANCEMENT

Examples of Extrinsic Rewards
The pink luxury cars driven by the "superstars" of **Mary Kay Cosmetics, Inc.,** are almost legendary in some parts of the United States. Founder Mary Kay Ash's skill at using recognition and rewards to motivate employees is also becoming legendary in management circles. The sales force pursues a program structured with many contests and rewards in addition to regular income. Recognition for outstanding performance ranges from photos in monthly magazines to incentive gifts such as cars, vacation trips, and diamond jewelry.
(Source: Wendy Zellner, "Mary Kay Is Singing I Feel Pretty," *Business Week*, December 2, 1991, p. 102).

        3.   **Intrinsic rewards** are self-administered; they occur "naturally" as a person performs a task. Major sources of intrinsic rewards are the feelings of competency, personal development, and self-control people experience in their work. The stimulus is *internal* and does not depend on the actions of others.

ENHANCEMENT

A nice way to involve students in the discussion of **work-related rewards** is to ask them to identify as many different types of rewards as possible that managers can use to motivate subordinates. While students are typically able to quickly list a large variety of rewards, they also usually overlook some more subtle rewards such as an enriched job or training opportunities. You may want to wrap up this discussion by presenting the following table and complimenting the students on the number of rewards they named.

Sources of Intrinsic Rewards	Extrinsic Rewards
Participation in decision making	Performance bonuses
Increased responsibility	Overtime and holiday premiums
Opportunities for personal growth	Profit sharing
Greater job freedom and discretion	Stock options
More interesting work	Impressive titles
Diversity of activities	Preferred work assignments
Training opportunities	Praise and recognition

D. *Rewards and Performance*

1. **If used well,** both intrinsic and extrinsic rewards can help the manager to lead effectively through motivation.

2. To achieve **maximum motivational impact**, it is necessary to:

   a) Respect diversity and individual differences.
   b) Clearly understand what people want from work.
   c) Allocate rewards to satisfy the interests of both individuals and the organization.

3. **Three Types of Motivation Theories**

   a) Content theories: Try to help managers understand human "needs" and how people with different needs may respond to different work situations. In essence, content theories focus on *what* motivates an individual.

   b) Process theories: Try to help managers understand *how* people give meaning to rewards and the work opportunities available to them.

   c) Reinforcement theory: Try to help managers understand how people's behavior is influenced by its *environmental consequences*. Its central thesis is reflected in the equation $B = F(C)$, which states that behavior is a function of its consequences.

II. Content Theories of Motivation

 A. *Needs* are physiological and psychological deficiencies that an individual feels some compulsion to eliminate.

 B. *Hierarchy of Needs Theory*   **FIGURE 14.1**

   1. **Lower-order needs** include physiological, safety and social concerns; **higher-order needs** include esteem and self-actualization concerns.

   2. The **deficit principle** holds that a satisfied need is not a motivator of behavior; people act to satisfy needs in which a deficit exists.

   3. The **progression principle** holds that the five needs exist in a strict hierarchy of prepotency such that a need at one level doesn't become activated until the next lower-level need is satisfied. People are expected to advance step by step up the hierarchy.

   4. **Managerial Implications:** While there is no consistent research evidence in support of Maslow's theory, his hierarchy is helpful for understanding people's needs and what can be done to satisfy them. You can generate discussion by asking students to identify the types of rewards that could be used to satisfy the various needs.

 C. *ERG Theory*

   1. Clayton Alderfer's ERG theory is an **extension** of Maslow's theory.

   2. Instead of five needs, Alderfer proposes **three needs**, the first letters of which are identified by the name of the theory itself - ERG.

     a) <u>Existence needs</u>: Desires for physiological and material well-being.

     b) <u>Relatedness needs</u>: Desires for satisfying interpersonal relationships.

     c) <u>Growth needs</u>: Desires for continued psychological growth and development.

   3. ERG theory does **not assume that lower-level needs must be satisfied before higher-level needs become activated.**

4. ERG theory includes a unique **"frustration-regression"** principle whereby an already satisfied lower-level need becomes reactivated when a higher-level need is frustrated.

ENHANCEMENT

A discussion of the **Body Shop** can be included at this point to illustrate how need fulfillment can serve as the basis for a successful business. The company founder, *Anita Roddick,* feels a need to make a personal contribution to preserving the environment. This need led her to establish this unusual and highly successful business. The Body Shop is a cosmetics retailer whose products only contain natural biodegradable ingredients that have not been tested on animals. Packaging is kept to a minimum and employs recycled materials. In choosing franchisees and store managers, Roddick pays more attention to applicants' interests and needs, than she does to their experience. She favors people who share her concern for the environment. Applicants must take personality tests, spend a trial period working in a store, be evaluated by other employees, and pass through a series of interviews with Body Shop executives. Through these practices, Roddick has built an empire of people who share her needs.

(Source: "Dwarfs, and How Not to Be One," *The Economist,* October 12, 1991, p. 92).

D. *Two-Factor Theory* **FIGURE 14.2**

ENHANCEMENT

To make the discussion of **Herzberg's two factor theory** more personally meaningful for students, assign them the *Assessment* which appears in the *Career Readiness Workbook* titled, **Two-Factor Profile**. It will provide them with an indication of how important both *satisfiers* and *hygiene factors* are for them. For most students, the satisfiers, which are part of the *job content* will provide a greater source of *job satisfaction* and *motivation*.

---

1. *Frederick Herzberg* is a psychologist who concluded with his associates after examining nearly 4000 responses of people to questions about their work, that different factors were sources of **job satisfaction** and **job dissatisfaction.**

2. **Hygiene Factors: Sources of Job *Dissatisfaction***

   a) <u>Hygiene factors</u> are elements of the <u>job context</u> which serve as sources of <u>job dissatisfaction</u>.

   b) <u>Types of Hygiene Factors</u>

     (1) Working conditions.
     (2) Interpersonal relations.
     (3) Organizational policies and administration.
     (4) Technical quality of supervision.
     (5) Base wage or salary.

   c) <u>Improvements in hygiene factors can prevent and/or eliminate job dissatisfaction</u>; they will not improve job satisfaction.

  3. **Satisfier Factors: Sources of Job Satisfaction**

   a) <u>Satisfier factors</u> are elements of the <u>job content</u> which serve as sources of <u>job satisfaction</u>.

   b) <u>Types of Satisfier Factors</u>

     (1) Sense of achievement.
     (2) Feelings of recognition.
     (3) Sense of responsibility.
     (4) Opportunity for advancement.
     (5) Feelings of personal growth.

   c) <u>Improvements in satisfier factors can increase job satisfaction</u>; they will not prevent job dissatisfaction.

  4. **Managerial Implications**

   a) Elements of the <u>job context</u> must be maintained at <u>acceptable</u> levels to avoid job dissatisfaction; improvements in hygiene factors above acceptable levels, however, will have no affect on job satisfaction.

   b) To increase job satisfaction, improvements must be made in the <u>job content</u>.

E. *Acquired-Needs Theory*

  1. *David McClelland* proposes that people **acquire** needs through their life experiences.

  2. McClelland uses a **Thematic Apperception Test (TAT)** to measure the strengths of three acquired needs:

   a) <u>Need for achievement (nAch)</u>: The desire to do something better or more efficiently, to solve problems, or to master complex tasks.

b) <u>Need for power (nPower)</u>: The desire to control other persons, to influence their behavior, or to be responsible for other people. A finer distinction can be made between:

* The **need for "personal" power,** which is exploitative and concerned with manipulation and power for the pure sake of personal gratification; and

* The **need for "social" power,** which is socially responsible and directed toward organizational rather than personal objectives.

c) <u>Need for affiliation (nAff)</u>: The desire to establish and maintain friendly and warm relations with other persons.

ENHANCEMENT

Thematic Apperception Test Questions
To help students understand how the TAT works, you may want to describe to them some sample questions. In one case, McClelland tested three executives using a photograph that showed a man sitting down and looking at family photos arranged on his work desk. One executive wrote of an engineer who was daydreaming about a family outing scheduled for the next day (nAff). Another described a designer who had picked up an idea for a new gadget from remarks made by his family (nPow). The third saw an engineer who was intently working on a bridge-stress problem that he seemed sure to solve because of his confident look (nAch).

3. **High need achievers** prefer work that...

   ... involves individual responsibility for results.
   ... involves achievable but challenging goals.
   ... provides feedback on performance.

   Example: A computer scientist responsible for software design and technical problem solving in support of a MIS.

4. **People high in need for power** prefer work that...

   ... involves control over other persons.
   ... has an impact on people and events.
   ... brings public recognition and attention.

   Example: An audit manager in charge of a group of newly-hired junior accountants assigned to complete a complex audit of a bank.

5.   **People high in need for affiliation** prefer work that...

... involves interpersonal relationships.
... provides for companionship.
... brings social approval.

Example: A human resources specialist responsible for employee relations, college recruiting, and management development programs.

ENHANCEMENT

Before presenting the following **need profile of successful executives**, you may want to ask students to indicate which needs they think will be most pronounced among executives. This can provide a nice introduction of the following points and serve to highlight the surprising fact that **need for achievement** is not always and solely associated with executive success.

6.   **The Need Profile of Successful Executives** - Based on his research on the needs of executives, McClelland concluded that:

a)   The most important need for executive success is the need for social power.

b)   While nPower was often accompanied by a high need for achievement, the later need in itself was not consistently associated with executive success.

c)   Persons with a high need for affiliation may not make the best managers, since their desire to be liked could get in the way of effective decision making.

d)   The successful executive is likely to possess a high need for social power that is greater than an otherwise strong need for affiliation.

F.   *Questions and Answers on Individual Needs at Work*   **FIGURE 14.3**

1.   Use **Figure 14.3** to compare and contrast the three content theories and as a tool in answering the following questions.

a)   "How many different individual needs are there?" Research has not yet determined a complete list of work-related needs. Each of the needs identified by Maslow, Alderfer and McClelland can help managers understand the needs of people at work.

354

b) "Can a work outcome or reward satisfy more than one need?" Yes. Pay, for example, can be used to satisfy existence, achievement and social needs.

c) "Is there a hierarchy of needs?" Research supports the flexible hierarchy suggested by Alderfer more than the five-step hierarchy postulated by Maslow. The distinction between lower-level and higher-level needs does appear to be useful.

d) How important are the various needs?" Research is inclusive as to the importance of different needs. Individuals vary widely. Managers should use the insights of the content theories to best understand the differing needs of people at work.

III. Process Theories of Motivation   FIGURE 14.4

A. *Equity Theory*

1. *J. Stacy Adams* advanced the theory that **perceived inequity can be a motivating state.**

2. **Equity theory** asserts that when people believe that they have been treated inequitably in comparison to others, they try to eliminate the discomfort and restore equity.

ENHANCEMENT

Relate this discussion of **equity theory** to the **psychological contract** concept presented earlier. Basically, the *contributions* offered by the individual are *inputs*, while the *inducements* provided by the organization are *rewards*. If an *imbalance* occurs, the individual may experience *perceived inequity*. In reviewing the psychological contract, you may ask students to think about a job they have held or currently hold. Next, ask them if they feel they were rewarded fairly. Many are likely to say that they were not paid enough, or that the work was not challenging enough. From here on, you can use these students as examples of people who have experienced negative inequity. Be sure to ask them how they responded to the inequity. In nearly all cases, students will indicate that they exhibited one of the responses to perceived inequity listed below.

3. **Perceived equity** occurs whenever a person perceives that their personal rewards/inputs ratio is equivalent to the rewards/inputs ratio of a **comparison other** ($R_p/I_p = R_o/I_o$). Under these circumstances, the individual is satisfied and is not motivated to change the situation or their behavior.

4.   **Perceived inequity** occurs whenever one's rewards/inputs ratio is perceived to be unequal to the rewards/inputs ratio of a comparison other ($R_p/I_p \neq R_o/I_o$).

    a)   <u>Positive inequity</u> occurs when a person feels overrewarded, given their relative inputs.

    b)   <u>Negative inequity</u> occurs when a person feels underrewarded, given their relative inputs.

ENHANCEMENT

Examples of Equity and Inequity
Hewlett-Packard recently closed a plant because of heavy snow. Salaried workers were paid. Hourly workers had to make up the time. Honeywell, Inc. operates similarly. In contrast, Polaroid pays everyone kept from work by inclement weather. Given the inconsistency of this policy at Hewlett-Packard and Honeywell, it is quite possible that their hourly workers experience negative inequity whenever a plant is snowed in.

---

5.   **Possible Responses to Perceived Inequity**

    a)   Change their work inputs.
    b)   Change the rewards received.
    c)   Change the comparison points.
    d)   Change the situation.

6.   For example, a person experiencing a **positive inequity** in which $R_p/I_p > R_o/I_o$, may respond by increasing the quantity or quality of their work inputs.

ENHANCEMENT

Point out to students that Adams' theory predicts that people who are overpaid will experience **positive inequity**. While many will not doubt scoff at this possibility, it is useful to explore how a person who encountered a positive inequity is likely to respond. Two possible, though unlikely options, are to ask for a pay cut or quit their job. Another, more realistic option, is to exert greater effort. Finally, the individual can develop a rationalization to justify receiving a relatively high level of pay.

---

7.   In contrast, a person encountering **negative inequity** in which $R_p/R_p < R_o/I_o$, may respond by reducing their work efforts or quitting.

8. Managers are responsible for **minimizing inequities** by:

   a) <u>Recognizing that equity comparisons are likely</u> whenever highly visible rewards such as pay and promotions are allocated.

   b) <u>Anticipating felt negative inequities</u>.

   c) <u>Communicating</u> the intended value of the reward, the performance on which it is based, and the appropriate comparison points.

9. Equity dynamics are apparent in the issue of **comparable worth,** the principle that people doing jobs of similar value should receive equal pay, i.e., *"Equal pay for equal work."*

ENHANCEMENT

Example of Comparable Worth
"Equal pay for equal work" is becoming a reality as the Toronto Sun Publishing Corp.'s employees experience the effects of Ontario's new law on pay equity. A comprehensive review of all jobs was conducted and points assigned to each according to set criteria. Where less-paid but equivalent jobs performed mostly by women were found equivalent to others performed mostly by men, salary adjustments were made.

B. *Expectancy Theory*   **FIGURE 14.5**

   1. **Expectancy theory** asserts that: "People will do what they can do when they want to."

   2. **Three Fey Factors in Expectancy Theory**

      a) <u>Expectancy (Effort --> Performance Expectancy)</u>: A person's belief that working hard will result in a desired level of task performance.

      b) <u>Instrumentality (Performance --> Work-Outcome Expectancy)</u>: A person's belief that successful task performance will be followed by rewards and other potential outcomes.

      c) <u>Valence</u>: The value a person assigns to possible rewards and other work-related outcomes.

3.　**Multiplier Effects**

   a)　The relationship between motivation and these factors can be expressed as an <u>equation</u>:

$$M = E \times I \times V$$

   b)　The <u>multiplier effect</u> implies that for motivation to be high, expectancy, instrumentality and valence must be high. Conversely, if <u>expectancy is low</u> (the person feels he or she can't perform), <u>instrumentality is low</u> (the person is not confident performance will be rewarded), and/or <u>valence is low</u> (the reward is not valued), <u>motivation will be low</u>.

ENHANCEMENT

A useful way to help students understand the **multiplier effect of expectancy theory**, is to relate it to their own academic experiences. Ask students to think about their motivation in their various classes. Do they believe that if they work hard, they will be able to achieve a high level of performance (expectancy)? If they succeed in performing well, do they expect to be rewarded with a high grade (instrumentality)? Finally, do they value a high grade (valence)? If the answer to any of these questions is "No," their motivation will suffer.

4.　**Managerial Implications**　　　　　　　　　　**FIGURE 14.6**

   a)　Basically, the theory suggests managers can motivate employees by <u>ensuring that E, I and V are high and positive</u>.

   b)　<u>To maximize</u>:

   　(1)　*Expectancy*

   　　*　Select workers with ability.
   　　*　Train workers to use ability.
   　　*　Support work efforts.
   　　*　Clarify performance goals.

   　(2)　*Instrumentality*

   　　*　Clarify psychological contracts.
   　　*　Communicate performance-outcome possibilities.
   　　*　Demonstrate what rewards are contingent on performance.

(3)   *Valence*

    *   Identify individual needs.

    *   Adjust rewards to match these needs.

IV. Goal-Setting Theory

A.   The basic premise of *goal setting theory*, as developed by *Edwin Locke*, is that well-set and well-managed *task goals* are important sources for motivation.

B.   *Task goals,* in the form of clear and desirable performance targets, provide direction, energize persistent long-term work efforts, clarify performance expectations, and serve as a basis for feedback.

C.   *How to Make Goal-setting Work for You*   **MANAGER'S NOTEPAD 14.1**

1.   **Set specific goals:** Specific goals, such as "increase sales by six percent over the next three months," lead to higher performance than more generally stated ones, such as "do your best."

2.   **Set challenging goals:** As long as they are viewed as realistic and attainable, more difficult goals lead to higher performance than easy goals.

3.   **Build goal acceptance and commitment:** People work harder for goals that they accept as their own and truly believe in; they tend to resist goals that seem inappropriately forced on them.

4.   **Clarify goal priorities:** Make sure that expectations are clear as to which goals should be accomplished first, and why.

5.   **Reward goal accomplishment:** Don't let positive accomplishments go unnoticed; reward people for doing what they set out to do.

D.   *Management-by-objectives (MBO)* is one example of a goal-setting system which promotes participation.

V.   Reinforcement Theory

A.   Unlike the prior motivation theories which rely on *cognitive explanations of behavior*, reinforcement theory focuses instead on the impact which *external environmental consequences* have on behavior. This premise is reflected in the following equation:

Behavior = Function (Consequences) or B = F(C)

ENHANCEMENT

An excellent way to introduce the material on **reinforcement theory** is to conduct a "shaping exercise." This exercise involves the following steps:
1. Solicit a volunteer from the class to serve as an "employee."
2. Ask the volunteer if he or she has ever seen or heard of the "shaping exercise" before; if he/she has, find a new volunteer.
3. Explain to the class that the volunteer will be the "employee" and the class will serve as a composite manager/supervisor. The "manager" will try to shape the employee's behavior by yelling "hot, hot" whenever the "employee" engages in a behavior which approximates the desired response. Conversely, whenever the "employee" engages in a behavior which does not resemble the desired behavior, the "manager" will say "cold, cold."
4. Ask the volunteer to leave the room for a few minutes.
5. Tell the class that they want the "employee" to **walk backwards.**
6. Ask the "employee" to step back into the room.
7. Run the exercise!

You will find that the class is usually able to shape up the desired response with remarkable speed. The entire class gets a real kick out of this exercise, and it provides an excellent lead into the discussion of **shaping** and the **law of effect**, since "hot, hot" was as a positive outcome which increased the desired response, while "cold, cold, cold" served as a negative outcome which effectively decreased undesirable responses.

    B.   *Thorndike's Law of Effect:* Behavior that results in a pleasant outcome is likely to be repeated; behavior that results in an unpleasant outcome is not likely to be repeated.

    C.   *Reinforcement Strategies*   **FIGURE 14.7**

        1.   **Operant conditioning**, a term popularized *B. F. Skinner,* is the process of controlling behavior by manipulating its consequences; i.e., learning by reinforcement.

        2.   **Organizational behavior modification**, or "OB Mod", involves the application of operant conditioning techniques to influence human behavior in work settings. It is achieved by systematically reinforcing desirable organizational behavior while denying reinforcement for unwanted organizational behavior.

        3.   By definition, **reinforcement** is anything that *increases* the frequency of, or strengthens, a behavior. There are two types of reinforcement:

            a)   <u>Positive reinforcement</u> increases the frequency of a behavior through the contingent *presentation* of a *desirable* consequence.

Example of OB Mod
The customer is always right at Nordstrom's -- a Seattle-based department store chain. The chain pays its employees 20 percent more than competitors and deliberately congratulates and encourages them for good work. If customers complain, employees are instructed to replace anything on demand, no questions asked. Workers have "learned" through the positive consequences of their behavior to continue to do the right things.

Example: A manager compliments a salesperson who lands a new account.

b) <u>Negative reinforcement</u> increases the frequency of a behavior through the contingent *removal* of an *undesirable* consequence.

Example: A manager who has been consistently scolding an employee for poor quality work, doesn't say anything when the employee's work meets the quality standard one day.

4. **Punishment** decreases the frequency of a behavior through the contingent *presentation* of an *unpleasant* consequence.

Example: A manager gives a written reprimand to an employee for fighting.

5. **Extinction** decreases the frequency of a behavior through the contingent *removal* of a *pleasant* consequence.

Example: A manager notices that the more he listens to an employee's complaints, the more the employee complains. The manager decides his attentive listening may be reinforcing the complaints. He ignores subsequent complaints and finds that they decline (extinction).

6. The distinctions between the **four OB Mod strategies** can be usefully summarized by the following chart:

	Desirable Consequence	**Undesirable Consequence**
Presentation of the Consequence	Positive Reinforcement	Punishment
Removal of the Consequence	Negative Reinforcement	Extinction

D.   *Positive Reinforcement*

1.   Two laws should guide a managers' actions in using positive reinforcement:

a)   <u>Law of contingent reinforcement</u>: In order for a reward to have maximum reinforcing value, it must be delivered only if the desired behavior is exhibited.

b)   <u>Law of immediate reinforcement</u>: The more immediate the delivery of a reward after the occurrence of a desirable behavior, the greater the reinforcing value of the reward.

2.   **Shaping** is the creation of a new behavior by the positive reinforcement of successive approximations of the desired behavior.

Example: A manager compliments a new employee each time his output gets closer to the production quota by telling him he is doing "better"; output levels below the employee's previous high are not reinforced. Gradually the employee's performance rises to meet the standard.

3.   **Schedules of Reinforcement**

a)   <u>Continuous reinforcement</u> administers a reward each time a desired behavior occurs.

b)   <u>Intermittent reinforcement</u> only rewards behavior periodically.

c)   A manager can expect that:

   *   *Continuous reinforcement* will draw forth a desired behavior *more quickly* than intermittent reinforcement.

   *   Behavior acquired under an *intermittent schedule* will be *more permanent* than behavior acquired under a continuous schedule.

4.   **Guidelines for Positive**   **MANAGER'S NOTEPAD 14.2**
      Reinforcement

a)   Clearly identify desired work behaviors.
b)   Maintain diverse inventory of rewards.
c)   Inform everyone what must be done to get rewards.
d)   Recognize individual differences when allocating rewards.

e) Follow the laws of immediate and contingent reinforcement.

E. *Punishment*

1. To punish an employee, a manager may **deny the person a valued reward** such as verbal praise or pay, or the manager may **administer an aversive stimulus** such as a verbal reprimand, pay reduction or demotion.

ENHANCEMENT

Example of Punishment

At Tampa Electric, a paid day off is used as punishment. The company gives an oral "reminder" to employees who come in late, mistreat a colleague, or do a sloppy job. Next comes a written reminder. Then a paid day off is scheduled-- called a "decision-making leave day." After this day off employees must agree orally or in writing that they will be on their best behavior for **the** next year. This is an all-or-nothing chance to reform; employees who don't shape up are fired. And since the process is documented, it's perfectly legal.

---

2. **Guidelines for Punishment**   **MANAGER'S NOTEPAD 14.2**

   a) Tell the person what is being done wrong.
   b) Tell the person what is right.
   c) Make sure the punishment matches the behavior.
   d) Administer the punishment in private.
   e) Follow the laws of immediate and contingent reinforcement.

3. **Punishment and Positive Reinforcement** - Managers often use these two strategies in combination; punishment is used to remove the undesirable behavior and positive reinforcement is used to shape up more desirable behaviors.

F. *Ethical Issues in Reinforcement*

1. The power of reinforcement theory is dramatically illustrated by a number of "success stories" at corporations such as GE, B.F. Goodrich, Michigan Bell and Emery Air Freight, where **improvements in safety, absenteeism, tardiness and productivity** have been reported.

2. There is considerable debate over the **ethicality** of using OB Mod to influence behavior. But as the text notes, "the real question may be not whether it is ethical to control behavior, but whether it is ethical *not* to control behavior well enough

363

that the goals of both the organization *and* the individual are well served."

G.   *An Integrated Model of Individual Motivation*   **FIGURE 14.8**

1.   The **integrated model** combines the above perspectives to gain useful insights for **managing motivational dynamics.**

2.   **Motivation** leads to **effort** which, along with appropriate **abilities** and **organizational support**, leads to **performance.**

3.   The model illustrates how **rewards** for performance, when they are perceived as **equitable** and possess **reinforcement value**, can produce **satisfaction.**

VI.   Motivation and Compensation

A.   *Pay for Performance*

1.   **Merit pay** is a system of awarding pay increases in proportion to performance contributions.

2.   Merit pay serves to motivate employees by providing **performance contingent reinforcements.**

3.   **Example:** IBM uses merit pay to allow its employees to directly influence their earnings through sustained and improved job performance.

B.   *Incentive Compensation Systems*

1.   **Incentive compensation systems** are bonus systems in which employees at all levels participate.

a)   Bonus pay plans provide bonuses to employees based on the accomplishment of performance targets.

Example: Nucor Corporation divides production crews into bonus groups consisting of 25-35 employees. Bonuses are earned by exceeding performance standards for the group. Workers wait no more than a week to receive them. Many employees double their pay through bonuses.

b)   Profit-sharing plans distribute to some or all employees a proportion of net profits earned during a time period.

Lincoln Electric pioneered *profit sharing*. In addition to paying its workers on a piece-rate basis, Lincoln Electric rewards employees with year-end bonuses which are contingent on their merit ratings and the firm's profits. The average profit sharing bonus is approximately equal to the employee's annual salary. The motivating power of Lincoln's compensation policies are readily apparent from the fact that its workers produce about three times as much as other American workers in the same categories.

(Source: Restoring Competitive Luster to American Industries: An Agenda for Success, Cleveland: The Lincoln Electric Company).

c) <u>Gain-sharing plans</u> extend the profit-sharing concept by allowing groups of employees to share in any savings or "gains" realized through their efforts to reduce costs of increase productivity.

<u>Example</u>: The *Scanlon Plan* usually results in 75% of gains going to workers.

Long John Silver's uses a **gain-sharing plan** which is targeted at the firm's 16,000 hourly workers and each restaurant's "bottom-line." The program gives workers quarterly bonuses according to improvements made in their restaurant's revenues and profits. James E. Stahl, a restaurant manager in Austin, Texas, says the plan has made employees more sales oriented. For managers like James, however, annual bonuses are also tied to improvements in the company's stock price.

(Sources: Business Ethics, vol. 5, no. 4, 1991; Joann S. Lubin, "Managing Employee Stock Plans Run into Snags," The Wall Street Journal, September 16, 1991, p. B1; Business Week, January 27, 1991, pp. 90-95).

d) <u>Employee stock ownership plans</u> involve employees in ownership through the purchase of company stock.

* Some firms provide employees with *stock options*, which give the option holder the right to buy stock at a future date at a fixed price.

* *Stock option plans* provide employees with an incentive to work hard to raise the firm's stock price, so that they can purchase it at a discount in the future.

<u>Example</u>: More than 140,000 Pepsico employees have access to stock options. In a program called, "sharepower," workers get options equal to 10% of their compensation.

e) <u>Pay for Knowledge</u>

* *Skills-based pay* ties pay to the number of job-relevant skills an employee masters.

  Example: Federal Express' pay-for-knowledge reward system requires customer-contact to periodically take -- and pass -- written job-knowledge tests. Scores are incorporated into employees' performance appraisals, and pay can be increased if employees score highly.

* *Entrepreneurial pay* requires individuals to put part of their pay at risk, in return for the right to pursue entrepreneurial ideas, and share in any resulting profits.

  Example: Some employees at AT&T have contributed from 12 to 15% of their salaries for the opportunity to pursue entrepreneurial ideas in this way.

ENHANCEMENT

To help students acquire in depth knowledge about a controversial aspect of **incentive pay**, assign the *Research Project* titled, **CEO Pay -- Is it Too High?** from the *Career Readiness Workbook*. Further discussion of this assignment is provided in Unit 9 of this *Manual*.

CHAPTER 14 SUMMARY

Why is motivation important?
* Motivation involves the level, direction, and persistence of effort expended at work; a highly motivated person works hard.
* Extrinsic rewards are given by another person; intrinsic rewards derive from the work itself.
* To maximize the motivational impact of rewards, managers must allocate them in ways that respond to both individual and organizational needs.
* The three major types of motivation theories are the content, process, and reinforcement theories.

What are the different types of individual needs?
* Maslow's hierarchy of human needs suggests a progression from lower-order physiological, safety, and social needs, to higher-order ego and self-actualization needs.
* Alderfer's ERG theory identifies existence, relatedness, and growth needs.
* Herzberg's two-factor theory points out the importance of both job content and job context factors in satisfying human needs.
* McClelland's acquired needs theory identifies the needs for achievement, affiliation, and power, all of which may influence what a person desires from work.
* Managers should respect individual differences and diversity to create motivating work environments.

What are the insights of process theories of motivation?
* Adam's equity theory recognizes that social comparisons take place when rewards are distributed in the workplace.
* People who feel inequitably treated are motivated to act in ways that reduce the sense of inequity.
* Perceived *negative* inequity may result in someone working less hard in the future.
* Vroom's expectancy theory states that Motivation = Expectancy x Instrumentality x Valence.
* Expectancy theory encourages managers to make sure that any rewards offered for motivational purposes are achievable and individually valued.
* Locke's goal-setting theory emphasizes the motivational power of goals; people tend to be highly motivated when task goals are specific rather than ambiguous, difficult but achievable, and set through participatory means.

What role does reinforcement play in motivation?
* Reinforcement theory recognizes that human behavior is influenced by its environmental consequences.
* The law of effect states that behavior followed by a pleasant consequence is likely to be repeated; behavior followed by an unpleasant consequence is unlikely to be repeated.
* Reinforcement strategies used by managers include positive reinforcement, negative reinforcement, punishment, and extinction.

* Positive reinforcement works best when applied according to the laws of contingent and immediate reinforcement.

What are the trends in motivation and compensation?

* The area of compensation is a good test of a manager's ability to integrate and apply the various insights of motivation theories.
* Pay for performance in the form of merit pay plans ties pay to performance increases.
* Various incentive compensation programs, such as gain sharing and profit sharing, allow workers to benefit materially from improvements in profits and productivity.
* Pay for knowledge systems link pay typically to the mastery of job relevant skills.

CHAPTER 14 KEY TERMS

Bonus pay plans Incentive compensation plans that provide cash bonuses to employees based on the achievement of specific performance targets.

Employee stock ownership plans Incentive compensation plans that allow employees to share ownership of their employing organization through the purchase of stock.

Entrepreneurial pay A pay for knowledge plan that involves workers putting part of their compensation at risk in return for the right to pursue entrepreneurial ideas and share in any resulting profits.

Expectancy A person's belief that working hard will enable various levels of task performance to be achieved.

Extinction Discouraging a behavior by making the removal of a desirable consequence contingent on the occurrence of the behavior.

Extrinsic rewards Rewards given as a motivational stimulus to a person usually by a superior.

Gain-sharing An incentive compensation plan that allows employees to share in any savings or gains realized through their efforts to reduce costs and increase productivity.

Higher order needs Esteem and self-actualization needs in Maslow's hierarchy.

Hygiene factors Factors in the work setting, such as working conditions, interpersonal relations, organizational policies, and administration, supervision, and salary.

Instrumentality A person's belief that various work-related outcomes will occur as a result of task performance.

Intrinsic rewards Rewards that occurs naturally as a person performs a task or job.

Law of effect A law of human behavior which states that behavior followed by unpleasant consequences is likely to be repeated while behavior followed by unpleasant consequences is not likely to be repeated.

Lower order needs Physiological, safety, and social needs in Maslow's hierarchy.

Merit pay A system of awarding pay increases in proportion to performance contributions.

Motivation A term used in management theory to describe forces within the individual that account for the level, direction, and persistence of effort expended at work.

Natural rewards Rewards that occurs naturally as a person performs a task or job.

Need A physiological or psychological deficiency a person feels the compulsion to satisfy.

Need for Achievement The desire to do something better or more efficiently, to solve problems, or to master complex tasks.

Need for Affiliation The desire to establish and maintain friendly and warm relations with other people.

Need for Power The desire to control, influence, or be responsible for other people.

Negative reinforcement Strengthening a behavior by making the avoidance of an undesirable consequence contingent on the occurrence of the behavior.

Operant conditioning The process of controlling behavior by manipulating its consequences.

O B Mod The application of operant conditioning techniques to influence human behavior in work settings.

Positive reinforcement Strengthening a behavior by making a desirable consequence contingent on the occurrence of the behavior.

Profit-sharing An incentive compensation program that distributes a proportion of net profits to employees during a stated performance period.

Punishment Discouraging a behavior by making an unpleasant consequence contingent on the occurrence of that behavior.

Reward A work outcome of positive value to the individual.

Satisfier factors Factors in the job content, such as a sense of achievement, recognition, responsibility, advancement, or personal growth, experienced as a result of task performance.

Shaping Positive reinforcement of successive approximations to the desired behavior.

Skills-based pay A system of paying workers according to the number of job-relevant skills they master.

Task goals Performance targets for individuals and/or groups.

Valence The value a person assigns to work-related outcomes.

CHAPTER 15: INDIVIDUAL PERFORMANCE AND JOB DESIGN

CHAPTER 15 STUDY QUESTIONS

o   What is the meaning of work?
o   What are important issues in job design?
o   How can jobs be enriched?
o   Why are alternative work arrangements?
o   How can job and workplace stress be managed?

CHAPTER 15 LEARNING OBJECTIVES

After completing this chapter, students should be able to:

1.   Discuss the meaning of work, the psychological contract, and the significance of work to the quality of life.
2.   Define the terms job and job design.
3.   Define job satisfaction and discuss its relationship to job performance.
4.   Compare and contrast the alternative job design strategies available to managers.
5.   Explain the job characteristics model and its implications for job design.
6.   Provide answers to common questions about job enrichment.
7.   Discuss the impact of technology on job enrichment, including socio-technical systems and robotics.
8.   Identify and explain the alternative work schedules that are available in the flexible workplace.
9.   Define stress, identify potential sources of stress, and discuss the consequences of stress.
10.   Discuss alternative approaches to stress management.

CHAPTER 15 OVERVIEW

A fundamental task for any organization is the design of work for individuals and teams. Effective work design applies a contingency perspective in choosing the appropriate task attributes and work setting to achieve high levels of task performance and job satisfaction. This chapter presents key work design issues, strategies, and applications of importance to the manager in achieving productivity.

The chapter begins with a discussion of the meaning of work, including the psychological contracts between organizations and employees, and the importance of work to the quality of life. After considering the various aspects of job satisfaction and its relationship to job performance, specific strategies of job design are explored, along with the job characteristics model. The importance of designing jobs to fit the requirements of the situation is stressed. The chapter's focus then shifts to a discussion of alternative work schedules available to managers as means of creating a flexible workplace which is conducive to productivity.

The chapter concludes by focusing on work-related stress and stress management skills. The discussion of stress identifies its major sources and distinguishes between constructive and destructive stress. After exploring the relationship between stress and health, several stress management alternatives are described, including stress prevention, stress coping and personal wellness. From a manager's perspective, it is important to practice stress management while helping colleagues and subordinates to do likewise.

CHAPTER 15 LECTURE OUTLINE

Purpose: The purpose of this chapter is provide students with an appreciation for the principles and practices of work design. To achieve this goal, the critical issues and strategies of work design at the individual and team levels are presented.

Suggested Time: Two hours are recommended to present the material on work design. More time may be needed if multiple enhancements are used.

The Meaning of Work
        Psychological Contracts
        Work and the Quality of Life

Job Design Issues
        Job Satisfaction
        Job Performance
        Job Design Alternatives
        Job Simplification
        Job Rotation and Job Enlargement
        Job Enrichment

Directions in Job Enrichment
        The Job Characteristics Model
        Technology and Job Enrichment
        Questions and Answers on Job Enrichment

Alternative Work Arrangements
        The Compressed Workweek
        Flexible Working Hours
        Job Sharing
        Telecommuting
        Part-Time Work

Job Stress and Stress Management
        Sources of Stress
        Consequences of Stress
        Stress Management Strategies

CHAPTER 15 SUPPORTING MATERIALS

Textbook Inserts

Headline: Unlock Everyone's Performance Potential
Margin Photos: Marriott Hotels, International Survey Research, Lotus Development
    Corporation, Catalyst
Embedded Box: Hewitt Associates, Boeing Company,
    Aetna Life & Casualty Company
Manager's Notepad 15.1: Job Enrichment Checklist
Manager's Notepad 15.2: How to Cope with Workplace Stress

Multi-Media Resources

NBR Video Report:
    Boeing (Available on Video Supplement & Video Cases CD-ROM)

PowerPoint Presentations (Website):
    Figures 15. 1 to 15.4 from Textbook plus Supplemental Figures
    NBR Viewing Questions: Boeing & UPS

In-Class Activities

Cases for Critical Thinking (Career Readiness Workbook & Website):
    Boeing (Primary Case)
    UPS (Alternate Case)

Exercises:
    The Case of the Contingency Workforce (Career Readiness Workbook)
    The "Best" Job Design (Career Readiness Workbook)
    How Workers Feel (Website Quick Hitter)
    Happy Workers, High Returns (Website Quick Hitter)
    International Morale Watch (Website Quick Hitter)

Assessments:
    Job Design Preferences (Career Readiness Workbook)
    Stress Self-Test (Career Readiness Workbook)

Research and Presentation Project:
    Job Satisfaction in Our Community (Website)

Self-Test 15 (Textbook and Website)

CHAPTER 15 LECTURE NOTES

I.   The Meaning of Work

To introduce this chapter, consider assigning the *Exercise* titled, **Why Do We Work?** from the *Career Readiness Workbook*. The exercise demonstrates that, while some people view work as drudgery, others may define the same tasks in terms of a higher purpose. Further discussion of this exercise is available in Unit 9 of this manual.

      A.   *Psychological Contracts*   **FIGURE 15.1**

        1.   A **psychological contract** is a person's expectations about what will be given and received from an organization as a part of the employment relationship.

        2.   As part of the psychological contract, a person offers **contributions** or valued work activities to the organization, such as...

... effort.	... cooperation.
... time.	... commitment.
... creativity.	... expertise.

        3.   **Inducements** are things of value that the organization gives to the individual in return for these contributions, such as...

... pay.	... opportunity.
... fringe benefits.	... respect.
... training.	... security.

One way to enhance the discussion of the **psychological contract** is to ask students to think of a job they have held or currently hold. Select one student and ask this individual to describe the nature of his or her job. With this job as an example, you can use **Figure 15.1** as a framework for identifying the **inducements** offered by the organization and the **contributions** made by the student. Alternatively, you may ask the student to identify these factors. To wrap up this discussion, ask the student if he or she feels that a healthy **balance** exists between the inducements and contributions for this job. Follow this question up by asking the student how he or she feels about their job. If the student indicates a balance exists, they will typically feel satisfied with the job. If an imbalance is perceived, the student usually experiences some dissatisfaction, especially if the imbalance is in the organization's favor. At this point you can stress the importance of equity in the psychological contract.

B. *Work and the Quality of Life*

1. Work is an important component of the **quality of life**. For some people, jobs are a source of pleasure; for others work is sheer drudgery.

2. The term **work-life balance** refers to the fit between one's job or work responsibilities an personal or family needs.

II. Job Design Issues

A. A *job* is a collection of tasks performed in support of organizational objectives.

B. *Job design* is the process of creating or defining jobs by assigning specific work tasks to individuals or groups.

C. *Job Satisfaction*

1. **Job satisfaction** is the degree to which an individual feels positively or negatively about various aspects of the job.

2. **Common Aspects of Job Satisfaction**

a) Satisfaction with pay.
b) Satisfaction with tasks.
c) Satisfaction with supervision.
d) Satisfaction with coworkers.
e) Satisfaction with the work setting.
f) Satisfaction with advancement opportunities.

ENHANCEMENT

The **Management 6/E Website** provides four *Quick Hitters* and one *Project* that are relevant to the current material on job satisfaction. These include: a) **How Workers Feel**, b) **Happy Workers, High Returns**, c) **International Morale Watch**, and d) **Job Satisfaction in Our Community**. Consider including one or more of these activities to illustrate the importance of job satisfaction and employee morale to organizational performance.

---

3. Research has demonstrated a strong and positive relationship between job satisfaction and **absenteeism** and **turnover;** workers who are satisfied with their jobs come more often, and are more likely to stay with an organization.

4. **Job involvement** is defined the extent to which an individual is dedicated to a job.

5. **Organizational commitment** is defined as the loyalty of an individual to the organization itself.

D. *Job Performance*

1. **Job performance** is the quantity and quality of task accomplishments by an individual or group at work.

2. A **value-added criterion** is being used in many organizations to evaluate the merits of jobs and/or job holders.

3. All managers should see **job performance** and **job satisfaction** as *key* results to be achieved by people at work.

4. **High-Performance Equation**

   Performance = Ability X Support X Effort

   a) <u>Performance begins with ability</u>: Ability establishes an individual's capacity to perform at a high level of accomplishment.

   b) <u>Performance requires support</u>: To fully utilize their abilities workers need sufficient resources, clear goals and directions, freedom from unnecessary rules and job constraints, appropriate technologies, and performance feedback.

   c) <u>Performance involves effort</u>: Even the most capable, well supported workers won't achieve the highest performance levels unless they are willing to work hard.

E. *Job Design Alternatives*   **FIGURE 15.2**

ENHANCEMENT

Before presenting the Continuum of *Job Design Strategies* (**Figure 15.2**) described below, assign the initial part of the *Exercise* titled **Job Design Preferences** from *Career Readiness Workbook*. During class, students can complete the activities designated for work groups. Their individual and group preferences can then be discussed with the class as a whole, and referred to throughout the discussion of job design approaches. Further discussion of this exercise is provided in Unit 9 of this *Manual*.

1. **Job design strategies** vary along a **continuum** ranging from high to low levels of **task specialization**, as follows.

	Job Simplification	**Job Rotation and Enlargement**	**Job Enrichment**
Job Scope	Narrow	Wide	Wide
Job Depth	Low	Low	High
High task Specialization	<-->		Low task Specialization

2. The amount of **task specialization** is a function of the:

    a) <u>Job scope</u>: The number and combination of different tasks an individual is asked to perform; and

    b) <u>Job depth</u>: The extent of planning and evaluating duties performed by the worker rather than the supervisor.

F. Job Simplification

ENHANCEMENT

To introduce the **job simplification** strategy, ask students if they have ever had a job in which this strategy was employed. If any respond yes, ask them to describe their job. You can use one of these jobs to illustrate the characteristics of this strategy. Next, ask what these students thought of their jobs and why they no longer hold them. Students will typically respond that they found the job to be boring so they quit. Responses such as these reflect the problems of **boredom** and **turnover** which are commonly associated with job simplification. Thus, they provide a nice introduction into a discussion of the expected advantages and potential disadvantages of this strategy, which are summarized below.

1. **Job simplification** involves standardizing work procedures and employing people in clearly defined and highly specialized jobs; this strategy creates a **narrow job scope**. A few, simple tasks are performed repeatedly as follows:

    Task 1---->Task 2---->Task 3
    <--------------------------

2. **Automation,** or the total mechanization of a job, represents the most extreme form of job simplification.

3.   **Expected Advantages of Job Simplification**

   a)   Unskilled labor can be employed.
   b)   Easier and quicker training of workers.
   c)   Interchangeable workers.
   d)   Workers become good at performing repetitive tasks.

4.   **Potential Disadvantages of Job Simplification**

   a)   Poor worker morale.
   b)   High absenteeism and turnover.
   c)   Worker boredom and alienation.
   d)   Low quality and job performance.

G.   *Job Rotation and Job Enlargement*

1.   **Job rotation and job enlargement** are job design strategies that expand the **job scope** to offset some of the disadvantages of job simplification.

2.   **Job rotation** increases task variety by periodically shifting workers among jobs involving different sets of assignments.

3.   **Job enlargement** increases task variety by combining into one job two or more tasks that were assigned to separate workers. This strategy can be depicted as follows:

   Task 1---->Task 2---->Task 3---->Task 4---->Task 5
   <--

4.   **Horizontal loading** can be used to enlarge jobs by pulling prework and/or later work stages into the job.

5.   **Figure 15.3** schematically depicts the process of horizontal loading.

6.   Because job enlargement and job rotation can reduce some of the monotony of simplified jobs, an increase in job satisfaction and performance should result.

ENHANCEMENT

Ask students what they think of the **job rotation** and **job enlargement** strategies. Usually, they respond correctly that, while these strategies may reduce some of the monotony of highly simplified jobs, their benefits are likely to be limited. In the words of Frederick Herzberg, "Why should a worker become motivated when one or more 'meaningless' tasks are added to previously existing ones or when work assignments are rotated among equally 'meaningless' tasks?" This point provides a nice lead into the material on **job enrichment** which follows.

H.   *Job Enrichment*

1.   **Job enrichment** increases job depth by adding work planning and evaluating duties normally performed by the supervisor.

2.   Job enrichment seeks to expand both **job scope** and **job depth**. This strategy can be depicted as follows:

```
Planning     A┐
                │
   &            │  B   Task 1---->Task 2----->Task 3---->Task 4---->Task 5
                │      <------------------------------------------------
Evaluating   C┘
```

3.   *Herzberg* advocates this approach, arguing that "If you want people to do a good job, give them a good job to do."

4.   Changes designed to increase job depth are sometimes referred to as **vertical loading.**

5.   **Figure 15.3** schematically illustrates the process of vertical loading.

ENHANCEMENT

Point out to students that in recent years, technological changes have enriched secretarial jobs. You may want to ask students to identify these changes and explain their impact on secretarial work. The integration of personal computers into the modern office is the cause of many of these changes. For example, personal computers have reduced the number of simplified and repetitive tasks performed by secretaries. In addition, the **scope** and **depth** of many secretarial jobs have been expanded to include such responsibilities as word processing and the monitoring of budgets.

---

6.   **Job Enrichment Checklist**   MANAGER'S NOTEPAD 15.1

Check 1:   Remove controls that limit people's discretion in their work.

Check 2:   Grant people authority to make decisions about their work.

Check 3:   Make people understand their accountability for results.

Check 4:   Allow people to do "whole" tasks or complete units of work.

Check 5:   Make performance feedback available to people doing the work.

ENHANCEMENT

Example of Job Enrichment
Jim Thorneberg, owner and CEO of Thorneberg Hosiery, called a meeting to tell his workers that, if the firm was to survive, drastic changes had to be made, and that if these changes didn't work within two years, he would sell the firm. Under the new system, each employee was held accountable for both the quality and quantity of his or her own work; supervisors became "servants of the worker." Not only did Thorneberg end up keeping the firm, but sales continue to increase.

III. Directions in Job Enrichment

> A. *A Contingency Perspective of Job Design* - Modern management theory recognizes that the appropriateness of this strategy depends upon the situation.

> B. *The Job Characteristics Model*   **FIGURE 15.4**

ENHANCEMENT

Ask a student who has worked in a fast-food restaurant, assembly line, or some other type of simplified job to rate the job on a scale from 1 to 5 on each of the five core job characteristics; then ask someone who has had a more enriched job to do the same. Finally, ask each person how they felt about their work. Their responses are typically very consistent with the predictions of the job characteristics model.

> 1. **Core Job Characteristics**

>> a) <u>Skill variety</u>: The degree to which a job requires a variety of activities and skills in carrying out the work and involves the use of a number of different skills and talents of the individual.

>> b) <u>Task identity</u>: The degree to which the job requires the completion of a "whole" and identifiable piece of work-- that is, one that involves doing a job from beginning to end with a visible outcome.

>> c) <u>Task significance</u>: The degree to which the job has a substantial impact on the lives or work of other people in the organization or in the external environment.

>> d) <u>Autonomy</u>: The degree to which the job gives the individual substantial freedom, independence, and discretion in scheduling the work and in determining the procedures to be used in carrying it out.

       e)   <u>Feedback (from the job itself)</u>: The degree to which carrying out the work activities required by the job results in the individual obtaining direct and clear information on the results of his or her performance.

2.   **Critical Psychological States** - The core job characteristics directly impact the following critical psychological states:

    a)   Experienced meaningfulness of work.
    b)   Experienced responsibility for the outcomes of the work.
    c)   Knowledge of actual results of work activities.

3.   **Individual Work Outcomes** - The critical psychological states, in turn, influence the following individual work outcomes:

    a)   High internal work motivation.
    b)   High growth satisfaction.
    c)   High general job satisfaction.
    d)   High work effectiveness.

4.   **Growth Need Strength (GNS)**

    a)   <u>Growth need strength</u> is the individual's desire to achieve a sense of psychological growth, is the key contingency variable moderating these relationship.

    b)   People <u>high in GNS</u> will respond <u>positively to enriched jobs</u> whereas those with <u>low GNS</u> will respond <u>negatively</u>.

5.   **Ways to Improve Core Job Characteristics**

    a)   <u>Form natural units of work</u>: Make sure that the tasks people perform are logically related to one another and provide a clear and meaningful task identity.

    b)   <u>Combining tasks</u>: Expand job responsibilities by pulling together into one larger job a number of smaller tasks previously done by others.

    c)   <u>Establishing client relationships</u>: Allow people to maintain contact with other persons who, as clients inside and/or outside the organization, use the results of his or her work.

    d)   <u>Open feedback channels</u>: Provide opportunities for people to receive performance feedback as they work, and to learn how this performance is changing over time.

e) <u>Practice Vertical loading</u>: Give people more control over their work by increasing authority for planning and controlling activities previously done by supervisors.

C. *Technology and Job Enrichment*

1. **Socio-technical systems** are job designs that use technology to best advantage while still treating people with respect, and allowing their human talents to be applied to the fullest potential.

2. **Robotics** involves the use of computer-controlled machines to completely automate work tasks previously performed by hand.

3. Despite a rapid rise in industrial applications of robotics, this technology still has its limitations.

4. In service industries, people often miss the "human touch" when being served by a computer rather than a person (e.g., an automated teller).

ENHANCEMENT

The *Photo Essay* on the **Boeing Company** describes one application of **socio-technical systems theory**. At Boeing, design of the new 777 widebody plane uses the latest computer assisted techniques and is largely paperless. Engineers work out problems on powerful computers, including all the coordinating details of some 130,000+ engineered parts and 3+ million rivets, screws, and fasteners. Says Allan R. Mulally, the vice-president in charge of the project: "The magic is, you can simulate assembly before you actually do it." But technology isn't the only key; people count too. Mulally's engineers work in cross-functional "design-build" teams which include representatives from all critical areas. Design and manufacturing problems are solved by the teams *before* production starts. This discussion can provide a nice introduction into the following section on job design for work teams.

D. *Questions and Answers about Job Enrichment*

1. **Question: "Is it expensive to do job enrichment?"** - It depends. The cost of job enrichment grows as the required changes in the work flow technology and physical setting increase.

2. **Question: "Will people demand more pay for doing enriched jobs?"** - Herzberg argues that if people are being paid competitive wages, the satisfaction of performing enriched tasks will be adequate compensation for the increased work involved. Nevertheless, any manager who employs job

enrichment should recognize that pay may be an important issue for the people involved.

3. **Question: "What do the unions say about job enrichment?"** - At least some union officials consider wages and benefits to be more important issues than job enrichment.

4. **Question: Should everyone's job be enriched?"** - No. Job enrichment is most appropriate for high GNS workers who have the training, education and ability to do the enriched job.

V. **Alternative Work Arrangements**

A. Not only is the *content* of jobs changing in today's workplace, the *job context* is changing as well. To deal with the needs and interests of a *diverse workforce,* a more *"flexible" workplace* with *alternative work schedules* has emerged.

B. *Types of Alternative Work Schedules*
1. Compressed workweek.
2. Flexible working hours.
3. Job sharing.
4. Telecommuting.
5. Part-time work.

C. *The Compressed Workweek*

1. The **compressed workweek** is any work schedule that allows a full-time job to be completed in less than the standard five days of eight-hour shifts.

2. Its most common form is a **"4-40" schedule** -- that is, 40 hours of work accomplished in four 10 hour days. This provides 3 consecutive days off.

3. **Benefits for the Individual**

    a) More leisure time.
    b) Lower commuting costs.

4. **Benefits for the Organization**

    a) Lower absenteeism.
    b) Potentially higher performance.

5. **Potential Disadvantages**

    a) Increased fatigue.
    b) Family adjustment problems.
    c) Increased scheduling problems.

d) Possible customer complaints.

e) Union opposition.

D. *Flexible Working Hours*   **FIGURE 15.5**

1. The terms **flexible working hours**, **flextime**, or **flexitime**, describe any work schedule that gives employees some choice in the pattern of daily work hours.

2. **Figure 15.5** provides an example of "flextime" in which all employees work four hours of **"core time"** between 9 and 11 AM and 1 and 3 PM. They are free to choose another four work hours from "flextime" blocks. Sample schedules include 7:00 AM to 3:00 PM (No lunch), 8:00 AM to 4:30 PM (30 minutes lunch), and 9:00 AM to 5:30 PM (30 minutes lunch).

3. Flexible working hours give people **greater autonomy** in work scheduling. Early risers and late sleepers can adjust their schedules accordingly. Employees are also provided with flexibility to attend to personal affairs during the day.

4. Flextime enables organizations to attract and retain members of a **diverse workforce**, such as **single parents with young children**, and **employees with elder-care responsibilities**.

5. Flextime can also boost **worker morale**.

E. *Job Sharing*

1. **Job sharing** involves a work schedule wherein one full-time job is split between two persons.

2. Job-sharing often occurs where each person works one-half day, although it can also be done on a weekly or monthly basis.

3. Job sharing can benefit organizations by enabling them to employ talented people who would otherwise be unable to work.

4. **Example:** A qualified specialist who is also a parent may be unable to work a full day, but able to work a half day.

F. *Telecommuting*

1. **Work-at-home** encompasses all work scheduling options that allow individuals to spend all or part of their time at home. These options include:

a) Self-employment.

b) Entrepreneurship.

      c)   *Telecommuting:* Work done at home using computers and information technology with links to the home office, central computers, external data bases, and other places of work.

      d)   Employees with a *virtual office* who work from home and/or their automobiles, and do so without permanent office space provided by the employer.

2.   **Potential Advantages of Work-at-Home**

      a)   Freedom from the constraints of commuting, fixed hours, special work attire, and even direct contact with supervisors.

      b)   Increased productivity.

      c)   Fewer distractions.

      d)   Being one's own boss.

      e)   More time for oneself.

3.   **Potential Disadvantages of Work-At-Home**

      a)   Working too much.

      b)   Less time to oneself.

      c)   Difficulty in separating work and personal life.

      d)   Less time for family.

      e)   Feelings of isolation.

      f)   Loss of visibility for promotion.

      g)   Managers may experience difficulties in supervising work-at-home employees from a distance.

G.   *Part-Time Work*

1.   **Part-time work** is work done on any schedule less than the standard 40-hour work week; this means the worker is not scheduled as a full-time employee.

2.   Employers are often relying on **contingency workers** -- part-timers and temporaries -- to supplement a permanent workforce.

3.   It is now possible to hire on a part-time basis everything from secretaries and unskilled laborers, to engineers, computer programmers, and even executives.

4.   Because contingency workers can be easily hired, contracted, and terminated as needed, many employers like the **flexibility** they offer in controlling labor costs.

5.   Contingency workers are often **paid less**, and they typically **fail to receive important benefits** such as health care, life insurance, pension plans, and paid vacations.

To stimulate a lively discussion of the issues involved with **contingency workers**, assign the *Exercise* titled, **The Case of the Contingency Workforce** from *Career Readiness Workbook*. Further discussion of this exercise is provided in Unit 9 of this *Manual*.

VI.   **Job Stress and Stress Management**

    A.   *Stress* is a state of tension experienced by individuals facing extraordinary demands, constraints, or opportunities.

    B.   *Job-related stress* goes hand in hand with the *dynamic* and sometimes *uncertain* nature of the *manager's role*.

    C.   *Sources of Stress*

        1.   **Stressors** are things that cause stress.

        2.   **Potential Work, Personal, and Non-work Stressors**

            a)   <u>Work factors</u> include task demands, role dynamics, interpersonal relationships and career progress.

Example of Work-Related Stressors
Union officials complain about the stress caused by automated equipment and restrictive rules at the U.S. Postal Service. "There's a rule for everything," says one shop steward, "if a supervisor wants to get you, he'll get you." In response to new equipment requiring mail sorters to work faster, another union official says, "The stress is tremendous."

            b)   <u>Personal factors</u> include needs, capabilities and personality.

               (1)   For a person with a *Type A personality*, for example, stressful behavior patterns such as those summarized below are commonplace.

                   *   Always moving, walking and eating rapidly.
                   *   Acting impatient, hurrying others, disliking waiting.
                   *   Doing, or trying to do, several things at once.
                   *   Feeling guilty when relaxing.

> * Trying to schedule more in less time.
> * Using nervous gestures such as clenched fist.
> * Hurrying or interrupting the speech of others.

ENHANCEMENT

You may want to assign the *Exercise* titled, **Stress Self-Test**, which appears in *Career Readiness Workbook*, to be completed prior to the class period in which you intend to cover stress. This self-test provides a measure of students' tendencies toward **Type A behaviors**. Knowing their own tendencies will naturally make your presentation on this topic much more relevant and interesting to students. During your discussion of **Type A personalities**, you may want to ask for a show of hands to see how many students score as Type A. You could also share with them your own score. Students usually find the notion of a Type A personality fascinating because it helps them to learn something about themselves. Further discussion of this exercise is provided in Unit 9 of this *Manual*.

---

    c)   <u>Nonwork factors</u> include family, economics and personal affairs which can "spill over" and influence the stress an individual experiences at work.

ENHANCEMENT

Example of Nonwork Stressors
A survey was conducted at AT&T among managers and top executives to investigate major sources of stress. The survey found that parenting and the difficulties of dealing with children caused respondents more stress and worry than anything else.

    D.   *Consequences of Stress*

        1.   **Constructive stress** acts in a positive or energizing way to increase effort, stimulate creativity, and encourage diligence in one's work.

        2.   **Eustress** is stress that is constructive for the individual, and which helps them to achieve a positive balance with their environments (e.g., studying hard for an exam).

        3.   **Destructive stress** is dysfunctional for the individual and/or the organization. It results from excessively high levels of stressors.

4. Managers must know how to **maintain the positive edge of constructive stress while avoiding destructive stress.**

5. Multiple and varied **symptoms of excessive stress** include changes in eating habits, restlessness, irritability and stomach upset.

ENHANCEMENT

If you used the **Self-Stress Test** exercise described earlier, you may want to ask some of the students who scored as *Type A*, if they are experiencing any of the above indicators of stress. In addition, since this is likely to be the end of the semester and many students may be cramming for exams, writing term papers, etc., you may want to ask the class as a whole this question. Many students who are under stress usually laugh nervously and respond in the affirmative. From here, you can move on to a discussion of *stress management alternatives.* This is a good way to point out the relevance of this material.

E. *Stress Management Strategies*

1. There are several **reasons why managers should be alert to signs of excessive stress** in themselves and their coworkers, including:

    a) <u>Humanitarianism</u> -- Managers should enhance and protect employee health to the extent possible.

    b) <u>Productivity</u> -- Healthy employees are more productive than unhealthy employees.

    c) <u>Creativity</u> -- Unhealthy persons are less creative and less willing to take reasonable risks than healthy persons.

    d) <u>Return on investment</u> -- When poor health reduces or removes an individual's contributions to the organization, the return on the investment in human resources is lost.

2. **Stress prevention** -- The best way to manage stress is to prevent it from reaching excessive levels.

    a) Persons with <u>Type A personalities</u> must exercise self-discipline; managers of Type A employees may try to model a more relaxed approach to work.

    b) <u>Family difficulties</u> may be relieved by a change in assignments or schedules, or an empathetic supervisor.

389

      c)   <u>Role ambiguities</u>, <u>conflicts</u>, <u>underloads</u> and <u>overloads</u> can be reduced through <u>role clarification</u> techniques such as MBO.

      d)   Formal programs can be developed to help people cope with the <u>survivor syndrome</u>, the stress experienced by persons who fear for their jobs in organizations that are reducing staffs through downsizing or layoffs.

3.   **How to Cope Better with**   **MANAGER'S NOTEPAD 15.2**
      Workplace Stress

      a)   Take control of the situation.
      b)   Pace yourself.
      c)   Open up to others.
      d)   Do things for others.
      e)   Exercise and work off stress.
      f)   Balance work and recreation.

ENHANCEMENT

Example of Stress Management Techniques
Among the techniques described by five executives for handling stress are morning exercise, listening to meditation tapes while commuting, and exercising in the gym after work.

(Source: "Oh, What a Relief It Is: Managing Without Stress," *Business Month,* August 1990, p. 25).

4.   **Personal wellness** is a term used to describe the pursuit of one's physical and mental potential through a personal health-promotion program. Managers should (a) practice personal wellness and (b) encourage subordinates to do likewise.

ENHANCEMENT

To integrate and build upon the chapter's discussion of **using positive influence**, **managing conflict**, *successful negotiation*, and **managing stress**, assign the *Research and Presentation Project* titled, **How to Manage Your Boss** from *Career Readiness Workbook*. Since most students find the concept of "managing one's boss" to be original and intriguing, they typically enjoy this research project. Moreover, by requiring them to consider how various power and influence, conflict management, and stress management strategies can be used to "manage" one's boss, their learning regarding these topics can be reinforced and broadened. Thus this research project should provide students with considerable insight into the ways in which interpersonal skills can be employed to ensure that their relationship with their boss is a positive one. Additional discussion of this assignment is available in Unit 9 of this *Manual*.

CHAPTER 11 SUMMARY

What is the meaning of work?

* Work is an activity that produces value for other people; it is something people do to "earn a living."
* Work is an exchange of values between individuals who offer contributions such as time and effort to organizations who offer monetary and other inducements in return.
* A healthy psychological contract occurs when a person believes that his or her contributions and inducements are in balance; it is one component of a high quality of work life.
* Quality of work life is one component in the quality of a person's life overall.

What are important issues in job design?

* Job design is the process of creating or defining jobs by assigning specific work tasks to individuals and groups.
* Jobs should be designed so workers enjoy high levels of job performance and job satisfaction.
* Job simplification creates narrow and repetitive jobs consisting of well-defined tasks with many routine operations, such as the typical assembly line job.
* Job enlargement allows individuals to perform a broader range of simplified tasks; job rotation allows individuals to transfer among different jobs of similar skill levels on a rotating basis.
* Job enrichment results in more meaningful jobs involving more autonomy in making decisions and broader task responsibilities.

How can jobs be enriched?

* The diagnostic approach to job enrichment involves analyzing jobs according to five core characteristics: skill variety, task identity, task significance, autonomy, and feedback.
* Jobs deficient on one or more of the prior "core" characteristics can be redesigned to improve their level of enrichment.
* Job can be enriched by forming natural work units, combining tasks, establishing client relationships, opening feedback channels, and vertically loading to allow more planning and controlling responsibilities.
* Job enrichment does not work for everyone; it works best for people with a high growth-need strength---the desire to achieve psychological growth in their work.

What are alternative work arrangements?

* Alternative work schedules can make work hours less inconvenient for people and respond better to a wide range of individual needs and personal responsibilities.
* The compressed workweek allows 40 hours to be completed in only 4 days' time.
* Flexible working hours allow people to adjust daily schedules in terms of starting and ending times.

* Job sharing allows two people to share one job.
* Telecommuting allows people to work at home or in mobile offices through computer links with their employers and/or customers.
* An increasing number of people work on part-time schedules; more and more organizations are employing part-timers or contingency workers to reduce their commitments to full-time employees.

How can job and work stress be managed?
* Stress occurs as tension accompanying extraordinary demands, constraints, or opportunities.
* Stress can be destructive or constructive; a moderate level of stress typically has a positive impact on performance.
* Stressors are found in a variety of work, personal, and nonwork situations.
* For some people, having a Type A personality creates stress due to continual feelings of impatience and pressure.
* Stress can be effectively managed through prevention and coping strategies, including a commitment to personal wellness.

CHAPTER 15 KEY TERMS

Compressed workweek Any work schedule that allows a full-time job to be completed in less than the standard 5 days of 8-hour shifts.

Constructive stress Stress that acts in a positive or energizing way to increase effort, stimulate creativity, and encourage diligence in one's work.

Contingency workers Workers employed on a part-time and temporary basis to supplement a permanent workforce.

Destructive stress Stress that is dysfunctional for the individual and/or the organization.

Flexible working hours Work schedules that give employees some choice in the pattern of daily work hours.

Growth-need strength An individual's desire to achieve a sense of psychological growth in her or his work.

Job The collection of tasks a person performs in support of organizational objectives.

Job design The allocation of specific work tasks to individuals and groups.

Job enlargement A job-design strategy that increases task variety by combining into one job two or more tasks that were previously assigned to separate workers.

Job enrichment A job-design strategy that increases job depth by adding to a job some of the planning and evaluating duties normally performed by the supervisor.

Job performance The quantity and quality of task accomplishment by an individual or group at work.

Job rotation A job-design strategy that increases task variety by periodically shifting workers among jobs involving different tasks.

Job satisfaction The degree to which an individual feels positively or negatively about various aspects of the job, including assigned tasks, work setting, and relationships with coworkers.

Job scope The number and combination of tasks an individual or group is asked to perform.

Job sharing An arrangement that splits one job between two people.

Job simplification A job-design strategy that involves standardizing work procedures and employing people in clearly defined and specialized tasks.

Part-time work Work done on a basis that classifies the employee as "temporary" and requires less than the standard 40-hour workweek.

Personal wellness The pursuit of one's physical and mental potential through a personal-health promotion program.

Psychological contract A person's expectations about what will be given and received from an organization as a part of the employment relationship.

Sociotechnical system Designing jobs so that technology and human resources are well integrated in high-performance systems with maximum opportunities for individual satisfaction.

Stress A state of tension experienced by individuals facing extraordinary demands, constraints, or opportunities.

Stressors Sources of stress.

Telecommuting Working at home using a computer terminal with links to the office or other places of work.

Type A personality A person oriented toward extreme achievement, impatience, and perfectionism and who may find stress in circumstances others find relatively stress-free.

Work-at-home Accomplishing a job while spending all or part of one's work time in the home.

CHAPTER 16: COMMUNICATION AND INTERPERSONAL SKILLS

CHAPTER 16 STUDY QUESTIONS

o   What is the communication process?
o   How can communication be improved?
o   How does perception influence behavior?
o   How can conflict be constructively managed?
o   How can agreements be negotiated successfully?

CHAPTER 16 LEARNING OBJECTIVES

After completing this chapter, students should be able to:

1.   Define communication, describe communication as an interpersonal process, and explain the difference between effective and efficient communication.
2.   Identify and discuss five barriers to effective communication.
3.   List and discuss the guidelines for making a successful oral presentation.
4.   Discuss six means of improving the communication process, including active listening, constructive feedback, open communication channels, proxemics and space design, technology utilization, and valuing culture and diversity.
5.   Define perception and explain how perception acts as an information screen or filter that influences the communication process.
6.   Discuss four perceptual distortions, explain their impact on the communication process.
7.   Define conflict, distinguish between substantive versus emotional conflicts, and explain the relationship between conflict and performance.
8.   Discuss and provide examples of the major types of conflict antecedents.
9.   Define conflict resolution, describe alternative approaches to conflict resolution, and discuss the five alternative conflict management styles and their associated outcomes.
10.   Define negotiation and discuss the major goals of negotiation, criteria of effective negation, and negotiation approaches.
11.   List and explain the four rules of principled negotiation; describe the key elements of the negotiation process, including the information foundations, initial offer, minimum and maximum reservation points, and bargaining zone.
12.   Identify and describe common negotiation pitfalls, negotiation goals and approaches, and the ethical aspects of negotiation.

CHAPTER 16 OVERVIEW

Communication is a fundamental element of organizations and managerial work. Communication is especially important to the leading function, since the manager depends on communication to inform followers of performance objectives and elicit their enthusiasm to achieve them.

This chapter focuses on the basic principles of interpersonal and organizational communication. It begins by examining the process of interpersonal communication, and distinguishing between effective and efficient communication. Next, various barriers to effective communication are described in detail, including poor use of channels, semantic problems, absence of feedback, physical distractions, and status effects. Specific means of improving communication are then presented, including active listening, constructive feedback, proxemics and space design, technology utilization, and valuing culture and diversity. The influence of perception on the communication process is explored next. Particular attention is devoted to potential perceptual distortions such as stereotypes, halo effects, selective perception, and projection, which can bias managerial communications and decisions.

The focus then shifts to the importance of conflict management skills to interpersonal relations is examined. Conflict is defined, the curvilinear relationship between conflict and performance is described, different types of conflict situations are presented, and structural and interpersonal approaches to conflict management are discussed. The value of collaborative, win-win methods of achieving conflict resolution is emphasized. The subsequent section on the goals, approaches, process, potential pitfalls, and ethical aspects of negotiation, likewise emphasizes the pursuit of win-win outcomes through integrative agreements.

The chapter concludes with a discussion of the negotiation process. Negotiation goals and approaches, the importance of principled negotiation to gaining integrative agreements and avoiding negotiating pitfalls, and ethical issues in negotiation are specifically examined.

CHAPTER 16 LECTURE OUTLINE

Teaching Objective: To thoroughly familiarize students with the interpersonal communication and the importance of interpersonal skills. To achieve this, the communication, perception, conflict management and negotiation processes,

Suggested Time: Three hours of class time are recommended to present this chapter. However, the material can be covered in less time through the use of the summary transparencies provided.

The Communication Process
        What is Effective Communication?
        Barriers to Effective Communication

Improving Communication
        Active Listening
        Constructive Feedback
        Open Communication Channels
        Proxemics and Space Design
        Technology Utilization
        Valuing Culture and Diversity

Perception, Communication, and Behavior
        Attribution Errors
        Perceptual Tendencies and Distortions

Communication and Conflict Management
        Functional and Dysfunctional Conflict
        Conflict Antecedents
        Conflict Resolution
        Conflict Management Styles

Communication and Negotiation
        Negotiation Goals and Approaches
        Gaining Integrative Agreements
        Avoiding Negotiation Pitfalls
        Ethical Issues in Negotiation

CHAPTER 16 SUPPORTING MATERIALS

Textbook Inserts

Headline: When in Doubt, Communicate
Margin Photos: BankBoston, Scott Co., Alcoa, McGraw-Hill
Embedded Box: Sam Walton, Hyatt, IBM
Manager's Notepad 16.1: How to Make a Successful Oral Presentation
Manager's Notepad 16.2: Ten Steps to Good Listening

Multi-Media Resources

NBR Video Report:
> Southwest Airlines (Available on Video Supplement & Video CD-ROM)

PowerPoint Presentations (Website):
> Figures 16.1 to 16.5 from Textbook plus Supplemental Figures
> NBR Viewing Questions: Southwest Airlines & Ben and Jerry's Ice Cream

In-Class Activities

Cases for Critical Thinking (Career Readiness Workbook & Website):
> Southwest Airlines (Primary Case)
> Ben and Jerry's Ice Cream (Alternative Case)

Exercises:
> Upward Appraisal (Career Readiness Workbook)
> Feedback and Assertiveness (Career Readiness Workbook)
> How to Give, and Take Criticism (Career Readiness Workbook)

Assessments:
> Facts and Inferences (Career Readiness Workbook)
> Conflict Management Styles (Career Readiness Workbook)

Self-Test 16 (Textbook and Website)

CHAPTER 16 LECTURE NOTES

I.   **The Communication Process**

A.   *Communication* is an interpersonal process of sending and receiving symbols with meanings attached to them.

One way to enhance the discussion of the **communication process** note that, as the lecturer, you are occupying the role of sender, whereas the students are receivers. To communicate with them, you use a variety of symbols including spoken and written words, transparencies, and gestures to send them messages. As receivers, the students decode these messages into perceived meanings which may or may not be the same as the intended meanings. Continuing with this example, you can introduce the concepts of effective and efficient communication by noting that while you can communicate quite *efficiently* with students through straight lectures, their involvement and feedback is needed to insure *effective* communication. Finally, you can preview the discussion of communication barriers by asking students to identify sources of "noise" which sometimes interfere with the effectiveness of lectures. An added benefit of this discussion is that instructors often obtain valuable feedback on their lecture style.

B.   *Elements of the Communication Process*   **FIGURE 16.1**

1.   The **sender** is the person who is responsible for encoding an intended **message** into meaningful symbols -- both verbal and nonverbal.

2.   The message is sent through a **channel**, written or oral, to a **receiver**, who then decodes or interprets its meaning -- which may or may not match the sender's intentions.

3.   **Feedback**, when present, reverses the process and conveys the receiver's response to the sender.

C.   *What is Effective Communication?*

1.   **Effective communication** occurs when the intended meaning of the sender and the perceived meaning of the receiver are one and the same.

Example: Face-to-face communication tends to be more effective than written memos, letters or posted bulletins.

2.   **Efficient communication** occurs at minimum cost in terms of resources (particularly time) expended.

Example: In communicating to many people, written memos, letters, bulletins and "E-mail" messages are more efficient than face-to-face communication.

3. Efficient communications are not always effective. Good managers know how to **maximize effectiveness while maintaining reasonable efficiency.**

D. *Barriers to Effective Communication*

1. **Noise** is anything that interferes with the effectiveness of the communication process.

ENHANCEMENT

You can demonstrate the impact of **noise** on the communication process by having five or six students play a round of "Telephone" in class. The first student should read a selected written paragraph, whispering to the second student. The second student should repeat the message from memory, as accurately as possible, whispering to the third student, and so on. Compare the message, as recited by the last student, to the original paragraph.

---

2. **Poor Choice of Channels**

    a) A <u>communication channel</u> is the medium through which a message is conveyed from sender to receiver.

    b) <u>Oral communication</u> takes place via the spoken word in telephone calls, face-to-face meetings, formal briefings, videotape messages, and the like.

    c) Oral channels work best for <u>complex and difficult-to-convey messages</u> where immediate feedback to the sender is valuable.

    d) <u>Written communication</u> has the advantage of being able to reach many people in a cost-efficient manner.

    e) Written channels are acceptable for <u>simple and easy-to--convey messages</u>, for those that require <u>extensive dissemination quickly</u>, and when <u>formal policy or authoritative directives</u> are being conveyed.

3. **Poor Written or Oral Expression**

    a) <u>Semantic barriers</u> occur as encoding and decoding errors and as mixed messages. <u>Example</u>: "Eat Here and Get Gas."

399

        b)   Managers need to speak and write clearly to avoid "<u>bafflegab</u>."

ENHANCEMENT

Additional examples of semantic problems include amusing advertisements or signs, such as, "Clean and decent dancing every night except Sunday," and "Shoes are required to eat in the cafeteria."

        c)   <u>How to Make a Successful Presentation</u>   **MANAGER'S NOTEPAD: 16.1**

* Be prepared.
* Set the right tone.
* Sequence points.
* Support your points.
* Accent the presentation.
* Add the right amount of polish.
* Check your technology.
* Don't bet on the Internet.
* Be professional.

4.   **Failure to Recognize Nonverbal Signals**

        a)   <u>Nonverbal communication</u> takes place through such things as hand movements, facial expressions, posture, eye contact, and the use of interpersonal space.

ENHANCEMENT

A fun way to illustrate the power of **non-verbal communication**, is to call on volunteers to "act out" various emotions without speaking verbally. Specifically, you may whisper to one volunteer to "act angry," another to "be sad," another to "be happy," etc. Alternatively, you may ask one student to portray all of these emotions, plus any others that you choose. Then you can ask the student's classmates to guess which emotion is being portrayed.

        b)   A <u>mixed message</u> occurs when a person's words communicate one message while actions, body language, or appearance communicate something else.

        c)   One potential side effect of electronic mail, computer networking, and other communication technologies is that nonverbal communication -- signals that may add important meaning -- are lost.

5. **Physical Distractions**

   a) <u>Physical distractions</u> such as interruptions from telephone calls, drop-in visitors, etc. can interfere with the effectiveness of a communication attempt.

   b) Many physical distractions can be avoided or at least minimized through <u>proper managerial attention</u>.

   c) <u>Examples</u>: Asking one's secretary to screen calls and visitors.

6. **Status Effects**

   a) <u>Status effects</u> involve noise which arises from an organization's hierarchy of authority.

   b) <u>Filtering</u> is the intentional distortion of information to make it appear most favorable to the recipient.

   c) When subordinates act as "yes men," the manager receiving filtered communications may make <u>poor decisions</u> because of a biased or inaccurate information base.

   d) Given the authority of their position, managers may be inclined to do a lot of "<u>telling</u>" but not much "<u>listening</u>."

II. **Improving Communication**

   A. *Active Listening*

   1. **Active listening** means taking action to help the source of a message say what he or she really means.

   2. **Rules for Active Listening**

      a) <u>Rule 1</u>: Listen for message content.
      b) <u>Rule 2</u>: Listen for feelings.
      c) <u>Rule 3</u>: Respond to feelings.
      d) <u>Rule 4</u>: Note all cues, verbal and nonverbal.
      e) <u>Rule 5</u>: Reflect back to the source what you think you are hearing.

3.   **Ten Steps for Good Listening**   MANAGER'S NOTEPAD 16.2

     a)   Stop talking.
     b)   Put the other person at ease.
     c)   Show that you want to listen.
     d)   Remove any potential distractions.
     e)   Empathize with the other person.
     f)   Don't respond too quickly, be patient.
     g)   Don't get mad, hold your temper.
     h)   Go easy on argument and criticism.
     i)   Ask questions.
     j)   Stop talking.

B.   *Constructive Feedback*

ENHANCEMENT

To personalize the following material on **feedback** for students, assign the *Exercise* titled, **Feedback and Assertiveness** which appears in *Career Readiness Workbook*. The preparation portion of the exercise includes a questionnaire which can be assigned to be completed before class. The questionnaire asks questions about managerial situations in which students may be uncomfortable giving feedback or being assertive. The in-class portion of the exercise requires students to practice with another student and an observer, the three behaviors that they are most uncomfortable exhibiting. The observer provides feedback and the students try again. This exercise provides students with a genuine opportunity to refine their skills at giving feedback. Further discussion of this exercise is provided in Unit 9 of this *Manual*.

1.   **Feedback** is the process of telling others how you feel about something they did or said, or about the situation in general.

2.   **Constructive Feedback Guidelines**

     a)   Give feedback directly and with real feeling, based on trust between you and the receiver.

     b)   Make feedback specific rather than general, using good, clear, and preferably recent examples.

     c)   Give at a time when the receiver appears willing or able to accept it.

     d)   Make sure the feedback is valid, and limit it to things the receiver can be expected to do something about.

e) Give feedback in small doses; never give more than the receiver can handle at any particular time.

ENHANCEMENT

To provide students with experience in giving and receiving **constructive feedback**, assign the *Exercise* titled, **How to Give, and Take, Criticism** from *Career Readiness Workbook*. Further discussion of this exercise is provided in Unit 9 of this *Manual*.

C. *Open Communication Channels*

1. **Management by Wandering Around (MBWA)** -- Dealing directly with subordinates by regularly spending time walking around and talking with them about a variety of work-related matters.

2. **Open Office Hours** -- Setting aside time for walk-in visitors during certain hours each week.

3. **Employee Group Meetings** -- A rotating schedule of "shirt-sleeve" meetings which bring top managers into face-to-face contact with mixed employee groups throughout the organization.

4. **Employee Advisory Councils** -- A council of employees elected by their fellow employees who meet with top management on a regular basis to discuss and react to new policies and programs that will affect employees.

5. **Suggestions Boxes** -- Physical or electronic "boxes," through which employees may anonymously communicate, sometimes anonymously, ideas or complaints.

6. **360-Degree Feedback** or **Multirater Assessment** -- involves upward appraisals from subordinates, as well as additional feedback from peers, internal and external customers, and higher managers.

D. *Proxemics and Space Design*

1. **Proxemics** is the use of interpersonal space; the distance between people conveys varying intentions in terms of intimacy, openness, and status.

2. The proxemics or **physical layout** of an office is an often overlooked form of nonverbal communication.

403

3. Office or workspace architecture is becoming increasingly recognized for its important influence on communication and behavior.

E. *Technology Utilization*

1. New information technologies, such as electronic mail systems (E-mail), videoconferencing, computer-mediated meetings, voice mail, and Intranets, facilitate **upward communication** and **flatter organizational structures**.

2. The rise of **information centers and departments** reflects the growing importance of information technology to organizations.

3. Computers can **empower lower-level personnel** with more and better information.

4. Computer technology enables managers to achieve **improved control and accountability**.

5. While computer technology allows people to work together across great distances through **"electronic networks"** the "personal" side of group decision making may be lost.

6. *New* managers must be able to **use new information technologies** while preserving a leadership edge based on **good interpersonal relations**.

F. *Valuing Culture and Diversity*

1. **Ethnocentrism** is the tendency to consider one's culture superior to any and all others.

2. Ethnocentrism can adversely affect **cross-cultural communication** by causing someone to...

... <u>not listen</u> to others, especially when they give feedback.

... address or speak to others in ways that <u>alienate</u> them.

... use <u>inappropriate stereotypes</u> which interfere with the development of good working relations.

3. The importance of **cross-cultural communication skills** apply at home just as well as abroad.

III. Perception, Communication, and Behavior   **FIGURE 16.2**

> A. *Perception* is the process through which people receive and interpret information from the environment.
>
> B. *Understanding Different Perceptions*
>
> > 1. **Figure 16.2** illustrates how perceptions influence the communication process by serving as an **information screen** or **filter**.
> >
> > 2. Depending on individual values, needs, cultural background, and other circumstances of the moment, **people can perceive the same situation quite differently**.

ENHANCEMENT
_____

A good illustration of how perceptual differences can cause different people to interpret the same information in different ways can be provided by a discussion of the **Nature Company**. The Nature Company consists of 70 shops and a catalogue business, all selling gifts and children's merchandise that promote an interest in the environment. When the company signed an agreement to open a chain of stores in Japan, the *San Francisco Chronicle* questioned the firm's ethics, noting that Japan has historically been behind the times environmentally. The Nature Company responded by pointing out that many of its executives had travelled throughout Japan, and concluded that things were changing dramatically. The firm felt that the presence of its stores would help to educate the Japanese public regarding environmental issues.

(Source: Success, April 1988, p. 16; Business Week, October 25, 1991, p. 16).
_____

> C. *Attribution Errors*
>
> > 1. **Attribution** is the process of developing explanations for events.
> >
> > 2. **Attribution theory** describes how people try to explain the behavior of themselves and other people.
> >
> > 3. The fundamental **attribution error** overestimates internal factors and underestimates external factors as influences on someone's behavior.
> >
> > 4. The **self-serving bias** occurs because individuals tend to blame their personal failures or problems on external causes and attribute their successes to internal causes.

D.   *Perceptual Tendencies and Distortions*

    1.   **Stereotypes**

        a)   A <u>stereotype</u> occurs when someone is identified with a group or category, and then oversimplified attributes associated with the group or category are assigned to the individual.

        b)   The influence of stereotypes in organizations, may account for the <u>glass ceiling</u>, an invisible barrier that limits the advancement of women and minorities to higher-level responsibilities in organizations.

        c)   <u>Racial stereotypes</u> are still pervasive in the workplace. This may explain why the number of African-American executives remains disappointingly low.

        d)   While <u>gender stereotypes</u> are falling, women may still suffer from false impressions and biases.

        e)   <u>Age stereotypes</u> may likewise place older workers at a unfair disadvantage in various work settings.

            <u>Example</u>: Because a manager assumes older workers lack creativity, are cautious and tend to avoid risks, a highly qualified older worker is not considered for a promotion.

        f)   Stereotypes prevent managers from <u>accurately assessing individual differences</u> at work, leading to <u>poor decision making</u> and <u>underutilization of human resources</u>.

    2.   **Halo Effects**

        a)   A <u>halo effect</u> occurs when one attribute is used to develop an overall impression of a person or situation.

        b)   <u>Example</u>: An employee is occasionally late for work but is otherwise a good performer; the manager concludes that the employee's overall performance is poor.

    3.   **Selectivity**

        a)   <u>Selective perception</u> is the tendency to single out for attention those aspects of a situation or attributes of a person that reinforce one's existing beliefs, values or needs.

      b)   <u>Example</u>: People from different departments or functions tend to see things from their own viewpoints -- and tend not to recognize other points of view.

   4.   **Projection**

      a)   <u>Projection</u> is the assignment of personal attributes to others.

      b)   <u>Example</u>: A manager assumes that subordinates have the same needs to achieve as she does.

IV.   Communication and Conflict Management

   A.   *Conflict* involves disagreements between people on issues of substance or emotion.

ENHANCEMENT

One way to get students highly involved in your discussion of conflict is to ask them to note on a piece of paper a situation where they were involved in a conflict at work. You can either (a) collect and sort through these papers to find good conflict examples (in which case you may suggest that students write their names on their papers) or (b) simply ask students to share their experiences with the class. Regardless of the option you choose, you can count on this approach to supply you with numerous examples which you can then refer back to in presenting the different types of **conflict** and **conflict management** below.

   B.   *Substantive conflict* involves disagreements over such things as goals, the allocation of resources, distribution of rewards, policies and procedures, and job assignments.

   C.   *Emotional conflict* arises from feelings of anger, distrust, dislike, fear, and resentment, as well as from personality clashes.

   D.   *Functional versus Dysfunctional Conflict*   **FIGURE 16.3**

     1.   **Figure 16.3** depicts the curvilinear relationship between conflict and performance.

     2.   Conflicts of moderate intensity can be **functional** or **constructive** for organizations, whereas conflicts of low-intensity or very-high intensity can be **dysfunctional** or **destructive.**

     3.   **Functional conflict** is constructive and stimulates people toward greater work efforts, cooperation, and creativity.

4. **Dysfunctional conflict** is destructive and hurts task performance.

E. *Conflict Antecedents*

1. Role ambiguities
2. Resource scarcities
3. Task interdependencies
4. Competing objectives
5. Structural differentiation
6. Unresolved prior conflicts

F. *Conflict Resolution*

1. **Conflict resolution** involves the elimination of the underlying causes for a conflict and removal of any lingering conditions which may rekindle the conflict again sometime in the future.

2. Managers may choose one of the following **structural approaches to resolve conflicts.**

   a) *Appeal to superordinate goals* that focus the attention of the conflicting parties on one mutually desirable end state.

   b) *Expanding the resources available* to everyone.

   c) *Altering one or more human variables* by replacing or transferring one or more of the conflicting parties.

   d) *Altering the physical environment* by rearranging facilities, workspace, and workflows to reduce opportunities for conflict.

   e) *Use of integrating devices* such as liaisons, special task forces, cross-functional teams, or a matrix organization.

   f) *Changes in reward systems* to reduce competition among individuals and groups for rewards.

   g) *Policies and procedures* may be used to direct behavior in appropriate ways.

G.   *Conflict Management Style*   **FIGURE 16.4**

ENHANCEMENT

To increase the relevance of *conflict management style* for students, assign the *Assessment* titled, **Conflict Management Styles**, from *Career Readiness Workbook*. It helps students gain some valuable personal insights about the ways in which they tend to manage conflict. Further discussion of this assessment is available in Unit 9 of this *Manual*.

1.   Conflict management varies along the **underlying dimensions** of:

    a)   <u>Cooperativeness</u> -- The desire to satisfy the other person's needs and concerns.

    b)   <u>Assertiveness</u> -- The desire to satisfy one's own needs and concerns.

2.   The various combinations of these dimensions result in the following **styles of conflict management:**

    a)   <u>Avoidance</u> -- Being uncooperative and unassertive; downplaying disagreement, withdrawing from the situation, and/or staying neutral at all costs.

    b)   <u>Accommodation or smoothing</u> -- Being cooperative but unassertive; letting the other's wishes rule; smoothing over differences to maintain superficial harmony.

    c)   <u>Competition or authoritative command</u> -- Being uncooperative but assertive; working against the wishes of the other party, fighting to dominate in win-lose competition, and/or forcing things to conclusion through the exercise of authority.

    d)   <u>Compromise</u> -- Being moderately cooperative and assertive, but not to either extreme; working toward partial satisfaction of everyone's concerns; bargaining or negotiating for "acceptable" solutions where each party wins a bit and loses a bit.

    e)   <u>Collaboration or problem solving</u> -- Being both cooperative and assertive; seeking true satisfaction of everyone's concerns by working through differences; finding and solving problems so everyone gains.

ENHANCEMENT

Note that each of the five **conflict management styles** has some value. For example, *avoidance* is appropriate when an issue is trivial or there is no chance of resolution. *Accommodation* has merit when issues are more important to others than yourself or when you realize you are wrong. Finally, *authoritative command* is useful in situations where quick, decisive action is vital.

     3.   **Lose-lose conflict** occurs when no one achieves his or her true desires, and the underlying reasons for conflict remain unaffected. This is common when conflict is managed by <u>avoidance</u> and <u>accommodation</u> or <u>smoothing</u>.

     4.   **Win-lose conflict** occurs when one party gains at another's expense, e.g., <u>competition</u> or <u>authoritative command</u> and <u>compromise</u>.

     5.   **Win-win conflict** is resolved to the mutual benefit of both parties, e.g., <u>collaboration</u> or <u>problem solving</u>.

V.   Communication and Negotiation

   A.   *Negotiation* is the process of making joint decisions when the parties involved have different preferences; that is, it is a way of reaching agreements when decisions involve more than one person or group.

   B.   *Issues people negotiate* include salary, merit raises and performance evaluations, job assignments, work schedules, work locations, etc.

   C.   *Negotiation Goals and Approaches*

     1.   **Substance goals** are concerned with outcomes; they are tied to the "content" issues of the negotiation.

     2.   **Relationship goals** are concerned with processes; they are tied to the way people work together while negotiating, and how they (and any constituencies they represent) will be able to work together again in the future.

     3.   **Effective negotiation** occurs when issues of substance are resolved *and* working relationships among the negotiating parties are maintained or even improved in the process.

4. **Three Criteria for Effective Negotiation**

   a) <u>Quality</u> -- Effective negotiation produces a "wise" agreement that is truly satisfactory to all sides.

   b) <u>Cost</u> -- Effective negotiation is "efficient;" it is no more time consuming or costly than absolutely necessary.

   c) <u>Harmony</u> -- Effective negotiation is "harmonious" and fosters, rather than inhibits, interpersonal relationships.

5. **Distributive negotiation** focuses on "claims" made by each party for certain preferred outcomes; such negotiations can become competitive and lead to "win-lose" outcomes.

6. **Principled negotiation** often called **integrative negotiation**, is based on a "win-win" orientation; the goal is to base the final outcome on the merits of individual claims, and to find a way for all claims to be satisfied.

D. *Gaining Integrative Agreements*

   1. **Four Rules for Integrative Agreements**

      a) Separate the people from the problem.
      b) Focus on interests, not on positions.
      c) Generate many alternatives before deciding what to do.
      d) Insist that results are based on some objective standard.

   2. The **attitudinal foundations of integrative agreements** involve each party approaching the negotiation with a willingness to trust, share information with, and ask reasonable questions of the other party.

   3. The **information foundations of integrative agreements** involve each party knowing:

      a) What is really important to each party; and
      b) His or her personal <u>Best Alternative To A Negotiated Agreement</u> (BATNA).

   4. **Figure 16.5** depicts a **classic two-party negotiation** for a typical case of labor-management negotiation.

      a) Note that both parties make "<u>initial offers</u>".

      b) The union negotiator has in mind a <u>minimum reservation point</u> -- the minimum wage she is willing to accept.

c)   Similarly, the management negotiator possesses a <u>maximum reservation point</u> -- the highest wage that he is prepared to eventually offer to the union.

5.   The **bargaining zone** in a classic two-party negotiation, is defined as the zone between one party's minimum reservation point and the other party's maximum reservation point.

a)   A "<u>positive</u>" <u>bargaining zone</u> exists whenever the reservation points of the two bargaining parties overlap.

b)   A "<u>negative</u>" <u>bargaining zone</u> exists when they do not.

E.   *Avoiding Negotiation Pitfalls*

1.   **Common Negotiation Pitfalls**

a)   Falling prey to the myth of the "fixed pie."
b)   Nonrational escalation of conflict.
c)   Overconfidence and ignoring others' needs.
d)   Too much "telling" and too little "hearing."

2.   **Approaches to Avoiding Negotiation Pitfalls**

a)   <u>Mediation</u> involves a neutral third party who tries to improve communication among negotiating parties and keep them focused on relevant issues.

b)   The <u>mediator</u> does not issue a ruling or make a decision, but can take an active role in discussions, such as making suggestions in an attempt to move the parties toward agreement.

c)   <u>Arbitration</u> is a still stronger form of dispute resolution which involves a neutral third party -- the <u>arbitrator</u> -- as a "judge" who issues a binding decision.

d)   Arbitration usually includes a <u>formal hearing</u> where the arbitrator listens to both sides and reviews all facets of the case in coming to a ruling.

e)   <u>Alternative dispute resolution</u> utilizes mediation and/or arbitration, but only after direct attempts to negotiate agreements among conflicting parties have failed; often an <u>ombudsperson</u>, or designated neutral third party, listens to complaints and disputes and plays a key role in the process.

F.   *Ethical Issues in Negotiation*

    1.   Managers, and other negotiators, should maintain **high ethical standards** when negotiating.

    2.   **Motives for Unethical Negotiation**

        a)   Overemphasis of the profit motive.
        b)   Competitive desire to "win" a negotiation.

    3.   While **acceptance** and **rationalizations of unethical negotiating behavior** can lead to **short-run gains, long-run losses** may also accrue as the other parties lose their trust in the negotiator or seek revenge.

CHAPTER 16 REVIEW

What is the communication process?
* Communication is the interpersonal process of sending and receiving symbols with messages attached to them.
* Effective communication occurs when the sender and the receiver of a message both interpret it in the same way; efficient communication occurs when the message is sent at low cost --- time and effort --- by the sender.
* Noise is anything that interferes with the effectiveness of communication; it occurs in the form of poor utilization of channels, poor written or oral expression, physical distractions, and status effects, among other possibilities.

How can communication be improved?
* Active listening, through reflecting back and paraphrasing, can help to overcome communication barriers.
* Upward communication may be improved through techniques such as MBWA, managing by wandering around, and by the use of structured meetings, suggestions systems, advisory councils, and the like.
* Space can be used and designed to improve communication in organizations.
* The appropriate use of information technology, such as E-mail and Intranets, can improve communication in organizations.

How does perception influence communication?
* Perception acts as a filter through which all communication passes as it travels from one person to the next.
* Because people tend to perceive things differently, the same message may be interpreted quite differently by different people.
* Attribution is the process of assigning explanations to events. Attribution theory identifies tendencies toward fundamental attribution errors when judging the performance of others and self-serving biases when judging the performance of ourselves.
* Common perceptual distortions that may reduce communication effectiveness include stereotypes, projections, halo effects, and selective perception.

How can managers deal positively with conflict?
* Conflict occurs as disagreements over substantive or emotional issues.
* Managers should support functional conflict that facilitates a high performance edge and creativity; they should avoid the harmful effects of too little or too much conflict that becomes dysfunctional.
* Conflict may be managed through structural approaches that involve changing people, goals, resources, or work arrangements.
* Personal conflict management "styles" include avoidance, accommodation, compromise, competition, and collaboration.
* True conflict resolution involves problem-solving through a collaborative approach.

How can managers negotiate agreements?

* Negotiation is the process of making decisions in situations in which the participants have different preferences.
* Both substance goals---concerned with outcomes, and relationship goals---concerned with processes, are important in successful negotiation.
* Effective negotiation occurs when issues of substance are resolved and good working relationships result.
* Distributive approaches to negotiation emphasize win-lose outcomes, and are usually harmful to relationships.
* Integrative approaches to negotiation emphasize win-win outcomes and the interests of all parties.

CHAPTER 16 KEY TERMS

Accommodation Playing down differences among conflicting parties and highlighting similarities and areas of agreement.

Active Listening The process of taking action to help the source of a message say exactly what he or she really means.

Arbitration The process by which parties to a dispute agree to abide by the decision of a neutral and independent third party called an arbitrator.

Attribution error Overestimating internal factors and underestimating external factors as influences on someone's behavior.

Authoritative command When a conflict victory is achieved through force, superior skill, or domination of one party by another.

Avoidance Pretending that a conflict doesn't really exist or hoping that a conflict will simply go away.

BATNA The "*best alternative to a negotiated agreement*," or what can be done if an agreement cannot be reached.

Collaboration Working through conflict differences and solving problems so everyone wins as a result.

Communication An interpersonal process of sending and receiving symbols with meanings attached to them.

Communication channel The medium through which a message is conveyed from sender to receiver.

Competition When a conflict victory is achieved through force, superior skill, or domination of one party by another.

Compromise When accommodations are made such that each party to the conflict gives up something of value to the other.

Conflict A disagreement over issues of substance and/or emotional antagonism.

Conflict resolution The removal of the reasons "substantial and/or emotional" for a conflict.

Distributive negotiation Negotiation that focuses on "claims" made by each party for certain preferred outcomes.

Dysfunctional conflict Conflict that works to the disadvantage of the individual(s) and/or organization(s) involved.

Effective communication Communication that occurs when the intended meaning of the source and the perceived meaning of the receiver are identical.

Efficient communication Communication that occurs at minimum cost in terms of resources expended.

Emotional conflict Conflict resulting from feelings of anger, distrusts, dislike, fear, and resentment, as well as from personality clashes.

Feedback The process of telling someone else how you feel about something that person did or said or about the situation in general.

Filtering The intentional distortion of information to make it appear most favorable to the recipient.

Functional conflict Conflict that results in benefits for the individual(s) and/or organization(s) involved.

Integrative negotiation A negotiation process that seeks a way for all claims to be satisfied if at all possible.

Halo Effect A perceptual bias that occurs when one attribute is used to develop an overall impression of a person or situation.

Lose-lose conflict When no one achieves his or her true desires and the underlying reasons for conflict remain unaffected.

Management by wandering around (MBWA) Dealing directly with subordinates by regularly walking around and talking with them about a variety of work-related matters.

Mediation When a neutral party engages in substantive discussions with conflicting parties in the hope that the dispute can be resolved.

Mixed message A barrier to communication that results when a person's words communicate one message while actions, body language, or appearance communicate something else.

Negotiation The process of making joint decisions when the parties involved have different preferences.

Noise Anything that interferes with the effectiveness of the communication process.

Nonverbal communication Communication that takes place through channels such as body language and the use of interpersonal space.

Perception The process through which people receive, organize, and interpret information from the environment.

Principled negotiation A negotiation process that seeks a way for all claims to be satisfied if at all possible.

Problem solving Working through conflict differences and solving problems so everyone wins as a result.

Projection The assignment of personal attributes to other individuals.

Proxemics The use of interpersonal space, such as in the process of interpersonal communication.

Selective perception The tendency to define problems from one's own point of view or to single out for attention things consistent with one's existing beliefs, values, or needs.

Self-serving bias The tendency for individuals tend to blame their personal failures or problems on external causes and attribute their successes to internal causes.

Smoothing Playing down differences among conflicting parties and highlighting similarities and areas of agreement.

Stereotype When an individual is assigned to a group or category and then the attributes commonly associates with the group or category are assigned to the individual in question.

Substantive conflict A disagreement over such things as goals, the allocation of resources, distribution of rewards, policies, and procedures, and job assignments.

360-degree feedback An upward communication approach that involves upward appraisals done by a manager's subordinates, as well as additional feedback from peers, internal and external customers, and higher-ups.

Win-lose conflict When one party achieves its desires at the expense and exclusion of the other party's desires.

Win-win conflict When conflict is resolved to the mutual benefit of all concerned parties.

CHAPTER 17: TEAMS AND TEAMWORK

CHAPTER 17 STUDY QUESTIONS

o   How do teams contribute to organizations?
o   Why are current directions in the use of teams?
o   How do teams work?
o   How do teams make decisions?
o   How can leaders build high performance teams?

CHAPTER 17 LEARNING OBJECTIVES

After completing this chapter, students should be able to:

1.   Define team and teamwork, and discuss the concept of synergy and usefulness of teams in organizations.
2.   Define social learning and discuss the things that can go wrong in teams.
3.   Explain the differences between formal and informal teams in organizations and provide examples of each.
4.   Identify and discuss current trends in the use of teams in organizations, including committees and task forces, cross-functional teams, employee involvement teams, and virtual teams
5.   Summarize the guidelines for managing a task force.
6.   Define self-managing team and discuss the characteristics of self-managing teams.
7.   Define the terms human resource maintenance, effective team, and group process and describe the team as an open system; identify and discuss specific inputs, throughputs and outputs of teams.
8.   Describe the five stages of team development.
9.   Define the terms norm and performance norm, and describe how managers can build positive norms.
10.   Define the term cohesiveness and explain how managers can increase team cohesiveness.
11.   Explain the interaction that occurs between performance norms and team cohesiveness and its effects on team performance.
12.   Define and provide examples of task activities, maintenance activities, and disruptive activities of team members; explain the concept of distributed leadership and its importance to team effectiveness.
13.   Identify and discuss alternative interaction patterns and communication networks in teams; explain the types of tasks for which particular networks are most appropriate.
14.   Describe various approaches whereby teams make decisions, and discuss the assets and liabilities of group decision making.
15.   Define "groupthink, describe its symptoms, and indicate what managers can do to deal with this phenomenon.
16.   Discuss specific techniques for group decision making that are designed to increase creativity.
17.   Discuss the purpose of team building and the steps involved in this process.
18.   Identify the characteristics of high performing teams and discuss the role which leadership plays in creating high performing teams.

CHAPTER 17 OVERVIEW

Work teams are an essential organizational resource that all members, and managers in particular, must understand in order to tap their full potential. The chapter begins by describing the concept of synergy and the usefulness of teams in organizations. Next, things that can go wrong in teams are discussed, followed by an examination of the distinction between formal teams and informal groups. Current trends in the use of teams in organizations, including committees and task forces, employee involvement teams, virtual teams, and self-managing work teams, are then discussed. The focus of the chapter subsequently shifts to developing an understanding of the foundations of team effectiveness. An open systems model of teams is presented and specific inputs, group processes, and the critical team outputs of task performance and human resource maintenance are explored. Next, the five stages of team development are described followed by a discussion of the impact of norms, cohesiveness, task and maintenance activities, and communication networks on team productivity. Decision making in teams, including various approaches to making decisions, assets and liabilities of group decision making, groupthink, and techniques for improving team creativity are then described. The chapter concludes by considering the importance of team building to the long-term survival and effectiveness of teams.

CHAPTER 17 LECTURE OUTLINE

Teaching Objective: To provide students with a basic understanding of team dynamics and their impact on organizational productivity.

Suggested Time: While three hours are recommended for presenting this chapter, the material can be presented in less time by using the open systems model of teams as a general framework for describing group processes.

Teams in Organizations
> Synergy and Usefulness of Teams
> What Can Go Wrong in Teams?
> Formal Work Teams
> Informal Teams

Trends in the Use of Teams
> Committees and Task Forces
> Cross-Functional Teams
> Employee Involvement Teams
> Virtual Teams
> Self-Managing Work Teams

How Teams Work
> Team Effectiveness
> Stages of Team Development
> Norms and Cohesiveness
> Task and Maintenance Needs
> Communication Networks

Decision Making in Teams
> How Teams Make Decisions
> Assets and Liabilities of Team Decisions
> Groupthink
> Creativity and Team Decision Making

Leadership and High Performance Teams
> The Team-Building Process
> Leadership Challenges

CHAPTER 17 SUPPORTING MATERIALS

Textbook Inserts

Headline: Teams are Worth the Hard Work
Margin Photos: Rockport Company, Telespan, Goodyear, Worhtington Industries
Embedded Box: American Express, Ford Motor Company, Motorola
Manager's Notepad 17.1: Guidelines for Managing a Task Force
Manager's Notepad 17.2: How to Avoid Groupthink

Multi-Media Resources

NBR Video Report:
Steinway (Available on Video Supplement & Video Cases CD-ROM)

PowerPoint Presentations (Website):
Figures 17.1 to Figure 17.7 from Textbook plus Supplemental Figures
NBR Viewing Questions: Steinway & Nucor

In-Class Activities

Cases for Critical Thinking (Career Readiness Workbook & Website):
Steinway (Primary Case)
Nucor (Alternate Case)

Exercises:
Work Team Dynamics (Career Readiness Workbook)
Lost at Sea (Career Readiness Workbook)

Research and Presentation Project:
Self-Managing Teams -- How Good Are They?(Career Readiness Workbook)
Virtual Teams -- Does Groupware Work?(Career Readiness Workbook)

Self-Test 17 (Textbook and Website)

CHAPTER 17 LECTURE NOTES

I.   Team in Organizations

ENHANCEMENT

A good way to introduce this chapter is to ask students how they feel about participating in teams. You will usually receive both highly positive and negative opinions. Students who have been members of successful athletic, social, extracurricular and/or work teams may have quite positive attitudes. Those with less favorable experiences, such as students who have encountered nonproductive work teams in their classes, may be more skeptical of the utility of teams. For these students, the quip "A camel is a horse designed by a committee" may ring true. Point out that despite their potential drawbacks, work teams are an essential organizational resource that all organizational members, and managers in particular, must understand in order to tap their full potential.

A.   A *team* is a collection of people who regularly interact to pursue common goals.

B.   *Teamwork* is the process of people actively working together to accomplish common goals.

C.   *Synergy and Usefulness of Teams*

1.   **Synergy** is the creation of a whole that is greater than the sum of its parts.

2.   **Team synergy** means that a team is using its membership resources to the fullest, and is achieving through collective performance far more than could be otherwise achieved.

ENHANCEMENT

Example of Team Synergy
The Rocky Hill, Connecticut office of Aetna Life uses 12-person teams to do all claims handling functions previously assigned to different departments. The team members manage their own work flow, do their own scheduling, divide up overtime, and evaluate one another's performance.

3. **How Teams Help Organizations**

   a) Increasing resources for problem solving.
   b) Fostering creativity and innovation.
   c) Improving quality of decision making.
   d) Enhancing members' commitments to tasks.
   e) Raising motivation through collective action.
   f) Helping control and discipline members.
   g) Satisfying individual needs as organizations grow in size.

D. *What Can Go Wrong in Teams?*

   1. **Social loafing** is the tendency of some people to avoid responsibility or engage in "free riding" in teams.

   2. **Common Problems in Teams**

      a) <u>Personality conflicts</u>: Individual differences in personality and work style can disrupt the team.

      b) <u>Task ambiguity</u>: Unclear agendas and/or ill-defined problems can cause teams to work too long on the wrong things.

      c) <u>Poor readiness to work</u>: Time can be wasted because meetings lack purpose and structure, and because members come unprepared.

      d) <u>Poor teamwork</u>: Failures in communication, conflict, and decision making may limit performance and/or hurt morale.

ENHANCEMENT

Discuss the **"Ringleman Effect,"** the theory that people may not work as hard in teams as they would have individually. Relate Ringleman's experiment in which people were asked to pull as hard as they could on a rope, first alone and then in a team; average productivity dropped as more people joined the rope pulling task. Ask the class why this might occur. Their answers should include the notion that an individual's contribution is less noticeable in a team, and that members may wish to see others carry the work load.

3. The first part of a manager's job in dealing with teams is to know **WHEN a team is the best choice** for applying human resources to a task.

4. The second is knowing **HOW to work with and manage the team** to best accomplish that task.

423

    D.   Formal Work Teams

ENHANCEMENT

An easy way to really get students involved in the following discussion of various types of organizational teams, is to ask them to identify as many different teams to which they belonged while working for a particular organization as possible. When you present the different types of **formal and informal groups** described below, you can ask students for examples of that type of group from the lists they generated. This exercise helps students relate to the material and recognize its relevance to their own experiences.

1.   **Formal teams** are officially designated by the organization, and may appear on organization charts; they are specifically created to perform tasks considered essential to the accomplishment of key operating objectives.

    a)   A <u>functional team</u> is a formal work unit consisting of a manager and his or her subordinates; it is a basic building block of organizations.

    b)   <u>Examples</u>: Functional teams are often called *departments* (e.g., market research department), *units* (e.g., product assembly team), or *divisions* (e.g., office products division).

    c)   **Figure 17.1** shows how organizations can be viewed as an <u>interlocking network of formal work teams</u>.

    d)   *Rensis Likert* identified an important "<u>linking pin</u>" role of managers who <u>vertically and horizontally link</u> organizational levels together, by acting as *superiors* at one level, while serving as *subordinates* who interact with their "boss" and "peers" at the next higher level.

2.   **Informal groups** are not officially created to serve an organizational purpose, and are not recognized on organization charts; they are part of the informal structure and flows of informal communications that emerge from "natural" or "spontaneous" relationships among people.

    a)   <u>Interest groups</u> are informal groups in which workers band together to advance a common cause or special position.

    b)   <u>Friendship groups</u> are informal groups that spontaneously develop within and across formal groups for a wide variety of personal reasons.

c) <u>Support groups</u> are informal groups in which the members basically help one another do their jobs.

3. **Potential Benefits of Informal Teams**

a) Informal teams offer a network of interpersonal relations that may actually <u>speed the work flow</u> or allow people to "<u>get things done</u>" in ways that may not be possible within the formal structure.

ENHANCEMENT

A study conducted at Xerox provides an excellent example of this **potential benefit of informal groups,** which you may want to share with your students. Consultant David Nadler concluded from his study at Xerox's Palo Alto, California, research center, that informal "storytelling" by workers "standing around the watercooler" and in other such settings helped improve task performance. Says Nadler: "Most managers would say those guys were wasting their time." But he claims they actually shared and swapped information on fixing copiers, and that this information was often better than what was being provided in official manuals. He suggested that Xerox should create more opportunities for spontaneous and informal meetings of this type.

Xerox seems to have followed that advice in its international business. Through its Global Account Marketing Strategy, account managers champion their international accounts to the firm, while representing Xerox to their clients. Roger Ford, the president of AlphaGraphics Printshops of the Future -- a Tuscon-based print and copy shop franchiser with some 300 U.S. and 50 foreign stores -- reports that his firm has capitalized on this strategy by welcoming Xerox's account manager, Mike Wagoner, as "an extension of our team." AlphaGraphics was so satisfied with the relationship that in a single year it replaced competitors' machines with Xerox equipment in 22 stores in Great Britain.

(Source: Thomas A. Stewart, "Brainpower," *Fortune,* June 3, 1991, pp. 44-60; *Annual Report,* 1990).

---

b) Informal groups also help to <u>satisfy the personal needs of members</u>, including social satisfactions, security, support and a sense of belonging.

II. **Trends in the Use of Teams**

A. *Committees and Task Forces*

1. **Committees** and **task forces** bring people together in teams to apply their collective efforts toward a specific purpose; both usually operate with specific task agendas and are headed by a designated chairperson or leader.

2. A **committee** usually operates with an ongoing purpose, and its membership may change over time even as the committee remains in existence.

3. A **task force**, by contrast, usually operates on a temporary basis; it has a very specific task and time frame, and disbands when the stated purpose has been accomplished.

4. **Guidelines for Managing Task Forces   MANAGER'S NOTEPAD 17.1**

    a) Select appropriate task-force members.
    b) Clearly define the purpose and goals of the task force.
    c) Carefully select a task-force leader.
    d) Periodically review progress.

B. *Cross-Functional Teams*

1. A **cross-functional team** is a team whose members come from different functional units and part of an organization.

2. Such teams are specifically created to **knock down the "walls"** separating departments within the firm; representation on a team might consist, for example, of engineers, buyers, assemblers, and shipping clerks.

3. Typically, members of a cross-functional team, task force or **committee come together to work on a specific problem** or task and to do so with the **needs of the whole organization in mind.**

C. *Employee Involvement Teams*

1. **Employee involvement teams** are groups of workers who meet on a regular basis outside their functional teams, and with the goal of applying their expertise and attention to important workplaces matters.

2. **Example:** Phillips Corporation, a building materials producer, uses employee involvement teams in a "How-can-we-save-money?" program. The five-member teams work together for a week to improve products and cut costs. Vice-president Bill Roberts says that all of the 150 teams created thus far have yielded savings.

3. **Quality circles** represent a common form of involvement team in which a small team of employees meet periodically to discuss ways of improving the quality of their performance.

ENHANCEMENT

AT&T's quality circles and management councils to illustrate how these teams can be used to promote innovation. AT&T Microelectronics in Reading supports two business units, each of which forms Quality Improvement Teams (QITs) as needed. Each QIT is empowered to work on a problem, find a solution, and implement it. They consist not only of engineering and management members, but also non-management members. In addition, new "management councils" have been formed to deal with manufacturing, quality, and human resources matters that cover both business units in the entire facility. The three councils report to a Leadership Council, which includes representatives from all parts of the Reading Works and is the overall decision making body.

Central to the Reading-style of participatory management are "quality circles" made up primarily of nonmanagement volunteers. Members meet once a week to identify, analyze, and solve any problems they perceive as hampering or restricting effective job performance. Operator Dottie Hanson, a quality circle member, says: "Before I got involved with the circle, if I noticed a problem I'd think, `That's wrong; why don't *they* fix it?' But now, working with the circle, I know there's no such thing as 1-2-3 and it's fixed. I've seen, first-hand, the dedication and work it takes to solve even the simplest problems. I have a lot of respect for the people in the quality circles and ... I also like the fact that, through the circle, management is saying that when it comes to doing my job, I'm the expert, and my ideas are valuable."

(Source: AT&T Magazine, Vol. 1, no. 2, 1985; *Business Week,* March 31, 1988, special advertising supplement; Emily T. Smith, "Why AT&T Is Dialing 1 800 Go Green," *Business Week,* October 25, 1991, p. 49).

D. *Virtual Teams*

1. **Virtual teams**, which are sometimes called, *computer-mediated groups,* or *electronic group networks,* are groups of people who interact through computer-based communications rather than face-to-face interactions.

    a) <u>Local-area networks</u> link computers and offices or buildings that are close to one another.

    b) <u>Wide-area networks</u> link computers across large geographic distances.

    c) <u>Example</u>: At Digital Equipment Corporation (DEC) employees use, Easynet, a WAN linking operations in 26 countries, to form teams which share information, help solve problems, and generally speed up operations.

    d) Some organizations use <u>electronic meeting rooms</u> where team members sit at computer terminals, are guided by special software -- or <u>groupware</u> and perhaps trained team facilitators, and address problems and seek consensus on how to deal with them.

e) <u>Example</u>: In two months of operation, Marriott's electronic meeting room was used by over 1000 people who identified over 10,000 ideas as they worked on problems via computer mediation.

ENHANCEMENT

Research on Virtual Teams

When team members engage in computer-mediated communications, many social context and nonverbal cues (e.g., status, gender, appearance, demeanor, facial expressions, eye contact, body movements) are filtered out. As a result, computer network users sometimes experience feelings of depersonalization and alienation. Thus, while there are many benefits of computer network teams, they can also produce some unintended and undesirable consequences.

(Source: Sara Kiesler, J. Siegel, & T. W. McGuire, "Social Psychological Aspects of Computer-Mediated Communication, *American Psychologist,* 1984, Volume 39, pp. 1123-1134).

E. *Self-Managing Work Teams*   **FIGURE 17.1**

1. **Self-managing work teams** or **autonomous work groups** are work teams whose members are empowered to perform many duties previously done by the supervisor.

2. The **"self-management"** responsibilities include planning and scheduling work, training members in various tasks, sharing tasks, ensuring quality, handling day-to-day operating problems and, in some cases, "hiring" and "firing" its members.

3. An elected or appointed **"team leader"** serves in the **linking-pin role,** and represents the team to the next level of management.

4. A true self-managing team emphasizes **participative decision making**, **shared tasks**, and **member responsibility** for many tasks performed by supervisors in more traditional work teams.

5. **Characteristics of Self-managing Teams**

a) Members are held collectively accountable for performance results.
b) Members have discretion in distributing tasks within the team.
c) Members have discretion in scheduling work within the team.
d) Members are able to perform more than one job on the team.
e) Members train one another to develop multiple job skills.

f) Members evaluate one another's performance contributions.

g) Members are responsible for the total quality of team products.

6. **Example:** At Colgate-Palmolive's Cambridge, Ohio, liquid detergent plant, self-managing work teams operate the entire production process -- empty bottle to finished shipping. The teams have output targets, and members decide among themselves on work assignments, schedules and production goals.

ENHANCEMENT

To provide students with more in-depth knowledge regarding the strengths and limitations of **self-managing teams**, assign the *Research Project* titled, **How Good are Self-Managing Teams?** from the *Career Readiness Workbook*. Further discussion of this assignment is provided in Unit 9 of this *Manual*.

III. **How Teams Work**

A. Two *key results* of any team are: a) *task performance*, and b) *human resource maintenance*.

B. *Human resource maintenance* is the ability of the team to maintain its social fabric and capabilities of its members to work well together over time.

C. *Team Effectiveness*   **FIGURE 17.2**

1. An **effective team** is defined as one that achieves and maintains high levels of *both* task performance *and* human resource maintenance.

2. **Figure 17.2** illustrates that any team may be viewed as an **open system** that *transforms* various *inputs* into *two key outputs*, *task performance* and *human resource maintenance* -- the ultimate *criteria of team effectiveness*.

3. **Group process** is the means through which multiple and varied resource inputs are combined and transformed into team outputs; it includes the ways in which members communicate with one another, make decisions, and handle conflicts.

ENHANCEMENT

If you have assigned group projects to your students, be sure to relate the **open systems model** to their group experiences. Throughout your discussion, ask students to indicate how the various group inputs (e.g., organization setting, nature of the task, size, membership characteristics) and processes (e.g., stages of group development, norms and cohesiveness, and task and maintenance activities) impacted on their group performance and human resource maintenance.

4. Important **team inputs** include the:

   a) <u>Organizational setting</u> -- resources, technology, structures and rewards.

   b) <u>Nature of the task</u> -- clarity and complexity.

   c) <u>Team size</u> -- number of members, even-odd members.

   d) <u>Membership characteristics</u> -- abilities, values and personalities.

D. *Stages of Team Development*

1. **Forming:** A stage of initial orientation and interpersonal testing.

   a) Members begin to identify with other members and the team itself.

   b) Members are concerned about getting acquainted, establishing relationships, identifying acceptable behavior, and learning how others perceive the task.

2. **Storming:** A stage of conflict over tasks and ways of operating as a team.

   a) Members may become highly emotional and subgroups form as tension over task and interpersonal concerns emerges.

   b) Task agendas become clarified, and members begin to clarify one another's interpersonal styles.

   c) Efforts are made to find ways to meet team goals while also satisfying individual needs.

3. **Norming:** A stage of consolidation around task and operating agendas.

   a) The team begins to become coordinated as a working unit, and tends to operate with shared rules of conduct.

   b) The team feels a sense of leadership, with each member starting to play useful roles.

   c) Harmony and cooperation are emphasized, but minority viewpoints may be discouraged.

   d) Members are likely to develop initial feelings of closeness, a division of labor, and a sense of shared expectations.

4. **Performing:** A stage of teamwork and focused task performance.

   a) The team becomes mature, organized and well-functioning.

   b) Members perform complex tasks and deal with conflict in creative ways.

   c) The team operates with a clear and stable structure, and members are motivated by team goals.

   d) **Figure 17.3** contrasts the <u>characteristics of mature versus less mature teams</u>.

5. **Adjourning:** A stage of task accomplishment and eventual disengagement.

   a) Members prepare for and eventually implement the team's disbandment.

   b) Adjourning is especially common for temporary teams that operate in the form of committees, task forces, and projects.

   c) Ideally, the team disbands with a sense that important goals have been accomplished.

E. *Norms and Cohesiveness*

   1. A **norm** is a behavior expected of team members; it is a "rule" or "standard" that guides the behavior of team members.

   2. Violations of norms may result in **team sanctions** such as reprimands or social ostracization.

3.　　A **performance norm** defines the level of work effort and performance that members are expected to contribute to the team task; it can be positive or negative.

Example: At Steelcase, Inc. a Michigan-based office furniture company, many workers are on "piecework" incentives. In some cases, team norms seem to go against the system. Says one worker, "There's an unspoken law. You don't turn in too much."

ENHANCEMENT

Ask students to provide examples of both **positive and negative team norms** for the following areas: organizational pride; performance; leadership; profitability; teamwork.

4.　　**How to Build Norms**

　　a)　Acting as a positive role model.
　　b)　Reinforcing the desired behaviors via rewards.
　　c)　Controlling results by performance reviews and feedback.
　　d)　Training and orienting new members to adopt desired behaviors.
　　e)　Recruiting and selecting new members who exhibit desired behaviors.
　　f)　Holding regular meetings to discuss group progress and ways of improving.
　　g)　Using group decision-making methods to reach agreement.

5.　　**Team cohesiveness** is the degree to which members are attracted to and motivated to remain part of a team.

6.　　Persons in **highly cohesive teams** tend to value membership and strive to maintain positive relations with other team members; they also tend to conform to norms as a result.

ENHANCEMENT

Discuss the sources of team cohesiveness, such as size; interdependency of tasks; homogeneity of members; and physical placement.

7.　　**Figure 17.4** illustrates the impact of various **combinations of team cohesiveness and performance norms on productivity**.

　　a)　<u>Positive norms in combination with high cohesiveness</u> leads to the <u>highest</u> level of team productivity.

　　b)　<u>Positive norms in combination with low cohesiveness</u> leads to a <u>moderate</u> level of team productivity.

    c)   <u>Negative norms in combination with low cohesiveness</u> leads to a <u>moderate to low level</u> of team productivity.

    d)   <u>Negative norms in combination with high cohesiveness</u> leads to the <u>lowest</u> level of team productivity.

8.   **How to Increase Team Cohesiveness**

    a)   Induce agreement on team goals.
    b)   Increase membership homogeneity.
    c)   Increase interactions among members.
    d)   Decrease team size.
    e)   Introduce competition with other teams.
    f)   Reward team rather than individual results.
    g)   Provide physical isolation from other teams.

9.   If a **highly cohesive team** is supporting **negative performance norms,** the manager may want to **decrease cohesion** by reversing the steps summarized above.

F.   *Task and Maintenance Needs*

1.   **Task activities** are actions by team members that contribute to the team's performance purpose. They include:
    a)   Initiating
    b)   Information sharing
    c)   Summarizing
    d)   Elaborating
    e)   Opinion giving

2.   **Maintenance activities** support the emotional life of the team as an ongoing social system. They include:
    a)   Gatekeeping
    b)   Encouraging
    c)   Following
    d)   Harmonizing
    e)   Reducing tension

3.   **Distributed leadership in group dynamics** makes every team member responsible for:

    a)   <u>Correctly recognizing</u> when task and/or maintenance activities are needed; and

    b)   <u>Responding appropriately</u> by providing or helping others to perform them.

4.   **Leading through team task activities** involves making an effort to define and solve problems and apply work efforts in support of task accomplishment.

5. **Leading through maintenance activities** helps strengthen and perpetuate the team as a social entity.

6. The **disruptive activities** of team members summarized in **Figure 17.5** and below detract from team effectiveness.
    a) Being aggressive.   f) Competing.
    b) Blocking.   g) Special pleading.
    c) Self-confessing.   h) Horsing around.
    d) Seeking sympathy.   i) Seeking recognition.
    e) Withdrawal.

7. Everyone shares in the responsibility for minimizing its occurrence and meeting the distributed leadership needs expressed in this equation:

Team results = Task Gains + Maintenance Gains - Self-serving losses

G. *Communication Networks*   **Figure 17.6**

1. **Figure 17.6** depicts three interaction patterns and communication networks that are common in teams.

2. A **decentralized network**, sometimes called an_all-channel network_ or _star_ communication structure, is a network in which all members communicate directly with one another; it is most appropriate when teams are interacting intensively and their members are working closely together on tasks.

3. A **centralized network**, sometimes called a _wheel_ or _chain_ communication structure, is a network in which activities are coordinated and results pooled by a central point of control; it is most appropriate when team members work on tasks independently with the required work being divided up among them.

4. A **restricted communication network** is one in which polarized subgroups contest one another and engage in sometimes antagonistic relations; communication between subgroups is often limited and biased, with the result that problems can easily occur.

5. In general, **centralized networks** seem to work better on **simple tasks** that require little creativity, information processing, and problem solving.

6. **Decentralized networks** work well for more complex tasks, where interacting groups do better, because they are able to support the more intense interactions and information sharing required.

IV. **Decision Making in Teams**

    A. *How Teams Make Decisions*

        1. In **decision by lack of response**, one idea after another is suggested without any discussion taking place. When the team finally accepts an idea, all others have been bypassed and discarded by simple lack of response rather than by critical evaluation.

        2. In **decision by authority rule**, the leader, manager, committee head, or some other authority figure makes a decision for the team.

        3. In **decision by minority rule,** two or three people are able to dominate or "railroad" the team into making a mutually agreeable decision.

        4. In **decision by majority rule**, formal voting may take place, or members may be polled to find the majority viewpoint; this is one of the most common ways teams make decisions.

        5. In **decision by consensus**, discussion leads to one alternative being favored by most members and the other members agreeing to support it; when consensus is reached, even persons who may have opposed the course of action know they have been heard and had an opportunity to influence the decision.

        6. In **decision by unanimity**, team members agree on the course of action to be taken; this may be the ideal state of affairs — it is the "logically perfect" method for decision making in teams, but it is also extremely difficult to attain.

    B. *Assets and Liabilities of Group Decisions*

        1. **Potential Assets of Team Decisions**

            a) Greater sum total of knowledge and information.
            b) Increased acceptance of the final decision.
            c) Better understanding of the final decision.

        2. **Potential Liabilities of Team Problem-solving**

            a) Social pressure to conform.
            b) Individual domination.
            c) Time requirements.

The *Exercise* titled, **Lost At Sea** which appears in the *Career Readiness Workbook*, can be used to demonstrate the challenges involved in achieving team consensus. A discussion of this exercise and an ideal solution to this exercise is included in in Unit 9 of this *Manual*.

F.   *Groupthink*

1.   **"Groupthink"** is a tendency for highly cohesive groups to lose their critical evaluative capabilities.

2.   Psychologist, *Irving Janis,* identified groupthink after studying **historical blunders** such as the Bay of Pigs incident, and U.S. involvement in Vietnam.

3.   **Symptoms of Groupthink**

   a)   Illusions of group invulnerability.
   b)   Rationalizing unpleasant of disconfirming data.
   c)   Belief in inherent group morality.
   d)   Stereotyping competitors as weak, evil, and stupid.
   e)   Applying direct pressure to deviants to conform to group wishes.
   f)   Self-censorship of members.
   g)   Illusions of unanimity.
   h)   Mind guarding.

4.   **How to Deal with Groupthink**   **MANAGER'S NOTEPAD 17.2**

   a)   Assign the role of critical evaluator to each group member; encourage a sharing of viewpoints.
   b)   Don't, as a leader, seem partial to one course of action; do absent yourself on occasion to allow free discussion.
   c)   Create subgroups to work on the same problems and then share their proposed solutions.
   d)   Invite outside experts to observe group activities and react to group processes and decisions.
   e)   Assign one member to play a "devil's advocate" role at each group meeting.
   f)   Hold a "second-chance" meeting after consensus is apparently achieved, to review the decision once again.

G.   *Creativity Team Decision Making*

1.   **Brainstorming** is a group technique for generating a large quantity of ideas by freewheeling contributions made without criticism.

2. **Rules for "Brainstorming" in Groups**

    a) All criticism is ruled out.
    b) "Freewheeling" is welcomed.
    c) Quantity is important.
    d) Building on one another's ideas is encouraged.

3. **Nominal group technique** is a group technique for generating ideas by following a structured format of individual response, group sharing without criticism, and written balloting.

4. **Steps in the Nominal Group Technique**

    a) Participants <u>work alone</u> and write out possible solutions to a stated problem.
    b) Ideas are then <u>read aloud</u> in a round-robin fashion *without* any criticism or discussion; all ideas are <u>recorded</u> on a flipchart or blackboard as they are read.
    c) Ideas are <u>discussed and clarified</u> in round-robin sequence, with no evaluative comments allowed.
    d) Members individually and silently follow a <u>written voting procedure</u> which allows for alternatives to be rated or ranked in priority order.
    e) The last two steps are <u>repeated as needed</u> to further clarify the process.

V. **Leadership and High Performance Teams**

    A. *Team-building* is a sequence of planned activities to gather and analyze data on the functioning of a team and implement constructive changes to increase its operating effectiveness.

    B. *The Team-Building Process*   **FIGURE 17.7**

        1. **Steps in the Team-building Process**
            a) <u>Step 1</u>: Problem awareness.
            b) <u>Step 2</u>: Data gathering.
            c) <u>Step 3</u>: Data analysis and diagnosis.
            d) <u>Step 4</u>: Action planning.
            e) <u>Step 5</u>: Action implementation.
            f) <u>Step 6</u>: Evaluation.

ENHANCEMENT

The hospital administration case included in the text provides an excellent example of the **team-building process** depicted in **Figure 17.7**. A quick overview of this case can serve to anchor your presentation of this process. Be sure to note that the top management team went through the following steps in this process:

Step 1: Problem awareness. The hospital president became aware that the team lacked cohesiveness and was not working well together.

Step 2: Data gathering. The consultant interviewed the president and other members of the team.

Step 3: Data analysis and diagnosis. The consultant and the hospital's top management went on a retreat to examine the data collected. They concluded that while the hospital's goals were understood by all, action priorities weren't clear. Interpersonal problems with two directors were also identified and attributed to friction between lower-level personnel.

Step 4: Action planning. The team decided to take action to clarify the hospital's mission and to identify priority objectives. The directors of the units experiencing inter-team problems agreed to work with the consultant, perhaps through a special retreat, to resolve the situation.

Step 5: Action implementation. The next step will be to carry out the plans developed in step 4.

Step 6: Evaluation. The hospital top management team agreed to a follow-up retreat to ensure that the problems identified are solved and to work toward continued team development.

2. The **data gathering** and **data analysis and diagnosis** steps are key elements of the team-building cycle.

    a) Structured and unstructured interviews, questionnaires, team meetings, and written records are some of the many <u>data collection approaches</u> that can be used.

    b) <u>Collaborative assessment</u> of this data is critical to team-building success.

C. *Leadership Challenges*

    1. To foster high performing teams, **effective team leaders** act to:

        a) Establish a clear vision.
        b) Create change.
        e) Unleash talent.

    2. **Characteristics of High Performing Teams**

        a) A clear and elevating goal.
        b) A task-driven, results-oriented structure.
        c) Competent and committed members who work hard.

d)   A collaborative climate.
e)   High standards of excellence.
f)   External support and recognition.
g)   Strong and principled leadership.

ENHANCEMENT

To increase the relevance of this material to students, assign the *Exercise* titled, **Work Team Dynamics** which is included in the *Career Readiness Workbook*. This exercise is likely to be especially meaningful to students if they are members of work teams in your class.   Further discussion of this exercise is provided in Unit 9 of this *Manual*.

CHAPTER 17 SUMMARY

What is the role of teams in organizations?

* A team is a collection of people who work together to accomplish a common goal.
* Organizations operate as interlocking networks of teams, which offer many benefits to the organizations and to their members.
* Teams help satisfy important needs for their members, providing various types of support and social satisfactions.
* Social loafing and other problems can limit the performance of teams.

What are current trends in the use of teams?

* Teams are important mechanisms of empowerment and participation in the workplace.
* Committees and task forces are increasingly being used to facilitate cross-functional relations and allow special projects to be completed with creativity.
* Cross-functional teams bring members together from different departments and help improve lateral relations and integration in organizations.
* Employee involvement teams, such as the quality circle, are also creating opportunities for employees to provide important insights into daily problem solving.
* New developments in information technology are also making virtual teams, or computer-mediated groups, more commonplace.
* Self-managing teams are changing organizations by allowing team members to perform for themselves many tasks previously reserved for their supervisors.

How do teams work?

* An effective team is one that achieves high levels of both task performance and human resource maintenance.
* Important team input factors include the organizational setting, nature of the task, size, and membership characteristics.
* A team matures through various stages of development, including forming, storming, norming, performing, and adjourning.
* Norms are the standards or rules of conduct that influence the behavior of members; cohesion is the attractiveness of the team to its members.
* In highly cohesive teams, members tend to conform to norms; the best situation for any manager is a team with positive performance norms and high cohesiveness.
* Distributed leadership in serving a team's task and maintenance needs helps in achieving long term effectiveness.
* Effective teams make use of alternative communication networks to best complete tasks.

How do teams make decisions?

* Teams can make decisions by lack of response, authority rule, minority rule, majority rule, consensus, and unanimity.
* The potential advantages of more team decision making include having more information available and generating more understanding and commitment.

* The potential liabilities to team decision making include social pressures to conform and greater time requirements.
* Groupthink is a tendency of members of highly cohesive teams to lose their critical evaluative capabilities and make poor decisions.
* Techniques for improving creativity in team decision making include brainstorming and the nominal group technique.

How can leaders build high performance teams?
* Team-building helps team members develop action plans for improving the way they work together and the results they accomplish.
* The team-building process should be data based and collaborative, involving a high level of participation by all team members.
* High-performance work teams have a clear and shared sense of purpose, as well as strong internal commitment to its accomplishment.

CHAPTER 17 KEY TERMS

Centralized communication network A network in which activities are coordinated and results pooled by a central point of control.

Cohesiveness The degree to which members are attracted to and motivated to remain part of a team.

Committee A formal group designated to work on a special task on a continuing basis.

Decentralized network A network in which all members communicate directly with one another.

Effective team A team that achieves and maintains high levels of both task performance and membership satisfaction over time.

Employee involvement team A team of employees that meets on a regular basis with the goal of applying members' expertise to solve problems and achieve continuous improvement.

Formal team A team created by the formal authority within the organization.

Functional team A formally designated work team consisting of a manager and subordinates.

Group dynamics Forces operating in groups that affect task performance and membership satisfaction.

Group process The way group members work together to accomplish tasks.

Groupthink A tendency for highly cohesive groups to lose their critical evaluative capabilities.

Human resource maintenance A team's ability to maintain its social fabric and capabilities of its members to work well together over time.

Informal group A group that is not officially created and emerges based on relationships and shared interests among members.

Maintenance activities Actions taken by team members that support the emotional life of the team as a social system.

Norm A behavior, rule, or standard expected to be followed by group members.

Quality circle A team of employees who meet periodically to discuss ways of improving the quality of their products or services.

Self-managing team Teams whose members are empowered to perform many duties previously done by the supervisor.

Social loafing The tendency of some people to avoid or engage in "free riding" in teams.

Synergy The creation of a whole that is greater than the sum of its individual parts.

Task activities Actions taken by team members that contribute directly to the team's performance purpose.

Taskforce A formal team convened for a specific purpose and expected to disband when that purpose is achieved.

Team A collection of people who regularly interact with one another over time and in respect to the pursuit of one or more common goals.

Team-building A sequence of planned activities to gather and analyze data on the functioning of a group and implement constructive changes to increase its operating effectiveness.

Teamwork The process of people working together in groups to accomplish common goals.

Virtual team A group of people who work together and solve problems through computer-based rather than face-to-face interactions.

CHAPTER 18: INNOVATION AND CHANGE MANAGEMENT

CHAPTER 18 STUDY QUESTIONS

o   What is the nature of innovation?
o   What are the challenges of organizational change?
o   How can planned organizational change be managed?
o   What is organization development?
o   How do you build career readiness in a change environment?

CHAPTER 18 LEARNING OBJECTIVES

After completing this chapter, students should be able to:

1.   Define the terms learning organization, creativity, and innovation and discuss their importance to organizations.
2.   Explain the innovation process, the characteristics of innovative organizations, and the critical innovation roles.
3.   Discuss the role of organizational change agent.
4.   Distinguish between planned and unplanned change and identify organizational forces and targets for change.
5.   List and explain the phases of the planned change process.
6.   Compare and contrast power bases, managerial behaviors, and advantages and disadvantages associated with alternative planned change strategies.
7.   Identify the major reasons why people resist change and discuss methods for dealing with such resistance.
8.   Present a general model of the organizational development (OD) process.
9.   Explain the action research foundations of organizational development and identify specific types of OD interventions.
10.   Discuss how one can build career readiness in a change environment.

CHAPTER 18 OVERVIEW

In dealing with innovation and organizational change, managers pursue the common goal of "constructive change." Indeed, it is important for managers to facilitate and manage change to insure organizational survival and growth. The benefits of such change are readily apparent from the chapter opener titled, **Innovation = Competitive Advantage**, which describes how Mitsubishi developed a new car that can travel 900 miles on a single tank of gas!

The chapter picks up on this theme by first considering the importance of creativity and innovation to organizational success. The innovation process and characteristics or innovative organizations are considered next. The focus then shifts to the manager's role as a change agent. A distinction between planned and unplanned change is made and forces and targets for organizational change are identified. Particular attention is devoted to the planned change process and strategies available to managers. Reasons why people often resist change and ways in which managers can deal with such resistance are also presented. Next, the chapter looks at the organizational development (OD) process, including its action research foundations and specific OD interventions. The chapter concludes with advice to students for building "the brand called 'you'"!

CHAPTER 18 LECTURE OUTLINE

Purpose: To familiarize students with the importance and means of managing innovation and change in organizations.

Suggested Time: Two hours of class time are recommended for presenting the material in this chapter.

The Nature of Innovation
    Creativity
    The Innovation Process
    Characteristics of Innovative Organizations

Challenges of Organizational Change
    Change Leadership
    Planned versus Unplanned Change
    Forces and Targets for Change

Managing Planned Change
    The Phases of Planned Change
    Choosing a Change Strategy
    Dealing with Resistance to Change
    Technological Change

Organization Development (OD)
    A General Model of OD
    Types of OD Interventions
    OD and Continuous Improvement

Change and Career Readiness
    Early Career Advice
    Building the Brand Called "You"

CHAPTER 18 SUPPORTING MATERIALS

Textbook Inserts

Headline: Innovation = Competitive Advantage
Margin Photos: Olympus Optical, Toro, Hyatt Hotels, Motorola, Clorox
Embedded Box: Rubbermaid, Mellon Bank
Manager's Notepad 18.1: Ten Ways to Increase Creativity
Manager's Notepad 18.2: Spotting Barriers to Innovation
Manager's Notepad 18.3: Why People May Resist Change

Multi-Media Resources

NBR Video Report:
     Disney/ABC (Available on Video Supplement & Video CD-ROM)

PowerPoint Presentations (Website):
     Figures 18.1 to 18.6 from Textbook plus Supplemental Figures
     NBR Viewing Questions: Disney/ABC & Boeing

In-Class Activities

Cases for Critical Thinking (Career Readiness Workbook & Website):
     Disney/ABC (Primary Case)
     Boeing (Alternative Case)

Exercises:
     Creative Solutions (Career Readiness Workbook)
     Force-Field Analysis (Career Readiness Workbook)

Assessments:
     Stress Self-Test (Career Readiness Workbook)

Self-Test 18 (Textbook and Website)

CHAPTER 18 LECTURE NOTES

I.   **Introduction**

    A.   A *learning organization* is one in which people, values, and systems support continuous change and improvement based upon the lessons of experience.

    B.   *Innovation* and *organizational change* are important topics because organizations and their managers must continually adapt to new situations if they are to survive and prosper over the long run.

ENHANCEMENT

Point out to students that the topics of **innovation**, **planned change** and **organizational development** (OD) share the underlying theme of "constructive change." That is, all three reflect a need to adapt to changing circumstances, be it through (a) creative innovations in which the organization serves as the impetus for change, (b) planned change efforts to respond to a performance gap, or (c) the comprehensive organizational change interventions which constitute OD.

II.   **The Nature of Innovation**

    A.   *Creativity*

        1.   **Creativity** involves the display or use of ingenuity and imagination to create a novel approach to things or a unique solution to a problem.

        2.   Creativity is very important to organizations struggling to meet the demands of a **complex, ever-changing environment.**

        3.   **Ten Ways to Increase Creativity**   **MANAGER'S NOTEPAD 18.1**

            a)   Look for more than one "right" answer or "one best way."
            b)   Avoid being too logical; let your thinking roam.
            c)   Challenge rules; ask "why"; don't settle for the status quo.
            d)   Ask "what if" questions.
            e)   Let ambiguity help you and others see things differently.
            f)   Don't be afraid of error; let trial and error be a path to success.
            g)   Take time to play and experiment; let them be paths to discovery.
            h)   Open up to other viewpoints and perspectives.
            i)   Support nonconformity; let differences exist.
            j)   Believe in creativity; make it a self-fulfilling prophecy.

B.   *The Innovation Process*

1.   **Innovation** is the process of creating new ideas and putting them in practice as part of the organization's normal operating procedures.

   a)   <u>Process innovations</u> result in better ways of doing things.

   b)   <u>Product innovations</u> result in the creation of new or improved goods and services.

   c)   *Innovation = Invention + Application*

   d)   <u>Invention</u> relates to the act of discovery and the development of new ideas.

   e)   <u>Application</u> deals with the utilization of inventions to take best advantage of their value.

ENHANCEMENT
___

To illustrate the value of *creativity and innovation* to organizations, share with students the classic story on the origins of "post-it" in the **3M Corporation**. To embellish the information provided, explain how Art Fry, a 3M employee got the idea for "post-it" notes while attempting to mark pages in his Sunday hymnal. He found that a light adhesive developed by a colleague, Spencer Silver, was perfect for the task. To this point, Spencer's adhesive had been considered a failure because it wasn't sticky enough. Even after the "post-it" application of the adhesive was identified, Fry had trouble getting the full support of management. To win them over, he distributed "post-it" notes throughout the company. Within a short-time, top executives were hooked on them. When market tests proved successful, the product received the green light. Ultimately, "post-it" notes became one of the five best selling office products in history. Innovations such as this are encouraged at 3M through formal practices such as "bootlegging" in which small groups of researchers and marketers work together to bring new products to market.

(Source: A Passion for Excellence, New York: Random House, 1985; *Breakthroughs!,* New York: Rawson Associates, 1986; Christopher Knowlton, "What Makes America Best, *Fortune,* March 28, 1988, pp. 40-54; Brian Dumaine, "Ability to Innovate," *Fortune,* January 29, 1990; pp. 43, 46; Steve Weiner, "A Hard Way to Make a Buck," *Forbes,* April 29, 1991, pp. 134-137; *The Economist,* November 30, 1991, pp. 70-72).
___

2.   **Four Steps in Product Innovation**

   a)   <u>Idea creation</u> - New knowledge forms around basic discoveries, extensions of existing understandings or spontaneous creativity made possible by individual ingenuity and communication with others.

b) <u>Initial experimentation</u> - Ideas are tested in concept through discussions with others; referrals to customers, clients, or technical experts; and/or in the form of prototypes or samples.

c) <u>Feasibility determination</u> - Practicality and financial value are examined in formal feasibility studies, which also identify potential costs, benefits, markets and/or applications.

d) <u>Final application</u> - A new product is finally commercialized or put on sale in the open market, or a new process is implemented as part of normal operating routines.

3. **Commercializing innovations** is the process of turning new ideas into products or processes that can make a difference in sales, profits, and/or costs; the entire process must be related to the needs of the organization and its marketplace.

4. **Example:** Sony Corporation's innovative engineers create an average of four new products per day, causing *Fortune* to call it "the most consistently inventive consumer electronics enterprise on the planet." For example, Sony's new "palmtop" is a computerized pocket secretary created by engineer Tomoshi Hirayama to help Japanese business people better manage their time. The palmtop took 2 years to develop and has been a smashing success.

C. *Characteristics of Innovative Organizations*

1. **The corporate strategy and culture support innovation**, e.g., 3M's "bootlegging" practice and acceptance of failures as a inevitable consequence of risk-taking behavior.

2. **The organization structure supports innovation**, e.g., firms use structures such as "skunkworks," intrapreneurial new ventures, and cross-functional R & D teams to promote innovation.

3. **The organization's staffing supports innovation.** Creative personnel are needed for such critical innovation roles as:

a) <u>Idea generators</u> -- People who create new insights from internal discovery or external awareness, or both.

b) <u>Information gatekeepers</u> -- People who serve as links between people and groups within the organization, and with external sources.

  c) <u>Product champions</u> -- People who advocate and push for change and innovation in general, and for the adoption of specific product or process ideas in particular.

  d) <u>Project managers</u> -- People who perform the technical functions needed to keep an innovative project on track with all needed resource support.

  e) <u>Leaders</u> -- People who encourage, sponsor, and coach to keep the values and goals in place, and the all-important psychic energies and commitments to innovation channeled in the right directions.

4. **Top management supports innovation.** Effective managers understand the innovation process, welcome differences of opinion, keep pressure on, and remove obstacles to success.

5. **Spotting Barriers to Innovation** **MANAGER'S NOTEPAD 18.2**

  a) Top management isolation.
  b) Intolerance of differences.
  c) Vested interests.
  d) Short time horizons.
  e) Narrow accounting practices.
  f) Overly rational thinking.
  h) Inappropriate incentives.
  i) Excessive bureaucracy.

III. Challenges of Organizational Change   FIGURE 18.2

 A. *Change Leadership*

  1. A **change agent** is a person or group taking responsibility for changing the existing pattern of behavior of another person or social system.

  2. **Figure 18.2** illustrates the process of **top-down change**, which is initiated and directed by top management; strategic and comprehensive changes typically follow this pattern.

  3. **Bottom-up change** may also occur in which initiatives for change come from lower levels and are supported by lower and middle level managers acting as change agents.

 B. *Planned versus Unplanned Change*

  1. **Planned change** happens as a result of specific efforts by a change agent to respond to a performance gap, i.e., a discrepancy between the desired and actual state of affairs.

2. **Unplanned change** occurs spontaneously or at random and without a change agent's attention (e.g., interpersonal conflict).

C. *Forces and Targets for Change*

1. **External forces for change** including the global economy and market competition, local economic conditions, government laws and regulations, technological developments, market trends, and social forces, can serve as the impetus for performance gaps and change in any of these areas.

2. **Internal forces for change** may arise from a change in another part of the organizational system; changes initiated in response to one or more of the external forces can often create the need for change in another part of the system.

3. **Organizational Targets for Planned Change**

a) <u>Tasks</u>: The nature of work as represented by organizational mission, objectives and strategy, and job designs for individuals and groups.

b) <u>People</u>: The attitudes and competencies of employees and the human resource systems that support them.

c) <u>Culture</u>: The value system for the organization as a whole, the norms guiding individual and group behavior.

d) <u>Technology</u>: The operations technology used to support job designs, arrange work flows, and integrate people and machines in systems.

e) <u>Structure</u>: The configuration of the organization as a complex system, including its bureaucratic features, and lines of authority and communications.

VI. **Managing Planned Change**

A. *The Phases of Planned Change*

1. **Figure 18.3** depicts **Lewin's three phases of planned change.**

a) <u>Unfreezing</u>: Preparing a system for change; creating a felt need for change. This is done by:

(1) Establishing a good relationship with the people involved.
(2) Helping others realize that present behaviors are not effective.
(3) Minimizing expressed resistance to change.

451

Example: At TJ International, CEO Walt Minnick waits until an economic downturn to introduce major changes in technology. Recently, he invested millions in a new milling process to more efficiently manufacture lumber products. He notes that it is much easier to experiment when there is idle machinery, than when production is at full capacity.

b)   Changing: Making actual changes in the system. This is done by:

(1)   Identifying new, more effective ways of behaving.
(2)   Choosing appropriate changes in tasks, people, culture, technology, and/or structure.
(3)   Taking action to put these changes into place.

c)   Refreezing: Stabilizing the system after change. This is done by:

(1)   Creating acceptance and continuity for the new behaviors.
(2)   Providing any necessary resource support.
(3)   Using performance-contingent rewards and positive reinforcement.

B.   Choosing a Change Strategy   **FIGURE 18.4**

1.   **Figure 18.4** compares and contrasts the **power bases, managerial behaviors**, and likely results associated with the following **planned change strategies**.

a)   A force-coercion strategy uses position power to create change by decree of formal authority.

b)   An empirical-rational strategy involves an attempt to bring about change through persuasion backed by special knowledge and rational argument.

c)   A shared power strategy (or normative-reeducative strategy) identifies or establishes values and assumptions from which support for a proposed change will naturally emerge.

C.   Dealing with Resistance to Change   **MANAGER'S NOTEPAD 18.3**

1.   **Why People May Resist Change**

a)   Fear of the unknown: Not understanding what is happening or why.

452

b)   <u>Disrupted habits</u>: Feeling upset when you can't follow the old ways of doing things.

c)   <u>Loss of confidence</u>: Feeling incapable of performing well under the new ways of doing things.

d)   <u>Loss of control</u>: Feeling that things are being done "to" you rather than "by" or "with" you.

e)   <u>Poor timing</u>: Feeling overwhelmed and that things are moving too fast.

f)   <u>Work overload</u>: Not having the energy, physical or psychic, to commit to the change.

g)   <u>Loss of face</u>: Feeling inadequate or humiliated because the "old" ways apparently weren't "good" ways.

h)   <u>Lack of purpose</u>: Not seeing any reason for the change and/or not understanding its benefits.

2.   **Six Ways to Deal with Resistance to Change**

a)   <u>Education and communication</u>: Using discussions, presentations, and demonstrations to educate people about a change.

b)   <u>Participation and involvement</u>: Allowing others to contribute ideas and help design and implement change.

c)   <u>Facilitation and support</u>: Providing encouragement and training, actively listening to problems and complaints, and helping overcome performance pressures.

d)   <u>Facilitation and agreement</u>: Offering incentives to actual or potential resistors; making trade-offs in exchange for assurance that the change will not be blocked.

e)   <u>Manipulation and co-optation</u>: Using covert attempts to influence others by providing information selectively and structuring events in favor of the desired change.

f)   <u>Explicit and implicit coercion</u>: Force people to accept change by threatening resistors with a variety of undesirable consequences if they do not go along as planned.

D.   *Technological Change*

    1.   Technological change brings special challenges; for the full advantages to be realized, **a good fit with work needs, practices and people** is requried.

    2.   Technological change may best be approached as an ongoing process that will inevitably require improvisation as things are being implemented.

V.   Organizational Development (OD)

A.   *Organizational development (OD) is the application of behavioral science knowledge in a systematic and long-range effort to improve organizational effectiveness.*

B.   *Goals of Organizational Development*

    1.   **Outcome goals of OD** seek to improve the performance of individuals, groups and the organization as a whole.

    2.   **Process goals of OD** seek to improve interpersonal relationships, communications and decision-making processes among members.

    3.   **OD = planned change PLUS.** The **plus** is the goal of developing the organization's capacity for self-renewal.

    4.   The **core values of OD** include improving the organization by:

        a)   <u>Freedom of choice</u>: OD believes in providing people with choices about matters affecting their work.

        b)   <u>Shared power</u>: OD believes in involving organizational members in participative problem-solving.

        c)   <u>Self-reliance</u>: OD believes in leaving people and systems capable of self-renewal and continued development.

C.   *A General Model of OD*   **FIGURE 18.5**

    1.   **Figure 18.5** depicts the following **general model of the OD and planned change process**:

        a)   <u>Establish a working relationship</u>: Create links with members of the client system.

        b)   <u>Diagnosis</u>: Gathering and analyzing data, setting change objectives.

     c)   <u>Intervention</u>: Taking collaborative action to implement desired changes.

     d)   <u>Evaluation</u>: Following up to reinforce and support change.

     e)   <u>Achieve a terminal relationship</u>: Withdraw to leave members of client system on their own.

ENHANCEMENT

To clarify the **OD process**, give the example of a small firm that was experiencing a performance gap. Management perceived the problem and hired a consultant, who interviewed key people and planned a problem-solving workshop. Participants in the workshop were coached on how to analyze data and determine appropriate action directions; they also received information on group process techniques. The consultant continued to meet periodically with the group to review progress and additional help was given when needed. The problem-solving workshops became an annual event for the firm.

    D.   *Action Research Foundations of OD*   **FIGURE 18.6**

    1.   **Action research** is a process of systematically collecting data on an organization, feeding it back to the members for more action planning, and evaluating results by collecting more data and repeating the process as necessary.

    2.   **Figure 18.6** illustrates the following steps in the **action research process**.

     a)   Perception of the problem.
     b)   Data gathering.
     c)   Data analysis and feedback.
     d)   Action planning.
     e)   Action implementation.
     f)   Evaluation and follow-up.

    E.   *Organization Development Interventions*

    1.   **OD Interventions** are activities initiated by consultants or managers in support of a comprehensive OD program.

    2.   **Individual Interventions**

     a)   Sensitivity training (T-groups).
     b)   Management training.
     c)   Role negotiations.
     d)   Job redesign.
     e)   Career planning.

3. **Team Interventions**

    a)   Team building.
    b)   Process consultation.
    c)   Intergroup team building.

ENHANCEMENT

Example of Team Building
Hundreds of organizations offer executive retreat programs for building teamwork and reinvigorating managers, with programs ranging from physical trials to cheerleading sessions and new age spiritualism.

(Source: "A Team Builder's Guide to the Galaxy," *Business Month*, March 1990, p. 66).

---

4. **Organization-wide Interventions**

    a)   Survey feedback.
    b)   Confrontation meeting.
    c)   Structural redesign.
    d)   Management by objectives.

VI. **Change and Career Readiness**

A.   *Early Career Advice*

    1.   The best early career advice returns to the same message: **"What happens is up to YOU!"** Don't let yourself down.

    2.   Begin building what Tom Peters calls, "A brand called 'YOU.'"

    3.   To do so, be prepared to step forward in a career and always:

        a)   Behave like an entrepreneur.
        b)   Seek feedback on your performance.
        c)   Set up your own mentoring systems.
        d)   Get comfortable with teamwork.
        e)   Take risks to gain experience and learn new skills.
        f)   Be a problem solver.
        g)   Keep your life in balance.

B.   *Building the Brand Called "YOU"*

    1.   Point out to students that the **career readiness workbook** is designed to help them begin the process of brand building.

    2.   A **career portfolio** documents academic and personal accomplishments for external review.

3.   The workbook is intended to help students to develop this portfolio.

4.   Urge students to use the insights, examples, and concepts from *Management 6/E* and their introductory management course as a strong foundation for life-long personal developments and career advancement.

CHAPTER 18 SUMMARY

How does creativity and innovation occur in organizations?
* A learning organization is one in which people, values, and systems support continuous change and improvement based upon the lessons of experience.
* Creativity, essential to a learning organization, is the use of ingenuity and imagination to uniquely solve problems.
* Innovation allows creative ideas to be turned into products and/or processes that benefit organizations and their customers.
* Product innovation involves idea creation, initial experimentation, feasibility determination, and final application.
* Highly innovative organizations tend to have supportive strategies, structures, staffing, and top management.
* The possible barriers to successful innovation in organizations include a lack of top management support, excessive bureaucracy, short time horizons, and vested interests.

What are the challenges of organizational change?
* A change agent is someone who takes leadership responsibility for helping to change the behavior of people and organizational systems.
* Managers should be able to spot change opportunities and lead the process of planned change in their areas of work responsibilities.
* Although organizational change may proceed with a top-down emphasis, inputs from all levels of responsibility are essential to achieve successful implementation.
* The many possible targets for change include organizational tasks, people, cultures, technologies, and structures.

How can planned change be managed?
* Lewin identified three phases of planned change: (1) unfreezing---preparing a system for change; (2) changing---making a change; and (3) refreezing---stabilizing the system with a new change in place.
* Good change agents understand the force--coercion, rational persuasion, and shared power change strategies, and they use these strategies well in appropriate circumstances.
* People resist change for a variety of reasons, including fear of the unknown and force of habit.
* Good change agents deal with resistance in a variety of ways, including education, participation, facilitation, manipulation, and coercion.

What is organization development?
* Organization development (OD) is a comprehensive approach to planned organization change that uses behavioral science principles to improve organizational effectiveness over the long term.
* OD has both outcome goals, with a focus on improved task accomplishment--and process goals, with a focus on improvements in the way people work together to accomplish important tasks.
* The OD process involves action research wherein people work together to collect and analyze data on system performance, and decide what actions to

take in order to improve things.
* OD interventions are structured activities used to help people work together to accomplish change; they may be implemented at the individual, group, and/or organizational levels.

How do you build career readiness in a change environment?
* What happens in your career is up to you; take responsibility for building and maintaining a competitive "brand called you."
* Take charge of your learning; create a career portfolio that documents at all times your career readiness by displaying critical skills and accomplishments.
* Use the insights, examples, and concepts from *Management 6/E* and your introductory management course as a strong foundation for life-long personal developments and career advancement.

CHAPTER 18 KEY TERMS

Action research A collaborative process of systematically collecting data on an organization, feeding it back for action planning, and evaluating results.

Career portfolio A document that summarizes an individual's academic and personal accomplishments for external review.

Change agent A person or group that takes leadership responsibility for changing the existing pattern of behavior of another person or social system.

Changing The central phase in the planned-change process in which the manager actually implements the change.

Creativity An application of ingenuity and imagination that results in a novel approach or unique solution to a problem.

Force-coercion strategy A planned change strategy which attempts to bring about change through formal authority and/or the use of rewards or punishments.

Innovation The process of taking a new idea and putting it into practice as part of the organization's normal operating routines.

Learning organization An organization in which people, values, and systems support continuous change and improvement based upon the lessons of experience.

OD interventions Structured activities initiated by consultants or managers that directly assist in a comprehensive organizational development program.

Organization development (OD) The application of behavioral science knowledge in a long-range effort to improve an organization's ability to cope with change in its external environment and increase its internal problem-solving capabilities.

Performance gap A discrepancy between the desired and actual status of performance affairs.

Planned change Change that occurs as a result of specific efforts in its behalf by a change agent.

Rational persuasion strategy A planned change strategy that attempts to bring about change through persuasion backed by special knowledge, empirical data, and rational argument.

Refreezing The final stage in the planned-change process during which the manager is concerned with stabilizing the change and creating the conditions for its long-term continuity.

Shared power strategy A participative change strategy that relies on involving others to examine values, needs, and goals in relationship to an issue at hand.

Unfreezing The initial phase in the planned-change process during which the manager prepares a situation for change.

Unplanned change Change that occurs spontaneously or at random and without a change agent's direction.

Unit 9

THE CAREER READINESS WORKBOOK: INSTRUCTOR'S NOTES

In this unit, we provide instructor's notes for the *Career Readiness Workbook* included in the text. The specific sections of this workbook for which instructional support is provided include:

Cases for Critical Thinking

Integrative Activities

   In Basket Exercise: Broadway Management Company

   Integrated Cross-Functional Case:
      Outback Steakhouse, Inc. -- Fueling the Fast-Growth Company

Exercises in Teamwork

Management Skills Assessment

Research and Presentation Projects

CASES FOR CRITICAL THINKING

ANSWERS TO REVIEW QUESTIONS FOR CASE 1
THE COCA-COLA: A GLOBAL PRESENCE

1. **What are the management functions performed by Mr. Goizueta, Mr. Hunter, and Mr. Ivester? How do their responsibilities differ?**

    Mr. Goizueta, the former chief executive officer (CEO), and Mr. Ivester, the chief operating officer (COO) are both top managers. They are responsible for planning the future directions of the company and for seeing that objectives are achieved. Their responsibility is to oversee the entire Coca-Cola Corporation.

    Mr. Hunter is also a top manager, since he is the head of all international operations. He reports to Mr. Ivester, the COO, but is accountable for operations in more than 195 countries, including many of the areas that Coke is counting on as sources of future growth and profits. Mr. Hunter started as a regional manager. This could be considered either top management or middle management. It is potentially a top management position, since he was responsible for a significant part of the organization, the Philippines. He had to pay attention to the external environment, as shown by his calling attention to the bottler's concentrating on its other products. He developed a plan to improve this situation. In his approach, Coke as the controlling partner in a joint venture with an anchor bottler, was used as the model for future international expansion in other regions. Students may see "regional manager" as a middle manager, because he reports to top management and oversees only one or a few work groups. However, in comparison with some of the examples of middle managers in Chapter 1, Mr. Hunter appears to have been in charge of a much larger operation, and to have had considerable authority. For example, he reported directly to Mr. Goizueta with his plan for the joint venture. This ambiguity between middle and top management may be due to the large size of Coca-Cola, compared with the chapter's examples.

    Mr. Goizueta is the only one who isn't both a supervisor and a subordinate. As CEO, he is the top level of management, and has no supervisors, except to the extent that he is appointed by the Board of Directors of the company and could be removed by them (the role of the Board of Directors is not explicitly discussed in the case). He is accountable to the Board for the actions of the entire company. All three are line managers and general (as opposed to functional) managers.

    Mr. Goizueta's job, as CEO, should involve primarily strategic planning and leading. Examples of leading include challenging Mr. Ivester to rejuvenate the Coke brand, giving Mr. Hunter the authority to develop a new form of partnership in the Philippines, and sharing his vision of the company's future direction by emphasizing the importance of international markets. The Chief Operating Officer, Mr. Ivester, is also involved in planning for the future directions of the company.

    However, as the person accountable for all operations of the company, he is somewhat more concerned with organizing than Mr. Goizueta (although Mr. Goizueta is quoted as saying "what I really do is allocate resources," which is a good description of the organizing function). This is illustrated in the discussion of rejuvenation of the Coke brand, where he selected a new head of marketing and formulated new guidelines for advertising (in this case, the possibility of different messages for different target markets of consumers). However, he still primarily served in a leadership role for this project, leaving the specific details to Sergio Zyman, his new head of marketing. Both men are concerned with results, and monitor brand success and per capita consumption, among other factors, but their concern is less with controlling than with watching for the need for further planning, resources, or leadership. Mr. Hunter's managerial roles are less fully described. As the head of international operations, he undoubtedly has planning and leading responsibilities. Organizing is also an important part of his job. He is ultimately responsible for all resources within his part of the company, which may involve decisions on how to allocate among new markets to be developed, which bottling companies to work in partnership with, etc. He also needs to monitor results and push for the achievement of goals, both aspects of controlling, since he is accountable for the success of the entire international operations. However, as a top manager, he is less likely to focus on control and more likely, like Mr. Ivester and Mr. Goizueta, to use it as an indicator of when changes need to be made in his other functions.

As the Philippines regional manager, controlling was clearly important, and led Mr. Hunter to recognize a performance problem with his leading bottler and to take corrective action. This is consistent with the chapter's conclusion that more time is spent on planning at higher levels and on controlling at lower levels of management. In this case, since "regional manager" is still a fairly high level position, the effort devoted to organizing may or may not be about the same. Although this question only called for students to consider managers' functions, they could also be asked to speculate on the roles played by the three Coke executives. All three are likely to perform interpersonal roles, particularly since all three are in the position of working with people outside of their work units. All three have informational roles, although these differ in content. Mr. Goizueta is the most concerned with gathering and analyzing information from the external environment. Mr. Ivester most likely is also involved in the analysis, and in sharing information with the rest of the organization. Mr. Hunter's role is a combination of the two - collecting and interpreting the external environments for his sphere of operations, and sharing information and setting the direction for his subordinates. All three have decisional roles, but again the types of their decisions will be somewhat different.

2. **Describe the changes in Coca-Cola's environment since Mr. Goizueta became CEO and after his death.**

In 1980, when Mr. Goizueta became CEO, competition in the U.S. market consisted primarily of arch-rival Pepsi Cola. Diet drinks were the fastest growing part of the market, and cola was the most preferred flavor. Coke was available in many foreign markets. It served these markets by selling its syrup or concentrate to independent bottlers, who added standard ingredients (these are not discussed in the case but are water and carbonation and, possibly, sweetener), bottled, marketed and distributed the products.

One important change in Coke's external environment was in consumers' preferences. Demand for diet drinks leveled off. Consumers began to drink other carbonated products, such as seltzers and flavored waters. They also began to drink more juices and teas. "All-natural" products also became more popular.

This change in consumer habits was partly due to new technology - not high-tech computerization, but the development of new types of single serving containers. This enabled a thirsty person to buy iced tea or cranapple drinks from the same distribution channels as sodas (including vending machines and convenience stores such as those at Rutgers University).

As a result, Coca-Cola had many new competitors in the U.S. market, which was already very well developed. It had to consider competitors far different from Pepsi, both national and regional, and with a variety of convenience drink products. By contrast, in 1980 neither Coke nor Pepsi was even concerned about competition from other soft drink companies. The rate of new product introductions was staggering by 1991 when 1800 new beverages were marketed, and even Pepsi was experimenting with new products such as Crystal Pepsi.

Globally, competition had also increased, although this was not discussed in the case. The case does talk about the growth in global markets. It appears that, although Diet Coke was the world's leading low calorie soda, its primary market was still highly concentrated in four English-speaking countries. 80% of sales came from 16 markets which represented only 20% of the world's population. Coke was less widely distributed in 1980, but this was not a primary concern, probably because of the rapid growth still occurring in the U.S. The chapter discusses several regions which are developing particularly rapidly, notably Asia and the Pacific Rim, central Europe, and Latin America. Africa may also represent a potential growth market for Coke products.

Diversity in the workplace was valued by society in 1980, but is even more of a consideration in the 1990's, as discussed in Chapter 1. The main forces of diversity mentioned in the Coca-Cola case are international, but this appears to have been a long-term strength, as Mr. Goizueta himself, CEO since 1980 and promoted from within the company, is a Cuban-American. Ethical and social responsibilities are not discussed in the case. However, one trend that students may identify is environmentalism and the strong importance of recycling now, compared with 1980. The trend to convenience and single serving containers is also a trend toward increased trash. Ask students what, if anything, competitors in the beverage industries have done to alleviate this concern.

3. **How has the Coca-Cola Company changed to adapt to its environment?**

Coca-Cola's purpose does not appear to have changed significantly since 1980. It was, and is, a large, global, and for-profit corporation, whose purpose is to provide beverages and juices for consumers worldwide. During the 1980's, it appears that the company tried to diversify, through the purchase of Columbia Pictures, but has since sold this operation and returned to concentrating on beverages and juices. The company continued to target Pepsi as its chief competitor, but was not always successful - as illustrated by New Coke. However, Diet Coke, introduced in the early 1980's, was very successful. In response to the slowdown in diet drinks in the early 1990's, Mr. Ivestar was charged with rejuvenating Diet Coke which had become the company's most important brand. Several changes were developed in response to this challenge, including new ways to make Coke products more convenient for customers to purchase. No new technologies of packaging were described, but the "fast lane merchandisers" and exclusive supplier relationships were designed to help Coke compete more effectively for the thirsty customer, particularly in the younger age group that had been attracted to alternative products.

Coke also began to develop and promote new products, in several categories. A sports drink, a lightly carbonated soda (to compete with the waters and seltzers) and Fruitopia mixed-fruit drinks were aimed directly at the growth in the alternative beverage market. The company acquired canned coffee and tea products through a joint venture with Nestle, a multinational firm.

The Coca-Cola Company also increased its emphasis on international markets. One of the first changes was taking a more active role in international bottling, marketing, and distribution by becoming the controlling partner in joint ventures with key bottlers. This gave Coke more control over how its products were promoted and sold. It also enabled Coke to enter new markets with a minimum of "cultural bias" because of its relationship with knowledgeable local businesses and its local workforce. Coke would start by identifying key population centers and retail channels and make its products available through them, while it looked for a strong local business partner. These companies, such as Coca-Cola Amatil and Ringnes, were also key partners in identifying new business opportunities such as Warsaw and other Eastern European markets. Coke actively anticipated the opening of new markets and was able to move rapidly, such as when Vietnam was reopened to U.S. companies.

Coca-Cola was already a diverse company when Mr. Goizueta became CEO in 1980. Diversity has been increased in upper management; the case names regional and area heads from Turkey and Ireland. The company appears to offer good opportunities for promotion from within, regardless of national origin (at least for men). This will continue to be important as the company receives more of its sales and profits from non-U.S. sources.

4. **Find 5 Internet sites discussing Coca-Cola or its competitors.**

Here are five pertinent internet sites that students may locate; of course, they may also identify many other relevant sites.

http://www.bevnet.com/" *Bev Net*
http://www.beverageworld.com/welcome.html *Beverage World*
http://www.7up.com/index.html *7 UP*
http://www.drmedia.com/tops.html *1995 Soft Drink Market Shares*
http://www.gds.co.za/klerksdorp/coca-cola/origin.html
    The Origin of Soft Drinks

ANSWERS TO REVIEW QUESTIONS FOR CASE 2
Saturn: A New Kind of Car

1.   **Describe the changes that G.M. is trying to implement at Saturn Corp.**

G.M. management is trying to change its management style from one of administrative policy based on rules and procedures to one based on democratic participation between employees and management. The company realized that the former organization structure, decision making style, and labor relations were not adequate to meet global competition. The quality of G.M. products was perceived by customers to be low relative to foreign auto makers. Moreover, management had come to the realization that the company was unable to develop new products as rapidly as Japanese manufacturers.

Management at G.M. had decided that a totally different type of organization was needed if the company were to survive in the long run. They decided that, since the firm needed to develop a new, low priced compact car, they would adopt a management and organizational style similar to the form described by Peters and Waterman. Ask students which of their eight attributes of performance excellence G.M. was using. They will most likely mention productivity through people, hands-on and value driven (because of the emphasis on quality and on cross-training, and because top management agreed to accept the financial consequences of Saturn's initially less-than-satisfactory performance), and a bias toward action (developing an entirely new form of organization in order to compete). The Saturn plant also illustrates simultaneous loose-tight properties (flexibility but under tight control, particularly of quality) and sticking to the knitting, or possibly returning to the knitting G.M.'s long-time ability to produce cars that Americans would demand.

General Motors top management was trying to get greater involvement of people at all levels. The organization, in an attempt to gain greater efficiency and quality in the production process, had instituted several changes in the decision making process during the development of the Saturn project. This included the development of group decision making processes with the formation of the "Group of 99" described in the case. A major change in the formation of this group was the inclusion of the United Auto Workers (UAW) as part of the planning team. This quickly led to the realization that good labor relations would be critical to the success of the Saturn project. This is akin to participative and human resources theories of management. It should be noted that the UAW workers are already highly paid and are probably longing for higher order needs in the Maslow hierarchy. This appears, at the time of the case, to have succeeded, since the quality of the new Saturn was perceived to be high, and the plant had recently gone to a third shift to increase production.

2.   **What are the critical factors in developing the management of the Saturn Corp. plants?**

The first critical factor is the involvement of the UAW in the decision process. Labor and management had traditionally taken on an adversarial relationship at G.M. There was little trust between the two groups. The UAW agreed to participate in this experiment to try to retain jobs and job security in the U.S. and among its members.

At the end of the case, G.M. management had to change the method by which Saturn hourly employees were paid, since the previously agreed upon plan would have left them receiving approximately 85% of what UAW members at other G.M. plants would normally receive on an annual basis. It is interesting to note that G.M. management felt compelled to do this despite the fact that Saturn employees had greater job and wage security than other G.M. hourly employees. Management felt that wage parity with other G.M. employees was important. This would prevent Saturn employees from feeling that this experiment was just another way of getting employees to work harder for less pay. Clearly, the trust issue and the human relations aspect of the new management procedures at G.M. felt to be critical to the success of the Saturn project.

Another critical factor is the ability of G.M. to be able to gain acceptance of the shared decision making process by first and second level supervisors and managers. For the kind of democratic management style involved at Saturn to be successful, these managers would have to change their methods. In the past, these low level managers operated under the administrative principle of clearly defined rules and regulations. Under the new model, rules were to be made by individual work units. Moreover, small groups could select their own leaders. They could also change the rules without having to go through contract negotiations with the union.

Workers were expected to be cross trained in several different tasks. This was designed to add flexibility in the production process. This required a better trained employee. It also required better trained and more responsible supervisory ranks. The supervisors would have to be able to understand the interaction required of the various tasks. They would now have to become more generalist in their supervisory approach, rather than be task specialists.

The changes G.M. has proposed for the Saturn organization, essentially, require different forms of training for both hourly workers and management and supervisory personnel. All need to be willing to work closely with each other. Trust in the participative process will be necessary for all concerned.

3. **What problems might G.M. management face in trying to transplant the Saturn concept to other G.M. units?**

The first potential problem is that the Saturn project might not succeed to the degree felt necessary by the Board of Directors to justify its use throughout the rest of the company. This is important, since this program requires a sizable commitment of resources for both new plant redesign as well as wage and job security guarantees. This kind of organizational change, from administrative to human relations and participative styles of management focusing on a total quality program, requires commitment from top management to succeed.

A major problem that will need to be overcome involves the suspicions of ardent and long time union members. The Saturn plants were staffed primarily with new employees; the case describes later hires as being transfers from closed G.M. plants. If your students do not have a lot of prior knowledge about unions, help them to realize that, while the original employees became union members upon starting work, many did not belong to the UAW prior to joining this G.M. project. Transforming existing plants will require the cooperation of older UAW members. This may be difficult since there is a great deal of distrust between both

467

management and labor. Previous changes have been viewed as means by which productivity was to be raised with no perceived benefit to labor, in either wages or job security.

Many employees, both hourly workers and supervisors, may feel threatened by these changes. Supervisors may not feel capable of developing participative or democratic styles of management, even with proper training. Some workers may be resistant to being required to cross train in several tasks. Moreover, they may also find it difficult to adapt to a democratic form of management. Some of the older workers, especially, have spent much of their working lives following clearly defined rules and roles. The open systems format developed for the Saturn plants may be quite threatening for these workers.

Changes of this nature require a great deal of time and financial resources. Organizations are not changed overnight. By 1994, the addition of a third shift indicates that the Saturn car is a success with customers. However, the initial investment has not yet been recovered. Although the product has been a success, it may be that the cost is too high to be worth attempting at other plants.

ANSWERS TO REVIEW QUESTIONS FOR CASE 3

Netscape: Taking on Goliath

1. **What was Netscape's impact on the Internet in particular, and the business community in general?**

   Netscape contributed in two fundamental ways to popularizing the Internet. First, it provided one of the first alternatives to Mosaic, one of the first Internet browsers. Mosaic was not user friendly and left the general user unable to make full use of the Internet and its many locations. Andreesson's choice to go to Illinois and recruit many of the developers of Mosaic turned out to be an excellent decision. While the World Wide Web and the Internet had been around for some time, it took Netscape's web browser to bring a critical mass of people online to popularize the Net.

   Secondly, Netscape pioneered downloading software over the Internet. This may actually be its more lasting legacy, as web downloads now dominate software distribution. In addition, all kinds of items are now distributed over the web, from music to graphics. E Commerce, expected to grow from $4 billion in 1997 to $120 billion in 10 years may revolutionize consumer behavior in the next decade.

   Microsoft, a pioneer in software development, was caught off guard by Netscape. Bill Gates did not take the Net seriously when Netscape first appeared on the scene. Only after they started to grow did Gates decide to move into Internet-related software in a large way. With Microsoft's huge resources, Gates was able to close the technology gap relatively quickly. It can be said without hesitation that Netscape's impact on business has been profound and lasting.

2. **Can Netscape survive as an independent entity?**

Many Internet-related firms have come and gone relatively quickly. They attract a lot of early capital as people rush into their Initial Public Offerings (IPOs), but once revenue realities set in, they tend to lose value. Netscape is an excellent example of this phenomenon, as its stock has fluctuated between $80 and $17, after debuting at $27 in 1995.

One difficulty with Internet firms is that their early success attracts imitators, imitators with deeper pockets and better capitalization. In its efforts to diversify its product offerings, Netscape is moving away from its innovative browser and into areas where other firms have greater technical knowledge. As Gates notes, these firms will lose money for long periods of time if necessary to attain adequate market share.

It becomes increasingly difficult for upstarts, even successful ones, to compete against firms such as Microsoft and Oracle with such deep pockets. The two Internet "blue-chip" name brands that have been successful include America Online and Yahoo, the search directory. Yahoo, in particular, has been very adept at developing brand recognition as a "portal" or entry point for web users. Advertisers pay Yahoo to list on their site, in addition to Yahoo receiving a share of commerce activities that originate on its location.

3. **Can Netscape continue by giving away its primary product?**

In response to Microsoft's continued erosion of Netscape's Communicator with its Microsoft Explorer browser, Netscape's reaction in late 1997 was to offer its browser free to users. This was not new to Netscape, as they had originally given away over 6 million copies of their browser, but this new strategy necessitates the evolution of Netscape into a "portal" location on the Net. Web users travel though "portals", so such sites are valuable to advertisers and web commerce.

Much of the difficulty with the Internet is the concept of "free" information. Many providers, such as CNNfn.com (http://cnnfn.com), Kelly Blue Book (http://kbb.com), and others now give away information for which they formerly charged. Advertisers and other providers usually provide the support for this "free" information. Netscape's Netcenter, its attempt at becoming a portal for Internet users, now becomes the primary source of revenue for the firm.

While Netscape's Communicator software propelled it into a major player on the Internet, the firm must "remake" itself to continue as an independent entity. It is highly possible that Netscape will end up in alliance or ownership by another player in the Web drama.

ANSWERS TO REVIEW QUESTIONS FOR CASE 4

Harley-Davidson: The Harley Way of Life

1. **Describe Harley-Davidson's international business strategy. Would you consider Harley to be a multinational corporation?**

   Harley's approach to international business can be described as a market entry strategy, rather than a direct investment strategy. Harley organizes promotional activities such as its European H.O.G., and has learned the value of customizing ads and promotional activities for local markets. Despite substantial sales abroad, the company has made very little investment in foreign facilities, only buying a Japanese distribution center and building a parts warehouse to serve foreign dealers. Its approach is to export from its U.S. plants to meet foreign demand. It also uses franchising. It has an extensive series of franchise dealers, who are independent business people in their own countries. It does not plan to manufacture abroad, since the company feels that the American image is an important part of the motorcycles' appeal.

   Harley is definitely not a multinational corporation. Its strategy is not world-wide in scope. Foreign demand is high and foreign sales contribute extensively to revenues, but the company produces only in the U.S., and has put a limit on overseas sales in order to provide more motorcycles for the U.S. market.

2. **If you were Harley's top management, in which regions of the world would you consider expanding?**

   Demand for Harleys is growing rapidly in Japan, and European dealers are also eager for more bikes to sell. Both of these markets could be very attractive for Harley's top management. The European Community now represents the world's largest market. It has many potential customers who can afford the $25,000 or more for a Harley bike. Motorcycles may also be an efficient form of transportation, being quick and able to handle crowded streets, as well as highways and mountains. Harley does not want to produce overseas, as stated by Mr. Teerlink; however, the text points out that EC companies may improve their positions relative to foreign competitors (not in the text: there may be barriers to entry, such as tariffs or quotas, for non-EC companies). Harley may eventually feel that it has to produce, or at least assemble, in Europe to stay competitive in the European market. Its history of concern for quality should mean that ISO 9000 certification would not be too big a problem.

   Japan represents another potential growth market for Harley. Again, motorcycles may be an efficient form of transportation, and there are a large number of potential customers with enough income for a Harley. Producing in Japan would probably be very expensive, however. Several other Asian countries present potential market opportunities - in particular South Korea and Taiwan. Harley should watch Malaysia, Thailand, Indonesia, and the Philippines. Each of these countries is a very large market, although as yet there may not be a large pool of interested customers with sufficient incomes. The "piece of the American dream" image is an advantage, but also potentially a drawback, if anti-American attitudes re-emerge in these, or any other foreign markets. China, at the present time, probably does not present many opportunities for Harley, as incomes are still relatively low, and the text implies that it is easier to sell there if you manufacture there. If Harley chooses to manufacture in Asia, to serve the potentially huge Pacific Rim markets and take advantage of low wage workers, it would do better to pick a country with fewer political issues.

Eastern Europe is easily reached from the EC, both by distributors and media, and represents a potential market. However, the number of customers per country is still relatively small. Harley could reach these people by encouraging its nearest dealers to export.

Africa and Latin America also have potential, but as yet, relatively few potential customers per country. Latin America has higher average incomes, and is providing a welcoming environment, according to the text. It will certainly become a market opportunity if an agreement similar to NAFTA is reached among Latin American countries. South Africa, now that it has been re-integrated into the world's economy, is growing and relatively affluent, and could probably support Harley dealerships. However, most other African countries do not have enough potential customers.

However, despite the potentials, Harley has given no indication that it wants to expand production, let alone overseas. If the company does not expand capacity, it does not need to consider new markets. If it does expand production, it would be simplest to do so in the U.S., as discussed in question 3, and where there is still more demand than the company can supply.

3. **Evaluate Harley-Davidson's decision not to produce overseas. What would be the advantages of overseas production? What problems might the company encounter if it does manufacture abroad?**

Overseas production, particularly in a country which is a member of the European Community, would enable Harley to expand output and meet European demand. Choice of an EC country would eliminate barriers and tariffs on bikes sold within Europe. Delivery time might be quicker and parts would be more readily available. Producing in Japan would have similar advantages for selling in the Japanese market, and would be a base from which to export to the Pacific rim. Production in Latin America or Africa would perhaps be lower-cost, but the market for Harleys is not well developed and the company would have substantial transportation costs to reach areas of current demand.

The problems that Harley would most likely encounter if it produced abroad include quality and costs. The European Community and Japan both have relatively high labor cost, and access to land and investment capital may also be similar to the U.S. In lower labor cost areas in Southeast Asia, Africa, and Latin America, the skill level may not be high enough, without extensive worker training. The company also has little expertise in operating abroad. It would most likely have to find joint venture partners who understand the local environment, including laws, labor markets, and economic differences.

Harley has chosen to produce only in the U.S. This is essential for the culture it has created, including the emphasis that both company and employees place on quality. It would be difficult to reproduce this culture in another location, possibly even within the U.S. and

471

particularly in another environment. Quality is very important to the company, and might be more difficult to maintain if Harley operated additional plants, particularly at a distance; a foreign culture would make this more difficult. Also, part of Harley's appeal may be its limited availability - a large increase in production, at any location, might have an adverse impact on demand.

ANSWERS TO REVIEW QUESTIONS FOR CASE 5

Eastman Kodak: A Company in Transition

1. **What strategy has Kodak adopted to enter the global arena?**

   Kodak has relied strongly on its brand image, with its yellow box of film recognized the world over. As the leading producer of film products, Kodak long enjoyed a virtual monopoly in film and film processing. With its simple, low-cost cameras in the 1970s, Kodak concentrated on expanding film usage among consumers. At the beginning, they were highly successful, marketing their products around the world. Kodak primarily produces their product in their home country of the United States and exports overseas.

   Difficulties arose in two areas. First, Fuji from Japan has grown to be a formidable competitor in film products. Fuji enjoys a 30% advantage in costs compared to Kodak, so they can offer their film at a lower price. At the 1997 Stockholders meeting, all the photographers taking pictures at Kodak's meeting were using Fuji film in their cameras. Fuji has been extremely aggressive in battling Kodak for market share in the United States market, Kodak's home territory.

   Secondly, due to changes in technology, Kodak has been forced to enter an arena that is less familiar to it - digital cameras. Such devices require a deep knowledge of optics and computer chips, areas that are relatively new to Kodak. In addition, it forces Kodak to confront an entirely new set of competitors, such as Canon and Sony, that have not historically competed with Kodak in film. Ironically, digital cameras do not need the one item that Kodak has historically excelled at - film.

2. **How has Kodak reacted to their global competition?**

   Kodak has been slow to react to changes in global competition. They filed a complaint with the World Trade Organization regarding barriers in Japanese markets for film, claiming that these barriers allowed Fuji to enjoy an unfair advantage in its home market. In late 1977, the WTO ruled that Kodak was not being harmed by any such barriers. This result has forced Kodak to rethink its strategy of competing with Fuji.

   Fisher was specifically brought in from Motorola to help re-establish Kodak as the dominant player in its market. While the formula Fisher used at Motorola was most successful, he has been far less successful at Kodak. He has resisted large cost-cutting moves until recently in early 1998. Kodak retains its large, bloated bureaucracy that raises costs and lowers decision making speed. Such an organizational structure worked well when Kodak dominated the film industry, but works to their disadvantage now that the marketplace is more dynamic.

Fisher has received some sharp criticism for being slow to inject cost cuts into Kodak's system. The old culture of decision by committees and protected employment does not work in the new marketplace. It does appear that Fisher is finally making the harder decisions to reduce workforce numbers and improve margins on film. It remains to be seen if he can turn Kodak into a dominant player in the digital arena.

3. **An October 20, 1997 Business Week cover story asked the question: Can George Fisher Fix Kodak? How would you respond to that question?**

    From a high of $94, Kodak stock price dropped to $63 by late 1997. Wall Street has finally taken notice of Kodak's bloated bureaucracy and high costs. Much of Fisher's problem appears to be in a paternalistic, with a mind-set left over from an earlier manufacturing age. Kodak's original intention was to use profits from the mature film industry to enter younger, more high-growth markets. The company tried everything from drugs to copiers with little success.

    Fisher arrived and announced that Kodak would become a digital company, moving from film to imaging as its engine of growth. The question becomes, can Fisher move Kodak into an arena that requires a blistering pace for innovation and change? Can he remake Kodak's culture into one that fosters initiative and risk?

ANSWERS TO REVIEW QUESTIONS FOR CASE 6

Tom's of Maine: Not Your Average Toothpaste

1. **Which way of thinking about ethical behavior best describes Tom's of Maine and its founder, Tom Chappell?**

    Tom's of Maine has a strong code of moral principles that set standards of appropriate behavior for its employees. Although not specifically mentioned in the case, this most likely includes obeying legal requirements, but numerous examples show that it goes beyond mere adherence to the law.

    The best fit with the chapter's views of ethical behavior is with the Moral-rights view. The company's mission statement talks about respect for employees and the need for meaningful work and fair pay. It is also concerned with the quality of their work life, through such programs as flexible scheduling, subsidized day care, individual assistance in education and training, and even healthy snacks. The emphasis on voluntary volunteer work could be seen as an extension of workers' right to feel that they are making a meaningful contribution to society. The company takes its philosophy a step further, believing that customers also have rights - to a high quality, effective product (the recall of honeysuckle deodorant may be used as an example: it didn't hurt anyone, and it worked for half the customers, but the company felt that this was not sufficient, despite the costs and potential negative publicity of a recall).

Students may also advocate the Utilitarian view. Tom's is providing the greatest good for the greatest number of people. Its concern is not necessarily for current profits (the financial good of the owners). It is willing to provide support services for employees which may or may not be paid for by improved productivity. In particular, the volunteer program had no direct link with improving revenues or productivity, but did have substantial costs (20 employee-days/month, as well as the position of Vice President for Community Life). The company also looks at benefits to customers, and to the physical environment (which affects us all) in developing its products. The "good" to a variety of stakeholders is considered.

Tom Chappell can be seen as having the Individualism view of ethical behavior, both for himself and for his company. He takes the long-term view of what's best for the company, as in the case of the product recall - an ineffective product does no harm in the short run, but potentially could affect consumers' views of other new products as ineffective. Neither Tom nor the company is following a pecuniary ethic, although most of the time his ideas are very successful and do make money for the company. He sees his long-term self-interest as succeeding in business without compromising his principles. The company also takes a long-term view. It, however, is concerned with being a good citizen of society rather than with more typical corporate behavior of self-interest.

There is not much evidence in the case on the Justice view of ethical behavior, particularly in an employee justice sense. The company does not, in fact, practice distributive justice. People with different needs are treated differently - given individualized help in getting their high school equivalency, provided with subsidized daycare (probably of little benefit to a 50-year-old employee), encouraged to take paid time to volunteer if, and only if, they desired. The company probably does display procedural justice, fair administration of policies and rules, but there are no specifics in the case to back this up.

Although discussed above under the individualism ethic, students may argue that Tom Chappell's personal view is either based on moral rights or is utilitarian, for reasons very similar to the arguments concerning the company's views.

2. **What potential dilemma did Tom Chappell face in the mid-1980's?**

Tom did not face an issue of "right or wrong", "legal or illegal." However, he did face a situation which forced him to decide between two courses of action or sets of values. On the one side was the company's growth potential. Sales had been increasing 16% yearly in the early 1980's. Tom could continue to "grow" the company, to achieve more market share and profits. He was actively thinking about expanding into new regions of the country, and potentially into channels in addition to health-food stores. He had even hired a marketing team with the necessary experience.

On the other side were Tom's own feelings. He was providing environmentally friendly products, and had proved that he could succeed as a business person. However, he was increasingly unhappy, and felt that growth and making money were not enough for him, personally. He wanted to do more with his life than make money. From his later actions (after Divinity school), we can infer that he wanted to be able to do business according to his values and to have a socially responsible impact on society.

As of 1986, Tom and his company had not done anything unethical. The pivotal event was the baking soda toothpaste, which was very unlike other companies' products. It fit the company's product line of all natural ingredients, and students will probably know that baking soda was known to be effective in cleaning teeth (the product's benefits are not described in the case, but have been advertised by competitors in the early 1990's). However, his marketing manager was concerned that it would not be a commercial success. Tom realized that, for his company, commercial success was becoming more important than the benefits of the product. Since he was the company's founder, and CEO, he may have been afraid that his own values were changing also. Using the engineering manager's definition from Chapter 5 ("I define an unethical situation as one in which I have to do something I don't feel good about"), Tom was faced with an ethical dilemma between the company's growth and his personal values.

3. **How important were Tom Chappell's personal views in helping Tom's of Maine to be successful?**

Tom's personal views formed the basis of the company's product line. His (and his wife's) concern for effective, natural, environmentally friendly products created the rapid growth of the 1970's and 80's. These views of the company's product line have continued to the present, as evidenced by their inclusion in the mission statement.

Tom's time at the Harvard Divinity School did not appear to change his personal values, but did enable him to express them in ways that could be communicated more effectively to his employees. The mission statement for Tom's of Maine was a formal document which the company's responsibilities to its employees, customers, owners, and the community and world. It serves as a formal code of ethics. It is consistent with the information about the company's behavior prior to 1986. It is also consistent with Tom's personal concern for succeeding as a business, by operating according to his principles. There are several quotes in the second half of the case that students may cite as evidence that he understands the business implications of his (and the company's) decisions, but would rather have a smaller group of customers that appreciate the benefits to themselves and society, instead of changing his product or marketing to reach a wider market.

Tom, and his top management, also lead by example. His business decisions, as discussed above, reflect both his personal values and the company's mission statement. As CEO, he has created a position at the top level of the company (vice president) to coordinate and develop Tom's of Maine's role in the outside community. He and top management also set examples for employees: by corporate donations, by decorating with products of volunteer activities (the totem pole), and by providing tangible benefits designed to meet employees' needs. They set an example also with the joint CVS promotion - with the message that something can be good for business and good for the community. As the company begins to compete nation-wide and in distribution channels used by the major personal care products companies, Tom's values for success are also going to be important.

ANSWERS TO REVIEW QUESTIONS FOR CASE 7

Wal-Mart: Always the Low Price

1. **Who are Wal Mart's major external stakeholders?**

   Students may find this question difficult to answer. They may even wonder why it is being asked. A strategic constituencies analysis is critical to understanding Wal Mart's success, since the firm has based its strategy on an analysis of the external environment and on developing ways to meet the needs of its external stakeholders, or overcoming their threats.

   The first, and most obvious, stakeholder is the customer base. Sam Walton realized early on that there was a group of customers that felt that they were being ignored by large and small retailers alike. These were the middle class customers who desired high quality and good service, all at a low price. Wal Mart has followed a focused strategy of providing those factors to its customers. Among other factors, Wal Mart decided that it had to follow a business strategy to meet customer needs. This included cost leadership, differentiation and technological development. More will be said about each of these in the following responses.

   A second group of external stakeholders was comprised of suppliers. Wal Mart knew that without the full cooperation of this critical group, the success of its strategy was questionable. Wal Mart decided early on that it would work closely with a small number of suppliers for each of its needs. Wal Mart buyers became expert at understanding the technical demands of their suppliers. They also became highly skilled negotiators. Wal Mart buyers looked for the lowest possible cost, but not at the expense of quality or on time delivery. Moreover, in line with the knowledge of the values of their middle class customers, Wal Mart buyers sought out American suppliers of as many of the products as possible. In this manner, company management was following a strategy that integrated its mission, corporate objectives and values, and actions. This was done in a manner that met customer needs and overcame competitive threats.

   Competitors became another set of stakeholders. Wal Mart realized that it needed to somehow differentiate itself from a variety of competitors to be successful. Wal Mart management felt that nation-wide retail chains such as Sears, and J.C. Penney's were alienating their traditional customer base. This left the field wide open to discounters like KMart and Target. Wal Mart felt that the growth potential was available for another major player. Moreover, it saw that potential as greatest in smaller towns and cities where the market was now being served by small specialty retailers who provided quality and service but at a relatively high price. This group of competitor stakeholders, therefore, presents both threats and opportunities in the environment. Competition was also intensifying in the warehouse club market, where smaller competitors were merging and moving into many of Sam's Wholesale Club's markets.

   The local communities have also become important stakeholders. Increasingly, Wal-Mart is meeting resistance, and has even been forced to change its plans to locate in several new markets. This resistance will add to the cost of opening new stores. It will also make the company's growth goals more difficult to achieve.

2. Do a SWOT analysis of Wal Mart. What are the company's distinctive competencies?

The company has a clear strength in its dominance of its market. Not only is it the top selling retailer in the United States, as of 1994, but it is dominant in most of the regions in which it operates. This has developed as a result of many of the policies noted above. These have led to high customer loyalty for Wal Mart.

Management at the company has taken the lead in developing a strong information network linking all its stores, warehouses, and even many of its suppliers with its headquarters in Arkansas. This allows the firm to maintain a minimum level of inventory and follow something quite close to just in time supplier inventory management. This also has helped the firm keep track of sales in the regions in which it operates, allowing the firm to react rapidly to changing demand patterns. All of this allows the firm to maintain sales growth while keeping costs and financial needs low.

Wal Mart maintains a relatively low management staff at its headquarters. Moreover, headquarters was maintained in Arkansas. Both of these factors lead to a relatively low overhead structure for the company.

All of these factors have allowed Wal Mart to reduce prices on the products it sells while retaining profit margins at or above industry averages. Its financial health, therefore, is another strength of the company.

Wal-Mart's distinctive competencies are its ability to provide customers with value (the products they want at reasonable prices), its relations with its employees, and its combination of supplier relationships and advanced technology which leads to low cost, efficient operations.

Many analysts would say that the company has no obvious weaknesses. However, its growth goals are very demanding, and one could question whether Mr. Glass, or anyone for that matter, will be able to continue Sam Walton's entrepreneurial zeal and vision, to achieve the desired growth rates. Internal conflicts with its "Made in the U.S.A." program has caused embarrassment in the past, even though a company official had checked the Bangladesh factory. The increasing number of layers of management may make it more difficult to coordinate activities, and runs counter to the current trend of downsizing corporate management.

A threat to the firm is the fact that it is rapidly approaching saturation of its stores in its traditional markets. Unfortunately, the markets that are left are those that do not match the traditional demographics of the firm. this includes the middle Atlantic, northeast, and west coast states. These new markets have a much higher population density and concentration of medium to large size cities than the traditional geographic markets served by Wal Mart. Moreover, these markets are already heavily populated by major competitors such as K-Mart and Target discount department stores as well as several smaller, regional chains. These are also the areas where resistance to Wal-Mart has been strongest.

The firm is also committed to expanding continuing sales growth as well as opening new stores in the midst of a recession. This has led to increased competitive pressures. Moreover, given the number of stores currently in operation, there is a need to constantly increase the number and size of new stores opened in any year. This is a further drain on the corporate management staff at headquarters. Moreover, given Sam Walton's stated objectives of achieving $125 billion in sales by the year 2000, sales at the firm will have to triple over that period.

There are several opportunities available to Wal Mart. The most populated areas of the country are still open to expansion. Moreover, many of its competitors have been weakened by poor differentiation strategies and a variety of price wars. The economy may actually work to Wal Mart's favor. Despite the fact that, by 1994, the U.S. was in an economic expansion, many consumers were still looking to save money in their spending. Many workers still did not feel secure in their jobs, and a number of Fortune 500 firms were still downsizing. Discount stores like Wal Mart continued growing in popularity, as they had during the recession. People also feared that jobs were being exported to countries with lower labor costs. Wal Mart was also appealing to the renewed patriotism brought on by the job outflow, the Gulf War and other events. The Buy American policy is in line with this set of external values.

Sam Walton's relinquishing of control created an opportunity, as well. This opened up the company to new thoughts and planning. It provided another avenue for advancement within the company. It also allowed for the development of professional managers to help guide the firm as it continues its growth. It is often difficult for the entrepreneurs who found firms such as Wal Mart to maintain that growth as the competitive pressures on the firm increase. While Sam's death was an important loss to the company, the ability to professionalize and expand management opportunities would continue to help the company grow.

3. **How would you describe Wal Mart's "Grand" strategy for the next decade? In terms of Porter's generic strategies? In Miles and Snow's adaptive model?**

Wal-Mart is following a grand strategy of growth, primarily through concentration. It continues moving both Wal-Marts and Sam's Warehouse Club stores into new areas. It is also pursuing growth through diversification into supercenters and in international markets, including both Canada and Mexico. Wal-Mart is attempting to follow an opportunistic, focus strategy based on geographic expansion and diversification. In many respects, this strategy can be viewed as a form of logical incrementalism.

The company is continuing to do what it does best. It is sticking to its tried and proven strategy of focusing on middle America. It provides quality and service at a low cost. It is not trying to radically change its image, as did Sears and Penney's. It is clearly building on its strengths of customer and employee loyalty. It continues to provide good quality and service at a reasonable price. It also has developed good supplier relationships as a means to maintain cost leadership while retaining its high profit margins.

In terms of Porter's generic strategies, Wal Mart has clearly placed the needs and demands of the customers at the top of its corporate objectives. As such, the firm is providing cost leadership. It is very difficult to differentiate on the basis of products, for the most part. Other firms, such as K Mart and Target, sell many of the same products. Despite this,

Wal Mart has differentiated itself somewhat through the "Bring it Home to the U.S.A." campaign. Calling employees "associates" has led to the development of a special corporate culture. This is seen by the customers and viewed positively from a service perspective.

Wal-Mart viewed its competition as vulnerable to a concerted attack from the flanks. The strategy essentially uses parts of all three generic strategies. The firm focused on developing a cost leadership position through maintaining strong supplier relations that led to lower costs, and prices, while allowing Wal Mart to maintain reasonable profit margins. As noted, it also differentiated, somewhat, by developing the Buy American program. To some extent, this was viewed as successful, as noted by articles in business publications.

While some may argue that the firm is trying to appeal to a mass market, it is really focusing on the middle American, price conscious market. The company is now spreading from its geographic market focus, however. It is hoping that the current price and service strategy will continue to be effective in its new geographic markets. The central focus of the strategy continues to be the successful implementation of a cost leadership strategy.

Miles & Snow's adaptive strategy calls for firms to pursue strategies that match their external environments. Wal-Mart can be viewed as having either a prospector strategy or an analyzer strategy. There is risk in entering the new markets that Wal-Mart has been counting on for growth. The Northeast U.S. and the West Coast are already heavily competitive retail markets. Mexican consumers may, or may not, be as value-conscious as those in the U.S. In addition, they may have different buying habits and product preferences. This fits the Prospector definition of "using existing technology to new advantage", although it is not "creating new products to which competitors must respond." The Analyzer strategy may be closer - seeking "to maintain stability of a core business while selectively responding to opportunities for innovation and change."

4.   **Would you consider Wal-Mart to be an entrepreneurial organization? Why or why not?**

Under Sam Walton, Wal-Mart clearly had an entrepreneurial spirit. "Mr. Sam" is cited in this chapter as an example of a successful entrepreneur. The ideas of the small-town focus, high level of customer service, and importance of employee "associates" were all part of Sam's original concept. These values have been institutionalized in the organization, as shown by the fact that Wal-Mart has continued to grow without changing its philosophy or objectives, since Mr. Walton's death in the early 1990s.

Entrepreneurship is defined in Chapter 7 as "risk taking behavior that results in the creation of new opportunities for individuals and/or organizations." The company has attempted to overcome the disadvantages of large size and multiple levels of management by decentralizing decision-making power to individual stores. This creates the opportunity for store managers to be entrepreneurial. An entrepreneurial manager "seizes opportunities for innovation and not only expects surprises, but capitalizes on them." The company does not want trustee managers, who react and who prefer the status quo. However, students may argue that the scope of decision making allowed to store managers is not enough to make them true entrepreneurs. The company decides on locations and on the basic types of services to offer; the manager has the ability to customize to fit her/his individual market, but does he/she really create "new opportunities?" A good question! Is Wal-Mart itself entrepreneurial? It does not appear so at this time. Its growth strategy does not involve doing anything really new. However, "Mr. Sam's" culture and values should permit the company to recognize and act on entrepreneurial ideas, if they are presented to it.

ANSWERS TO REVIEW QUESTIONS FOR CASE 8

Can Nucor Handle Growth and Control?

1. **Evaluate Nucor's strategy using Porter's Competitive Strategy Framework.**

As a *rival* in the steel industry, Nucor faced competitors much larger than itself in the form of US Steel and Bethlehem Steel. However, by introducing the use of mini-mill technology that melts scrap metal in electric furnaces, Nucor was able to produce steel at a much lower cost than its more highly integrated competitors. Previously, steel manufacturers had to use iron ore and coke to produce steel. Economies of scale supported the *vertical integration* of these operations. Nucor upset the balance in the industry by introducing a new, more cost-efficient technology.

The primary *suppliers* that Nucor depends on are scrap metal dealers. When Nucor first introduced mini-mill technology, there was an abundance of scrap metal available on the open market. As Nucor grew, scrap has become increasingly difficult to acquire. As a result, Nucor has been a leader in the attempt to develop iron carbide as an alternative to scrap as a source for its manufacturing process. It has not chosen to duplicate the steel manufacturers and *backward integrate* into the scrap steel market.

Nucor has been diligent in the development of new *buyers* for its steel. Originally, it produced steel for less value-added products as steel beams and girders. However, by refining the mini-mill process, Nucor was able to enter more lucrative markets such as flat rolled sheet, a primary product for the automotive industry. By diversifying its buyer group, Nucor retains more market power.

Substitute products represent a possible threat to the entire steel industry. Plastics, aluminum, and other composite materials offer a very real alternative to steel. However, by lowering the cost of producing steel, Nucor has reinvigorated the industry, keeping steel competitive in the marketplace. It continues to innovate on a regular basis.

Threat of New Entrants has increased as the mini-mill technology is largely available to anyone. Competition in the steel industry remains high as foreign producers continue to seek out the American market. However, Nucor does not follow the industry custom of calling for tariffs on imported steel products. One indication of Nucor's success is imitation on the part of its larger competitors.

2. **Evaluate Nucor based on Miles and Snow's Adaptive Model.**

Miles and Snow offer four alternative product/market strategies consistent with their industry environment:

Defender - an organization that emphasizes current products and markets without seeking growth

Prospector - firms seeking innovation and growth in the face of risk

Analyzer - a combination of defender in its core product lines and prospector in new opportunities

Reactor - no specific strategy, the firm just reacts to environmental imperatives

Nucor's present strategy appears to best represent the *analyzer* approach. As the second largest steel producer in the US, they have a large core product line. However, they continue to innovate in new areas, as reflected in their research on iron carbide as a raw material source. Consistent with the analyzer model, Nucor maintains stability in their core product line while continuing to seek opportunities in other areas.

3. **Is Nucor capable of continuing its entrepreneurial spirit as it grows larger?**

Nucor, through its use of incentives, offers an interesting contrast to the *bureaucratic imperative* (do firms have to adopt more bureaucratic structures as they get larger?). By tying performance standards to rewards across the entire organization, Nucor attempts to substitute rewards in the place of additional structures. Nucor president, John Correnti, recognizes this when he states: "My biggest fear is even though we're now a $3.3 billion company, we've still got to act, feel, and smell like a $300 million company (1)."

By rewarding its employees directly for performance, Nucor provides *control* without the expense of costly new structures and management layers. The rewards have the effect of employees identifying directly with the organization's goals and objectives. In addtion, by making sure that upper managers share in the pain when the market turns down, Nucor sets an excellent example of performance-based pay.

ANSWERS TO REVIEW QUESTIONS FOR CASE 9

United Parcel Service: Technology to the Rescue

1. **How does performance appraisal assist control and how does it relate to UPS?**

   Performance appraisal can be used for two different purposes-evaluation and development. Evaluation involves letting people know where they stand relative to objectives and standards. Development by contrast involves assisting in training and continued personal development of people. When done well, performance appraisal facilities control through both purposes.

   In respect to the *evaluation* role performance appraisal focuses on *past* performance and measurement of results against standards. It documents performance for administrative record and provides a basis for allocating performance-contingent rewards. This is largely a form of prostaction and external control. In respect to *development* performance appraisal focuses on *future* performance and helps to clarify expectations and standards of success. It is an opportunity for both the manager and the subordinate to discover any performance obstacles and identify training needs. When done properly, this is a form of preliminary control that can enhance a person's ability and willingness to express internal control in the future.

   In relation to UPS, Casey evaluated the US Postal service and developed UPS with efficiency as a focus. Jim's slogan is "Best service lowest rates". To keep a slogan such as this and to have efficiency in mind, it is quite obvious that UPS uses performance appraisal in assisting with control.

2. **How has UPS implemented the use of the Internet and how does it apply to control.**

   UPSnet provides an informational processing pipeline for international package processing and delivery. UPS has over 500,000 miles of communication lines, a UPS satellite, and links to 1,300 distribution sites in 46 countries. The system tracks 821,000 packages daily. This specifically relates to concurrent controls. The focus is on what happens during the work process. UPS monitors ongoing operations and activities to make sure things are done correctly. Ideally, these controls allow for corrective actions to be taken while the work is being done. This helps to avoid the waste and misfortunes of creating finished products of services that are unacceptable.

   UPS Document Exchange, a suite of document delivery and management services, will be available to the public in the second quarter. It provides state-of-the-art technology to alleviate customer anxiety over performing critical business practices over the Internet by providing maximum encryption levels, as well as user authentication, proof of delivery and archiving.

"This is an exciting juncture for UPS," said Mark Rhoney, UPS marketing vice president of electronic commerce. "We are the first delivery company to provide reliable and secure service for both the Internet and traditional ground and air delivery. It is also a significant milestone for electronic commerce. NetDox and Tumbleweed are providing the technology that makes UPS Document Exchange easy to use, reliable, secure and universally compatible so that UPS customers around the world can confidently use the Internet 24 hours a day to send and receive confidential information."

Expanding the company's service portfolio to include electronic document delivery is the latest electronic commerce initiative undertaken by the company. UPS, which launched its Web site (www.ups.com) in December 1994, now has one of the most interactive sites available, allowing users to track packages, request a pickup, calculate and compare rates, locate drop-off centers, prepare international documentation and download software. Recently, UPS has formed alliances with leading electronic commerce providers such as IBM, Open Market, Lotus, Pandesic and Harbinger, as well as several search engine companies to embed UPS tracking and other functionality into the products they are developing that meet a variety of logistics management needs.

3. **The fourth management function is controlling, explain and relate to UPS.**

Controlling sees to it that the right things happen, in the right way, and at the right time. Done well, control helps ensure that overall direction of individuals and groups are consistent with short and long-range organizational plans. It helps ensure that objectives and accomplishments are consistent with one another throughout an organization in proper means-end fashion. And, it helps maintain compliance with essential organizational rules and policies. The following restrictions are stated on the UPS web page regarding the carrying of packages.

No service shall be rendered in the transportation of articles of unusual value. The maximum value or declared value per package is $50,000 and the maximum UPS liability per package is $50,000.

No service shall be rendered in the transportation of any package or article weighing more than 150 pounds, or exceeding 108 inches in length, or exceeding a total of 130 inches in length and girth combined. Each package or article shall be considered as a separate and distinct shipment.

The maximum weight for a hazardous materials package is 70 pounds unless further restricted in the UPS Guide for Shipping Ground and Air Hazardous Materials.

Hazardous Materials packages requiring shipping papers as described under Title 49 C.F.R. Section 172.200 are not accepted in Hundredweight Ground Service.

UPS does not provide a protective service for the transportation of perishable commodities or of commodities requiring protection from heat or cold. Such commodities will be accepted for transportation solely at the shipper's risk for damage occasioned by exposure to heat or cold.

Each of the shipping categories, <u>International</u>, <u>Air</u>, <u>3-Day Select</u>, and <u>Ground</u>, has these restrictions. Further explanation for each category is given as well. Through this it is very obvious that UPS has a sincere dedication to control.

Many firms have difficulties maintaining an entrepreneurial spirit as they grow larger. Entrepreneurism is defined as strategic thinking and risk-taking behavior that results in the creation of new opportunities for individuals and/or organizations. As firms get larger, they many grow more bureaucratic in structure, a situation that can often stymie innovation.

ANSWERS TO REVIEW QUESTIONS FOR CASE 10

AT&T: Reorganization for Performance

1. **Analyze AT&T's organization based on functional and divisional structures.**

    Prior to deregulation in the long distance market, AT&T, known widely then as Ma Bell, exhibited a largely *functional structure*, exactly appropriate for the stable environment in which the firm found itself. The company was very *paternalistic*, allowing lifetime employment to many of its employees. Employees with similar skills and responsibilities were grouped together into the same departments, encouraging an efficient use of scarce system resources.

    Upon deregulation in 1984, AT&T faced an increasingly dynamic marketplace, as new competitors armed with new technologies invaded the formerly safe haven of long distance. As a result, AT&T has chosen to restructure itself a number of times in an attempt to shift to a structure that supports its shifting focus. Many top executives stepped down or retired rather than adjust to the new realities of unrestricted competition.

    AT&T made a number of new acquisitions, including NCR in computers, and McCaw Cellular in mobile phones. Because of these new businesses, AT&T has increasingly moved toward a more divisional structure. However, each time the company restructured in an attempt to find an efficient and effective operating structure, but each time the expected efficiencies failed to evolve. The computer industry proved hard for AT&T to acquire a competitive advantage in and cellular prices are dropping as the number of competitors increases. As an example of the increasing competition in the industry, since 1984, long-distance prices in the U.S. have plummeted 60 percent, driven down by the growing number of long-distance companies, which now number more than 400 (1).

    In its most recent restructuring on September 20, 1995, AT&T announced that it would be splitting into three companies over the subsequent fifteen months. These companies are: today's AT&T, which provides communication services; Lucent Technologies, a systems and technology company, which provides communications products; and NCR Corp., in the computer business. The company hopes that splitting into these component parts will encourage more focus among its managers.

2.   Would a matrix structure be more effective for AT&T?

Matrix structures utilize permanent cross-functional teams to blend the technical strengths of functional structures with the integrating potential of divisional structures. They are most appropriate in very dynamic environments when large amounts of expertise are needed to complete the task. The difficulty in matrix structures is that each member belongs to two formal groups, one being functional and the other representing a project group.

With the increasing impact of new technologies on AT&T's core business of voice and data communication, a matrix structure might afford some benefits not presently available from the divisionalized structure. The telecommunications market is converging with the computer market at an ever increasing rate. Depending on the *project-orientation* of the businesses, a matrix structure might be more effective.

3.   What is the purpose of the headquarters staff now that AT&T has split into three businesses?

The most recent reorganization of AT&T is an attempt to focus resources within each division. Upper management concluded that the businesses were too diverse to support any particular synergy possible by keeping the divisions consolidated. The primary purpose of the headquarters at AT&T becomes coordination and overall resource allocation among the three groupings.

This may be a preview of things to come in the more modern organizational field. With the advent of new technologies and communication options, many firms may find this arrangement more advantageous. Coordination activities, previously accomplished through organizational structure, may now be possible through the application of sophisticated communication systems. Groupware systems such as Lotus Notes and the increasing use of the Internet may portend huge changes in structural options for managers.

Review Nucor's use of incentives discussed in the previous chapter as another means of compensating for less structure. Structure, primarily with the use of middle managers, is an expensive proposition. Less costly alternatives available with the advances in communication technology offer the 21st century manager some intriguing options.

ANSWERS TO REVIEW QUESTIONS FOR CASE 11

Price Waterhouse and Coopers and Lybrand

1. **Compare the cultures between Price and Coopers. Are there differences?**

    Organizational culture is defined as a systems of shared beliefs and values that develops within an organization and guides the behavior of its members. It is important not only for managers to recognize the existence of culture within organizations, but also to manage it so as to support organizational goals and objectives. The case clearly identifies significant differences between the two cultures as a major problem to the merger.

    Price Waterhouse is described as more "pristine" and dignified. Price has long been identified as one of the more "classy" operations of the old Big Six firms. Howard Schilit, an accounting professor, argues that "Price Waterhouse always tried to create a special image that there was Price Waterhouse and then there was everybody else. They relished being different from the others" (3). Price even had its own version of the auditor's report that appears the the financial statements of each audited firm, with a length of one paragraph instead of the three standardized paragraphs used by the other firms (3).

    In contrast, Coopers is viewed as much less disciplined and competitive for new business. The partners' support of "unbridled commercialism" flies in the face of Price's partners, who exist more as administrators, rather than winners of new business (5). In addition, the old Price represented a loose federal structure of devolved groups of a few large partnerships. This may not sit well with the combined firm.

    Lastly, the existence of worldwide operations for both firms further complicates the cultural differences. European partners are not so eager to assume the liability problems of their more liability-prone American partners. With over 8500 partners between the two firms, integrating them into the new organization will be interesting.

2. **What pressure does this merger put on the rest of the industry?**

    By moving from a Big Six to a Big Five configuration, many experts in the accounting/consulting field argue that there are unlikely to be any further mergers. Consolidation occurs in a number of industries, including telecommunications, banking, tire manufacturing, computer production, and others. It is common in areas where size and economies of scale provide a competitive advantage.

    As accounting and consulting become the two main areas of operations in the large, public accounting firms, global reach has become a necessity. As firms become increasingly multinational in scope, they require accounting and consulting practices that mirror this global perspective. Alone, both Price and Coopers represented the smallest global firms in the market. Since they faced the danger of falling out of the Big Six category, it made sense for them to merge.

However, several members of the industry plan to "raid" partners from the new entity. Individuals not happy with the merger often flee to other competitors, sometimes in large numbers. Competitors often use the opportunity of a merger to entice dissatisfied partners to bring talented subordinates with them. This is a situation that Price/Coopers will have to confront as the merger proceeds.

3. **Would you classify the accounting/consulting work design as small batch, mass production, or continuous process according to Joan Woodward's classification?**

Small batch processes, a variety of custom products are tailor-made to order. Each customer may be slightly different, and a high level of worker skill is needed. *Mass production* produces a large number of uniform products in an assembly -line process, with the products passed from stage to stage until its completion. *Continuous process* products a large quantity of product by passing a continuous stream of raw material through a highly automated system.

It appears that the accounting/consulting field most closely represents the small batch process. While many of the services are standardized, they still require a customized approach for each client. Accountants and consultants must spend large amounts of time on the premises of their client gathering information that is specific to each entity. This process is highly time-consuming and requires a high degree of education and skill among the individuals.

The small batch imperative causes problems for the firms. It is difficult to control costs when you must supply large numbers of highly-trained individuals at remote locations. Computer experts are expensive and require high interaction with individuals from the customer firms. This action is time-consuming and costly. It may be time for the accounting firms to contemplate changing some of their technology to mass production, through the use of computers and the application of telecommunications. Video-conferencing might be able to replace some of the face-to-face time needed to complete their services.

ANSWERS TO REVIEW QUESTIONS FOR CASE 12

Ben and Jerry's Ice Cream: Leading with Values

1.   **What HRM policies does Ben & Jerry's employ to gain acceptance and commitment of improved quality within the work force?**

One of the main aspects of the HRM policies in force at Ben & Jerry's has been the development of an open system of communications within the company. As part of this process, employees are expected to evaluate their supervisors on an annual basis. While the supervisors are expected to provide a similar process for their subordinates in an open and positive basis, it is unusual for the opposite to occur. The HRM department perceived this addition as gaining commitment from the employees. The workers felt that they had a clear determination in the way that the firm would be directed. The employees appeared to feel that their comments had an impact on the future of the firm. Students might be asked to compare this process with the course evaluations that are typically completed by students at the end of each semester. It should be noted that B&J's sets up sessions to help train the employees to effectively carry out this process.

Employees are also set up in self-structured work teams to perform many of the tasks within the firm. The members of the teams are expected to design their own work procedures. This was extended to seeking employee team inputs into the design and implementation of new facilities. This process was also used in the design and development of the employee benefits programs offered by the company. This had led to such benefits as an employee day care center, flexible benefits and flexible work scheduling.

The purpose of all of these policies was to encourage employees to take ownership in their decisions and work processes. It was hoped that, in this manner, they would take greater pride in the quality of their work and their products. It was also hoped that these policies would lead to a greater commitment by the employees to their jobs and to the company.

2.   **What recruiting and staffing innovations does Ben & Jerry's use to improve employee morale and motivation?**

One of the major innovations that the HRM department had instituted at Ben and Jerry's was to fully involve employees in the recruitment, selection, and training process within the company. Members of the team where there might be an opening were expected to assist in the recruitment process. While this is fairly common in US companies, B&J's involved the team members at all phases of the process. Prospective new employees were interviewed not only by members of the HRM department and managers, but also by members of the team with which they would be working if they were to be hired. This process was even extended to including an employee who was to be replaced in the interview process.

As noted by Jerry Greenfield, co-founder of the firm, "the new person would be surrounded by people who would have a vested interest in his or her success." The employee, moreover, would feel accepted by the people with whom s/he was working. Therefore, it was hoped that there would be a greater mutual commitment between the new employee and his/her fellow workers.

3. **What reactions might occur as the founders turn over operation control to a new CEO from outside the company?**

The employees of B&J's had come to expect look to the founders for consistency and commitment to the goals and objectives of the firm. With at least one the founders around at most times, the employees would probably feel assured that the policies of the firm would continue. Especially, the counter culture aspect and feel of the company would be a concern of the employees. It was common for the founders to come to work in tie dyed tee shirts.

The new CEO, while having been educated and matured during the sixties, as well as being a member of a minority (Robert Holland is an African American) had also been an employee at McKinsey and Company, a traditional, old line management consulting firm. There was probably some concern among some employees that the "suits" were coming in to take over. This would probably be exacerbated by a salary that would undoubtedly exceed the former cap of 7 times that of the average salary of the lowest level employee within the company.

These concerns were heightened by the first quarterly loss incurred by the company since going public. Employees appeared to feel that Holland might reduce the independence enjoyed by the employees of B&J's.

Employees would also be concerned over the fact that Chuck Lacy, the President of B&J's had been passed over for CEO. While most analysts, apparently including Lacy himself, conceded that Lacy was a good operating officer, but lacked the characteristics needed for a CEO to lead the company into an expansionary strategy both in the US and abroad. Lacy had played a major role in developing some of the more innovative aspects of the HRM policies in place at B&J's.

Overall, analysts were concerned that Holland might implement a more traditional and hierarchical organizational and decision making structure at B&J's. This kind of structure could easily undo the benefits of employee commitment and morale that had been developed within the company through the implementation of innovative HRM.

ANSWERS TO REVIEW QUESTIONS FOR CASE 13

Mike Krzyzewski: No-nonsense Leader

1. **Describe Coach Krzyzewski's leadership style according to House's Path-Goal Leadership Theory.**

    House's Theory suggests four possible leadership roles: directive, supportive, participative, or achievement oriented. The choice of leader behavior is contingent on situational contingencies, including task structure, work group, subordinates' abilities and experience. It appears that Coach K practices this approach when leading his basketball team.

    Depending on the make-up of his basketball team, particularly in regard to the number of freshmen or seniors that he has available to him, Coach K would need to adjust his leadership style accordingly. With more seniors, he can adopt a more achievement oriented approach, allowing his seniors to direct the game on the floor. During the time that he started three freshmen, it is likely that the coach needed to be more directive, providing more exact instructions to his players.

    As his younger players receive more court time, the coach can gradually become more supportive, allowing the players more and more decision making. As the players mature, he can adopt a more participative style, taking input from his more veteran players. His style must be *contingent on* his players, the specific team he is playing, whether it is a home or away game, and a variety of other factors.

2. **Analyze Coach K's leadership approach using Blake and Mouton's Managerial Grid and the Hershey-Blanchard Situational Leadership Theory. Which of the two models provides more insight in this case?**

    Under Blake and Mouton's model, Coach K might represent five different leader behaviors:

    1. Impoverished - exertion of minimal effort
    2. Authority-obedience - efficiency in operations with a minimum of human interference
    3. Country Club - thoughtful attention to needs of people
    4. Organization Man - balance of concern for people with concern for production
    5. Team - work accomplishment from committed people with a "common stake"

    The authors of the model clearly argue that highest performance is attained through acceptance of the Team Leadership behavior. This is not a contingency approach, but relies on one-best-way for its value-added.

    It does appear from the article that Coach K has developed a Team emphasis in his approach to leading. However, given that his players turn over every four years, this approach might result in problems as his basketball team changes. If you assume that Coach K *cannot change his leader behavior*, then this model provides insight.

Conversely, the Hershey-Blanchard approach is a contingency model that *does assume that people can change their leadership styles*. Follower readiness or maturity is the primary factor that influences the choice of leader behaviors. With a young, inexperienced team, Coach K would likely choose a more "*selling*" approach, explaining decisions and providing opportunity for clarification.

As his players mature, he can move to a "*participating*" style, sharing ideas and asking for input. With a more experienced team dominated by seniors, the coach would do better to concentrate more on "*delegation*" as the primary means to lead. In this mode, he depends on a great deal of leadership from his senior, experienced players.

Once again, this model assumes the ability of the leader to change behaviors as the situation dictates. Coach K does appear capable of this approach, as the case suggests. This model might show more insight to the situation and provide a better means of analysis to the student - provided they state their assumption that Coach K can switch styles.

3. **Would you describe Coach K's style as more representative of transactional or transformational?**

It appears that Coach K is very much capable of inspiring his players to perform at or above their natural abilities. He describes motivation "as my passion", indicating that he is interested in high performance from his players. A transformational leader is defined as "someone who uses charisma and related qualities to raise aspirations and shift people and organizational systems into t new high performance patterns". Coach K appears to represent the transformational form of leadership.

Interestingly, he does so with a very quiet and reserved approach to the game of basketball. The case points out the difference in approaches between Coach K and Coach Bobby Knight of Indiana. Coach Knight is much more demonstrative and aggressive on the court, a leadership style that is both admired and ridiculed. Coach K chooses a different approach that represents a more controlled demeanor.

Transformation leadership goes beyond merely diagnosing a situation and choosing a leader style. The transformational leader must provide a strong aura of vision and contagious enthusiasm. When Coach K suffered back problems, it did not appear possible for him to exhibit the level of energy necessary to maintain this approach. As a result, the team suffered. Upon his return, the team reacted in a positive manner and played at or above their abilities.

ANSWERS TO REVIEW QUESTIONS FOR CASE 14

Black Entertainment Television (BET): Rags to Riches

1. **How does motivation influence performance and is this evident in BET?**

   Motivation does not directly affect performance. It affects effort. Highly motivated persons are those who put forth a lot of effort in their work; they work hard. Whether or not they achieve high performance, however, is determined not just by the amount of effort they put forth but by their abilities and the available support as well. This is the lesson to the individual performance equation: Performance = Ability x Support x Effort. The following two paragraphs will show how Robert Johnson was motivated to found BET and continues to help its success.

   Robert Johnson, born the ninth of ten children in Hickory, Mississippi, is a true rags-to-riches success story. His father, Archie, chopped wood while his mother taught school, and their search for a better life led them to Freeport, Illinois, a predominantly white working-class neighborhood. Archie supplemented his factory jobs by operating his own junkyard on the predominantly black East Side of town. Edna Johnson got a job at Burgess Battery, and although she eventually secured a job for her son Robert at the battery firm, he knew it wasn't for him.

   Johnson lives on a $4.3 million, 133-acre horse farm in Virginia, and while he supports a large number of black causes, he declines to be identified as a role model. "I don't want to be seen as a hero to younger people. I want to be seen as a good solid business guy who goes out and does a job, and the job is to build a business ... What are my responsibilities to black people at large? If I help my family get over and deal with the problems they might confront, then I have achieved that one goal that is my responsibility to society at large".

   Johnson appears to have a high *need for achievement* described in McClelland's Needs Theory. The need for personal achievement and personal feedback drives Johnson to be successful.

2. **What role does reinforcement play in motivation?**

   Skinner's work introduced to the field of management the power of operant conditioning that is, controlling behavior by manipulating its consequences. A behavior followed by a pleasant consequence is likely to be repeated; a behavior followed by an unpleasant consequence is unlikely to be repeated. Using this principle, managers are especially advised to use positive reinforcement to raise the level of motivation in the workplace. When people perform or behave in desirable ways, the reinforcement advice is to make sure they are positively reinforced. The most powerful reinforcement, furthermore, is delivered immediately and continently.

   Robert Johnson continues to have grand plans for BET, wanting to turn the enterprise into what marketers call an umbrella brand. The firm publishes two national magazines that reach 250,000 readers: Young Sisters and Brothers for teens and Emerge for affluent adults, and it has interests in film production, electronic retailing, and radio. The first <u>BET SoundStage</u>

restaurant opened in suburban Washington, with another opening in Disney World in Orlando. With Hilton as a partner, Johnson hopes to open a casino in Las Vegas, Nevada.

Johnson wants to capture some of the black consumers' disposable income - valued at $425 billion annually. To do this, he partners primarily with such big names as Disney, Hilton, Blockbuster, Microsoft and others. "You simply cannot get big anymore by being 100 percent black-owned anything " Johnson claims. Reaching 98% of all black cable homes, his BET cable station provides the perfect medium to influence this increasingly affluent black audience.

3. **What is happening in the area of motivation and compensation?**

New developments in compensation are having many positive impacts on the workplace. More and more workers now have access to special incentive programs in the cases, the attempt is to allow the worker to benefit materially form improvements in productivity resulting form their individual and/or group efforts. In creatively, but always with an attempt to tie rewards and performance. This is a special application of all motivation principles available in many theories introduced in this chapter.

The first show bounced off an RCA satellite and into 3.8 million homes served by Rosencran's franchises. Johnson received his first crucial financing from John Malone of TCI for a $380,000 loan plus $120,000 to purchase 20% of BET To raise capital in the 1980s, Johnson sold off pieces of BET to Time Inc. and Taft Broadcasting for over $10 million. However, controversy over programming has followed Johnson from the start, with his heavy reliance on music videos (60% of total programming), gospel and religious programs, infomercials, and reruns of older shows such as Sanford and Son and "227".

In September, 1997, Delano E. Lewis, a director of BET, was appointed to serve as a Special Independent Committee of the BET Board of Directors to consider and make recommendations to the Board concerning a September 10, 1997 proposal by Mr. Robert L. Johnson and TCI's Liberty Media Group to purchase all of the outstanding shares of BET common stock not already owned by them for a price of $48.00 per share. In early 1998, Lewis reported that the $48/share offer was inadequate.

ANSWERS TO REVIEW QUESTIONS FOR CASE 15

Boeing: Faster-Better-Cheaper

1. **Interpret Boeing's work design based on the core job characteristics of the Job Characteristics Model presented in this chapter.**

    The five core job characteristics are *skill variety, task identity, task significance, autonomy* and *feedback*. A job high in the core characteristics is considered to be *enriched* - it offers more opportunities for satisfaction into the job. As an assembly line system, Boeing depends on specialization of labor to allow efficient assembly of its airplanes. This arrangement may lead to lower opportunities for skill variety, task identity, and autonomy for the individual worker.

    The effort by Yoshiki Iwata, the former Toyota engineer, to adopt many of the principles of the automotive assembly operations into Boeing's situation may help to alleviate some of these problems. The *accelerated improvement workshops* mentioned in the case allow workers a greater input into the system and concurrently a greater feedback from the job itself. Workers may feel in better control of a situation where they have precise input, supporting greater task identity and and task significance.

    One option Boeing has at its disposal is the grouping of work design in *self-managed work teams*. This allows for both *job enlargement* and *job enrichment* as workers divide the task among themselves. *Skill variety* is heightened and workers avoid tedium and boredom from doing the same tasks repeatedly. All of these factors join to encourage a greater level of satisfaction - all hopefully, effort - in their job.

2. **Interpret "old" versus "new" trends in the workplace in regard to Boeing's shift away from 1940s methods to new, more modern work designs.**

    The purpose of work design is to create opportunities for individuals both to achieve high levels of job "performance" and to experience high levels of job "satisfaction". The shutdowns of Boeing's assembly lines due to parts shortages and safety concerns are clues to a wider problem. The pressure on its production process through continuing high plane orders exposes the weaknesses of a production process that has not materially changed since the 1940s.

    The new trend on job design where workers "think" and "do" does appear to be taking hold at Boeing. Ideas from the shop floor are being integrated into the work flow design. The example of the ladder, although small, shows the attention to detail that manufacturing such a complex product such as an airplane must include.

    By introducing production methods developed and refined on automobile assembly plants, Boeing is hoping to benefit from innovations introduced by the Japanese and others. The impact of technology on the workplace, a common theme throughout this text, is amply evident in this case. Computers impact every area of design and assembly from inventory control to marketing.

3. **Do environmental conditions assist or hinder Boeing's attempts to restructure its work force?**

The statement at the end of the case points out numerous, simultaneous problems facing Boeing. Boeing's takeover of McDonnell Douglas complicates its hopes to streamline its assembly processes, as these new workers are integrated into the Boeing workplace. In addition, the high number of plane orders, while good for the firm, significantly complicate its hopes of re-engineering itself. New workers must be trained and inculcated into the work flow representing an increasingly complex and technical nature.

Quality control is particularly important to airplane production, where even minor design or assembly problems can lead to catastrophic results. Boeing appears to be in transition from the *old trends* to *new trends* in the workplace. Its stated purpose of reducing development costs and development time must place a greater emphasis on individual and group job design. Moving from 18 to 43 jets per month requires a monumental overhaul of the production process, from start to finish.

All this must be accomplished with an increasing emphasis on lowering costs. Airbus provides a meaningful competitor for Boeing that forces it to innovate. The ACPS system supports modular development that works across aircraft types, thereby reducing inventory and design costs. With its emphasis on "lean manufacturing", Boeing must put all its attention on supporting job design on its shop floor.

ANSWERS TO REVIEW QUESTIONS FOR CASE 16

Having Fun at Southwest Airlines

1. **What needs were Southwest's employees able to meet through their jobs?**

Maslow's hierarchy of needs can be applied to the Southwest case. Lower order needs are not discussed; students will assume that physiological and safety needs have been met. There are a number of examples of employees meeting social needs, such as welcoming new colleagues from the acquired airline: The "Culture Committee's" purpose is to find opportunities to maintain Southwest's corporate spirit. An important part of the manager's job is to meet and talk to employees. Esteem needs are also being met - examples such as "customer of the month" and employee-written letters of commendation indicate a culture strong on providing rewards to increase esteem. Jobs have been structured so as to allow some opportunities for employees to work toward promotion and increased pay. Meeting self-actualization needs is also possible. Working at the Ronald McDonald House should give individuals a feeling of personal satisfaction. Supporting the company via donations for fuel during the Gulf War showed the importance of the company to individuals, and their willingness to go beyond their job descriptions. Employees are also encouraged to use their own creativity to find solutions for customer issues. The progression principle appears to apply. Employees are working on meeting self-actualization needs, and appear to have ample opportunities to satisfy needs at all lower levels. Self actualization can be achieved in a variety of ways, as the examples show - and, fortunately for Southwest, as employees work toward satisfying this need, it appears to grow stronger, further motivating them.

Alderfer's ERG theory condenses Maslow's hierarchy into three levels: existence needs; relatedness needs; and growth needs. As discussed above, Southwest enables employees to meet their existence needs, but the specifics are not described in the case. The discussion of social needs also applies to Alderfer's "relatedness", while growth needs include personal growth and satisfaction, reflected both in others' esteem and in one's own feelings of accomplishment and development. Alderfer, however, states that it isn't necessary to completely satisfy one level before moving on to the next. A person can be influenced by any or all three at the same time. The "Frustration - regression" principle reminds us, and Southwest, that employees can again become worried, or unmotivated, by lower order needs.

Herzberg's two-factor theory talks about satisfier factors and hygiene factors. The hygiene factors, which come from the job context, are not discussed in the case. However, since workers don't appear to be dissatisfied, the hygiene factors can be assumed to be adequate.

Satisfiers, which do provide job satisfaction and motivation, include a sense of achievement, feelings of recognition, a sense of responsibility, opportunity for advancement, and feelings of personal growth. All of these are present, as already discussed.

McClelland's acquired needs theory is more complex to apply. Southwest appears to be looking for people who are high in need for achievement. They like to put their competencies to work; they are willing to take moderate risks - both business and personal (jumping out of an overhead luggage bin could be perceived as somewhat abnormal behavior); while they don't necessarily work alone, they often work as individual specialists on a team (gate personnel, for example), and much of their reward comes from the task itself - successfully creating satisfied customers. There is an element of the need for social power - taking responsibility and influencing others. Employees are encouraged to satisfy customers, using their own initiative, and to reward others via letters and awards. Southwest's hiring policies and its limited opportunities for promotion make the need for personal power an unlikely interest. Many employees also may have a need for affiliation; they appear to enjoy the interpersonal relationships and the social interaction. As with Herzberg and particularly Alderfer, these needs can co-exist, and an employee may be able to meet more than one need in a particular situation.

2.   **How did Southwest motivate its employees?**

Motivation is described in Chapter 14 as "forces within the individual that account for the level, direction and persistence of effort expended at work."

Rewards are defined as "a work outcome of positive value to the individual." Southwest uses both extrinsic and intrinsic rewards. One extrinsic reward, given to employees by the organization, is profit sharing; if the company is successful, 15% of its net profits is distributed to employees. Another may be employee stock ownership -again, the employee benefits from his or her efforts because if the company does well, the stock price should rise. If the stock, or options to buy, are given as a reward for performance, this is clearly a source of extrinsic motivation (the case doesn't specify how employees own the stock, so it is possibly via pension plans). The company also uses special assignments such as the "culture committee" to involve employees. To the extent possible, "job families" were created to allow opportunities for promotion. Managers were encouraged to interact with their subordinates and to understand (and occasionally do) their jobs. Departments within Southwest also use extrinsic motivations, through techniques such as "customer of the month" and writing letters to praise other employees or departments. All of these are external sources of recognition.

As covered in question 1 in the discussion of meeting personal needs, the company also makes it possible for employees to receive internal or intrinsic rewards. Southwest selected its employees for their attitude, specifically looking for humor, desire to achieve, and ability to work with others, in other words for employees who were capable of self-motivation. Gate and flight attendants were encouraged to use their creativity to provide superior customer service, through games, impersonations, or any other technique. All employees were encouraged to anticipate customer needs and fill them.

The case doesn't have enough information to discuss process theories of motivation such as equity theory and expectancy theory. The reinforcement theory of motivation can be applied. Southwest uses, and encourages its employees to use, positive reinforcement through letters, pizza, profit sharing, and listening to employees (examples include both the expectation that managers will interact with employees and the use of cross-functional teams such as the "culture committee").

3. **What are the principle motivational problems facing Southwest as it continues to expand?**

Expansion could create problems for Southwest in several ways. First, there is the need to hire many additional people. These new employees should have the same characteristics as current employees, in particular enthusiasm and the willingness to work hard. This should not pose a serious problem as the hiring process has been successful in the past.

A more serious problem is stated in the last paragraph: "how to maintain the culture of caring and fun while expanding rapidly into new markets." This is further complicated by the distances that are now involved - it is difficult to involve employees in Baltimore or Cleveland in home office activities. They are less likely to serve on the Culture Committee, or to know anyone in the company above the level of their own operations. They may not have the same degree of close contact with other departments. As a result they may not be as enthusiastic about Southwest as employees located physically closer. They also may have fewer opportunities to interact with colleagues, and learn from each other.

These are not insurmountable problems. The company's "internal customer" approach can be still be rewarded. Values such as caring can be encouraged - many cities have Ronald McDonald Houses, for example. Ask students to come up with ways to overcome potential problems caused by distance and increasing size.

ANSWERS TO REVIEW QUESTIONS FOR CASE 17
Steinway: A History of Quality

1.   **How have group norms developed in Steinway?**

"Norming" is the process which involves developing shared rules of conduct and lerning to coordinate indivdiduals as part of a working unit. Group members develop roles and learn to work together in harmony. They come to experience feelings of closeness and shared expectations.

The impact of history has had a profound effect on the development of manufacturing norms for Steinway and Sons. The importance of quality and craftsmanship is deeply embedded in the 150-year history of the firm. The early work of Henry Engelhard Steinway serves as a reminder of the importance of every detail of a Steinway piano. The company's 114 patents serve as tangible proof f the importance that Steinway has had on the piano market.

Many of the employees of Steinway appear to work for the company for most of their lives. This consistency allows powerful group norms to develop and carry on from one group to the next. The groups appear to represent formal, functional groups responsible for different assembly processes involved in piano manufacturing. The piano is handed off from one group to the next, creating interdependence among the groups. Each depends on the other to correctly complete their task assignment so the next group can proceed.

2.   **How does Steinway's piano manufacturing process exhibit the need for teamwork?**

The case states that it takes up to one year to manufacture a piano in the Steinway method. Task specialization allows the various craftspeople to concentrate their energies on the numerous processes involved in the manufacture of a grand piano. It is highly likely that the many groups in Steinway represent self-managed work groups, where teams plan, schedule, and train members in the various tasks.

As new members become more experienced, they support more participative decision making representative of self-managed teams. With its constant emphasis on quality, Steinway encourages close-knit relationships among its employees. Due to the close working relationships among its members, it is likely that many of the formal work groups in the plant continue as informal friendship groups outside the work environment.

A Steinway grand piano moves between a number of assembly stations as it proceeds from soundboard to finished piano. Each step requires a substantially different set of skills, but each adds its own unique contribution to the overall process. As an example, early in the manufacturing process, the rim of the piano is formed. "18 hard-rock maple layers, each twenty-two feet long, are used to construct the rim of a concert grand piano. The layers are first coated with glue and stacked. The stacked layers are then glued into a single form of wood by bending on the rim-bending press, a giant piano-shaped vise. The rim-bending team centers the layers on the press and wrestles the wood into place with the aid of clamps" (1).

The piano then moves along the manufacturing process as subsequent assembly operations are completed. "The voicing process involves minute adjustments to the hammer, which are critical to the piano's sound and the distinctive personality of each Steinway. A master voicer makes adjustments to the hammer's resiliency by sticking the hammer's felt with a small row of needles, reducing its stiffness and thereby mellowing its tone" (1). This is then followed by a tone regulator, who listens intently to the piano's pitch and turns the tuning pins with a tuning hammer to adjust string tension. This is followed by a final inspection.

3. **Suggest how a new employee might work his or her way through the Stages of Group Development.**

Steinway employees would first face the forming stage where initial orientation and interpersonal testing by other members occurs. Identification with the group evolves as new members develop relationships, identify acceptable behavior and learn how others perceive the task at hand.

The storming stage requires that members confront conflict as they form subgroups and status considerations come to the front. Personal agendas become more transparent and various interpersonal styles become more evident. If new members cannot move through this stage, they likely will not stay with their new employment.

The norming stage represents a consolidation around task requirements and operating agendas as appropriate behaviors are accepted. Craft skills that have been handed down form generations become the preferred means of accomplishing the task of building a high-quality piano. The various roles consistent with all groups, including leadership, counseling, and presider of rituals evolve.

Performing represents a mature group stage that emphasizes task accomplishment and high group cohesiveness. Conflict is dealt with in innovative and creative ways - in a functional versus dysfunctional manner. Members identify highly with group goals and the organization of the group represents a stable structure that encourages high performance.

Adjourning represents group death. Employees at Steinway may only experience this sensation in rare occasions, as craftspeople work at the organization for much of their life. Elaborate ceremonies often accompany this stage, as organizations incorporate rites and rituals to mark departure from the group.

ANSWERS TO REVIEW QUESTIONS FOR CASE 18

The Walt Disney Company: Undergoing Change

1. **Examine the internal and external forces for change faced by Disney.**

    The Walt Disney Company has undergone a number of changes since its inception in 1923. Beginning largely as cartoon production company, it has branched out into a large number of new ventures, including feature films, theme parks, retail outlets, and network television. Much of this came as a result of external forces for change, from competitors including Paramount and Fox, and environmental forces, including cable television, video rentals and purchases, and increases in leisure time and the recreation dollar present both opportunities and threats to the company.

    Perhaps the greatest change involved the hiring of Michael Eisner as President of Disney. Eisner brought an enhanced desire to change the rather staid corporate culture exhibited by Disney executives. *Low performance* of the stock led Eisner to look towards new avenues to drive earnings. Disney had been the target of greenmail and an attempted hostile takeover. In response to these actions, Eisner was brought in to enhance shareholder value.

    Eisner's strategy was to bring Disney into a number of new ventures, including Touchstone Productions, EuroDisney, video distribution, Disney stores, and eventually the purchase of ABC/Capital Cities Network. Eisner recognized a valuable but largely underutilized brand image founded on family values. His actions have resulted in a tremendous increase in shareholder value, in addition to his own personal wealth.

    The transformation of Disney from a sleepy cartoon/theme park operator into one of the world's premier entertainment companies has not come without controversy. Several groups, including the Southern Baptists and some Catholic groups are <u>boycotting</u> Disney regarding the company's stand on gay rights.

2. **How have external forces in the Entertainment Industry affected Disney's need for change?**

    The Entertainment Industry has undergone a tremendous upheaval in the last 20 years. Changes in technologies, including cable and satellite TV, video distribution through chains such as Blockbuster Video, and increasing competition for the leisure dollar, confronted Disney simultaneously with tremendous opportunities and threats. Multiple industries are merging, including television, telephone, and computer, to create global players driven by size and reach.
    Disney now reaches into an amazing number of markets. Entertainment now includes an incredibly wide range of activities, and Disney is interested in capturing as much revenue as possible by branching into new ventures. In this way, they hope to *leverage their brand name* across a wide group of consumers. If they can get loyal followers to buy their movies, television programs, theme park admissions, videos, toys, cruises, and other items marketed by Disney, then the firm can experience economies of scale in its operations.

500

Eisner feels that if Disney is to remain a major player in the entertainment industry, then they have no choice but to grow larger. Size becomes a necessary component to success in this market. Eisner's choice to buy ABC network is recognition of the importance of controlling distribution channels in the entertainment market. By adding ABC to his movies and cable holdings, Eisner can reach hundreds of millions of potential buyers of Disney products and services.

3. **What changes do you foresee in the Entertainment Industry in the next five years?**

Much of the *driving forces* in the last few years in the Entertainment Industry has been consolidation of firms into increasingly larger entities. Viacom, Rupert Murdoch, and others are building entertainment mega-companies. Eisner reacted to this situation by buying ABC/Capital Cities in an effort to keep up. The primary argument comes down to what is more important - content or distribution. Disney is hedging its bets by involvement in both areas.

Technology will have a profound effect on this industry in the next few years. Satellite television broadcasts, companies running cable to homes through phone lines, cable companies offering internet access, and other developments will have monumental impact on this industry. No one can be sure of the dominant paradigm that will emerge as computers, telecommunications, and cable/television broadcasting all merge into a single industry.

High-definition television, DVD technology, increased leisure dollars among the aging baby boomers - all these factors offer both opportunities and threats to players in the entertainment industry. Disney is attempting to reach the maximum number of people with the maximum number of products and services. Whether Eisner is correct in his assessment of the industry remains to be seen.

INTEGRATIVE ACTIVITIES

INSTRUCTOR'S NOTES: IN-BASKET EXERCISE

Broadway Management Company

Bonnie Fremgen, Ph.D.
Associate Professor
Department of Management
University of Notre Dame

The in-basket exercise is designed to give students a taste of a "real-life" business activity. The exercise is deliberately written about a business that few students know—the Broadway music industry. The students will not be able to research their answers and must, therefore, draw upon their own problem-solving skills to solve the exercise. In order to promote student creativity in problem-solving, the instructor may wish to give minimal instructions on how to proceed with the exercise. However background information on such topics as budgeting, legal/illegal questions relating to employee confidentiality, business ethics, and handling employee grievances may be discussed in class before assigning the exercise. It is worthwhile to show the class at least one example of a well-structured memo response. This can be enlarged onto a transparency, if desired.

The exercise is structured to encourage the student to respond with a written comment for each memo since there is a power failure, the telephones are down, there is no computer code, and the files are locked. However the instructor can change the assignment and have students provide their solutions via e-mail if desired.

Students should be encouraged to read all memos through very quickly before writing any responses. In some cases one memo will be related to another (eg., Memos 15 and 20).

The author's sample solutions (see Exhibit 1) are only meant as possible suggestions. Individual instructors may have a solution to the memos that they prefer other than the author's. In some cases, the instructor may wish to have the students use specific material that has been covered in class, such as employment regulations, when working through solutions to the exercise.

TYPE OF ASSIGNMENTS

Individual Assignment

This exercise can be assigned as homework that is turned in by each student. If solutions to the entire project are to be submitted to the instructor, then it is advisable to have each student use a TO DO list on which he or she lists the tasks that need to be accomplished for each memo. Responses to the memos should be written directly on the memo.

Another option is to have the students read over the entire exercise, work out solutions before coming to class, and then provide their responses during a class discussion. If this option is selected then it is still advisable to have the student turn in a written solution to Memos 4 (potential grievance), Memo 5 (budget), Memo 20 (time chart), and Memo 27 (employee reference). These four memos seem to give the beginning management student the most difficulty.

Group or Team Assignment

This exercise can also be assigned to small groups of 4 to 6 students. The students must come to a consensus on how to handle each memo. The group then presents their findings to the class as a whole. It is interesting to compare the memos written by one group or team against those of another group. The teams should be encouraged to make their presentation to the class as interesting as possible. The rationale behind each solution should also be given.

Grading for the In-Basket Exercise

Each instructor will have areas he or she wishes to concentrate on when grading an exercise such as this. In general, the type of wording that is contained in each memo and the overall solution are the two most important points to consider. For example, when handling a potential employee grievance (memo 4) the student should avoid making promises to the employee such as "You clearly deserve to have the position. I'll do everything in my power to right this wrong." When handling the memo asking for confidential employee information (eg., Memo 27) the student's response should indicate to the instructor that the student understands what kind of employee information can be placed in writing. When handling the memo relating to the budget (Memo 5) the student should be able to calculate how much budget money is allocated for each line item per quarter, determine if the budget is over or under at the end of the 2nd quarter, and estimate, based on current spending, if enough money remains for the fiscal year.

Grading for this exercise can be handled in a number of ways. A grade sheet can be prepared with a space to grade each memo listed (see exhibit 2). The totals are then calculated for an overall grade. The student should handle each memo. If there is no response to a particular memo then the grade for that memo is zero.

If the assignment is just discussed in class, without handing in any portion of the assignment, the instructor can move through the class and check off that the assignment has been completed.

When appropriate, students may write their responses directly on each memo if they turn in the entire assignment for grading. If the memo requires a written letter response, such as in memos 4 and 27, the student should type this response before turning it in.

EXHIBIT 1

SAMPLE MEMORANDUM RESPONSES

Memo 1: Welcome Back!

Guidelines: This memo illustrates the importance of establishing a good relationship with one's secretary. Mitch needs to leave a brief memo for the temporary secretary, Alice, welcoming her and indicating how he wishes his work to be handled in his absence. Students lose credit for this memo if they fail to welcome Alice and merely give her orders.

Response:

TO: Alice

Welcome! I really regret not being able to meet you in person but I will be in touch with you by phone as soon as I arrive in Toronto. I will be staying at the Toronto Plaza Hotel the first week and then at Seattle Inn the second week. I can always be reached by leaving a message with the front desk. Please handle the attached memos by noting the instructions on each memo. You can send all typed letters by overnight mail for me to personally sign unless I indicate otherwise on the memo.

Thanks so much for all your help.

Memo 2: Employee Complaint

Guidelines: This memo relates to memo 4. The fact that Mitch received two memos in one day concerning this matter should indicate its importance. See solution in memo 4

Memo 3: Broker

Guidelines: Many students have a tendency to place great importance on this memo and to handle it first. Since it relates to a personal matter, Mitch's own financial investments, it should be handled on Mitch's personal time. He can place a call to his broker when he leaves the office.

Memo 4: Betty Black Letter

Guidelines: Memos 2 and 4 both deal with an important memo relating to an employee grievance. What the student does not know is that Betty has not been able to keep up with new technology in the field of costume design. Lee Adams was hired because she has superior skills in this area. The fact that she is a personal friend of another employee, Diane Friend, meant that she most likely had a recommendation from within the organization. As in most organizations, the Human Resources Department posts all positions internally so that current employees can apply first before the position is advertised externally. The instructor may wish to share this information with the students before they respond to this memo. However, the student response should be the same whether they have this information or not.

The student should be able to read between the lines and know that this situation may result in a lawsuit. Betty's 25 years with the company indicates that she is over 40 years of age and has some protection from the law (e.g., Age Discrimination in Employment Act of 1967, Equal Employment Opportunity Act of 1972). Before reacting to this memo the student needs to be aware that Mitch has no background information concerning the recent hiring situation since Bob Boyd, VP for Human Resources, has provided no supporting information relating to this situation other than attaching Betty Black's letter.

The language used in Mitch's response to Betty has to be carefully worded. The tendency of students is to apologize to Betty. While this is a courteous response, it, nevertheless, can indicate guilt if entered into a court proceeding. A response does need to be made so that Betty will not think her concerns are being ignored. The best response is a minimal response. The student should draft a separate memo to Bob Boyd asking him to investigate the hiring procedures concerning the head costume designer position.

This memo response should be in the form of a letter since it will be sent to the residence of the employee. Mitch may wish to have the corporate attorney review his response before it is sent to Betty.

Response: (Written in letter format)

Dear Betty,

Thank you for you recent letter. Our company policy is to hire the most qualified person for available positions.

We do appreciate your long years of service and hope that you will continue your dedicated work for the Broadway Management Company.

Sincerely,

Mitch Morris

Vice-President

Memo to Bob Boyd: Could you send me material relating to the advertising and hiring of the head costume designer position.

Memo 5: Budget

Guidelines: Students may need an explanation of line item budgeting before handling this memo. A line item budget is set up with an individual account in each line (eg., salaries, travel, supplies). Monies cannot be moved from one line to another if there is an overexpenditure in one line and an underexpenditure in another. The budget is developed by each Vice President or department head for his or her own area based on previous budgets and projected expenditures. The Budget For Year Ending December 31, 1997 CANNOT be changed by the student. This has already been approved.

The Cumulative Actual Expenditures to June 30, 1997 indicates the amount of money already spent in the first half of the year. The Budget For Year Ending December 31, 1997 is the amount of money that is available in each line for the entire year. Mitch must stay within this proposed and approved amount. The student should begin by calculating the amount that is needed for each quarter (divided budgeted amount by 4). This amount is then doubled to determine if there has been an over- or under-expenditure at the end of the second quarter (June 30, 1997). Each line should be calculated in this manner. Salaries do not increase over the projected year-end budget amount during the year unless a new employee is hired. Rent should remain the same for each year since rent is generally only raised once a year, if at all. The Broadway music industry has large expenses for advertising, travel, and communications, hence the large budgeted amounts.

Response:

Item	Need per quarter	Amount over/under budget
Salaries	$800,000/4 = 200,000	--
Benefits	150,000/4 = 37,500	--
Travel	80,000/4 = 20,000	over $20,000 (60,000 - 40,000)
Advertising	600,000/4 = 150,000	over 150,00 (450,000-300,000)
Training	50,000/4 = 12,500	over 20,000 (45,000 -25,000)
Supplies	40,000/4 = 10,000	under 10,000 (20,000-10,000)
Maintenance & Repairs	60,000/4 = 15,000	under 10,000 (30,00-20,000)
Communications	42,000/4 = 10,500	over 9000 (30,000-21,000)
Rent	120,000/4 = 30,000	--

Memo 6: Confidential Memo

Guidelines: This memo should be a "red flag" concerning ethics in general and Bob Boyd's in particular. The candidate may be qualified but she should be placed in the pool with all the other candidates. Bringing her salary up 8% would be in conflict with a concern for budget overruns. Also there is no budget excess for salaries (Memo 5). Bob Boyd's previous personal relationship with the candidate should also be a "red flag" for the student. Confidential memos are not generally handled by secretaries. Therefore the response to this memo may have to be stapled shut with Bob Boyd's name on the front.

The student should be advised that information such as is found in this memo should not be placed in writing.

Response:

TO: Bob Boyd

Thanks for your suggestion regarding the candidate for the manager position in "Charlie." Unfortunately I have no budget flexibility for salaries so the 8% increase is out of the question at this time. Please have your friend interview for the position along with the other candidates.

Memo 7: Revenue Projections

Guidelines: This is an important memo since it comes from the president. This memo is related to memo 12. Mitch should take the time now to complete a time chart for this musical since that can help to allay the fears of the investors regarding the opening of the musical. Since Mitch is going out of town he will have to delegate the task of providing revenue projections to Richard to others. Both John Brown, VP for Finance, and Amy McBride, manager of "Charlie," can assist with this.

Response:

TO: Richard Reynolds

Attached is the time chart estimation for "Charlie" (see Memo 12). As you can tell, we plan to be on target. I have asked John Brown and Amy McBride to work together and send you the revenue projections on Monday since I will be in Toronto. Please feel free to call me in Toronto for any additional information.

Memo to John Brown:

John, I'm on my way out of town and need to ask your assistance on some financial projections for "Charlie" that Richard needs ASAP—on Monday, if at all possible. I have asked Amy McBride to call you early Monday morning and give you all of her projections. Can you FAX me a copy of these projections before turning them into Richard. My secretary, Alice, has my address in Toronto.

Thanks so much, John, for all your help on this. As you can imagine Richard and his investors are concerned about the finances.

Memo To Alice: Please call Amy McBride and have her contact John ASAP on Monday morning. He is going to work with her on putting together a report for Richard Reynolds on financial projections for "Charlie." She will need to have all the financial figures for "Charlie" with her when she talks with John. Please stress the importance of calling John ASAP.

Memo 8: Mack Aldridge

Guidelines: This memo needs careful attention. Mitch needs to encourage his managers to be able to handle their own problems. Mack seems to be "dumping" his problems onto Mitch's shoulders. Managers need to make their own decision even if it entails making an occasional mistake. However, in the case of the first situation in Mack's memo regarding employee threats to file grievances, Mitch may need to get involved. Mitch's memo to Mack should be worded to let Mack know that Mitch understands Mack's problems but that he will not solve them for Mack.

Response:

TO: Mack Aldridge

Thanks for keeping me informed. I trust your good judgment when handling these problems. I have found that it is always beneficial to communicate openly and let the musicians and performers know about the budget constraints we have in order to head off employee grievances. You might talk to the Red Road Inn manager and see if conditions can't be improved somewhat. Of course, let the employees know about your efforts on their behalf. Let me know how this works out.

I trust your judgment relating to the transport firm. You might drop me a copy of the criteria that you use to select a transport company.

Memo 9: Financial Analyst

Guidelines: Jay Craig appears to be able to provide valuable assistance to Mitch since he has a broad accounting background. Mitch will need to meet with Jay as soon as he returns from Seattle. Mitch should ask Alice to make an appointment for him with Jay.

Response:

TO: Jay Craig

Good to hear from you! I look forward to meeting you and working together as soon as I return from Seattle. I have asked my secretary, Alice, to set up an appointment with you. You might review our budgets over the past five years and take a look at our budget projections for this year as preparation for this meeting.

Thanks so much.

Memo 10: Performance Evaluation

Guidelines: The instructor may wish to provide the students with additional information regarding performance evaluations such as Management by Objectives (MBO). This task has to be delegated to each manager by Mitch. He should also indicate to each manager the importance of a timely report. The student should be aware of the chain of command and send the managers' responses to Mitch rather than directly to Richard. Mitch will then communicate the master report to Richard.

Response:

TO: Alice

Please type and send the following memo to all my managers. Could you FAX me their reports to Toronto or Seattle as soon as they come in.

Thanks.

TO: Company Managers

RE: Performance Evaluations

Richard has asked me to compile a report for him on the steps we have taken to implement the new employee performance evaluation system. Can you summarize the steps you have taken within your own group and give this report to Alice before the end of the week.

Thanks for your continued assistance during this busy season.

Memo 11: Bob Boyd

Guidelines: Once again Bob Boyd is flying a "red flag" of ethics for the students. He mentions that he is promoting an indoor track at work so he can save money on a club membership. This is certainly at least of "suspect ethics."

Employees are interested in much more than simply money. The students should tactfully respond to Bob about methods to determine what the employees really want. One of these methods is through the use of an employee survey tool. Bob should probably get assistance in the development of this tool since his views are biased.

Response:

TO: Bob Boyd

Thanks for asking my opinion about employee satisfaction. I've always found that the best way to find out about what people want is to ask them. Why not work with a consultant to develop a survey questionnaire that we can give to all the employees. We can actually gather information relating to a lot of the issues we've been discussing during the past year. I would be happy to work with you on this project.

Memo 12: Time Chart

Guidelines: The instructor may wish to give the students a format to follow for developing a time chart or graph. The key feature of this type of exercise is that the student should work backwards from the date when the project is due to open on August 1st. The date of Richard's memo June 20th can be used since the production is already under way.

The students should use creative thinking when working on a time line. They have to deal with a holiday (July 4th). This can cause a delay in any work done that week. If they wish to have anyone work on the holiday, such as the carpenters, it will result in having to pay them time-and-one-half wages. The student should allow some overlap between the carpenters and when the set is needed in case there are necessary alterations. Safety checks and inspections may require more time than originally allowed. The student should allow extra time for problems in these areas to be corrected.

Unit 9: The Career Readiness Notebook — Instructor's Notes

Response:

TO: Richard Reynolds

RE: Time Chart for "Charlie"

Dates by Week

Week	1	2	3	4	5	6	OPEN
	June 20th	June 27th	July 4th	July 11th	July 18th	July 25th	Aug. 1st

```
Advertising***********************************************************

Tickets *****

Contracts signed                       *******

Carpentry work for set ********

Assembly of set            *********

Ticket Pre-sales           ********************************************

Telephone installation              **

Electrical work                                ******

Dress rehearsal                                          *******

Inspection                                          ****

Safety check                                        ****
```

Memo 13: Emily Andrews

Guidelines: The student should note that this manager, Emily Andrews, seems to be on top of management issues that need to be addressed. Mitch should encourage her initiative by setting up a meeting as soon as he returns from Seattle.

Response:

TO: Emily Andrews

I'm delighted to hear of your interest in helping us move ahead with our hiring of minority personnel. Please call my secretary, Alice, to set up an appointment for us so we can discuss this further. I will be in Toronto and then on to Seattle for the next couple of weeks. Feel free to FAX me your ideas to Toronto or Seattle so that I have time to review them before our meeting.

Thanks so much.

Memo 14: Diane Friend

Guidelines: This memo should be another "red flag" for the students. Diane is asking for a "good" reference from Mitch when she knows that she won't get one from her boss, Richard Reynolds. The student should relate this back to memo 4 in which Diane Friend may have caused problems by supporting Grace Foster. Mitch may have difficulty placing in writing that Diane is "fair." Mitch can indicate to Diane that he might not be the best one to write a letter for her since he is not her immediate boss. If he does write a letter it will have to be vague and just state the time frame during which he has known her and in what capacity.

Response: CONFIDENTIAL

TO: Diane Friend

I wish you all the best of luck with your recent job opportunity. While I consider you a friend, I may not be the best person to write a letter of recommendation for you since you report to Richard and not to me. Why don't you discuss this with Richard?

Again, I wish you the best of luck!

Memo 15: Budget Forecast

Guidelines: If the students have read through all of the memos before beginning to respond to this one they will know that this memo is related to memo 20. In memo 20, John Brown indicates that his staff has put in overtime to develop the budget figures that Reynolds is congratulating Mitch for. Mitch needs to give the proper credit to John's staff.

Response:

TO: Richard Reynolds

I'm glad to hear that the budget forecast met your needs. It was accomplished due to the hard work of a lot people and, in particular, John Brown's staff.

CC: John Brown

Memo 16: Federal Regulations

Guidelines: The instructor may ask students to use the federal regulations that are discussed in class when writing this memo. The responses will be varied but might include: Occupational Safety and Health Act (OSHA) of 1970, Title VII of the Civil Rights Act of 1964, Civil Rights Act of 1991, Wagner Act of 1935, Taft-Hartley Act of 1947, Equal Employment Opportunity Act of 1972, Pregnancy Discrimination Act of 1978, Age Discrimination in Employment Act of 1967, American with Disabilities Act of 1990, Fair Labor Standards Act (FLSA) of 1938, Equal Pay Act of 1963, Federal Insurance Contribution Act of 1935, Health Maintenance Organization Act of 1973, Consolidated Omnibus Budget Reconciliation Act (COBRA) of 1985, Worker's Compensation Act, Employee Retirement Income Security Act (ERISA) of 1974, and the Family and Medical Leave Act of 1994.

Response:

TO: Richard Reynolds

I am in total agreement with your planned seminars relating to the federal regulations. I believe the following should be included:

(Student responses may vary)

Memo 17: Public Relations

Guidelines: Managers must avoid having work "dumped" on them that could be more appropriately handled by others. In this case, Diane Friend, as Vice-President for marketing, is asking Mitch to do her job. Mitch needs to gently, but firmly, let her know that she must handle overcharges that relate to public relations. The students must keep in mind the chain of command and note that Diane does not report to Mitch. She is his equal and reports directly to Richard Reynolds. However, it is not appropriate for Mitch to cause trouble for Diane by going over her head and complaining to Richard.

Response:

TO: Diane Friend

Sorry to hear about your problems with the PR firm and overcharges for the musical "Mortgage." I'm confident that you will convince them of their error.

I'm on my way out of town for a couple of weeks but I would appreciate an update on the closure of this problem when I return.

Memo 18: Late delivery

Guidelines: Once again Mack Aldridge is demonstrating a reluctance to accept his responsibilities as a manager. Mitch will have to diplomatically let him know that this is his job.

Response:

TO: Mack Aldridge

Sorry to hear about your problem. I know how frustrating this must be for you and that you will want to resolve the problem as soon as possible.

Why don't you FAX me in Toronto next week with your solution. We can then discuss your progress when I return from Seattle in two weeks.

Memo 19: Fred Stauffer

Guidelines: This manager is demonstrating a proactive approach to management. He is also keeping his boss up to date by enclosing recent newspaper clips (not included in the case). Mitch should acknowledge his good work and circulate the two articles to the other managers since the topic applies to all of them.

Response:

TO: Fred Stauffer

Thanks so much for the update on the situation with music lyrics. I'm delighted to hear that the local news media has treated us favorably. I'm sending a copy of the articles you attached out to all my managers for their review. Would you be prepared to discuss the handling of this situation at our next management meeting?

Memo 20: Five-year Budget Forecast

Guidelines: See memo 15

Response:

TO: John Brown

Please extend my thanks to your staff for all their hard work on the budget forecast. It is greatly appreciated.

Memo 21: Journal Article

Guidelines: Anything sent from the president to one of his or employees should be taken seriously. It's always appropriate to indicate that one has received material. In addition, Mitch might want to take this article along with him to read on the flight to Toronto. It is also important for his managers to read the article since they are involved in unionized industry.

Response:

TO: Richard

Thanks for the article. I have sent it to my managers to read as well.

TO: Alice

Could you send a copy of the article "Union Negotiations" to each of my managers. Attached a cover memo asking them to read the article and be ready to discuss it at our next management meeting. I am taking my copy with me but you can obtain another copy from Richard's secretary.

Thanks.

Memo 22: Gunpowder Incident

Guidelines: This is a potential legal problem that may result in a fine or closure of the musical "Charlie." Even though students will be unfamiliar with the musical industry, they should consider the seriousness of a violation of a federal regulation such as the Clean Air Act. Responses to this memo may vary from asking Amy McBride, manager of "Charlie," to temporarily cease the use of gunpowder until the matter can be resolved to getting the company's attorney immediately involved. The student should also note the date of this memo was three weeks ago (June 6). Mitch should have been informed of this issue immediately by his secretary and/or Amy McBride (manager of "Charlie").

Response:

July 1

TO: Richard Reynolds

I just received your memo relating to the gunpowder situation in Madrid, Illinois. I'll get onto this matter immediately.

I will get in touch with our attorney tomorrow morning to seek her opinion. I am also asking Amy McBride to temporarily cease the use of gunpowder until we can determine the facts.

Memo To Amy McBride:

Please call me in Toronto tomorrow morning (July 2nd) to discuss the use of gunpowder in "Charlie." I believe that we should stop using gunpowder until the facts can be gathered regarding the Clean Air Act. I will be in Seattle the following week for the opening of "Charlie" and we can discuss this more fully after we have reviewed all the facts.

Memo 23: Japanese Management

Guidelines: Emily Andrews appears to be a proactive manager who has proposed a plan to adopt some of the Japanese management practices when taking a musical production to Japan. Mitch will want to encourage such initiative even though not all of the practices may be feasible. For example, the company may not be able to pay bonuses for extraordinary performances since all the performers are covered by union rules. A bonus would have to be given to ALL performers both in and out of Japan according to union rules. His memo should reflect that he

517

supports Emily's initiative but that she must be able to implement a plan to put the feasible ideas into practice.

Response:

Emily,

Thanks so much for your interesting thoughts regarding Japanese management practices. I would like to discuss this further with you. Please set up an appointment through my secretary, Alice, for the week when I return from Seattle.

In the meantime, would you draft your thoughts on a workable plan of action for implementing the feasible management practices.

Once again, thanks for your innovative ideas!

Memo 24: Budget Concerns

Guidelines: This is an important memo and demonstrates the need for students to read all the memos before writing a response to any one memo. This memo indicates that the company is having a financially difficult year and everyone must make a budget cut for the next fiscal year.   This does not mean that this year's budget is reduced (Memo 5). The students do not have the budget for next year in this exercise. However, Mitch should reinforce the memo from Richard Reynolds to all his department heads and managers. He should copy (cc) Richard Reynolds on the memo he sends.

Response:

TO: Amy McBride, Mack Aldridge, Fred Stauffer, and Emily Andrews

RE: Budget Concerns

As a follow-up to Richard Reynold's memo directive about 10% across-the-board budget cuts for the next fiscal year, would you send me your revised budgets by August 1st. I appreciate your support in this matter and know that if we all pull together we can end up on a positive note by the end of the next fiscal year.

cc: Richard Reynolds

Memo 25: Speaking Engagement

Guidelines: This is another example of a memo that is coming through to Mitch at a very late date. He receives the memo on July 1st and is leaving on a two week business trip. Therefore he will miss the speaking engagement at his alma mater. He will most likely want to speak to his secretary, Jean, about a better method for reminding him about engagements when he returns from his Seattle trip. He can put this item on his TO DO list.

Mitch will need to draft a letter for his secretary to type, sign, and send for him if he wishes to cancel this speaking engagement. If he is going to make arrangements to fly in for the weekend to speak at his alma mater then he does not have to draft a letter. However he will need to make flight reservations. Either way, the student will have to handle this memo immediately.

Response: (Alice—Please type this letter for me, sign my name and send on Monday.)

Broadway Management Productions

1212 Broadway

New York, New York 10011

(123) 555-1000

Sylvia Brennan

Director

MBA Program

University of _____

Home Town, USA

July 1, 1997

Dear Sylvia,

Due to an unexpected business trip I find that I will be in Seattle on the date of your MBA conference. Since I am unable to arrange to get back to the East coast in time for your conference, I deeply regret that I will have to cancel. Fortunately there are many other very capable speakers lined up for our panel discussion that can carry on without me. However I am very sorry to miss this opportunity to take part in the conference.

Please keep me in mind for next year's conference. Feel free to call upon me to assist my alma mater in any other way I can.

Sincerely,

Mitch Morris

Memo 26: Legal Problem

Guidelines: Copyright research is the process of examining all the existing titles for such things as musicals, songs, and books to determine if a name or title has already been used. Since copyright research has already been conducted about the title "Charlie", Mitch will need further clarification from the legal department on this issue. Students should learn to use the services of support departments and consultants. As managers, they should always ask for recommendations from support departments and their staff.

Response:

TO: John Brown

Your memo regarding the use of the title "Charlie" is confusing since we had already done such a thorough search. Could you ask the legal department to give us the details regarding this issue. Then I would like to meet with you to discuss a plan of action.

Thanks.

Memo 27: Employee Reference

Guidelines: Employee references need to be written very cautiously. The employee's confidentiality must be protected at all times. In addition, the employer cannot make a statement regarding the employee, such as "He is stable emotionally," or "He always pays his debts," which may ultimately reflect negatively on the person providing the reference. For example, an employer cannot know if an employee is always stable or always pays his or her debts. The student should also sense an undertone in this letter that suggests that Frank Lynch is misusing his business relationship (financing of a new musical) when asking for confidential information about an employee.

The student can assume that Fred Stauffer knows that Frank Lynch is making the inquiry since Fred would have had to provide the name and address of a contact person at his place of employment. This would be an even more serious violation of confidentiality if Fred did not know about the request. Mitch may still wish to let Fred Stauffer know that he was asked to submit a recommendation.

Human Resource Departments will only state the dates of employment and the employee's salary when asked for references. Mitch should do the same.

Response: Written in letter format

Frank Lynch
Vice-President
First National Mortgage Bank
111 Finance Way
New York, NY 10011

Dear Frank,

This letter is in reference to your recent inquiry about our employee, Fred Stauffer. According to our personnel policy we provide information relating to dates of employment and salary for any employee if they make this request.

Fred has been employed as a company manager from _____ to the present time. His salary is $ _____.

Sincerely,

Mitch Morris
Vice-President

EXHIBIT 2

GRADING FORM FOR IN-BASKET EXERCISE

MEMO #/TOPIC	1	2	3	4	5
1. Welcome Back!					
2. Employee Complaint					
3. Broker					
4. Betty Black Letter					
5. Budget					
6. Confidential Memo					
7. Revenue Projections					
8. Mack Aldridge					
9. Financial Analyst					
10. Performance Evaluations					
11. Bob Boyd					
12. Time Chart					
13. Emily Andrews					
14. Diane Friend					
15. Budget Forecast					
16. Federal Regulations					
17. Public Relations					
18. Late Delivery					
19. Fred Stauffer					
20. Five-year Budget Forecast					
21. Journal Article					
22. Gunpowder Incident					
23. Japanese Management					
24. Budget Concerns					
25. Speaking Engagement					
26. Legal Problem					
27. Employee Reference					

Grading Scale

1 = Does not meet expectations: indicates the student has made NO response to a memo.
2 = Barely meets expectations: indicates that a minimal attempt has been made to respond to some of the memos
3 = Average responses: indicates that all memos have responses with only 4-6 errors
4 = Above average: indicates that all memos have responses with fewer than 3 errors.
5 = Above average in critical thinking: demonstrates a unique solution to a difficult problem using correct management language with NO errors.

INTEGRATIVE ACTIVITIES

INSTRUCTOR'S NOTES: INTEGRATED CROSS-FUNCTIONAL CASE

Outback Steakhouse, Inc. — Fueling the Fast-Growth Company

Marilyn L Taylor

Bloch School of Business and Public Administration

University of Missouri at Kansas City

George M. Puia

College of Business Administration

University of Tampa

Krishnan Ramaya

School of Business

University of Kansas

Madelyn Gengelbach

Bloch School of Business and Public Administration

University of Missouri at Kansas City

Support for the development of this case was provided by:

Center for Entrepreneurial Leadership

Ewing Marion Kauffman Foundation

Kansas City, MO

GENERAL CASE NOTES

Case Overview

Outback Steakhouse is a high-growth company in the casual dining segment of the restaurant industry. Using a strategy that defies the conventional wisdom, Outback Steakhouse has grown from 1 location to its current size of 243 restaurants in just seven years. In 1995, the Outback management team won the prestigious "Entrepreneur of the Year" award from the Ewing Kauffman Foundation.

The values of the Outback top management strongly influence the company's strategy. In particular, the founders believe their success is the result of two deliberate actions, exceeding customer expectations and creating great work environments for its employees.

The case presents ways in which Outback strives to operationalize its core value. Outback has the highest food cost as a percentage of gross revenues in the casual dining industry. Its managers are preoccupied with the small details of food preparation (they spend three hours a day on croutons). Outback has over-designed the kitchen space. Proprietors inspect every dish before it is seen by the customers. Restaurants serve dinner only so their staff can be "fresh" to service customers, and offer employees a stake in the outcomes of the restaurant and the company.

While the company has been very successful to this point, Outback's dramatic growth could grind to a standstill if they do not successfully develop new restaurant concepts. Since the company is publicly traded, it faces pressure from its board of directors to continue its growth.

A follow-up case is provided that explores Outback's international potential. This case assumes some knowledge of Outback or familiarity with the first case. A separate teaching note is provided for the case.

Teaching Materials

There is a separate teaching note for each section of the case. The notes included discussion questions for each chapter in the section. Each question is briefly answered. Some of the answers include aids to differentiate top students from average students. Additional teaching ideas (role-play, simulation, WWW exercises, etc.) are also provided. In addition, there are two complete self-contained supplements provided to adopters of this text: a video case study and a follow-up case study. The video was professionally produced from original and archival material. It is approximately 20 minutes long and is divided into three sections to facilitate class discussion. The follow-up case is approximately 6 pages in length. It addresses Outback's decision to internationalize its operations. The case is an abbreviated version of Outback Goes International, published in the Case Research Journal. The video and two cases have been field-tested and peer reviewed.

Case Background

This case was developed using original field-research, archival materials and secondary sources. As part of Outback's Entrepreneur of the Year award, the Kauffman Foundation requested that Outback allow a team to 1) write a case study for use in the classroom and 2) participate in the production of a video case study. The authors received a grant from the foundation to develop both the case and video.

Several rounds of interviews were conducted over a month long period. All interviews were taped on either an audio or video format. Tapes were fully transcribed. The research team then constructed a draft case from the interviews. This generated additional questions that were handled largely by phone interviews. The case was then reviewed at a NACRA workshop. Improvements were made to the case as the result of the comments of anonymous reviewers and a public review panel. The purpose of the case is to stimulate student discussion, not to portray effective or ineffective management techniques.

INTEGRATING THE OUTBACK CASE WITH PART 1:

MANAGEMENT TODAY

General Overview: Part 1

Outback Steakhouse is a high-growth company in the casual dining segment of the restaurant industry. Using a strategy that defied the conventional wisdom, Outback Steakhouse had grown from 1 location to 243 restaurants in just seven years. In 1995, the Outback management team won the prestigious "Entrepreneur of the Year" award from the Ewing Kauffman Foundation.

The values of the Outback top management strongly influence the company's strategy. In particular, the founders believed their success to be the result of two deliberate actions: exceeding customer expectations and creating great work environments for its employees.

The case traces the value adding chain of Outback Steakhouse and shows the shared values of the founders, executives, managers and employees.

Outback Teaching Suggestions: Part 1

Class discussions are most effective when students are equally prepared. You can bring students to a common level of preparation by having them type their answer to one of the discussion questions. This will require them to have read the case and familiarized themselves with the case. The remaining questions can then be discussed in class.

Sample class discussion questions are identified below. An alternative to a teacher-controlled discussion is to assign student teams to answer one of the questions or sections below. Each team can prepare one overhead and lead a discussion of that section.

Two additional teaching ideas follow the discussion questions: A WWW scavenger hunt and a career search. Both can be used as original assignments or as a follow-up to class discussion.

Outback Discussion Questions and Answers: Part 1

Answers to Outback Review Questions for Chapter 1:

The Dynamic New Workplace

1. **How many levels of management can you find in the Outback Case?**

    There are four to five levels mentioned: Sullivan, CEO; Basham, VP; Proprietor-managers; and Assistant managers. In franchising, there is an additional level of multi-store franchise holders.

2. **How do managerial roles differ across levels at Outback?**

    Top level managers are more long term (strategic) in their orientation. Proprietors deal with day to day operations. For example, Gannon is working on new menu items; the stores do not control their own menus. Sharp students may refer to the Manager's notepad 1.1 to identify the eight responsibilities of team leaders and supervisors.

3. **What management skills and competencies did the Outback founders bring to their new venture?**

    They brought differing skills and backgrounds. Gannon was an experienced chef with international experience; Basham is a master at operations management and site selection; Sullivan is a strong general manager. They all had long careers in food service and hospitality management. Each had started at the bottom and worked their way up (Gannon cooking, Sullivan washing dishes; Basham serving tables). They had worked in small and large restaurants and in corporate restaurant positions. Then had been franchise holders. In essence, they had trained their whole career to become founders of Outback. In addition to their rich and diverse experiences, they seemed close to the customer—they had a proven intuition about customer preferences. They were also in touch with the research in their field.

Answers to Outback Review Questions for Chapter 2:

Environment and Competitive Advantage

1. **What environmental factors may have influenced Outback's success?**

    The anti-red meat craze may have worked to Outback's advantage. People were buying less red meat at the supermarkets but more in restaurants. There were few restaurateurs that wanted to enter the market, reducing potential competition. Culturally, the US market had become more casual - office workers were required to dress less formally. There was a competitive niche that was under-serviced by competitors; fine food but a casual atmosphere. The economy was strong. Unemployment was relatively low. Baby boomers were reaching peak income producing years. Two income families made food preparation time more scares; dining became a larger part of boomer's food budgets.

2. **What evidence can you find in the case to suggest Outback steakhouse is committed to quality?**

Outback has the highest food cost as a percentage of gross revenues in the casual dining industry. They seem preoccupied with the small details of food preparation (they spend three hours a day on croutons). Outback has been over-designing the kitchen space, making their kitchens larger than their competitors. Management inspects every dish before it is seen by the customers. The company serves dinner only so their staff can be "fresh" to service customers.

3. **To what extent is Outback a customer driven organization?**

All of the quality examples above are also examples of Outback's commitment to customers. In addition, students might note the nature of casual dining; customers need not "dress-up" to enjoy a fine meal. Bright students however will note areas where Outback seems to lack commitment to customers including the long wait that customers often face. In addition to examples of failing to meet customer expectations, the case is silent about a number of issues. For example there is no mention of on-going customer satisfaction surveys, etc.

4. **Describe the culture of Outback Steakhouse?**

Outback's founders have strong values and have worked hard to influence their organization to retain those values. Outback is described as a fun place to work. There is an emphasis on being and remaining casual. There is a strong commitment to quality in both food and service.

Answers to Outback Review Questions for Chapter 3:

Information Technology and Decision Making

1. **If you were an executive at Outback what information would you want available on a regular basis?**

(Speculative discussion question; the case is not needed to specifically answer this question). Students will likely want every piece of information externally and internally; they typically ask for more information then is manageable. Key external information requirements relate to demand and competition: Is their anything happening in the external environment that would result in an increase or decrease in demand for fine steak in a casual setting. Key competitive information might include restaurant start-ups, competitive advertising efforts, etc. Key internal information might include performance measures like "same store sales." If students ask for obtuse information, you might wish to probe their answer with one or more of the following questions. What would you do with that information?   What measure would you use to determine if there is a problem?

2.   **Is Outback a "learning organization"? Defend your answer?**

The text utilizes Senge's six ingredients of a learning organization: Mental models, personal mastery, systems thinking, shared vision and team learning.   Certainly at its founding Outback utilized mental models.   CEO Sullivan notes his need for (open to his teams ideas) his management team - a form of personal mastery, there is some evidence of systems thinking (food sourcing, size of kitchen, etc.), clearly there is a shared vision throughout the organization.   The training and start-up of each new restaurant requires team teaching and learning.   Therefore, based on Senge's model, Outback could be considered a learning organization.

Additional Outback Teaching Suggestions: Part 1

WWW Scavenger Hunt

1.   **Send your students on an Outback scavenger hunt.   Students are asked to search the web and bring one printout for each example below.**

An outback home page

A home page from one of Outback's direct competitors

An article from a trade publication

U.S. Government information on the restaurant market

A recent story or press release about Outback from anywhere in the world.

2.   **Have your students discuss what they found.   You can probe with the following questions?**

How easy is it to find information about the restaurant industry? Outback?

If you were one of Outback's competitors, how easy would it be for you to track their actions?

Career Search

Students are often unaware that restaurant management and multi-store management are high paying jobs. Have the students look at trade publications to find salary information on restaurant careers. Have your students imagine that they are applying for an assistant manager position at Outback Steakhouse (either the front of the house or kitchen). What types of experiences, knowledge and skills might help them land a position? What steps might they take now to enhance their resumes?

INTEGRATING THE OUTBACK CASE WITH PART 2:

CONTEXT

General Overview: Part 2

Outback Steakhouse is a high-growth company in the casual dining segment of the restaurant industry. Using a strategy that defied the conventional wisdom, Outback Steakhouse had grown from 1 location to 243 restaurants in just seven years. In 1995, the Outback management team won the prestigious "Entrepreneur of the Year" award from the Ewing Kauffman Foundation.

The case provides information about the context of management: management history, global issues, ethics and social responsibility.

Outback Teaching Suggestions: Part 2

Class discussions are most effective when students are equally prepared. You can bring students to a common level of preparation by having them type their answer to one of the discussion questions. This will require them to have read the case and familiarized themselves with the case. The remaining questions can then be discussed in class.

Sample class discussion questions are identified below. An alternative to a teacher-controlled discussion is to assign student teams to answer one of the questions or sections below. Each team can prepare one overhead and lead a discussion of that section.

Outback Discussion Questions and Answers: Part 2

Answers to Outback Review Questions for Chapter 4:

Historical Foundations of Management

1. **What examples can you find in Outback Steakhouse of systems thinking? Contingency thinking?**

    The Outback case has several examples of systems thinking. In particular, for Outback to be successful in breaking one of the cardinal rules of the restaurant business, location is everything, it had to view the entire customer satisfaction system. Examples include: over-sizing the kitchen at the expense of seating area; preparing food by hand; training without a training staff; focusing on dinner only, etc. The text defines contingency thinking as maintaining that, "there is no one best way to manage and what is best depends in any given circumstance on the nature of the situation." Outback in general operates with the same management system in all of its restaurants. Good students will note that for the most part, Outback does not employ contingency management. The local managers however do have some discretion. Outback wants managers involved in the community, but the type of involvement is up to the manager. The style of management employed by the local proprietor is also beyond Outback's direct control, allowing for some contingency thinking. However, Outback does screen potential managers to see if there is a general match with their philosophy.

2. **To what extent does Outback employ a quality management philosophy?**

The text defines quality as the ability to meet customer needs 100% of the time. Outback goes a step beyond this and talks of exceeding customer expectations. Examples of concerns with quality can be divided into four areas: management values; restaurant design, food quality and service quality. The managers in this case seem clearly influenced by the desire for top quality. The restaurant is designed to provide optimum cook times during peak periods. The owners insist on ingredients from only the best sources: a single steak provided, Parmesan cheese from Parma Italy, etc. Every dish coming out of the restaurant is inspected. The hours of operations are designed to improve service quality. Outback is very systematic in its approach to quality. Good students might note however that Outback managers do not invoke the quality literature (there is no mention of Juran, Deming or the Baldrige award). A good follow up question might be to ask if companies achieve high quality without studying TQM?

Answers to Outback Review Questions for Chapter 5:

Global Dimensions of Management

1. **In what ways are Outback restaurants and international business?**

Average students may suggest that Outback is a domestic business because that is where their current stores are located. More sophisticated students will note that many of Outback's suppliers are offshore. The best students will likely note that Outback has some international competitors. Further, for Outback to continue to grow at its current rate, it will need to find new markets.

2. **What part of Outback's success might be unique to US culture?**

Students will likely note that Outback, with its Australian theme, clearly has U.S. values. In particular, Outback appeals to an American's sense of individualism (Hofstede). Consider their advertising message, "no rules, just right." It is clearly an example of individualism. The large kitchen size is easier to accomplish in the US, where big is often considered better. Our culture accepts chain restaurants better (our population is more mobile than many - people want the same quality at each location). The U.S. has strong national advertising outlets that make it easier for large companies to establish an identity with a customer segment. American's have an affinity for steak that is not shared in many countries. Casual dining of high quality food is consistent with America's sense of individualism (why do I have to play by someone else's rules and dress for dinner).

3. **What difficulties might Outback face in further internationalizing its operations?**

In addition to the issue of management values, one must address international experience; Outback's top managers have international restaurant experience. Another issue is the menu; Outback's menu would fail in many countries (students will likely invoke selling beef in Hindu countries). The size of the restaurant and size of the portions may be addressed (especially if you have Asian students - Outback's kitchen size might be prohibitively expensive in cities like Tokyo or Hong Kong). Casual fine dining may not translate culturally. The Australian theme may not translate to Australia.

Answers to Outback Review Questions for Chapter 6:

Ethical Behavior and Social Responsibility

1. **What examples of corporate social responsibility are evident at Outback?**

Students will likely identify several issues including corporate giving, employee ownership and employee benefits. Outback's charitable giving includes charitable golf tournaments, sponsorship of collegiate sporting events and local charity events. Employee ownership provides the opportunity for a larger number of employees to share the company's wealth creation. The employee benefits program is aimed at helping lower level employees achieve financial security. Sharp students might also note Outback's commitment to quality of worklife, including longer-term management contracts, dinner only hours and limiting the number of tables served.

2. **What benefits might Outback accrue by virtue of their socially responsible performance?**

Outback should be able to attract the best human resources as the offer better compensation, benefits and quality of worklife. If this is true, than Outback should find it easier to gain and sustain competitive advantage. The charitable activities of Outback are also promotional activities at two levels. Outback gains support from the staff, board and friends of the organization it supports, and it will also likely receive free positive coverage in the local media. This results in a positive image for Outback and greater awareness of their presence in the community.

3. **Open discussion (not supported in one way of another by the case data). Do you feel Outback's managers would make social responsible decisions if they were not also profitable?**

The class will likely divide on this issue. Some will say no, that it would not be logical for Outback to lose money for the sake of doing good. Other students may note that Outback's benefit program was rolled out after they hired many of their employees; it was not used to recruit the best.

Additional Outback Teaching Suggestions

Taking Outback Abroad

A complete supplemental case is provided for instructors who wish to investigate international issues in more depth. The second case, approximately six pages, allows students to consider whether Outback would be successful overseas. To resolve that issue students may explore several questions: Should Outback take its business abroad? What skills should Outback posses if it wants to be successful internationally? Does Outback posses those skills? If you were Outback and wanted to internationalize your operations, in what country would you start?

Corporate Code of Ethics

Have students work in teams to develop a code of ethics for Outback's employees. Each code must address the following stakeholders: Customers, employees, shareholders, suppliers and the local community. Have each team present their code of ethics and then ask the following discussion questions:

1. How will you measure adherence to your code?

2. How difficult will your code be to enforce?

3. What possible conflicts of interest might occur between differing stakeholders (e.g., stockholders and customers)? With what stakeholder group if any should Outback be most concerned?

INTEGRATING THE OUTBACK CASE WITH PART 3:

MISSION

General Overview: Part 3

Outback Steakhouse is a high-growth company in the casual dining segment of the restaurant industry. Using a strategy that defied the conventional wisdom, Outback Steakhouse had grown from 1 location to 243 restaurants in just seven years. In 1995, the Outback management team won the prestigious "Entrepreneur of the Year" award from the Ewing Kauffman Foundation.

The values of the Outback top management strongly influence the company's strategy. In particular, the founders believed their success to be the result of two deliberate actions: exceeding customer expectations and creating great work environments for its employees. The case includes especially rich examples of Outback's entrepreneurial actions and spirit. The case includes rich information about Outback's environments including the general external and competitive environment. Students should be able to make a rudimentary analysis of the environment from information in the case. It also can be used a strategic management case to demonstrate the need to "fit" and organization to its environment.

Outback Teaching Suggestions: Part 3

Class discussions are most effective when students are equally prepared. You can bring students to a common level of preparation by having them type their answer to one of the discussion questions. This will require them to have read the case and familiarized themselves with the case. The remaining questions can then be discussed in class.

Sample class discussion questions are identified below. An alternative to a teacher-controlled discussion is to assign student teams to answer one of the questions or sections below. Each team can prepare one overhead and lead a discussion of that section.

Outback Discussion Questions and Answers: Part 3

Answers to Outback Review Questions for Chapter 7:

Planning - To Set Direction

1. **Describe the different types of planning evident at Outback?**

    Students should be able to find evidence in the case for strategic planning (comprehensive actions and directions) using examples like Carrabbas and internationalization; operational plans are represented by restaurant opening plans, location plans, etc. Standing plans/policies are represented by Outback's ownership strategy and HR policies. Single use plans might be represented by the PR strategy for a new store opening. Project schedules are used extensively in the opening of a new restaurant. Students should be able to identify all levels of planning either implicitly or explicitly. A good exercise here is to use probing questions to link this chapter with earlier materials. For example, you might ask the students to link the planning activities in this chapter with the levels of management in Chapter 1. This will help students to become less compartmentalized in their knowledge of management.

Answers to Outback Review Questions for Chapter 8:

Strategic Management and Entrepreneurship

1. **What examples of "levels of strategies" can you find in the Outback case?**

    The corporate level Outback is pursuing a second Italian restaurant concept and international activities. Outback has a business level strategy (focused differentiation) centered on the issues of casual dining and high food quality. An example of a functional strategy is Outback's HR policies of providing benefits to lower level employees. Students will also likely note that Outback has clearly chosen a growth strategy.

2. **Perform a SWOT analysis on Outback?**

    This question will work equally well for individuals or for teams. Students will likely find it easier to identify strengths and opportunities (which are noted in the case) than weaknesses and threats (which are largely inferred in the case). Look for student perspectives. Make sure they are including shareholder interests as well as those or customers. *Strengths* include top management experience and expertise, commitment to quality, use of highest quality ingredients, design of restaurants, quality of food, ability to recruit strong employees and solid record of profitability. *Weaknesses* include customer waiting-time, lack of international presence, lack of presence in large cities, uneven geographic presence, and a menu that favors one demographic segment. *Opportunities* include international operations, second restaurant concepts (like Carrabas Italian Grill) and franchise operations in larger cities. *Threats* include news competitors, the ability of competitors to imitate Outback's menu and or processes, lack of growth opportunities for Outback restaurants (market saturation) and the aging of Outback's primary target market.

Answers to Outback Review Questions for Chapter 9:

Controlling - To Ensure Results

1. What types of controls are used at Outback?

The book notes several types of controls including feedforward controls, concurrent controls, feedback controls, internal and external controls. Examples of feedforward controls might include Outback's selection process for suppliers and some of its hiring practices. Concurrent controls include management's inspections of plates as they leave the kitchen. Feedback controls include customer feedback (which is noted directly in the text on this section). It also includes proxy measures like improvements in same-store sales (is customer volume increasing at a specific location). At the management level, internal control is clearly prevalent at Outback. Outback aggressively recruits top talent and then lets them manage the local operation. (Clearly indicative of the Theory Y management style noted in this section of the text). Sharp students may note that lower level employees may face more external control (the chef has his work directly inspected, the manager does not).

2. In your opinion, how effective are Outback's control methods?

The text includes criteria for control effectiveness. Top students will likely reflect on these seven criteria: Controls should be strategic and results oriented; controls should be understandable, controls should encourage self-control; controls should be timely and exception oriented; controls should be positive in nature; controls should be fair and objective; and controls should be flexible. The case will provide grounds for discussion on all seven criteria save timely and exception oriented (the case simply does not provide sufficient data to allow an informed guess). Some students will skip the model and go directly to Outback's strong results. Students should be encouraged to think of the model, as Outback might merely be successful as the result of some externally relevant factors.

Additional Outback Teaching Suggestions: Part 3

Video Case

A complete video case is available to adopters of this text. The video case includes interviews with the founders of Outback: Sullivan, Basham and Gannon; as well as with executives, managers and employees. Students will be able to see the shared mission and values of Outback employees and get a sense of their entrepreneurial spirit. A complete instructors note is included. The video case is approximately 20 minutes long and is divided into three sections. The sections can be used as a stand-alone resource.

New Venture Scenario

To better expose students to the strategy making process, you may have them prepare a brief plan or plan outline to meet the following scenario. Outback has decided it can capitalize on its history of involvement with collegiate sports by developing a chain of sports bars. Have the students work in small groups or teams to address the following issues:

1. What synergies (shared resources, skills, assets or knowledge) might be shared between Outback and the new venture?

2. Who would be Outback's major competitors?

INTEGRATING THE OUTBACK CASE WITH PART 4:

ORGANIZATION

General Overview: Part 4

Outback Steakhouse is a high-growth company in the casual dining segment of the restaurant industry. Using a strategy that defied the conventional wisdom, Outback Steakhouse had grown from 1 location to 243 restaurants in just seven years. In 1995, the Outback management team won the prestigious "Entrepreneur of the Year" award from the Ewing Kauffman Foundation.

The traditional restaurant uses a hierarchical structure. Successful managers are promoted to larger stores and then to positions as area managers and then regional managers. The higher in the organization they rise, the less contact managers have with customers. Outback deliberately chose an alternative organization. Managers are given longer-term contracts. They are compensated at a level that allows them to have a successful career without loosing customer contact. Outback has no middle management field structure. The result is a very flat structure with very direct communication to top management.

Outback Teaching Suggestions

Class discussions are most effective when students are equally prepared. You can bring students to a common level of preparation by having them type their answer to one of the discussion questions. This will require them to have read the case and familiarized themselves with the case. The remaining questions can then be discussed in class.

Sample class discussion questions are identified below. An alternative to a teacher-controlled discussion is to assign students teams to answer one of the questions or sections below. Each team can prepare one overhead and lead a discussion of that section.

Two additional teaching ideas follow the discussion questions. The first is a separate case, "Taking Outback Abroad", is available as a supplement. The case can be provided as a handout to students for either individual and team assignments. The second is a competitive comparison that can be accomplished via the Internet.

Outback Discussion Questions and Answers: Part 4

Answers to Outback Review Questions for Chapter 10:

Organizing - To Create Structures

1. **Based on information in the case, draw an organization chart for Outback. Try to include as many positions as possible. Based on your diagram, describe Outback's structure?**

   At the top of the chart is CEO, Chris Sullivan. Reporting to Sullivan are the Executive VP: Basham, Gannon, Marketing VP, Nancy Schneid. Proprietors report to Basham. Assistant managers report to the proprietors. Employees report to an assistant manager. There are only three levels of management separating a bus person or server from corporate CEO.

2. **In what ways does Outback reflect the new developments in organizational structure.**

   The text notes four trends: increasing complexity and change; teams and networks; horizontal cooperation; boundaryless organizations. The pace of change at Outback can be best understood when one considers the pace of change they have undergone. Seven years ago they were a single restaurant, now they are a large publicly traded organization. There are several examples of teams, the most salient of which is the top management team. Sullivan, Basham and Gannon have brought together their unique skills into one management package. Horizontal team building is evidenced in the training function at Outback. The function is accomplished without the addition of additional staff by instead networking internally. Finally, there is an element of the boundaryless organization when one considers Outback's relationship to its suppliers. Brust, the meat supplier, is an integral part of Outback's operations.

Answers to Outback Review Questions for Chapter 11:

Organizational Design and Work Processes

1. **Would you consider Outback an Organic or Mechanistic structure?**

   Organic structures work best in a rapidly changing environment. Given the rapid growth at Outback, a bureaucratic organization would not have been able to manage the degree of change. Figure 11.1 notes more organic designs. Consistent with these designs, Outback displays more decentralized authority (no regional managers following up on the local manager), fewer rules and procedures (Outback flaunts this in their advertising, "no rules, just right"); wider spans of control and more personal means of coordination.

Answers to Outback Review Questions for Chapter 12:

Human Resource Management

1. What steps does Outback undertake to assure it attracts and retains top quality employees and managers?

Outback has a fairly sophisticated set of policies that are designed to attract quality employees. These policies can be divided into two broad categories: quality of work life and compensation. In terms of quality of worklife, Outback has some unique attributes. First, Outback provides its managers with long term contracts. This allows managers to become a part of the community. (In private conversations in the research, managers commented on their ability to own their own home — in the past they moved so much this was not possible). Dinner only allows employees to make more money in tips and work fewer hours. Managers work a much more "normal" work schedule. Servers work only three tables, making their work easier to manage. Cooks have a high quality kitchen work environment. In terms of compensation, Outback pays more than its competitors, it offers significant performance incentives, and even offers its employees the opportunity of ownership. Further, they have a competitive benefits program that is available to all employees. The program is subsidized to provide more affordable insurance benefits to lower level employees.

2. What steps does Outback take to ensure its employees are properly trained?

Bright students will note that Outback hires employees with experience, reducing some need for training. In addition, Outback uses three training elements: field experienced trainers, dress rehearsals and learning through teaching. Instead of having a training staff, Outback identifies high performing individuals within their organization (e.g., best server, best front of the house manager, etc.) and has them conduct the training. This assures that the trainers are well respected and that training focuses on field tested skills. Outback also uses "dress rehearsals" when it opens a new restaurant. For a week before its opening, restaurants have private dinners. One night is for family and friends, another night or two are for a charitable organization and the third is for the local media. All food is provided for free. This gives Outback a chance to work out their operational difficulties with a friendly audience before they open their doors to the public.

Additional Outback Teaching Suggestions: Part 4

Taking Outback Abroad

Use the supplemental case to explore Outback's international operations. Assume Outback decides to do business in North America, Latin America, Asia and Europe. Ask the student teams to develop an appropriate structure for the organization. Have them check their design against the summary at the end of Chapter 11 (What contingency factors influence environmental design? To what extent has their design taken into account these factors?)

Competitor's Structure

Have teams choose one of the publicly traded restaurant companies. Use the WWW to find the structure of a competitor. Have the students describe the difference between Outback's structure and its competitor. [Outback prides itself in a very flat structure. By having store managers become proprietors (owners), Outback is assured of strong local control. This ownership, along with its compensation strategy for employees, minimizes Outback's control costs. Outback then has no middle management of area and regional managers common to chains like Ruby Tuesday. Ask if the students think the structure at Outback is different because of its external contingencies or its strategy?

INTEGRATING THE OUTBACK CASE WITH PART 5:

LEADERSHIP

General Overview: Part 5

Outback Steakhouse is a high-growth company in the casual dining segment of the restaurant industry. Using a strategy that defied the conventional wisdom, Outback Steakhouse had grown from 1 location to 243 restaurants in just seven years. In 1995, the Outback management team won the prestigious "Entrepreneur of the Year" award from the Ewing Kauffman Foundation.

Outback's success can be clearly attributed to the vision and values of its founders and to their leadership skill in bringing that vision to reality. The case provides ample examples of leadership skills and activities. There is also an abundance of information to support a discussion on motivation and rewards. The case also explores the issues of innovation and change. A supplemental case, Taking Outback Abroad, addresses further issues of innovation and change.

Outback Teaching Suggestions: Part 5

Class discussions are most effective when students are equally prepared. You can bring students to a common level of preparation by having them type their answer to one of the discussion questions. This will require them to have read the case and familiarized themselves with the case. The remaining questions can then be discussed in class.

Sample class discussion questions are identified below. An alternative to a teacher-controlled discussion is to assign students teams to answer one of the questions or sections below. Each team can prepare one overhead and lead a discussion of that section.

Two additional teaching ideas follow the discussion questions: First, the supplemental video case can be used to explore issues of leadership and communication. Second, a group project is suggested that facilitate an in-depth discussion of change management. The supplemental case, Taking Outback Abroad can also be used to discuss issues of change management.

Outback Discussion Questions and Answers: Part 5

Answers to Outback Review Questions for Chapter 13:

Leading - To Inspire Effort

1. **What types of power are evident at Outback? How is power utilized?**

    The book notes two bases of power: position power and personal power. Position power is based on rewards, coercion and legitimacy. Outback's leaders clearly have legitimate authority from the shareholders. They also clearly use rewards to guide action toward shared goals. Personal power is based on expertise and reference. Interviewed employees consider the founders and leaders of Outback to be true experts in their field. Further, they identify with them, want to be with them or even be like them (reference). In addition the book notes that effective leaders empower others. Outback has clearly done this through the sharing of ownership (granting of legitimate authority).

Answers to Outback Review Questions for Chapter 14:

Motivation and Rewards

1. **What insights from the process theories of motivation shed light on the leadership of Outback?**

    Three of the theoretical insights from the text seem to be reflected in the case: Vroom's expectancy theory, Locke's goal setting and the specificity of goals. Expectancy theory encourages managers to make sure that any rewards offered are achievable and individually valued. Outback's compensation and quality of work life systems seem to match both these requirements. Locke's theory emphasizes the motivational quality of goals. Outback's performance incentives from ownership, performance bonuses and stock options all rely on the motivational quality of goals. Finally for goals to be meaningful they need to be specific and achievable and set through participatory means. The case provides insight into all three. Bright students will note the participatory team nature of top management. There is little in the case to support discussion on goal setting or participation at the lower levels of the organization. Bright students might also add that there might be an over-reward inequity. Outback employees may be aware that they have better compensation and working conditions than do other restaurant employees. They may be motivated to protect their jobs by working harder.

Answers to Outback Review Questions for Chapter 15:

Individual Performance and Job Design

1. **In your opinion, to what extent can Outback's employees sustain high performance?**

    The high performance equation in the text is Performance = ability x support x effort. Outback recruits only employees with high potential and experience. Their employees start with a high level of ability, especially at the management level. Outback supports this level with effective training and supervision. Finally, Outback has a motivational structure that encourages effort. This structure includes reward systems and quality of worklife components. Reward systems include bonuses, ownership incentives and stock options. Quality of worklife issues includes well-designed working spaces, better work hours, less stressful work environments and longer-term commitments.

Answers to Outback Review Questions for Chapter 16:

Communication and Interpersonal Skills

1. **Prior to reading the Outback case what stereotypes did you have about the restaurant industry? How have those stereotypes changed since you read the case?**

    Students will likely identify the following stereotypes: poor pay, poor working conditions, not professionally managed, and little career opportunity among others. Students typically note surprise at the compensation levels and in particular the management salaries. It is valuable to probe how those stereotypes were formed. Sometimes a student worked part time in a poorly managed restaurant. In many cases, the information the used to form their opinion is second hand or from the media. A good follow-up question to have students to consider is: If you were wrong about the hospitality industry because of stereotyping, might you also be wrong about steel? Construction? Health care? How might your career choices be influenced by stereotyping? This can lead to a fruitful discussion of peer pressure, group influence, halo effect, selection bias and stereotyping.

Answers to Outback Review Questions for Chapter 17:

Group Process and Teamwork

1. **To what extent does a single Outback restaurant operate as a self-directed work team?**

    Figure 17.2 notes seven characteristics of self-managing teams. At first glance, most of the characteristics in that table seem to provide evidence for a self-directed team environment. Average students may feel that this is a self-directed work team environment. There are some major exceptions. Outback employees tend to have limited jobs. For example, servers do not work in the kitchen, bus people do not work as servers, etc. This limitation infringes on the other areas; scheduling is less flexible as a result of single purpose jobs, as is the distribution of jobs within the team. There is no information in the case on the extent to which employees evaluate one another. After some discussion, students should realize that while Outback has effective work teams, they are not the self-directed teams noted in 17.2.

2. **How might the group life cycle effect the performance of a company like Outback Steakhouse?**

    Outback starts each restaurant from scratch with an entirely new group of employees. That group must go through the group formation process of forming, storming, norming, performing and adjourning. It is critical for Outback as a company to have a strong hand in the forming through norming stages. Outback wishes for the norm to be outstanding performance. It uses its motivational resources to influence the norming process. Further, Outback uses its recruiting and selection process to have a group that is more likely to accept its norms. If Outback were to fail at this process and have a team that developed a lower set of standards, then management would be faced with a very difficult set of problems. It is much easier for Outback to establish clear standards from the beginning than to change an ineffective team.

Answers to Outback Review Questions for Chapter 18:

Change Management and Innovation

1.   In what ways might Outback have to change in order to serve customers overseas? How should they manage that change?

(This question can be asked directly from this case or you may wish to use the supplemental case, Taking Outback Abroad). Students will likely note some of the following changes: Hours, compensation, menu, location planning, the role of women, and suppliers. In short, this one change in operations would generate cascading levels of change throughout the organization. Especially bright students might also note things like changes in structure and in management roles. The chapter summary provides an effective five-point outline of the change process. You may wish to write students' ideas on the board under five categories without naming the categories in advance. When there is something in each category, put the title on the board and refer them to the summary. This will help them discover the value of the model presented in the text.

Additional Teaching Suggestions: Part 5

Two additional reaching ideas are discussed below. In addition, you may substitute Taking Outback Abroad for a discussion of leadership or change.

Outback Video Case

Have the students review the Outback video case with two questions in mind. The first is to write down every example of leadership behavior in the organization. The second is to note any example of direct communication between the CEO and the other Outback employees. In the first case, there will be ample examples of leadership behavior at all levels of the organization. For the second question, students will likely be surprised by the amount of direct communication between CEO Sullivan and the other employees. The students should find a clear picture of an active, aggressive and personal communication presence.

The Restaurant of 2010

Ask the students to work in teams (either in class or as a take-home assignment). Each team should develop a list of the ten to fifteen major changes that will occur in restaurants by the year 2010. Ask the students to then identify how those trends will change management at Outback. Finally, ask them what they feel Outback's response should be. You may wish to have them summarize their findings in a table.

Major Factor	Effect on Outback	Proposed response
1. High tech food preparation	May make other restaurants able to compete with Outback with less qualified staff	Give up
		Develop more sophisticated foods that require hand preparation
		Reduce their costs by adopting the same type of system.
1. Next items …	Effects	Responses

VIDEO CASE NOTES:

OUTBACK STEAKHOUSE, INC.

Case Overview

Outback Steakhouse is a high-growth company in the casual dining segment of the restaurant industry. Using a strategy that defies the conventional wisdom, Outback Steakhouse has grown from 1 location to its current size of 243 restaurants in just seven years. In 1995, the Outback management team won the prestigious "Entrepreneur of the Year" award from the Ewing Kauffman Foundation.

The values of the Outback top management strongly influence the company's strategy. In particular, the founders believe their success is the result of two deliberate actions, exceeding customer expectations and creating great work environments for its employees.

The video presents ways in which Outback strives to operationalize its core value. Outback has the highest food cost as a percentage of gross revenues in the casual dining industry. Its managers are preoccupied with the small details of food preparation (they spend three hours a day on croutons). Outback has over-designing the kitchen space. Proprietors inspect every dish before it is seen by the customers. Restaurants serve dinner only so their staff can be "fresh" to service customers, and offer employees a stake in the outcomes of the restaurant and the company.

While the company has been very successful to this point, Outback's dramatic growth could grind to a standstill if they do not successfully develop new restaurant concepts. Since the company is publicly traded, it faces pressure from its board of directors to continue its growth. The students are asked to: 1) evaluate Outback's value chain to understand the keys to its success, 2) determine whether Outback possesses the knowledge skills and resources to be successful in new non-steakhouse restaurant concepts, and 3) envision the types of changes that may occur in Outback's management values and style as they become a larger and more diversified firm.

Objectives

1. Provide a vehicle for applying the value chain to determine Outback's knowledge, skills and resources.

2. Help students discover the different skills, knowledge and resources required to run a diversified firm.

3. Help students better understand the link between strategy and top management values.

Case Background

This case was developed using original research and original and archival video footage. As part of Outback's Entrepreneur of the Year award, the Kauffman Foundation requested that Outback allow a team to 1) write a case study for use in the classroom and 2) participate in the production of a video case study. The authors received a grant from the foundation to develop both the case and video. The video case study was intended for multiple uses including Kauffman seminars for entrepreneurs and use by the authors and hopefully other faculty members for use in undergraduate and graduate business classes as both a stand-alone case or as a supplement to a written Outback case study.

The video case was developed from approximately eleven hours of original video footage and one hour of archival footage. (In addition, several hours of additional audio-taped interviews were used for the written case study). The video was professionally shot by a Kauffman Foundation crew under the direction of a Kauffman Foundation producer. The case authors conducted the interviews (the questions are not heard on the tape), transcribed the tapes and developed a video script for the Kauffman Foundation. The Kauffman team edited the video to the authors' script, while reserving for them the creative freedom to substitute or select background footage (B-roll) that they considered most appropriate.

Discussion Questions: Outback Video Case

Undergraduate or Graduate

1. **Construct a value chain for Outback Steakhouse -- Does Outback possess the skills, knowledge and resources to continue growing for the next decade?**

2. **Will Outback's skills and resources assure that Carrabbas will also be a success?**

Discussion Questions and Answers

1. **Construct a value chain for Outback Steakhouse -- Does Outback possess the skills, knowledge and resources to continue growing for the next decade?**

   The primary value-chain elements referenced indirectly in the video include inbound logistics, operations, sales & marketing, franchise support and customer service. A discussion of inbound logistics might include the procurement of unique ingredients, quality control of ingredients. In the production/operations area students should be able to identify from the video: higher than average food costs, lots of food on the plate, not charging customers for extras (note Joe Cofer describing that competitors charge for every scoop of sour cream), strong menu, all products are considered important (not just the center of plate items) -- each restaurant spends 3.5 hours on croutons, etc. In sales and marketing, students might recall some of the creative TV advertising they have seen. (It is not mentioned in the video, but Outback does not employ print advertising), the product/concept is marketed as a quality product at a good value -- no couponing or discounting is allowed, and the company seems to rely heavily on repeat customers and word-of-mouth promotion to build its base. In terms of customer service the student analyst should note that servers need wait on only three tables, they are well paid relative to the industry, they have a better work schedule (dinner only), and that servers are encouraged to enjoy their work. Customers comment that the staff is energetic and enjoy their work.

Support activities in the value chain include: infrastructure, new product/concept development, real estate management/location planning, and human resource systems.

Little is said about the financial condition of the company other that to note its rapid growth in revenues. In terms of their management team, the students should be able to note the diversity of skills between Sullivan, Basham and Gannon (the three founders) and their compatibility of values. At the corporate level, Outback has developed an excellent franchising system. At the restaurant level, students will note that the facilities are designed to maximize product and service quality, not sales volume. Chris Sullivan notes that Bob Basham is an expert in finding the right location.

Strong students might note that Outback did not develop Carrabbas, they discovered it. This could lead to a good discussion as to which shill should be more highly valued. They may also note that although Outback has strong initial demand from overseas, they have yet to develop a single international operation.

At the human resource level, students will likely note the management equity program for store managers, the innovative health care plan and the comments on employee earning power.

2. **Will Outback's skills and resources assure that Carrabbas will also be a success?**

    The students should consider that Outback developed a venture with Carrabbas -- they did not develop Carrabbas. Areas where Outback can positively influence Carrabbas development include: skills at finding appropriate locations, franchising experience, menu planning and facilities design. Advanced students might make note of Nancy Schneid's comment that Outback will need to compete with Carrabbas in the future. In addition to competing for customers, Outback may also need to compete for management talent.

Areas where Outback may be unable to help are in menu planning (might not be able to translate their steakhouse success to Italian), food costs (not enough is known from the case to determine whether Carrabbas can maintain a high average food cost and still be profitable). Also, while Outback has built a strong reputation, their is nothing in the Carrabbas name or menu to link the two restaurants together. To the customer, Carrabbas is a new restaurant chain, therefore there are no economies of scale in advertising, no ability to transfer brand loyalty, etc.

3. **As Outback continues to grow by diversifying its product line through Carrabbas and by adding international distribution, will it be able to maintain its current management style and values?**

Bob Merrit mentions in the video that maintaining the culture will be Outback's biggest challenge -- strong students should note therefore that Outback views this as a potential problem. Several forces favor a change in culture. First, shareholder pressures to continue growing at their current pace. When the growth in revenue from new restaurants slows, individual stores would need to increase profits to keep investor income growth at a constant rate. This in turn might pressure local restaurants to cut food costs. Another way to increase revenue would be to stop serving dinner only, increasing the return on assets employed. The growth of the Carrabbas concept may also add pressure for change, as Carrabbas and other concepts become a bigger part of the Outback revenue stream, differences in values might become more visible. Internationalization might also require change -- some countries might not allow Outback to use its current compensation system.

References:

1. Outback Steakhouse, Inc. is a publicly traded company. Ample information about its financial performance is available from traditional investment information sources including investment guides, Standard & Poors, Moody's Directory, etc. Industry information can be found for the casual dining segment of the restaurant industry from similar sources. For the written case study, the authors used the InvestText Online Database. InvestText includes full text reports on the company and industry for the last twelve-month period. Two Outback competitors worth noting are Brinker International (privately traded) -- owner of Chillis, Romano's Macaroni Grill, and several other successful chains and Morrisons (publicly traded) -- owner of Ruby Tuesday's, Tia's Tex Mex Cantina and other chains.

2. For the value chain, the author's recommend Michael Porter, (1985) and, *Competitive Advantage,* New York: Free Press. For additional techniques of resource analysis, see Grant, (1995). *Contemporary Strategy Analysis,* 2nd ed., Cambridge Mass: Blackwell.

EXERCISES IN TEAMWORK

EXERCISE --- MY BEST MANAGER

Preparation

Working alone, make a list of the *behavioral attributes* that describe the *best* manager you have ever worked for. This could be someone you worked for in a full-time or part-time job, summer job, volunteer job, student organization, or whatever. If you have trouble identifying an actual manager, make a list of behavioral attributes of the type of manager you would most like to work for in your next job.

Instructions

Form into groups as assigned by your instructor, or work with a nearby classmate. Share your list of attributes, and listen to the lists of others. Be sure to ask questions and make comments on items of special interest. Work together to create a master list that combines the unique attributes of the "best" managers experienced by members of your group. Have a spokesperson share that list with the rest of the class.

Instructor's Note

This exercise is designed to help break the ice in class and to get students thinking about what differentiates good managers from poor ones. Hopefully, they will develop a sense of purpose or directions through which their study of management and the total course experience become more personally meaningful.

The exercise can be done informally in smaller classes (up to 45-50) as stated. It can also be done in modified form in larger lecture settings. In the large lecture, we recommend that you not use small group discussions, but rather have all students answer question #1 at their seats. Then, your random questioning can create a master list on the blackboard. This list becomes a basis for total class discussion and your personal reactions.

In discussing the results, take advantage of the opportunity to convey the logic of your course outline as well as how you plan to use the book and other supporting materials. In smaller classes, have students introduce themselves in their work groups. Be comfortable with the "brainstorming" nature of the exercise. Don't overdo it by making it too complicated or overly definitive. It is simply a way to start students thinking and talking about being good managers. What follows is one instructor's report on using the exercise.

Exercise Report

Students were assigned into four groups to work on the exercise. Rather than follow exact exercise procedures, they were given the task to list ten characteristics that described the best managers group members have worked for. The group part of the exercise worked very well and took approximately 15 minutes to complete. At the conclusion of the group brainstorming stage, spokespersons were asked to report on each group's list. The meaning of each item was discussed as it was being presented. A total of eight items was obtained from the four groups in approximately 20 minutes.

(Source: Adapted form John R. Schermerhorn, Jr., James G. Hunt, and Richard N. Osborn, *Managing Organizational Behavior*, 3rd ed., New York: Wiley, 1988, pp. 32--33. Used by permission.)

EXERCISE --- WHAT MANAGERS DO

Preparation

Think about the questions that follow. Record your answers in the spaces provided.

1. How much of a typical manager's time would you expect to be allocated to these relationships? (total should = 100%)

    _____ %   of time working with subordinates

    _____ %   of time working with boss

    _____ %   of time working with peers and outsiders

2. How many hours per week does the average manager work? _____ hours

3. What amount of a manager's time is typically spent in the following activities? (total should = 100%)

    _____ %   in scheduled meetings

    _____ %   in unscheduled meetings

    _____ %   doing desk work

    _____ %   talking on the telephone

    _____ %   walking around the organization/work site

Instructions

Talk over your responses with a nearby classmate. Explore similarities and differences in your answers. Be prepared to participate in class discussion led by your instructor.

Instructor's Note

As with most exercises, this could be assigned as an out of class project, assigned to be prepared before a class session and discussed in class, or included totally in a class session. However it is assigned, the questions provide a logical sequence of instructions.

Exercises can be a valuable alternative method of teaching in that they require thought and application of ideas, theories, etc. As such, you could use this exercise when discussing "Managerial Activities."

Preparation: *Think about the questions that follow. Record your answers in the spaces provided.*

Provide students with about 5 to 10 minutes to respond to the questions presented in these step.

Instructions: *Talk over your responses with a nearby classmate. Explore similarities and differences in your answers. Try to understand each other's reasoning.*

Provide students with another 5 minutes for this step. If you are pressed for time, you may want to skip this step.

Be prepared to participate in class discussion led by your instructor.

It is a good idea to solicit individual responses to each of the questions. As you collect their answers, you may want to record these or perhaps the range of responses. Next, you can provide them with the findings listed below that have been obtained from research into managerial work.[14] Students enjoy seeing how close they come to being right. In presenting these results, however, be sure to point out that findings may vary across managerial levels and types of managers. For some of the answers, this variation is specifically indicated by supplying information for different types of managers.

---

[14]For a review article summarizing these results, see Mark J. Martinko and William L. Gardner, "Structured Observation of Managerial Work: A Replication and Synthesis," *Journal of Management Studies*, 1990, 3: 329-357.

1. How much of a typical manager's time would you expect to be allocated to these relationships? (total should = 100%)

    __48__ %   of time working with subordinates

    __8__ %   of time working with boss

    __44__ %   of time working with peers and outsiders

    100 % = total time

2. How many hours per week does the average manager work? _____ hours

    On the average, managers work about 55 to 60 hours a week. Of course, this will vary from individual to individual and across managerial positions and levels.

3. What amount of a manager's time is typically spent in the following activities? (total should = 100%)

    _____ %   in scheduled meetings

    _____ %   in unscheduled meetings

    _____ %   doing desk work

    _____ %   talking on the telephone

    _____ %   walking around the organization/work site

    The answer to this question depends on the type of manager. Below are sample percentages for CEO's, Police Chiefs and School Principals. Note that these are also top, middle and lower level managers, respectively. Percentages for the latter two types of managers do not add to %100 because the researchers also included other categories of activities.

	CEO's	Police Chiefs	School Principals
Scheduled meetings	59	24	14
Unscheduled meetings	10	26	29
Desk work	22	24	21
Telephone calls	6	8	6
Walking around the organization	3	2	15

After presenting this data, you may want to ask students if they see any trend to it. Students are usually quick to recognize that the managers' time becomes less scheduled as one moves down the hierarchy of authority. You may want to follow this up by asking students why they think this

553

occurs. Students typically respond correctly that upper level managers have more control over their time for a number of reasons (e.g., they can have a secretary screen their telephone calls and appointments).

You can wrap up this exercise by reviewing Mintzberg's conclusions about managerial work.

1. Managers work long hours.

2. Managers work at an intense pace.

3. Managers work at fragmented and varied tasks.

4. Managers work with many communication media.

5. Managers work largely through interpersonal relationships.

EXERCISE --- WHAT DO YOU VALUE IN WORK?

Preparation

The following nine items are from a survey conducted by Nicholas J. Beutell and O.C. Brenner ("Sex Differences in Work Values," *Journal of Vocational Behavior,* vol. 28, 1986, pp. 29-41). Rank order the nine items in terms of how important they would be to you in a job.

How important is it to you to have a job that:

_____**1.** Is respected by other people?

_____**2.** Encourages continued development of knowledge and skills?

_____**3.** Provides job security?

_____**4.** Provides a feeling of accomplishment?

_____**5.** Provides the opportunity to earn a high income?

_____**6.** Is intellectually stimulating?

_____**7.** Rewards good performance with recognition?

_____**8.** Provides comfortable working conditions?

_____**9.** Permits advancement to high administrative responsibility?

Instructions

Form into groups as designated by your instructor. Within each group, the *men in the group* will meet to develop a consensus ranking of the items as they think the *women* in the Beutell and Brenner survey ranked them. The reasons for the rankings should be shared and discussed so they are clear to everyone. The *women in the group* should not participate in this ranking task. They should listen to the discussion and be prepared to comment later in class discussion. A spokesperson for the men in the group should share the group's rankings with the class.

Optional Instructions

Form into groups as designated by your instructor, but with each group consisting entirely of men or women. Each group should meet and decide which of the work values members of the *opposite* sex ranked first in the Beutell and Brenner survey. Do this again for the work value ranked last. The reasons should be discussed, along with reasons why each of the other values probably was not ranked first . . . or last. A spokesperson for each group should share group results with the rest of the class.

Instructor's Note

The following table shows the results form the Beutell and Brenner (1986) study. Men and women agreed on the most important characteristics of work; however, the largest difference on the five highest-rated dimensions occurred for the "high income" dimension, with men ranking it higher.

Results of the Beutell and Brenner Study

	Men (rank)	Women (rank)
Provides a feeling of accomplishment	1.0	1.0
Provides job security	2.5	2.0
Provides the opportunity to earn a high income	2.5	5.0
Permits advancement...responsibility	4.0	6.5
Is respected by other people	5.5	3.0
Provides comfortable working conditions	7.0	4.0
Rewards good performance with recognition	5.5	8.5
Encourages continued development...skills	8.0	6.5
Is intellectually stimulating	9.0	8.5

The experience of many instructors is that men tend to underestimate the importance of intrinsic rewards for women and are often wrong about their top-rated dimensions. This exercise is most involving when you emphasize sex-role issues. However, you may choose to play this aspect down in order to focus more clearly on the issue of motivation.

You may wish to conclude the exercise by posing the following thought-provoking questions to the class:

* Where do we get our ideas of what other people from work?

* Why is it important for managers to know what people want from work?

* To what extent do our personal expectations enter into our managerial decision-making?

(Source: Adapted from Roy J. Lewicki, Donald D. Bowen, Douglas T. Hall, and Francine S. Hall, *Custom Experiences in Management and Organizational Behavior.* 5th ed., New York: Wiley, 1995, pp. 7-10. Used by permission.)

EXERCISE --- **THE FUTURE WORKPLACE**

Instructions

Form groups as assigned by the instructor. Brainstorm to develop a master list of the major characteristics of the future workplace in the year 2010. Use this list as background for completing the following tasks:

1. Draw a "picture" representing what the "Workplace 2010 *manager"* will look like.

2. Draw a "picture" representing what the "Workplace 2010 *organization"* will look like.

Have a spokesperson prepared to share your list with the class as a whole, *and* to share and explain both "pictures"---that is, what each represents, why, and with what implications for the class members.

Instructor's Note

This exercise can be extremely useful for stimulating students to seriously consider what their future job and workplace may be like. While student "pictures" can and should vary depending upon their perspectives and their expectations for the future, their "picture" of the manager may reflect some of the following desirable **characteristics of the 21st-century executive** (see Chapter 3, page 64).

a) *Global strategist:* Who recognizes interconnections among nations, cultures, and economies in the world community, and is able to plan and act in due consideration of them.

b) *Master of technology:* Who is comfortable with existing high technology, who understands technological trends and their implications, and is able to use them to best individual and organizational advantage.

c) *Consummate politician:* Who understands the growing complexity of government regulations and the legal environment, and is able to work comfortably at the interface between them and organizational interests.

d) *Leader/motivator*: Who is able to attract highly talented workers, and enthuse them by creating a high performance climate for individuals and teams to do their best work.

Moreover, success for future managers will require the **personal competencies for managerial success** summarized in the **Manager's Notepad 1.2** and below.

a) *Leadership*: Ability to influence others to perform tasks.

b) *Self-objectivity*: Ability to realistically evaluate one's self.

c) *Analytic thinking*: Ability to interpret and explain patterns in information.

d) *Behavioral flexibility*: Ability to modify personal behavior to reach a goal.

e) *Oral communication*: Ability to clearly express one's ideas in oral presentations.

f) *Written communication*: Ability to clearly express one's ideas in writing.

g) *Personal impact*: Ability to create good impression and instill confidence.

h) *Resistance to stress*: Ability to perform under stressful conditions.

i) *Tolerance for uncertainty*: Ability to perform in unstructured and uncertain situations.

Finally, as the conclusion to Chapter 1 indicates, truly progressive managers are expected to fulfill **the manager's challenge** while fostering:

a) Self-fulfillment, employee involvement, participation, and creativity among their subordinates.

b) Coordination through cross-functional teams, task forces, and new forms of groupwork.

c) Meaningful work environments that respect individual differences, provide a high quality of work life, and build long-term commitments among employees.

The "picture" of the organization, may reflect the following **trends in workforce demographics**:

a) The size of the workforce is growing more slowly.

b) The available pool of younger workers is shrinking.

c) The average age of workers is rising.

d) More women are entering the workforce.

e) The proportion of ethnic minorities in the workforce is increasing.

f) The proportion of immigrants in the workforce is increasing.

Finally, the "picture" of the organization may reflect the following characteristics of **vanguard organizations:**

a) Vanguard organizations are people-oriented.

b) Vanguard organizations have visible leadership.

c) Vanguard organizations seek employment stability.

d) Vanguard organizations have a consumer orientation.

e) Vanguard organizations are future-oriented.

EXERCISE --- **DEFINING QUALITY**

Preparation

Write your definition of the word "quality" here.

QUALITY =

Instructions

Form groups as assigned by your instructor. (1) Have each group member present a definition of the word "quality." After everyone has presented, work to a consensus definition of "quality." That is, determine and write one definition of the word with which every member can agree. (2) Next, have the group assume the position of top manager in each of the following organizations. Use the group's "quality" definition to specifically state for each a *quality objective* that can guide the behavior of members in producing high "quality" goods and/or services for customers or clients. Have a spokesperson prepared to share group results with the class as a whole.

Organizations:

a. A college of business administration

b. A community hospital

c. A retail sporting goods store

d. A fast-food franchise restaurant

e. A U.S. Post Office

f. A full-service bank branch

g. A student-apartment rental company

h. A "tie-dye" t-shirt manufacturing company

i. A computer software manufacturing firm

Instructor's Note

Although student definitions of quality will clearly vary, some definitions from the text are provided below for comparative purposes.

Quality: A degree of excellence; often defined in managerial terms as being able to meet customer needs 100 percent of the time. Potential *quality objectives* for each of the organizations listed are presented below.

A college of business administration

*   To provide students with the conceptual, human and technical knowledge and skills necessary to excel at a career in business.

A community hospital

*   To provide an integrated, team approach that promotes wellness and meets the health care needs of the community -- be they physical or social.

A retail sporting goods store

*   To provide a complete array of sporting goods equipment, apparel, and instructional materials for popular sports and games.

A fast-food franchise restaurant

*   To fill standard customer orders within 1 minute, and special orders within 3 minutes, with 100% accuracy.

A full service bank branch

*   To respond to customer inquiries about accounts and/or bank services in a prompt and courteous manner.

A student-apartment rental company

*   To provide rodent and pest free rental apartments on a year-round basis.

A "tie-dye" t-shirt manufacturing company

*   To fill special orders for customized and personalized t-shirts within three working days.

A computer software manufacturing firm

*   To replace defective software within 24 hours of customer notification of the defect.

*   To provide comprehensive, 24-hour customer support for all software products.

EXERCISE --- **WHAT WOULD THE CLASSICS SAY?**

Preparation

Consider this situation:

> Six months after being hired, Bob, a laboratory worker, is performing just well enough to avoid being fired. He was carefully selected and had the abilities required to do it really well. At first Bob was enthusiastic about his new job, but now he isn't performing up to this high potential. Fran, his supervisor, is concerned, and wonders what can be done to improve this situation.

Instructions

Assume the identity of one of the following persons: Frederick Taylor, Henri Fayol, Max Weber, Abraham Maslow, Chris Argyris. (You choose, or have your instructor choose.) Assume next that *as this person* you have been asked by Fran for advice on the management situation just described. Answer these questions as you think your assumed identity would respond. Be prepared to share your answers in class, and to defend them based on text discussion of this person's views.

a. As *(your assumed identity)*, what are your basic beliefs about good management and organizational practices?

b. As *(your assumed identity)*, what might be wrong in this situation to account for Bob's low performance?

c. As *(your assumed identity)*, what could be done to improve Bob's future job performance?

Instructor's Note

This exercise can serve as experiential tool for teaching students about the ideas espoused by important management theorists. Likely responses for each of the theorists identified above are provided below.

Frederick Taylor: a) **Basic Beliefs** - Taylor argued that "The principle object of management should be to secure maximum prosperity for the employer, coupled with the maximum prosperity for the employee." b) **Problem Diagnosis** - Since Taylor felt that many workers perform below their true capacities, he would probably draw this conclusion in this instance as well. c) **Solution** - Taylor believed that the underutilization of workers could be corrected through **scientific management**, i.e., a systematic approach to management based on proper direction and support by supervisors, and monetary incentives for workers. He developed the following four principles for managers to follow:

(1) Developing a "science" for every job.

(2) Carefully selecting workers with the right abilities for the job.

(3) Carefully training these workers and providing proper incentives.

(4) Providing these workers with the necessary support.

In this case, he would probably recommend studying Bob's job to identify the one best way to perform it, providing Bob with training to teach him how do best do his job, and then offering Bob appropriate monetary incentives to perform the work. Doing so will enable Bob to maximize his performance and his rewards.

Henri Fayol: a) **Basic Beliefs** - Henry Fayol advanced five "rules" of management: **Foresight, organization, command, coordination, and control** which he considered to be the foundations for effective management. He also introduced 14 general **principles of management** such as division of work, scalar chain, unity of command and unity of direction. b) **Problem Diagnosis** - Fayol would probably conclude that Bob's deficient performance stemmed from a failure of command. He defined command as getting the best out of people working toward a plan; leading. Since the organization is clearly not getting the best out of Bob, Fran's "duty" to command is not being fulfilled. c) **Solution** - To solve this problem, Fran must find a way to lead and motivate Bob to perform his job. Thus the manager should provide Bob with better direction and more reasons to excel.

Max Weber: a) **Basic beliefs** - Max Weber introduced bureaucracy as an organizational structure which would promote efficiency and fairness. He viewed a **bureaucracy** as an **ideal organizational form**, which includes the following attributes: (1) a clear division of labor; (2) explicit duties and responsibilities, (3) standard rules and procedures; (4) a hierarchy of authority; (5) selection based on technical competence; and (6) career managers. b) **Problem Diagnosis** - Given his basic beliefs, Weber might conclude that Bob's marginal performance stems from a lack of explicit duties and responsibilities, as well as standard rules and procedures. c) **Solution** - Weber would recommend that Bob's duties and responsibilities be better defined, and standard rules and procedures introduced.

Abraham Maslow: a) **Basic Beliefs** - Maslow's hierarchy identifies five levels of human needs: **physiological, safety, social, esteem, and self-actualization.** His **deficit principle** states that people act to satisfy "deprived" needs - that is, needs for which a satisfaction "deficit" exists; conversely, *a satisfied need is not a motivator* of behavior. The **progression principle** states that the five needs exist in a *hierarchy of prepotency;* a need at any level only becomes activated once the next lower-level need is satisfied. b) **Problem Diagnosis** - Maslow would probably argue that Bob's job does not adequately satisfy his higher order needs for esteem and self-actualization; as such, Bob has reduced his efforts to attain these goals. c) **Solution** - Maslow would recommend that steps be taken to satisfy Bob's higher order needs. He should be provided with recognition for his achievements, and opportunities to perform more challenging work.

Chris Argyris: a) **Basic Beliefs** - Argyris asserts that some **classical management principles** such as task specialization, chain of command and unity of direction *inhibit worker maturation* by discouraging independence, initiative and self-actualization. b) **Problem Diagnosis** - Argyris would argue that the specialization of Bob's job and Fran's retention of authority, have inhibited his maturation and discouraged him from taking initiative and self-actualizing. c) **Solution** - Argyris advocates management practices which accommodate the mature personality by increasing (1) task responsibility and variety, and (2) participative decision making. Thus, Argyris would recommend delegating additional authority to Bob and providing him with more discretion in performing his duties. In addition, efforts to enrich Bob's job in other ways would be beneficial. In other words, Fran should take steps to empower Bob.

EXERCISE --- **THE GREAT MANAGEMENT HISTORY DEBATE**

Preparation

Consider the question: "What is the best thing a manager can do to improve productivity in his or her work unit?"

Instructions

The instructor will assign you, individually or in a group, to one of the following positions. Complete the missing information as if you were the management theorist referred to. Be prepared to argue and defend your position before the class.

Position A: "Frederick Taylor offers the best insight into the prior question. His advice would be to...." (advice to be filled in by you or the group)

Position B: "Max Weber's ideal bureaucracy offers the best insight into the prior question. His advice would be to...." (advice to be filled in by you or the group)

Position C: "Henri Fayol is the best insight into the prior question. His advice would be to...." (advice to be filled in by you or the group)

Position D: "The Hawthorne studies offer the best insight into the prior question. His advice would be to...." (advice to be filled in by you or the group)

Instructor's Note

This exercise can serve as a useful tool for increasing   student interest in management history. Indeed, some spirited and memorable debates can emerge which can make a lasting impression on students. Brief summaries of each position are included below.

Position A: Taylor argued that "The principle object of management should be to secure maximum prosperity for the employer, coupled with the maximum prosperity for the employee." In his opinion, many workers perform below there capacities. He believed that this underutilization of workers could be corrected through **scientific management**, i.e., a systematic approach to management based on proper direction and support by supervisors, and monetary incentives for workers. Accordingly, he developed the following four principles for managers to follow:

(1) Developing a "science" for every job.

(2) Carefully selecting workers with the right abilities for the job.

(3) Carefully training these workers and providing proper incentives.

(4) Providing these workers with the necessary support.

By following these principles, productivity in the manager's work unit can be substantially improved.

Position B: Max Weber introduced bureaucracy as an organizational structure which would promote efficiency and fairness. Indeed, he viewed a **bureaucracy** as an **ideal organizational form**, which includes the following attributes: (1) a clear division of labor; (2) explicit duties and responsibilities, (3) standard rules and procedures; (4) a hierarchy of authority; (5) selection based on technical competence; and (6) career managers. As such, he would argue that the best way to improve the productivity of the manager's work unit is to divide up the tasks to be done, clearly assign them to qualified individuals, introduce standard rules and procedures, and clarify the hierarchy of authority. These actions will facilitate the efficient operation of the work unit, and insure that all subordinates are treated fairly.

Position C: Henry Fayol advanced five "rules" of management: **Foresight, organization, command, coordination, and control** which he considered to be the foundations for effective management. He also introduced 14 general **principles of management** such as division of work, scalar chain, unity of command and unity of direction. Hence, he would assert that the best way to improve the productivity of the manager's work unit is to insure that these rules and principles are implemented. That is, the manager should: a) carefully plan (foresight) the work unit's activities, b) divide up the work and coordinate activities (organization and coordination), c) lead subordinates towards work unit goals (command), and d) measure work unit performance and take corrective action if necessary (control). To facilitate the execution of these functions, the manager should insure that the work is appropriate divided and assigned to subordinates (division of work), a clear and unbroken chain of command is established (scalar chain), the subordinates answer to one and only one boss (unity of command), and the subordinates work together to achieve common goals (unity of direction).

Position D: After years of studies, the Hawthorne researchers concluded that: a) people's **feelings, attitudes and relationships** with co-workers influence their performance, and therefore, b) managers who **maintain good human relations** will achieve productivity. Therefore, the Hawthorne researchers would recommend that the manager pay close attention to workers' feelings, attitudes, and work relationships, and take action to improve them where appropriate. By doing so, the morale of the workers, and hence their productivity, will be high.

EXERCISE: **CONFRONTING ETHICAL DILEMMAS**

Preparation

Read and indicate your response to each of the situations below.

a. Ron Jones, vice president of a large construction firm, receives in the mail a large envelope marked "personal." It contains a competitor's cost data for a project that both firms will be bidding on shortly. The data are accompanied by a note from one of Ron's subordinates saying: "This is the real thing!" Ron knows that data could be a major advantage to his firm in preparing a bid that can win the contract. *What should he do?*

b. Kay Smith is one of your top-performing subordinates. She has shared with you her desire to apply for promotion to a new position just announced in a different division of the company. This will be tough on you since recent budget cuts mean you will be unable to replace anyone who leaves, at least for quite some time. Kay knows this and in all fairness has asked your permission before she submits an application. It is rumored that the son of a good friend of your boss is going to apply for the job. Although his credentials are less impressive than Kay's, the likelihood is that he will get the job if she doesn't apply. *What will you do?*

c. Marty Jose got caught in a bind. She was pleased to represent her firm as head of the local community development committee. In fact, her supervisor's boss once held this position and told her in a hallway conversation, "Do your best and give them every support possible." Going along with this, Marty agreed to pick up the bill (several hundred dollars) for a dinner meeting with local civic and business leaders. Shortly thereafter, her supervisor informed everyone that the entertainment budget was being eliminated in a cost-saving effort. Marty, not wanting to renege on supporting the community development committee, was able to charge the dinner bill to an advertising budget. Eventually, an internal auditor discovered the mistake and reported it to you, the personnel director. Marty is scheduled to meet with you in a few minutes. *What will you do?*

Instructions

Working alone, make the requested decisions in each of these incidents. Think carefully about your justification for the decision. Meet in a group assigned by your instructor. Share your decisions and justifications in each case with other group members. Listen to theirs. Try to reach a group consensus on what to do in each situation, and why. Be prepared to share the group decisions, and any dissenting views, in general class discussion.

Instructor's Note

This is an extremely useful exercise for exposing students to the kinds of ethical dilemmas that they can expect to experience in their careers. As such, it provides them with an opportunity to consider how they will respond to such dilemmas. During in-class discussions of these dilemmas, allow all students to discuss their anticipated responses. There is likely to be considerable variability in their answers, with some students selecting much more "ethical" responses than others. During your discussion, emphasize the long-term advantages of selecting highly ethical responses (e.g., maintaining one's integrity, demonstrating to others that you can be trusted, having a clear conscience), since these advantages may not be immediately apparent to all members of the class. Finally, instruct students to use the following *checklist for making ethical decisions* to evaluate their initial responses to each of these dilemmas. Doing so should prove to be beneficial in separating unethical from ethical responses to these dilemmas.

A Checklist for Making Ethical Decisions   **MANAGER'S NOTEPAD 5.1**

1.   Recognize the ethical dilemma.

2.   Get the facts.

3.   Identify your options.

4.   Test each option:

     Is it legal?

     Is it right?

     Is it beneficial?

5.   Decide which option to follow.

6.   Double-check your decision by asking:

     "How will I feel if my family finds out about my decision?"

     "How will I feel if my decision is printed in the newspaper?"

7.   Take action.

EXERCISE: BEATING THE TIME WASTERS

Preparation

1. Make a list of all the things you need to do tomorrow. Prioritize each item in terms of *how important it is to creating outcomes that you really value.* Use this classification scheme:

    A: Most important, top priority

    B: Important, not top priority

    C: Least important, low priority

    Look again at all activities you have classified as B. Reclassify any that are really As or Cs. Look at your list of As. Reclassify any that are really Bs or Cs. Double check to make sure you are comfortable with your list of Cs.

2. Make a list of all the "time wasters" that you find often interfere with your ability to accomplish everything you want to on any given day.

Instructions

Form into groups as assigned by the instructor. Have each person in the group share their lists and their priority classifications. Other members of the group should politely "challenge" the classifications to make sure that only truly "high priority" items receive an A rating. They might also suggest that some C items are of such little consequence that they not be worth doing at all. After each member of the group revises their "to do" list based on this advice, go back and discuss the "time wasters" identified by group members. Develop a master list of time wasters and what to do about them. Have a group spokesperson prepared to share discussion highlights and "tips" on beating common time wasters with the rest of the class.

Instructor's Note

This is a fun exercise which is designed to provide students with valuable feedback and insights regarding the ways in which they set priorities, and various "time wasters" which may interfere with their efforts to achieve their objectives. Students' discussion with their classmates of their priorities is likely to be especially enlightening. Some supplemental information for Parts 1 and 2 of this exercise is provided below.

Part 1. The ABC system for establishing priorities and managing one's time which is reflected by this exercise is described by Alan Lakein (1973) in *How to Get Control of Your Time and Your Life.* Additional tips that Lakein provides for scheduling time and using it more efficiently are presented below.

1. Keep a daily "TO DO" list and review it each morning.

2. Block out time for priority activities -- either save a time slot in each day or set a day aside each week.

3. Don't let anything interfere with this time.

4. Use your time efficiently. Handle paper only once, don't keep reshuffling it. Don't procrastinate -- if something has to be done, do it immediately. Minimize the steps involved in what you do. Delegate as much as possible to others. Unless you absolutely have to do something, assign it to someone else.

5. Learn to know your "prime time." When do you work best? Save it for priority projects.

6. Try to be flexible. Always leave time in your schedule for emergencies or catch up.

7. Plan time to relax. If you are exhausted, you won't be able to work effectively or efficiently.

8. Learn to use transition time to get things done. For example, can you read, catch the news on the radio, or discuss matters with your partner or family while you dress, do your nails, or eat breakfast? How do you use time spent in commuting, coffee breaks, lunch hour, or waiting in offices? Do you carry your list with you so you can save time to plan? Do you carry paper and pencil for writing or have something along to read?

9. Finally, can you turn C activities into things that can be put off indefinitely? How many C activities do you do that, in the end, don't have to be done, or can be done later if they turn out to be important? Learn to discriminate and put them aside.

Part 2. Some or all of the following "time wasters" which Alex Mackenzie describes in his book, *The Time Trap* (New York: AMACOM, American Management Associations, 1972), as factors which interfere with people's work, are also likely to be mentioned by students.

Telephone interruptions

Unannounced drop-in visitors

Meetings, scheduled and unscheduled

Lack of objectives

Failure to delegate routine matters

Indecision and procrastination

Inability to say "no"

Fatigue

MacKenzie's suggestions for beating some of these "time wasters" follow.

Telephones

1. Always outline topics to discuss.

2. Group your calls and make those calls when you know people will be there.

3. Get through small talk as soon as possible. Get to the point of the call.

4. When appropriate, use telephone answering machines.

5. Tell long-winded callers you have an appointment or a deadline to meet.

6. As a last resort, try hanging up while you are talking.

7. Record your phone calls. Find out how "you" use the phone.

8. Have your secretary screen your calls and help on routine matters.

9. Have your secretary look up answers for return calls, so you are prepared.

10. Instead of being irritated when the phone rings, remind yourself that it is important to your job... you will be less frustrated.

Drop-In Visitors

1. Realize that interruptions are part of the job. Keep a positive attitude about them.

2. Don't constantly interrupt others needlessly throughout the day.

3. Allow time for interruptions and unscheduled events.

4. Regarding long-winded visitors, never let them get seated.

5. Close your door for quiet time.

6. Be careful when someone asks "Have a minute?" - say "Not right now."

7. Go to the other person when you can - you can leave when you want.

8. Rearrange you furniture so you're not in the traffic flow.

9. Meet visitors outside your place of business.

10. Learn to control the controllable and accept the uncontrollable.

Meetings

1. Be prepared for the meetings. Resist tangents.

2. Try to hold some meetings with everyone standing.

3. Have an agenda and stick to it.

4. Set a time limit. Start on time. Quit on time.

5. Make decisions without meetings. Never use a committee if it can be handled individually.

6. Have your secretary take concise notes. Distribute within 24 hours.

7. Discourage and discontinue unnecessary meetings.

8. Minimize small talk. Do not contribute to unnecessary conversation yourself.

9.   Critique the meeting at its conclusion.

10.   Read a good book on how to conduct meetings.

Objectives and Priorities

1.   First hour of every work day is your most productive.   Use it wisely.

2.   Distinguish between important and merely urgent.   Always do the important tasks.

3.   Don't do someone else's request at your expense.

4.   Set one major objective each day and achieve it.

5.   When conditions change, you change.

Planning

1.   Write out your plan each week for accomplishing significant items.

2.   Plan each day.

3.   Make sure your daily "To Do" list includes "priorities and "time estimates."

4.   Plan time in each day for you! - at least 15 minutes for personal objectives.

5.   Plan breaks for yourself so you can be refreshed.

Delegation

1.   Delegate. Delegate. Delegate. *Don't do it all yourself.*

2.   If you can't control it, don't delegate it.

3.   Delegate the right to be wrong.   Use mistakes as a learning process.

4.   Once you have delegated, leave the person alone.

5.   Take time to provide good instructions.

Indecision

1.   Don't waste time regretting your failures.

2.   Make important decisions in your prime time.

3.   If you are not making any mistakes, you are not doing anything worthwhile.

4.   Indecision is a form of procrastination.   Act with boldness.

5.   It is a time waster to deal with the past. Forget it. Use the past as a guide for the future.

(Source: Developed from Roy J. Lewicki, Donald D. Bowen, Douglas T. Hall, and Francine S. Hall, *Experiences in Management and Organizational Behavior,* Third Edition. New York: John Wiley & Sons, 1988, pp. 314-316).

EXERCISE: **PERSONAL CAREER PLANNING**

Preparation

Complete the following three activities, and bring the results to class. Your work should be in a written form suitable for review by the instructor.

Step 1: *Strengths and Weaknesses Inventory* Different occupations require special talents, abilities, and skills if people are to become really good in their work. Each of us, you included, has a repertoire of existing strengths and weaknesses that are "raw materials" we presently offer a potential employer. Of course actions can (and should!) be taken over time to further develop current strengths, and turn many weaknesses into strengths. Make a list that identifies your most important strengths and weaknesses at the moment, and in relation to the career direction you are most likely to pursue upon graduation. Place an "*" next to each item that you consider most important to address in your courses and student activities *before* graduation.

Step 2: *Five Year Career Objectives* Make a list of three to five career objectives that are appropriate given your list of personal strengths and weaknesses. Limit these objectives to ones that can be accomplished within five years of graduation.

Step 3: *Five Year Career Action Plans* Write an action plan for accomplishing each of the five objectives. Be specific. State exactly what you will do and by when in order to meet each objective. If you will need special support or assistance, identify it *and* state how you will obtain it. Remember, an outside observer should be able to read your action plan for each objective and end up feeling confident that a) they know exactly what you are going to do, and b) why.

Instructions

Form into groups as assigned by the instructor. Share your career planning analysis with the group; listen to those of others. Participate in a discussion that examines any common patterns and major differences among group members. Take advantage of any opportunities to gather feedback and advice from others. Have one member of the group prepared to summarize the group discussion for the class as a whole. Await further class discussion led by the instructor.

Instructor's Note

This exercise can be done with a minimum of at-home preparation time and in a normal class period. It forces students to be somewhat precise in looking five years ahead into their futures, and trying to anticipate not only their preferred work positions but also their strengths and weaknesses in being able to succeed in those positions. The exercise can be done as an individual written assignment to be turned in as a concluding requirement for the course. It is also very easy to turn the exercise into a short classroom activity. Students can convene in small groups to share career goals and discuss some of the problems and opportunities that are expected along the way. Brief classroom presentations by each group help bring a sense of closure to the course, and also help students explore some of the differences between their viewpoints, opinions and aspirations and those of their colleagues.

Most students find career planning activities to be valuable and interesting. For most of them (even part-time MBAs), this will be the first real attempt to set a specific career objective and develop a plan for reaching the objective. The exercise will have quite a different flavor, depending upon whether it is done with younger undergraduates or older participants already embarked on a career. Younger students need more help with the self-exploration aspects of the exercise. Older students may find it a little more difficult to be open about their weaknesses, depending on what the norms about openness are at your school.

If you are teaching an undergraduate course, you may do well to use this exercise toward the end of the course. You could assign it early in the year and point out that some students may want to use the library, visit the placement center, and perhaps interview people in the occupation they are considering. You can exercise some control over this by requiring that they write a "Career Plan" paper covering all aspects of their planning.

Possible Discussion Questions and Answers

a) *Why should a person plan their career now? Wouldn't it be better to wait until one needs to make changes?*

Changes should be planned for, if you want to make them work to your advantage. Unplanned changes may be crisis events that make planning difficult. Stress, insecurity, or uncertainty may cause a person to respond to strong (but temporary) needs, and make it difficult to think patiently and systematically about the future (*Source:* D.D. Bowen and D. T. Hall, "Career Planning for Employee Development: A Primer for Managers," *California Management Review*, Winter 1977, pp. 23-25).

b) *Is it better to plan your career by building on your strengths or by remedying your deficiencies?*

The primary focus should be on your strengths, since using your satisfying needs and abilities is enjoyable and likely to motivate you further. Attention should be paid to deficiencies only in those instances where the deficiency stands in the way of progress toward your objective.

c)   *How frequently should you revise your career plans?*

Clearly, any time your needs or circumstances change, you should revise your career plan. In addition, it is probably a good idea to systematically review your plan every two or three years, even if there have been no major changes to cause you to do it more often.

d)   *Is there any evidence that preparing career plans helps people to achieve their objectives?*

The research of Locke and his colleagues (Edwin A. Locke and Gary P. Latham, *Goal Setting: A Motivational Technique that Works!* Englewood Cliffs, NJ: Prentice-Hall, 1984) demonstrates clearly that goal-setting increases task performance. Mangers who set career goals seem to weather crises better and achieve greater success (Bowen and Hall, 1977).

e)   *Why might management want to provide a career planning service for employees?*

There are several reasons why a large number of more progressively managed organizations are providing career planning assistance to their employees. These include a recognition that an employee with a strong career commitment is likely to be more highly motivated to produce, a growing awareness that certain types of employees (college recruits, mid-career employees, and so forth) have special needs for career planning, and the desire to comply with court orders on affirmative action programs requiring career planning for minorities or women (Bowen and Hall, 1977).

(Source: Developed in part from Roy J. Lewicki, Donald D. Bowen, Douglas T. Hall, and Francine S. Hall, Experiences in Management and Organizational Behavior, Third Edition. New York: John Wiley & Sons, 1988, pp. 261-267).

EXERCISE: STRATEGIC SCENARIOS

Preparation

In today's turbulent environments, it is no longer safe to assume that an organization that was highly successful yesterday will continue to be so tomorrow -- or, that it will even be in existence. Changing times challenge the best from strategic planners. Think about the situations currently facing the following list of well-known organizations. Think, too, about the futures they may face.

McDonald's	Harvard University
Texaco	United Nations
Xerox	National Public Radio

Instructions

Form into groups as assigned by your instructor. Choose one or more organizations from the prior list (as assigned) and answer for that organization the following questions:

1. What in the future might seriously threaten the success, perhaps the very existence, of this organization? (As a group develop at least three such *future scenarios*.)

2. Estimate the probability (0 to 100%) that each future scenario might occur.

3. Develop a strategy for each scenario that will enable the organization to successfully deal with it.

Thoroughly discuss these questions within the group and arrive at your best possible consensus answers. Be prepared to share and defend your answers in general class discussion.

Instructor's Note

This is an excellent exercise for providing students with experiential learning at strategic planning and the generation of future scenarios. Encourage students to conduct library research on these organizations as a foundation for identifying possible environmental threats, future scenarios, and strategies. Consider assigning more than one group a particular organization(s) and have each group critique the analysis of the other. Explore the reasons for any discrepancies between the groups' analyses, and consider the implications of these differences for organizations that employ scenario planning.

(Source: Suggested by an exercise in John F. Veiga and John N. Yanouzas, *The Dynamics of Organization Theory: Gaining a Macro Perspective.* St. Paul, Mn.: West, 1979, pp. 69-71).

EXERCISE: INTERVIEWING JOB CANDIDATES

Preparation

Make a list of the "generic" questions you think any employment interviewer should ask any job candidate regardless of the specific job or situation. Then, place an X next to those of the following items you think represent additional important questions to ask.

7 questions

_____ How old are you?

_____ Where were you born?

_____ Where are you from?

_____ What religion are you?

_____ Are you married, single, or divorced?

_____ If not married, do you have a companion?

_____ Do you have any dependent children or elderly parents?

Instructions

Form work groups as assigned by your instructor. Share your responses with other group members, and listen to theirs. Develop group consensus on a list of "generic" interview questions you think any manager should be prepared to ask of job candidates. Also develop group consensus on which of the items on the prior list represent questions that an interviewer should ask. Have a spokesperson prepared to present group results to the class, along with the reasons for selecting these questions.

Instructor's Note

Use the following to provide students with feedback regarding the legality of these questions.

Interview Questions	Legal	Illegal
How old are you?	1	
Where were you born?		X
Where are you from?		X
What religion are you?		X
Are you married, single or divorced?		X
If not married, do you have a companion?		X
Do you have any dependent children or elderly parents?		2

1 - only if to establish proof of true age.

2 - illegal except if asked to clarify information for dependent benefits such as health care.

NOTE: Check with the EEO and Affirmative Action officer(s) at your college for more specifics. Generally, any information which tends to have an adverse impact on a particular group of people is illegal to obtain. That information illegally discriminates if it eliminates applicants based on their group membership and not on their qualifications.

EXERCISE: COMPENSATION AND BENEFITS DEBATE

Preparation

Consider the following quotes taken from text discussion in Chapter 12.

On compensation: "A basic rule of thumb should be---pay at least as much, and perhaps a bit more, in base wage or salary than what competitors are offering."

On benefits: "When benefits are attractive or at least adequate, the organization is in a better position to employ highly qualified people."

Instructions

Form groups as assigned by the instructor. Each will be given *either* one of the prior position statements, *or* one of these alternatives.

On compensation: Given the importance of controlling costs, organizations can benefit by paying as little as possible for labor.

On benefits: Given the rising cost of health-care and other benefit programs, and the increasing difficulty many organizations have with staying in business, the best thing is to eliminate or minimize paid benefits and let employees handle them on their own.

Each group should prepare to debate a counterpoint group on its assigned position. After time allocated to prepare for the debate, the instructor will have groups present their opening positions. Each will then be allowed one rebuttal period to respond to the other group. General class discussion on the role of compensation and benefits in the modern organization will follow.

Instructor's Note

This exercise can be quite effective at generating a lively debate about the appropriate levels of compensation and benefits. Students are likely to enjoy this debate, and learn more about the tradeoffs involved in determining the level at which to set base compensation and benefits for employees. Thus this exercise provides an excellent way for students to experientially learn about important issues surrounding compensation and benefits decisions.

EXERCISE: WORK AND FAMILY -- YOU BE THE JUDGE

1. *Read the following situation.*

    Joanna, a single parent, was hired to work 8:15 A.M. to 5:30 P.M. weekdays selling computers for a firm. Her employer extended her work day until 10 P.M. weekdays and from 8:15 A.M. — 5:30 P.M. on Saturdays. Joanna refused to work the extra hours, saying that she had a six-year old son and that so many work hours would lead to neglect. The employer said this was a special request during a difficult period and that all employees needed to share in helping out during the "crunch." Still refusing to work the extra hours, Joanna was fired. She sued the employer.

2. *You be the judge in this case. Take an individual position on the following questions:*

    Should Joanna be allowed to work only the hours agreed to when she was hired? Or, is the employer correct in asking all employees, regardless of family status, to work the extra hours? Why?

3. *Form into groups as assigned by the instructor. Share your responses to the questions and try to develop a group consensus. Be sure to have a rationale for the position the group adopts. Appoint a spokesperson who can share results with the class. Be prepared to participate in open class discussion.*

Instructor's Note

Clearly, this is not a black and white issue, since one can argue for both Joanna and the company's positions. With regards to Joanna, it is quite possible that she took the work hours into account before accepting this job, and found the position to be attractive because it allowed her to spend time with her son. When the employer changed the hours, it essentially became impossible for her to meet both her work and family responsibilities — through no fault of her own. On the other hand, her employer should normally have the right to set the hours of employment — within reason. Denial of this right would make it difficult for the firm to serve its clients, and could ultimately threaten its success.

Despite the merits of the firm's position, it does seem to be overly rigid in requiring Joanna to work hours that prohibit her from caring for her son. Indeed, since the hours of employment changed after she accepted the job, it seems only fair that some effort be made to accommodate Joanna's schedule. Ideally, an integrative solution should be explored that would allow Joanna to work additional hours -- perhaps by telecommuting -- without neglecting her son.

Regardless of the position taken by the students' groups, the key point of this exercise is to help students to recognize the real challenges that working parents face, while considering integrative solutions to these problems.

(*Source:* This case scenario is from Sue Shellenbarger, "Employees Challenges Policies on Family and Get Hard Lessons," *The Wall Street Journal*, December 17, 1997, p. B1.)

EXERCISE: SOURCES AND USES OF POWER

Preparation

Consider *the way you behaved* in each of the following situations. This may be from a full-time or part-time job, student organization or class group, sports team, or whatever. If you do not have an experience of the type described, try to imagine yourself in one. In this case, think about how you would expect yourself to behave.

1. You needed to get a peer to do something you wanted that person to do, but were worried he or she didn't want to do.

2. You needed to get a subordinate to do something you wanted him or her to do, but were worried the subordinate didn't want to do.

3. You needed to get your boss to do something you wanted him or her to do, but were worried the boss didn't want to do.

Instructions

Form into groups as assigned by the instructor. Start with situation 1 and have all members of the group share their approaches. Determine what specific sources of power (see Chapter 12) were used. Note any patterns in group members' responses. Discuss what is required to be successful in this situation. Do the same for situations 2 and 3. Note any special differences in how situations 1, 2, 3 should be or could be handled. Have a spokesperson prepared to share results in general class discussion.

Instructor's Note

The sources of power identified by students can be categorized into the following categories of position and personal power.

Position power is the degree to which a position in the organization's hierarchy of authority gives a person the power to reward and punish subordinates.

(a) *Reward power:* The capability to offer something of value -- a positive outcome -- as a means of controlling people.

(b) *Coercive power:* The capability to punish or withhold positive outcomes as a means of controlling people.

(c) *Legitimate power:* The capability to control other people by virtue of the rights of office. Legitimate power is equivalent to *formal authority*.

Personal power is power that the person brings to the situation in terms of unique personal attributes.

(a) *Expert power:* The capability to control other people because of specialized knowledge.

(b) *Reference power:* The capability to control other people because of their desires to identify personally and positively with the power source.

Students will typically report using personal sources of power to influence peers and supervisors, while drawing on their position power to influence subordinates. This is because they lack the position power required to influence peers and superiors; as such, they will draw on their expertise and referent power to influence these targets.

The **influence strategies** mentioned by students can also be typically classified into one or more of the categories listed below.

Retribution strategies rely on position power, and result in feelings of coercion or intimidation. These strategies include:

(a) *Assertiveness* -- Being directive and forceful in approach ("Everyone else is going along, why aren't you?")

(b) *Appeal to higher authority* -- Referring to higher-level support ("You know I have the support of "higher-ups" on this matter.")

(c) *Sanctions* -- Offering rewards or threatening punishments ("If you don't do what I want, you'll regret it.")

Reason strategies rely more on personal power and persuasion based on data, needs, or values. These strategies include:

(a) *Facts* -- Using facts and empirical data in a logical argument ("Look at these figures and I know you'll agree something needs to be changed here.")

(b) *Friendliness* -- Acting extra nice and using flattery ("Given your great strengths in this area, I know you'll agree with me that...")

(c) *Coalition* -- Forming relationships with other people ("I have already talked to Mary and Marvin, and they are ready to go. Can I count on you joining the team?")

Reciprocity strategies involve the mutual exchange of values and search for shared positive outcomes. These strategies include:

(a) *Bargaining* -- Using negotiation to exchange benefits ("If I could do this for you, would you be able to do what I need now?")

(b) *Involvement* -- Asking consultation and allowing participation ("Here's the situation, would you sit down with me and help decide what can be done about it?")

Research suggests that the type of strategy students report using will depend upon the **influence target**. If the target is a *superior,* people tend to rely on the facts. With *co-workers,* friendliness, bargaining, and appeals to higher authorities are commonly employed. When the target is a *subordinate,* assertiveness, friendliness, sanctions, bargaining, and upward appeals are favored. See if this is the case for your class. If so, ask students why this is true. The obvious reason is that while subordinates lack the position power to use retribution strategies to influence superiors, superiors are able to choose from the full range of tactics. If not, explore with students the reasons why their responses differ from those which are more typically obtained.

(Source: David Kipnis, Stuart M. Schmidt, and Ian Wilkinson, "Intraorganizational Influence Tactics: Explorations in Getting One's Way," *Journal of Applied Psychology,* August 1980, pp. 440-452).

EXERCISE: EMPOWERING OTHERS

Instructions

Think of times when you have been in charge of a group — this could be a full-time or part-time work situation, a student work group, or whatever. Complete the following questionnaire by recording how you feel about each statement according to this scale:

1 = Strongly   2 = Disagree   3 = Neutral   4 = Agree   5 = Strongly

　　Agree   Agree

When in charge of a group I find

_____ 1. Most of the time other people are too inexperienced to do things, so I prefer to do them myself.

_____ 2. It often takes more time to explain things to others than to just do them myself.

_____ 3. Mistakes made by others are costly, so I don't assign much work to them.

_____ 4. Some things simply should not be delegated to others.

_____ 5. I often get quicker action by doing a job myself.

_____ 6. Many people are good only at very specific tasks and so can't be assigned additional responsibilities.

_____ 7. Many people are too busy to take on additional work.

_____ 8. Most people just aren't ready to handle additional responsibilities.

_____ 9. In my position, I should be entitled to make my own decisions.

Scoring

Total your responses: enter the score here [_____].

Interpretation

This instrument gives an impression of your willingness to delegate. Possible scores range from 9 to 45. The higher your score, the more willing you appear to be to delegate to others. Willingness to delegate is an important managerial characteristic: it is essential if you — as a manager — are to "empower" others and give them opportunities to assume responsibility and exercise self-control in their work. With the growing importance of empowerment in the new workplace, your willingness to delegate is worth thinking about seriously.

Instructor's Note

The title of this exercise is misleading in one sense -- people with higher scores tend to be *more reluctant* to delegate to others, rather than more willing. Be sure to point this out to your students. This exercise can serve as a useful tool for providing students with insight into their willingness to delegate, and hence their capability or tendency to empower others. Since delegation and empowerment are becoming increasingly important in the modern workplace, students who score as being reluctant to delegate should be aware of the potential adverse consequences of such reluctance. Indeed, the items reflect many of the reasons that managers often give for not delegating tasks to subordinates. Unfortunately, such reluctance can seriously undermine managerial effectiveness, for a variety of reasons. First, managers may simply become overwhelmed with tasks that they cannot begin to effectively complete on their own. Second, they may become overworked and experience excessive stress due to their efforts to perform the work of multiple persons. Third, the quality and/or quantity of work done may suffer as a result. Fourth, they will fail to develop their subordinates; as a result, their employees will not be properly prepared for more challenging assignments, and may become bored or frustrated with the lack of opportunities for growth. Finally, when and if such managers leave their post, their subordinates are ill-equipped to pick up the slack by assuming the managers' responsibilities and duties, since they lack experience in completing these tasks. For all of these reasons, it is imperative for managers to properly delegate assignments and empower their direct reports in order for the subordinates — and the manager — to achieve their full potential.

To provide students with some suggestions for overcoming their reluctance to delegate, share with them the following *guidelines on how to empower others*:

1. Get others involved in selecting work assignments and the methods of accomplishing tasks.

2. Create an environment of cooperation, information sharing, discussion, and shared ownership of goals.

3. Encourage others to take initiative, make decisions, and use their knowledge.

4. When problems arise, find out what others think and let them help design the solution.

5. Stay out of the way; let others put their ideas and solutions into practice.

6. Maintain high morale and confidence by recognizing successes and encouraging high performance.

(*Source:* Questionnaire adapted from L. Steinmertz and R. Todd, *First Line Management*, 4th ed.,Homewood, Il: BPI/Irwin, 1986, pp. 64-67. Used by permission.)

EXERCISE: LEADING VIA PARTICIPATION

Preparation

Read each of the following vignettes. Write in the space to the left of each whether you think the leader should handle the situation by an individual decision (I), consultative decision (C), or group decision (G).

Vignette I

You are general supervisor in charge of a large gang laying an oil pipeline. It is now necessary to estimate your expected rate of progress in order to schedule material deliveries to the next field site. You know the nature of the terrain you will be traveling and have the historical data needed to compute the mean and variance in the rate of speed over that type of terrain. Given these two variables, it is a simple matter to calculate the earliest and latest times at which materials and support facilities will be needed at the next site. It is important that your estimate be reasonably accurate. Underestimates result in idle supervisors and workers, and an overestimate results in tying up materials for a period of time before they are to be used. Progress has been good and your five supervisors and other members of the gang stand to receive substantial bonuses if the project is completed ahead of schedule.

Vignette II

You are supervising the work of 12 engineers. Their formal training and work experience are very similar, permitting you to use them interchangeably on projects. Yesterday your manager informed you that a request had been received from an overseas affiliate for four engineers to go abroad on extended loan for a period of six to eight months. For a number of reasons, he argued and you agreed that this request should be met from your group. All your engineers are capable of handling this assignment, and from the standpoint of present and future projects there is no particular reason why any one should be retained over any other. The problem is complicated by the fact that the overseas assignment is in what is generally regarded in the company as an undesirable location.

Vignette III

You are the head of a staff unit reporting to the vice president of finance. He has asked you to provide a report on the firm's current portfolio to include recommendations for changes in the *selection* criteria currently employed. Doubts have been raised about the efficiency of the existing system in the current market conditions, and there is considerable dissatisfaction with prevailing rates of return. You plan to write the report, but at the moment you are quite perplexed about the approach to take. Your own specialty is the bond market and it is clear to you that a detailed knowledge of the equity market, which you lack, would greatly enhance the value of the report. Fortunately, four members of your staff are specialists in different segments of the equity market. Together, they possess a vast amount of knowledge about the intricacies of investment. However, they seldom agree on the best way to achieve anything when it comes to the stock market. While they are obviously conscientious as well as knowledgeable, they have major differences when it comes to investment philosophy and strategy. The report is due in six weeks. You have already begun to familiarize yourself with the firm's current portfolio and have been provided by management with a specific set of constraints that any portfolio must satisfy. Your immediate problem is to come up with some alternatives to the firm's present practices and select the most promising for detailed analysis in your report.

Vignette IV

You are on the division manager's staff and work on a wide variety of problems of both an administrative and technical nature. You have been given the assignment of developing a universal method to be used in each of the five plants in the division for manually reading equipment registers, recording the readings, and transmitting the scorings to a centralized information system. All plants are located in a relatively small geographical region. Until now there has been a high error rate in the reading and/or transmittal of the data. Some locations have considerably higher error rates than others, and the methods used to record and transmit the data vary between plants. It is probable, therefore, that part of the error variance is a function of specific local conditions rather than anything else, and this will complicate the establishment of any system common to all plants. You have the information on error rates but no information on the local practices which generate these errors or on the local conditions which necessitate the different practices. Everyone would benefit from an improvement in the quality of the data as it is used in a number of important decisions. Your contacts with the plants are through the quality-control supervisors who are responsible for collecting the data. They are a conscientious group committed to doing their jobs well, but are highly sensitive to interference on the part of higher management in their own operations. Any solution which does not receive the active support of the various plant supervisors is unlikely to reduce the error rate significantly.

Instructions

Form groups as assigned by the instructor. Share your choices with other group members and try to achieve a consensus on how the leader should best handle each situation. Refer back to the discussion of the Vroom-Jago "leader-participation" theory presented in Chapter 13. Analyze each vignette according to their ideas. Do you come to any different conclusions? If so, why? Have a spokesperson prepared to share results in general class discussion.

Instructor's Note

There are at least three alternative ways to use the above vignettes, depending upon the amount of time you want to devote to this exercise.

Option 1 *(Smallest time requirement):* Work through the following guidelines and/or the decision tree depicted below with students by asking them the diagnostic questions in sequence. As the students answer each question, follow the branches of the tree until the recommended decision method is revealed.

Participation Guidelines: In general, managers are advised to use a more group-oriented decision method and participative leadership style when:

* They lack sufficient information to solve a problem by themselves.

* The problem is unclear and help is needed to clarify the situation.

> * Acceptance of the decision by others is necessary for its implementation.
>
> * Adequate time is available to allow for true participation.

On the other hand, the model suggests that managers can make individual decisions and use a more authority-oriented leadership style when:

* They personally have the expertise needed to solve the problem.

* They are confident and capable of acting alone.

* Others are likely to accept the decision they make.

* Little or no time is available for discussion.

Option 2 *(Moderate time requirement):* Ask students to work through the guidelines and/or decision tree individually or in groups until they arrive at a recommended decision style. Then discuss the styles selected and work through the model with the class as a whole.

Option 3 *(Largest time requirement):* Ask students to work through the guidelines and/or decision tree individually until they arrive at a recommended decision. Next, break the students into groups and ask them to share the results of their individual analyses. Instruct the groups to work toward a consensus regarding the appropriate decision method. Next, give each group an opportunity to indicate their preferred decision method before working through the model with the class as a whole.

Vignette Analyses

Use the decision tree and/or guidelines to analyze the scenarios. For each vignette, the answers to the diagnostic questions and recommended style are indicated below.

Vignette I: *Answers to the Diagnostic Questions:* Quality Requirement (QR) – High; Commitment Requirement (CR) – High; Leader's Information (LI) – Yes; Commitment Probability (CP) – Yes.

Recommended Style: I – Individual Decision.

Vignette II: *Answers to the Diagnostic Questions:* Quality Requirement (QR) – Low; Commitment Requirement (CR) – High; Commitment Probability (CP) – No.

Recommended Style: G – Group Decision.

Vignette III: *Answers to the Diagnostic Questions:* Quality Requirement (QR) – High; Commitment Requirement (CR) – Low; Leader's Information (LI) – No; Problem Structure (ST) –Yes; Goal Congruence (GC) – Yes; Subordinate Conflict (CO) – Yes.

Recommended Style: C – Consultative Decision.

Vignette IV: *Answers to the Diagnostic Questions:* Quality Requirement (QR) - High; Commitment Requirement (CR) - High; Leader's Information (LI) - No; Problem Structure (ST) -Yes; Commitment Probability (CP) - No; Goal Congruence (GC) - Yes; Subordinate Conflict (CO) - Yes.

Recommended Style: G - Group Decision.

(Source: Victor H. Vroom and Arthur G. Jago, *The New Leadership.* Englewood Cliffs, NJ: Prentice Hall, 1988. Used by permission).

EXERCISE: GENDER DIFFERENCES IN MANAGEMENT

1. The question is "Do women or men make better managers?"

2. A research study by the Foundation for Future Leadership examined the management abilities of 645 men and 270 women in terms of supervisor, peer, and self-evaluations. Among the management skills studied were those listed below.

Skills	Women Higher	Men Higher	No Difference
Problem solving			
Planning			
Controlling			
Managing self			
Managing relationships			
Leading			
Communicating			

3. Indicate in the space provided whether you believe women scored higher on the average than men for each skill, men scored higher than women, or no difference in scores was found.

4. Meet in your discussion groups to share results and the rationale for your choices. Try to arrive at a group consensus regarding the likelihood of differences between women and men. Ask questions of one another:

    * What is your experience with men as bosses?

    * What is your experience with women as bosses?

    * Why exactly do you think women/men would score better on each dimension?

    * Is it useful to try and identify gender differences in management?

* Why is gender even relevant when it comes to questions about management skills?

5. Be prepared to summarize your results and participate in further class discussion lead by the instructor.

Instructor's Note

This exercise is designed to reveal popular conceptions of men and women as leaders, and to show the degree to which these conceptions may differ from reality. In many cases, students are likely to predict that men possess superior skills to women, due to common gender stereotypes. Alternatively, they may predict no gender-related differences. Importantly, the later prediction is consistent with most of the findings of prior research on male and female managers (see Gary N. Powell, *Women and Men in Management*, 2nd ed., Sage Publications, Newbury Park, California, 1993).

Surprisingly, the results from a 1996 study sponsored by the Foundation for Future Leadership's -- a non-profit organization dedicated to identifying tomorrow's leaders today -- tell a much different story. Specifically, they revealed that corporate women outperformed men in 29 of 31 categories, including maintaining high productivity, meeting schedules and deadlines, meeting commitments, recognizing trends and generating new ideas. Indeed, the study by Janet Irwin and Michael Perrault -- authorities in the field of executive assessment with over 20 years managerial experience -- strongly suggests that women tend to be more effective managers than men. Contrary to commonly held beliefs that women excel at supportive and cooperative roles only, Irwin concluded that, "We have seen the successful executive of the future and she is a woman. This report indicates that women are stronger than men overall in both interpersonal skills and managerial effectiveness." Female managers surpassed their male counterparts in 90% of the behaviors assessed, with statistically significant differences being obtained for 25 categories. "Traditionally women were thought to be good on the interpersonal side, but this study shows that women perform equally well in both interpersonal and intellectual capacities," said Ken Feltman, a trustee of the Foundation.

"The statistical significance of this data is almost unbelievable," said Irwin. "Men are not rated significantly higher in any of the areas measured." While male managers were rated higher (but not significantly) than their female counterparts for two behaviors, handling pressure and coping with (their) own frustration, and equal to women on another, delegating authority, women were rated higher on all of the remaining categories. These include motivating and inspiring others, resolving conflicts, adapting to change, producing high quality work, and developing their own capabilities. "This is evidence that women have the skills to be top managers and shows that a lot of America's best leaders are already women," said Feltman. Irwin concludes, "While there has been much speculation about the capabilities of female managers, this research shows that women managers are more competent across the board than their male counterparts. Because women have historically been expected to play a supportive and cooperative role, women have learned how to manage effectively without relying on the control of resources and power to motivate others."

586

"The best news is that this study is good news for men, too. To win the war for a stronger economy and better jobs, we need women in the command center of corporate America," said Dr. John Albertine, chairman of Albertine Enterprises, Inc. and past Reagan appointee on the Commission for Private Sector Initiatives. "Profitable companies understand the importance of successful teams — and many of those teams have women as quarterbacks. Bottom line — women managers make companies more profitable."

Share the results of this study with your students and ask them if they think they are valid. You may have them speculate on why these findings contradict those of prior studies, which revealed few gender-related differences in managerial behavior or performance. Finally, be sure to have them reflect on their own preconceived notions regarding the skills of male and female managers. Did their expectations reflect gender stereotypes? If so, what are the implications for women managers and their employers, particularly in light of the counterintuitive findings described above.

EXERCISE: UPWARD APPRAISAL

Instructions

Form into work groups as assigned by the instructor. The instructor will then leave the room. As a group, complete the following tasks:

1. Within each group create a master list of comments, problems, issues, and concerns about the course experience to date that members would like to communicate with the instructor.

2. Select one person from the group to act as spokesperson and give this feedback to the instructor upon his or her return to the classroom.

3. The spokespersons from each group should meet to decide how the room should be physically arranged (placement of tables, chairs, etc.) for the feedback session. This should allow spokespersons and instructor to communicate while being observed by other class members.

4. While the spokespersons are meeting, members remaining in the groups should discuss what they expect to observe during the feedback session.

5. The classroom should be rearranged. The instructor should be invited in.

6. Spokespersons should deliver feedback to the instructor, while observers make notes.

7. After the feedback session is complete, the instructor will call on observers for comments, ask the spokespersons for their reactions, and engage the class in general discussion of the exercise and its implications.

Instructor's Note

This is one of the most beneficial exercises that we have found in our experiences with management courses. The exercise has practical value in that it sensitizes students to the potential barriers associated with communications upward in an organizational hierarchy. It also provides direct feedback of potential value to the instructor in improving the course at the mid-semester point. Thus, it can be used by the instructor to demonstrate appropriate managerial behavior in the context of the course as a learning organization.

The procedures described in the text should be followed in implementing the exercise. They are straightforward and students have little difficulty following them. It is important to set the stage for the exercise properly. Students should be encouraged to be frank in communicating to the spokespersons the issues that they would like to have pointed out to the instructor. The instructor should be open and receptive, and carefully demonstrate good listening behavior while receiving the feedback in the class session. This point cannot be over-emphasized. This is where the instructor should be an active listener and show students how feedback can be received without defensiveness and in a manner that encourages the future flow of similar evaluative information.

We always take notes during the exercise and report back to students in a subsequent class period regarding our responses to the major points. Often you will find that students raise points that can be immediately and positively addressed. Other points may be ones that they and you must simply live with based upon the nature of the course or the administrative structure of the university. Nevertheless, students always feel good having had the chance to communicate with you. We have always felt good in return having had the benefit this mid-semester feedback. Listed below are some of the comments that we have received over the years regarding our courses. This listing may help you anticipate things students will say.

* Like the lectures.

* Use good examples in class.

* Know material well.

* Exams are too lengthy.

* Exams are graded too hard.

* A periodic summary of material to date and an integration of the material would be helpful.

* The timing of the term paper assignment is bad.

* Need more detail on how to handle case analyses.

* Grading criteria are not clear.

* The class is too large.

* You sometimes talk too fast.

* The course is well organized.

* You use diagrams well in class.

* We feel free to participate.

* You are hard to reach and have limited office hours.

In debriefing the exercise in class, be sure to emphasize your feelings regarding the roles of both the spokespersons and the instructor. Ask the observers what examples they can generate of good communication behavior on the part of the spokespersons, and perhaps some ideas of where the communication could have been better. Ask them to also indicate the things you did to serve as a good listener and perhaps some of the things that you did that might discourage the flow of information from which the communication event took place. We have experienced many different arrangements, from the instructor being in the center of a very large circle, to the instructor being in the front of the room behind the desk with all students lined up in front of him/her, to the instructor being included in a general circle. We like to emphasize the fact that the arrangement sets a tone and perhaps introduces a potential barrier to communication effectiveness.

(Source: Developed from Eugene Owens, "Upward Appraisal: An Exercise in Subordinate's Critique of Superior's Performance," *Exchange: The Organizational Behavior Teaching Journal,* Vol. 3, 1978, pp. 41-42).

EXERCISE: FEEDBACK AND ASSERTIVENESS

Preparation

Indicate the degree of discomfort you would feel in each situation given below, by circling the appropriate number:

1. high discomfort; 2. some discomfort; 3. undecided; 4. very little discomfort; 5. no discomfort.

1 2 3 4 5   **1.**   Telling an employee who is also a friend that he or she must stop coming to work late.

1 2 3 4 5   **2.**   Talking to an employee about his or her performance on the job.

1 2 3 4 5   **3.**   Asking an employee if he or she has any comments about your rating of his or her performance.

1 2 3 4 5   **4.**   Telling an employee who has problems in dealing with other employees that he or she should do something about it.

1 2 3 4 5   **5.**   Responding to an employee who is upset over your rating of his or her performance.

1 2 3 4 5   **6.**   An employee's becoming emotional and defensive when you tell him or her about mistakes in the job.

1 2 3 4 5   **7.**   Giving a rating that indicates improvement is needed to an employee who has failed to meet minimum requirements of the job.

1 2 3 4 5   **8.**   Letting a subordinate talk during an appraisal interview.

1 2 3 4 5 **9.** An employee's challenging you to justify your evaluation in the middle of an appraisal interview.

1 2 3 4 5 **10.** Recommending that an employee be discharged.

1 2 3 4 5 **11.** Telling an employee that you are uncomfortable in the role of having to judge his or her performance.

1 2 3 4 5 **12.** Telling an employee that his or her performance can be improved.

1 2 3 4 5 **13.** Telling an employee that you will not tolerate his or her taking extended coffee breaks.

1 2 3 4 5 **14.** Telling an employee that you will not tolerate his or her making personal telephone calls on company time.

Instructions

Form three-person teams as assigned by the instructor. In each team, have members identify the three behaviors with which they indicate the most discomfort. Then each member should practice doing these behaviors with another member, while the third member acts as an observer. Be direct, but try to perform the behavior in an appropriate manner. Listen to feedback from the observer and try the behaviors again, perhaps with different members of the group. When finished, discuss the exercise overall. Be prepared to participate in further class discussion.

Instructor's Note

The instrument presented above is intended to measure the levels of discomfort students anticipate they would feel in providing various forms of negative performance feedback to employees. Importantly, the exercise goes beyond assessing student assertiveness about giving feedback, by providing them with opportunities to practice giving feedback to subordinates in the three situations that they feel most uncomfortable with. As such, this exercise can provide them with some valuable training for assertively providing negative feedback. At the conclusion of the exercise, you may want to share with students the following **guidelines for giving constructive feedback.**

(a) Give feedback directly and with real feeling, based on trust between you and the receiver.

(b) Make feedback specific rather than general, using good, clear, and preferably recent examples.

(c) Give feedback at a time when the receiver seems most willing or able to accept it.

(d) Make sure the feedback is valid, and limit it to things the receiver can be expected to do something about.

(e) Give feedback in small doses; never give more than the receiver can handle at any particular time.

You can also present the following **guidelines for a productive criticism session:**

Step 1: Get to the Point - Don't evade the issue.

Step 2: Describe the Situation - Use a descriptive opening that is specific, not general. Avoid evaluative statements.

Step 3: Use Active Listening Techniques - Encourage the subordinate to tell his or her side of the story. Ask open-ended questions such as "what" or "how" which invite discussion.

Step 4: Agree on the Source of the Problem and Its Solution - Its essential that the subordinate agree there is a problem. Once the problem is identified and agreed upon, work together to identify the source and a solution.

Step 5: Summarizing the Meeting - Have the subordinate summarize the meeting to ensure that both the manager and the subordinate agree on what's been decided. Set a time for a follow-up meeting.

(*Source:* Feedback questionnaire is from Judith R. Gordon, *A Diagnostic Approach to Organizational Behavior,* Third Edition. Boston: Allyn and Bacon, 1991, p. 298. Used by permission).

EXERCISE: HOW TO GIVE---AND TAKE---CRITICISM

The "criticism session" may well be the toughest test of a manager's communication skills. Picture Setting 1---you and a subordinate, meeting to review a problem with the subordinate's performance. Now picture Setting 2---you and your boss, meeting to review a problem with *your* performance. Both situations require communication skills in giving and receiving feedback. Even the most experienced person can have difficulty and the situations can end as futile gripe sessions resulting in hard feelings. The question is: How can "criticism sessions" be handled in a positive manner that encourages improved performance . . . and good feelings?

Instructions

Form into groups as assigned by the instructor. Focus on either Setting #1 or Setting #2, or both, as also assigned by the instructor. First, answer the question from the assigned perspective. Second, develop a series of action guidelines that could be used to best handle situations of this type. Third, prepare and present a mini-management training session to demonstrate the (a) unsuccessful and (b) successful use of these guidelines.

If time permits outside of class, prepare a more extensive management training session that includes a videotape demonstration of your assigned criticism setting being handled poorly and then very well. Support the videotape with additional written handouts and an oral presentation to help your classmates better understand the communication skills needed to successfully give and take criticism in work settings.

Instructor's Note

This assignment can serve as an excellent tool for familiarizing students with the difficulties involved in giving and receiving performance feedback. Moreover, it can help them to learn about the best ways of handling these difficult situations. Since giving and receiving performance feedback are especially important aspects of manager's jobs, the benefits of this assignment can be considerable. In addition, the task of creating a management training session and videotape, should provide students with some practical knowledge about the preparation instructional materials.

EXERCISE: WHY DO WE WORK?

Preparation

Read the following "ancient story."

In days of old a wandering youth happened upon a group of men working in a quarry. Stopping by the first man he said: "What are you doing?" The worker grimaced and groaned as he replied: "I am trying to shape this stone, and it is backbreaking work." Moving to the next man he repeated the question. This man showed little emotion as he answered: "I am shaping a stone for a building." Moving to the third man, our traveler heard him singing as he worked. "What are you doing?" asked the youth. "I am helping to build a cathedral," the man proudly replied.

Instructions

In groups assigned by your instructor, discuss this short story. Ask and answer the question: "What are the lessons of this ancient story for (a) workers and (b) managers of today?" Ask members of the group to role play each of the stonecutters, respectively, while they answer a second question asked by the youth: "Why are you working?" Have someone in the group prepared to report and share the group's responses with the class as a whole.

Instructor's Note

This is a useful exercise which highlights the difference which one's outlook towards work can make. It typically stimulates interesting discussions among students of the reasons why people work. Point out that to the extent that managers can succeed in defining the work of their unit in terms of higher order goals (e.g., building a cathedral), the intrinsic satisfaction of the work will be elevated. Thus, this exercise has implications for the chapters on leadership and motivation that are included in *Part 5.*

(*Source:* Developed from Brian Dumaine, "Why do We Work," *Fortune,* December 26, 1994, pp. 196-204).

EXERCISE: THE CASE OF THE CONTINGENCY WORKFORCE

Preparation

Part-time and contingency work is a rising percentage of total employment in the United States. Go to the library and read about the current use of part-time and contingency workers in business and industry. Ideally, go to the Internet, enter a government data base, and locate some current statistics on the size of the contingent labor force, the proportion that is self-employed and part-time, and the proportion of part-timers who are voluntary and involuntary.

Instructions

In your assigned work group, pool the available information on the contingency workforce. Discuss the information. Discuss one another's viewpoints on the subject, as well as its personal and social implications. Be prepared to participate in a classroom "dialog session" in which your group will be asked to role-play one of the following positions:

(a)   Vice-president for human resources of a large discount retailer hiring contingency workers.

(b)   Owner of a local specialty music shop hiring contingency workers.

(c)   Recent graduate of your college or university, working as a contingency employee at the discount retailer in (a).

(d)   Single parent with two children in elementary school, working as a contingency employee of the music shop in (b).

The question to be answered by the (a) and (b) groups is: "What does the contingency workforce mean to me?" The question to be answered by the (c) and (d) groups is: "What does being a contingency worker mean to me?"

Instructor's Note

This exercise can be extremely useful in helping students to appreciate how contingency employers and employees think *and* feel about this type of work. For employers, the primary reasons for hiring contingency workers are practical: they need additional workers but can't guarantee or justify permanent employment. They are likely to argue that the relationship is beneficial for both parties: their work needs are meet, and while workers who might otherwise be unemployed, receive temporary employment. The workers may express appreciation for the opportunity to work, but anxiety about the temporary nature of their employment. In addition, contingency workers typically are not eligible for many of the benefits (e.g., health care, insurance) that permanent workers receive. As a result, some of the students who role play contingency employees may express feelings of being exploited by the employers -- a charge which the employers will most likely vehemently deny. Because of dynamics such as these, each role play can prove to be a spirited, informative and memorable learning experience for those involved. In addition, the use of the Internet as part of the preparation process, can provide students with a valuable learning experience as well.

EXERCISE: THE "BEST" JOB DESIGN

Preparation

Use the left column to rank the following job characteristics in the order most important *to you* (1 = highest to 10 = lowest). Then use the right column to rank them in the order you think they are most important *to others*.

_____ Variety of tasks   _____

_____ Performance feedback   _____

_____ Autonomy/freedom in work   _____

_____ Working on a team   _____

_____ Having responsibility   _____

_____ Making friends on the job   _____

_____ Doing all of a job, not part   _____

_____ Importance of job to others   _____

_____ Having resources to do well   _____

_____ Flexible work schedule   _____

Instructions

Form work groups as assigned by the instructor. Share your rankings with other group members. Discuss where you have different individual preferences and where your impressions differ to the preferences of others. Are there any major patterns in your group---for either the "personal" or the "other" rankings? Develop group consensus rankings for each column. Designate a spokesperson to share the group rankings and discussion with the rest of the class.

Instructor's Note

Job design is concerned with a number of attributes of a job. Among these attributes are the job itself, the requirements of the job, the interpersonal interaction opportunities on the job, and performance outcomes. There are certain attributes that are preferred by individuals. Some prefer job autonomy, while others prefer to be challenged by different tasks. It is obvious that individual differences in preferences would be an important consideration for managers. An exciting job for one person may be a demeaning and boring job for another individual. Managers could use this type of information in attempting to create job design conditions that allow organizational goals and individual goals and preferences to be matched.

Most of the job design characteristics listed above would be classified by Herzberg as satisfier factors, since they reflect various aspects of the job content. However, working on a team, making friends on the job, and a flexible work schedule are clearly examples of hygiene factors.

Students' rankings of these job design characteristics will reflect individual differences in their job design preferences. In addition, the differences between their "personal" and "other" rankings may reflect their assumptions about others' job design values. Students should discuss the reasons for these differences. Do they reflect actual or imagined differences? What are their implications for the students' managerial careers? Explore these and other issues with your students.

(Source: Developed from John M. Ivancevich and Michael T. Matteson, Organizational Behavior and Management, Second Edition. Homewood, IL: BPI/Irwin, 1990, p. 500. Used by permission).

EXERCISE: WORK TEAM DYNAMICS

Preparation

Think about your course work group, a work group you are involved in for another course, or any other group suggested by the instructor. Indicate how often each of the following statements accurately reflects your experience in the group. Use this scale:

1 = Always   2 = Frequently   3 = Sometimes   4 = Never

1. My ideas get a fair hearing.
2. I am encouraged for innovative ideas and risk taking.
3. Diverse opinions within the group are encouraged.
4. I have all the responsibility I want.
5. There is a lot of favoritism shown in the group.
6. Members trust one another to do their assigned work.
7. The group sets high standards of performance excellence.
8. People share and change jobs a lot in the group.
9. You can make mistakes and learn from them in this group.
10. This group has good operating rules.

Instructions

Form groups as assigned by your instructor. Ideally, this will be the group you have just rated. Have all group members share their ratings, and make one master rating for the group as a whole. Circle the items on which there are the biggest differences of opinion. Discuss those items and try to find out why they exist. In general, the better a group scores on this instrument the higher its creative potential. If everyone has rated the same group, make a list of the five most important things members can do to improve its operations in the future. Have a spokesperson prepared to summarize group discussion for the class as a whole.

Instructor's Note

This exercise can be extremely useful at providing work teams with valuable insights into the dynamics of their groups. It should be especially useful if you use work groups in your class, since the members are more likely to have considerable insight into their teams' processes. Moreover, by examining the items for which the biggest differences of opinion arise, team members should be able to quickly pinpoint and discuss problem areas for the group. Finally, by creating action plans for improving group processes, the stage can be set for improving the effectiveness of these groups. In essence, this exercise can serve to facilitate the data gathering, data analysis and diagnosis, and action planning steps of the team building process for your class' work teams.

(Source: Adapted from William Dyer, *Team Building,* Second Edition. Reading, MA: Addison-Wesley, 1987, pp. 123-125).

EXERCISE: LOST AT SEA

Consider this situation

You are adrift on a private yacht in the South Pacific when a fire of unknown origin destroys the yacht and most of its contents. You and a small group of survivors are now in a large raft with oars. Your location is unclear, but you estimate being about 1000 miles south--southwest of the nearest land. One person has just found in her pockets five $1 bills and a packet of matches. Everyone else's pockets are empty. The following items are available to you on the raft.

	A	B	C
Sextant	-------	-------	-------
Shaving mirror	-------	-------	-------
5 gallons water	-------	-------	-------
Mosquito netting	-------	-------	-------
1 survival meal	-------	-------	-------
Maps of Pacific Ocean	-------	-------	-------
Floatable seat cushion	-------	-------	-------
2 gallons oil--gas mix	-------	-------	-------
Small transistor radio	-------	-------	-------
Shark repellent	-------	-------	-------
20 square feet black plastic	-------	-------	-------
1 quart 20-proof rum	-------	-------	-------
15 feet nylon rope	-------	-------	-------
24 chocolate bars	-------	-------	-------
Fishing kit	-------	-------	-------

Instructions

1. *Working alone,* rank in Column **A** the 15 items in order of their importance to your survival ("1" is most important and "15" is least important).

2. *Working in an assigned group,* arrive at a "team" ranking of the 15 items, and record this ranking in Column **B**. Appoint one person as group spokesperson to report your group rankings to the class.

3. *Do not write in Column* **C** until further instructions are provided by your instructor.

Answers and Rationale

According to the "experts," the basic supplies needed when a person is stranded in mid ocean are articles to attract attention and articles to aid survival *until rescuers arrive.* Articles for navigation are of little importance: Even if a small life raft were capable of reaching land, it would be impossible to store enough food and water to subsist during that period of time. Therefore, of primary importance are the shaving mirror and the two-gallon can of oil-gas mixture. These items could be used for signaling air-sea rescue. Of secondary importance are items such as water and food, e.g., the survival meal. The "experts" rankings are provided below.

	Rank
Sextant	15
Shaving mirror	1
5 gallons of water	3
Mosquito netting	14
One survival meal	4
Maps of Pacific Ocean	13
Floatable seat cushion	9
2 gallons of oil-gas mix	2
Small transistor radio	12
Shark repellent	10
20 square feet black plastic	5
One quart 20-proof rum	11
15 feet nylon rope	8
24 chocolate bars	6
Fishing kit	7

Unit 9: The Career Readiness Notebook — Instructor's Notes

A brief rationale is provided for the ranking of each item. These brief explanations obviously do not represent all of the potential uses for the specified items but, rather, the primary importance of each.

1 - Shaving mirror

Critical for signaling air-sea rescue.

2 - Two-gallons oil-gas mix

Critical for signaling -- the oil-gas mixture will float on the water and could be ignited with a dollar bill and a match (obviously, outside the raft).

3 - Five gallons of water

Necessary to replenish loss by perspiring, etc.

4 - One survival meal

Provides basic food intake.

5 - Twenty square feet of black plastic

Utilized to collect rain water, provide shelter from the elements.

6 - Twenty-four chocolate bars

A reserve food supply.

7 - Fishing kit

Ranked lower than the candy bars because "one bird in the hand is worth two in the bush." There is no assurance that you will catch any fish.

8 - Fifteen feet of nylon rope

May be used to lash equipment together to prevent it from falling overboard.

10 - Shark repellent

Obvious.

11 - One quart of 20-proof rum

Contains alcohol -- enough to use as a potential antiseptic for any injuries incurred; of little value otherwise; will cause dehydration if ingested.

12 - Small transistor radio

Of little value since there is no transmitter (unfortunately, you are out of range of your favorite AM radio stations).

13 - Maps of the Pacific Ocean

Worthless without additional navigational equipment -- it does not really matter where you are but where the rescuers are.

14 - Mosquito netting

There are no mosquitoes in the mid-Pacific.

15 - Sextant

Without tables and a chronometer, relatively useless.

The basic rationale for ranking signaling devices above life-sustaining items (food and water) is that without signaling devices there is almost no chance of being spotted and rescued. Furthermore, most rescues occur during the first thirty-six hours, and one can survive without food and water during this period.

Instructor's Note

This exercise can be extremely useful at illustrating the importance of creativity to both individual and group decision making. As part of your discussion of this exercise, ask students to score their individual and group responses by summing their personal and group absolute deviations from the expert's rankings. Next instruct them to calculate the mean for the individual group members' responses. Typically, "the best individual" score will be superior to the group score; nevertheless, the group score is normally superior to the mean of the individual scores. These tendencies provide two important lessons. First, a creative individual, who may or may not have some relevant expertise, can often outperform a group on a problem solving task. Second, the group will typically obtain a superior solution than will *most* individuals. Thus, while some people are capable of outperforming a group on a task, the capability of groups to share information and varied perspectives typically results in some improvement in the quality of solutions generated by most individuals. As such, there are clearly benefits of both individual decision making (for creative or expert persons) and group decision making.

(Source: Adapted from "Lost at Sea: A Consensus-Seeking Task," in *The 1975 Handbook for Group Facilitators.* Used with permission of University Associates, Inc.)

***EXERCISE*: DOTS AND SQUARES PUZZLE**

Instructor's Note

1.   *Shown below is a collection of 16 dots. Study the figure to determine how many "squares" can be created by connecting the dots.*

   Students will probably find 10 squares. Some may find 9 based on the phrase "connecting the dots." They may not see the overall outline as connecting the dots.

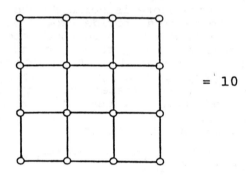

= 10

   On the other hand, some may use diagonal lines and find other squares.

2.   *Draw as many squares as you can find in the figure while making sure a dot is at every corner of every square. Count the squares and write this number in the margin to the right of the figure.*

   The second instruction may suggest that there are more squares. Some students may see squares in overlap, i.e.:

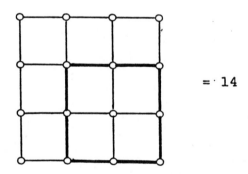

= 14

3.   *Share your results with those of a classmate sitting nearby. Explain the location of squares missed by either one of you.*

   While they may not call it this, students will begin seeing that their perception differs from others. This is really a way of defining the problem more accurately.

4. *Based on this discussion, redraw your figure to show the maximum number of possible squares.   Count them and write this number to the left of the figure.*

At this point, students will probably use diagonal lines in addition to the lines used in questions 1 and/or 2.   Several squares could be added:

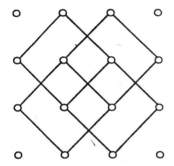

= 4 in addition to the above.

Also, if students ignored the stipulation about dots in the corners (5 more above), defined squares loosely to include rectangles (2 more above), or "went out of the lines" (as below), more squares could be added.

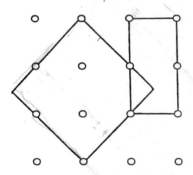

5. *Await further class discussion led by your instructor.*

This exercise can be used to demonstrate many issues related to defining the problem and to creativity.   Some students may define the problem too narrowly and not see the overall square or the overlapping squares. Others may define it too broadly, as noted above, by ignoring the "corner dot" requirement, including rectangles, or "going out of the lines." Relate this to perceptions and the ideas discussed regarding barriers to creativity.   In any case, point out how one's perceptions, and other influences, can greatly determine the definition of the problem.   Also, point out and discuss the effects of sharing information with others.   In this exercise, the sharing of information probably leads to better problem definition.   Relate this then to forms of group problem solving.

You may point out now, or later when you discuss power and influence, how if a person is allowed to define the problem, that person can greatly affect, or determine, what the group or organization works toward.

EXERCISE: CREATIVE SOLUTIONS

Instructions

Complete these five tasks while working alone. Be prepared to present and explain your responses in class.

1.   Divide the following shape into four pieces of exactly the same size.

   Task   Solution

   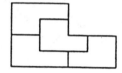

2.   Without lifting your pencil from the paper, draw no more than four lines that cross through all of the dots below.

   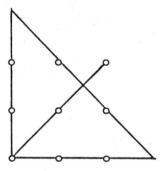

   This question can be used to demonstrate the tendency of some students to define the problem too narrowly and not see the overall problem. Indeed, some students unnecessarily make the limiting assumption that they cannot go outside the lines.

3.   Draw the design for a machine that will turn the pages of your textbook so that you can eat a snack while studying.

   Student drawings will vary. The key is for them to use their imagination to design such a machine.

4.   Why would a wheelbarrow ever be designed this way?

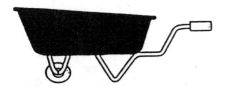

When an eminent student of creativity, Edward de Bono, asked this question of an audience of managers and management scientists, there was a good deal of squirming, murmuring, and embarrassed tittering, but no answer. After waiting a few minutes to let their discomfort grow, De Bono told his audience that he had recently asked the same question of a group of children and almost immediately one of them had rushed to the board and drawn a squiggly line such as that shown in below. "The wheelbarrow is for a bumpy road," the child said. At this point, the audience blushed and laughed self-consciously. This example demonstrates the unfortunate fact that the creativity of children is suppressed at home and at school; by the time one is an adult, only a fraction of one's innate creativity remains.

5.   Turn the following into words.

a. ____ program   *(space program)*

b. r\e\a\d\i\n\g *(reading between the lines)*

c. ECNALG *(backwards glance)*

d.   j   *(just between you and me)*

     u

   yousme

     t

e. stand   *(I understand)*

     i

Optional Instructions

After working alone, share your responses with a nearby classmate or with a group. See if you can develop different and/or better solutions based on this exchange of ideas.

Instructor's Note

Students typically find this exercise to be fun and informative. It provides them with an opportunity to test their personal creativity, and gain insights with regards to potential limiting assumptions that they may make. Moreover, point out that by sharing their responses with a classmate, they can typically achieve a better problem definition and solution.

*(Source: Ideas #2 and #5 found in Russell L. Ackoff, *The Art of Problem Solving*. New York: John Wiley & Sons, 1978; Ideas #1 and #4 found in Edward De Bono, *Lateral Thinking: Creativity Step by Step*. New York: Harper & Row, 1970; source unknown for #5).*

EXERCISE: FORCE-FIELD ANALYSIS

1.   Form into your class discussion groups.

2.   Review the concept of force-field analysis — the consideration of forces driving in support of a planned change and forces resisting change.

3.   Use this force-field analysis worksheet in the assignment:

List of Driving Forces (those supporting the change)

_____

_____ ... list as many as you can think of

List of Resisting Forces (those working against the change)

_____

_____ ... list as many as you can think of

3. Apply force-field analysis and make your lists of driving and resisting forces for one of the following situations:

   (a) Due to rapid advances in Web-based computer technologies, the possibility exists that the course you are presently taking could be in part offered "on-line." This would mean a reduction in the number of required class sessions, but an increase in students' responsibility for completing learning activities and assignments through computer mediation.

   (b) A new owner has just taken over a small walk-in-and buy-by-the-slice pizza shop in a college town. There are presently 8 employees, 3 of whom are full-time and 5 of whom are part-timers. The shop is presently open 7 days a week from 10:30 A.M. to 10:30 P.M. each day. The new owner believes there is a market niche available for late-night pizza and would like to stay open each night until 2 A.M.

   (c) A situation assigned by the instructor.

4. Choose the 3 driving forces that are most significant to the proposed change. For each force develop ideas on how it could be further increased or mobilized in support of the change.

5. Choose the 3 resisting forces that are most significant to the proposed change. For each force develop ideas on how it could be reduced or turned into a driving force.

6. Be prepared to participate in class discussion led by the instructor.

Instructor's Note

This exercise is designed to help students improve their analytical skills for addressing complex situations and show them how force-field analysis can aid the understanding of change. It allows them to take a current problem or situation and reflect upon how it can be changed.

This exercise can be done in its entirety in class, or steps 1 through 5 inclusive can be assigned as homework; then, if desired, step 6 could be done in class. In a large class, you may wish to choose a problem or situation and do the exercise with the class as a whole. Encourage students to brainstorm driving forces, thus bringing in other course concepts to this exercise.

MANAGEMENT SKILLS ASSESSMENTS

ASSESSMENT: WHAT ARE YOUR MANAGERIAL ASSUMPTIONS?

Instructions

Read the following statements. Use the space to the left to write "Yes" if you agree with the statement, or "No" if you disagree with it. Force yourself to take a "yes" or "no" position. Do this for every statement.

____ **1.** Are good pay and a secure job enough to satisfy most workers?

____ **2.** Should a manager help and coach subordinates in their work?

____ **3.** Do most people like real responsibility in their jobs?

____ **4.** Are most people afraid to learn new things in their jobs?

____ **5.** Should managers let subordinates to control the quality of their own work?

____ **6.** Do most people dislike work?

____ **7.** Are most people creative?

____ **8.** Should a manager closely supervise and direct work of subordinates?

____ **9.** Do most people tend to resist change?

____ **10.** Do most people work only as hard as they have to?

____ **11.** Should workers be allowed to set their own job goals?

____ **12.** Are most people happiest off the job?

____ **13.** Do most workers really care about the organization that they work for?

____ **14.** Should a manager help subordinates advance and grow in their jobs?

Scoring

Count the number of "Yes" responses to items # 1,4,6,8,9,10,12. Write that score here [**X** = _____]. Count the number of "Y" responses to items # 2,3,5,7,11,13,14. Write that score here [**Y** = _____].

Interpretation

This assessment offers a general look at how you fit into Douglas McGregor's Theory X and Theory Y concepts. If your **Y** score is greater, your tendency may be to approach people in the workplace with a positive point of view based on the Theory Y assumptions. If your **X** score is greater, your tendency may be to approach them with more negative Theory X assumptions. Developments in the new workplace are more consistent with Theory Y than with Theory X thinking.

Instructor's Note

The key to this assessment is for students to recognize the implications of their scores, particularly with respect to their behavior towards subordinates. You may want to provide students with an opportunity to discuss their scores with the classmate sitting next to them or in groups, before opening the discussion up to the class as a whole. Either way, its a good idea to tell students' that their scores are for their own benefit and it is not necessary to divulge them unless they want to do so. For those students who do wish to share their scores, however, be sure to ask them why they answered as they did. What kind of experiences have they had which lead to their assumptions about people? How might their scores affect them in their roles as group member? Leaders?

What would it take to change their assumptions?

Some students are likely to report mixed scores. These students will probably argue that their assumptions vary depending upon the types of people they would be managing. This provides you with a good opportunity to discuss the contingency approach to management. In other words, you might argue that the validity of Theory X and Theory Y assumptions, and the consequent ability of the manager to delegate depend upon the subordinates and the situation.

ASSESSMENT: A 21ST-CENTURY MANAGER?

Instructions

Rate yourself on the following personal characteristics. Use this scale.

S = Strong, I am very confident with this one

G = Good, but I still have room to grow

W = Weak, I really need work on this one

? = Unsure, I just don't know

1. **Resistance to stress:** The ability to get work done even under stressful conditions.

2. **Tolerance for uncertainty:** The ability to get work done even under ambiguous and uncertain conditions.

3. **Social objectivity:** The ability to act free of racial, ethnic, gender, and other prejudices or biases.

4. **Inner work standards:** The ability to personally set and work to high performance standards.

5. **Stamina:** The ability to sustain long work hours.

6.   **Adaptability:** The ability to be flexible and adapt to changes.

7.   **Self-confidence:** The ability to be consistently decisive and display one's personal presence.

8.   **Self-objectivity:** The ability to evaluate personal strengths and weaknesses, and understand one's motives and skills relative to a job.

9.   **Introspection:** The ability to learn from experience, awareness, and self-study.

10. **Entrepreneurism:** The ability to address problems and take advantage of opportunities for constructive change.

Scoring

Give yourself 1 point for each S, and 1/2 point for each G. Do not give yourself points for W and ? responses. Total your points and enter the result here [MF = _____].

Interpretation

This assessment offers a self-described profile of your **management foundations** *(MF)*. Are you a perfect 10, or is your MF score something less than that? There shouldn't be too many 10s around. Ask someone who knows you to assess you on this instrument. You might be surprised at the differences between your MF score as self-described and your MF score as described by someone else. Most of us, realistically speaking, must work hard to continually grow and develop in these and related management foundations. This list is a good starting point as you consider where and how to further pursue the development of your managerial skills and competencies. The items on the list are recommended by the *American Assembly of Collegiate Schools of Business (AACSB)* as skills and personal characteristics that should be nurtured in college and university students of business administration. Their success---and yours---as 21st-century managers may well rest on: (a) an initial awareness of the importance of these basic management foundations, and (b) a willingness to continually strive to strengthen them throughout the work career.

Instructor's Note

This is an excellent self-assessment instrument for students. Consider using it in conjunction with the **Personal Career Planning** exercise included in *Career Readiness Workbook,* as well as the *Career Advancement Portfolio.* Ask students -- either as individuals or in groups -- to identify specific means whereby one could develop one's skills or personal characteristics with regards to each of these areas. If this assessment is used with the **Personal Career Planning** exercise, you may want to require students to include specific action plans for overcoming their weaknesses in their report.

(Source: See Outcome Measurement Project, Phase I and Phase II Reports. St. Louis: American Assembly of Collegiate Schools of Business, 1986 & 1987).

ASSESSMENT --- DIVERSITY AWARENESS

Instructions

Complete the following questionnaire.

II. Diversity Awareness Checklist

Consider where you work or go to school as the setting for the following questions. Indicate "O" for often, "S" for sometimes, and "N" for never, in response to each of the following questions as they pertain to the setting.

_____ 1. How often have you heard jokes or remarks about other people that you consider offensive?

_____ 2. How often do you hear men talk "down" to women in an attempt to keep them in an inferior status?

_____ 3. How often have you felt personal discomfort as the object of sexual harassment?

_____ 4. How often do you work or study with African-Americans or Hispanics?

_____ 5. How often have you felt disadvantaged because members of ethnic groups other than yours were given special treatment?

_____ 6. How often have you seen a woman put in an uncomfortable situation because of unwelcome advances by a man?

_____ 7. How often does it seem that African-Americans, Hispanics, Caucasians, women, men, and members of other minority demographic groups seem to "stick together" during work breaks or other leisure situations?

_____ 8. How often do you feel uncomfortable about something you did and/or said to someone of the opposite sex or member of an ethnic or racial group other than yours?

_____ 9. How often do you feel efforts are made in this setting to raise the level of cross-cultural understanding among people who work and/or study together?

_____10. How often do you step in to communicate concerns to others when you feel actions and/or words are used to the disadvantage of minorities?

Scoring

There are no correct answers for the Diversity Awareness Checklist.

Interpretation

In the diversity checklist, the key issue is the extent to which you are "sensitive" to diversity issues in the workplace or university. Are you comfortable with your responses? How do you think others in your class responded? Why not share your responses with others and examine different viewpoints on this important issue?

Instructor's Note

This quiz can be useful for providing many students with insight into their limited awareness of other cultures -- even regional subcultures within the United States. Moreover, *the Diversity Awareness Checklist* can be used to provide students with insights into their "sensitivity" to diversity issues in the workplace or university. Responses of "Often" to these questions suggest that students are extremely sensitive to these issues, whereas responses of "Never" suggest that they are considerably less sensitive.

Explore with students their reasons for responding as they did, and consider their potential implications for their careers in the global marketplace.

(Source: Items for the *WV Cultural Awareness Quiz* selected from a longer version by James P. Morgan, Jr., and published by University Associates, 1987. Used by permission).

ASSESSMENT: YOUR INTUITIVE ABILITY

Instructions

Complete this survey as quickly as you can. Be honest with yourself. For each question, select the response that most appeals to you.

1. When working on a project, do you prefer to:

   a. be told what the problem is, but be left free to decide how to solve it?

   b. get very clear instructions about how to go about solving the problem before you start?

2. When working on a project, do you prefer to work with colleagues who are:

   a. realistic?

   b. imaginative?

3. Do you most admire people who are:

   a. creative?

   b. careful?

4. Do the friends you choose tend to be:

   a. serious and hard working?

   b. exciting and often emotional?

5. When you ask a colleague for advice on a problem you have, do you:

    a. seldom or never get upset if he or she questions your basic assumptions?

    b. often get upset if he or she questions your basic assumptions?

6. When you start your day, do you:

    a. seldom make or follow a specific plan?

    b. usually first make a plan to follow?

7. When working with numbers do you find that you:

    a. seldom or never make factual errors?

    b. often make factual errors?

8. Do you find that you:

    a. seldom daydream during the day and really don't enjoy doing so when you do it?

    b. frequently daydream during the day and enjoy doing so?

9. When working on a problem, do you:

    a. prefer to follow the instructions or rules when they are given to you?

    b. often enjoy circumventing the instructions or rules when they are given to you?

10. When you are trying to put something together, do you prefer to have:

    a. step-by-step written instructions on how to assemble the item?

    b. a picture of how the item is supposed to look once assembled?

11. Do you find that the person who irritates you *the most* is the one who appears to be:

    a. disorganized?

    b. organized?

12. When an unexpected crisis comes up that you have to deal with, do you:

    a. feel anxious about the situation?

    b. feel excited by the challenge of the situation?

Scoring

Total the number of "a" responses circled for questions 1, 3, 5, 6, 11; enter the score here [**A** = _____]. Total the number of "b" responses for questions 2, 4, 7, 8, 9, 10, 12; enter the score here [**B** = _____]. Add your "a" and "b" scores and enter the sum here [**A+B** = _____]. This is your *intuitive score.* The highest possible intuitive score is 12; the lowest is 0.

Interpretation

In his book *Intuition in Organizations* (Newbury Park, CA: Sage, 1989), pp. 10--11, Weston H. Agor states: "Traditional analytical techniques . . . are not as useful as they once were for guiding major decisions. . . . If you hope to be better prepared for tomorrow, then it only seems logical to pay some attention to the use and development of intuitive skills for decision making." Agor developed the prior survey to help people assess their tendencies to use intuition in decision making. Your score offers a general impression of your strength in this area. It may also suggest a need to further develop your skill and comfort with more intuitive decision approaches.

Instructor's Note

According to Agor, students with high *intuitive scores* have the ability to base their decisions on unknowns and possibilities. They are capable of applying ingenuity to problems to see how best to prepare for the future, and can tackle difficulties with zest. They are also more likely to prefer management situations that are unstructured, fluid and spontaneous. Indeed, they have the potential ability to function best in occupations that are characterized by crisis or rapid change and where they are asked to chart new, emerging trends from data including unknowns. Finally, they prefer to solve new and different problems versus the same or similar problems time after time.

Questions for Class Discussion

* Can intuition be developed? Explain.

* What are the limitations of intuition? How can they be overcome?

* What types of professions would best suit someone scoring high on intuition? Low?

(Source: AIM Survey. El Paso, TX: ENFP Enterprises, 1989. Copyright c 1989 by Weston H. Agor. Used by permission).

***ASSESSMENT*: DECISION-MAKING BIASES**

Instructions

How good are you at avoiding potential decision-making biases? Test yourself by answering the following questions:

1. Which is riskier:

    a. Driving a car on a 400-mile trip?

    b. Flying on a 400-mile commercial airline flight?

2. Are there more words in the English language:

    a. that begin with "r"?

    b. that have "r" as the third letter?

3. Mark is finishing his MBA at a prestigious university. He is very interested in the arts and at one time considered a career as a musician. Is Mark more likely to take a job:

    a. in the management of the arts?

    b. with a management consulting firm?

4. You are about to hire a new central-region sales director for the fifth time this year. You predict that the next director should work out reasonably well, since the last four were "lemons" and the odds favor hiring at least one good sales director in five tries. Is this thinking:

    a. correct?

    b. incorrect?

5. A newly hired engineer for a computer firm in the Boston metropolitan area has 4 years' experience and good all-around qualifications. When asked to estimate the starting salary for this employee, a chemist with very little knowledge about the profession or industry guessed an annual salary of $35,000. What is your estimate?

    $ _____ per year

Scoring

Your instructor will provide answers and explanations for the assessment questions.

Interpretation

Each of the prior questions examines your tendency to use a different judgmental heuristic. In his book *Judgment in Managerial Decision Making,* 2nd ed. (New York: John Wiley & Sons, 1990), pp. 5--6, Max Bazerman calls these heuristics "simplifying strategies, or rules of thumb" used in making decisions. He states: "In general, heuristics are helpful, but their use can sometimes lead to severe errors. . . . If we can make managers aware of the potential adverse impacts of using heuristics, they can then decide when and where to use them." This assessment offers an initial insight into your use of such heuristics. An informed decision maker understands the heuristics, is able to recognize when they appear, and eliminates any that may inappropriately bias decision making. Test yourself further. Before hearing from your instructor, go back and write next to each item the name of the judgmental heuristic (see Chapter 5 text discussion) that you think applies.

Use this space to identify a situation that you have experienced and in which some decision making bias may have occurred. Be prepared to share and discuss this incident with the class.

Answers

1. **Availability Heuristic** - Many people respond that flying in a commercial airliner is far riskier than driving a car. The media's tendency to sensationalize airplane crashes contributes to this perception. In actuality, the safety record for flying is far better than that for driving. Thus, this example demonstrates that a particularly **vivid** event will systematically influence the probability assigned to that type of event by an individual in the future. This bias is an example of the *availability heuristic*; it occurs because vivid events are more easily remembered and consequently more available when making judgements.

2. **Availability Heuristic** - If you responded "start with an r," you have joined the majority. Unfortunately this is the incorrect answer. People typically solve this problem by first recalling words that begin with r and words that have an r as the third letter. The relative difficulty of generating words in each of these two categories is then assessed. If we think of our minds as being organized like a dictionary, it is easier to find lots of words that start with an r -- they are more readily *available*. The dictionary, and our minds, are less efficient at finding words that follow a rule that is inconsistent with the organizing structure - like words that have an r as the third letter.

3. **Representativeness Heuristic** - Most people will choose "a" because they approach the problem by analyzing the degree to which Mark is *representative* of their image of individuals who take jobs in each of the two areas. However, when you reconsider the problem in light of the fact that a much larger number of MBAs take jobs in management consulting - relevant information that should enter into any reasonable prediction of Mark's career path - then it is only reasonable to pick "b."

4. **Representativeness Heuristic** - Many people pick "a" despite the fact that the performance of the first four sales directors will not directly affect the performance of the fifth. Most individuals frequently rely upon their intuition and the representativeness heuristic and incorrectly conclude that a poor performance is unlikely because the probability of getting five "lemons" in a row is extremely low. Unfortunately, this logic ignores the fact that we have already witnessed four "lemons" (an unlikely occurrence) and the performance of the fifth sales director is independent of that of the first four.

5. **Anchoring and Adjustment Heuristic** - Was your answer affected by the chemist's response? Although most people will deny that it did, individuals are generally affected by the fairly irrelevant information given by the chemist. Reconsider how you would have responded if the chemist's estimate was $85,000. Studies have found that people develop estimates by starting from an initial anchor, based on whatever information is provided, and adjusting from there to yield a final answer.

Instructor's Note

There is no better way to teach students about judgmental heuristics than through experiential activities such as those provided in this assessment. Students can readily understand these biases when they witness themselves exhibiting them. From here, you can explore the implications of these biases for decision making in organizations. For instance, the **anchoring and adjustment heuristic** illustrated by question 5 often influences managers' merit pay decisions. Too often, an underpaid employee who achieves a high level of performance, receives a merit pay increase as an added percentage of his or her salary. As such, the existing salary serves as an anchor which is then adjusted. However, since the initial salary was too low to begin with, the adjusted salary is also likely to be too low as well. A practical example of the **availability heuristic** is provided by the manager who decides not to invest in a new product because it is somewhat similar to a product which sold poorly in the past. Since failure of the prior product could have been caused by a number of factors, such as poor promotion or introduction into the market during the wrong time of the year, a decision based solely on product attributes may be inappropriate. Finally, an example of the **representativeness heuristic** is provided by a manager's decision to hire someone because he or she attended the same university as the firm's most successful occupant of this job. Since this criterion does not accurately assess the abilities of the current candidate, it could lead to an inferior decision.

(*Source:* Incidents from Max H. Bazerman, *Judgement in Managerial Decision Making, Second Edition.* New York: John Wiley & Sons, 1990, pp. 13-14. Used by permission).

Assessment: **FACTS & INFERENCES**

Preparation

Read the following report:

> Often, when we listen or speak, we don't distinguish between statements of fact and those of inference. Yet, there are great differences between the two. We create barriers to clear thinking when we treat inferences (guesses, opinions) as if they are facts. You may wish at this point to test your ability to distinguish facts from inferences by taking the accompanying fact-inference test based on those by Haney (1973).

Instructions

Carefully read the following report and the observations based on it. Indicate whether you think the observations are true, false, or doubtful on the basis of the information presented in the report. Write T if the observation is definitely true, F if the observation is definitely false, and ? if the observation may be either true or false. Judge each observation in order. Do not reread the observations after you have indicated your judgement, and do not change any of your answers.

A well-liked college professor had just completed making up the final examinations and had turned off the lights in the office. Just then a tall, dark, broad figure appeared and demanded the examination. The professor opened the drawer. Everything in the drawer was picked up and individual ran down the corridor. The Dean was notified immediately.

_____ 1. The thief was tall, dark, and broad.

_____ 2. The professor turned off the lights.

_____ 3. A tall figure demanded the examination.

_____ 4. The examination was picked up by someone.

_____ 5. The examination was picked up by the professor.

_____ 6. A tall, dark figure appeared after the professor turned off the lights in the office.

_____ 7. The man who opened the drawer was the professor.

_____ 8. The professor ran down the corridor.

_____ 9. The drawer was never actually opened.

_____ 10. In this report three persons are referred to.

When told to do so by your instructor, join a small work group. Now, help the group complete the same task by making a consensus decision on each item. Be sure to keep a separate record of the group's responses and your original individual responses.

Scoring

Your instructor will read the correct answers. Score both your individual and group responses.

Interpretation

To begin ask yourself if there was a difference between your answers and those of the group for each item. Why? Why do you think people, individually or in groups, may answer these questions incorrectly? Good planning depends on good decision making by the people doing the planning. Being able to distinguish "facts" and understand one's "inferences" can be important steps toward improving the planning process. Involving others to help do the same can frequently assist in this process.

Answers

1. "?" - We are not sure that the "tall, dark and broad figure" is a thief; it could be a secretary demanding the exam to make copies, or a student who is taking the test early. For that matter, we don't even know for sure that the figure is a person. Could it be the professor's shadow, and he or she is only jokingly demanding the exam? The text does not provide enough information for us to know who or what the "figure" is with certainty.

2. "T" - The text specifically says the professor turned off the lights.

3. "T" - The text specifically says that a tall figure demanded the exam.

4. "?" - The text never says that the exam was picked up -- only that everything in the drawer was picked up. The exam may not have been in the drawer.

5. "?" - Again, the text never says the exam was picked up, let alone by the professor.

6. "T" - The text clearly says that just after the professor turned of the lights in the office, a tall, dark and broad figure appeared.

7. "?" - The text does not say that the professor is a *man!*

8. "?" - We do not know who ran down the hall, only that it was an "individual."

9. "F" - The text specifically says that the drawer was opened by the professor.

10. "?" - We don't know how many people are referred to, for a number of reasons. First, as indicated we don't know for sure that the "figure" is a person. Second, a "professor," "figure," "individual," and "dean" are mentioned. However, we don't know if the professor and individual are the same or different persons. Third and similarly, we don't know if the "figure" or individual are the same or different persons. Fourth, it is possible that the dean is either the individual or the "figure."

(*Source:* Joseph A. Devito, *General Semantics: Guide and Workbook*, Rev. Ed. Deland, Fl.: Everett/Edwards, 1974, p. 55. Reprinted by permission).

ASSESSMENT: CULTURAL ATTITUDES INVENTORY

Instructions

Complete this inventory by circling the number that indicates the extent to which you agree or disagree with each of the following statements.

Strongly   **Strongly**

Disagree   **Agree**

1. Meetings are usually run more effectively when they are chaired by a man.

    1   2   3   4   5

2. It is more important for men to have a professional career than it is for women to have a professional career.

    1   2   3   4   5

3. Women do not value recognition and promotion in their work as much as men do.

    1   2   3   4   5

4. Women value working in a friendly atmosphere more than men do.

    1   2   3   4   5

5. Men usually solve problems with logical analysis; women usually solve problems with intuition.

    1   2   3   4   5

6. Solving organizational problems usually requires the active, forcible approach that is typical of men.

    1   2   3   4   5

7. It is preferable to have a man in a high-level position rather than a woman.

    1   2   3   4   5

8. There are some jobs in which a man can always do better than a woman.

    1   2   3   4   5

9. Women are more concerned with the social aspects of their job than they are with getting ahead.

    1   2   3   4   5

10. An individual should not pursue his or her own goals without considering the welfare of the group.

    1   2   3   4   5

11. It is important for a manager to encourage loyalty and a sense of duty in the group.

    1   2   3   4   5

12. Being accepted by the group is more important than working on your own.

    1   2   3   4   5

13. Individual rewards are not as important as group welfare.

    1   2   3   4   5

14. Group success is more important than individual success.

    1   2   3   4   5

15. It is important to have job requirements and instructions spelled out in detail so that people always know what they are expected to do.

    1   2   3   4   5

16. Managers expect workers to closely follow instructions and procedures.

    1   2   3   4   5

17. Rules and regulations are important because they inform workers what the organization expects of them.

    1   2   3   4   5

18. Standard operating procedures are helpful to workers on the job.

    1   2   3   4   5

19. Instructions for operations are important for workers on the job.

    1   2   3   4   5

20. It is often necessary for a supervisor to emphasize his or her authority and power when dealing with subordinates.

    1   2   3   4   5

21. Managers should be careful not to ask the opinions of subordinates too frequently.

    1   2   3   4   5

22. A manager should avoid socializing with his or her subordinates off the job.

    1   2   3   4   5

23. Subordinates should not disagree with their manager's decisions.

    1   2   3   4   5

24. Managers should not delegate difficult and important tasks to his or her subordinates.

    1   2   3   4   5

25. Managers should make most decisions without consulting subordinates.

    1   2   3   4   5

Scoring

Add up your responses to items 1--9 and divide by 9; record the score here [MF = ____]. Sum items 10--14 and divide by 5; record the score here [IC = ____]. Sum items 15--19 and divide by 5; record the score here [UA = ____]. Sum items 20--25 and divide by 6; record the score here [PD = ____].

Interpretation

Each of these scores corresponds to one of Hofstede's (see Chapter 2) dimensions of national culture: MF = masculinity--femininity; IC = individualism--collectivism; UA = uncertainty avoidance; PD = power distance. His research shows that various "national" cultures of the world score differently on these dimensions. Consider how closely *your* scores may represent *your* national culture. What are the implications of your score for your future work as a manager?

Compare yourself to these scores from a sample of U.S. and Mexican students; MF---U.S. = 2.78 and Mexico = 2.75; IC---U.S. = 2.19 and Mexico = 3.33; UA---U.S. = 3.41 and Mexico = 4.15; PD---U.S. = 1.86 and Mexico = 2.22. Are there any surprises in this comparison?

Instructor's Note

This assessment can be an extremely useful tool for providing students with insights into their cultural values and the manner in which differ from their own and other "national" cultures. As such, the exercise can substantially increase the perceived relevance of Hofstede's research to students. The comparison of the mean scores for the U.S. and Mexico reveal that Mexican students tend to be more collectivistic, less willing to tolerate uncertainty, and more willing to tolerate power distance. Explore with students the implications of these cultural differences.

(Source: Items are part of a larger instrument developed by Peter W. Dorfman and Jon P. Howell, New Mexico State University. Used by permission. The comparative data are from Stephen P. Robbins, *Management,* 3rd ed. Englewood Cliffs, NJ: Prentice Hall, 1990, p. 670).

ASSESSMENT: GLOBAL READINESS INDEX

Instructions

Rate yourself on each of the following items to establish a baseline measurement of your readiness to participate in the global work environment.

Rating Scale:

1 = Very Poor

2 = Poor

3 = Acceptable

4 = Good

5 = Very Good

_____ 1. I understand my own culture in terms of its expectations, values, and influence on communication and relationships.

_____ 2. When someone presents me with a different point of view, I try to understand it rather than attack it.

_____ 3. I am comfortable dealing with situations where the available information is incomplete and the outcomes unpredictable.

_____ 4. I am open to new situations and am always looking for new information and learning opportunities.

_____ 5. I have a good understanding of the attitudes and perceptions toward my culture as they are held by people from other cultures.

_____ 6. I am always gathering information about other countries and cultures and trying to learn from them.

_____ 7. I am well informed regarding the major differences in government, political, and economic systems around the world.

_____ 8. I work hard to increase my understanding of people from other countries.

_____ 9. I am able to adjust my communication style to work effectively with people from different cultures.

_____ 10. I can recognize when cultural differences are influencing working relationships and adjust my attitudes and behavior accordingly.

Interpretation

To be successful in the 21st-century work environment, you must be comfortable with the global economy and the cultural diversity that it holds. This requires a *global mind-set* that is receptive to and respectful of cultural differences, *global knowledge* that includes the continuing quest to know and learn more about other nations and cultures, and *global work skills* that allow you to work effectively across cultures.

Scoring

The goal is to score as close to a perfect "5" as possible on each of the three dimensions of global readiness. Develop your scores as follows:

Items (1 + 2 + 3 + 4)/4 = _____ Global Mind-set Score

Items (5 + 6 + 7)/3 = _____ Global Knowledge Score

Items (8 + 9 + 10) = _____ Global Work Skills Score

Instructor's Note

Through this self-assessment, students can reflect on their readiness to interact and work with persons from other cultures. A high score would suggest that they deem themselves to be well-prepared for intercultural relations; a low score would reveal a need to better prepare themselves for the global workplace. Such insights can be very useful for students as they consider their preparedness for their careers, and identify areas for self-improvement.

(Source: Developed from "Is Your Company Really Global," *Business Week,* December 1, 1997).

ASSESSMENT: **TIME MANAGEMENT PROFILE**

Instructions

Complete the following questionnaire by indicating "Y" (yes) or "N" (no) for each item. Force yourself to respond with a yes or no. Be frank and allow your responses to create an accurate picture of how you tend to respond to these kinds of situations.

_____ 1. When confronted with several items of similar urgency and importance, I tend to do the easiest one first.

_____ 2. I do the most important things during that part of the day when I know I perform best.

_____ 3. Most of the time I don't do things someone else can do; I delegate this type of work to others.

_____ 4. Even though meetings without a clear and useful purpose upset me, I put up with them.

_____ 5. I skim documents before reading them, and don't read further any that offer a low return on my time investment.

_____ 6. I don't worry much if I don't accomplish at least one significant task each day.

_____ 7. I save the most trivial tasks for that time of day when my creative energy is at its lowest.

_____ 8. My workspace is neat and organized.

_____ 9. My office door is always "open," I never work in complete privacy.

_____ 10. I schedule my time completely from start-to-finish every workday.

_____ 11. I don't like "to do" lists, preferring to respond to daily events as they occur.

_____ 12. I "block" a certain amount of time each day or week that is dedicated to high-priority activities.

Scoring

Count the number of "Y" responses to items # 2,3,5,7,8,12. [Enter that score here _____]. Count the number of "N" responses to items # 1,4,6,9,10,11. [Enter that score here _____]. Add the two scores together.

Interpretation

The higher the total score, the closer your behavior matches recommended time management guidelines. Reread those items where your response did not match the desired one. Why don't they match? Do you have reasons why your behavior in this instance should be different from the time management guideline? Think about what you can do (and how easily it can be done) to adjust your behavior to be more consistent with these guidelines. For further reading Alan Lakein, *How to Control Your Time and Your Life* (New York: David McKay, no date), and William Oncken, *Managing Management Time* (Englewood Cliffs, N.J.: Prentice-Hall, 1984).

Instructor's Note

Consider using this assessment in conjunction with the exercise that follows titled, "Beating the Time Wasters." They both deal with time management skills and complement one another. If you decide to use this assessment, but not the exercise, you may still want to present some or all of the suggestions for "beating the time wasters" which are provided as part of the instructor's note for the exercise.

(Source: Suggested by a discussion in Robert E. Quinn, Sue R. Faerman, Michael P. Thompson, and Michael R. McGrath, *Becoming a Master Manager: A Contemporary Framework.* New York: John Wiley & Sons, 1990, pp. 75-76).

ASSESSMENT: INTERNAL/EXTERNAL CONTROL

Instructions

Circle either "a" or "b" to indicate the item you most agree within each pair of the following statements.

1. **a.** Promotions are earned through hard work and persistence.

   b. Making a lot of money is largely a matter of breaks.

2. **a.** In my experience I have noticed that there is usually a direct connection between how hard I study and the grades I get.

   b. Many times the reactions of teachers seem haphazard to me.

3. **a.** The number of divorces indicates that more and more people are not trying to make their marriages work.

   b. Marriage is largely a gamble.

4. **a.** When I am right I can convince others.

   b. It is silly to think that one can really change another person's basic attitudes.

5. **a.** In our society an individual's future earning power is dependent upon his or her ability.

   b. Getting promoted is really a matter of being a little luckier than the next guy.

6.　**a.**　If one knows how to deal with people, they are really quite easily led.

　　b.　I have little influence over the way other people behave.

7.　**a.**　In my case the grades I make are the results of my own efforts; luck has little or nothing to do with it.

　　b.　Sometimes I feel that I have little to do with the grades I get.

8.　**a.**　People like me can change the course of world affairs if we make ourselves heard.

　　b.　It is only wishful thinking to believe that one can really influence what happens in society at large.

9.　**a.**　I am the master of my fate.

　　b.　Much of what happens to me is probably a matter of chance.

10.　**a.**　Getting along with people is a skill that must be practiced.

　　b.　It is almost impossible to figure out how to please some people.

Scoring

Count the number of times you circled the "a" alternative for these items; enter that total here [**IC** = _____]. Subtract that total from 10; enter that result here [**EC** = _____].

Interpretation

This instrument offers an impression of your tendency toward an **internal locus of control** or **external locus of control**. Persons with a high internal locus of control (IC score above 5) tend to believe they have control over their own destinies. They may be most responsive to opportunities for greater self-control in the workplace. Persons with a high external locus of control (EC score below 5) tend to believe that what happens to them is largely in the hands of external people or forces. They may be less comfortable with self-control and more responsive to external controls in the workplace.

Instructor's Note

By providing students with insight into their locus of control, this assessment can serve as a valuable tool for increasing their self-awareness. You can supplement your discussion of locus of control with the following summary of key research findings regarding the differences between internals and externals.

Some Ways in Which Internals Differ from Externals

Information processing	Internals make more attempts to acquire information, are less satisfied with the amount of information they possess, and are better at utilizing information.
Job satisfaction	Internals are generally more satisfied, less alienated, less rootless, and there is a stronger job satisfaction/performance relationship for them.
Performance	Internals perform better on learning and problem-solving tasks, when performance leads to valued rewards.
Self-control, risk, and anxiety	Internals exhibit greater self-control, are more cautious, engage in less risky behavior, and are less anxious.
Motivation, expectancies and results	Internals display greater work motivation, see a stronger relationship between what they do and what happens to them, expect that working hard leads to good performance, feel more control over their time.
Response to others	Internals are more independent, more reliant on their own judgement, and less susceptible to the influence of others; they are more likely to accept information on its merit.

(*Source:* Instrument from Julian P. Rotter, "External Control and Internal Control," *Psychology Today*, June 1971, p. 42. Used by permission).

ASSESSMENT: **ENTREPRENEURSHIP ORIENTATION**

Instructions

Answer the following questions.

1. What portion of your college expenses did you earn (or are you earning)?

    a. 50 percent or more

    b. less than 50 percent

    c. none

2. In college, your academic performance was/is:

    a. above average

    b. average

    c. below average

3. What is your basic reason for considering opening a business?

    a. I want to make money.

    b. I want to control my own destiny.

    c. I hate the frustration of working for someone else.

4. Which phrase best describes your attitude toward work?

    a. I can keep going as long as I need to; I don't mind working for something I want.

    b. I can work hard for a while, but when I've had enough, I quit.

    c. Hard work really doesn't get you anywhere.

5. How would you rate your organizing skills?

    a. superorganized

    b. above average

    c. average

    d. I do well to find half the things I look for.

6. You are primarily a(n):

    a. optimist

    b. pessimist

    c. neither

7. You are faced with a challenging problem. As you work, you realize you are stuck. You will most likely:

    a. give up

    b. ask for help

    c. keep plugging; you'll figure it out

8. You are playing a game with a group of friends. You are most interested in:

    a. winning

    b. playing well

    c. making sure that everyone has a good time

    d. cheating as much as possible

9. How would you describe your feelings toward failure?

    a. Fear of failure paralyzes me.

    b. Failure can be a good learning experience.

    c. Knowing that I might fail motivates me to work even harder.

    d. "Damn the torpedoes! Full speed ahead."

10. Which phrase best describes you?

    a. I need constant encouragement to get anything done.

    b. If someone gets me started, I can keep going.

    c. I am energetic and hard-working---a self-starter.

11. Which bet would you most likely accept?

    a. a wager on a dog race

    b. a wager on a racquetball game in which you play an opponent

    c. Neither. I never make wagers.

12. At the Kentucky Derby, you would bet on:

    a. the 100-to-1 long shot

    b. the odds-on favorite

    c. the 3-to-1 shot

    d. none of the above

Scoring

Give yourself 10 points for each of the following answers: 1a, 2a, 3c, 4a, 5a, 6a, 7c, 8a, 9c, 10c, 11b, 12c; total the scores and enter the results here [I = _____]. Give yourself 8 points for each of the following answers: 3b, 8b, 9b; total the scores and enter the results here [II = _____]. Give yourself 6 points for each of the following answers: 2b, 5b; total the scores and enter the results here [III = _____]. Give yourself 5 points for this answer: 1b; enter the result here [IV = _____]. Give yourself 4 points for this answer: 5c; enter the result here [V = _____]. Give yourself 2 points for each of the following answers: 2c, 3a, 4b, 6c, 9d, 10b, 11a, 12b; total the scores and enter the results here [VI = _____]. Any other scores are worth 0 points. Total your summary scores for I + II + III + IV + V + VI and enter the result here [EP = _____].

Interpretation

This assessment offers an impression of your **entrepreneurial profile**, or **EP**. It compares your characteristics with those of typical entrepreneurs. Your instructor can provide further information on each question, as well as some additional insights into the backgrounds of entrepreneurs. You may locate your EP score on the following grid.

> 100+ = Entrepreneur extraordinaire
>
> 80--99 = Entrepreneur
>
> 60--79 = Potential entrepreneur
>
> 0--59 = Entrepreneur in the rough

Instructor's Note

In discussing this assessment, emphasize that "capitalist societies depend on entrepreneurs to provide the drive and risk-taking necessary for the system to supply people with the goods and services they need." Point out that "entrepreneurs have some common characteristics, including independence, willingness to take risks, self-confidence, eagerness to see results, energy, and good organizational abilities. In a phrase, they are high achievers. Driven by these personal characteristics, entrepreneurs establish and manage small businesses in order to gain control over their lives, become self-fulfilled, reap unlimited profits, and gain recognition from society."

"Although most entrepreneurs are men, U.S. Department of Labor statistics show that women are opening businesses at a rate five times faster than men. Many of these women entrepreneurs are 'baby boomers,' frustrated with the discrimination and the barriers of corporate cultures. Curiously, entrepreneurs -- both men and women -- tend to be shorter than average. The average age of entrepreneurs has declined steadily over the last two decades. Most launch their business when they reach their 30s, after gaining enough capital and experience to step out on their own. The National Federation of Independent Businesses (NGIB) found that 45 percent of all new businesses were started by people 30 years old or younger. Most studies found that 75 percent of all entrepreneurs are married. Some researchers conclude that successful entrepreneurs must have very supportive spouses. Studies also show that entrepreneurs are often the oldest children in their families. Only children also rank high in entrepreneurial potential."

"Survey results support the stereotype of the immigrant entrepreneur who has come to 'the land of opportunity' to build a business. Often, immigrants believe they do not fit in with American culture, and business ownership can help bridge the cultural gap. Furthermore, entrepreneurs often come from backgrounds where the family struggled to make ends meet. Perhaps this is how many entrepreneurs acquired the ability to gain maximum benefits from limited resources. It appears that meager beginnings are a source of motivation for many. Entrepreneurs also appear to learn by example. Children whose parents (or at least one parent) are self-employed are much more likely to create businesses of their own. In the 'nature vs. nurture' argument in entrepreneurship, 'nurture' wins hands down."

"Most entrepreneurs complete four years of college. Although the stereotype of the high school dropout who builds a business empire is popular, it is not usually true. In fact, a growing number of entrepreneurs have earned master's degrees. Entrepreneurs appear to recognize the value of an education in helping them launch their businesses" (Scarborough and Zimmerer, 1991).

Relevant information on each question included in this assessment is provided below.

1. "Most entrepreneurs work while in school, earning at least one-half of their college expenses. Not only do they work while attending school, many head their own business ventures. Campus entrepreneurship has become so popular that students have formed a national Association of Collegiate Entrepreneurs, and its ranks are swelling."

2. "Despite their busy work schedules in school, entrepreneurs manage to keep their grades up. One recent survey found that only 38 percent were average or below-average performers."

3. "It is a myth that the primary motivating force behind most entrepreneurs is profit. Of course, earning a profit is necessary for business survival, but it is not the driving force. Today, entrepreneurs are most likely to cite dissatisfaction with working for someone else or lack of control over their lives as key reasons for starting businesses."

4. "Entrepreneurs are not afraid of hard work. They are willing to do whatever it takes to get the job done. Further, entrepreneurs do not separate work and play. Their work is a source of fun and excitement."

5. "Entrepreneurs usually are good organizers. Building a business from scratch requires valuable organizing skills. Putting together the pieces of a business puzzle -- employees, financing, inventory, and so on -- requires someone who can visualize the proper way to organize them."

6. "No doubt about it, entrepreneurs are optimistic. Sometimes, however, their excessive optimism gets them into trouble."

7. "Entrepreneurs are fiercely independent. They are extremely reluctant to ask for outside professional help. When faced with a difficult problem, most entrepreneurs simply roll up their sleeves and get to work. And, they don't quit until the problem has been solved."

8. "Entrepreneurs are intense competitors, and losing is *not* an acceptable outcome. Many embrace the feeling expressed by Vince Lombardi, who said 'Winning isn't everything; it's the only thing.' Of course, entrepreneurs don't always win, but when they fail, they tend to view it as a learning experience. Many owners of successful businesses failed at least once

before establishing a foothold. The threat of failure seems to motivate many entrepreneurs to do everything in their power to avoid it."

9. "Entrepreneurs are risk-takers, and they recognize that failure is a possibility (although most believe it a small one)."

10. "Entrepreneurs are definitely self-starters. They are much more energetic and enthusiastic than average, especially where their work is concerned."

11. "Entrepreneurs have a need to be in control of a situation. They are much more likely to take a chance on events they can affect themselves rather than on some externally imposed situation. Bold self-confidence allows an entrepreneur to believe that she can turn the odds in her favor if given the opportunity."

12. "Despite widely held beliefs to the contrary, entrepreneurs are not extreme risk-takers. Studies show that they set reasonable, attainable goals and take calculated risks to reach them. They gamble only when they believe the odds of winning are in their favor."

(Source: Instrument adapted from Norman M. Scarborough and Thomas W. Zimmerer, *Effective Small Business Management,* Third Edition. Columbus: Merrill, 1991, pp. 26--27. Used by permission).

ASSESSMENT: ORGANIZATIONAL DESIGN PREFERENCE

Instructions

To the left of each item, write the number from the following scale that shows the extent to which the statement accurately describes your views.

> 5 = strongly agree
>
> 4 = agree somewhat
>
> 3 = undecided
>
> 2 = disagree somewhat
>
> 1 = strongly disagree

I prefer to work in an organization where:

1. Goals are defined by those in higher-level positions.
2. Work methods and procedures are specified for me.
3. Top management makes important decisions.
4. My loyalty counts as much as my ability to do the job.
5. Clear lines of authority and responsibility are established.
6. Top management is decisive and firm.
7. My career is pretty well planned out for me.
8. I can specialize.
9. My length of service is almost as important as my level of performance.
10. Management is able to provide the information I need to do my job well.
11. A chain of command is well established.
12. Rules and procedures are adhered to equally by everyone.
13. People accept the authority of the leader's position.
14. People are loyal to their boss.
15. People do as they have been instructed.
16. People clear things with their boss before going over his or her head.

Scoring

Total your scores for all questions. Enter the score here [_____].

Interpretation

This assessment measures your preference for working in an organization designed along "organic" or "mechanistic" lines (see Chapter 7). The higher your score (above 64), the more comfortable you are with a mechanistic design; the lower your score (below 48), the more comfortable you are with an organic design. Scores between 48--64 can go either way. This organizational design preference represents an important issue in the new workplace. Indications are that today's organizations are taking on more and more organic characteristics. Presumably, those of us who work in them will need to be comfortable with such designs.

Instructor's Note

By providing students with some personal insights into their organizational design preferences, this assessment can make the discussion of mechanistic and organic designs more relevant to them. Students who have strong and definite preferences for one type of design or another, should probably not take a job in an organization with an opposite design. Instead, they should look for an organization where they will "fit" in better.

Questions for Class Discussion

1. What kinds of experiences are individuals with preferences for organic designs likely to have in mechanistic organizations? Can they be successful in this setting? If so, how? If not, why not?

2. What kinds of experiences are individuals with preferences for mechanistic designs likely to have in organic firms? Can they be successful in this setting? If so, how? If not, why not?

3. What, if anything, can organizations with mechanistic or organic designs do to help people with preferences for the alternative design configuration adjust to their job and work environment?

(*Source:* John F. Veiga and John N. Yanouzas, *The Dynamics of Organization Theory: Gaining a Macro Perspective.* St. Paul, MN: West, 1979, pp. 158--160. Used by permission).

ASSESSMENT: WHICH ORGANIZATIONAL CULTURE FITS YOU?

Instructions

Check one of the following organization "cultures" in which you feel most comfortable working.

1.   A culture that values talent and entrepreneurial activity, and values performance over commitment; one that offers large financial rewards and individual recognition.

2.   A culture that stresses loyalty, working for the good of the group, and getting to know the right people; one that believes in "generalists" and step-by-step career progress.

3.   A culture that offers little job security; one that operates with a survival mentality, stresses that every individual can make a difference, and focuses attention on "turn-around" opportunities.

4.   A culture that values long-term relationships; one that emphasizes systematic career development, regular training, and advancement based on gaining of functional expertise.

Scoring

These labels identify the four different cultures: 1 = "the baseball team," 2 = "the club," 3 = "the fortress," and 4 = "the academy."

Interpretation

To some extent, your future career success may depend on working for an organization in which there is a good fit between you and the prevailing corporate culture. It can help to learn how to recognize various cultures, evaluate how well they can serve your needs, and recognize how they may change with time. A risk-taker, for example, may be out of place in a "club," but fit right in with a "baseball team." Someone who wants to seek opportunities wherever they may occur may be out of place in an "academy," but fit right in with a "fortress." Although this assessment gives just a first impression of your preferences for organizational cultures, the topic is worth thinking more about.

Instructor's Note

You may want to provide students with the following more detailed set of descriptions of the four organizational cultures identified above.

1. ***Academies*** -- in which new hires are carefully moved through a series of training programs and a series of well-defined and specialized jobs. IBM is an "academy" that requires all managers to attend management training each year and carefully grooms fast-trackers to become functional experts.

2. ***Fortresses*** -- in which corporate survival is an overriding concern. These firms are struggling in competitive markets and can't promise much job security. What they do offer is the chance to participate in a "turn-around" and experience the sense of really making a difference.

3. ***Clubs*** -- which are driven by seniority, loyalty, commitment, and working for the good of the group. Moving quickly up the ladder doesn't happen; in the "club" you're supposed to work your way up. It counts who you know, and people are concerned about "fitting in." Career progress often means becoming more of a generalist by working across functions in different jobs.

4. ***Baseball teams*** -- which are entrepreneurial, place a high premium on talent and performance, and reward people very well financially when they produce. Commitment isn't as important as daily performance, and job-hopping from one "baseball team" to the next is fairly common. They are common in such areas as advertising, software development, and consulting.

These descriptions provide some indication of the types of career experiences that students could expect after joining an organization with these cultures. The key thing, of course, is to try and achieve a good fit between individual desires and capabilities and what the culture may expect of the newcomer. Then, too, it should be remembered that cultures can and do change over time.

(Source: Developed from Carol Hymowitz, "Which Corporate Culture Fits You?" *The Wall Street Journal,* July 17, 1989, p. B1).

ASSESSMENT: **PERFORMANCE APPRAISAL ASSUMPTIONS**

Instructions

In each of the following pairs of statements, check off the statement that best reflects your assumptions about performance evaluation.

Performance evaluation is:

1.   **a.**   A formal process that is done annually.

     b.   An informal process that is done continuously.

2.   **a.**   A process that is planned for subordinates.

     b.   A process that is planned with subordinates.

3.   **a.**   A required organizational procedure.

     b.   A process done regardless of requirements.

4.   **a.**   A time to evaluate subordinate performance.

     b.   A time for subordinates to evaluate the manager.

5.   **a.**   A time to clarify standards.

     b.   A time to clarify the subordinate's career needs.

6.   **a.**   A time to confront poor performance.

     b.   A time to express appreciation.

7.   **a.**   An opportunity to clarify issues and provide direction and control.

     b.   An opportunity to increase enthusiasm and commitment.

8.   **a.**   Only as good as the organization's forms.

     b.   Only as good as the manager's coaching skills.

Scoring

There is no formal scoring for this assessment, but there may be a pattern to your responses. Check them again.

Interpretation

In general, the "a" responses represent a more traditional approach to performance appraisal that emphasizes its *evaluation* function. This role largely puts the supervisor in the role of documenting a subordinate's performance for control and administrative purposes. The "b" responses represent a more progressive approach that includes a strong emphasis on the *counseling* or *development* role. Here, the supervisor is concerned to help the subordinate do better and to learn from the subordinate what he or she needs to be able to do better. There is more of an element of reciprocity in this role. It is quite consistent with new directions and values emerging in today's organizations.

Instructor's Note

Discuss with students the circumstances under which they believe that the evaluation and development functions are most appropriate for a manager to fulfill. Under what circumstances, if any, would each of these functions be inappropriate? What are the implications of the students' performance appraisal assumptions for their potential careers as managers? Explore these and other issues with your students.

(Source: Developed in part from Robert E. Quinn, Sue R. Faerman, Michael P. Thompson, and Michael R. McGrath, *Becoming a Master Manager: A Contemporary Framework.* New York: John Wiley & Sons, 1990, p. 187. Used by permission).

ASSESSMENT: "T-P" LEADERSHIP QUESTIONNAIRE

Instructions

The following items describe aspects of leadership behavior. Respond to each item according to the way you would most likely act if you were the leader of a work group. Circle whether you would most likely behave in the described way: always (A), frequently (F), occasionally (O), seldom (S), or never (N).

A F O S N	1.	I would most likely act as the spokesperson of the group.
A F O S N	2.	I would encourage overtime work.
A F O S N	3.	I would allow members complete freedom in their work.
A F O S N	4.	I would encourage the use of uniform procedures.
A F O S N	5.	I would permit the members to use their own judgement in solving problems.
A F O S N	6.	I would stress being ahead of competing groups.
A F O S N	7.	I would speak as a representative of the group.
A F O S N	8.	I would push members for greater effort.

A F O S N   9.   I would try out my ideas in the group.

A F O S N   10.   I would let the members do their work the way they think best.

A F O S N   11.   I would be working hard for a promotion.

A F O S N   12.   I would tolerate postponement and uncertainty.

A F O S N   13.   I would speak for the group if there were visitors present.

A F O S N   14.   I would keep the work moving at a rapid pace.

A F O S N   15.   I would turn the members loose on a job and let them go to it.

A F O S N   16.   I would settle conflicts when they occur in the group.

A F O S N   17.   I would get swamped by details.

A F O S N   18.   I would represent the group at outside meetings.

A F O S N   19.   I would be reluctant to allow the members any freedom of action.

A F O S N   20.   I would decide what should be done and how it should be done.

A F O S N   21.   I would push for increased performance.

A F O S N   22.   I would let some members have authority which I could otherwise keep.

A F O S N   23.   Things would usually turn out as I had predicted.

A F O S N   24.   I would allow the group a high degree of initiative.

A F O S N   25.   I would assign group members to particular tasks.

A F O S N   26.   I would be willing to make changes.

A F O S N   27.   I would ask the members to work harder.

A F O S N   28.   I would trust the group members to exercise good judgement.

A F O S N   29.   I would schedule the work to be done.

A F O S N   30.   I would refuse to explain my actions.

A F O S N   31.   I would persuade others that my ideas are to their advantage.

A F O S N   32.   I would permit the group to set its own pace.

A F O S N   33.   I would urge the group to beat its previous record.

A F O S N   34.   I would act without consulting the group.

A F O S N   35.   I would ask that group members follow standard rules and regulations.

Interpretation

Score the instrument as follows.

    a. Write a "1" next to each of the following items if you scored them as S (seldom) or N (never).

    8, 12, 17, 18, 19, 30, 34, 35

    b. Write a "1" next to each of the following items if you scored them as A (always) or F (frequently).

    1, 2, 3, 4, 5, 6, 7, 9, 10, 11, 13, 14, 15, 16, 20, 21, 22, 23, 24, 25, 26, 27, 28, 29, 31, 32, 33

    c. Circle the "1" scores for the following items, and then add them up to get your TOTAL "P" SCORE = _____.

    3, 5, 8, 10, 15, 18, 19, 22, 23, 26, 28, 30, 32, 34, 35

    d. Circle the "1" scores for the following items, and then add them up to get your TOTAL "T" SCORE = _____.

    1, 2, 4, 6, 7, 9, 11, 12, 13, 14, 16, 17, 20, 21, 23, 25, 27, 29, 31, 33

    e. Record your scales on the following graph to develop an indication of your tendencies toward task-oriented leadership, people-oriented leadership, and shared leadership. Mark your T and P scores on the appropriate lines, then draw a line between these two points to determine your shared leadership score.

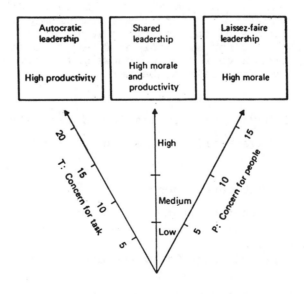

Instructor's Note

This instrument can serve as a particularly useful tool for helping students to distinguish between the styles of leadership that emerge from various combinations of task- and people-oriented leadership. The insights they gain regarding their own leadership styles, also serve to enhance the personal relevance of the material. Finally, a discussion of the limitations of this instrument can serve as a useful segue into your coverage of the contingency theories of leadership. Specifically, you can ask students if they think the instrument correctly identified their leadership style. Invariably, some will feel it did not. Follow up on their comments by asking them if there is anything about the instrument that they believe may have biased their scores. Many students astutely observe that "occasionally" responses are scored as neither task- or people-oriented leadership. As a result, students who frequently chose this response would fall short of the ideal "team leader" approach. In reality, however, such responses are quite consistent with the contingency perspectives that assert the effectiveness of task- versus people-oriented leadership depends upon the situation. You can conclude this discussion by reassuring such students that their style is not necessarily deficient; instead, it may be reflective of a more sophisticated contingency approach to leadership. From here, you can move into the specifics of the contingency perspectives advanced by Fiedler, House, Hersey and Planchard, and Vroom and Jago.

(Source: Modified slightly from "T-P Leadership Questionnaire," University Associates, Inc. 1987. Used by permission.)

ASSESSMENT: "T-T" LEADERSHIP STYLE

Instructions

For each of the following 10 pairs of statements, divide 5 points between the two according to your beliefs, perceptions of yourself, or according to which of the two statements characterizes you better. The 5 points may be divided between the a and b statements in any one of the following ways: 5 for a, 0 for b; 4 for a, 1 for b; 3 for a, 2 for b; 1 for a, 4 for b; 0 for a, 5 for b, but not equally 2-1/2 between the two. Weigh your choices between the two according to the one that characterizes you or your beliefs better.

1.   **a.**   As leader I have a primary mission of maintaining stability.

     b.   As leader I have a primary mission of change.

2.   **a.**   As leader I must cause events.

     b.   As leader I must facilitate events.

3.   **a.**   I am concerned that my followers are rewarded equitably for their work.

     b.   I am concerned about what my followers want in life.

4.   **a.**   My preference is to think long-range: what might be.

       b.   My preference is to think short-range: what is realistic.

5.   **a.**   As a leader I spend considerable energy in managing separate but related goals.

       b.   As a leader I spend considerable energy in arousing hopes, expectations, and aspirations among my followers.

6.   **a.**   While not in a formal classroom sense, I believe that a significant part of my leadership is that of teacher.

       b.   I believe that a significant part of my leadership is that of facilitator.

7.   **a.**   As leader I must engage with followers at an equal level of morality.

       b.   As leader I must represent a higher morality.

8.   **a.**   I enjoy stimulating followers to want to do more.

       b.   I enjoy rewarding followers for a job well done.

9.   **a.**   Leadership should be practical.

       b.   Leadership should be inspirational.

10.   **a.**   What power I have to influence others comes primarily from my ability to get people to identify with me and my ideas.

       b.   What power I have to influence others comes primarily from my status and position.

Scoring

Circle your points for items 1B, 2A, 3B, 4A, 5B, 6A, 7B, 8A, 9B, 10A, and sum the total points you allocated to these items; enter the score here [**T** = _____]. Next, sum the total points given to the uncircled items 1A, 2B, 3A, 4B, 5A, 6B, 7A, 8B, 9A, 10B; enter the score here [T = _____].

Interpretation

This instrument gives an impression of your tendencies toward "transformational" leadership (your **T** score) and "transactional" leadership (your T score). You might refer to the discussion of these concepts in Chapter 12. Today, a lot of attention is being given to the transformational aspects of leadership---those personal qualities that inspire a sense of vision and desire for extraordinary accomplishment in followers. The most successful leaders of the future will most likely be strong in both *Ts*.

Instructor's Note

This assessment can be used for two primary purposes. First, it illustrates one way of measuring the transactional and transformational styles of leadership. Accordingly, you could ask students to assess the instrument's accuracy in measuring their leadership style. Some students will undoubtedly report that they consider the results to be inaccurate. Follow up on these remarks by asking students why they think this inaccuracy occurred. You can then ask them to identify some of the challenges and limitations inherent in designing an instrument to measure leadership style. While it is important to address some attention to these issues, be careful not to give students the impression that leader style cannot be measured. Most of the class will probably agree with the results. Make sure that these persons express this agreement. You can then stress that while no measurement instrument is perfect and all are susceptible to certain biases, well designed measures can provide a good indication of leader style for most of the people, most of the time.

Once the limitations of the instrument are apparent, this assessment can be used for a second purpose -- to provide students with some potential insights into their leadership style and its implications for their managerial careers. For persons who score as having transactional leadership tendencies, the major implications are that they may have a tendency to emphasize exchange relationships with others. That is, they may tend to view leadership as a process of providing rewards and desired outcomes to others in exchange for certain behaviors and levels of performance. Given this perspective, such leaders look for followers to uphold their end of the bargain; that is, to provide a level of contributions commensurate with the rewards they receive. They would not, however, ask followers to provide more than this level since there would be an imbalance in the exchange. Because of their vested interests, familiarity and comfort with the status quo, transactional leaders see their role in organizations as one of maintaining the system at a high level of efficiency and effectiveness. It is important to emphasize that persons with these tendencies are an important component of organizations. Indeed, one could view these leaders as the "backbone" of our social institutions.

Transformational leaders are a rather rare bred; they are charismatic individuals who possess vision and the ability to inspire others to contribute above and beyond the level at which they expected to give. In essence, these leaders transform followers who in turn transform the organization into something new, and hopefully better, than it was before. A recent example of such an individual would be Lee Iacocca. Students who have tendencies toward transformational leadership may be highly successful at changing the status quo and eliciting unusually high levels of performance from followers. Such individuals should seriously consider pursuing careers which will enable them to tap this potential.

Before leaving this exercise, you may want to again assure students that there is no right or wrong style; both are critical to organizational success. Transformational leadership may be more glamorous and unusual, but transactional leaders are a key component of any organization's long term success.

(Source: Questionnaire by W. Warner Burke, PhD. Used by permission.)

ASSESSMENT: **LEAST-PREFERRED COWORKER SCALE**

Instructions

Think of all the different people with whom you have ever worked---in jobs, in social clubs, in student projects, or whatever. Next think of the *one person* with whom you could work *least* well---that is, the person with whom you had the most difficulty getting a job done. This is the one person---a peer, boss, or subordinate---with whom you would least want to work. Describe this person by circling numbers at the appropriate points on each of the following pairs of bipolar adjectives. Work rapidly. There are no right or wrong answers.

Pleasant	8	7	6	5	4	3	2	1	Unpleasant
Friendly	8	7	6	5	4	3	2	1	Unfriendly
Rejecting	1	2	3	4	5	6	7	8	Accepting
Tense	1	2	3	4	5	6	7	8	Relaxed
Distant	1	2	3	4	5	6	7	8	Close
Cold	1	2	3	4	5	6	7	8	Warm
Supportive	8	7	6	5	4	3	2	1	Hostile
Boring	1	2	3	4	5	6	7	8	Interesting
Quarrelsome	1	2	3	4	5	6	7	8	Harmonious
Gloomy	1	2	3	4	5	6	7	8	Cheerful
Open	8	7	6	5	4	3	2	1	Guarded
Backbiting	1	2	3	4	5	6	7	8	Loyal
Untrustworthy	1	2	3	4	5	6	7	8	Trustworthy
Considerate	8	7	6	5	4	3	2	1	Inconsiderate
Nasty	1	2	3	4	5	6	7	8	Nice
Agreeable	8	7	6	5	4	3	2	1	Disagreeable
Insincere	1	2	3	4	5	6	7	8	Sincere
Kind	8	7	6	5	4	3	2	1	Unkind

Scoring

This is called the "least-preferred coworker scale" (LPC). Compute your LPC score by totaling all the numbers you circled; enter that score here [LPC = _____].

Interpretation

The LPC scale is used by Fred Fiedler to identify a person's dominant leadership style (see Chapter 12). Fiedler believes that this style is a relatively fixed part of one's personality, and is therefore difficult to change. This leads Fiedler to his contingency views, which suggest that the key to leadership success is finding (or creating) good "matches" between style and situation. If your score is 73 or above, Fiedler considers you a "relationship-motivated" leader; if your score is 64 and below, he considers you a "task-motivated" leader. If your score is 65--72, Fiedler leaves it up to you to determine which leadership style is most like yours.

Instructor's Note

To conserve class time, consider assigning the LPC Scale as homework prior to the period in which you intend to discuss Fiedler's theory. During your lecture on the theory, ask for a show of hands of students who scored as relationship-oriented, task-oriented or somewhere in between. You may also want to ask students if they feel the LPC accurately measured their leadership style. While many will believe that it has, at least a few will usually think otherwise. At this point you can point out that the skepticism of these students is shared by critics of Fiedler's theory, who contend that one's score on the LPC Scale is not necessarily indicative of leadership style. It is also important to note, however, that Fiedler has obtained empirical support for his theory. You can then present the following propositions regarding the situations in which Fiedler asserts that task- and relationships-oriented leaders are most effective.

* *Proposition No. 1:* A task-oriented leader will be most successful in either very favorable (high control) or very unfavorable (low control) situations.

* *Proposition No. 2:* A relationship-oriented leader will be most successful in situations of moderate control.

Based on these conclusions, Fiedler recommends that prospective leaders should actively seek situations which *match* their leadership style. When a *mismatch* occurs, he asserts that leaders should first engage in *situational engineering;* this involves changing the situational characteristics to better match one's leadership style. Only as a last resort should they *change their leadership style* to match the situation; Fiedler feels this would be difficult because leadership style is strongly tied to personality factors that are hard to change.

(*Source:* Fred E. Fiedler and Martin M. Chemers, *Improving Leadership Effectiveness: The Leader Match Concept,* Second Edition. New York: John Wiley & Sons, 1984. Used by permission).

ASSESSMENT: CONFLICT MANAGEMENT STYLES

Instructions

Think of how you behave in conflict situations in which your wishes differ from those of one or more other persons. In the space to the left of each statement below, write the number from the following scale that indicates how likely you are to respond that way in a conflict situation.

1 = very unlikely   2 = unlikely   3 = likely   4 = very likely

1. I am usually firm in pursuing my goals.

2. I try to win my position.

3. I give up some points in exchange for others.

4. I feel that differences are not always worth worrying about.

5. I try to find a position that is intermediate between the other person's and mine.

6. In approaching negotiations, I try to be considerate of the other person's wishes.

7. I try to show the logic and benefits of my positions.

8. I always lean toward a direct discussion of the problem.

9. I try to find a fair combination of gains and losses for both of us.

10. I attempt to immediately work through our differences.

11. I try to avoid creating unpleasantness for myself.

12. I try to soothe the other's feelings and preserve our relationships.

13. I attempt to get all concerns and issues immediately out in the open.

14. I sometimes avoid taking positions that would create controversy.

15. I try not to hurt others' feelings.

Scoring

Total your scores for items 1, 2, 7; enter that score here [*Competing* = _____]. Total your scores for items 8, 10, 13; enter that score here [*Collaborating* = _____]. Total your scores for items 3, 5, 9; enter that score here [*Compromising* = _____]. Total your scores for items 4, 11, 14; enter that score here [*Avoiding* = _____]. Total your scores for items 6, 12, 15; enter that score here [*Accommodating* = _____].

Interpretation

Each of the scores above corresponds to one of the conflict management styles discussed in Chapter 15. Research indicates that each style has a role to play in management, but that the best overall conflict management approach is collaboration. Only it can lead to problem-solving and true conflict resolution. You should consider any patterns that may be evident in your scores, and think about how to best handle conflict situations in which you become involved.

Instructor's Note

You may want to supplemental your discussion of conflict management styles with the following information on the circumstances under which each tend to be useful.

Competing is useful:

    (a) When quick, decisive action is vital -- e.g., emergencies.

    (b) On important issues where unpopular courses of action need implementing -- e.g., cost cutting, enforcing unpopular rules, discipline.

    (c) On issues vital to company welfare when you know you're right.

    (d) To protect yourself against people who take advantage of noncompetitive behavior.

Collaborating is useful:

    (a) To find an integrative solution when both sets of concerns are too important to be compromised.

    (b) When your objective is to learn -- e.g., testing your own assumptions, understanding the views of others.

    (c) To merge insights from people with different perspectives on a problem.

    (d) To gain commitment by incorporating others' concerns into a consensual decision.

    (e) To work through hard feelings which have been interfering with an interpersonal relationship.

Compromising is useful:

    (a) When goals are moderately important, but not worth the effort or potential disruption of more assertive modes.

    (b) When two opponents with equal power are strongly committed to mutually exclusive goals -- e.g., labor-management bargaining.

    (c) To achieve temporary settlements to complex issues.

    (d) To arrive at expedient solutions under time pressure.

    (e) As a backup mode when collaboration or competition fails to be successful.

Avoiding is useful:

(a) When an issue is trivial, of only passing importance, or when other more important issues are pressing.

(b) When you perceive no chance of satisfying your concerns -- e.g., when you have low power or you are frustrated by something which would be very difficult to change (national policies, someone's personality structure, etc.).

(c) When the potential damage of confronting a conflict outweighs the benefits of its resolution.

(d) To let people cool down -- to reduce tensions to a productive level and to regain perspective and composure.

(e) When gathering more information outweighs the advantages of an immediate decision.

(f) When others can resolve the conflict more effectively.

(g) When the issue seems tangential or symptomatic of another more basic issue.

Accommodating is useful:

(a) When you realize that you are wrong -- to allow a better position to be heard, to learn from others, and to show that you are reasonable.

(b) When the issue is much more important to the other person than to yourself -- to satisfy the needs of others, and as a goodwill gesture to help maintain a cooperative relationship.

(c) To build up social credits for later issues which are important to you.

(d) When continued competition would only damage your cause -- when you are outmatched and losing.

(e) When preserving harmony and avoiding disruption are especially important.

(f) To aid in the managerial development of subordinates by allowing them to experiment and learn from their own mistakes.

(*Source:* Adapted from Thomas-Kilmann, *Conflict Mode Instrument*, copyright 1974, Xicom, Inc., Tuxedo, NY 10987. Used by permission).

ASSESSMENT: TWO-FACTOR PROFILE

Instructions

On each of the following dimensions, distribute a total of "10" points between the two options. For example:

Summer Weather	(7)..................(3)	Winter weather
1. Very responsible job	(___)..................(___)	Job security
2. Recognition for work accomplishments	(___)..................(___)	Good relations with coworkers
3. Advancement opportunities at work	(___)..................(___)	A boss who knows his/her job well
4. Opportunities to grow and learn on the job	(___)..................(___)	Good working conditions
5. A job that I can do well	(___)..................(___)	Supportive rules, policies of employer
6. A prestigious of high status job	(___)..................(___)	A high base wage or salary

Scoring

Summarize your total scores for all items in the *left-hand column* and write it here: MF = _____.

Summarize your total scores for all items in the *right-hand column* and write it here: HF = _____.

Interpretation

The "MF" score indicates the relative importance that you place on motivating or satisfier factors in Herzberg's two-factor theory. This shows how important job content is to you.

The "HF" score indicates the relative importance that you place on hygiene or dissatisfier factors in Herzberg's two-factor theory. This shows how important job context is to you.

Instructor's Note

This exercise can be used to "personalize" Herzberg's two-factor theory of motivation by helping students to determine the extent to which they value motivators as opposed to hygiene factors. As part of a general discussion of his theory, ask students to consider the implications of their scores for their careers and their efforts to secure jobs that are satisfying and motivating. Follow up by asking students to critically assess the validity of Herzberg's model. If most rate motivating factors as being more important than satisfiers, you can point out that Herzberg's predictions were basically supported in your class. If, in contrast, many students rate hygiene factors as being important, ask them to explain why this discrepancy from his predictions occurred. At a more basic level, you can solicit feedback on the basic distinction he makes between these two groups of factors. Many students are likely to strongly contest his notion that money is a hygiene factor, rather than a motivator, in particular. To summarize, this exercise can serve as a useful vehicle for making Herzberg's ideas more personally relevant to students and, in the process, identifying the strengths and weaknesses of the two-factor theory.

EXERCISE: JOB DESIGN PREFERENCE

Instructions

People differ in what they like and dislike about their jobs. Listed below are 12 pairs of jobs. For each pair, indicate which job you would prefer. Assume that everything else about the jobs is the same — pay attention only to the characteristics actually listed for each pair of jobs. If you would prefer the job in Column A, indicate how much you prefer it by putting a check mark in a blank to the left of the Neutral point. If you prefer the job in Column B, check one of the blanks to the right of Neutral. Check the Neutral blank only if you find the two jobs equally attractive or unattractive. Try to use the Neutral blank sparingly.

Column A

Column B

1. A job that offers little or no challenge.

|__|__|__|__|__|__|__|
Strongly Neutral Strongly
Prefer A   Prefer B

A job with excellent vacation and fringe benefits.

2. A job that pays well.

|__|__|__|__|__|__|__|
Strongly Neutral Strongly
Prefer A   Prefer B

A job that allows considerable opportunity to be creative and innovative.

3. A job that often requires you to make important decisions.

|__|__|__|__|__|__|__|
Strongly Neutral Strongly
Prefer A   Prefer B

A job in which there are many pleasant people to work with.

4. A job with little security in a somewhat unstable organization.

|__|__|__|__|__|__|__|
Strongly   Neutral   Strongly
Prefer A   Prefer B

A job in which you have opportunity to participate in decisions that affect your work.

5. A job in which greater responsibility is given to those who do the best work.

|__|__|__|__|__|__|__|
Strongly   Neutral   Strongly
Prefer A   Prefer B

A job in which greater responsibility is given to loyal employees who have the most *seniority*.

6. A job with a supervisor who sometimes is highly critical.

|__|__|__|__|__|__|__|
Strongly   Neutral   Strongly
Prefer A   Prefer B

A job that does not require you to use much of your talent.

7. A very routine job.

|__|__|__|__|__|__|__|
Strongly   Neutral   Strongly
Prefer A   Prefer B

A job in which your coworkers are not very friendly.

8. A job with a supervisor who respects you and treats you fairly.

|__|__|__|__|__|__|__|
Strongly   Neutral   Strongly
Prefer A   Prefer B

A job that provides constant opportunities for you to learn new And interesting things.

9. A job that gives you a real chance to develop yourself personally.

|__|__|__|__|__|__|__|
Strongly   Neutral   Strongly
Prefer A   Prefer B

A job with excellent vacation and fringe benefits.

10. A job in which there is a real chance you could be laid off.

|__|__|__|__|__|__|__|
Strongly   Neutral   Strongly
Prefer A   Prefer B

A job that offers very little chance to do challenging work.

11. A job that gives you little freedom and independence to do your work in the way you think is best.

|__|__|__|__|__|__|__|
Strongly   Neutral   Strongly
Prefer A   Prefer B

A job with poor working conditions.

12. A job with very satisfying teamwork.

|__|__|__|__|__|__|__|
Strongly   Neutral   Strongly
Prefer A   Prefer B

A job that allows you to use your skills and abilities to the fullest extent.

Interpretation

People differ in their need for psychological growth at work. This instrument measures the degree to which you seek growth need satisfaction. Score your responses as follows:

For items 1, 2, 7, 8, 11, and 12 give yourself the following points for each item:

```
| 1 | 2 | 3 | 4 | 5 | 6 | 7 |
```

Strongly   Neutral   Strongly
Prefer A   Prefer B

For items 3, 4, 5, 6, 9, and 10 give yourself the following points for each item.

```
| 7 | 6 | 5 | 4 | 3 | 2 | 1 |
```

Strongly   Neutral   Strongly
Prefer A   Prefer B

Add up all of your sources and divide by 12 to find the average. If you score above 4.0 your desire for growth need satisfaction through work tends to be high and you are likely to prefer an enriched job. If you score below 4.0 your desire for growth need satisfaction through work tends to be low and you are likely to not be satisfied or motivated with an enriched job.

Instructor's Note

This assessment can serve as an excellent tool for helping students to personalize the *Job Characteristics Model* presented in the text. In particular, it makes the importance of the contingency variable included in that model — Growth Need Strength (GNS) — much more salient. Based on the predictions of this model, students who score high in terms of GNS will greatly prefer jobs in which the core characteristics of skill variety, task identity, task significance, autonomy, and feedback are high; in addition, when these characteristics are low, they respond more favorably to efforts to enrich the job by incorporating these characteristics, as suggested above. In contrast, students who score low with respect to GNS are likely to react negatively to efforts to enrich their job. Ask your students to comment on the accuracy of the model's predictions for them as individuals. Most are likely to agree with its basic precepts. By demonstrating the personal relevance of this model for your students, its utility and implications for their careers -- as well as those of workers in general -- should become clear.

(Source: Reprinted by permission from J. R. Hackman and G. R. Oldham, The Job Diagnostic Survey: An Instrument for the Diagnosis of Jobs and the Evaluation of Job Redesign Projects, Technical Report 4, New Haven, CT: Yale University, Department of Administrative Sciences, 1974).

ASSESSMENT: STRESS SELF-TEST

Instructions

Complete the following questionnaire. Circle the number that best represents your tendency to behave on each bipolar dimension.

Am casual about appointments	1	2	3	4	5	6	7	8	Never late for appointments
Am not competitive	1	2	3	4	5	6	7	8	Very competitive
Never feel rushed, even under pressure	1	2	3	4	5	6	7	8	Always feel rushed
Take things one at a time	1	2	3	4	5	6	7	8	Try to do many things at once
Do things slowly	1	2	3	4	5	6	7	8	Do things fast (eating, walking, etc.)
Express feelings	1	2	3	4	5	6	7	8	"Sit" on feelings
Have many interests	1	2	3	4	5	6	7	8	Few outside interests

Scoring

Total the numbers circled for all items, and multiply this by 3; enter the result here [_____].

Interpretation

This scale is designed to measure your personality tendency toward Type A or Type B behaviors. Scores of 100 and above are considered Type A; scores under 100 are considered Type B. As described in Chapter 15, a Type A personality is associated with high stress. Persons who are Type A tend to bring stress on themselves even in situations where others are relatively stress-free. This is an important characteristics to be able to identify in yourself and in others.

Instructor's Note

Encourage students to think seriously about the implications of their personality type. Certainly, other things will affect the stress they experience on the job, as discussed in the chapter. However, be sure they consider the affect of personality type on stress.

(*Source:* Adapted from R. W. Bortner, "A Short Rating Scale as a Potential Measure of Type A Behavior," *Journal of Chronic Diseases*, Vol. 22, 1966, pp. 87-91. Used by permission).

RESEARCH AND PRESENTATION PROJECTS

PROJECT 1: DIVERSITY LESSONS -- "WHAT HAVE WE LEARNED?"

There are many reports out there -- *Workforce 2020, Workforce 2000,* and *Opportunity 2000,* among several others. Diversity in the workplace is clearly the subject of significant attention. Managers and employers are being urged to recognize and value diversity, and many are pursuing active programs to improve the environment for diversity in the workplace. Yet "glass ceilings" remain obstacles to career and personal accomplishment for too many females, African Americans, and other minorities.

Question

What are the "facts" in terms of progress for minorities in the workplace? What lessons of diversity have been learned? What are the "best" employers doing?

Instructions

Use research sources at your disposal to complete a project report addressing this question. Specific topics for consideration might include the following:

*   Case studies of employers reported as having strong diversity programs. What do they have in common? What do they do differently? Is there a "model" that could be followed by managers in other settings?

*   Investigation of diversity in specific respect to how well people of different facial, ethnic, gender and generational groups work together. What do we know about this, if anything? What are the common problems, if any? What concerns do managers and workers have?

*   Analysis of survey reports on the "glass ceiling" as it may affect the careers of women and minorities in various occupational settings. Get specific data, analyze them, and develop their implications. Prepare a report that summarizes your research.

*   A critical look at the substance of diversity training. What do these programs try to accomplish, and how? Are they working of not, and how do we know? Is there a good model of diversity training that others may use?

*   Look at where we go from here. What diversity issues lie ahead to be successfully mastered by the *new* managers of tomorrow?

Instructor's Note

Chapter 1 does an excellent job of alerting students to the growing importance of workforce diversity to managers and organizations. This research project can serve to build on this knowledge by guiding students toward much more detailed information on the trends in this area. Given the increasing amount of attention which this topic has received in recent years, students should have little trouble locating practitioner-oriented and academic publications on diversity. A good starting point is provided by Taylor Cox, Jr.'s 1993 book titled, *Cultural Diversity in Organizations: Theory, Research and Practice* (San Francisco: Berrett-Koehler). By examining resources such as this, students can acquire a stronger appreciation of the challenges and opportunities created by workforce diversity which they may face as *new* managers in the 21st century.

PROJECT 2: TOTAL QUALITY MANAGEMENT — "IS IT WORKING?"

Business Week once went so far as to state, "Quality, in short, may be the biggest competitive issue of the late 20th and early 21st centuries." The textbook has introduced total quality management (TQM) as a general concept; now it's time to look further at what the "real world" is doing with it.

Question

What are the "best of the best" doing in respect to total quality management, and where will they go from here? Is "TQM" working?

Instructions

Use the library and other research sources at your disposal to complete and submit a written report addressing this question. Specific topics for consideration might include:

*   Every so often, business periodicals such as *Business Week* and *Fortune* publish special issues on quality. Examine some of these reports, as well as other sources. Choose examples that you feel meet the standards of "best" of the best. Try to cover both manufacturing and services, and business as well as non-profits. Analyze the examples and identify common patterns as well as differences. Use the analysis for a report on "Total Quality Management: What It Takes to Succeed."

*   Look again at your research to identify examples where technology makes a significant difference. Try to be specific about how managers can use technology to the best quality advantage. Again, be sensitive to potential differences in manufacturing versus services, and businesses versus non-profits. What patterns do you see, and what positive examples can you find?

*   Look also at human resource issues and developments. What roles do people play in an organization's total quality movement? What are highly progressive organizations doing to ensure that they have a workforce that is both capable of and supportive of a total quality management approach? What lessons are we learning in this respect? What patterns do you see, and what positive examples can you find?

*   Examine the research literature. What do the researchers say? Does total quality management work? How do we know? What do we know? What don't we know?

*   Prepare a "practitioner's" bibliography of recommended books and readings on total quality management. Annotate the bibliography to give management readers some insight as to what is covered in a particular reference, and to help them set priorities as to what to read first.

*   Where does the total quality movement go from here? What new directions or steps are on the horizon? What should a truly informed manager be aware of in order to meet the leadership challenge of helping organizations achieve competitive advantage through quality products and services?

Instructor's Note

Because total quality management (TQM) represents one of the most important means whereby modern organizations can gain a competitive advantage, students can benefit greatly from developing an in-depth understanding of TQM. This research project directs students to examine both the academic and practitioner literatures to identify the keys to TQM success, including the full utilization of technological and human resources. In addition, they are asked to speculate on the new directions or steps for TQM which lie on the horizon. After studying these issues, students are likely to find themselves in a much better position to truly apply the principles of TQM in their careers and gain competitive advantages for their organizations.

PROJECT 3: CORPORATE SOCIAL RESPONSIBILITY -- "WHAT'S THE STATUS?"

The average fast food restaurant generates enormous waste each day. Actions taken to reduce this waste are applauded. The U.S. Food and Drug Administration monitors food labeling to guard against inappropriate claims. Firms sanctioned by the FDA often pay a price in negative publicity. Waste management and product labeling are but two of a growing range of activities by businesses and other organizations that are being publicly scrutinized for their social responsibility implications.

Question

Where do businesses stand today with respect to the criteria for evaluating social responsibility discussed in the textbook?

Instructions

Use research sources at your disposal to complete a project report on this question. Specific topics for consideration might include the following:

*   Research and evaluate the "status" of McDonald's and Proctor & Gamble on a variety of social responsibility performance matters. How well are they doing? Would you use them as "models" of social responsibility for others to follow, or not?

*   Conduct research to identify current examples of the "best" and the "worst" organizations in terms of social responsibility performance. Pursue this investigation on an a) international, b) national, and/or c) local scale.

*   Choose an issue -- for example, environmental protection or product labeling. Conduct research to identify the "best" and the "worst" organizations in terms of social responsibility performance in these specific matters. Again, consider looking at this issue on an a) international, b) national, and/or c) local scale.

* Create a "scale" that could be used to measure the social responsibility performance of an organization. Review the scholarly research in this area, but use your own judgement. Test your scale by applying it to two or three local organizations.

Instructor's Note

With increasing public awareness of environmental, health, and social issues, expectations regarding the social responsibility of organizations continue to rise. Such expectations served as the impetus for McDonald's efforts to reduce waste at its restaurants, as well as P&Gs embarrassment over its false "no-cholesterol" claim. Since many students likewise possess high expectations for socially responsible behavior, they are likely to relish the opportunity to learn more about the actual levels of social responsibility exhibited by prominent organizations. This research project can serve as a vehicle for obtaining such knowledge. By directing students to identify the "best" and "worst" examples of social responsibility displayed by organizations operating on an international, national, and/or local scale -- both in general and for specific issues -- this assignment should provide students with valuable insight into the extent to which societal expectations can and are being met and/or violated. In addition, by requiring students to create a scale for measuring social responsibility, they should become more aware of the appropriate criteria for evaluating organizational performance in this area. Ultimately, this assignment may provide students with a valuable set of guidelines for ensuring that they behave in an ethical and socially responsible fashion throughout their careers.

PROJECT 4: FOREIGN INVESTMENT IN AMERICA — "WHAT ARE THE IMPLICATIONS?"

Foreign investment in the United States is high and growing. For example, there are more than 1500 Japanese manufacturing companies in the United States. The number of Americans employed in these firms is 300,000+ and growing. In smaller communities like Marysville, Ohio, and Smyrna, Tennessee, the presence of a Honda or Nissan plant has extensive implications for the local economy -- and for the local way of life in general. Indeed, some Americans view the growing Japanese investment in the United States as a cause for concern, not jubilation.

Question

Which is it? Is foreign investment in the United States a cause for concern, or is it something to be welcomed?

Instructions

Use research sources at your disposal to complete and submit a written report on this question. Specific topics for consideration might include the following:

* The status of current foreign investment in the United States. How much is there, how fast is it growing, in what major industries is it found, and where is it located?

* The primary benefits and costs of this investment for the local communities and regions in which Japanese firms operate. What do the communities gain from the Japanese presence? What price do they pay?

* The effects of Japanese *keiretsu*. Do these linkages within business groups "spill over" to influence how Japanese firms operate in American? Do the *keiretsu* work to the disadvantage of non-Japanese firms wanting to do business with them in the United States? What do we really know about these issues? What positions do American corporate executives and government leaders take? What is your position?

* How do Americans feel about working for foreign employers. Do the Americans have opportunities for career advancement in the foreign firms? Do these opportunities vary for men and women? Are the foreign companies considered to be "good" employers? Why or why not?

Instructor's Note

There can be little doubt that people have very mixed reactions to the recent increase in foreign investment in America. From an economic and cultural perspective, there are some notable advantages of these trends. First, the presence of foreign manufacturing firms provides direct and indirect employment for many Americans. Second, since these firms typically produce affordable and high quality goods, the American consumer benefits. Third, foreign competition has spurred many U.S. manufacturers to improve their manufacturing processes and the quality of their goods, thereby making them more competitive in the global marketplace. Fourth, the presence of foreign firms in the U.S. helps employees, business associates, and local residents to better understand and appreciate Japan's unique culture. Disadvantages of foreign investment stem from the syphoning off of profits to other countries, and the limited advancement opportunities that are available to American employees. Women, in particular, are viewed as unsuited for executive positions in Japanese firms. Completion of this research project should provide students with in-depth insights into these and other issues associated with Japanese investment in the U.S. Since many students are likely to have opportunities to work and/or interact with foreign firms following their graduation, such insights could prove to be beneficial to their careers.

PROJECT 5: FRINGE BENEFITS — "CAN THEY BE MANAGED?"

Good compensation and benefits systems can help organizations attract and retain talented workers. But an increasingly diverse workforce is placing new and ever-greater demands on employers to provide benefits. Rising costs are making it ever more difficult for cost-conscious employers to maintain their benefits programs.

Questions

How can organizations best deal with the looming fringe benefits crisis? Can benefits programs be developed to both fit the needs of a diverse workforce and satisfy cost control needs of employers?

Instructions

Use research sources at your disposal to complete and submit a written report addressing this question. Specific topics for consideration might include the following:

* Look at the data on health care costs. How are rising costs of health care affecting employers . . . and their employees? Look at the special problems of those workers who may not be covered at all by employer-sponsored health insurance programs. Find some positive examples of organizations that are trying new and promising approaches to deal with rising costs of health-care related fringe benefits while still treating their employees well in the process.

* Shift the focus to pension plans and related matters. Look at the growing complexity of financial planning alternatives and tax laws. How are progressive organizations coping? What are the implications for employees? Try to come up with a series of "pension awareness guidelines" that could be offered to anyone entering the workforce today.

* Focus on the fringe benefits that best meet the needs of a diverse workforce. What special "needs" are appearing with greater frequency and sense of importance? Again, try to find examples of progressive employers who may be doing things that others could use as "benchmarks" for their own fringe benefit programs.

* Try to find surveys that report on workers' views of their fringe benefits. Look for similar reports on employer views. Examine the patterns and compare the perceptions. What are the implications for managers who want to establish the best support systems for employees in tomorrow's organizations?

Instructor's Note

The issue of who pays for fringe benefits is becoming increasingly important as organization's attempt to deal with rising benefits costs, while demands from a diverse workforce with varied needs expand. Since most students know little about the complexity of this issue or its implications for organizations and managers, this research project can serve as an excellent tool for increasing their awareness. Many students are likely to be shocked by the soaring costs of medical, retirement, and other benefits which organizations have traditionally shouldered. They are also likely to be torn between the two sides of this debate. As future employees, they will be sympathetic to individuals who argue that they simply cannot afford to bear these costs. However, as aspiring managers, they may have to see these benefits as a drain on organizational performance which many firms will likewise be unable to bear. Given this fact, the innovative approaches to providing fringe benefits which students are instructed to search for, become increasingly important. Thus, this research project may provide students with some invaluable ideas for helping individuals and organizations cope with this emerging crisis.

PROJECT 6: REENGINEERING -- "DOES IT WORK?"

Reports of reengineering are still in the news as many organizations try to improve performance through various forms of restructuring. Reengineering offers the potential advantages of streamlined operations, but may also affect careers, jobs, and worker loyalties. The impression remains that since so many organizations are doing it, reengineering must work. Its benefits must be greater than its costs.

Question

Do the benefits of reengineering outweigh its costs? What do we really know about the results of corporate reengineering organizations?

Instructions

Use research sources at your disposal to complete and submit a written report addressing this question. Specific topics for consideration might include the following:

* An examination of the issues from workers' perspectives. Look for reports on worker responses to reengineering programs. Try to find case examples that document how this type of organizational change affects people. Look, in particular, for both "success" and "failure" stories.

* An examination of organizational performance results. Try to find reports on how reengineering affects corporate profits, productivity, competitive advantage, and other success indicators. Look for case examples that document the impact of reengineering on performance---both positively and negatively.

* A review of the scholarly literature for empirical research on this and related topics. Summarize the findings. Identify questions for further study.

* Patterns from your analysis. Can you show when and in under what conditions reengineering can succeed? Can you identify guidelines for managerial decision making and action that may increase the likelihood that it can be successful? Be diligent, persistent, frank, and inquisitive.

Instructor's Note

This research project can be extremely useful for making students think more seriously about the plusses and minuses of reengineering. While the potential benefits in terms of increased operating efficiency are readily apparent, there are also some hidden costs to both the organization and society, such as a loss of expertise, a decline in morale and loyalty among retained employees, a damaged public image, increased unemployment, etc. Thus, the assignment of this research project can force students to critically evaluate the true benefits and costs of current trends in organizing.

PROJECT 7: CORPORATE CULTURE — "CAN IT BE CHANGED?"

"Culture" is a popular topic these days in management circles. Conventional wisdom holds that strong cultures can bond employees to a common sense of mission, and reinforce work habits needed to serve customers well and maintain productivity. The implication is that cultures in organizations can and should be changed when necessary to improve performance. Skeptics, by contrast, seem to believe that it may be better to work with, get the best out of, an existing culture than try to change it.

Question

What do you think? Can an organization's culture be changed? Should managers consider attempts to change the culture when an organization or work unit is not performing up to expectations?

Instructions

Use research sources at your disposal to complete and submit a written report addressing this question. Specific topics for consideration might include the following:

* Look for the latest thinking of management scholars and consultants on the role of "corporate culture" in successful organizations. Many case examples and reports should be available on this topic. Look for success stories, and try to interpret them in the context of the research question.

* Make a list, from your research, of things that can be done to change the culture of an organization or work unit. Critically evaluate each of these items in terms of these action criteria: (a) feasibility of dealing with the item, (b) length of time needed to achieve impact on the item, and (c) the follow-up or reinforcement that will be needed to maintain this impact. Review your entire analysis, and answer this question: "Can the recommended things really be accomplished by (a) a CEO, (b) a middle manager, and (c) a team leader?"

* Place the issue of corporate culture in the context of the growing number of international mergers, joint ventures, and strategic alliances found in the global economy. What is the importance of differences in "corporate cultures" as organizations of different "national cultures" try to work with one another? What do management consultants and scholars know or have to say about managing the problems of culture in this specific arena of business activity?

Instructor's Note

This research project can be extremely useful in stimulating students to critically evaluate the malleability of organizational cultures. While it is becoming increasingly popular to recommend that organization's change their cultures when things are going poorly, such actions may not always be realistic or desirable. Because there is much written on this topic, students should be able to collect a wealth of highly relevant and current information on the issues involved. What they are likely to find is that organizational cultures are highly complex, and often extremely resistant to change. When this is the case, management may be well advised to work with the culture to enlist its support, rather than attempting to dramatically alter it. However, when an existing culture is totally nonconducive to the achievement of a firm's objectives, management may have no choice but to radically alter the culture and replace it with one which provides a healthy climate for goal accomplishment. In sum, students who work on this research project should be able to obtain informed insights regarding the issues involved in managing organizational culture, and the circumstances under which change of the culture is required.

PROJECT 8: AFFIRMATIVE ACTION — "WHERE DO WE GO FROM HERE?"

In a *Harvard Business Review* article ("From Affirmative Action to Affirming Diversity," March-April 1990), R. Roosevelt Thomas makes the following statement: "Sooner or later, affirmative action will die a natural death." He goes on to praise its accomplishments, but then argues that it is time to "move beyond affirmative action" and learn how to "manage diversity." There are a lot of issues that may be raised in this context---issues of equal employment opportunity, hiring quotas, reverse discrimination, and others.

Question

What about it? Where do we stand with affirmative action today and where are we going?

Instructions

Use research sources at your disposal to complete and submit a written report addressing this question. Specific topics for consideration might include the following:

*   Read the Thomas article. Make sure you are clear on the term "affirmative action" and its legal underpinnings. Research the topic, identify the relevant laws, and make a history line to chart its development over time.

*   Examine current debates on "affirmative action" at the level of national policy? What are the issues? How are the "for" and "against" positions being argued?

*   Consider "reverse discrimination." Is there any pattern to employment situations in which it emerges as a management concern? Identify cases where reverse discrimination has been charged. How have they been resolved, and with what apparent human resource management implications?

*   Examine current controversies over hiring "quotas." Is this what affirmative action is all about? What are the arguments pro and con? What do the "experts" say about it? Where do we seem to be headed in this area?

*   Look at organizational policies that deal with diversity matters. Find what you consider to be the "best" examples. Analyze them and identify the common ground. Prepare a summary that could be used as a policy-development guideline for human resource directors who want to make sure their organizations truly support and value diversity in the workforce.

*   Try to look at all of these issues and controversies from different perspectives. Talk to people of different "majority" and "minority" groups in your college or university. Find out how---and why---they view these things. What are the implications for human resource management today?

Instructor's Note

This research project can be useful in stimulating students to seriously consider the issue of affirmative action from several different perspectives. Affirmative action is a complicated but important issue, which merits their attention. By enabling students to develop an appreciation of the controversy surrounding affirmative action, this assignment helps to prepare them to effectively and ethically deal with this issue during their careers.

PROJECT 9: SELF-MANAGING TEAMS -- "HOW GOOD ARE THEY?"

In Geert Hofstede's framework for describing national cultures (see Chapter 5), the United States is described as an "individualistic" country in his research sample. Americans, he suggests, are a people motivated by self-interests and opportunities for personal accomplishment and gain. This seems somewhat contrary to the growing emphasis on "teamwork" and increasing use of self-managing teams and various types of employee involvement groups in organizations.

Question

How well are self-managing teams working in the American workplace? What is the future of this approach?

Instructions

Use research sources at your disposal to complete a project report addressing this question. Specific topics for consideration might include the following:

* Check the research on self-managing teams. Where have they been tried, and with what success? Look for empirical data, not just theoretical arguments. Are there any patterns? What open questions remain to be answered?

* Look at the management guidelines for self-managing teams. What is the advice on how to ensure their success? What are the potential pitfalls in workplaces where one is changing *to* self-managing teams from other more traditional methods?

* Address the individualism issue. Can self-managing teams work with the highly individualistic American workers? What advice is available on how to deal with this individualism issue if, indeed, it is an issue at all?

* Address the organization structure issue. How must an organization's structure change in order to best support the activities of self-managing teams? What advice is available on handling these structural issues?

* Look more broadly at employee involvement groups in general. What do we know about the effectiveness of quality circles and other types? Are there any patterns that indicate when and under what conditions they tend to work best?

* Assume you have to give a formal briefing to a senior executive trying to decide if her organization should try self-managing teams and employee involvement groups. Based on your research, what will you say?

Instructor's Note

With the growing importance of self-managing teams, it is important for students to fully appreciate what's involved in utilizing them. Given the rugged individualism of American workers, one might expect that they would have difficulty embracing the team approach. However, through this research project, students are likely to conclude that self-managing teams and individualism are *not* necessary incongruent, since most self-managing teams provide the individual with more discretion and responsibility in performing his or her job. That is, such teams give members more say in conducting their work than many traditional management approaches. Most Americans are very willing to be part of a team, as long as their individual rights and identity are respected and recognized, and the team facilitates the achievement of their personal goals. Thus, this research project can help students to recognize the potential problems that may arise when forming self-managing teams of American workers, as well as the keys to avoiding these pitfalls.

PROJECT 10: CEO PAY — "IS IT TOO HIGH?"

The high, sometimes extremely high, pay of CEOs in many American corporations has caught the public's eye. Many people aren't very happy with what they are discovering. One report states that CEOs take home, on average, 160 times the pay of their employees, and earn three to six times what their counterpart CEOs in Japanese and European companies earn. It is not only the magnitude of the pay that is bothersome. Controversial too is the belief that many CEOs' pay goes up even when their firms' performances go down.

Question

What is happening in the area of executive compensation? Are CEOs paid too much? Are CEO's paid for "performance," or are they paid for something else?

Instructions

Use research sources at your disposal to complete a project report addressing this question. Specific topics for consideration might include the following:

* Check the latest reports on CEO pay. Try to get the facts. Prepare a briefing report as if you were writing a short informative article for *Fortune* magazine. The title of your article should be: "Status Report: Where We Stand Today on CEO Pay."

* Address the pay-for-performance issue. Do corporate CEOs get paid for performance, or for something else? What do the researchers say? What do the business periodicals say? Find some examples to explain and defend your answers to these questions.

* Find some positive cases where you consider a CEO's pay to be justified. What criteria are you using to justify it?

* Take a position: Should a limit be set on CEO pay? If no, why not? If yes, what type of limit do we set? Should we deal with an absolute dollar limit, a multiple of what the lowest-paid worker in a firm earns, or some other guideline? Why? Who, if anyone, should set these limits---Congress, company boards of directors, or someone else?

* Take a poll on campus. What do other students think about CEO pay? Do they think limits should be set? Take a poll in your local community. What does the public-at-large think? How does the public feel about limits to CEO pay? How about you---what is your conclusion? Is the "attack" on CEO pay justified?

Instructor's Note

Since many students are likely to consider current salaries of CEO's to be outrageously high, this research project can generate a considerable amount of interest and emotion. Perhaps the most important points for students to realize are that CEO salaries, like anyone else's, should be equitably administered, and contingent upon their performance. When CEO's are paid exorbitant salaries, perceived negative inequities among employees are unavoidable. These feelings may have a decidedly negative impact on the motivation and performance of lower-level personnel. Moreover, when a CEO's salary increases, despite poor or mediocre performance by the firm, these feelings of inequity are compounded, and the CEO is reinforced for actions which may have contributed to the firm's poor showing. On the other hand, high salaries may be viewed as appropriate when the CEO is clearly responsible for a dramatic improvement in the company's performance. In sum, this exercise should get students thinking about how the motivational principles discussed in this chapter should be applied to the issue of executive salaries. As a result, they will learn more about motivation theory, while gaining new insights into the complicated issue of executive salaries.

PROJECT 11: MANAGING YOUR BOSS — "POSSIBLE OR NOT?"

Today's workers must consider managing their relationships with "the boss" as part of their everyday job. It is no longer sufficient for a manager to be good only at dealing with subordinates. Increasingly, the network aspects of organizations require that managers do a good job of managing relationships with peers and bosses. But when it comes to the "bosses" in particular, one has to wonder about the guidelines.

Question

What do we really know about the techniques of "managing one's boss?"

Instructions

Use research sources at your disposal to complete a project report addressing this question. Specific topics for consideration might include the following:

* Start with a *Harvard Business Review* article by John J. Gabarro and John P. Kotter entitled "How to Manage Your Boss" (January-February 1980, pp. 92-100). Analyze its main points and summarize them to create an initial set of guidelines. Check the literature further. Add to your list based on other useful insights that might be available.

* Examine the literature on power and influence. What do we know about how someone can use power to influence people at higher levels in organizations? Draft a set of guidelines that could be useful to a new college graduate who wants to be able to "manage" her new boss.

* Identify three or more conflict situations a manager may typically become involved in with her boss. Show how these situations might develop into "win--lose" or "lose--lose" outcomes. Show how "win--win" outcomes might be more likely *if* the manager takes appropriate action in each situation.

* Identify three or more negotiation situations a manager may typically become involved in with her boss. How do the Fisher and Ury ideas on "principled negotiation" apply in these situations? Read further on the subject of negotiation. What additional insights on handling these situations are available?

* Examine the literature on stress. What do researchers say and studies report on the role of "bosses" as sources of workplace stress for their subordinates? Is there anything that the subordinate can do to deal with a "high stress" boss? What about the boss? What can he or she do to minimize the impact of their high-stress styles on others?

Instructor's Note

Since most students find the concept of "managing one's boss" to be original and intriguing, they typically enjoy this research project. Moreover, by requiring them to consider how various power and influence, conflict management, and stress management strategies can be used to "manage" one's boss, their learning regarding these topics can be reinforced and broadened. Thus this research project should provide students with considerable insight into the ways in which interpersonal skills can be employed to ensure that their relationship with their boss is a positive one.

PROJECT 12: **ENTREPRENEURSHIP — "IS IT FOR YOU?"**

Entrepreneurship offers unusual career opportunities in today's complex business environment. But entrepreneurship involves taking risk. There are rewards to be gained and potential costs to be borne.

Question

Is entrepreneurship for you?

Instructions

Use the library and other research sources at your disposal to complete and submit a written report addressing this question. Specific topics for consideration might include the following:

* Start with *Fortune, Business Week,* and other business periodicals. Then hit the Internet. What are the opportunities for entrepreneurs today? Find some directions for further research and investigation.

* Find some success stories. Use them as examples to explain what can be done to encourage and sustain entrepreneurship — by yourself and others. Are there any patterns in evidence that can explain entrepreneurship success?

* Consider the "entrepreneurial personality." Is there such a thing? What is it? Do you have it? What are the implications of having or not having this personality?

* Interview one or more local entrepreneurs to inquire into their "stories" — where did they start, what did they do, what mistakes did they make, what did they learn, what would they recommend?

Prepare a report that could be used for a formal briefing to a group of high school students on the topic — "Opportunities for career success through entrepreneurship."

Instructor's Note

Entrepreneurship is a career path which many students may not consider as an option — both because it is somewhat unconventional, and because it is risky. This assignment can help students to gain a greater appreciation for both the pros and cons of entrepreneurship — the tremendous opportunities that entrepreneurs pursue, as well as the risks that they incur. By asking students to also take a look at their personal attributes and then assess the extent to which they possess those that have been shown to be characteristic of entrepreneurs, this project can help students to make a much more informed decision on the viability of this option for their careers.

PROJECT 13: VIRTUAL TEAMS -- "DOES GROUPWARE WORK?"

There are many reports on the growing use of "virtual teams" in organizations. These involve a range of technologies, with a growing emphasis on "groupware" that allows the computer mediation of relationships between group members. Clearly this is a pathway to the future. But skeptics remain.

Question

What do we know about virtual teams? What is the current status of "groupware" alternatives and does it really work? How far should we go in letting computers mediate relationships between work team members?

Instructions

Use research sources at your disposal to complete a project report addressing this question. Specific topics for consideration might include the following:

* An inventory of current groupware alternatives. What is available, from what sources, at what costs? Are there any alternatives that seem to be more popular than others, and/or that represent the most likely alternatives to be found in your workplace of the future?

* Consider the argument about "depersonalizing" teamwork when you move it into the virtual environment. Start with the academic literature. What are the researchers saying? Look at the applied literature and news reports. What are they saying, and what do the workers themselves appear to be saying? Are there any patterns in these sources that shed light on the research question?

* Take a look at organizations operating in your area. Talk to managers and workers. Spend some time with those in charge of the organizations' information services function. Is virtual teamwork making its way into

your community? If so, what is happening? What are the trends in the use of groupware? Do the people involved like it or not, and why?

Prepare a report on the future of virtual teamwork. Include in this report your prediction regarding the "best" available groupware applications and specific guidelines for using virtual teams to best advantage in organizations. Be sure to address the potential limits of this technology as well as its advantages.

Instructor's Note

For many students, the concepts of "virtual teams" and "groupware" may sound like science fiction. The reality is, however, that the "future is now," since these technologies are becoming more and more common in today's workplace. This assignment can go a long ways towards familiarizing students with these technologies and new types of teams, and stimulating them to reflect on the applications for which they can be applied, as well as their utility. In the process, they'll learn that the brave new world of computer-mediated communication is already upon us, while increasing their awareness of, and preparation for, the roles of virtual teams and groupware in the workplace of the future.

Unit 10

NIGHTLY BUSINESS REPORT VIDEO SERIES: INSTRUCTOR'S NOTES

The *Nightly Business Report (NBR) Video Series* includes video segments from the highly respected business news program *Nightly Business Report*. These video clips tie directly to the textbook theme of the management mosaic and bring to life many of the case examples used in the text as well as others from outside sources. Descriptions of each video segment and the relevant course concepts are summarized below. A set of discussion questions for each segment is also provided.

Segment Number	Featured Company	Segment Location in Minutes	Segment Duration in Minutes	Video Description	Relevant Course Concepts
1.	Coca-Cola	1:19	5:10	Interview with the late Robert Goizueta regarding the leadership challenges he faced and accomplishments Coca-Cola achieved during his 17 year tenure as CEO.	Leadership, international business and management, strategic management, competitive advantage
2.	Saturn	6:29	3:08	Explains General Motors' efforts to reinvent the manner in which automobiles are manufactured and marketed, with an emphasis on employee/management cooperation and consensus decision making.	Historical foundations of management, self-managing work teams, organizational design and work systems, human resource management, motivation and rewards, individual performance and job design

670

Segment Number	Featured Company	Segment Location in Minutes	Segment Duration in Minutes	Video Description	Relevant Course Concepts
3.	Netscape	9:37	4:23	Analyzes the evolution and development of a legendary Silicon Valley startup, in addition to competitive challenges posed by Microsoft's entry into the Internet browser market.	Dynamic new workplace, planning, strategic management, competitive advantage, leading, innovation and change management
4.	Harley-Davidson	14:00	3:28	Describes the history and competitive strategies of Harley-Davidson, and the increasing appeal of its motorcycles — and the accompanying lifestyle and image — in Japan	Competitive advantage, global economy, strategic management, innovation and change
5.	Kodak	17:28	3:02	Describes Kodak's difficulties in meeting international competition from Fuji, including its frustrated efforts to penetrate the Japanese film market.	Global economy, international business and management, strategic management, innovation and change management

Segment Number	Featured Company	Segment Location in Minutes	Segment Duration in Minutes	Video Description	Relevant Course Concepts
6.	Inland Steel	20:30	5:00	Describes the cooperative efforts of unionized workers at Inland Steel to improve the productivity and competitive posture of the firm.	Innovation and change management, human resource management, participative decision making, strategic management, competitive advantage, controlling
7.	UPS	25:30	3:19	Describes union-management relations at UPS, where 200,000 employees went on strike in 1997 over higher wages, better pensions, and fewer part-time workers	Human resource management, motivation and rewards, controlling, full-time and part-time employment
8.	AT&T	28:49	5:16	Looks at the difficulties AT&T has experienced in moving from a regulated monopoly to an extremely competitive marketplace for communication services.	Dynamic new workplace, global economy, strategic management, leading, innovation and change
9.	Price Waterhouse /Coopers & Lybrand	34:05	4:53	Analyzes the mega-merger between the two accounting firms and suggests consequences for the accounting/ consulting industry.	Competitive advantage, global economy, strategic management, competitive advantage, organizational culture

Segment Number	Featured Company	Segment Location in Minutes	Segment Duration in Minutes	Video Description	Relevant Course Concepts
10.	Black Entertainment Television (BET)	38:55	4:27	Chronicles Robert John's rise from poverty to the head of the largest African-American cable company in America.	Planning, strategic management, innovation, organizing, motivation
11.	Boeing	43:22	3:04	Describes the efforts of Boeing to fill record orders for aircraft through the acquisition of McDonnell Douglas, and improvement of its production processes	Strategic management, planning, organizing, operations management, teams, innovation and change, controlling
12.	Southwest Airlines & Home Depot	46:26	4:02	Describes the unique organizational culture of Southwest Airlines and Home Depot, including the ways management motivates its employees	Organizational culture, dynamic new workplace, motivation and rewards, strategic management, leading, communication and interpersonal skills
13.	Disney/ABC	50:28	2:41	Follows the evolution of Disney from a small production company into one of the largest integrated entertainment firms in the world today.	Dynamic new workplace, strategic management, planning, competitive advantage, organizing, leading, change management

Viewing Questions for NBR Videos

Segment 1: Coca-Cola Company

- What was Goizueta's unique "leadership" contribution to Coke?
- How does Goizueta personally differentiate "management" and "leadership"?
- What did being an "international" company mean to Goizueta?
- According to Goizueta, what are the responsibilities of business leadership?
- What is Coke's future without Goizueta as leader?

Segment 2: Saturn

- What was unique about the Saturn experiment in automobile manufacturing?
- In what ways does the Saturn operation respect the needs and talents of workers?
- Why is the time required to make consensus decisions considered to be worth it at Saturn?
- Is Saturn sustainable in the long run in this highly competitive industry?
- Will problems in labor-management relations eventually undermine the Saturn experiment?

Segment 3: Netscape

- Can Netscape compete with Microsoft?
- What is your position on the Justice Department's lawsuit against Microsoft?
- Why has Netscape been such an innovator?
- If you were CEO, what would you do to ensure the firm's future success?

Segment 4: Harley Davidson

- What is Harley's competitive strategy in Japan?
- What barriers to Harley's success are evident in the Japanese setting?
- Can Harley stay competitive over the long run in Japan?
- Should Harley even be worrying about success in the Japanese market?

Segment 5: Kodak

- What is Kodak's complaint against Fuji and the competitive environment in Japan?
- Is Kodak trying to find excuses for its own lack of ability to break the Japanese market?
- How does the WTO decision affect Kodak's future in the global economy?

Segment 6: Inland Steel

- What is unique about Nucor and other mini-mills in the steel industry?
- What was labor proposing to Inland's management?
- What are the potential costs of labor-management conflict to a firm in this industry?
- Should the steel workers be involved in "management" decisions?
- What do unions really want from management?
- What does management really want from unions?

Segment 7: UPS

- Was there a "winner" in the UPS/union conflict?
- What did labor gain in the conflict?
- What did management gain in the conflict?
- What did labor and management lose in the conflict?
- How can labor management relations become a source of competitive advantage?

Segment 8: AT&T

- What are the potential advantages of appointing an "outsider" as CEO?
- Are there any possible disadvantages?
- What is Armstrong's basic strategy in trying to revitalize AT&T?
- What does Armstrong mean when saying AT&T has "cost structure" and "cycle time" problems?
- How is AT&T doing today?

Segment 9: Price Waterhouse/Coopers Lybrand

- Are mergers in any industry good for... society, customers, employees, shareholders?
- Is PW/CL prepared to handle employee problems associated with this merger?
- How can PW/CL or any merger entity deal with the problem of "redundant" workers?

Segment 10: Home Depot

- Would you want to work for Home Depot? Why or why not?
- What role do these quarterly employee meetings play in Home Depot's success?
- What is the leadership style and corporate culture of this company?
- How does Home Depot build employee loyalty?
- Can good employee relations create long-term productivity?

Segment 11: Black Entertainment Television (BET)

▸ What is the growth strategy? How is BET trying to grow?
▸ Is this strategy doable?
▸ What are the potential risks of this growth strategy?
▸ Is CEO Johnson an innovator or a copycat?
▸ What are the advantages for Johnson and BET in taking the company private again?

Segment 12: Boeing

▸ What are the unique problems of manufacturing this type of product?
▸ Can Airbus compete with Boeing?
▸ Was the merger with McDonnell Douglas a good idea?
▸ What are the challenges now facing Boeing?

Segment 13: Disney

▸ What was the special "vision" Michael Eisner brought to Disney as CEO?
▸ What are the challenges of expansion by this company?
▸ Is Disney now getting too big and too diversified to remain successful?
▸ Could Disney go back to its core business — theme parks, and survive successfully?

Unit 11

USING THE *MANAGEMENT 6/E* WEB SITE

An extensive Web Site has been developed in support of **Management 6/e**. This site is available at *http://www.wiley.com/college/scherman6e*, and includes the following special resources for instructional enrichment of both instructors and students using the book.

* PowerPoint downloads for text figures and supplementary figures and special class activities and presentations

* Interactive on-line versions of cases

* Interactive on-line versions of skills assessments

* Supplementary in-class exercises and activities

* Special "quick-hitters" for use with various chapters, and with special value for large-section class sizes

* Internet links to organizations and information sites relevant to chapter materials

* A full electronic version of the Career Advancement Portfolio

* An on-line study guide for students

Additionally, the web site features a truly unique and highly valuable resource — "The Author's Classroom." This feature takes the instructor inside the author's own classroom to find additional teaching ideas and resources for each chapter. A supplement to this *Manual*, this on-line resource provides teaching tips and class enhancements for treating the core topics of each chapter. By using this resource, the instructor has access to John Schermerhorn's personal PowerPoint presentations, special in-class activities, unique web sites for browsing during class, and more.

Site Organization

This **Management 6/e Web Site** is designed to support excellence in teaching. It will be updated regularly to provide enrichment opportunities for students and instructors alike. The site is organized as follows.

   Getting Started: Overview of all Web Site features.

   Study Guide: Chapter-by-chapter online study guide with detailed PowerPoint reviews of chapter highlights and self-testing. The *On-Line Study Guide* provides a way for students to study, review and test themselves on the chapter material from the text. Each chapter is outlined in PowerPoint slide format which can be downloaded, and printed if desired, for note-taking and review. In addition, students can test their knowledge of the chapter content by taking interactive self-tests.

   Online Cases: Interactive, hyperlinked and updated versions of cases provided in the textbook.

   Self Assessments: Skills building assessments to be completed online and with immediate feedback of scores and comparisons.

   Career Portfolio: Template for students to build unique electronic career portfolios that include professional homepages, resumes, course work samples, and other demonstrations of competencies and accomplishments. The *Career Portfolio* provides a means for students to develop professional-looking electronic portfolios and make them available to prospective employers via the Internet.

   Author's Classroom: Chapter-by-chapter instructor's guide to teaching management as the authors do, utilizing special classroom resources and materials, PowerPoint presentations, videotapes, quick-hitting activities, special Web links, and more.

   Instructor Contributions to this Site: We welcome contributions that would like to share with other management educators. All submissions will be peer-reviewed by our special editorial team. Those accepted will be published on the Web site with full recognition to the contributors. Instructions for contributors are found on the Author's Classroon/User Contributions page for each chapter.

On-Line Cases

The *Online Cases* are updated versions of the textbook case studies, with Web links to a variety of Internet sites and information sources. A suggested Primary Case and Alternate Case are indicated for each chapter. A listing of these cases is provided below.

Chapter 1: The Dynamic New Workplace
      The Coca-Cola Company (Primary Case)
      Kodak (Alternate Case)

Chapter 2: Environment and Competitive Advantage
      Saturn (Primary Case)
      Tom's of Maine (Alternate Case)

Chapter 3: Information, Technology & Decision-Making
      Netscape (Primary Case)
      Boeing (Alternate Case)

Chapter 4: Historical Foundations of Management
      Harley Davidson (Primary Case)
      UPS (Alternate Case)

Chapter 5: Global Dimensions of Management
      Kodak (Primary Case)
      Harley Davidson (Alternate Case)

Chapter 6: Ethical Behavior and Social Responsibility
      Tom's of Maine (Primary Case)
      Ben and Jerry's Ice Cream (Alternate Case)

Chapter 7: Planning - To Set Direction
      Wal-Mart (Primary Case)
      Boeing (Alternate Case)

Chapter 8: Strategic Management and Entrepreneurship
      Nucor (Primary Case)
      Tom's of Maine (Alternate Case)

Chapter 9: Controlling - To Ensure Results
      UPS (Primary Case)
      Nucor (Alternate Case)

Chapter 10: Organizing - To Build Structures
      AT&T (Primary Case)
      UPS (Alternate Case)

Chapter 11: Organizational Design and Work Processes
　　　Price Waterhouse/Coopers and Lybrand (Primary Case)
　　　Boeing (Alternate Case)

Chapter 12: Human Resource Management
　　　Ben & Jerry's Ice Cream (Primary Case)
　　　Nucor (Alternate Case)

Chapter 13: Leading - To Inspire Effort
　　　Mike Krzyzewski: A No-Nonsense Leader (Primary Case)
　　　Tom's of Maine (Alternate Case)

Chapter 14: Motivation and Rewards
　　　Black Entertiainment Television (Primary Case)
　　　Nucor (Alternate Case)

Chapter 15: Individual Performance and Job Design
　　　Boeing (Primary Case)
　　　UPS (Alternate Case)

Chapter 16: Communication and Interpersonal Skills
　　　SouthWest Airlines (Primary Case)
　　　Ben and Jerry's Ice Cream (Alternate Case)

Chapter 17: Teams and Teamwork
　　　Steinway (Primary Case)
　　　Nucor (Alternate Case)

Chapter 18: Innovation & Change Management
　　　Disney/ABC (Primary Case)
　　　Boeing (Alternate Case)

Self-Assessments

Self-Assessments provide students with unique insights into their managerial style. Results and interpretations are returned to them instantly. A listing of the *Self-Assessments* available on-line follows.

Assessment #1: *A 21st Century Manager*

Assessment #2: *Cultural Attitudes Inventory*

Assessment #3: *Your Intuitive Ability*

Assessment #4: *Time Management Profile*

Assessment #5: *Entrepeneurship Orientation*

Assessment #6: *Organizational Design Preference*

Assessment #7: *T-T Leadership Style*

Assessment #8: *Least Preferred Coworker*

Assessment #9: *Stress Self-Test*

Assessment #10: *Who's In Control*

Career Portfolio

The *Career Portfolio* provides a means for students to develop professional-looking electronic portfolios and make them available to prospective employers via the Internet. The *on-line instructions* for using this component of the *Management 6/e Web Site* are reproduced below.

System Requirements

To complete the Career Portfolio, you will require the following:

★ Access to a personal website. Many universities provide Web server space to students, check with your local web administrator.

★ Access to either **Microsoft Word 97, Microsoft Explorer 4.0 or later, or Netscape 4.0** or later. Each of these provides a web editor that creates HTML (HyperText Markup Language) documents viewable on the web. Once documentation is created, it can be uploaded to the student's personal web space through the use of an FTP program such as WS-FTP (Winsock File Transfer Protocol).

Portfolio Preparation

Prepare your portfolio using two templates:

★ <u>Resume</u>

The Resume template provides the main, front page for the portfolio, in addition to access to the coursework section. The template can be downloaded to a student's disk or edited within Netscape or Explorer and then saved to the student's disk. The student makes editing changes in the template, just as they would with a normal word processing document. Directions are as follows:

Word 97 - <u>Click Here</u> to go to the resume template. In your web browser (Netscape or Microsoft Explorer) select **File**, and **Save As.** Save the file to a drive on your computer. Launch Word 97 and open the file from your selected drive. It is now editable just like any normal document; however, Word 97 will create the HTML programming language for you as you type. Save the file often.

Netscape Communicator 4.0 or higher - <u>Click Here</u> to go to the resume template. Select **File**, **Edit Page** and Netscape will capture the file from the web and open it in its text editor.

You may now manipulate the document as you would any word processing item. Save the file often.

Microsoft Explorer 4.0 or higher - <u>Click Here</u> to go to the resume template. Select File, Edit and Explorer will capture the file from the web and open it in its own text editor. You may now manipulate the document as you would any word processing item. Save the file often.

You can bold, underline, italicize and manipulate the resume template in any manner. Create hyperlinks in your document as follows:

Word 97 - Highlight (or "paint") the text you wish to hyperlink by holding down the left mouse button and "dragging" it across the selection. Select **Insert** and **Hyperlink** (usually the bottom choice) in the drop-down menu. You will be prompted for a Uniform Resource Locator (URL) or web address. It should be similar to: http:// followed by an address. An example is Wiley's homepage at http://www.wiley.com. Once you have typed the address, enter Finish and you will see the text highlighted, signifying it as a hyperlink.

Netscape and Explorer - Highlight (or "paint") the text you wish to hyperlink by holding down the left mouse button and "dragging" it across the selection. Select **Link** on the button menu. You will be prompted for a Uniform Resource Locator (URL) or web address. It should be similar to: http:// followed by an address. An example is Wiley's homepage at http://www.wiley.com. Once you have typed the address, enter Finish and you will see the text highlighted, signifying it as a hyperlink.

Email addresses are a special type of hyperlink. In the address box, type mail to: followed by the email address. This will cause the browser mail program to launch when this hyperlink is selected.

The remainder of the editing occurs like any other word processing document. You can change font sizes, colors, and other special formatting by use of the text editing tools. Save you work often. The file should be saved as resume (program will name it resume.htm) when you are finished.

★ <u>Course Work</u>

The Course Work page should be considered optional and only attempted when the student feels comfortable enough with the web to edit classroom assignments for posting on their web page. Any Microsoft Office 97 documents, including Word,

Excel, and Powerpoint can be saved in HTML format for display on the web. "Deliverables" such as memo assignments, project reports, Excel spreadsheets, are a few examples of items that can be displayed to "showcase" the student's potential. Viewable "outcome documents" provide a more useful evaluation of the student's potential than the sheer reliance on a resume. Student's can provide evidence of their unique skills.

<u>Click Here</u> to view the coursework template. You can choose to post a variety of coursework examples in your portfolio. The template provides a format for the student to use in order to provide access to examples of their work. Microsoft Word 97 provides a useful vehicle to develop web-based documents. In Word 97, choose File and New and you can choose a Web option. The document developed in this manner will be HTML ready and can be uploaded to the student's web address with the use of WS-FTP.

Going Live

★ <u>Instructions</u>.

File Transfer Protocol (FTP) - You have your file saved on your disk, but it must be loaded onto a SERVER in order for people to view it. You must get the file from your local computer onto your server space.

    * Start program **WS_FTP**
    * You will see a session window as below. You must fill in the following information:

Host Name/Address:	The domain name of your server. Ex: www.wiley.com
Host Type:	Automatic Detect
User ID:	Your username (email username)
Password:	Your password (email password)

    * Select OK and you will enter a window area that has your <u>local computer</u> in the left-hand window and your <u>public_html directory</u> (this is your "web page" area) in the right-hand window
    * **Double-click** the directory "public_html" in the right window.
    * In the left window, choose **ChgDir** (Changes the directory) and type in your desired directory address. Hit enter.
    * Select the file you want to transfer: highlight it
    * Click on the appropriate arrow key to transfer files: (right arrow)
    * Your file should now show up in the right-hand window.

Common Mistakes:

* People think their local computer is their server. People cannot view files from the web on your local computer. You must upload files onto the oak server in CSC for people to view them.
* File names are upper and lower case specific. Spelling must be exact.

The Author's Classroom: A Sample Chapter

To illustrate the types of instructional support provided for each chapter through *The Author's Classroom*, a sample on-line teaching outline for Chapter 1, which references the materials available, is provided below.

Chapter 1: The Dynamic New Workplace

Teaching Outline

Organizations and the New Workplace

What Is an Organization?

Organizations as Systems [Use Ppt 1.2]

Productivity And Organizational Performance

The Changing Nature of Organizations

Managers and the New Workplace

* Online Case

Review and discuss the range of issues covered in the *Chapter 1 Coca Cola Case* [available as *Coca-Cola Online Case* and as text case in the **Career Readiness Workbook**, p. 414].

Areas of emphasis in case:

1. Focus on shareholder value

2. Globalization

3. Organizational change

4. Management roles and activities

* Web Site Browsing

Introduce the *New Workplace* by browsing a current issue of the **Fast Company Magazine** as featured in the *Chapter 1 Opener*, "*Smart People Create Their Own Futures.*"

What is a manager?

Types and Levels of Managers

Accountability and Managerial Performance

The Changing Nature of Managerial Work

The Management Process

* NBR Video

Show the *Coca-Cola Video* and discuss challenges managers face in this organization.

Viewing Questions:

1. How is Coke meeting the challenge of the global economy?

2. What are the implications of Coke's change in leadership?

3. What is Coke's competitive strategy?

* Power Point Presentations

Manager's and Team Leader's Challenge

★ Discuss the concept of the *"Manager's Challenge"* in <u>Ppt 1.2</u> by pointing out issues of accountability, dependency, and performance.

★ Show *"Team Leader's Challenge"* in <u>Ppt 1.3</u> to point out how same concepts apply in this management context.

* In-Class Activity

Do *My Best Manager Exercise* [from the **Career Readiness Workbook**, p. 476].

Functions of Management

Managerial Activities and Roles

Managerial Agendas and Networks

Managerial Skills and Competencies

* Power Point Presentations

Managerial Work Power Points

★ Show <u>Ppt 1.4</u> and discuss the various *Ways of Thinking about the Management Process*

★ Show <u>Ppt 1.5</u> to Discuss *Mintzberg's View of Managerial Roles*

★ Show <u>Ppt 1.6</u> *to* discuss *Katz's Notion of Essential Managerial Skills*

* Focus throughout on highlighting needs to develop personal managerial competencies

* In-Class Activity

Have students complete the *Personal Managerial Skills Assessment* [*Career Readiness Workbook*].

* Note that this could be a homework assignment with the results brought to class for follow-up discussion.

* Follow-up Assignment

Assign the project *What Do Managers Really Do?* from the *Web Site*, asking students to interview a manager and report back to the class.

The Challenges Ahead

A Global Economy

Ethics and Social Responsibility

Workforce Diversity

Employment Values and Human Rights

Information and Technological Change

Portfolio Careers [*Bookmark*: See Also Career Advice in Chapter 12 Classroom Notes]

Management/6e: A Learning Framework

* Web Site Browsing

Focus on Diversity and Ethical Issues

★ Visit the *Society for Human Resource Management's* Listing of Diversity Links

★ Access the *Women's Wire* Homepage for Web Site Browsing

★ Ethics Resources on the Web

* In-Class Activity

Do *A 21st Century Manager?* Assessment [from **Career Readiness Workbook**, p. 494].

* Follow-up Assignment

You can also have the students do *A 21st Century Manager?* Assessment from the Web Site as homework and bring the results to class

An option is to have students write a short memorandum summarizing the implications of their score for personal and professional development as managers.

* Personal Career Readiness -- Special Emphasis

Emphasize need for proactive career approach, including use of WWW resources

Show and discuss career site at *Arthur Andersen*

Introduce Charles Handy's notion of *"Portfolio Careers"* using Ppt. 1.8.

Introduce the *Career Portfolio* concept from the **Career Readiness Workbook**, p. 407

Emphasize the opportunity in developing an *Electronic Career Portfolio* using Web Site resources with the book. Ideally, introduce the electronic career portfolio as course project -- have students prepare their portfolio for course-long use.

As an introduction to *Internet Career Resources* go to *Career Advice* section in Chapter 18

PowerPoint Presentations

Author's PowerPoint File:

1.1 Management 6/e Conceptual Framework

1.2 Organizations as Open Systems

1.3 The Manager's Challenge

1.4 The Team Leader's Challenge

1.5 Nature of Managerial Work

1.6 Mintzberg's Managerial Roles

1.7 Katz's managerial skills

1.8 Handy's Shamrock organization

Text Figures PowerPoint File

Figure 1.1 Organizations as Open Systems

Figure 1.2 Productivity

Figure 1.3 Upside-Down Pyramid

Figure 1.4 Functions of Management

Chapter Outline PowerPoint File

(Open or Save the Chapter Outline
PowerPoint file for Chapter 1)

Notes

Notes

Notes

Notes

Notes

Notes

Notes

Notes